Rational Emotive Behavioral Approaches to Childhood Disorders

Theory, Practice and Research

Rational Emotive Behavioral Approaches to Childhood Disorders

Theory, Practice and Research

Edited by:

Albert Ellis, Ph.D.
Albert Ellis Institute
New York, NY

and

Michael E. Bernard, Ph.D.
University of Melbourne
Victoria, Australia

Library of Congress Control Number: 2005928175

ISBN-10:0-387-26374-8 ISBN 0-387-26375-6 (eBook)
ISBN-13:978-0-387-26374-8

Printed on acid-free paper.

Printed in the United States of America. (SPI/MVY)

9 8 7 6 5 4 3 2 1

springeronline.com

About the Editors

Dr. Albert Ellis holds a Ph.D. in Clinical Psychology from Columbia University and is President of the Institute for Rational-Emotive Therapy in New York City. He is the founder of rational-emotive therapy (RET) and the grandfather of cognitive-behavior therapy (CBT). Several professional societies have honored him: He holds the Humanist of the Year Award of the American Humanist Association, the Distinguished Psychologist Award of the Academy of Psychologists in Marital and Family Therapy, and the Distinguished Practitioner Award of the American Association of Sex Educators, Counselors and Therapists. The American Psychological Association has given him its major award for Distinguished Professional Contributions to Knowledge (and the American Association for Counseling and Development has given him its major Professional Development Award.) He has published more than 70 books and over 700 articles on psychotherapy, sex, love, and marital relationships. Still going strong, he sees about 70 individual clients and conducts 5 group therapy sessions each week at the psychotherapy clinic of the Institute, supervises interns, and postdoctoral fellows, and gives numerous talks and workshops in the United States and abroad.

Professor Michael E. Bernard is the Founder of You Can Do It! Education, a program for promoting student social-emotional well-being and achievement that is being used in over 6000 schools in Australia, New Zealand, England, and North America. After receiving his doctorate in educational psychology from the University of Wisconsin, Madison, he worked for 18 years in the College of Education, University of Melbourne, Australia. In 1983, he was appointed as Reader and Coordinator of the Master of Educational Psychology Program. From 1995–2005, he was a tenured professor in the Department of Educational Psychology, Administration and Counseling, College of Education, at California State University, Long Beach. Professor Bernard has worked as a consultant school psychologist helping families and schools address the educational and mental health needs of school-age children. He has spent extensive time counseling children with emotional, behavioral or academic difficulties. Professor Bernard is a co-founder of the Australian Institute for Rational Emotive Behavior

Therapy and is the author of many books on REBT. For eight years, he was the editor-in-chief of the *Journal of Rational-Emotive and Cognitive-Behavior Therapy*. He is the author of over 50 books, 15 book chapters, and 30 journal articles in the area of children's early childhood development, learning, and social-emotional well-being as well as parent education, teacher professional development, and school improvement. Today, Professor Bernard is an international consultant to universities, educational authorities, organizations, and government. He is a professor at the University of Melbourne, Faculty of Education.

Contributors

Michael E. Bernard, Ph.D., Faculty of Education, University of Melbourne, Victoria Australia

John Boyd, Private Practice, Charlottesville, Virginia, USA

Raymond DiGiuseppe, Department of Psychology, St. John's University, Jamaica, New York, USA

Kristene Doyle, Ph.D., Associate Director, Albert Ellis Institute, New York, New York, USA

Albert Ellis, Ph.D., Albert Ellis Institute, New York, New York, USA

Maria A. Esposito, Department of Psychology, St. John's University, Jamaica, New York, USA

Russell Grieger, Ph.D., Private Practice, Charlottesville, Virginia, USA

Marie R. Joyce, Ph.D., Australian Catholic University, Institute for the Advancement of Research, St. Patrick's Campus, Fitzroy, Australia

Jill Kelter, Ph.D., Department of Psychology, St. John's University, Jamaica, New York, USA

William J. Knaus, Ed.D., Adjunct Professor, American International University, Longmeadow, Massachusetts, USA

Bridget McInerney, M.Ed., Clinical Social Worker, Philadelphia, Pennsylvania, USA

John McInerney, Ph.D., Private Practice, Cape May Court House, New Jersey, USA

Daniela Pires, M. Ed., Department of Educational Psychology, Administration & Counseling, California State University, Long Beach, California, USA

Mark Terjesen, Ph.D., Program Director, Graduate Programs in School Psychology, St. John's University, Jamaica, New York, USA

Ann Vernon, Ph.D., Department of Educational Administration and Counseling, University of Northern Iowa, Waterloo, Iowa, USA

Howard Young, (deceased) Former Staff Therapist, Hibbard Psychiatric Clinic, Huntington, West Virginia

Preface

It is now over 20 years since the publication of the first edition of this book and almost 50 years since the first use of rational-emotive behavior therapy (REBT) with a young person was described in the literature. Throughout these years, child-REBT and adolescent–REBT practice has existed in many parts of the world.

I (A.E.) have always believed in the potential of REBT to be used in schools as a form of mental health promotion and with young people experiencing developmental problems. After all, irrational thinking both in children and as it manifests itself in adolescence contributes to a bewildering array of emotional problems (e.g., childhood depression, anger), behavior problems (e.g., anger, oppositional defiance, conduct disorders), and academic problems (e.g., underachievement).

Over the past six decades, REBT and its educational derivative, Rational Emotive Education, has been embraced by a wide variety of child-oriented and adolescent-oriented mental health practitioners. Those who incorporate and integrate REBT in their individual work with young people have seen that REBT's essentials enhance their practice.

What are the essentials of REBT when applied to young people? Which aspects of cognitive-behavior, child and adolescent therapy (CBT) as currently practiced do we believe are founded on these essentials? How will you know that you are practicing REBT as you embrace the CBT orientation? Today, CBT is practiced as the treatment of choice by many and we would like REBT's distinctive contributions to the practice of CBT not to be lost. Moreover, we believe that there are distinctive aspects of REBT that add value to the practice of CBT. For example, there is little question in our minds that REBT's espousement of a core set of rational beliefs that contribute to mental health of young people (e.g., self-acceptance, high frustration tolerance, unconditional acceptance of others) as well as its focus on core irrational beliefs that contribute to psychosocial and mental health problems (e.g., needs for approval/achievement, self-depreciation, low frustration tolerance, demands for consideration, justice, fairness, respect, global rating of others, world) adds value to our understanding and treatment of the problems of young people. We believe that CBTers may underestimate the strength of children's irrational beliefs when they instruct children and adolescents in the use of positive self-talk and verbal self-instructions without working on the deeper level of helping them gain insight on and change their more powerful irrational beliefs and self-talk. We believe that layering positive self-talk on pre-existing irrational beliefs can in many instances be palliative.

REBT's differentiation of "hot cognitions" associated with very unhealthy emotions and dysfunctional behaviors found in absolutes, awfulizing, I can't-stand-it-itis, global rating of self, others, world from "warm cognitions" (e.g., perceptions, conclusions, predictions) that give rise to less extreme emotional intensity is distinctive to REBT's approach to assessment and treatment.

We believe the essentials of child and adolescent REBT practice can first be found in its theory that distinguishes rational from irrational aspects of the psyche of young people and directs the practitioner to distinguish in their assessment rational from irrational thoughts. Also, its theory of emotional upset (see Chapter 1) directs the practitioner though REBT hypothesis-driven questioning to root out both *automatic thoughts* that reflect distortions of reality (e.g., "I have failed and will always fail") *and* what REBT considers to be thoughts that are deeper and less accessible to introspection; namely, irrational evaluations and beliefs ("I should be successful, it's awful that I am not, I can't stand it, I'm a loser."). REBT's theory of different irrational beliefs that give rise to different problems of childhood provides the practitioners with advanced accurate empathy. REBT helps you to anticipate likely cognitions of the young person depending on the presenting problem. This is one of the most "appealing" aspects of the practice of REBT.

Other distinctive aspects of child-REBT and adolescent-REBT practice some of which have helped define the field of CBT include:

1. Teaching young people an *emotional vocabulary* and an *emotional schema* (feelings vary in intensity from strong to weak) and that they have behavioral and emotional options when something bad happens.
2. Using the ABC framework (sometimes revised as Happenings→ Thoughts→Feelings→Behaviors) to help young people conceptualize relationships among thinking, feeling, and behaving and for the purpose of assessment and intervention.
3. Explicit teaching of "emotional responsibility"; namely, you, not others, are the major influence on how you feel and behave.
4. Using disputing/challenging strategies to help identify and change irrational, negative thinking/self-talk *before* moving to instruction in rational, positive thinking/self-talk (for children older that 6 years of age).
5. Instructing young people in rational self-statements.
6. Through homework assignments, practicing new ways of thinking, feeling and behaving in the "real world."
7. Perhaps, the most unique aspects of REBT with young people is how it advances the argument that young people will be happier and more ful-

filled when they are taught (in therapy, in the classroom, at home) rational beliefs including *self-acceptance*, *high frustration tolerance*, and *unconditional acceptance of others*.

There are several misconceptions about REBT and its practice with young people that we believe this book helps to correct. Some of these include:

REBT when practiced with young people is simply a downward extension of REBT adult methods. It is not as many of its methods and activities have evolved from the pioneering work done at the Living School where REBT was taught by teachers in the form of REE to all children. Moreover, as discussed in Chapter 1 of this book, child-REBT and adolescent-REBT takes into account the developmental level of the child in prioritizing problems and selecting assessment and treatment methods.

REBT and REE focus too much on intellectual insight and change. REBT has always considered that beliefs be they rational or irrational never exist on their own but rather are intimately connected to emotions and behaviors. As such, when irrational and rational beliefs are discussed with young people, their impact on emotions and behaviors, and the reciprocal impact of emotions and behaviors on beliefs are always emphasized. Moreover, REBT always has used not only cognitive change methods (e.g., disputing, rational self-statements), but emotive (e.g., rational-emotive imagery, forceful, evocative repetition of rational self-statements) and behavior methods (cognitive-behavioral role play/rehearsal, homework assignments including practicing new behavior in difficult circumstances).

There is no research supporting the efficacy of REBT with younger populations. As Chapters 1, 8 and 13 reveal in this volume, since the 1970s, numerous individual studies and several important meta-analyses have been conducted. While the quality of studies has varied and the studies represented in meta-analyses have been selective (have not included all available studies), it will be seen that there is sufficient array of studies that demonstrate the positive effects of REBT and REE to qualify it as an evidence-based practice.

Now to this book. We have asked many of the original contributors to the first edition to update their work. Furthermore, we have identified some new contributors and new topics relevant to child-REBT and adolescent-REBT practice.

Section I of the book contains chapters addressing the history, rationale, practice, and issues surrounding the use of REBT to treat disorders of childhood. The opening chapter presents the most up-to-date statement of the theory and practice of REBT as applied to younger populations and includes the latest meta-analysis of available studies. In the second and third chapters, special considerations in using REBT with children and adolescents are reviewed. The author of Chapter 3, Howard Young, is now deceased and we reproduce his original chapter in its entirety as it is still today an excellent exposition of ways to effectively use REBT with adolescents. Chapter 4 by

Bill Knaus reviews for the reader one of REBT's cornerstone "constructs" for understanding childhood disorders; namely, low frustration tolerance. Chapter 5 presents recent child developmental research and practice addressing emotional resilience and coping skills training and discusses how it can be integrated in REBT.

Section II contains specialized chapters by leading REBT practitioners on the treatment of depression, anxiety/fears/phobias, aggressive, ADHD, and under-achievement. It will be clear that REBT is now being integrated with other CBT and ecological approaches (e.g., family therapy) in the treatment of childhood disorders.

Section III contains chapters addressing the use of REBT with parents as well as with the parents and teachers of exceptional children. The final two chapters discuss the applications of REBT in group work and in the schools in the form of prevention, promotion, and intervention mental health programs.

Finally, we would like to acknowledge a number of REBT scholars who over the years have helped to demarcate REBT's use with younger populations. There is little doubt that Ray DiGiuseppe has made enormous contributions to its clinical practice and Ann Vernon to the practice of REE in schools in the form of developmental curriculum. Bill Knaus continues the work he initiated in writing "the manual" describing the applications of REBT in educational settings by teachers (Rational Emotive Education). Over the years, Paul Hauck has been very instrumental in outlining the use of REBT with parents. In the early 1980s, Virginia Waters helped pave the road for the use of REBT with children and their parents while Howard Young did the same for working with adolescents. Many others (Jay and Harriet Barrish, Terry London, Jerry Wilde, John McInerney, Marie Joyce) have embellished the REBT field with their stimulating ideas and child-friendly and family-friendly practice.

Albert Ellis
Michael E. Bernard

Contents

Section I. Introduction, Rationale, and Basic Issues **1**

Chapter 1: Rational-Emotive Behavioral Approaches to Childhood Disorders: History, Theory, Practice and Research 3
Michael E. Bernard, Albert Ellis and Mark Terjesen

Chapter 2: REBT Assessment and Treatment with Children 85
Raymond DiGiuseppe and Michael E. Bernard

Chapter 3: REBT Assessment and Treatment with Adolescents 115
Howard Young

Chapter 4: Frustration Tolerance Training for Children 133
William J. Knaus

Chapter 5: Emotional Resilience in Children and Adolescence: Implications for Rational-Emotive Behavior Therapy 156
Michael E. Bernard and Daniela Pires

Section II. Disorders of Childhood **175**

Chapter 6: A Developmental, Rational-Emotive Behavioral Approach for Working with Parents 177
Marie R. Joyce

Chapter 7: Depression in Children and Adolescents: REBT Approaches to Assessment and Treatment 212
Ann Vernon

Chapter 8: Childhood Anxieties, Fears, and Phobias: A Cognitive-Behavioral, Psychosituational Approach 232
Russell M. Grieger and John D. Boyd

Chapter 9: Treating Aggressive Children: A Rational-Emotive Behavior Systems Approach 257
Raymond DiGiuseppe and Jill Kelter

Chapter 10: Rational-Emotive Behavior Therapy and Attention Deficit Hyperactivity Disorder 281
Kristene A. Doyle and Mark D. Terjesen

Chapter 11: Working with the Educational Underachiever: A Social and Emotional Developmental Approach 310
Michael E. Bernard

Section III. Applications **367**

Chapter 12: Working with the Parents and Teachers of Exceptional Children 369
John F. McInerney and Bridget C.M. McInerney

Chapter 13: Rational-Emotive Behavior Group Therapy with Children and Adolescents 385
Mark D. Terjesen and Maria A. Esposito

Chapter 14: Applications of REBT in Schools: Prevention, Promotion, Intervention 415
Ann Vernon and Michael E. Bernard

INDEX **461**

Section I

Introduction, Rationale, and Basic Issues

1

Rational-Emotive Behavioral Approaches to Childhood Disorders: History, Theory, Practice and Research

MICHAEL E. BERNARD, ALBERT ELLIS AND MARK TERJESEN

The history of cognitive restructuring with children and youth doubtless goes back many centuries and may be traced to early philosophers and religious preachers. Socrates, let us remember, was persecuted by the Athenians for supposedly corrupting the youth of that ancient city. And the Greek–Roman Stoic Epictetus, who is often acknowledged as one of the main philosophical fathers of rational-emotive-behavior therapy (REBT) and cognitive-behavior therapy (CBT), pioneered in conveying significant cognitive teachings to the young people as well as the adults of his time. Because of his influence, some 2,000 years ago, the Roman Emperor Marcus Aurelius was raised from childhood in the Stoic tradition and consequently was later led to write his famous *Meditations*, one of the most influential books of all time, outlining the principles and practice of cognitive restructuring.

In modern times, methods of teaching children and adolescents to talk more sensibly to themselves, and thereby to make themselves individually and socially more effective, were pioneered by Alfred Adler. Not only was Adler (1927) one of the first cognitive therapists to specialize in direct psychological approaches to youngsters, but he and his associates, starting in the 1920s, saw the importance of using cognitive approaches in the school system and of teaching them to parents to employ in the rearing of children. Today, the field of child therapy and adolescent therapy has embraced the cognitive model and, indeed, therapy has been operationalized as any intervention designed to alter the attitudes, thoughts, feelings and actions of the young person who has sought or been brought to treatment with distress and/or maladaptive behavior (Weisz et al., 1995).

History of Rational-Emotive-Behavior Therapy with Children and Adolescents

It is interesting to note that although many behavior therapists (Craighead, 1982) appear to date the beginnings of the cognitive-behavioral movement around the late 1960s and the early 1970s, the application of cognitive methods in the form of REBT to parenting and to the psychological treatment of youngsters was pioneered by Ellis in the mid-1950s. Soon after he started to use REBT with adults, at the beginning of 1955, he saw that it could also be employed with children either directly by a therapist or indirectly by a REBT practitioner working with the children's parents. He therefore included some cognitive parenting techniques in his first book on REBT, "How to Live with a "Neurotic" (Ellis, 1957). When he began making tape recordings of REBT sessions, he recorded a series of sessions with an 8-year-old female bed wetter (Ellis, 1959), which were widely circulated and encouraged many other therapists to use RET methods with children. In the 1960s, cognitive restructuring with youngsters was promoted by a number of REBT-oriented writers who showed how it could be effectively employed by therapists, parents, and school personnel (Doress, 1967; Ellis, 1967; Ellis et al., 1966; Glicken, 1967, 1968; Hauck, 1967; Lafferty et al., 1964; McGory, 1967; Wagner, 1966).

By and large, the only cognitive restructuring approach being employed with school-age children through the late 1960s was REBT. By the late 1960s, behavior therapists began to open their minds to cognition, and as a consequence, widely practiced and researched behavioral methods of helping youngsters overcome their emotional and behavioral problems began to be combined with REBT and other cognitive methods.

During the 1970s, a large number of articles, chapters, and manuals appeared that explained the use of REBT with children and adolescents (Bedford, 1974; Blanco and Rosenfeld, 1978; Brown, 1974, 1977, 1979; Daly, 1971; DiGiuseppe, 1975a,b; Edwards, 1977; Ellis, 1971a,b, 1972a, 1973a, 1975a,b, 1980b; Grieger et al., 1979; Hauck, 1974, 1977; Knaus, 1974, 1977; Knaus and McKeever, 1977; Kranzler, 1974; Maultsby, 1974, 1975; McMullin et al., 1978; Miller, 1978; Nardi, 1981; Protinsky, 1976; Rand; 1970; Rossi, 1977; Sachs, 1971; Smith, 1979; Staggs, 1979; Waters, 1980a,b, 1981; Young 1974a,b, 1977).

Indeed, because of the observed success of REBT that was found in early clinical and experimental investigations, the Institute for Rational-Emotive Therapy in New York started the Living School in 1970, a small private grade school where all the children were taught REBT along with the usual elementary-school curriculum. The school flourished for five years, in the course of which it was found that teachers (not therapists) could teach young children REBT in the regular classroom situation and thereby help them (and their parents) improve their emotional health and live more happily and efficiently. Publications on the use of REBT in this school setting have been published by DiNubile and Wessler (1974), Ellis (1971a, b, 1972b, 1973b, 1975b), Gerald and Eyman (1981), Knaus (1974), Sachs (1971), and Wolfe and staff (1970). In order to have a greater impact in classrooms both in the community and across the country, the Living School was transformed in 1975 into the Rational-Emotive Education Consultation Service, which provides (1) in-service workshops for teachers and counselors; (2) consultations to schools, classes, and teachers wishing to implement a program of RET; and (3) materials and techniques for use in classrooms and/or school counseling settings (Waters, 1981).

In the 1970s, large number of case studies and quasi-experimental and experimental outcome studies have appeared in the REBT literature (Agosto and Solomon, 1978; Albert, 1972; Bernard, 1979; Block, 1978; Bokor, 1972; Brody, 1974; Cangelosi et al., 1980; Costello and Dougherty, 1977; D'Angelo, 1977; DeVoge, 1974; DiGiuseppe, 1975a; DiGiuseppe and Kassinove, 1976; Forman and Forman, 1978; Harris, 1976; Jacobs, 1977; Katz, 1974; Knaus and Bokor, 1975; Kujoth, 1976; Maes and Heinman, 1970; Maultsby et al., 1974; Miller, 1978; Ritchie, 1978; Sharma, 1970; Solomon, 1978; Sydel, 1972; Taylor, 1975; Wagner, 1966; Warren et al., 1976; Zelie et al., 1980). A review of many of these studies by DiGiuseppe, Miller, and Trexler (1979) led to the following conclusion:

> These studies provide support for the hypothesis that elementary school children are capable of acquiring knowledge of rational-emotive principles and that the modification of a child's self-verbalizations or irrational self-statements can have a positive effect on emotional adjustment and behavior. Certain critical factors relevant to rational-emotive therapy procedures have not been thoroughly investigated. These include the specification of the relative contributions of the behavioral components within rational-emotive therapy (i.e., behavioral rehearsal and written homework assignments) and the degree to which a child's intellectual ability is related to his acquisition of the cognitively oriented principles of rational-emotive therapy. (p. 225)

From the early 1980s with the publication of the first edition of this book, *Rational-Emotive Approaches to the Problems of Childhood* (Ellis and Bernard, 1983) and Bernard and Joyce's (1984) *Rational-Emotive Therapy with Children and Adolescents*, through the 1990s and early part of the twenty-first century, clinical and educational applications of REBT have been written about extensively (Barnes, 2000; Barrish and Barrish, 1985, 1989; Bernard et al., 1983; Bernard, 1990; Bernard, 2004a,b,c, and Wilde, Bernard and Joyce, 1993; Bernard, 2004a; Burnett, 1994, 1996; DiGiuseppe, 1981; Ellis and Wilde, 2002; Kelly, 1996; Lucey, 1995; Shannon and Allen, 1998; Vernon, 1980, 1983, 1989a, b, c, 1990, 1993a, 1997, 1998a, b, c, 1999, 2000, 2002, 2004a, b, 2006a, b; Warren et al., 1988; Wilde, 1992; Zionts and Zionts, 1997). A special issue of the School Psychology Review was devoted to the implications of REBT and Rational-

Emotive Education (REE) for the role of school psychologists (Bernard and DiGiuseppe, 1991). Bernard and DiGiuseppe's book (1993) *Rational-Emotive Consultation in Applied Settings* contained a variety of chapters detailing ways in which REBT could be used by practitioners to address the mental health needs of primary caregivers of young people (parents, teachers) with emotional and behavioral disorders as well as ways in which the ABCs and rational beliefs could be introduced by primary caregivers to young people. Hajzler and Bernard's (1991) review of research concluded that REBT leads to decreases in irrationality, anxiety and disruptive behavior among students in 88, 80 and 56% of the studies, respectively. Internal locus of control and self-esteem increased in 71 and 57% of the studies, respectively. Gonzalez et al. (2004) found in their meta-analysis of 19 REBT studies with children and adolescents that the overall mean weighted effect of REBT was positive and significant with the largest effect of REBT found for disruptive behaviors and children benefiting more from REBT than adolescents (see final section of this chapter).

Today, it is abundantly clear that within the fields of school psychology, school counseling and guidance, REBT is a preferred methodology incorporated within the tool boxes of counselors and psychologists who work with children and adolescents. In the field of school-wide prevention and promotion programming, REBT in the form of You Can Do It! Education (YCDI) (Bernard, 2001a, 2002, 2005, 2006) in a preferred theoretical framework in Australia with over 5,000 primary and secondary schools employing YCDI programs (see last chapter of this book). Over 50,000 four to six-year-old children are learning rational, positive beliefs as a result of participating in the REBT-based YCDI early childhood program (Bernard, 2004b). Over the past several decades, the Albert Ellis Institute in New York and affiliated training REBT centers throughout the world have offered the Child and Adolescent Certificate in Rational-Emotive-Behavior Therapy to a large number of practitioners. Additionally, professors throughout the world who have received training in child-oriented and adolescent-oriented REBT, incorporate REBT in their counseling, counseling psychology, clinical and school psychology, clinical psychology, and social work graduate programs. In the field of cognitive-behavioral child treatment, clinical psychologists have not embraced REBT as extensively as in other mental health professions due in part to a perception that REBT has no research base to speak of and, as a consequence, REBT has been ignored by CBTers (Reinecke, 2005). Hopefully, the material presented later on in this chapter will dispel this notion.

As shown in this book and revealed in the results of meta-analytic studies reported later on in this chapter, REBT is being used to treat a variety of emotional, behavioral and achievement-related problems of children. This chapter will now present an overview of the existing REBT child and adolescent treatment literature pertaining to the theory and practice of REBT with younger populations.

Theoretical Considerations in Applications of Rebt to Childhood Disorders

In this section, we examine important theoretical foundations that underpin the practice of REBT with younger populations.

REBT Developmental Model of Childhood Disorders

There is little question that REBT is developmentally oriented and meets existing criteria for establishing a therapy's developmental credentials (Holmbeck et al., 2003; Holmbeck and Updegrove, 1995; Shirk, 2001; Weisz and Hawley, 2002). REBTers who work with children and adolescents strive to stay current with the developmental literature (Vernon, 2004c), take into account the critical developmental tasks and milestones relevant to a particular child's or adolescent's presenting problem and have the flexibility to be able to choose which presenting symptoms to prioritize, depending on the degree to which each of the symptoms is developmentally atypical. REBT is developmentally sensitive with its assessment and treatment methods tailored to take into account the developmental levels of the child or adolescent (Bernard and Joyce, 1984). For example, REBT does little disputing of irrational beliefs in children younger than six and reserves more sophisticated disputing of general beliefs until after the age of 11 or 12. As can be seen in the chapters of this book, REBT has always thought *multisystemically* and always considers the need to involve peers, teachers, parents, and the whole family (Woulff, 1983) while treating the child. A final point concerning the REBT therapeutic methods employed with children and adolescents. Rather than being merely downward refinements of REBT verbal techniques used with adults such as Socratic disputing, the tool box of thinking, feeling and behaving methods, activities and techniques used with younger populations have been either developed in consultation with teachers of children and adlescents.

Ellis and other REBT theorists (Bernard and Joyce, 1984; Ellis and Bernard, 1983; Vernon, 1993b) have adopted the perspective of *interactionism* in conceptualizing the origins of childhood maladjustment. As reflected in this volume, REBT practitioners believe that emotional disorders and abnormal behavior in childhood can be best understood in terms of an interaction between "person" and environmental (e.g., parenting, peer) variables. Bernard and Joyce (1984) characterized this perspective as follows:

> Children demonstrate characteristic ways of thinking about and relating to their environment which exert an influence on their environment. Similarly, situations themselves modify the behavior and attitudes of people by providing (or not providing) appropriate learning experiences and enrichment opportunities as well as rewarding and punishing consequences for behavior within certain contexts. We believe that there is an almost inexorable reciprocal relationship between abnormal behavior and

a deviant environment such that abnormalities in either the person or the environment of the person tend to bring out abnormalities in the other. It would seem, therefore, necessary to determine how persons and environments interact and covary together in analyzing childhood psychopathology.

Similar sentiments are expressed by Bernard (2004a).

The extent to which children's thinking and associated beliefs are dominated by irrationality rather than rationality depends upon their age, their biological temperament (e.g., feisty, fearful, flexible), their home environment including their parent's style of parenting (e.g., firm/not firm, kind/unkind), the extent to which their parents model, and communicate irrational or rational beliefs and whether there are negative events present in their lives (e.g., divorce, persecution). Children who manifest social-emotional-behavioral and achievement problems often present with developmental delays in their capacity to think rationally and logically concerning affective-interpersonal issues (e.g., have difficulty keeping things in perspective, personalize negative experiences) as well as in the development of other emotional self-management skills (e.g., relaxation, finding someone to talk with). They also are dominated by a range of irrational beliefs including self-downing, low frustration tolerance, and the lack of acceptance by others.

Child Factors

According to REBT theory, children are born with an innate capacity to think irrationally and illogically. This human disposition exerts its influence across the life span and precludes the possibility of perfect mental health. What moderates the influence of irrationality is the development of rationality and logical reasoning abilities which emerge around the age of six (Piaget's concrete operational stage of development) with abstract reasoning abilities developing more fully around the age of 11 or 12 (Piaget's formal operational stage of development). There are relationships between a child's level of cognitive development as defined by Piaget's stages and REBT therapeutic methods. Whereas we employ rational self-statements with children of all ages, we generally do not dispute irrational beliefs with children who are less than 7-year-old, and we do not often logically dispute irrational beliefs in the abstract with children much below the age of 11 or 12.

There are a number of interesting overlaps between the theories of Ellis and those of Piaget. Both share the assumption of constructivism. They also place great "faith" in the scientific method of investigation and the power of formal logical reasoning. Both appear to be in agreement concerning the importance of cognition in the experience and expression of emotions. Piaget (1952) wrote that "it is, in fact, only a romantic prejudice that makes us suppose that affective phenomena constitute immediate givens or innate and ready-made feelings similar to Rousseau's 'conscience"' (p. 12).

In his writings, Ellis (1994) discusses the idea that the strength of one's propensity for irrational thought and the strength of conviction one has in one's irrational beliefs is heavily influenced by genetics. That is, while parenting practices as well as the influence of peers and one's culture definitely condition the beliefs of young people through modeling and direct communication, the tendency for beliefs be they rational or irrational to be fully integrated within a young person's phenomenology or view of the world and the extent to which a young person's cognitive processing is characterized by absolutism is not learned but is biologically determined. The evidence provided by Ellis to substantiate nature over nurture when it comes to the origins of an individual's irrational thinking is partly found in the many instances of families seen by Ellis where only one child is presented with an internalizing or externalizing problem. In these families, other siblings of the referred child presented as problem free while the parenting styles of parents remained constant and there was no evidence that the parents or family experienced unusual upheavals during the developmental years of the referred child. Some children who experience distress and demonstrate maladaptive behaviors have parents who appear to be reasonably well adjusted, who have positive attitudes toward their child, and whose child-rearing practices appear to be sound. We also do not receive referrals for well-adjusted children whose parents, because of their problems, would back at long odds to produce disturbed offspring. Research (Kagan, 1998; Rothbard and Bates, 1998) indicates temperamentally difficult children who, as a result of their frustrating behavior, literally create conditions that drive their parents to distraction.

As already indicated, REBT has historically recognized the importance of the young person's cognitive developmental level of maturity in treatment. On the assessment side, a recognition of child development enables the practitioner to judge whether a presenting problem is a transient and/or a normal developmental phenomenon (i.e., fear of the dark) or whether it represents something more serious. The level at which the REBT intervention is used (rational self-statements, disputing of inferences, or abstract disputing of irrational beliefs) depends on the linguistic and cognitive maturity of the young client.

Rational Emotive Behavior Therapy recognizes, as do the proponents of many different approaches to childhood psychopathology, that there is a reciprocal relationship between mental and emotional development. When children are very young, the quality of their subjective emotional experience is very much limited by their capacity to think about and understand the meaning of experience. The cognitive limitations of the early childhood period can often result in children acquiring beliefs about themselves and their surrounding world that are untrue and irrational and that if not corrected can have an extremely deleterious effect on their future well-being. That is, children construct their own theories and arrive at their own conclusions based on inferences from what they have observed. The child's conception of the world is idiosyncratically organized and derives from the child's limited capacity to make observations and draw logical conclusions.

In working with children, we are struck by the pervasive influence that their ideas and beliefs have on their emotions and behavior. These beliefs are often implicit and frequently result from the child having formed a conclusion based on limited evidence and having used the conclusion as an "unquestioned" rule for guiding subsequent behavior. The beliefs, be they rational, or irrational, that are formed early in life may become firmly fixed, and they represent part of the, phenomenological framework of children that provides the basis for self-evaluation, for the demands they place on others, and for the interpretation they make of the behavior of others. Young children's incapacity for rational and logical thought limits the types of ideas that they acquire and frequently reinforces a variety of irrational beliefs which take many years to overcome.

A cognitive analysis of maladjustment in children and adolescents frequently reveals beliefs about themselves, others, and the world, as well as logical reasoning processes that appear to be either a holdover from or a regression to preconcrete operational levels of thinking and primitive belief systems. Characteristics of preconcrete operational thought include:

1. Drawing arbitrary inferences—conclusions not based on evidence or when evidence contradicts conclusion
2. Selective abstraction—focusing on a detail taken out of context, ignoring salient features of the situation
3. Magnification/minimization—errors in evaluating significance of event
4. Personalization—tendency to relate external events to themselves when no basis for making connection
5. Overgeneralization—drawing a conclusion based on limited and isolated events
6. Dichotomous thinking—tendency to place events into opposite categories (e.g., good-bad)

The advent of formal operational thought capacities in adolescents also brings with it its own problems. Adolescents in their early teens begin to experience a form of egocentrism, a "naive, idealism" (not dissimilar in effect from the egocentrism of the early childhood period), that frequently leads to a variety of emotional and behavioral problems. The struggle for a personal identity and for new definitions of social relationships that accompanies the increased capacity for reflective and abstract thought often results in adolescents' acquiring sets of beliefs concerning themselves (self-rating) and others (demandingness) that accompany some people throughout life.

Parental Factors

According to REBT, parents as role models and reinforcing-punishing agents can play a major part in preventing, minimizing, or exacerbating emotional and behavioral problems in their children. As indicated earlier, this is not to say that poor parenting is the only cause of psychological maladjustment in children. We agree with Bard's (1980) comments:

Some children seem especially prone to make themselves miserable about their parent's relatively minor imperfections. I emphasize this point at the onset to attack the myth that parents are always to blame and to alert practitioners to the fact that parent-child problems may be extremely complex. (p. 93)

Ellis has consistently maintained that the worst thing that parents can do to their children is to blame them for their mistake making and wrongdoing. Such blaming encourages children to continue to blame themselves and inevitably leads to chronic feelings of anxiety, guilt, and low self-esteem for some children and hostility and bigotry in others. Ellis (1973c) wrote:

Parents or other early teachers usually help a child plummet down the toboggan slide toward disturbed feelings and behavior by doing two things when he does something that displeases them: (a) they tell him that he is wrong for acting in this displeasing manner; and (b) they strongly indicate to him that he is a worthless individual for being wrong, and that he therefore deserves to be severely punished for his wrongdoing.... For if they were really sensible about bringing up their children, they would obviously show their child that: (a) she is wrong when she engages in activities that displease them and other members of their social group, and that (b) she is still a highly worthwhile individual who will merely, if she wants to get along well in the community, eventually have to discipline herself and learn to be less wrong in the future. (pp. 239–240).

Irrational beliefs of parents can influence their behavior in two basic ways. One is through their emotions.

Parents frequently get very upset when their child breaks a rule because they believe that: (a) "My child must be good all the time"; (b) "I find it awful or horrible when my child is not—I can't stand it," and (c) "My child deserves punishment because he has made me so angry and for being such a bad child." The belief that children must never break a rule leads to extreme anger which produces intense and non-constructive disciplinary action. (Bernard and Joyce, 1984)

Alternatively, parents may employ inappropriate and counterproductive methods of child management because of ignorance. That is, they believe that what they are doing is the correct thing to do, and often, it is the only way that they can conceptualize relating to their children. Their maladaptive behavior is not associated with extreme emotional arousal but motivated directly by their "unjustified" and "outdated" assumptions. Bernard and Joyce (1984) have noted:

We have worked with several fathers who would administer physical consequences to their children whenever they caught them misbehaving. At these times, they were not particularly angry though they may have felt mildly irritated. These fathers held the simple belief that "children who break rules need to be punished severely to learn a lesson" and employed this rule as a basis for knowing what to do in problematic situations.

Irrational beliefs of parents can, therefore, lead directly to behavior without the intervention of significant emotional arousal. The practitioner can help objectively to dispute the rationality and adaptiveness of these beliefs without considering the emotional involvement. This is not to say, of course, that there are not more pervasive, absolutistic beliefs underlying these parenting beliefs that do occasion high degrees of emotionality, such as, "To be a perfect parent and a worthwhile person, my child must be totally obedient at all times." Both types of influences had better be considered in understanding the role of parental beliefs.

Paul Hauck (1967, 1977) is a REBT practitioner who has written extensively regarding irrational beliefs that underlie ineffective parenting. REBT practitioners have followed his lead in identifying a number of erroneous parental beliefs concerning child management that are irrational not only because they are inaccurate and empirically unsupportable, but also because they lead to dysfunctional styles of parenting. Also Hauck and others have discussed how destructive extreme parental emotional upset can have on parent-child relationships and the ability of parents to parent effectively including the teaching of socialization and self-management skills.

According to Hauck, the *Unkind and firm pattern* ("unquestioning obedience toward authority combined with a kick in the ego) involve parental behavior of setting of rigid rules, never letting their child question their authority, focusing on the wrongdoing of their child, attacking the personality of their child, strictness and little praise ("Children must never disagree with their superiors"). As a response to this style, children may come to regard themselves as worthless and inferior and view everyone else as superior; they experience feelings of anxiety, insecurity and guilt and may demonstrate avoidant, dependent and submissive behavior.

The parental beliefs that underlay an overly strict and harsh style of parenting

1. Getting angry is an effective way to modify my child's behavior.
2. Anger helps get things done.
3. Children are naturally undisciplined and behave like wild beasts. Parents must beat them into shape to make them civilized.
4. A child and his behavior are the same.
5. Since a child should do well, praise and reward are unnecessary and spoil the child.
6. A parent is always correct and, therefore, children must never question or disagree with them.
7. As a parent, I have the power to make my children do whatever I want.

The *kind and not firm* child-rearing practice involve parents who while showing love and affection makes few demands and set few limits. Parents who demonstrate this pattern appear to do so out of either not wanting to frustrate their child ("Children must not be frustrated") or out of guilt ("I am responsible for all my child's problems and, therefore, I am hopeless.").

Children of such parents may become "goofers" who are weak, egocentric, emotionally infantile and dependent, have low frustration tolerance, and shirk responsibility.

The parental beliefs that underlay an overly permissive and undemanding style of parenting include:

1. Children must not be frustrated.
2. All punishment is wrong.
3. Children should be free to express themselves.
4. Parenting should be fun and easy.
5. Whatever feels right is right.
6. I'm too weak and helpless to know what is the right thing to do, so I'll leave it to the moment.

With the *unkind and not firm* child-rearing practice, parents harshly criticize their children for misbehavior and hardly ever praise them when they behave well.

As a result, their may become chronic rule breakers, trouble with law, angry and frustrated for never being able to please parents, test limits to get parents to show they care.

Hauck has written that the *kind and firm* child-rearing practice is the preferred and skilled form of parenting. Parents who raise their children in this fashion talk and reason with them about objectionable behavior, focus on the behavior but do not blame the child, set limits with clear consequences for rule violations, set punishment that is related to rule learning, not blame, sometimes frustrate their child when necessary, apply reasonable pressure to teach self-discipline and delay of gratification, never punish out of anger and frequently praise and show love. Children raised under this regime often experience positive social-emotional well-being and achieve to the best of their ability.

REBT Conceptualization of an Emotional Episode

Incidents of emotional upset are complicated psychological phenomena. Ellis (1994) has provided his now famous ABC model to help clients grasp the role of their thoughts in causing emotional disturbance. Wessler and Wessler (1980) expanded the ABC model to help therapists to a fuller understanding of these complex psychological events. At the start of every emotional event, a stimulus is presented to the child:

Step 1: Stimuli are then sensed by the person's eyes, ears, sense of smell, touch, etc.

Step 2: Sensory neurons process the stimuli and transmit them to the CNS.

Step 3: Not all sensations enter consciousness. Some are filtered out and others are perceived. Perception is Step 3. Perception, however, is not an exact replication of reality. Perceptions consist of equal parts of information provided by the senses and information provided by the brain. At this point, all information is organized, categorized, and defined. Perception is as much a peripheral as a CNS function.

Step 4: People usually do not stop thinking after they have perceived information. In most cases, they attempt to extract more information than is present in the perception, so some interpretations or inferences are likely to follow perceptions.

Step 5: Humans are not just passive processors of information. Inferences and conclusions usually have some further meaning associated with them. Conclusions and inferences may vary in their importance to an individual. Almost all inferences are appraised by the person either positively or negatively in relation to the person's life. Irrational appraisals consists of *absolutes* (shoulds, oughts, musts, needs) and *evaluations* (awfulizing, I can't standit-it-is, global rating of self, others, the world).

Step 6: According to rational-emotive behavior therapy, affect or emotion accompanies appraisal. We feel happy or sad or mad at Step 6, after we have appraised something as being beneficial, threatening, etc.

Step 7: Emotional states are not separate psychological phenomena. Emotions have evolved as part of the flight-fight mechanism and exist primarily to motivate adaptive behavior. Therefore, emotions usually include not only the reactions of the autonomic nervous system and the phenomenological sensations, but action tendencies or behavioral response sets that are learned.

Step 8: Responses, once they are made, usually have some impact on the external world. This effect can be desirable or undesirable, and feedback of our action tendencies serves as a reward to strengthen or extinguish a response set.

Elements of the Emotional Episode:

(1) Stimulus,
(2) Sensation,
(3) Perception,
(4) Inference,
(5) Appraisal,
(6) Affect,
(7) Action tendency, and
(8) Feedback

Given this model, emotional disturbance develops because of one or two types of cognitive errors: empirical distortions of reality that occur at Step 4 (inferences) and irrational, exaggerated and distorted appraisals of inferences at Step 5. According to REBT, it is primarily the appraisal that is necessary for emotional disturbance. This is the B in Ellis's ABC. Ellis has noted, however, that, many times, the appraisals are about distortions of reality. Faulty inferences usually do accompany exaggerated appraisal, but the appraisal alone is sufficient to arouse disturbed affect.

Let us take a hypothetical clinical example to explain how these two cognitions operate. George, a 14-year-old, has moved to a new neighborhood and has not met new friends. He is sitting quietly in the neighborhood playground while the other teenagers are talking amongst themselves or playing basketball. He feels very anxious and his associated action potential is withdrawal. He sits alone leaning up against a wall, reading a book. As he sees others gather nearby, George thinks, "They'll never like me, they'll think I'm weird, and they won't want to speak with me no matter what I do." George has drawn these inferences from his peer's behavior. In fact, they are predictions about what might happen but never actually has happened. Inferences alone are not sufficient to arouse high levels of anxiety. Some adolescents, although not George, might be perfectly happy to sit by themselves and read books, but George appraises this situation quite negatively and irrationally. His implicit absolute "I need people to like and approve of me" leads him to catastrophize "It's awful that I don't have anyone to play with" and, then, to put himself down "I must be a jerk if they won't play with me."

Defining "Beliefs"

In REBT, the terms *belief* and *belief system* refer to that aspect of human cognition that is responsible for the mental health and the psychological well-being of the individual. Beliefs are a central explanatory construct of REBT, and it is important that the meaning of the term be as clear as possible.

Ellis (1977) has elaborated an ABC (DE) theory of emotional disturbance that describes how a person becomes upset. REBT starts with an emotional and behavioral consequence (C) and seeks to identify the activating event (A) that appears to have precipitated (C). While the commonly accepted viewpoint is that, (A) caused (C), REBT steadfastly maintains that it is the individual's beliefs (B) about what happened at (A) that more directly "create" (C). Disputation (D), one of the cornerstones of the RET practice of therapeutic change, involves employing the scientific method of challenging and questioning anti-empirical and untenable hypotheses, as well as imperative and absolutistic assumptions (irrational beliefs) that individuals may hold about themselves, about others, and about the world, which lead to the particular interpretations and appraisals that the individual forms about the activating event. When individuals who hold irrational beliefs begin to change their unsound assumptions, to reformulate them into more empirically valid statements, and to believe strongly in the validity of the new ideas, they wind up with new cognitive (philosophical), emotive, and behavioral effects (E's).

Belief may be viewed as a very broad hypothetical construct that embraces at least three distinct subclasses of cognitive phenomena: (1) thoughts that an individual is thinking and is aware of at a given time about A; (2) thoughts about A that the individual is not immediately aware of; and (3) more abstract beliefs that the individual may hold in general (Bernard, 1981). Eschenroeder (1982) was in essential agreement with this analysis when he wrote that the ABC scheme is a simplification of the complex processes of the perception, interpretation, and evaluation of events and the activation of emotional reactions and behavioral responses:

> The B-element of the ABC refers to rather different phenomena: (1) *thoughts and images*, which can be observed through introspection by the individual; (2) *unconscious processes*, which can be inferred post hoc from the individual's. feelings and behavior ("unconscious verbalizations"); (3) the *belief system* underlying the person's thoughts, emotions, and behaviors. (p. 275)

The more abstract beliefs that people hold are unspoken and constitute the assumptive framework by which they evaluate, appraise, and form conclusions about what they observe to be happening to themselves, to others, and in the world around them. These abstract beliefs are not expressed in the self-talk of people but can be considered relatively enduring personality traits that affect people's interpretations of reality and often, in so doing, guide subsequent behavior. They are inferred from the types of thought statements that clients are able to articulate to themselves and to the practitioner as well as from their pattern of behavior. For example, people who strongly hold the belief that they desperately need others to depend and rely on tend to interpret situations in terms of whether they offer particular sorts of personal security and also search for environments and relationships that satisfy this self-perceived need.

Abstract beliefs can be differentiated on the basis of whether they reflect absolutistic and imperative qualities (irrational) or relativistic and conditional qualities (rational). Those beliefs that lead to self-defeating emotional and behavioral consequences are almost always expressed as unqualified should's, ought's, must's, command's, and demand's and are deemed "irrational." Ellis, who has referred to these beliefs as a form of "musturbatory thinking," has indicated that if people hold rigid views and beliefs about how they, others, and the world should or must be under all circumstances, then they are likely to experience some form of disturbance. Beliefs that are expressed not as commands but as preferences and that are viewed as' conditional on and relative to a set of circumstances are defined as rational and lead to more adaptive levels of emotionality and appropriate behavior.

In terms of the ABC model, rational beliefs generally lead to moderate emotions that enable clients to achieve their future goals by facilitating constructive behavior, although rational beliefs may result in extreme levels of some emotions that are appropriate, such as extreme sadness and regret. Irrational beliefs lead to extremely stressful emotional consequences (intense anxiety, anger, or depression) and behavioral reactions (aggression or withdrawal), which make it quite difficult for the individual to improve the situation (see Figure 1).

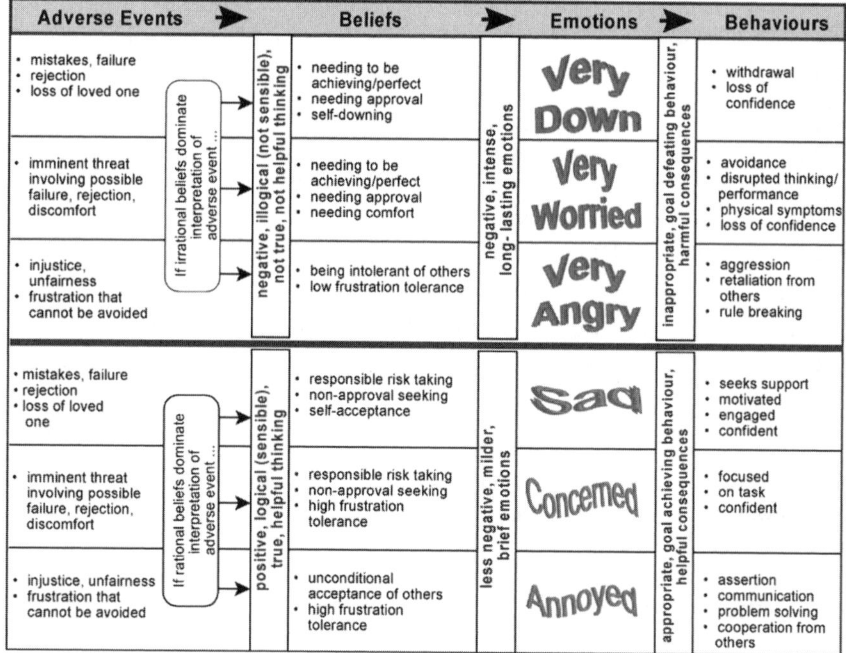

Adverse Events
Beliefs
Emotions
Behaviours
• mistakes, failure
• rejection
• loss of loved one
• imminent threat involving possible failure, rejection, discomfort
• injustice, unfairness
• frustration that cannot be avoided
If irrational beliefs dominate interpretation of adverse event ...
negative, illogical (not sensible), not true, not helpful thinking
• needing to be achieving/perfect
• needing approval
• self-downing
• needing to be achieving/perfect
• needing approval
• needing comfort
• being intolerant of others
• low frustration tolerance
negative, intense, long- lasting emotions
Very Down
Very Worried
Very Angry
inappropriate, goal defeating behaviour, harmful consequences
• withdrawal
• loss of confidence
• avoidance
• disrupted thinking/ performance
• physical symptoms
• loss of confidence
• aggression
• retaliation from others
• rule breaking
• mistakes, failure
• rejection
• loss of loved one
• imminent threat involving possible failure, rejection, discomfort
• injustice, unfairness
• frustration that cannot be avoided
If rational beliefs dominate interpretation of adverse event ...
positive, logical (sensible), true, helpful thinking
• responsible risk taking
• non-approval seeking
• self-acceptance
• responsible risk taking
• non-approval seeking
• high frustration tolerance
• unconditional acceptance of others
• high frustration tolerance
less negative, milder, brief emotions
Sad
Concerned
Annoyed
appropriate, goal achieving behaviour, helpful consequences
• seeks support
• motivated
• engaged
• confident
• focused
• on task
• confident
• assertion
• communication
• problem solving
• cooperation from others

FIGURE 1. The relationship of children's irrational beliefs to their emotions and behaviors (Bernard, 2004c)

Rational-emotive behavior theory states that irrational beliefs in the form of *absolutes* (shoulds, oughts, musts, needs) are the psychological core of children and adolescent emotional and behavioral problems (see Bernard, 2004a). For example,

- I must be successful.
- I need love and approval.
- The world should give me what I want comfortably, quickly and easily.
- People must treat me fairly and considerately.

Ellis indicates that there are a number of derivatives of absolutes that also contribute to the intensity of emotional problems including *awfulizing, I can't-stand-it-it is* and *global rating* (self, others, world). For example,

- It's awful to make mistakes.
- I can't stand to be criticized.
- I can't stand having to do boring homework.
- People who treat me badly are bad people and deserve severe punishment.
- School is stupid.
- I'm stupid.

As a result of their irrational beliefs, young people are prone to misrepresent reality (errors of inference including faulty conclusions, predictions). Sometimes, inferences are referred to as *automatic thoughts*. For example,

- I will always make mistakes.
- My teacher doesn't like me.
- All homework is boring.
- People always act unfairly to me.
- I'm a hopeless student.

The tendency for young people to selectively attend to and remain overfocused on the negative aspects of their environment is strongly influenced by their core irrational beliefs and feelings. For example, they pay attention to:

- Children who are not wanting to play with them
- Mistakes and other negative comments offered by their teacher concerning school work
- The boring aspects of homework
- Classmates who are mean to them
- Negative aspects of the way they look

Common Irrational Beliefs of Children include (Waters, 1982)

1. It's awful if others don't like me.
2. I'm bad if I make a mistake.
3. Everything should always do my way: I should always get what I want.
4. Things should come easy to me.
5. The world should be fair and bad people should be punished.
6. I shouldn't show my feelings.
7. Adults should be perfect.
8. There's only one right answer.
9. I must win.
10. I shouldn't have to wait for anything.

Common irrational beliefs of adolescents include (Waters, 1982):

1. It would be awful if my peers did not like me. It would be awful to be a social loser.
2. I should not make mistakes, especially social mistakes.
3. It's my parents' fault I am so miserable.
4. I can't help it. That is just the way I am, and I guess I'll always be this way.
5. The world should be fair and just.
6. It's awful when things don't go my way.
7. It's better to avoid challenges rather than risk failure.
8. I must conform to my peers.
9. I can't stand to be criticized.
10. Others should always be responsible.

Appendix A provides an analysis of common problems of childhood in terms characteristic irrational beliefs.

Bernard and Joyce (1984) have offered the view that the irrational tendency of self-downing/self-depreciation rather than being derivative of core absolutes is primary and that children and adolescents who have this trait put themselves down when they are faced with a variety of negative events be they mistakes, rejection, unfairness of "bad hair" days. A factor analysis of the Child and Adolescent Scale of Irrationality (Bernard and Cronan, 1999) yielded "Self-Downing" as one of a number distinct factors representing different patterns of irrational thinking.

TABLE 1. Results of a principal components analysis of the child and adolescent scale of irrationality (Bernard and Cronan, 1999).

Factor 1. Self-Downing (eigenvalue = 7.4)

2. People would act more fairly around me if I wasn't such a hopeless person. (.69)
6. I'm a failure when I don't succeed. (.66)
10. When things are boring, I think I'm a dull and uninteresting person. (.62)
14. I think I'm worthless if someone disapproves or rejects me. (.61)
18. If I wasn't so weak, things in my life would be easier. (.59)
22. When I feel nervous, uncomfortable or tense, I think it just goes to show what a hopeless person I am. (.59)
25. I think I'm a total fool when I fail at something important. (.57)
28. I think I'm hopeless when people reject me. (.46)

Factor 2. Intolerance of Frustrating Rules (eigenvalue = 3.9)

3. I can't stand having to behave well and follow rules. (.67)
7. I can't stand classmates who always follow the rules and behave well. (.65)
11. I think it's horrible to have to behave well all the time. (.60)
15. I shouldn't have to obey rules and behave well. (.54)
19. Classmates who always follow rules and behave well are jerks. (.54)
23. It's terrible to have to behave well all the time. (.54)
26. People shouldn't always have to obey rules and behave well. (.51)

Factor 3. Intolerance of Work Frustration (eigenvalue = 2.0)

1. When I start getting tired doing homework, I think I shouldn't have to do any more. (.56)
5. When I get frustrated with homework which is hard, I think it's unfair and that I shouldn't have to do anymore. (.56)
9. When it's time to get started with my homework, I think I need more time to get in the right mood. (.50)
13. The worst thing in life is having to work on things which are boring. (.48)
17. It's really awful to have lots of homework to do. (.43)
21. What I find impossible to put up with is having to do chores around the house when I could be having fun. (.43)
24. It's awful to have too much work to do and not enough time to do it. (.42)
27. I need to be rested and relaxed before I can work hard. (.40)

Factor 4. Demands for Fairness (eigenvalue = 1.6)

4. It's really horrible to be unfairly picked on by a teacher. (.54)
8. A teacher who unfairly picks on a student is totally rotten. (.50)
12. I can't stand classmates who act inconsiderately. (.40)
16. Teachers should really act fairly all the time.(.40)
20. A parent who acts negatively or critically toward his or her kids is totally rotten. (.40)

The Child and Adolescent Scale of Irrationality (CASI) (Bernard and Cronan, 1999) validated on 567 children and adolescents delimited through a principal components factor analysis four distinct dimensions of childhood irrationality (Cronbach alphas, internal reliabilities appear in parentheses): Total Irrationality (.90), Self-Downing (.84), Intolerance of Frustrating Rules (.82), Intolerance of Work Frustration (.72) and Demands for Fairness (.60) (see Table 2). The 28 items on the CASI (see Table 1) were worded in the form of statements and young people express the extent of their agreement or disagreement using a 5-point Likert scale, from 1 to 5 (1=strongly disagree, 2=disagree, 3=not sure, 4=agree, 5=strongly agree). Other statistical analyses of the CASI revealed: Total Irrationality correlated with Trait Anxiety (.40) and Trait Anger (.38); Self-Downing with Trait Anxiety (.55); Demands for Fairness with Trait Anger (.27); Intolerance of Frustrating Rules with Trait Anger (.38). Total Irrationality correlated with teacher ratings of student emotional problems (.30) while Intolerance of Frustrating Rules correlated with teacher ratings of student low effort on schoolwork (.32), behavior problems (.30) and emotional problems (.27).

Allied Cognitive-Behavioral Theories

Rational-Emotive Behavior Therapy practitioners who work with young people are cognizant of complimentary cognitive-behavioral theories and techniques (covered later in the chapter) that help define additional aspects of cognitive processing and functioning of young people that influence their mental health.

The Interpersonal Cognitive Problem Solving View of Maladjustment

While REBT views irrational beliefs and cognitive processing errors as the source of childhood disorders, other cognitive-behavior theorists have taken a different perspective and see emotional disturbance as resulting from a deficit in the cognitions that are usually present in well-functioning children. Spivack, Platt, and Shure (1976) and Shure (1996) have identified several interpersonal cognitive problem-solving skills. Their research focused on developing psychometric measures of these skills and correlating them with child psychopathology. Their research identified several skills in solving social problems that consistently distinguish psychopathological from normal populations. The most important skill they have uncovered is alternative-solution thinking (i.e., the number of different solutions that a child can generate to solve a specific practical problem). The second most important skill, consequential thinking, measures children's ability to predict the social consequences or results of their actions. Once children can generate alternatives and predict sequences, the next skills that seem to be important are the ability to anticipate problems and the implementation of a solution to plan around them. Spivak and his colleagues have termed these "means-end thinking."

Research suggests that attempts to teach children interpersonal, cognitive problem-solving skills can lead to reduced emotional upset and more adaptive behavior (Urbain and Kendall, 1980). Interpersonal, cognitive problem-solving skills can be effective for several reasons within the context of Wessler and Wessler's emotional episode model. Problem solving could occur after the inferences, the appraisals, or the affect. Effective problem-solvers may experience disturbed affect less often because (1) they distract themselves from the appraisal and thereby lift affect—as long as one is thinking about how to go about solving a problem, one is less likely to be entertaining catastrophizing ideas and therefore to become upset; (2) social-problem solving may bring about solutions to change the activating event and thereby eliminate the problem in the first place; and (3) thinking of alternative solutions may help one change one's appraisal of a negative event. People who believe they have options may be less likely to view events as awful or catastrophic.

Behavioral Disorders as Verbal Mediational Deficits

A variety of childhood disorders (e.g., aggression, hyperactivity, and impulsivity) have been characterized in the CBT literature in terms of verbal mediational deficits. Inappropriate behavior (excessive or insufficient action tendencies) is seen as deriving from the child's either thinking too quickly or not thinking at all. Meichenbaum (1977) characterized the thinking styles of these children in terms of three mediational deficiencies: (1) they may not comprehend the nature of the problem or the task and thus cannot discover what mediators to produce—a "comprehension" deficiency; (2) they may have the correct mediators within their repertoire but may fail to produce them spontaneously and appropriately—a "production" deficiency; and (3) the mediators that children produce may not guide their ongoing behavior—what a "mediational" deficiency.

There is evidence that verbal self-control strategies can be utilized by children to guide their ongoing behavior (Urbain and Kendall, 1980). Cognitive self-verbalization treatment programs are being designed to foster the acquisition both of specific skills and of more general reflective thinking strategies including those processes involved in the treatment of a variety of behavior disorders such as attention deficit/hyperactivity disorder (Hinshaw, 2000) and aggression (Lochman et al., 2000). By providing the child with skills that can be employed in problem situations, these programs appear to influence the inferences made (Step 4) by the child when initially faced with a difficult impersonal or interpersonal task. Equipped with a task-specific skill, the child may no longer underestimate his or her coping resources; a result would be a reduction in the affective stress that presumably would previously have been experienced (Step 6). Alternatively, adaptive task performance brings about self-perceived "need satisfaction," thereby reducing the frequency with which the child's demands are not fulfilled. It can be seen that both the interpersonal cognitive problem-solving and the verbal mediational perspectives tend to emphasize direct cognitive-behavioral solutions to childhood problems, whereas REBT is very much oriented toward emotional problem solving.

REBT Versus CBT

Is the use of REBT synonymous with the use of CBT when they are employed with children and adolescents? Not exactly, because, as has been shown in a paper, "Rational-Emotive Therapy and Cognitive Behavior Therapy: Similarities and Differences" (Ellis, 1980c), although general or non-preferential REBT is virtually synonymous with CBT, specific or preferential REBT is not. Preferential RET is what RET practitioners usually prefer to use, particularly with relatively bright, neurotic, and reasonably well-motivated clients. It includes a deep philosophical emphasis, a humanistic outlook, the seeking of a profound and maintained personality change, the use of active disputing techniques, the teaching of clients how to give up any kind of rating of their egos or their selves (and, instead, only how to rate their acts and performances), and the getting at and eliminating of secondary as well as primary sources of anxiety, anger and depression.

Although preferential REBT is highly suitable for many bright adolescents, it may require too much philosophical analysis and more of an application of rigorous scientific method than many average youngsters, not to mention most young children, is capable of fulfilling. In the case of younger children, non-preferential REBT, or general cognitive-behavior therapy, is usually employed. These clients are shown how they upset themselves with irrational and unrealistic beliefs; and they are sometimes taught how to actively dispute these beliefs and to figure out more rational philosophies by which to run their lives. But as they often resist this kind of teaching, and especially the internalization of a thoroughgoing scientific way of thinking, they are frequently provided with rational or coping statements (as explained in several succeeding chapters of this book) and are encouraged and reinforced for believing these more sensible beliefs.

Cognitive-behavior therapy subsumes a variety of methods that attempt to modify cognitive content and processes that support problem behavior. The main difference between CBT and REBT is that CBT does not attempt to modify the overall philosophy and assumptive world of clients through the use of disputational methods and other more didactic forms of direct discussion and psychoeducation. It appears that CBT is more problem-focused (or behavior-focused) and defines goals of treatment in terms of specifiable behavior change. REBT views problem behavior (and emotions) as symptomatic of an underlying belief system that constitutes the core of maladjustment. An elegant RET solution is conceived of as having been achieved when the client has adopted a more flexible, relativistic, and conditional outlook on life, which manifests itself in a more objective and empirically based reality-testing approach, in emotional reactions that are consistent with reality, and in self-enhancing, goal-directed behavior.

An elegant CBT solution involves the client's acquiring cognitive and metacognitive strategies not only for dealing with a presenting problem, but also for dealing with a range of stressful situations that may confront the client in the future. These general and conceptually based strategies may involve the client's learning to think (and act) more reflectively and to adopt a more systematic problem-solving approach to life's difficulties.

As emphasized in *Rational-Emotive Therapy and Cognitive Behavior Therapy* (Ellis, 1984), REBT is not only a form of psychological treatment (or training) that is comprehensive and multimodal, and that is cognitive, emotive, and behavioral (and not *strictly* cognitive) in its methods, but it is also wedded to an interactional theory of human personality and personality disturbance. It emphasizes that humans, especially when they once acquire language and internalized speech, almost never experience *pure* thoughts, feelings, or actions. What we (somewhat arbitrarily) *call* their thinking, their emoting, and their behaving invariably seems to coalesce and interact, so that their ideations influence their feelings and behaviors, their emotions influence their thoughts and behaviors, and their behaviors influence their thoughts and feelings. Therefore, to help effect both moderate symptom removal and profound personality transformation, REBT encourages the use of a wide variety of intellectual, affective, and activity-oriented techniques. And it assumes that although youngsters, because of their relatively immature stage of development, are especially influenced by affective and behavioral interventions, they are also highly susceptible to didactic, persuasive, information-giving, and other cognitive appeals. Showing the reader how to understand and use children's and adolescents' intellectual susceptibility to change is one of the main-though hardly the only-purposes of the material in this book.

Practical Considerations In The Application Of Rebt To Childhood Disorders

This section provides many insights and advice that has emerged over the years from the REBT literature on how to use REBT with young populations.

It Is Not Just About Disputing Irrational Beliefs

Much of the focus of REBT treatment is focused on disputing irrational beliefs and developing rational beliefs/self-statements. While this approach sounds "one eyed" cognitive to the exclusion of emotions and behaviors it is not. Practitioners need to be aware that Ellis and REBT have always recognized that there is no such thing as pure cognition and that there is an organic interrelatedness of cognition, emotion and behavior; they are interdependent and one rarely occurs without the other.

When disputing irrational beliefs that contribute to underachievement, anxiety, unhappiness, anger and/or work avoidance, the REBT practitioner is equally concerned with changes in the young person's emotions and behaviors. For example, let us suppose you have identified that a core belief an underachiever you are working with is low frustration tolerance; namely, "Everything I do in school should be fun and exciting and if it isn't, I shouldn't have to do it." This belief results not only in work avoidance, but when forced to have to do school work, the young person can experience high degrees of anger. When disputing LFT, you will also want to target emotional and behavioral change. It is important to teach young people the link between their beliefs/thoughts and their emotions and behaviors in order for the disputing of irrational beliefs not to merely result in intellectual insight and understanding ("I understand what you are saying but I still don't feel any differently about doing homework."). In disputing, it is very important to always discuss with young people the empowering aspects of their thinking and self-talk on their emotions and behaviors and how rational thinking goes along with healthy emotions and goal-directed behavior.

The REBT goal when working with young people with psychosocial and mental health problems is not only the elimination of irrational beliefs (and associated unhealthy emotions and self-defeating behaviors), it is also in helping the young person acquire, strengthen and practice rational beliefs. In the ABCDE model of REBT, the "D" stands for dispute and the "E" stands for a new rational effect that includes rational beliefs and rational self-statements. Sometimes, this phase of REBT, psycho-education that supports rational beliefs, is not sufficiently incorporated in practice. This author has spent hours discussing with Albert Ellis whether, indeed, REBT's goal is eliminating the irrational or developing the rational (Bernard, 2001). In initial discussions with Ellis, he expressed the view that since young people receive constant reinforcement of rational beliefs from parents and teachers, the greater need was to eliminate through discussions and disputing irrational beliefs which he considers to be the barriers to learning and well-being. We discussed at length the idea that in today's irrational world with academic standards and grades are muscling out teachers' and parents' time for instilling rational messages in young people. I asserted that many of today's children are being underexposed to rational beliefs and, as a consequence, their rational beliefs tend to be lightly held and their irrational beliefs are the more strongly held ones. At the end of our discussions, we agreed that in therapy as well as in our daily interactions with young people, we need to help eliminate the irrational *and* develop the rational. Three of the core rational beliefs that REBT puts forward as central to mental health, success in school and life and positive relationships are:

1. Self-Acceptance

Teach children to never rate themselves in terms of their behavior and to separate judgments of their actions from judgments of self-worth. Encourage them to acknowledge and accept responsibility for their *traits* and *behaviors*—both good and bad—without evaluating *themselves* as good or bad. Help combat children's tendencies towards self-downing by reminding them they are made up of many good qualities (and some that are not so helpful) and that they do not lose their good qualities when bad things happen. Explain to children that all human beings are capable and likeable in their unique ways and, therefore, it is good for children to accept themselves unconditionally without having to prove themselves.

2. High Frustration Tolerance

Teach children that in order to be successful, they will sometimes have to do things that are unpleasant and not fun. Explain that frustration and obstacles are a normal part of life and that it is not helpful for them to think that life including school and homework should always be fun and exciting. Help children combat their belief that they cannot stand things they do not like and that they must have what they want immediately. Reinforce them for frustration tolerance and delay of gratification.

3. Acceptance of Others

Teach children never to rate people by their actions and to separate judgments of people's actions from judgments about their self-worth. This does not mean they like everything another person does. It means disliking another person's *traits* and *behaviors* without judging the whole of the *person* as bad. Help children develop the attitude of *preferring* for people to behave fairly and considerately but never to demand and insist that people *must* act that way every minute of the day. Explain that people make mistakes.

It also needs to be emphasized in this discussion that when discussing rational beliefs with young people, it is most important to, again, bring to their attention how their rational thinking and self-talk are psychologically linked to their feelings and behaviors. Again, in order to avoid making REBT merely an intellectual exercise, in elaborating on rational beliefs and in your selection of homework activities, you will want to provide young people with opportunities for understanding and integrating cognitive change, with emotional and behavioral change (e.g., "When you think this way, what impact does it have on how you feel and behave?").

Emotional Versus Practical-Problem Solving

There are two types of problems that young people can experience: emotional and practical. Waters (1982) differentiates between these problems as follows:

> Emotional problems are generated by self and goal defeating belief systems and are characterized by extremely uncomfortable, stagnated feelings, while practical problems are realistic difficulties in the environment resulting in unsatisfactory situations, which one wishes to change (p. 570).

In children and adolescents, common emotional difficulties include anger, anxiety, and self-downing (depression), and practical problems are not having enough friends, getting into fights, being teased and not knowing what to do. It is frequently but not always the case that practical problems are accompanied by emotional problems and that, indeed, emotional problems often originate in practical problems.

By way of example, let us see the variety of ways of helping George, who has no friends. There are several ways. The first would be to play camp counselor and introduce George to new friends. This would be very helpful to George and he would probably greatly appreciate it. However, it would not help George to learn to cope with fearful situations. This approach is called in REBT the *practical solution.* On its own, it is usually inadvisable because it in no way helps the young person to develop psychological coping mechanisms for managing his anxiety when facing difficult problems in the future, as he or she most certainly will. Practical solutions change the stimuli or activating event. Although they are often effective in changing children's specific emotional episodes, they are palliative. If George were again in a strange environment, he would have the same problem and become upset once again. Stop and think of your own interventions with young people and those of your colleagues. How often have you seen therapists opt for the practical solutions and miss the opportunity to teach the child how to learn emotional self-management and rational thinking skills. Practical-problem solving assumes that the child cannot learn to deal with the adversity on her or his own. Carried to extremes, it could become a self-fulfilling prophecy because the child would get no practice in solving emotional problems.

A second strategy to help George in the situation mentioned above is to reduce his anxiety. There are two primary ways that REBT teaches a young client to resolve emotional difficulties. At the inferential stage in Wessler and Wessler's diagram of emotions, George believes that the other young people will never like him. How does he know this to be true? He did not try to meet them. He most probably has had other friends in other places. Few kids in his past have actively disliked him. One could go on eliciting from George reasons that others would not like him and put these to the empirical test. If George became convinced that others would like him if he introduced himself, there would be no reason for him to be anxious. He might then attempt to behave differently and actively initiate social contact. We call this the *empirical solution* because it attempts to test empirically the truth of inferential thinking by collecting data. George is probably distorting reality in believing that others would have such a negative view of him, and the therapist could show George how his thinking in this manner is untrue. Although the empirical solution deals with changing George's emotional reaction to the situation, it is considered, in REBT, an inelegant solution. It is considered inelegant because it challenges the inferences and not the appraisal (absolute and evaluations). George's inferences could be true—if not this time, maybe the next. Suppose that in his next move he encounters peers who dislike him for his race, creed, color, or any other characteristic.

No amount of empirical challenging may change his emotional devastation at being disliked if the other children's negative prejudice against him is real. The *elegant solution* in REBT challenges the appraisal, the evaluation, or the meaning that a person applies to the inferences and conclusions he or she draws. In this way, George can learn to reduce his anxiety in this situation and other like situations that may occur. We would dispute his absolute that he needs his peers to like and approve of him all the time and help him shirt his appraisal to one of preferring but never needing approval to survive. We would challenge his evaluation that it is awful if others do not like him and teach him not to blow the hassles and misfortunes of life out of proportion. Even if he would rather be with them, he can go about his business, do the next most enjoyable thing, and not catastrophize and not put himself down. If George believes that it would not be terrible if others did not like him and that his value as a person cannot be defined by his peer popularity, he might also take the risk of asking them to play with him because the stakes would be lowered considerably for rejection.

Building the Therapeutic Alliance/Working Relationship

It has always been recognized by child-oriented and adolescent-oriented REBT practitioners that a warm, supportive, empathic relationship with young people is a necessary condition for the full benefits of REBT interventions to be realized. REBTers do not jump in and start disputing before some time has been spent getting to know the young person, listening, and offering unconditional positive regard. While REBT practitioners hold firm hypotheses concerning the types of cognitive issues that are involved in specific problems, they gently and tactfully "school" young people as to the role of their thinking in their feelings and behaviors. For example, we avoid as much as possible telling the angry adolescent that all their problems are a result of their "attitudes" and if only they would change their attitudes, their problems would evaporate. (See Table 2 for suggestions culled from the REBT literature of building rapport when using REBT).

Rapport building and developing the therapeutic alliance are keys to effective REBT practice. REBT practitioners are quite explicit in explaining their roles, the goals of therapy/counseling as well as the tasks each party (practitioner and young person) have responsibility for.

In REBT, the practitioner is conscious of the need to establish a therapeutic alliance (Bordin, 1979; Dryden, 1987) between practitioner and the young person. The three components of the therapeutic alliance are incorporated in REBT work with young people are found in a) the bond established between practitioner and client, b) the goals set jointly by them, and c) the tasks undertaken by each to bring about change (Bernard and Joyce, 1993).

DiGiuseppe and his colleagues (DiGiuseppe, 1995; DiGiuseppe et al., 1996) presented a cognitive behavioral approach to establishing the therapeutic alliance in those children and adolescents who begin therapy in what Prochaska and DiClemente's (1981) refer to as the precontemplative stage. In this stage, the

TABLE 2. Suggestions for developing a positive relationship with younger clients (Bernard, 2004a).

1. Be empathic no matter how trivial child's concern/problem appears to be ("That must be hard."). Do not be too quick to move into problem analysis/solving.
2. Be non-judgmental (unconditional acceptance) of client when you hear about problem even when you disapprove of their behavior (if client broke law, engaged in sexual behavior). Do not feel you are judging them.
3. Respect resistance and move forward to build trust. When experienced, move slower and back off from interpretation. Use more indirect methods (e.g., puppets; reference to problems of a friend).
4. Be patient as trust can be a slow process.
5. Show genuine interest in them. Ask them to share personal stories. Ask them to bring in work and other prize possessions to show you (e.g., CDs, books, yearbooks, artwork).
6. Do not act like a teacher or parent. For example, do not communicate a negative tone about their behavioral infractions. Do not try to coerce change.
7. Build trust through mutual self-disclosure.
8. In early sessions, listen, listen and reflect back feelings and information.
9. Do not become over-involved emotionally; maintain objectivity.
10. As a rule, do not give treats.
11. Especially with adolescents, work on winning their respect rather than their approval. You may have to ask them to do things they do not want to do.
12. Do not be afraid to communicate with humor (e.g., exaggeration); OK to laugh about a client's or your own behavior, but never at the client.
13. Help client develop sense that you are on their side (not side of parents or teachers).

child does not see the need to change. According to DiGiuseppe, unless the practitioner can move the young person to thinking about change and, then, taking action, cognitive behavioral interventions are doomed. DiGiuseppe advocates asking clients in a Socratic fashion to assess the consequences of their emotional and behavioral responses. This helps clients identify the negative consequences for their maladaptive emotions and behaviors. A technique called the motivational syllogism may be then used to reach agreement on the goals of therapy. The elements of this motivational syllogism are as follows:

1. My present emotion is dysfunctional (for aggressive children, the dysfunctional emotion is primarily their anger).
2. An acceptable alternative emotional script exists for this type of activating event (e.g., annoyance).
3. Giving up the dysfunctional emotion and working toward feeling the alternative one is better for me.
4. My beliefs cause my emotions; therefore, I will work at changing my beliefs to change my emotions.

The initial sessions of REBT with young people combine relationship building with data gathering concerning the young person's issues. The key ingredient to success during the initial stages of REBT work is for the young person to know you are on their side. Once your trust is gained, it is much easier to educate young people concerning power of their thinking including the difficult process of identifying, challenging and changing irrational self-talk and beliefs. Table 3 presents some suggestions for the content of Session 1 that incorporates elements discussed above.

Principles of Assessment

RET assessment can be seen as being composed of a *problem identification* and a *problem analysis* phase. Problem identification involves determining whether, in fact, a problem exists and, if it does, who owns it. Children and

TABLE 3. Suggestions for session one (Bernard, 2004a).

1. Define role of counselor (problem solver: "I am good at helping you if you have hassles with others, worries about the future, hurt feelings.") Reassure clients that they are not crazy and that having a problem is not "bad"—everyone has problems—especially when growing up. Explain that just as they go to a medical doctor when they have a cold, break a leg, they go to a counselor when they have a social, behavioral or emotional problem. Explain that counseling is a safe place to explore feelings and thoughts.
2. Establish confidentiality limits with parents and child. Ask young clients whether there is anything they have shared with you that they do not want someone else to know.
3. Share reason for referral.
4. If you sense child's reluctance/resistance to being referred, normalize feelings ("I sense that you don't want to be here and that's all right. But because someone else thinks there is something wrong, maybe I can help.")
5. Share information about the counseling process you are using. Explain that the two of you will be working together helping the young person deal with particular problems. Indicate that for most sessions, you will be asking them to talk about their thoughts, feelings, behaviors and you will be showing them different ways to manage their feelings so that when something bad happens, they do not feel so upset and how to feel better. Indicate you will be asking them to perform various "experiments" during the week that can provide them with additional ways to solve problems. Stress that it is very important that the young client carry through with the practice involved in conducting the experiments. Indicate the number of counseling sessions.
6. Normalize problem and communicate hope ("Lots of kids lose their temper a lot, have big worries, get very down." "And lots of kids as learn how to feel better and not be so upset. We can come up with some ideas to deal with this. (With adolescents, share information about typical adolescent development).
7. Start off by finding out about interest/hobbies/skills/talents of client including pets/family members ("teach me about you"). Ways to do this: write a story; draw a picture if family, and acrostic poem. Consider using a "get acquainted" structured activity (share something personal).
8. Ask one question about presenting problem ("I heard you are being treated badly by a classmate?") and then paraphrase/summarize answer. Gain agreement. Do not minimize problem nor dramatize.
9. Ask: "How does that make you feel?" Have client put into words his/her feelings and reflect feelings. Offer emotional labels when client seems unable to put feelings into words.
10. Summarize happening and feelings/behaviors. Gain agreement. Indicate that you would like to be able to talk with client about ways to make things better.
11. Review what clients can say to their classmates in response to the question: "Where were you?" during time client was with you (possible answer: "I was getting extra help with my homework"). Have client select what she/he feels comfortable saying.

adolescents are frequently referred to a practitioner by their parents (or teachers). The initial task of the practitioner is to determine whether the youngster, the parents, and/or the teachers are actually demonstrating an emotional or a behavioral problem. During problem identification, it is important for the practitioner to be aware of developmental, peer, and cultural-familial norms in the area of concern. It is quite common for the problem to be shared by both a child and his or her significant others.

Once it has been established that a problem does exist and the problem ownership has been determined, the problem analysis phase of REBT assessment takes place. The practitioner may interview the children, the parents, and the teachers to determine the extent of their respective cognitive, emotive, and behavioral disturbance including a delimitation of emotional and practical problems.

Different Targets of Emotional Assessment

Different problematic emotions and concomitant behaviors typically examined in REBT child assessment include:

- feeling down (including feeling angry with self)
- feeling anxious (worried)
  - social anxiety
  - performance anxiety (including perfectionism, test anxiety)
  - discomfort anxiety (anxious about feeling anxious-physiological arousal)
- feeling angry with another
- low frustration tolerance/procrastination (work avoidance, angry about having to do something that is boring)
- relationship problems
- secondary emotional problems
  - feeling down about primary emotional/behavioral problem (e.g., being down, procrastination)

Typical questions that REBT practitioners put to young clients to assess their feelings include:

- When _____ happened, what did you feel?
- What else did you feel?
- Using your Emotional Thermometer, when was the last time you got very angry/down/worried?
- What were you feeling inside when you felt very angry/down/worried?
- When you were very angry/down/worried, what did you do, how did you behave?
- What happened to you after you behaved in that way? What did other people say or do?

Sometimes, when you ask young clients about the degree of emotional upset they experienced when they were confronted with a negative event in the recent past, they might say: "Medium upset. Maybe a 5 out of 10 on the Emotional Thermometer." Unless you can identify a time when your client was extremely upset (e.g., 8–10 on the Emotional Thermometer) it is unwise to conclude that the client has an emotional problem or harbors irrational beliefs. To "get at" a more extreme emotional reaction of young clients, ask: "When was the last time you got extremely upset (really angry, anxious or down)—a time when you were getting close to the top of the Emotional Thermometer?"

In assessing dysfunctional cognitions in both children and their parents and teachers, interpretations of reality as well as appraisals of interpretations are examined. Waters (1982) suggested four main problem areas to assess:

1. Is the client distorting reality?
2. Is the client evaluating situations in a self-defeating way?
3. Does the client lack appropriate cognitions?
4. Does the client lack practical problem-solving skills?

With younger clients, instead of using the traditional ABC framework to represent and explain important relationships, the HTFB framework is frequently employed to make more concrete these same relationships in both REBT assessment and treatment:

Happening ⟶ Thinking ⟶ Feeling ⟶ Behaving

It is often a good idea to write down for young clients a summary of the assessment data you are gathering. The following headings that can be written on the board or a piece of paper:

Happening ⟶	Thinking ⟶	Feeling ⟶	Behaving
John teases me	Everyone teases me. I have no friends. I'll never have friends. This is terrible. I'm a loser	down (9/10)	withdraw
John teases me	This is unfair. He shouldn't do this. I can't stand this. He's a real _____.	anger (10/10)	fight

The order of assessment questions using the HTFB framework is as follows:

1. Identify a specific Happening (day, place, person, task).
2. Assess different feelings client had about the Happening and assess using the Emotional Thermometer, the intensity of each.
3. Assess behavioral reactions that accompany feelings.

4. Select one feeling at a time to work on. Then, assess what client was thinking looking for errors of inference (faulty conclusions, predictions), absolutes (shoulds, oughts, musts, needs) and derivative evaluations (awfulizing, I-can't-stand-it-it is, global rating). Be thorough in eliciting absolutes and derivative evaluations using *inference chaining* and *deductive interpretation* questioning.

Once you have assessed the full range of inferences, absolutes and evaluations, summarize and validate the information you have gathered. Say: "So let me get this straight, you have said that when __________ happens and you think __________, __________, __________, and __________, you get very __________ (feeling) and you behave __________." Is that right?

If young client does not agree with your summary, return to conduct further assessment.

The chapters that follow reveal a variety of elicitational techniques that child-oriented REBT practitioners have developed to assess problem cognitions, emotions, and behavior of children as young as 4-year-old. Problem identification and analysis result in a specification and ordering of the goals of therapy; of the types of cognitive, emotive, and behavioral changes to be made; and of who will participate in therapy (one or both parents, child, parents and child) (Waters, 1982).

Treatment Goals and Methods

REBT is primarily oriented to teaching skills for the solving of emotional problems. Its aim is to have clients of all ages acquire an attitude of emotional responsibility, that is, to take manage their emotions through the operation of rational thinking and logical reasoning. The main goal of emotional problem solving is, to teach children and adolescents how to change unhealthy to healthy feelings.

REBT accomplishes this goal for younger children by helping them to become more aware of their emotions and thoughts and to develop a conceptual-linguistic system for expressing their emotions. They are taught to differentiate between feelings and thoughts and are given practice in verbalizing sets of rational self-statements. Older children and adolescents are taught the ABC's of REBT and the difference between rational and irrational beliefs, as well as how to dispute irrational concepts and beliefs. In addition, the practitioner helps young clients to correct their perceptions of reality.

Waters (1982) has made the following suggestions for working with young clients who have emotional problems.

1. Determine whether the client wishes to keep or give up the feeling and point out the consequences of each.
2. Have the client keep track of the frequency, location, and outcome of emotional reactions.

3. Challenge and dispute irrational beliefs, concepts, and self-statements and generate rational alternatives.
4. Discuss REBT concepts of self-acceptance, demandingness, approval-seeking, catastrophizing, intolerance, and condemnation.
5. Use rational-emotive imagery to practice changing the feeling.
6. Encourage client to focus on the present and avoid focusing on the past or future.
7. Encourage client to answer the question: "Where does this negative thought get me?"
8. Brainstorm with the client about other options in handling feelings.
9. Encourage client to observe how others handle their emotions.
10. Encourage client to reward herself or himself for handling problem emotions.
11. Teach relaxation, assertion, and prosocial skills. (pp. 242–245)

There are five main REBT intervention strategies used with young clients to restructure faulty inferences (predictions, conclusions), absolutes (shoulds, oughts, needs, musts) and evaluations (awfulizing, I can't stand it, global rating of self, other, world) (Bernard, 2004a) including (a) empirical disputation, (b) logical disputation, (c) semantic disputation, (d) rational self-statements (with/without disputing), and (e) rational-emotive imagery. Each of these cognitive change methods will now be described.

Empirical disputation involves an examination of evidence to determine whether the client's inferences and evaluation are reality based "Where is the evidence to support your idea that no one likes you?" "Where is the evidence that you are an idiot because you received a poor grade?" "Where is it written that you must do everything perfectly?" "Is it true that you must?" *Empirical analysis* is a common form of empirical disputation and involves you and the young client designing a simple experiment to gather data to test the client's interpretation of reality (conclusions, predictions). For example, in the case of George, a 10–year-old, who is quite down about being teased by a few of his classmates, one of his faulty inferences contributing to him feeling so down is: "No one likes me."

To use empirical disputation, you can provide George with a class list and have him go down the list noting those classmates whom he thinks like him or could be friends with him. If the list contains a few check marks, such data provides the evidence to George that his assumption of "No one likes me" is false. He can then be helped to generate a new rational self-statement such as: "Even though people are teasing me, I still have friends."

Another example of *empirical analysis and disputation* that you could utilize to help George cope with teasing and his belief "No one likes me" is as follows. You could have George conduct the following experiment. You could generate a list of common peer behaviors that are indicative that someone is liked (e.g. people say hello, invited to play at recess, someone helps you with your work, someone sits by you at lunch). You could then assign George the task of recording each instance during the ensuing week when he notices one of his classmates engaging in behaviors on the list. If over a week's time, George has recorded instances of positive peer behavior directed towards him, he would, once again, have evidence to dispute his thinking that "No one likes me." You would then go on to dispute his deeper irrational evaluations: "I need to be liked by everyone. It is awful to be teased. I can't stand it. I'm a nobody."

Logical disputation involves an examination of whether the conclusions the client is drawing and the expectations clients formulate are sensible and logically follow from the facts ("Does it make sense to conclude you are never going to be able to pass a math exam?" "Does it follow that because someone acts badly towards you from time to time that he is a totally bad person in every respect?" "Just because to want to succeed in your schoolwork, does it follow logically that it must happen?").

Semantic disputation involves you providing young clients with an objective definition of the words and phrases they employ in thinking about and evaluating their world. For example, if you have determined through your assessment that your client believes that "It is awful to be thought badly of by my peers," you can semantically dispute this using a Socratic style as follows: "Well, 'awful' really means the very worst things that could happen to you. Is being thought badly of by one or more of your classmates really the worst thing that could happen to you?" Another example of *semantic disputation* is seen in the following exchange between a therapist and young client.

T: So, let me get this straight. When, you were not invited to the party at Mary's house and your friend was, you thought of yourself as a 'loser.' Is that what you thought?

C: Yeah, I mean like Dina and Stephanie were invited.

T: Well, I would upset myself about what happened, too. But, if you don't want to get so down, let's examine what you were telling yourself and see if it is rational.

C: OK.

T: When you think of yourself as a loser, the word 'loser' means more than "I am not popular enough with Mary to get invited to her party."

The word 'loser' means loser in everything you have done, are doing and will be doing. It means your total essence is one of being a loser. Now, is your use of the word "loser" really true to this meaning?

Empirical, logical and semantic disputing can be used to dispute both inferences and evaluations.

In teaching your young clients about the process of disputing, you can explain that disputing involves asking three questions about one's thinking:

1. Is what I am thinking true? Is there evidence to support what I am thinking?
2. Is my thinking logical? Does it make sense to think this way?
3. Does it help me to think this way? Does my thought help me to achieve my goals and manage my emotions?

You can explain that when a client answers "No" to any one of these questions, she/he should with your help, try to change the thought to one that is true, sensible and helpful.

There are two main disputational styles you can use to help young clients change their irrational beliefs into more rational ones. Using a *didactic style,* the therapist directly explaining to young clients where their emotions come from and the differences between rational and irrational beliefs. This will include a mini-lecture as to why a belief is irrational. An example of a didactic dispute is as follows:

"You are saying that you can't stand it when your brother chooses not to play with you. Now, you have survived up into today even after being excluded by your brother. I think you can see there is no evidence to support your idea."

The *Socratic style* involves the therapist drawing information from young clients using a series of leading questions rather than by direct lecturing. This method helps young clients think through things themselves rather than just accept the therapist's viewpoint. Examples of such questions are: "In looking over your 12 years of life, is there any evidence you can think of that shows that you cannot stand it when your brother chooses not to play with you? If there is no evidence, what can you conclude? As clients become familiar with disputing, move from a didactic style of disputing where you explain to the client why his/her thinking is irrational, to a more Socratic style of disputing.

Be clear that the irrational beliefs (inferences, absolutes, evaluations) that you dispute are only those that you have initially identified and validated when you assessed your young client's thinking. Make sure your young client accepts that she/he possesses the specific irrational belief you are disputing.

In disputing young clients' "shoulds", validate their "preferences." Say, for example, 'While I quite agree with you that it is preferable that your brother treats you nicely, I'm not sure that it makes sense to believe he should and must always be that way and that you can't stand it when he is unfair." Avoid the mistake of providing clients with new rational self-statements and beliefs without first showing them how their original irrational thoughts and beliefs were not true, sensible and helpful. What follows are suggestions for disputing different irrational beliefs of children and adolescents.

Disputing "Needs"

Young clients prone to anxiety oftentimes mistakenly believe that they *need* to be successful and/or *need* the approval of others. As success and acceptance ebbs and flows, such clients will experience frequent periods of uncertainty and anxiety in growing up. And if they have a tendency to put themselves down, they will also experience episodic periods of feeling down and depressed. A standard REBT didactic dispute used with these clients involves you explaining the difference between "wants" and "needs." You can ask your client to identify real human needs (e.g., food, water, clothing, shelter). You can ask young clients whether achievement and approval are things people need for survival or are merely desirable.

Once your client can differentiate true needs from wants, you can help them restructure their beliefs to:

While I would prefer to be successful, I don't need to be successful.

While I prefer to be liked and approved of, I don't need to be liked and approved of.

Disputing "Self-Downing"

To dispute self-downing, you will want to show young clients how their thinking "I'm hopeless, a loser" does not make sense and is not true. You can begin by having your young client come up with a range of positive and negative traits using a self-concept circle divided into segments with pluses and minuses in each segment. Once completed, ask young client "Does it make sense to think because something bad happened (e.g., poor grade, teased, rejection) that you are totally bad?" "Do you lose all your positive qualities when you make something bad happen?"

Discuss the concept of *human fallibility*. Indicate that everyone is born as a mistake maker and, as such, it never makes sense to think "I must not make mistakes" as mistakes are inevitable.

Teach the following ideas to help engender both *self-acceptance* and *other-acceptance*: (1) Every person is complex, not simple, (2) I am complex, not simple, (3) Every person is made up of many positive and negative qualities, (4) I am made up of many positive and negative qualities, (5) A person is not all good or all bad because of some of his or her characteristics, (6) I am not all good or all bad, (7) When I only focus on the negative characteristics of a person, I feel worse about the person, (8) When I only focus on my negative qualities, I feel worse about myself, (9) Focusing only on the negative qualities of someone else and thinking he is totally bad is irrational. People who do the wrong thing also have other positive qualities. (10) Only focusing on my negative qualities and concluding 'I am hopeless' is irrational. Even when I do the wrong thing, I still retain my positive qualities."

Another successful technique for disputing self-downing is to ask a young client: "Would you put a friend of yours down because she didn't do well in a subject or wasn't invited to a party? Would it make sense to think that she was a total loser?" Once young client agrees ask: "Well then, why are you putting yourself down because of what happened. If you would not put your friend down, does it make sense to put yourself down?" Explain that a person's worth cannot be calculated from a person's performance.

You can also use an analogy to make a similar point. Ask: "Would you junk a car if it had a flat tire?" When the young client can see that it would not make sense to do so, you can help him begin to see that junking himself when something bad happens does not make sense.

For children who are depressed due to perceived loss of love from a parent through divorce, abuse or abandonment, gather evidence (instances of loving behavior) to prove or disprove the automatic thoughts "My parent doesn't love me." If it appears that there is no evidence of loving behavior on the part of the child's parent, be prepared to dispute the child's irrational belief that he needs his parent's love, that he will not be able to be happy without it and that he **is unlovable.**

Disputing "Low Frustration Tolerance/I Can't Stand-it-It-Is"

If you discover in your assessment that your client believes she/cannot stand an event occurring (e.g., specific homework to be done, being criticized by a teacher, staying in on a Saturday night), combine semantic with empirical disputing.

Semantic disputing: Explain to your client that "I can't stand it" literally means—dictionary definition—that she/he cannot exist, live in the presence of the negative activating event. Combine with Empirical Disputing: "Now, do you have any evidence that you cannot survive in the presence of _____? Will it kill you? Will you have a heart attack? Will your eyeballs fall out? Will you faint? Have you survived so far?"

Discuss with your young client that thinking "I can't stand it" often enough creates a situation where she/he starts believing it without question. You can say: "Sometimes, you react physically as though you will actually die. Now, where is the evidence you cannot stand it? How often have you said 'I can't stand it'—and yet you're still alive?" Explain to your young client that if the statement "I can't stand it" is repeated often enough, she/he may feel something awful is going to happen. Indicate that she/he cannot trust this feeling or feeling you cannot stand it.

Help your young clients come up with rational self-statements to replace their "I can't-stand-it-it is": "Even though I do not like this, I can put up with the situation and feeling this way." Use the phrase, "end of the world" to show the client she/he is awfulizing. Ask: "Would it be the end of the world?" results in young clients seeing that while the event might be bad and a disadvantage, it is not the worst thing that could happen. And "It's awful" means that it is <u>so</u> bad that it absolutely must not happen. But it <u>must</u> happen if it actually does happen, no matter how bad it is.

Disputing "Awfulizing"

The tendency to blow things out of proportion, to make mountains out of molehills, is characteristic of people of all ages. Make young clients aware that they are "awfulizing". Use the "catastrophe scale" exercise (see Table 4). On a blackboard or large sheet of paper, have the young client list all the catastrophes she/he can think of (given the current state of catastrophic events in the world, this should be easy). After listing, 9/11, other terrorist attacks, war, natural disasters, you can bring up one more event; the young client's complaint (e.g., Horace called my mother a bad name). It may not be necessary to point out that the event while bad, does not belong on the same list.

Disputing "Global Rating of Another Person"

There are a number of irrational beliefs of young clients that contain the component of "mistake-making" ("I'm a failure if I make a mistake." "Adults should be perfect." "I shouldn't make mistakes, especially social mistakes."). It is often the case that young clients referred for anger management and behavioral problems believe that people who are in positions of authority (parents, teachers) *should* never make mistakes (act unfairly). Any child referred for perfectionism and low self-esteem mistakenly equate mistakes with self-worth.

TABLE 4. The catastrophe scale (Bernard, 2004a).

Directions: Think back to the last time you were *extremely* angry, worried, and/or down about something that had happened or was about to happen. Using your Emotional Thermometer, think of a time when you were 8, 9 or 10. Write the event in the space below:

____

____

At the time you were extremely upset, how bad was it for you that the event or situation had happened or was about to happen? Place a mark to show how you were thinking *at the time* you were very upset. On a scale of 1 to 100, how bad was it for you at the time the bad event was happening or was about to happen?

____

0 10 20 30 40 50 60 70 80 90 100

not bad bit bad bad very bad awful, terrible

Now, come up with a list of things that could happen to you or in the world that you would consider to be: catastrophic (awful terrible), very bad, bad, and a bit bad. Write them in the spaces below.

"Catastrophic" Events	"Very Bad" Events	"Bad" Events	"A Bit Bad" Events

Think again about the bad event that you listed in the first part of this activity. Which category would you now place it in? – catastrophic, very bad, bad, a bit bad

Important Point: We all sometimes make things worse than they are in our own thinking. Learning to keep things in perspective by not thinking that something is worse than it is helps you cope with bad events that can happen to you.

You will want to explain what Ellis calls "human fallibility" by making the following points: (a) All human being including adults and young people make mistakes, (b) No one is perfect, (c) Mistakes do not take away from a person's good qualities, (d) A person is not the same as his/her performance, (e) People are not totally bad because they make mistakes, (f) People who make mistakes do not deserve to be blamed and punished as people, and (g) The reasons why people make mistakes are: lack of skill, carelessness or poor judgment, not having enough information, unsound assumptions, feeling tired or ill, different opinion, and their own irrational thinking.

Draw a circle and divide it into eight pie-shaped wedges. Label every other pie wedge with a (+) or a minus (–). Have your young client complete this circle with regards to someone who they believe is a total no-good nik for acting so badly. Once completed, discuss whether having one or more (–)s indicates that the person is *totally* bad. Explain that it does not make sense to think that because a person acts badly, she/he is without any positive qualities. Encourage the young client to separate judgments of another person's behavior from judgments of their overall worth and value as a human being.

Helping Young Clients Deal with Difficult Parents

You will sometimes be working with a young client who is living with a parent who engages in highly critical behavior towards your young client. For example, I worked with a 17-year-old girl whose father (when drunk) would accuse her of sleeping around and being loose (which she was not). Now the issue here is that many young people will become understandably enraged with their parent for their disrespectful behavior. This rage often carries over to all aspects of the parent-child interaction. Also, when young people are enraged with one of their parents, they find it literally impossible to feel any love towards the parent. This can be quite damaging to the emotional health of the young person.

The REBT goal for helping young clients live with highly critical parents is, on the one hand, to help empower them to take any and all steps necessary to remove themselves from the environment where the abuse is likely to occur and to through assertion and other means, put an end to the abuse. As well, through teaching young people "other acceptance," you help the young person not rate their parent as totally bad for their bad behavior.

You can also dispute the young client's belief "My parent should act better" by asking the young client to provide an explanation for their parent's bad behavior. The explanations the young client generally comes up with (e.g., difficult childhood, poor relationship with parents, alcohol problems) can be used as evidence to dispute the young client's assertion that his/her parent *should* be any other way than she/he is. The elegant REBT solution is for the young client to adopt the view that "I would prefer better behavior from my parent and I will work hard to change the behavior and to protect myself. However, I will not condemn and punish my parent for his/her behavior."

The following is a list of "Tips for Disputing" culled from the REBT child therapy and adolescent therapy literature.

1. Be animated when disputing.
2. For children ages 8–12 years-old, make sure your disputes are concrete and tied to specific events. Rather than asking: "Where is the evidence you cannot stand people's disapproval?', it is more developmentally appropriate to ask: "Where is the evidence that you cannot stand being teased by Warren at 8.30am on Thursday morning?").
3. You will need to go over the same disputes over successive sessions.
4. Be patient. Sometimes, it takes a client three sessions before he can employ a dispute and new rational effect to modify his feelings in a problematic situation.
5. Check to make sure that your young client is not just agreeing with you for the sake of agreeing.
6. Ask young clients to put in their own words their understanding of one of your didactic disputes.

Rational self-statements are generated through a collaborative effort of the therapist and client and are provided to young clients for rehearsal and for use in subsequent situations that tend to occasion in the young client high levels of emotionality. The use of rational self-statements is the preferred cognitive intervention for use with clients younger than the age of 8. For young clients, you can use "green light" and "red light" or "positive thinking" and "negative thinking" rather than "rational thinking" and "irrational thinking."

For clients older than 8, rational self-statements also are generated collaboratively between you and your client after disputing has occurred and are the main technique for developing in clients new rational Effects (beliefs).

Examples of rational self-statements a young client can use to modify anger include: "People make mistakes. I can stand it when people call me names. It's not the end of the world. I don't have to get angry even though someone is angry with me or is acting badly. Nobody makes me angry. I make myself angry—when I could only make myself sorry with people's behavior. Anger is not cool."

Examples of rational self-statements a young client can use to modify feeling down include: "I have talent and am capable. I have friends. I am still me even when bad stuff happens. I don't need to be successful in everything I do. I'll just do the best I can. I don't need everyone to like me all the time. I can survive and still be happy."

Examples of rational self-statements a young client can use to modify anxiety include: "It's OK to mistakes. It does not have to be perfect. It's not the end of the world if someone does not want to play with me. I can handle getting nervous."

Examples of rational self-statements a young client can use to modify fear include: "I can be brave. I can take care of myself in the dark. The dark is a fun place to be. There are many good things in the dark."

Examples of rational self-statements to help a young client cope with a difficult teacher: "Oh well, there is my teacher acting stupidly again. I wish he was more fair. I'm irritated that he does not believe me when I tell him I've left my homework at home. He's probably having a bad day. No point in getting too angry."

Rational-emotive imagery (REI) involves asking the young client to recreate as vividly as possible in his/her mind a mental picture of a situation in which she/he experiences a very strong emotional response. When the feeling is as strong as possible, the young client is asked to change the feeling from being extreme (8, 9 or 10 on the Emotional Thermometer) to a more moderate level (3, 4 or 5); for example, from extreme worry to moderate worry and concern.

When the young client indicates he was able to reduce the intensity of his emotional response, you can ask: "How were you able to do so?" (For example): "What did you do to change your anger to feeling sorry or disappointed about the bad things that people did?" Emphasize how changes in thinking helped the young client reduce the level of upset.

Cognitive Behavior Rehearsal and Role Play

No matter how effective you have been in disputing, many clients of any age when they return to their real world tend to fall back into using their old habitual irrational beliefs and self-talk when confronted with difficulty. To assist clients to be successful in applying new rational beliefs and self-talk in their problematic environment between sessions, it is good for you to give them practice in role-playing their use within the therapy session.

If you are working on helping a young client manage his anger when being teased by a classmate, you could have the young client pretend to verbally harass you and you, playing the role of your client, would think out loud rational self-statements (e.g., "I prefer him not to act this way. I don't like this but I can stand it. This isn't the worst thing that could happen. I can tolerate this. He's not a totally no good kid.") while at the same time ignoring him. You can then reverse roles with you playing the role of the "teaser" and your client thinking out loud the rational self-statements while ignoring you. This can be repeated with the client progressively internalizing the rational self-statements into his/her thinking.

Practical-Problem Solving

Many young clients are in trouble or are less than happy because they do not have the skills to handle a situation. If someone teases them, they may not know of any way to handle the situation than to fight. Many young clients would like to make more friends but do not know how to get them. Clients who would like to achieve better results in school may be lacking in academic confidence, persistence and organizational skills. In your REBT assessment, you will want to assess deficits in their practical skills and spend time during your sessions developing them.

Rational-Emotive-Behavior Therapy is deemed successful when the client is successful in solving emotional and practical problems. Younger clients can be expected to solve independently a more limited range of problems than older and more capable clients. The degree of emotional responsibility that a young client is able to assume is also bound by cognitive-affective developmental limitations.

Working with Parents

When family dysfunction is contributing to specific problems in children, REBTers through various forms of psychoeducation work on developing parent's sense of how effective families operate.

> Well-functioning families are able to accomplish the task of aiding the personality and social development of their offspring. This difficult task is hampered when the system has unclear or inappropriate rules, boundaries, and/or hierarchy.
> In an effective family system the parents comprise a cooperative working team that operate as the "executive" unit of the system and the children are a subsystem of clearly secondary power and status. The tasks of the parental subsystem are to work cooperatively in socializing the children and to be able to modify rules and expectations as children grow older. The task of the sibling system is to offer its members the opportunity to negotiate, cooperate, share, compete and make friends with peers. (Woulff, 1983)

There are many ways in which REBT can be incorporated in work with parents. The type of involvement depends on multiple factors including age of child, developmental maturity, type of problem and family dynamics. From an REBT perspective, the goals for your work with parents of young clients with achievement, emotional, social and/or behavior problems may include:

1. Discussing with parents the importance of maintaining distinct boundaries in their family between the parental "executive" system who work together in socializing children and modifying rules and expectations as children get older and the "child-sibling" subsystem that offers its members opportunities to learn how to negotiate, compete and get along with each other and peers.
2. Discussing with parents different types of child-rearing practices including the importance of being kind and firm and the negative child outcomes associated with unkind/harsh and not firm parenting styles.
3. Discussing basic child management skills (e.g., positive reinforcement, use of rules, consequences).
4. Teaching parents the ABCs of emotions so that they can manage their own emotions (e.g., anger, anxiety, guilt, low frustration tolerance) including how to calm down.

5. Providing parents with suggestions for how they can influence their own child's problems (e.g., anger, down/depression, anxiety, perfectionism, fear, underachievement).
6. Discussing with parents the desirability of and methodology for teaching their children rational beliefs including self-acceptance, high frustration tolerance and acceptance of others.

Many parents are sensitive to what they perceive as criticism of themselves or their child. We recommend that you be careful to build positive relationships before being too confrontational and directive with parents. That being said, some parents appreciate being given directive advice in the first session. A quick way to make parents feel comfortable with you and to alleviate their guilt about their child's problem is to explain the following if appropriate. As we indicated earlier, we believe that 80 percent of children and adolescent's tendency to engage in irrational thinking and as a consequence hold on strongly to irrational beliefs may be biological and 20 percent may be environmental. When parents blame themselves for their children's problems, you can indicate that the reason why one child in the family seems to have many more problems than other children of the same parents is evidence that the propensity for problems observed in a child is oftentimes a function of the child's biological-genetic make-up inherited from members in the child's extended biological family. Therefore, parents shouldn't automatically think it is their fault that their child has a problem.

Still, some parents will offer resistance to discussing their problems with their child and becoming involved in interventions. Common beliefs leading to resistance include: (a) When my child hears us discussing problems, he becomes more upset and we cannot bear it when he is upset, (b) My child's problems are all my fault and responsibility and this proves I am a terrible parent, and (c) It is a sign of complete failure to have to come for help with family members.

A collaborative relationship with parents designed to explore the causes of their child's problems and collectively investigates solutions is a good first step in developing rapport. It is suggested that you explain to parents that over the years it has been found that people do not do difficult jobs well when they are very upset. Indicate that the job as a parent is very difficult. Propose that parents will do an even better job if they learn some ways to manage their own emotions relative to their child. Make the point that the more parents get upset with their children, the harder it is for them to change their behavior and overcome their problems. Suggest that you are going to help parents learn some strategies for staying calm. You can help dispel parents' misconceptions about therapy such as viewing it as treatment for sick or mentally ill people. Also, initially it is best to accept parents' thoughts and feelings unconditionally and as facts which may be reexamined later on. Also express genuine concern about the parent and child's progress without being emotionally dependent on this progress.

It is advised that you see the parents of children with oppositional-defiant, non-compliant behavior separately from their children. If a child's problem is emotional (e.g., relationship, depression), the initial session can be held with parents and the child.

When assessing parents, first determine who owns the problem—child, parent, or both. Consider the following questions: (a) Are the parent's child management skills sufficient for them to solve their child's problems? (b) Is the style of parenting (warm/kind; authoritarian/authoritative/permissive) contributing to the child's problems? (c) Are the parent's emotional problems about their child's problems contributing to the problem (e.g., anger, low frustration tolerance, guilt)? (d) Is the parent's relationship supportive enough and relationship with their child differentiated enough to provide sufficient guidance and control?

There are two aspects of parent assessment that you need to concern yourself with in working with parents. *Problem identification* determines the types of problems that exist within the family and the service (advice, direct assistance, or psychotherapy) that will be most appropriate to the parents and child. *Problem analysis* involves a more detailed consideration of parental thinking-feeling patterns, child-rearing philosophies, dysfunctional behavioral-emotional habits, the parental use of structure as well as positive reinforcements and negative consequences.

The goals of parent *problem assessment* are:

1. gather relevant information about the child and his/her problems (antecedent events, emotions/behaviors, consequences).
2. gather information about the role parents play in creating or maintaining "the problem" including inappropriate reactions (emotional/behavioral) to their child's problem behavior as well as deficits in child management strategies.
3. uncover faulty inferences, irrational beliefs, emotions that are sustaining maladaptive parental emotions and behaviors.
4. settle on a goal for changing dysfunctional parental emotions and behaviors as well as formulate a plan for modifying the child's problem behavior including the use of behavior modification and a change in the way the child thinks and feels.

In assessing parental frustration tolerance, remind yourself that parents of children who present with a variety of problems (e.g., ADHD, oppositional, anxious) require high frustration tolerance. Rather than being on the lookout for those parents who get easily frustrated by their children's minor infractions, assess the extent of parental high frustration tolerance that often accompanies children's very difficult behavior. Explaining to parents that they may lack sufficient degrees of high frustration tolerance from time to time is often more palatable to parents as well as valid than being told they have low frustration tolerance.

A large part of REBT parent work involves helping parents to modify their general style of parenting, overcome their own emotional problems so that they can both effectively implement child management strategies as well as to help their children think rationally about problems they are having. It is not likely that a child who has learned rational thinking from you will continue to maintain this change when his parents and family members still strongly reinforce and/or model irrational beliefs, emotions and behavior. If you determine that parents are too permissive, punitive or inconsistent in the way they raise their children, it is important to dispel the irrational and erroneous beliefs that lie behind those practices. *It does not appear necessary for parents to resolve any and all outstanding personal or marital problems before they can use child management strategies.*

Oftentimes, a necessary beginning point for work with parents is teaching them where necessary that their strong emotional reactions to their child and their child's behavior had better be modified before they can make any real progress is getting their child to change. REBT's parental psychoeducation begins with teaching parents emotional responsibility including how their beliefs about their children, themselves and their child-rearing attitudes largely determine how they feel and behave towards their child. It is not the problem and their child's behavior that causes their emotions and behaviors. It is also important to convince parents of a philosophy of child rearing which emphasizes the desirability to teach frustration tolerance, the importance of setting limits and the advantage of inculcating appropriate social skills in compliance with the demands of others.

In motivating parents to work on their anger, it is sometimes better to introduce the topic after they have not been successful in implementing a behavior management program due to their own excessive emotionality. Examples of questions you might direct to parents at these times include: "What stopped you from rewarding Jane for having completed her homework?" "How do you feel when your son has not done his homework?" "What feeling prevented you from explaining to your son he had to do his schoolwork before he could play his computer games?"

Ellis, et. al, (1966) and other REBT practitioners have delimited a range of rational beliefs that can be shared with parents to be communicated to children who present with diverse emotional difficulties (see Appendix B).

Allied Cognitive-Behavioral Approaches

In working with both the emotional and the behavioral problems of childhood, the practitioner often combines several other important cognitive-behavioral approaches with REBT. In the main, they are designed to change negative to more sensible, positive thinking in an effort to reduce distress and develop adaptive skills and behavior.

Self-Instructional Training

Self-instructional training (SIT) is an educational procedure designed to teach clients both cognitive and behavioral skills for solving problems. Its application is based on a thorough cognitive-behavioral analysis of a task or situation that a client has not effectively dealt with and that may or may not be a source of unhappiness. There are two basic components of SIT. First, the practitioner analyzes behaviorally the performance skills that the client needs in order to demonstrate mastery of a task or a situation. Second, a cognitive-functional analysis is performed, which involves an inventory of the client's thinking (strategies, skills, and inner speech) as it relates to task performance and which seeks to answer the question: "In what psychological processes is the successfully achieving individual to engage, and in which of these is my subject failing?" (Meichenbaum, 1977). Once the task-appropriate mediators and performance skills are linked together and sequenced from simple to complex, the task of the practitioner is to instruct the client in how to employ the cognitive-behavior skills in relevant contexts.

The general outline for conducting think-aloud training programs for the teaching of performance-relevant skills is as follows:

> (a) problem identification and definition of self-interrogation skills ("What is it I have to do?"); (b) focusing attention and response guidance, which is usually the answer to the self-inquiry ("Now carefully stop and repeat the instructions"); (c) self-reinforcement involving standard-setting and self-evaluation ("Good, I'm doing fine."); and (d) coping skills and error-correcting options ("That's okay .... Even if I make an error I can go slowly."). (Meichenbaum and Asarnow, 1979, p. 13)

Self-instructional training (SIT) has been widely applied with school-age children. The training procedure is specifically designed to take into account and to specifically remediate the three major types of verbal mediation deficits that the child development literature has brought to light (Meichenbaum, 1977): (1) comprehension—understanding the nature of the problem, and therefore what mediators are required; (2) production—not only having the appropriate mediators in the repertoire, but producing them when needed; and (3) mediation—guiding one's behavior by means of the mediating process.

Initially developed to teach hyperactive, aggressive, and impulsive children to think reflectively (to "stop, look, and listen"), SIT is now being increasingly applied to academic tasks. SIT makes it possible "for students to do a kind of thinking they could not, or would not, otherwise do" (Meichenbaum and Asarnow, 1979, p. 18). In seeking to promote the wider use of reflective self-control thinking skills in children, Kendall and Finch (1979) have proposed that children can be taught a more "conceptual" set of self-instructions that can be applied both to a specific training task and to other tasks and in other situations. This strategy represents an effort to obtain a more general and elegant solution.

Bernard, Kratochwill, and Keefauver (1983) illustrated how REBT and SIT can be combined effectively in the treatment of chronic hair-pulling in a 17-year-old girl. The initial therapy sessions made extensive use of disputational techniques in order to deal with the client's obsessional anxieties. SIT, which was introduced during the middle treatment sessions, consisted of the therapist modeling a problem-solving dialogue that the client progressively internalized. An example of the SIT dialogue that the client was to employ while she was doing her homework was as follows: (1) *problem definition*: "What am I supposed to do?"; (2) *problem approach*: "I'd better pay attention to my assignment. What is the next thing I have to do?"; (3) *coping statements*: "Oh, I'm starting to get worried about school . . . and I just pulled out a hair. I know if I just relax and focus on my work that I won't worry"; and (4) *self-reinforcement*: "Hey, that's great. I finished that bit of work. I didn't worry. And I didn't pull my hair. You knew you could do it." Reviews of SIT research (Hobbs et al., 1980; Urbain and Kendall, 1980) indicate that SIT holds great promise for helping to change dysfunctional thinking-behavioral patterns in younger populations.

Although stress inoculation has been employed primarily in the treatment of adult disorders, its potential use with younger populations is becoming increasingly recognized. The stress inoculation approach was formulated by Meichenbaum and Cameron (1973) and has been used to help people cope with anxiety (Kendall, 1977; Kendall et al., 2003; Kendall et al., 2002; Meichenbaum and Cameron, 1973; Meichenbaum, 1987) and anger (Novaco, 1978, 1985). Thus, it can be conceived of as an approach to solving emotional problems rather than practical problems. It shares with RET the assumption that a person's thoughts and beliefs can lead to emotional difficulties and, as a consequence, behavioral problems. Additionally, stress inoculation attempts to alter emotional consequences through the altering of the client's cognitions.

When stress inoculation is being used within an REBT framework, both the cognitive preparation phase and the rehearsal phase contain strong REBT elements (e.g., understanding one's own role in triggering the maladaptive emotions by irrational self-statements; exploring the beliefs underlying the self-statements; generating new rational self-statements; and affirming one's ability to cope).

Interpersonal Cognitive Problem Solving

An extremely popular and influential cognitive-behavioral approach that has been developed specifically for children and adolescents who have problems in social relationships is interpersonal cognitive-problem solving (ICPS) (Spivack and Shure, 1974; Spivack et al., 1976), which has been developed at the Hahnemann Medical College and Hospital in Philadelphia, Pennsylvania. Spivack and Shure (1974) define their approach in this way:

The philosophy implicit in the program is that if one wishes to affect the behavior of people one must affect the specific (cognitive) abilities that mediate the behavior in question. The search has been, and still is, to discover the mediating cognitions intimately affecting social adjustment. (p. 131)

In their clinical work and research with younger populations, Spivack and his colleagues have identified a number of cognitive skills or types of thinking that are thought to mediate social behavior:

1. *Sensitivity or perspective thinking* is the awareness that there are difficulties or "problems" in human interactions and that other people may have different thoughts and feelings from one's own.
2. *Alternative thinking* is the generation of a variety of possible ways of dealing with a problem situation. By implication, the greater the number of possible alternative solutions a person can evolve, the more likely he or she is to come up with the best possible solution.
3. *Means-ends thinking* is the conceptualization of the step-by-step means needed to reach a specific objective. Knowing a solution is of little help if one cannot devise the way to reach it.
4. *Consequential thinking* involves the "thinking through" of the likely consequences of each alternative. An alternative that may initially look promising may, on reflection, turn out to have undesirable or have uncertain consequences if carried out.
5. *Causal thinking* is the spontaneous linking of cause and effect. Awareness of the connections between events and emotional states may be a prelude to identifying elements of the problem situation and generating solutions.

These cognitive processes are not thought of as personality traits or facets of general intelligence (as measured by an IQ score) but as skills that emerge at different developmental ages and are often acquired as a result of modeling by parents and other adults in real problem situations. Spivack and his colleagues have researched the relationship between ICPS skills and general intelligence measures and claim to have demonstrated a relationship between ICPS and social adjustment that is not accounted for by general intelligence.

Interpersonal cognitive-problem solving is used to help children and adolescents to think before they act. In a counseling-therapy context, it teaches young clients the importance of exploring alternatives for handling difficult situations, of thinking how they will go about realizing desired goals, and, equally important, of exploring the positive and negative consequences of alternatives before selecting one. In younger children (4-year old and 5-year-olds), alternative and consequential thinking is generally illustrated concretely; that is, the practitioner helps the child to solve a particular problem. Children in the 6-year-old to 12-year-old age group can be taught to apply alternative and consequential thinking skills across situations, as well as how to generate step-by-step plans to reach solutions to problems (means-ends thinking). With adolescents, the practitioner is able to combine work on alternative, consequential, and means-ends thinking skills with an emphasis on increasing the ability of adolescents to understand the thoughts and feelings of other individuals in the problem situation (perspective taking).

While ICPS emphasizes the resolving of practical and behavioral problems, the ICPS skills acquired may both lead to the reduction of emotional stress and facilitate the effectiveness of RET. On the one hand, when a young client learns to overcome an interpersonal obstacle, the emotions that had previously surrounded the source of frustration abate. A more reflective problem-solving approach to life enables children to deal more effectively with situations at home and at school that had previously led (via cognition) to emotional upset. On the other hand, ICPS skills may facilitate the process of therapeutic change. For example, exercises in alternative thinking may expedite the giving up of established maladaptive thinking habits. Or to take another example, as causal thinking appears to play a role in identifying one's irrational beliefs, training in causal thinking may aid in the process of disputation:

Attributional Retraining

As we have indicated in our discussion of the psychological conditions that influence childhood adjustment, the explanation that children "construct" and believe concerning the causes of events in their lives may play a strong role in determining their adaptive behavior and emotional well-being. Statements such as "It was my lucky day" and "My teacher must have favored me" reflect attributional beliefs about why a child received a good grade on a test that are different from statements such as "I got to the top because I worked extra hard" or "This is my special field. I'm good at maths." Individual differences in attributional beliefs have been the target of the theoretical and research interests of workers in several different fields. Personality theorists (Weiner, 1974), social learning psychologists (Rotter, 1966), and cognitive theorists (Dweck, 1975) have all approached this area, and although they may have used slightly different linguistic labels (e.g., *causal attribution*, *locus of control*, or *personal causation*), the overlap is marked (for an excellent review of theory and research from the attributional perspective, see Metalsky and Abramson, 1981).

Rotter (1966) has explored two dimensions of causal attributions that influence how these beliefs influence behavior: the *stability* of the factors that the individual has identified as causes, and the *internal versus external origin* of these factors. Stable causes are those that the individual believes persist over time. "Internal" attributions center on the individual's belief that effort is largely responsible for behavior and that he or she has control over what happens. "External" attributions are environmental factors the individual believes he or she has little control over. Four combinations that emerge from these two dimensions have been proposed to explain how a student may view his or her success and failure experiences in school: (1) stable-internal (e.g., ability); (2) unstable-internal (e.g., effort); (3) stable-external (e.g., task difficulty); and (4) unstable-external (e.g., luck). The force of these beliefs is evidenced in students' expectation of future success or failure, as well as their self-acceptance, their feelings of power or helplessness, and their achievement motivation.

Early work with attribution constructs examined the consistency with which the person holds attributions across situations and time (i.e., the construct was accorded a trait status). Continued research, however, has indicated that a person's attributional thinking varies with the situation. For example, different causal attributions may be made for success and for failure by the same individual, who may assume he or she has control over success but may ascribe failure to external factors (Crandall et al., 1965; Mischel et al., 1974).

The attributions of children appear to influence both behavior and emotion. The literature on the contributions of children's attributions to "learned helplessness" (Dweck and Reppucci, 1973) suggests that children who believe that their personal failures are related to internal conditions and their successes to external factors are likely to give up in the face of failure and to feel depressed.

The procedures used to retrain attributional thinking have been of two kinds: (1) contingent feedback in conjunction with manipulation of tasks and the environment, especially success, and failure (2) self-instructional training.

Although there has been increasing interest in the role that attributional beliefs play in influencing the school performance and efforts of children, there has been little work in the cognitive-behavioral area, to our knowledge, that has looked at the effects of attributional retraining on social behavior and emotional stability. It appears that REBT practitioners who are working with children and parents would do well to tap into those attributional beliefs that are at odds with reality and that appear to lead to a variety of cognitive errors (e.g., errors of insertion and errors of discounting). The detailed analysis of the attributional dimension has close links with RET, and the assessment methods that have been developed (e.g., locus of control inventories-Crandall et al., 1965) can readily be utilized in conjunction with rational-emotive methods.

Research

Now that the theoretical rationale of REBT with children and adolescents has been explained and techniques have been offered, we would like to briefly discuss what we do know about what works with this population. Psychotherapy with children has received comparatively less research attention than that given to adult psychotherapy (Casey and Berman, 1985). A landmark meta-analysis by Casey and Berman (1985) examined 75 studies which compared children under 13 years of age who were receiving psychotherapy with either another treatment or a control group. Effect size is the metric typically used in meta-analyses to quantitatively assess the amount of change in the targeted behavior in terms of standard deviation units. The most distinctive advantage of conducting a meta-analysis is that results from many different studies can be combined to give an effect size, which is an overall estimate of the intervention's effectiveness and a more powerful estimate than results from an individual study. Meta-analyses allow the field of psychotherapy outcome studies to overcome the problem of studies with small sample sizes, which we have found permeates the REBT literature and the work with children and adolescents in general. According to guidelines provided by Cohen (1977), a small effect size is around 0.2, a medium effect size is around 0.5, and a large effect size is around 0.8. The results reported by Casey and Berman (1985) indicated an overall effect size of 0.71 for all types of child therapies, compared with the effect size of 0.72 calculated by Shapiro and Shapiro (1982) in their review of adult therapy effectiveness. More recent meta-analyses with child and adolescent populations have demonstrated the efficacy of psychotherapy with effect sizes ranging from .54 to .88 (Weisz et al., 1995). As such, it appears that child psychotherapy is just as effective as adult psychotherapy.

Meta-analyses however are only as good as the studies that comprise them and are really based upon clearly described inclusionary criteria and the thoroughness of the search for studies to meet this criteria. White (1994) has described the conducting of an exhaustive literature review as "the reviewer's burden." Although it is impossible and unrealistic for a reviewer to find all of the studies related to a specific topic, the more exhaustive a review the more likely that its conclusions will avoid a bias from the selection and search procedures. The possibility exists that a review's findings "may say more about editorial preference, the politics of research finance, or the differential capabilities and biases of professionals and graduate students than about real treatment effects" (Bangert-Drowns, 1992, p. 460). White described 15 different search strategies for literature reviews and suggested that few reviewers actually perform an exhaustive search, and therefore, may have serious sampling problems by leaving out many studies.

The limitations of REBT outcome research seeking to determine the efficacy of REBT has frequently been discussed and debated in the literature (Bernard and DiGiuseppe, 1990; DiGiuseppe et al., 1979; Gossette and O'Brien, 1993; Gonzalez et al., 2004). Ellis (2001) in addressing the purported lack of research reported that over 250 outcome studies on REBT have been published since the early 1960's. Critics have argued that few of these studies actually test the distinctive components of REBT, with most studies involving a heterogeneous mix of cognitive-behavioral treatments (Gossette and O'Brien, 1992).

Before discussing specific research outcomes with regards to children and adolescents, we will briefly outline what the REBT meta-analytic outcome literature presently states with regards to its efficacy. DiGiuseppe, Terjesen, Goodman, Rose, Doyle and Vidalikis (1998) examined 13 reviews of the REBT outcome research for the period 1974–1996. The term REBT was cross-referenced with a number of related key words and synonyms. Each of the studies mentioned in each review was entered into a data base. Two research assistants and the first author read each review and searched the references of the reviews. The criteria for including articles in the final data base were: (a) REBT (or an appropriate synonym) was mentioned in the title of the article, (b) REBT interventions were mentioned in the method section of the article and (C) the study evaluated the effectiveness of treatments of REBT by either some control group or by a comparison of pretest and posttest scores. Unpublished doctoral dissertation reviews were included in this study. This strategy uncovered 69 additional studies not mentioned by the reviewers from 1957 until 1992, the time period covered by the reviews. Eighteen additional studies were uncovered from 1992 through 1998.

All of the newly uncovered studies were added to the data base and the number of times each study appeared in the following major reviews was calculated: DiGiuseppe, et al., 1977; Engels et al., 1993; Gossette and O'Brien, 1992, 1993; Haaga and Davison, 1989; Hajzler and Bernard, 1991; Jorm, 1989; Lyons and Woods, 1991; McGovern and Silverman, 1984; Silverman et al., 1992; Zettle and Hayes, 1980). The authors coded the types of studies included in the reviews as appearing in: (a) peer reviewed journals; (b) books; (c) unpublished dissertations; and (d) conference presentations and compared the number of studies each review included given the available pool included for the time period that the review sampled. The authors concluded that most reviewers of the REBT outcome research selectively reviewed the literature and missed a majority of studies available for the time period from which they sampled studies, with most studies being cited by only one reviewer. The majority of reviews supported the efficacy of REBT, reviewing 256 separate studies, but interestingly, the majority of studies were only mentioned once with little overlap over reviews. They reported that reviews that included significantly more dissertations reached more negative conclusions and that all reviews missed the majority of studies that had appeared in the years they included for review. Interestingly, substantial variability existed across reviews in the proportion of articles and dissertations. Specifically, the two reviews by Gossette and O'Brien (1992, 1993) that reached the most negative conclusions concerning REBT's effectiveness included not only the most dissertations but the fewest peer reviewed articles. It is possible that reviewing predominately unpublished dissertations resulted in more poorly done REBT which influenced their conclusions.

The researchers offered some interesting conclusions and questions for the field of REBT outcome literature to consider. First, the decision to include dissertations is highly variable among the outcome reviews and likely to increase the number of missing studies as dissertations are the most difficult documents to obtain. Including them in a review and not obtaining all of them may present a bias. The authors also express the concern about the "reviewer's burden" as the standard tactics of conducting searches by a few key words does not appear warranted. Additionally, some reviewers may have only reviewed studies with control groups and such a criterion may have led to a smaller sample and therefore more missed studies. The authors concluded by asking the question if the exclusion of so many studies is an artifact of the REBT literature or is this a problem in psychology as a whole?

What is even more problematic is that only two of those reviews (Hajzler and Bernard, 1991; Gossette and O'Brien, 1993) focused on children and adolescents with six of the reviews focusing on a mixture of REBT outcome studies with children and adolescents and adults only. This hampers the ability of the clinician to clearly know how effective REBT is for working with these populations. We will briefly describe the results of the two initial meta-analyses identified by DiGiuseppe et al. (1998) that examined the efficacy of REBT with children and adolescents exclusively, followed by a presentation of a more recent meta-analysis and some initial results of what we believe to be the largest meta-analytic review of REBT outcome literature to date. Table 5 presents a summary of all the meta-analytic reviews of REBT outcome research.

Summary of REBT Review and Meta-Outcome Studies with Children and Adolescents

While Bernard and Joyce (1984) provided a research review of REBT with children Hajzler and Bernard (1991) conducted one of the first reviews of the effects of REBT with children and adolescents published in a peer review journal. Actually, their review was of REE (Rational-Emotive Education) which is the educational derivative of REBT with school aged populations. Their review included 21 studies, seven of which included non-clinical populations with the remaining studies examining the effectiveness of REBT with anxious students (4 studies), learning disabled students (3 studies), high risk students ("out of control in the classroom") (3 studies), one study was with students with low self-esteem and 4 studies were of the single case design.

As one might expect. REE efficacy is greater on measures of irrationality, with 92% of studies that used such measures showing decreases. The next type of dependent measure showing the greatest change was the behavioral category, with 64% of the studies showing benefits of REE. Changes in anxiety were observed in 50% of the studies. Taken together, these three figures suggest that REE has its greatest effect on bringing about changes in irrationality and somewhat lesser and relatively equal effects in promoting emotional and behavioral changes. There was no hard evidence either for or against presented in any of the studies, however, that would allow us to infer that changes in emotions and behaviors were brought about by or correlated with cognitive changes.

Locus of control is a cognitive construct, although defined differently from rationality. REBT would argue that the teaching of emotional responsibility, which should lead to changes in rationality, should also bring about a change

TABLE 5. Reviews of the REBT outcome literature, Year Published, years spanned, focus, and conclusions.

Authors	Year published	Range of years of studies	Number of studies	Focus of the review	Conclusions
DiGiuseppe, Miller and Trexler	1977	1970–1977	26	Published and unpublished studies of children and adults.	Support for RET, "...appear(s) generally positive & promising, but far from conclusive." p.70.
McGovern and Silverman	1984	1977–1982	47	Published and unpublished studies of children and adults.	"...there were 31 studies favoring RET. In the remaining studies, the RET treatment groups all showed improvement and in no study was another treatment method significantly better than RET." p.16
Haaga & Davison	1989	1970–1987	69	Published and unpublished studies of children & adults.	Evidence for RET exists but the research is not very advanced.
Hajzler and Bernard	1991	1970–1982	45	Published and unpublished studies with children and adolescents.	"...support for the notion that changes in irrationality and changes in other dimension of psychological functioning." "..changes have been maintained at follow-up periods." p.31
Jorm	1989	1971–1986	16	Studies of any type of theory that included a measure of trait anxiety or neuroticism	" While RET and related therapies proved superior in the present meta-analysis (to other therapies),this conclusion is limited by the breath of studies available." p.25
Lyons and Woods	1991	1970–1988	70	Published and unpublished studies of children and adults.	"The results demonstrated that RET is an effective form of therapy. The efficacy was most clearly demonstrated when RET was compared to baseline or other forms of controls. Effect sizes were largest for dependent measures low in reactivity (i.e., low reactivity = behavioral or physiological measures; high reactivity = measures of irrational thinking)." p.36

Silverman, McCarthy and McGovern	1992	1982–1989	89	Published and Unpublished studies with children, adolescents and adults.	"...49 studies resulted in positive findings for RET." When compared to other treatments, "...no other treatments were found to be significantly better than RET." p.166.
Engels, Garnefski and Diekstra	1993	1970–1988	32	Published and unpublished studies of children and adults.	"RET on the whole was effective, compared with placebo and no treatment. Its effects were maintained over time, and it produced a delayed treatment effect with regard to behavioral outcome criteria." p.1088
Gossette and O'Brien	1993	1974–1992	36	Published and unpublished studies with children and adolescents.	RET has little or no practical benefit. "The most distinctive outcome of RET is a decrease in the endorsement of irrational beliefs."p.21. We can conclude that continued use of RET in the classroom is unjustified, in fact, contraindicated." p.23
Gonzalez, Nelson, Gutkin, Saunders, Galloway and Shwery	2004	1975–1998	19	Published studies with children and adolescents	Evaluation of REBT treatment indicated that, "the effects of psychotherapy with children and adolescents were beneficial and of a respectable magnitude" (p. 232).

TABLE 6. Significance between REE groups and no-treatment control groups in terms of numbers and percentage of dependent variables (Hajzler and Bernard, 1991).

Domain of dependent variable	Significant		Not significant	
	N	%	*N*	%
Irrationality	15	88	2	12
Anxiety	12	80	3	20
Locus of control	5	71	2	29
Neuroticism	2	67	1	33
Self-Esteem	12	57	9	43
Behavioral index	9	56	7	44

in locus of control. The fact that 64% of studies that included a locus of control measure showed increased internality suggests that REE does influence locus of control. Of the 19 studies that used a measure of self-esteem, half of them showed a benefit as a consequence of REE. This finding suggests that REE interventions need to be modified to bring about more consistent changes on this variable.

Adjustment and personality measures showed positive changes in 63% and 57% of studies, respectively. Changes in these more global measures suggest that REE has the potential to bring about general changes in adaptive functioning of school-age children rather than just resulting in specific behavioral changes.

While the Bernard and Hajzler results offer some interesting summaries of the positive impact of REBT on a variety of childhood problems and measures, we now turn to the findings of more recent meta-analytic studies concerning REBT's efficacy with younger populations.

In a select review of REBT outcome literature with children and adolescents, Gossette and O'Brien (1993) call into question the use of REBT with this population. The authors expressed concern over the fact that a REE/REBT curriculum package is being implemented in school settings and may be taking away from other academic instruction and that a thorough evaluation of this (and affective education programs) was warranted. The authors do question the earlier review of Hajzler and Bernard (1991), specifically their exclusion of some doctoral dissertations as well as the manner in which efficacy was calculated for the varied dependent measures. While the fact that methods for calculation of efficacy make it difficult for others to replicate conclusions, decisions to exclude/include unpublished doctoral dissertations should have a clear explanation. Interestingly, Gossette and O'Brien reviewed primarily unpublished dissertations (33) and only four published reports. Oftentimes, dissertations do have the advantage of a more complete description of the research design and treatment methods employed. However, according to DiGiuseppe et al. (1998), based on the review of available published articles at this time, Gossette and O'Brien missed approximately 70 percent of the available articles for review. Similar to the results obtained by Hajzler and Bernard, Gossette and O'Brien report that the most significant outcome is a change in irrationality. However, they point out that this change may not be a function of change but rather just students assimilating new information as they often do in classroom settings. This assertion implies that all of the studies utilized for their analysis were done in a classroom environment, however their methods fail to indicate whether or not they only included studies that took place in the school setting/classroom. Accompanying change in affective and behavioral states may lend further support to this philosophical change, something that Gossette and O'Brien report the extant literature does not demonstrate. They also point out some problems in the research that is consistent with concerns raised by Hajzler and Bernard (validity of measures; follow-up assessment).

In their meta-analysis of the use of REBT with children and adolescents, Gonzalez et al. (2004) looked at 19 studies and made several interesting conclusions. The authors' analyses revealed that, overall, REBT was more effective than an alternative treatment (Weighted Effect Size (WES) of .57) and more effective than a no-treatment control (WES of .49). The authors also discussed additional findings that we feel are pertinent to mention here and a few that are somewhat inconsistent with that of the results reported by Gossette and O'Brien (1993). First, REBT was most effective in its reduction of disruptive behaviors (WES of 1.15) followed by irrationality (WES of .51). While the fact that it was only based on 7 effect sizes is still problematic, perhaps researchers are finally catching on to the importance of having additional behavioral outcome measures. Interestingly, there was no significant difference between studies high and low in internal validity. That is, REBT was equally effective for those studies that were identified as well-designed (e.g., random assignment, sound instruments, low mortality rate) as those that were not with WES of .50 and .53 respectively. While the authors caution interpretation of these results based on the few number of studies included, they offer the suggested interpretation that the effects of REBT are robust against these methodological differences. In addition, the existence or lack of an identified problem did not change the effectiveness of REBT for children and adolescents. That is, REBT worked equally as well for students with an identified problem (e.g., test anxiety, behavior problems) as it did for students with no identifiable immediate behavioral problem but may be considered at risk (e.g., school failure, low self-esteem) with WES of .50 and .51 respectively. Children had better treatment results (WES of .70) than adolescents (WES of .51) which is consistent with results reported by Gossette and O'Brien (1993). Finally, the authors also state that REBT performed by non-mental health professionals led to greater effect sizes (.54) than those by health professionals (.36) and that children and adolescents receiving longer treatment durations showed the best results.

However, the analysis by Gonzalez et al. (2004) has a number of limitations, which may impact upon the social validity of their findings. Although they do address some of these limitations, including the small number of studies analyzed, the exclusion of all dissertations, the fact that the vast majority of the studies were conducted in the same setting (schools) and with students not referred for any treatment, another concern would be their inclusionary criteria. A review of the studies included in this meta-analysis, one study did not actually include REBT at all, as DeAnda (1998) performed relaxation and self-talk, but did not do any REBT. In addition, it appears that the authors compared effects across very different dependent measures, by creating five outcome domains (disruptive behavior, endorsement of irrationality, grade point average, self concept, and anxiety). This may not be able to offer a true evaluation of the efficacy of REBT as collapsing dependent measures into domains may misrepresent what the outcome measure is purporting to test.

As such, there appears to be a need to objectively evaluate the present research base regarding REBT. Acknowledging the recommendations and limitations of previous reviews, it is believed that a more comprehensive review of the existing research will provide not only support for the efficacy of REBT, but also a guideline for clinicians in the effective practice of scientifically supported strategies for working with children and adolescents. Additionally, it is posited that a thorough review of the extant literature will cogently demonstrate the limitations in the design of current REBT research, and point the way to more effective science.

Ford (2005) has been actively collecting and analyzing what we believe to be the most complete review of REBT outcome studies and a brief summary of his initial methodology and conclusions with regards to the efficacy of REBT with children and adolescents is presented below. Ford has updated a compendium of REBT studies compiled by DiGiuseppe, Goodman, Neva and Ford (2005) through October 2003 by conducting a literature search of *PsychInfo* using the following search words: "Rational-Emotive-Behavior Therapy," "Rational-Emotive Therapy," "RET," "REBT," "Cognitive Restructuring," and "Cognitive Therapy." In order for a journal article or dissertation to be included in the study, the words "rational," "rational-emotive," or "irrational" had to appear in either the title or the abstract. "Cognitive Therapy" as a search word was subsequently dropped due to the large number of articles identified (3324) and the relatively low number of usable articles (6 out of the first 1200 articles) obtained. A total of 441 studies were identified for potential inclusion in the meta-analysis. The following inclusion criteria were used: The study must (a) be a treatment outcome study, not a description of treatment; (b) contain at least one REBT treatment condition; (c) be published in English. Studies were excluded from the meta-analysis if they were a case study or included fewer than four subjects, or if the study failed to report adequate statistics to calculate an effect size.

Studies were scored according to a coding sheet developed by the researchers. The initial coding sheet was devised by DiGuiseppe but was revised and updated, to include the addition of a study statistics matrix, during the period September 2000 through June 2004. All studies were coded using the January 2004 version of the coding sheet, with a maximum of fifty-four variables, as well as effect sizes, calculated for each study. Studies that were determined to not be usable were not coded or included in the study. Five independent raters received 12 hours of training in coding outcome studies using a coding manual devised by the author. Additionally, all raters conjointly reviewed approximately 20 studies to ensure understanding of all coded items and to minimize rater bias, and weekly meetings were conducted with all raters to discuss questions and discrepancies with final conclusions agreed upon by consensus and precedent decisions incorporated into the coding manual as required.

Treatment efficacy was based on changes from pretreatment to posttreatments. Though the long-term effects of treatment are of importance in evaluating the effectiveness of treatment, the decision to not include results from treatment follow-up was based on the methodological difficulties of follow-up data (Baucom et al., 1998). Inconsistency in collecting follow-up data, widely varying lengths of follow-up periods, significant attrition during the follow-up period, which reduces statistical power, and failure to control for additional treatment during the follow-up period make drawing conclusions based on follow-up data difficult and subjective.

Additionally, Ford had the studies rated on quality based on the criteria for empirically supported treatments (Chambless and Hollon, 1998) by awarding points (0 or 1) for the absence or presence of the following study characteristics: (a) sample size greater than or equal to 30 subjects, (b) comparison to control condition, (c) comparison to alternative treatment condition, (d) use of a treatment manual, (e) random assignment of subjects, and (f) means and standard deviations of outcome measures reported in the study. Studies received 1 point if the outcome measure was a well established measure, 0.5 point if the dependent measure was created by the researchers for the study and they provided validity data for the measure, and 0 points if the dependent measure was created by the researchers for the study and no validity data was provided. The maximum number of quality points available per study was 7.

Data from each study was used to calculate effect sizes using the standardized mean gain for within group effects and the standardized mean difference for between group effects. Standardized mean gain values are calculated by dividing the difference between group pretreatment and post-treatment means by the pooled standard deviation of both means. These values can be conceptualized as the standardized difference between Time 1 and Time 2 means. Standardized mean difference values are calculated by dividing the difference between group means (i.e. REBT and Control and REBT and Alternative treatment) by the pooled standard deviation of both groups. These values can be conceptualized as the standardized difference between the two groups.

These effect sizes were used to compute the mean, median, 95% confidence interval of the effects sizes and the weighted mean effect size. The weighted mean effect size was calculated by weighting each effect size by value by the inverse squared variance, then dividing the sum of the weighted effect size values by the sum of the weights. This method of weighing is recommended by Lipsey and Wilson (2001) to give the optimal weight. To determine the overall (fixed effects) significance of the effects of REBT on the dependent measure, a direct test of the mean effect size was obtained by computing a *z-test*. The combined *Z* value was computed by dividing the absolute value of the mean effect size by the standard error of the effect size (Lipsey and Wilson, 2001). The result of this formula is distributed as a standard normal deviate. For groups of effect sizes that produced a significant combined *Z*, a *fail-safe N* (Rosenthal, 1979) (k_0) was calculated to estimate the number of studies reporting null results needed to reduce the combined effect size to the point of nonsignificance (d = 0.5).

To determine if the variation in the individual effect sizes averaged into the mean effect size value differed from the population mean effect size value by more than that expected from sampling error alone, a homogeneity test, *Q* (Hedges and Olkin, 1985), was calculated. The *Q* statistic is distributed as a chi-square with *k*-1 degrees of freedom where *k* is the number of effect sizes. If the combined effect size was determined to be heterogeneous, the random effects model of significance of the effects of REBT on the dependent measure will be computed to account for other sources of variability assumed to be random (Lipsey and Wilson, 2001).

Although not published yet, Ford reports data on REBT treatment effects for 2310 children and adolescents from 39 studies (22 peer reviewed journals and 17 dissertations). The mean quality rating for these studies was 4.87 and the average study sample consisted of 71 participants, with a mean age of 12.8 ± .95 years (range = 7–17 years).

Ford reports that just over 50 percent of the studies did pure REBT, with many integrating REBT with an alternative treatment (e.g., psychoeducation, systematic desensitization, relaxation) making it difficult to clearly ascertain how effective REBT in its pure form is.

Overall, REBT within group effects were moderate (WES = .62), with strong effects shown for self-concept (WES = 1.3) and GPA (WES = .74) and moderate effects for negative emotions (WES = .60) and Anxiety (WES = .55). This review is consistent with other reviews in that it identifies the paucity of behavioral outcome measures. Independent REBT versus control between group effect sizes were reported to be moderate in nature with a weighted mean effect size of .44, with all outcome measures being in the moderate range (.31 to .52). The was .44, which indicates a moderate effect. When REBT was compared to an alternative treatment group, the weighted mean effect size was -.16, which indicates that REBT is not only not more effective than some alternative treatments, but that in some instances it is actually less effective. Similar to the earlier comment about how pure is the REBT intervention, the question may also arise as to the purity of these alternative interventions.

Overall, the most cogent problem found in the REBT research with children and adolescents is the failure to report the specific characteristics of the study, the therapeutic setting, and the treatments utilized. Because the details of research are so poorly reported, it is difficult, if not impossible, to determine what is actually happening in therapy and what is influencing therapeutic change. While this may not be unique to REBT research literature, it is not good science.

REBT has been successfully applied to a wide array of psychological disturbances. However, the most frequent clinical problem treated in research studies is anxiety (33 percent in the children studies). This narrow focus of research on a single aspect of disturbance limits the empirical validity of generalizing REBT efficacy to other client problems.

A greater problem is the failure of most studies to adhere to the criteria defined by the Division 12 Task Force on Promotion and Dissemination of Psychological Procedures (1995) for efficacious and empirically supported treatments, frequently referred to as the "Chambless criteria." On almost every item coded, 18–78% of studies failed to include clear data describing the treated population.

An area of particular deficiency is treatment integrity, with just over half of studies reporting using a treatment manual and 26% report doing a treatment integrity check. Without a clear plan of treatment and verification to ensure that treatment is carried out consistent with a priori treatment objectives, the empirical validity and replicability of results is compromised.

Most therapy in REBT research is conducted by graduate students and pre-doctoral candidates. This is reflective of the number of pre-doctoral candidates collecting data for dissertation and the desirability of researchers in academia to use therapists and evaluators blind to the hypothesis of the study. The obvious weakness in this is the lack of experience of graduate student therapists. Several studies make vague reference to the experience of graduate student therapists, or mention training conducted prior to conducting therapy. However this does not remove the question of increased familiarity, application and effectiveness of techniques of a more experienced therapist.

A logical way to offset differences in therapists' experience levels would be through supervision by an experienced therapist. Unfortunately, only 18% of studies reporting any supervision of the therapists conducting the subject research, and over 82% failed to report data on supervision.

At the most fundamental level of therapist experience in REBT research is the absence of any indication that the researchers have had training in REBT. Fifty nine percent of the studies reviewed made no mention of REBT training by either the therapist or the supervisor. Within the 16 studies making some mention of REBT training, only two therapists had received a Primary Certificate in REBT. The effect of the infrequent use of supervision and evidence that fewer than about a quarter of studies conduct integrity checks is moot when considering the fact that even if integrity checks and supervision were conducted, the evaluators and supervisors aren't trained in REBT. As such, the accuracy and effectiveness of REBT techniques applied in therapy cannot be considered reliable.

These concerns are consistent with those raised by Terjesen et al. (1999) who surveyed a random list of members of the National Association of School Psychology (NASP) Association. Each member was sent a questionnaire regarding their graduate training, demographics, theoretical orientation, current job status, and therapeutic interventions utilized in their setting. Results indicated that REBT is used as a part of a treatment package for approximately 50% of the sample, however very few respondents identified REBT as their primary intervention. Cognitive-behavior therapy was the most frequently identified primary intervention strategy, however, they report that it was not clear whether respondents differentiated between CBT and REBT. Since 58% of those who described CBT as their primary intervention also reported some use of REBT, respondents may view REBT as a component of CBT rather than a distinct intervention. Terjesen et al. report that regardless of the disorder very few respondents used REBT exclusively and that REBT is used more frequently in combination with other interventions, and it is used more for internalizing disorders. The authors posit that perhaps one of the reasons that REBT is not used frequently with children and adolescents is that much of the REBT literature pertaining to children and adolescents is clinical in nature and that practitioners may not be aware of the empirical support of REBT with this population. Interestingly, 57% of the entire sample reported receiving training in REBT for working with children and adolescents and of those that received training, 63.6% report using REBT in the schools. The authors suggest that more research on the effects of training in REBT with children and adolescents (i.e., graduate programs and formal training institutes) for working with this population is warranted along with a more in-depth investigation as to what component of REBT these school psychologists are actually using, as it was not clear from this data how the respondents were using REBT. It is possible that they were using isolated components of REBT (e.g., coping skills, disputation). Additionally, an examination of the training in REBT of school-based practitioners and the type and quality of CBT and REBT being done in the school settings was recommended. Finally, they propose that further examination of the qualifications of REBT trainers in university settings be conducted to ascertain if REBT is being taught accurately.

Perhaps, the most fundamental flaw in REBT research with children, adolescents as well as adults is the failure of researchers to adequately report what therapeutic techniques they are applying in therapy. Due to the majority of researchers failing to report not only what techniques they used in therapy, but also what techniques they did not use, it is impossible to determine what REBT techniques are being applied in therapy, and in what frequency.

Of the studies included in this review, most integrated another form of therapy with REBT. While informal assessment of coded studies not yet included in this review indicate that this result is inflated, it nonetheless highlights the fact that REBT is frequently used in combination with other therapy techniques, further exacerbating the problem of determining what techniques are most effective. In most cases, the existing research does not clearly indicate or support which REBT interventions facilitate change. Ellis (2001) notes the inherent difficulty in testing the relative effectiveness of the different techniques used in REBT, due to the large number of cognitive, emotive, and behavioral techniques utilized.

Recommendations

Due to the inconsistent reporting of research study characteristics, it is difficult to determine whether research is poorly conducted, or poorly reported. Overall, greater meticulousness in reporting methodological and treatment characteristics in REBT research must be applied. Without a clear understanding of what is being done, and not done, and what works, and doesn't work, in therapy, research fails to provide the empirical link between theory and practice that research is intended to provide. Some specific recommendations for practice include:

1. Research needs to be conducted applying REBT to other clinical problems associated with childhood and adolescence, in addition to anxiety.
2. A clear articulation of the REBT techniques utilized and not utilized in therapy must be included in research results.
3. REBT researchers must be trained in the theory and techniques of REBT and clearly articulate their degree of training in study characteristics.
4. Supervision of therapists must be included in research as a means of insuring understanding and adherence to REBT treatment plans.

The Future

It is expected that the prevention and treatment of the emotional and behavioral problems of children and youth will influenced by REBT theory and practice. There are a number of trends we can anticipate in this area.

There is little question that the understanding of how the cognitive developmental status of children relates to maladjustment will serve as a background to determining the type of cognitive intervention that is best suited to children who manifest different levels of mental and emotional maturity. We still have a way to go in understanding the world from a child's perspective.

The use of cognitively-oriented preventive mental health programs such as REE and You Can Do It! Education will proliferate as the research presented in this chapter supports their use as an evidence-based intervention.

The extent to which faulty thinking processes and the irrational beliefs of parents and teachers influence childhood maladjustment will be more fully analyzed. The role that significant others can play in correcting the maladaptive thinking patterns and beliefs of younger populations will be of increasing interest. The popularity of cognitively oriented parent and teacher education programs will grow.

Behaviorally oriented cognitive practitioners will begin to recognize (assess and treat) more fully that children and their significant others have emotions that influence both behavioral dysfunctions and the potential effects of treatment. Cognitively oriented practitioners working with children in families and in classroom settings will conduct more systematic assessments of behavioral problems so that the benefits of treatment can be more fully and objectively verified. Child-oriented research scientists will begin to study more systematically how individual differences interact with cognitive treatments.

There will be an increasing cross-fertilization of cognitive approaches to the problems of childhood. As the contributors to this volume attest, there is a greater acceptance within the cognitive-behavioral school of the utility of cognitive practices that have originated in different psychological theories and traditions. It is hoped that this trend will continue.

Acknowledgment: The authors would like to acknowledge Patrick Ford for his help in coding and data analysis of research reported in the final section of this chapter.

References

Adler, A. (1927). *Understanding human nature*. New York: Garden City Publishing.

Agosto, R., and Solomon, H. (1978). Unclassified. *Rational Living*, *23*, 41–42.

Albert, S. (1972). *A study to determine the effectiveness of affective education with fifth grade students*. Unpublished master's thesis, Queens College.

Bangert-Drowns, R. L. (1992). Review of developments in meta-analytic method. In A. E. Kazdin (ed.). *Methodological Issues and Strategies in Clinical Research*. Washington, DC: American Psychological Association.

Bard, J. A. (1980). *Rational-emotive therapy in practice*. Champaign, Ill: Research Press.

Barnes, R. (2000). Mrs. Miggins in the classroom. *British Journal of Special Education, 27,* 22–28.

Barrish, H and Barrish, I. J. (1985). *Managing and Understanding Parental Anger*. Kansas City: Westport Publishers, Inc.

Barrish, H and Barrish, I. J. (1989). *Surviving and Enjoying your Adolescent*. Kansas City: Westport Publishers, Inc.

Baucom, D.H., Shoham, V., Mueser, K.T., Daiuto, A.D., and Stickle, T.R. (1998). Empirically supported couples and family therapies for adult problems. *Journal of Consulting and Clinical Psychology, 66,* 53–88.

Bedford, S. (1974). Instant replay: *A method of counseling and talking to little (and other) people*. New York: Institute for Rational Living.

Bernard, M. E. (1979). *Rational-emotive group counseling in a school setting*. Paper presented at the American Educational Research Association's Annual Meeting, San Francisco, April.

Bernard, M. E. (1981). Private thought in rational-emotive psychotherapy. *Cognitive Therapy and Research, 5*, 125–142.

Bernard, M. E. (1990). Rational-emotive therapy with children and adolescents: Treatment strategies. In M.E. Bernard and R. DiGiuseppe (eds.), *School Psychology Review* (Mini-Series): Rational-Emotive Therapy and School Psychology, *19,* 294–303.

Bernard, M. E. (2001). *Program achieve: A curriculum of lessons for teaching students how to achieve success and develop social-emotional-behavioral well-being,* 2nd ed., Vols. 1–6. Oakleigh, VIC (AUS): Australian Scholarships Group.

Bernard, M. E. (2001a). *Program achieve: A curriculum of lessons for teaching students how to achieve success and develop social-emotional-behavioral well-being,* 3rd ed., Vols. 1–6. Laguna Beach, CA: You Can Do It! Education.

Bernard, M. E. (2001b). Eliminate the negative or accentuate the positive? Paper presented at the Conference Honoring Albert Ellis, sponsored by the Albert Ellis Institute, June, Keystone, Colorado.

Bernard, M. E. (2002). *Providing all children with the foundation for achievement and social-emotional-behavioral well-being,* 2nd ed. Priorslee, Telford (UK): Time Marque.

Bernard, M.E. (2004a). *The REBT therapist's pocket companion for working with children and adolescents.* New York: Albert Ellis Institute.

Bernard, M. E. (2004b). *The You Can Do It! early childhood education program: A social-emotional learning curriculum (4–6 Year Olds).* Oakleigh, VIC (AUS): Australian Scholarships Group.

Bernard, M. E. (2004c). Emotional resilience in children: Implications for Rational Emotive Education. *Romanian Journal of Cognitive and Behavioral Psychotherapies, 4,* 39–52.

Bernard, M. E. (2005). Program achieve: A curriculum of lessons for teaching students how to achieve success and develop social-emotional-behavioral well-being, 3rd Ed., Vols. 1-6. Laguna Beach, CA: You Can Do It! Education.

Bernard, M. E. (2006). Its time we teach social and emotional competence as well as we teach academic competence. *Reading and Writing Quarterly,* in press.

Bernard, M. E., and Cronan, F. (1999). The child and adolescent scale of irrationality. Journal of Cognitive Psychotherapy, 13, 121–132.

Bernard, M.E. and DiGiuseppe, R. (eds.) (1990). Rational-emotive therapy and school psychology. *School Psychology Review* (Mini-Series), *19,* 267–321.

Bernard, M.E. and DiGiuseppe, R. (eds.) (1991). *Rational-emotive consultation in applied settings.* Hillsdale, NJ: Erlbaum, pp. 210.

Bernard, M. E., and Joyce, M. R. (1984). Rational emotive therapy with children and adolescents: Theory, *treatment strategies, preventative methods.* New York: Wiley.

Bernard, M. E., and Joyce, M. R. (1993). Rational-emotive therapy with children and adolescents. In T. R. Kratochwill and R. J. Morris (eds.), *Handbook of psychotherapy with children and adolescents.* Boston: Allyn and Bacon.

Bernard, M.E., Kratochwill, T.R., and Keefauver, L.W. (1983). The effects of rational-emotive therapy and self-instructional training on chronic hair-pulling. *Cognitive Therapy and Research, 7,* 273–280.

Blanco, R., and Rosenfield, J. (1978). *Case studies in clinical and school psychology,* Springfield, Ill: Thomas.

Block, J. (1978). Effects of a rational-emotive mental health program on poorly achieving, disruptive high school students. *Journal of Counseling Psychology, 25,* 61–65.

Bokor, S. (1972). *A study to determine the effects of a self-enhancement program in increasing self-concept in black, disadvantaged sixth-grade boys*, M.A. thesis, Queens College.

Bordin, E. S. (1979). The generalizability of the psychoanalytic concept of the working alliance. *Psychotherapy: Theory, research and practice, 16,* 252–260.

Brody, M. (1974). *The effect of the rational-emotive affective education approach on anxiety, frustration tolerance and self-esteem with fifth-grade students*. Ph.D. thesis, Temple University.

Brown, D. A. (1974). Rational success. *Art in Daily Living, 3,* 7.

Brown, D. A. (1977). The fourth "R": A school psychologist takes RSC to school. In J. Wolfe and E. Brand (eds.), *Twenty years of rational therapy*. New York: Institute for Rational Living.

Brown, D. A. (1979). Chad cannot be rotten. *Journal of School Health, 19,* 503–504.

Burnett, P. C. (1994). Self-talk in upper primary school children: Its relationship with irrational beliefs, self-esteem and depression. *Journal of Rational-Emotive and Cognitive-Behavior Therapy, 12,* 181–188.

Burnett, P. C. (1996). Children's self-talk and significant others' positive and negative statements. *Educational Psychology, 16,* 57–68.

Cangelosi, A., Gressard, C. V., and Mines, R. A. (1980).The effects of a rational thinking group on self-concepts in adolescents. *The School Counselor, 27,* 357–361.

Casey, R., and Berman, J. (1985). The outcome of psychotherapy with children. *Psychological Bulletin, 98,* 388–400.

Chambless, D. L., and Hollon, S. D. (1998). Defining empirically supported therapies. *Journal of Consulting and Clinical Psychology, 66*, 7–18.

Cohen, J. (1977). *Statistical power analysis for the behavioral sciences: Revised edition.* New York: Academic Press, Inc.

Costello, D. R. T., and Dougherty, D. (1977). Rational behavior training in the classroom. *Rational Living, 12,* 13–15.

Craighead, W. E. (1982). A brief clinical history of cognitive-behavior therapy with children. *The School Psychology Review, 11,* 5–13.

Crandall, V. C., Kratovsky, W., and Crandall, V. G, (1965). Children's beliefs in their own control of reinforcers in intellectual-academic achievement situations. *Child Development, 36,* 91–109.

Daly, S. (1971). Using reason with deprived preschool children. *Rational Living, 5,* 12–19.

D'Angelo, D. C. (1977). *The effects of locus of control and a program of rational principles on fear of negative evaluation*. Ed.D. thesis, West Virginia University.

DeVoge, C. (1974). A behavioral approach to RET with children. *Rational Living, 9,* 23–26.

DiGiuseppe, R. (1975a). A *developmental study of the efficacy of rational-emotive education*. Ph.D. dissertation, Hofstra University.

DiGiuseppe, R. (1975b). The use of behavioral modification to establish rational self-statements in children. *Rational Living, 1,* 18–20.

DiGiuseppe, R. (1981). Cognitive therapy with children. In G. Emery, S. D. Hollon, and R. C. Bedrosian (eds.), *New directions in cognitive therapy*. New York: Guilford Press.

DiGiuseppe, R. (1995). Developing the therapeutic alliance with angry clients. In H. Kassinove (ed.), *Anger disorders*. Washington, DC: Taylor and Francis.

DiGiuseppe, R., Goodman, R., Neva, S., and Ford, P. Outcome Studies. Retrieved March 15, 2005 from http://www.rebt.org/professionals/research2.asp

DiGiuseppe, R., and Kassinove, H. (1976). Effects of a rational-emotive school mental health program on children's' emotional adjustment. *Journal of Community Psychology, 4,* 382–387.

DiGiuseppe, R., Linscott, J., and Jilton, R. (1996). Developing the therapeutic alliance in child-adolescent psychotherapy. *Applied and Preventive Psychology, 5*(2), 85–100.

DiGiuseppe, R. A., Miller, N. J., and Trexler, L. D. (1977). A review of rational-emotive psychotherapy outcome studies. *The Counseling Psychologist, 7,* 64–72.

DiGiuseppe, R., Miller N. J., and Trexler, L. D. (1979). A review of rational-emotive psychotherapy outcome studies. In A. Ellis and J. M. Whiteley (eds.), *Theoretical and empirical foundations of rational-emotive therapy*. Monterey, CA: Brooks/Cole.

DiGiuseppe, R., Terjesen, M.D., Goodman, R., Rose, R., Doyle, K., and Vidalikis, N. (1998). *A Meta-Analytic Review of REBT Outcome Studies: A Comparative Investigation.* Poster presented at the 106th annual convention of the American Psychological Association (APA). San Francisco, CA.

DiNubile, L., and Wessler, R. (1974). Lessons from the living school. *Rational Living, 9,* 29–32.

Doress, I. (1967). The teacher as therapist. *Rational Living, 2,* 27.

Dryden, W. (1987). *Current issues in rational-emotive therapy*. London: Croon-Helm.

Dweck, C. (1975). The role of expectations and attributions in the alleviation of learned helplessness. *Journal of Personality and Social Psychology, 31,* 674–685.

Dweck, C., and Reppucci, N. (1973). Learned helplessness and reinforcement responsibility in children. *Journal of Personality and Social Psychology, 25,* 109–116.

Edwards, C, (1977). RET in high school. *Rational Living, 12,* 10–12.

Ellis, A. (1957). *How to live with a "neurotic."* New York: Crown, 1957. Revised edition, New York: Crown, 1975 and North Hollywood: Wilshire.

Ellis, A. (1959). *Psychotherapy session with an eight-year-old female bed wetter*. Cassette recording. New York: Institute for Rational-Emotive Therapy.

Ellis, A. (1967). Talking to adolescents about sex. *Rational Living,* 2, 7–12.

Ellis, A. (1971a). An experiment in emotional education. *Educational Technology, 11,* 61–64.

Ellis, A. (1971b). *Rational-emotive therapy and its application to emotional education.* New York: Institute for Rational-Emotive Therapy.

Ellis, A. (1972a). The contribution of psychotherapy to school psychology. *School Psychology Digest, 1*, 6–9.

Ellis, A. (1972b). Emotional education in the classroom: The living school. *Journal of Child Psychol*ogy, *1*, 19–22.

Ellis, A. (1973a). A *demonstration with an elementary school child.* Filmed psychotherapy session. Washington: American Personnel and Guidance Association, 1973.

Ellis, A. (1973b). Emotional education at the living school. In M. M. Ohlsen (ed.), *Counseling children in groups*. New York: Holt, Rinehart and Winston, 1973.

Ellis, A. (1973c). *Humanistic psychotherapy*. New York: McGraw-Hill.

Ellis, A.(1975a). *Raising an emotionally healthy, happy child.* Videotape. Austin Texas: Audio Visual Resource Center, School of Social Work, University of Texas.

Ellis, A. (1975b). Rational-emotive therapy and the school counselor. *School Counselor, 22,* 236–242.

Ellis, A. (1977). The basic clinical theory of rational-emotive therapy. In A. Ellis and R. Grieger (eds.), *Handbook of rational-emotive therapy*. New York: Springer, 1977.

Ellis, A. (1980b). The rational-emotive approach to childrens' and adolescents' sex problems. In J. M. Sampson (Ed.), *Childhood and sexuality: Proceedings of the International Symposium*. Montreal: Editions Etudes Vivantes.

Ellis, A. (1980c). Rational-emotive therapy and cognitive behavior therapy: Similarities and differences. *Cognitive Therapy and Research, 4*, 325–340.

Ellis, A. (1984). *Rational-emotive therapy and cognitive behavior therapy*. New York: Springer.

Ellis, A. (1994) *Reason and emotion in psychotherapy*. Revised edition. Secaucus, N.J.: Lyle Stuart and Citadel Press.

Ellis, A. (2001). Reasons why rational emotive behavior therapy is relatively neglected in the professional and scientific literature. *Journal of Rational-Emotive and Cognitive Behavior Therapy, 19*(1), 67–74.

Ellis, A., and Bernard, M. E. (1983). An overview of rational-emotive approaches to the problems of childhood. In A. Ellis and M. E. Bernard (eds.), *Rational-emotive approaches to the problems of childhood.* New York: Plenum Press.

Ellis, A, and Wilde, J. (eds.) (2002). *Case studies in rational emotive behavior therapy with children and adolescents*. Upper Saddle River, NJ: Prentice Hall.

Ellis, A., Wolfe, J. H., and Moseley, S. (1966). *How to raise an emotionally healthy, happy child.* New York: Crown; and Hollywood: Wilshire Books.

Engels, G. I., Garnefski, N. and Diekstra, R. F. W. (1993). Efficacy of rational-emotive therapy: A quantitative analysis. *Journal of Consulting and Clinical Psychology, 61,* 1083–1090.

Eschenroeder, C. (1982). How rational is rational-emotive therapy? A critical appraisal of its theoretical foundations and therapeutic methods. *Cognitive Therapy and Research, 6*, 274–282.

Ford, P. W. (2005). [A meta-analysis of REBT studies]. Unpublished raw data.

Forman, S. G., and Forman, B. D. (1978). A rational-emotive therapy approach to consultation. *Psychology in the Schools, 15,* 400-406.

Gerald, M., and Eyman, W. (1981). *Thinking straight and talking sense*. New York: Institute for Rational-Emotive Therapy.

Glicken, M. (1967). Counseling children: Two methods. *Rational Living, 1,* 27–30.

Glicken, M. D. (1968). Rational .counseling: A dynamic approach to children. *Elementary School Guidance and Counseling, 2,* 261–267.

Gonzalez, J. E., Nelson, J. R., Gutkin, T. B., Saunders, A., Galloway, A., and Shwery, C. S. (2004). Rational Emotive Therapy with children and adolescents: A meta-analysis. *Journal of Emotional and Behavioral Disorders, 12*, 222–235.

Gossette, R. L. and O'Brien, R. M. (1992). The efficacy of rational emotive therapy in adults: Clinical fact of psychometric artifact? *Journal of Behavior Therapy and Experimental Psychiatry, 23,* 9–24.

Gossette, R. L. and O'Brien, R. M. (1993). Efficacy of rational emotive therapy with children: A Critical Re-appraisal. *Journal of Behavior Therapy and Experimental Psychiatry, 24,* 15–25.

Grieger, R. M., Anderson, K., and Canino, F. (1979). Psychotherapeutic modes. In E. Ignas and R. Corsini (eds.), Alternative educational systems. Itasca, Ill: Peacock.

Haaga, D. A. and Davison, G. C. (1989). Outcome studies of rational-emotive therapy. In Bernard, M. E. and DiGiuseppe, R. (eds.), Inside rational-emotive therapy. A critical appraisal of the theory and therapy of Albert Ellis. San Diego, CA: Academic Press, Inc. pp. 155–197.

Hajzler, D. J., and Bernard, M. E. (1991). A review of rational emotive outcome studies. *School Psychology Quarterly, 6,* 27–49.

Harris, S. R. (1976). Rational-emotive education and the human development program: A guidance study. *Elementary School Guidance and Counseling, 11,* 113–123.

Hauck, P. A. (1967). The rational management of children. New York: Libra Publishers.

Hauck, P. A. (1974). Public forum: Eleven myths of child counseling. Rational Living, *9,* 38–43.

Hauck, P. A. (1977). Irrational parenting styles. In A. Ellis and R. Grieger (eds.), *Handbook of rational-emotive therapy*. New York: Springer.

Hedges L.V. and Olkin, I. (1985). *Statistical methods for meta-analysis*. Orlando: Academic Press.

Hinshaw, S. P. (2000). Attention deficit/hyperactivity disorder: The search for viable treatments. In P. C. Kendall (ed.), *Child and adolescent therapy,* 2nd ed. New York: Guilford Press.

Hobbs, S. A., Moguin, L. E., Tyroler, M., and Lahey, B. B. (1980). Cognitive behavior therapy with children: Has clinical utility been demonstrated? *Psychological Bulletin, 87,* 147–165.

Holmbeck, G. N., and Updegrove, A. L. (1995). Clinical-developmental interface: Implications of developmental research for adolescent psychotherapy. *Psychotherapy, 32,* 16–33.

Holmbeck, G. R., Greenley, R. N., and Franks, E. A. (2003). Developmental issues and considerations in research and practice. In A. E. Kazdin and J. R. Weisz (eds.), *Evidence-based psychotherapies for children and adolescents*. New York: Plenum Press.

Jacobs, E. E. (1977). The effects of a systematic teaching program for college undergraduates based on rational-emotive concepts and techniques. M.A. thesis, Florida State University.

Jorm, A. F. (1989). Modifiability of trait anxiety and neuroticism: A meta-analysis of the literature. *Australian and New Zealand Journal of Psychiatry, 23,* 21–29.

Kagan, J. (1998). Biology and the child. In W. Damon (Editor-in-Chief) and N. Eisenberg (Vol. Ed.), *Handbook of child psychology: Vol. 3. Social, emotional and personality development*(5th. Ed.). New York: Wiley.

Katz, S. (1974). The effects of emotional education on locus of control and self-concept. Unpublished doctoral dissertation, Hofstra University.

Kelly, F. (1996)."That's not fair!"—Using RET to address the issue of fairness in the classroom. *Elementary School Guidance and Counseling, 30,* 235–238.

Kendall, P. C. (1977). On the efficacious use of verbal self-instructional procedures with children. *Cognitive Therapy and Research, 1,* 331–341.

Kendall, P. C. and Finch, A.J., Jr. (1979). Developing nonimpulsive behavior in children. In P. C. Kendall and S. D. Hollon (eds.), *Cognitive Behavioral Interventions. Theory, Research and Procedures,* New York: Academic Press.

Kendall, P. C., Choudhury, M., Hudson, J., and Webb, A. (2002). *The C.A.T. project workbook for the cognitive-behavioral treatment of anxious adolescents*. Ardmore, PA: Workbook Publishing.

Kendall, P. C., Ascenbrand, S. G., and Hudson, J. L. (2003). Child-focused treatment of anxiety. In A. Kazdin and J. R. Weisz (eds.), *Evidence-based psychotherapies for children and adolescents*. New York: Guilford Press.

Knaus, W. J. (1974). *Rational-emotive education: A manual for elementary school teachers,* New York: Institute for Rational-Emotive Therapy.

Knaus, W. J. (1977). Rational-emotive education. In A. Ellis and R. Grieger (eds.), *Handbook of rational-emotive therapy*. New York: Springer Publishing Co.
Knaus, W., and Bokor, S. The effect of rational-emotive education on anxiety and self-concept. *Rational Living, 20*(2), 7–10.
Knaus, W., and McKeever, C. (1977). Rational-emotive education with learning-disabled children. *Journal of Learning Disabilities, 10,* 10–14.
Kranzler, C. (1974). *Emotional education exercises for children.* Eugene, Oregon: Cascade Press.
Kujoth, R. J. (1976). *The effects of teaching rational idea concepts vs. teaching insight concepts on community college students in a course in human relations.* Ed. D. dissertation, Marquette University.
Lafferty, G., Dennell, A., and Rettich, G. (1964). A creative school mental health program. *National Elementary Principal, 43,* 28–35.
Lipsey, M.W., and Wilson, D.B. (2001). *Practical Meta-Analysis.* Applied Social Research Methods Series (Vol. 49). Thousand Oaks, CA: SAGE Publications.
Lochman, J. E., Whidby, J. M., and FitzGerald, D. P. (2000). Cognitive-behavioral assessment and treatment with aggressive children. In P. C. Kendall (ed.), *Child and adolescent therapy,* 2nd ed. New York: Guilford Press.
Lyons, L. C. and Woods, P. J. (1991). The efficacy of rational-emotive therapy: A quantitative review of the outcome research. *Clinical Psychology Review, 11,* 357–369.
Maes, W., and Heinman, R. (1970). *The comparison of three approaches to the reduction of test anxiety in high school students.* Final report project 9-1-040. Washington, DC: Office of Education, U.S. Department of Health, Education and Welfare.
Maultsby, M. C., Jr. (1974). The classroom as an emotional health center. *The Educational Magazine, 32,* 8–11.
Maultsby, M. C., Jr. (1975). Rational behavior therapy for acting-out adolescents. *Social Casework, 56,* 35–43.
Maultsby, M. C., Knipping, P., and Carpenter, L. (1974). Teaching self-help in the classroom with rational self-counseling. *The Journal of School Health, 44,* 445–448.
McGovern, T. E. and Silverman, M. S. (1984). A review of outcome studies of rational-emotive therapy from 1977 to 1982. *Journal of Rational Emotive Therapy, 2*(1), 7–18.
McGory, J. E. (1967). Teaching introspection in the classroom. *Rational Living, 2,* 23–24.
McMullin, R., Asafi, I., and Chapman, S. (1978). *Straight talk to parents.* Lakewood, Colo.: Counseling Research Institute.
Meichenbaum, D. (1977). *Cognitive-behavior modification: An integrative approach.* New York: Plenum Press.
Meichenbaum, D. (1987). *Stress innoculation training: A practitioner's guidebook.* New York: Allyn and Bacon.
Meichenbaum, D., and Asarnow, J. (1979). Cognitive-behavioral modification and metacognitive development: Implications for the classroom. In P. C. Kendall and S. D. Hollon (eds.), *Cognitive-behavior interventions: Theory, research and procedures.* New York: Academic Press.
Meichenbaum, D., and Cameron, R. (1973). Training schizophrenics to talk to themselves: A means of developing attentional controls. *Behavior Therapy, 4,* 515–534.
Metalsky, G. I., and Abramson, L. Y. (1981). Attributional styles: Towards a framework for conceptualization and assessment. In P. C. Kendall and S. D. Hollon

(eds.), *Assessment strategies for cognitive-behavioral interventions*. New York: Academic Press.

Miller, N. J. (1978). *Effects of behavioral rehearsal, written homework and level of intelligence on the efficacy of rational-emotive education in elementary school children*. Ph.D. dissertation, Hofstra University.

Mischel, W., Zeiss, R., and Zeiss, A. (1974). Internal-external control and persistence: Validation and implications of the Stanford Preschool Internal-External Scale. *Journal of Personality and Social Psychology, 29,* 265–278.

Nardi, T. J. (1981). Irrational beliefs of an adopted child. *RETwork, 7,* 2–4.

Novaco, R. W. (1978). Anger and coping with stress. In J. Foreyt and D. Rathsen (eds.), *Cognitive behavior therapy: Therapy, research and practice*. New York: Plenum Press.

Novaco, R. W. (1985). Anger and its therapeutic regulation. In M. A. Chesney and R. H. Rosenman (eds.), *Anger and hostility in cardiovascular and behavioral disorders*. New York: Hemisphere.

Piaget, J. (1952). *The origins of intelligence*. New York: Norton.

Prochaska, J. and DiClemente, C. (1981). *The transtheoretical approach to therapy*. Chicago: Dorsey Press.

Protinsky, H. (1976). Rational counseling with the adolescents. School *Counselor, 23,* 240–246.

Rand, M. E. (1970). Rational-emotive approaches to academic underachievement. *Rational Living, 4,* 16–18.

Reinecke, M. A. (2005). Personal communication.

Ritchie, B. C. (1978). The effect of rational-emotive education on irrational beliefs, assertiveness and/or locus of control in fifth grade students. *Dissertation Abstracts International,* 39(4B), 2069–2070.

Rosenthal, R. (1979). The ''file drawer problem'' and tolerance for null results. *Psychological Bulletin, 86,* 638–641.

Rossi, A. S. (1977). RET with children: More than child's play. *Rational Living,* 1977, *12,* 21–24.

Rothbart, M. K., and Bates, J. E. (1998). Temperament. In W. Damon (Editor-in-Chief) and N. Eisenberg (Volume-Editor), *Handbook of child psychology: Vol. 3. Social, emotional and personality development*(5th ed.). New York: Wiley.

Rotter, J. B. (1966). Generalized expectancies for internal versus external control of reinforcement. *Psychological Monographs, 80,* 1–26.

Sachs, N. J. (1971). Planned emotional education: The living school. *Art in Daily Living, 1,* 8–13.

Shannon, H. D., Allen, T. W. (1998). The effectiveness of a REBT training program in increasing the performance of high school students in mathematics. *Journal of Rational-Emotive and Cognitive Behavior Therapy*, 16, 197–209.

Shapiro, D. A. and Shapiro, D. (1982). Meta-analysis of comparative therapy outcome studies: A replication and refinement. *Psychological Bulletin, 92,* 581–604.

Sharma, K. L. (1970). *The rational group therapy approach to counseling anxious underachievers*. Ph.D. thesis, University of Alberta.

Shirk, S. R. (2001). Development and cognitive therapy. *Journal of Cognitive Psychotherapy, 15,* 155–163.

Shure, M. (1996). *I can problem solve: An interpersonal cognitive problem-solving program*. Champaign, Ill: Research Press.

Silverman, M. S., McCarthy, M., and McGovern, T. (1992). A review of outcome studies of rational-emotive therapy from 1982–1989. *Journal of Rational-Emotive and Cognitive-Behavior Therapy, 10,* 111–175.

Smith, G. W. (1979). *A rational-emotive counseling approach to assist junior high school students with interpersonal anxiety*. Unpublished doctoral dissertation, University of Oregon.

Solomon, H. (1978). Unclassified. *Rational Living, 13*, 41–42.

Spivack, G., and Shure, M. B. (1974). *Social adjustment of young children: A cognitive approach to solving real-life problems,* San Francisco: Jossey-Bass.

Spivack, G., Platt, J., and Shure, M. (1976). *The problem-solving approach to adjustment*. San Francisco: Jossey-Bass.

Staggs, A. M. (1979). *Group counseling of learning disabled children in the intermediate grades enrolled in the public school special education program: Training in cognitive behavior modification*. Unpublished doctoral dissertation, University of Denver.

Sydel, A. (1972). A *study to determine the effects of emotional education on fifth grade children*. M.A. thesis, Queens College.

Task Force on Promotion and Dissemination of Psychological Procedures (1995). Training in and dissemination of empirically validated treatments: Report and recommendations. *The Clinical Psychologist, 48*(1), 3–23.

Taylor, M. H. (1975). A rational-emotive workshop on overcoming study blocks. *Personnel and Guidance Journal, 53,* 458–462.

Terjesen, M., Doyle, K., Rose, R., Sciutto, M., Iovine-Calabro, E. and Zampano, G. (1999). *REBT in the Schools: A Review and Implications for School Psychologists*. Poster presented at the 107th annual convention of the American Psychological Association (APA; Division 16). Boston, MA.

Urbain, E. S., and Kendall, P. C. (1980). Review of social-cognitive problem-solving interactions with children. *Psychological Bulletin, 88,* 109–143.

Vernon, A. (1980). *Help yourself to a healthier you: A handbook of emotional education exercises for children*. Boston, MA: University Press of America.

Vernon, A. (1983). Rational emotive education. In A. Ellis and M. Bernard (eds.), *Rational emotive approaches to the problems of childhood.* New York: Plenum Press.

Vernon, A. (1989a). *Thinking, feeling, behaving: An emotional education curriculum for children*. Champaign, IL: Research Press.

Vernon, A. (1989b). *Thinking, feeling, behaving: An emotional education curriculum for adolescents*. Champaign, IL: Research Press.

Vernon, A. (1989c). Assessment and treatment of childhood problems: Applications of rational-emotive therapy. *Counseling and Human Development, 22*(4), 2–12.

Vernon, A. (1990). The school psychologists' role in preventative education: Applications of rational-emotive education. *School Psychology Review, 19,* 322–330.

Vernon, A. (1993a). Rational-emotive consultation: A model for implementing rational-emotive education. In M. Bernard and R. DiGiuseppe (eds.), *Rational-emotive consultation in applied settings*. New York: Earlbaum.

Vernon, A. (1993b). *Developmental assessment with children and adolescents*. Alexandria, VA: American Counseling Association.

Vernon, A. (1997). Applications of REBT with children and adolescents. In J. Yankura and W. Dryden (eds.), *Special applications of REBT: A therapist's casebook*. New York, NY: Springer Publishing.

Vernon, A. (1998a). *The passport program: A journey through emotional, social, cognitive, and self-development* (Grades 1-5). Champaign, IL: Research Press.

Vernon, A. (1998b). *The passport program: A journey through emotional, social, cognitive and self-development* (Grades 6-8). Champaign, IL: Research Press.

Vernon, A. (1998c). *The passport program: A journey through emotional, social, cognitive, and self-development* (Grades 9-12). Champaign, IL: Research Press.

Vernon, A. (1999). Applications of rational-emotive behavior therapy with children and adolescents. In A. Vernon (Ed.), *Counseling children and adolescents* (2nd ed., pp. 140–157). Denver, CO: Love Publishing.

Vernon, A. (2000). Catastrophe continuum, Attacking anxiety, Zap the irrational beliefs, and Facts and beliefs. (Activities). In M. Bernard and J. Wolfe (eds.), *The REBT resource book for practitioners* (2nd edition). New York: Albert Ellis Institute.

Vernon, A. (2002). Philip: A third grader with anxiety. In A. Ellis and J. Wilde (eds.), *Case studies in rational emotive behavior therapy with children and adolescents*. Upper Saddle River, NJ: Prentice Hall.

Vernon, A. (2004a). Applications of rational emotive behavior therapy with children and adolescents. In A. Vernon (Ed.), *Counseling children and adolescents* (3rd ed., pp. 163–185). Denver, CO: Love Publishing.

Vernon, A. (2004b). Rational emotive education. *Romanian Journal of Cognitive and Behavioral Psychotherapies, IV,* 23–39.

Vernon, A. (2004c). Counseling children and adolescents: Developmental considerations. In A. Vernon (Ed.), *Counseling children and adolescents* (3rd ed., pp. 1–31). Denver, CO: Love Publishing.

Vernon, A. (2006a). Thinking, feeling, behaving: An emotional education curriculum for children (2nd ed.; Grades 1-6). Champaign, IL: Research Press.

Vernon, A. (2006b). Thinking, feeling, behaving: An emotional education curriculum for adolescents (2nd ed.; Grades 7-12). Champaign, IL: Research Press.

Wagner, E. E. (1966). Counseling children. *Rational Living, 1*, 26, 28.

Walen, S. R., DiGiuseppe, R. A., and Wessler, R. L. (1980). *A practitioner's guide to rational-emotive therapy*. New York: Oxford University Press.

Warren, R., Deffenbach, J., and Broding, P.(1976). Rational-emotive therapy and the reduction of test anxiety in elementary school students. *Rational Living,11*, 28–29.

Warren, R., McLellararn, R., and Ponzoha, C. (1988). Rational emotive therapy vs. general cognitive behavior therapy in the treatment of low self-esteem and related emotional disturbances. *Cognitive Therapy and Research, 12,* 21–38.

Waters, V. (1980a). Series of pamphlets on parenting: *Accepting yourself and your child; The anger trap and how to spring it; Building frustration tolerance in you and your children; Fear interferes; Rational problem solving skills; Teaching children to light up their lives*. New York: Institute for Rational Living.

Waters, V. (1980b). Series of stories for children: *Cornelia Cardinal learns to cope; Fasha, Dasha and Sasha Squirrel; Flora Farber's fear of failure; Freddie Flounder; Maxwell's magnificent monster*. New York: Institute for Rational Living.

Waters, V. (1981). The living school. *RETwork 1,* 1.

Waters, V. (1982). Therapies for children: Rational-emotive therapy. In C. R. Reynolds and T. B. Gutkin (eds.), *Handbook of school psychology*. New York: Wiley.

Weiner, B. (Ed.). (1974). *Achievement motivation and attribution theory*. Morristown, N.J.: General Learning Press.

Weisz, J. R., Weiss, B., Han, S. S., Granger, D. A., and Morton, T. (1995). Effects of psychotherapy with children and adolescents revisited: A meta-analysis of treatment outcome studies. *Psychological Bulletin, 117,* 450–468.

Weisz, J. R., and Hawley, K. M. (2002). Developmental factors in the treatment of adolescents. *Journal of Consulting and Clinical Psychology, 70,* 21–43.

Wessler, R. A., and Wessler, R. L. (1980). *The principles and practices of rational-emotive therapy*. San Francisco: Jossey-Bass.

White, H. D. (1994). Scientific communications and literature retrieval. In H. Coopers and L. Hedges (eds.) *The handbook of research synthesis*. New York: Russell Sage Foundation.

Wolfe, J., and Staff. (1970). Emotional education in the classroom: The living school. *Rational Living, 4,* 23–25.

Wilde, J. (1992). *Rational counseling with school-aged populations: A practical guide*. Bristol, PA: Accelerated Development Inc.

Woulff, N. (1983). Involving the family in the treatment of the child: A model for rational-emotive therapists. In A. Ellis and M. E. Bernard (eds.), *Rational-emotive approaches to the problems of childhood*. New York: Plenum Press.

Young, H. S. (1974a). A framework for working with adolescents. *Rational Living, 9,* 2–7.

Young, H. S. (1974b). *A rational counseling primer*. New York: Institute for Rational-Emotive Therapy.

Young, H. S. (1977). Counseling strategies with working class adolescents. In J. L. Wolfe and E. Brand (eds.), *Twenty years of rational therapy*. New York: Institute for Rational-Emotive Therapy.

Zelie,. K., Stone, C., and Lehr, E. (1980). Cognitive behavior intervention in school discipline: A preliminary study. *Personnel arid Guidance Journal, 59*, 80–83.

Zettle, R. and Hayes, S. (1980). Conceptual and empirical status of rational emotive therapy. *Progress in Behavior Modification, 9,* 125–166.

Zionts, P., and Zionts, L. (1997). *Journal of Emotional and Behavioral Problems, 6,* 103–108.

Appendix A: Typical ABCS of Common Childhood Problems (from Bernard, 2004a)

ABC's of Anger

Activating events: unfairness, inconsideration, disrespect, being picked on, not listened to, not getting one's way

Beliefs

Inferences (predictions, conclusions): This is unfair. I am never able to do what I want. Everyone else gets what he or she wants.

Absolutes (shoulds, oughts, musts, needs): People should treat me fairly, considerately and with respect. I must have what I want.

Evaluations (derivatives of the absolutes): This is awful, terrible . . . the worst thing in the world. I can't stand it . . . I shouldn't have to obey rules all the time. This person is totally bad and deserves to be punished.

Consequences (emotions, behaviors): anger, aggressive behavior (physical, verbal), rule breaking, power struggles, defiance, and procrastination

ABC's of Bullying

Type 1: Children Who Bully Because they Feel Inferior

Activating events: peers who cannot defend themselves

Beliefs:

Inferences (conclusions, predictions): I will be perceived by my peers as strong and "cool" if I can bully and intimidate others.

Absolutes (shoulds, oughts, musts, needs): To be approved of and to feel worthwhile, I must be the strongest. I need my peers to think highly of me.

Evaluations (derivatives of the absolutes): It is awful to be seen as weak. I can't stand it if my peers think they are stronger than me.

Consequences (emotions, behaviors): underlying inferiority, anger, verbal/physical abuse

Type 2: Children Who Bully Because they Need to Be Seen as the Best in Everything including having to Control Others

Activating events: peers who cannot defend themselves

Inferences (conclusions, predictions): Muscle power rather than brain power is the key to my success in school. The way to show others I am a man/woman is by showing my classmates through my fists and harsh words that I can control others and make the world run my way.

Absolutes (shoulds, oughts, musts, needs): I must be successful and all-powerful in all areas of my life. I must be the best in all my academic and social activities and be seen by others as the strongest too. People should do my bidding.

Evaluations (derivatives of the absolute): It is awful to be beaten by anyone. I can't stand losing. Coming in second means you are a loser.

Consequences (emotions, behaviors): over confidence, controlling behavior, victimization, and anger

ABC's of Cheating

Activating events: upcoming test, papers, assignments

Beliefs:

Inferences (conclusions, predictions): Because I have always cheated on tests and have somehow managed to pass and not get caught, I will never be able to pass unless I continue to cheat.

Absolutes (shoulds, oughts, musts, needs): I need to achieve well and be seen to be among the best in my schoolwork.

Evaluations (derivatives of the absolute): It is terrible and awful for me to fail on an exam. I would be a total idiot if I did fail.

Consequences (emotions, behaviors): anxiety, guilt, cheating, pressurizing friends to copy

ABC's of Feeling Down

Activating Events: loss of parental love through desertion/abandonment/neglect or death

Beliefs
Inferences (conclusions, predictions): My parent doesn't love me. It's my fault my parent never wants to see me. I cannot do anything to get his/her to love me. I cannot be happy without his/her love. Life is not worth living if I cannot have his/her love. Absolutes (shoulds, oughts, musts, needs): I need my parent's love.

Evaluations: I cannot bear to live without her love. This proves how unlovable and hopeless I am. This is terrible.

Consequence (emotional, behavioral): down, crying, periods of inactivity, avoidance of people and tasks, tiredness, irritability

Activating Events: poor school performance

Beliefs
Inferences (conclusions, predictions): I'm not good at any of my schoolwork and never will be. I am hopeless in everything I do.

Absolutes (shoulds, oughts, musts, needs): I should/must achieve in my schoolwork.

Evaluations: It is awful to make mistakes and do so poorly, I really can't stand it. This proves I am really a total failure.

Consequence (emotional, behavioral): down, crying, periods of inactivity, avoidance of people and tasks, tiredness, irritability

Activating events: social rejection, teasing, no one to play with, not being invited, loss of boyfriend/girlfriend

Beliefs
Inferences (conclusions, predictions): Everyone is against me. Everyone is teasing me. No one likes me. I'll never have any friends.

I can't be happy without his/her love or attention.

Absolutes (shoulds, oughts, musts, needs): I need people to like and approve of me.

Evaluations: It is awful to be criticized, laughed at and alone. I can't stand it. This proves that I really am a hopeless person.

Consequence (emotional, behavioral): down, crying, periods of inactivity, avoidance of people and tasks, tiredness, irritability

ABCs of Procrastination

Activating events: chores, homework

Beliefs:
Inferences (conclusions, predictions): Difficult tasks are impossible. Everything will turn out okay whether I work or not. To do this work would be a violation of my personal integrity. Nothing I do at school will benefit me.

Absolutes (shoulds, oughts, musts, needs): I shouldn't have to do things I do not feel like doing. Life should be comfortable and fun and never boring.

Evaluations: This work I have to do is the worst thing in the world. I can't stand having to do it. The world is crap in forcing me to do this work.

Consequences (emotions, behaviors): forgetfulness, daydreaming, delays in getting started and finishing schoolwork and chores, anger when forced to do things she/he doesn't feel like doing, impatience, impulsiveness, avoidance tactics, laziness, diffuse anxiety

ABCs of Perfectionism

Type 1: Compulsive Effort

Activating events: any work/activity/task deemed important to do and difficult to accomplish

Beliefs
Inferences (conclusions, predictions): I will not be able to do this successfully. By putting in maximum effort, I can be perfect. Mistakes show that I cannot do things perfectly.

Absolutes (shoulds, oughts, musts, needs): I really should do things perfectly.

Evaluations: It would be a catastrophe to not to be able to do this perfectly . . . too unbearable to tolerate. It is awful to make mistakes. To be imperfect would prove I am a failure.

Consequences (emotions, behaviors): generalized anxiety, excessive effort, depression when one fails

Type 2: Lack of Effort

Activating events: any work/activity/task deemed important to do and difficult to accomplish

Beliefs
Inferences (conclusions, predictions): I will not be able to do this perfectly. By putting in minimum effort, I have a ready-made excuse for not doing things perfectly (I didn't try). Why bother doing things if I cannot do them perfectly?

Absolutes (shoulds, oughts, musts, needs): I really should do things perfectly.

Evaluations: It would be a catastrophe to not to be able to do this perfectly . . . too unbearable to tolerate. It is awful to make mistakes. To be imperfect would prove I am a failure.

Consequences (emotions, behaviors): underlying anxiety, lack of effort, choosing not to participate in new activities where success is not guaranteed, choosing not to compete

ABCs of Social Anxiety

Activating events: being in social situations, meeting new people, having to give a speech

Beliefs:
Inferences (conclusions, predictions): I'll say something stupid or not know what to say. People will think I'm stupid. No one will want to speak with me. I'll be too uncomfortable.

Absolutes (shoulds, oughts, musts, needs): I need people to like and approve of me. I need to be comfortable.

Evaluations: It is awful to be laughed at or criticized by others.

Consequences (emotions, behaviors): social anxiety, discomfort anxiety, avoidance, blushing, physical signs of nervousness, stammering, mumbling

ABCs of Performance Anxiety

Activating events: having to take a test, give a speech

Beliefs:
Inferences (conclusions, predictions): I'll make mistakes. I have no talent in doing this and never will have.

Absolutes (shoulds, oughts, musts, needs): I must perform well at all times.

Evaluations (derivatives of the absolutes): It would be a catastrophe and intolerable not to not perform well.

Consequences (emotions, behaviors): tenseness, high anxiety/panic attack, forgetfulness, procrastination in preparation, shaky performance, careless mistakes, physical symptoms of nervousness (e.g., sweaty palms, muscle tenseness)

ABCs of School Phobia

Activating events: having to go to or stay at school

Beliefs:
Inferences (conclusions, predictions): Something bad will happen to me at school. I might even be killed. I will go to school and everyone will laugh at me. The teacher will think there is something wrong with me. I will not know what to do. I am too far behind to catch up. I will not understand what to do. It will be totally uncomfortable and unpleasant to be in class and with my classmates. They'll tease me and think I'm a total loser.

Absolutes (shoulds, oughts, musts, needs): I should/must achieve in my schoolwork. I need be to be liked and approved of. I need to be comfortable.

Evaluations: To be laughed at by my classmates and thought badly of by my teacher is awful and terrible. I cannot stand feeling so uncomfortable. Showing people how weak I am will prove that I am hopeless.

Consequences (emotions, behaviors): discomfort anxiety, social/performance anxiety, refusal to attend school or go to class, clinginess to mother, avoidance of children who attend school.

ABCs of Secondary Emotional Distress

Activating events: procrastination, depression, angry, anxiety
Inferences (conclusions, predictions): I am the only person with this problem. There must be something wrong with me. I'll always have this problem.
Absolutes (shoulds, oughts, musts, needs): I shouldn't have this problem.

I need people to think highly of me.

Evaluations: It's awful to have this problem. I can't stand it if people see I have a problem. I cannot stand myself for having this problem. I must be a real loser.

Consequences (emotions, behaviors): guilt, down, denial of primary problem

Appendix B: Tips to Share With Parents for Overcoming Different Problems of Childhood (Bernard, 2004a)

Tips to Share with Parents for Helping a Child Overcome Fear

1. If it is known that a child has a strong tendency to become frightened by dogs, the dark, loud noises or anything else, a special effort may be made to keep him/her out of the range of these things.
2. The easily upsettable child should preferably be kept away from excessively fearful adults and older children.
3. If you as a parent happen to be imbued with a great many intense fears, train yourself to suppress as thoroughly as possible these fears when you are with your child. Also work on minimizing them.

4. Children who are reasonably fearful of external events can frequently be talked out of fears (through repetition of rational explanations) if those who raise them will reason with them in a patient, kindly and persistent manner.
5. Blaming the child or making fun of him/her for fearfulness usually will not help but will tend to do more harm than good. The child had better clearly be shown that the fear is groundless and that other children do not have it but that there is nothing wrong with him/her because he/she now cannot handle him/herself in this area.
6. Getting children to laugh through the use of humor at their own and others' fears may be of value if it is directed at the child's panic rather than at him/her.
7. Calmness in dealing with a child's fears is one of the prime prerequisites for helping him/her overcome them.
8. Do not be deceived by a child's clever evasions of admitting his/her fears. If a child claims that she/he is not particularly afraid of other children or animals but simply dislikes them, ask yourself whether she/he is using dislike as a cover-up for his/her fears.

Tips to Share with Parents for Helping a Child Overcome Anxieties, Low Self-Esteem and Feeling Discouraged

1. Fully accept the fact that a child has not had time to learn all the strange rules of the adult world; consequently she/he is unusually fallible and will inevitably make mistakes that will bother his/her parents. Children will outlive their childishness only if they are allowed to act it out, to learn by making mistakes, rather than being warned of dire consequences, and berated for making mistakes.
2. Learn to tolerate normal inefficiencies (child unable to tie shoelaces) as they will always exist without getting angry. Displace the onus of mistakes and failures onto the task rather than the child.
3. Keep in mind that the cause of low self-esteem is the child's tendency to put him/herself down when something bad happens. Teach the child to never rate him/herself in terms of his/her behavior and to separate his/her actions from his/her judgments of his/her self-worth (teach self-acceptance).
4. Do not expect that a child prone to emotional lability will be problem free. Once a child feels that others do not like him/her and that it is horrible that they do not, she/he will frequently resort to testing procedures to see whether his/her peers and elders will accept him/her.
5. Show excitement and interest in the child's extracurricular activities.
6. Remind yourself that a young person's anxious-dependent behavior is often motivated out of the fear of making mistakes, the fear of disapproval and the need to manipulate his/her parents and others to help him with his/her work so that she/he does not make mistakes.
7. Do not allow yourself to be manipulated by your children into being overly supportive.

8. Use the Praise, Prompt and Leave procedure (e.g., allow the child to struggle with difficult activities without rescuing him/her).
9. Teach children not to judge or evaluate their schoolwork until after a certain period of time.
10. Communicate a belief that the child will be successful.
11. Evaluate the child's progress based on the amount she/he has learned rather than in comparison with other children.
12. Once you have ascertained that a child's behavior is poor, try to estimate what she/he is capable of doing and not doing and judge behavior, not himself/herself accordingly.
13. If you honestly believe that a child's behavior is correctable, keep in mind that change can be a very slow process; be patient and tolerant.
14. Keep in mind that the main reason for anyone's anxieties is his/her dire need to be accepted, approved, or loved by significant people in his life. Show your child by example that you do not need other's approval and that it is not the end of the world when others think poorly of you.
15. Do not give into an anxious child's desire to be pampered and protected.
16. Children who are anxious tend to become upset and put themselves down, become embarrassed, panicky and anxious about being seen as anxious. Tell children that it is not terrible to reveal to others how afraid one is.

Tips to Share with Parents for Helping a Child Overcome Perfectionism

1. Help the child become more aware of his/her perfectionism and the negative costs of anxiety and either excessive efforts on what she/he does or the lack of effort on tasks/activities that she/he anticipates not doing perfectly.
2. Teach the child about famous people (e.g., Thomas Edison) or role models who fumbled and stumbled their way to success. Point out that these individuals needed to make mistakes and take risks in order to succeed.
3. Have the child list the things she/he has always wanted to do but has been afraid of not doing perfectly. Have the child agree to do one of these activities.
4. Encourage the child to identify his/her areas of weakness. Have him/her agree to try activities in these areas. When the child has attempted such an activity, point out that she/he now has evidence that she/he can tolerate doing things imperfectly.
5. Encourage the child to stop ruminating about his/her grades. Encourage him/her to get involved in activities unrelated to school.
6. Teach the child there is a continuum of achievement; achievement is not an all (perfection) or nothing event (complete failure). Help the child set goals at a place on the achievement continuum where she/he does not have to be the best in order to learn something and have fun.
7. Constantly challenge the child's perfectionistic belief that she/he needs to do everything perfectly and that it is a catastrophe to make mistakes. Help the child to modify this belief to a desire to do the best she/he can and

appreciating that mistakes are not bad but are a natural part of learning something new. Encourage the child to give him/herself the permission to make mistakes.

8. Help the child to accept and be comfortable with doing things that are ambiguous and about which there is uncertainty about how to proceed.
9. For long-term projects and assignments, see if you can have your child to hand in the beginning portion (e.g., introductory paragraph, outline) well in advance. Explain that what is important is that she/he does some work, not that the work be done perfectly.
10. Help the child see tasks as a series of parts that have to be completed one after another rather than as a whole chunk that must be completed perfectly.
11. Reward the child as she/he completes each portion of an assignment and for not doing each part perfectly.
12. Point out to the child the pleasure of doing new activities.

Tips for Sharing with Parents for Helping Overcome their Child's Excessive Peer Conformity

1. Discuss with the child his/her long-term educational and occupational goals and the importance of successful school accomplishments in achieving these goals.
2. Offer the child an opportunity to express the desire to do well in school.
3. Point out the negative consequences on the child's effort and success in school that will ensue if the child continues to hang out with a peer group that lacks motivation and interest in doing well in school.
4. Ask the child what would happen if she/he started to work harder and do better in school. Establish that in the child's mind, his/her friends would reject him/her.
5. Explain to the child that his/her belief that his/her friends would reject him/her is probably erroneous even though they might hassle him/her for wanting to do better.
6. Ask the child if she/he would be willing to put this belief to the test by working harder and monitoring the effect that this has on his/her friends.
7. Ask the child what it would say about his/her peers if they did reject him/her simply because she/he chose to try hard to do well in school. Ask whether they would be "good" or true friends.
8. Point out to the child that his/her true friends will not reject him/her for working towards educational goals. State that if they do, it might be time for the child to look for different friends who will accept his/her right to decide how she/he approaches schoolwork.
9. Explore the possibility of alternative friendships and peer groups with the child.

Tips for Sharing with Parents for Helping a Child Overcome Lack of Motivation and Increase their Frustration Tolerance for Doing Schoolwork

1. Help organize the child's home and school activities by making a checklist of materials that need to be taken to school and home each day.
2. Check the child's notebooks on a daily basis to ensure that papers and work are correctly organized (e.g., filed).
3. Help the child breakdown long-term assignments and projects into easier, short-term steps.
4. Do not accept sub-standard homework from the child.
5. Provide strong and immediate feedback for the effort the child expends on work she/he finds hard or boring including the editing of schoolwork.
6. Communicate and model the belief that for people to be successful in the long-term, they sometimes have to do unpleasant things in the short-term.
7. Encourage the child to join a work-oriented peer study group.
8. As much as you can, help your child select classes and activities that accommodate his/her natural interests.
9. Provide real life examples that show how school learning relates to the real world and gives the child an advantage.
10. Explain to the child that things probably will not turn out OK for the child if she/he continues to put off doing schoolwork.
11. Identify a course, program or activity that a child would love to attend in the future that requires as an entry requirement a satisfactory performance in classes that the child is currently not applying him/herself.

Tips to Share with Parents for Helping a Child who Gets Angry and Rebels

1. As much as possible, stay calm when faced with a child who is misbehaving or disobedient. Convince yourself that the child sometimes will be misbehaving or disobedient, and that it is the child's natural nature.
2. Do not condemn or harshly punish a child for his/her hostility when she/he is unusually hostile.
3. Do not engage in a power struggle with the child (take your wind out of his/her sails).
4. Encourage siblings to support the child so that she/he does not feel alienated from the family.
5. Provide the child with opportunities to constructively contribute to the family.
6. Hold private rather than public discussions with the child.
7. Communicate, model and reinforce the belief that people make mistakes by acting unfairly and that the child should not judge their overall worth on the basis of their behavior.
8. Show the child that his/her anger comes from the rational idea "I don't like this thing

9. Help your child develop the belief that she/he can tolerate things she/he doesn't like.
10. When your child's behavior begins to get out of hand, use some kind of diversion as an effective means of calming him/her down.
11. Draw up a behavioral contract in which the child agrees to work on his/her assignments for a specific amount of time each week. Be sure the contract outlines the rewards for achieving the goal and the penalties for not achieving the goal. Ensure that the rewards and penalties proposed in the contract are sufficiently powerful to act as motivators of the child's behavior.
12. Explain to the child that she/he has choices in whether to act responsibly.
13. Remove unnecessary frustrations from the child.

2

REBT Assessment and Treatment with Children

RAYMOND DIGIUSEPPE AND MICHAEL E. BERNARD

Psychology has gone cognitive, and cognitive-behavior therapy has become the Zeitgeist in psychotherapy. Since the early 1980s, the cognitive orientation so popular with adults has filtered down to interventions with children (see Kendall, 2000). Today, many practitioners working with children use not only behavioral or family-systems conceptualizations to plan treatment but incorporate cognitive change as well. Cognitions have become viewed by many as the mediational variables by which these external factors (family systems and behavioral contingencies) have their effect. One can change children's behavior by restructuring systems or by rearranging contingencies or, more directly and, perhaps more efficiently, by attempting to change the child's cognitions directly.

As with adults, rational-emotive behavior therapy (REBT) hypothesizes that children's disturbed emotions are largely generated by their beliefs (Ellis, 1994). Irrational beliefs and distortions of reality are likely to create anger, anxiety, and depression in children just as they do with adults. In fact, because children are children—immature, less sophisticated, and less educated—one might expect them to make more cognitive errors than adults and to become upset more easily. There has been considerable research on the role of cognitions and irrational beliefs in particular in contributing to emotions not only in adults but in children (e.g., Bernard and Cronan, 1999).

Over the past 30 years, a variety of REBT-oriented publications have enabled cognitive behavior therapists and other child-oriented practitioners (school counselors, school psychologists, social workers) to integrate child-friendly REBT methods in their work with children. Chief amongst these publications has been Bill Knaus' (1974) book *Rational Emotive Education: A Manual for Elementary School Teachers* who for the first time, "translated" rational and irrational beliefs and disputing techniques into language and practices that could be understand and utilized by children as young as six. Child practitioners who discovered this resource found that their young clients readily understood relationships among Happenings→Thoughts→Feelings→Behaviors taught via "Mr. Head" and other child-friendly activities. Virginia Water's (1982) chapter on REBT with children appearing in the *School Psychology Handbook* outlined and discussed common irrational beliefs of children as well as outlined her common practice of always seeing the child with his/her parent(s) together in therapy in order for the parent(s) to learn how to support maintenance of the child's rational beliefs after therapy ceased. Ray DiGiuseppe (1981) pioneered the use of *rational self-statements* with young children (as distinct from positive self-statements). He also wrote about the use of *empirical disputation* as an easier form of disputing than logical disputing for children in the concrete stage of operational thought. Since the 1980s, REBT resources designed for children in the 6 to 12 year old age range have provided cognitively-oriented child practitioners with engaging activities that could be used in one-to-one child therapy to teach the basics of REBT instead of or having to rely on "talk therapy." Ann Vernon published "Thinking, Feeling, Behaving" (1989) and the "Passport Program" (1998) which have been extensively utilized at the elementary school level in individual and small group work. Michael Bernard's "Program Achieve" (2001a, b, c) a three volume curricula of personal development activities based on REBT is being used extensively throughout the world including many thousands of primary schools in Australia. Jerry Wilde published the popular board game for use with children "Let's Get Rational" in 1987. Finally, the publication in 1983 of the first edition of this book, in 1984 of Bernard and Joyce's "Rational Emotive Therapy with Children and Adolescents" and Bernard's 2004 book "The REBT Therapist's Pocket Companion for Working with Children and Adolescents", has provided cognitive behavior therapists with the theory and practice of REBT that applied to children and their parents.

This chapter outlines some of the ways in which REBT has been used over the past four decades to bring about cognitive changes and associated improvements in children's emotions and behaviors. This chapter addresses special aspects that need to be considered when using REBT with children ages six through twelve. Issues surrounding the use of REBT when working with the parents of children who present with depression, anger and anxiety are covered in the chapter by Marie Joyce that appears in the final section of this book.

Developmental Perspectives

Child-oriented REBT practice has always taken into account the child's cognitive-developmental status in selecting appropriate cognitive assessment and intervention procedures (e.g., Vernon and Clemente, 2006) and involving parents in child treatment (e.g., Waters, 1982). Armed with the knowledge that basic learning processes and abilities (e.g., attention, memory, verbal mediation, and cognitive strategies) appear to develop progressively over the childhood period, child-oriented practitioners have in the past few years begun to question the role of different developmental characteristics in determining the efficacy of cognitive-behavioral intervention (e.g., Cohen and Myers, 1983). Early work in this area focused in determining whether children's level of cognitive development influences their capacity to profit from self-instructional training (Meichenbaum, 1977), which is introduced at different levels of complexity employing different teaching formats. Schleser, Meyers, and Cohen (1981) suggested that pre-concrete-operational children may not have achieved a sufficient level of metacognitive development to profit from verbal self-instruction that employs directed discovery rather than direct expository methods. The related research of Cohen and Meyers (1983) indicated that preoperational children are unable to spontaneously generate cognitive self-guiding strategies.

REBT child-oriented practitioners employ several principles and guidelines when taking into account the child's cognitive status. We know from our review of Piaget that it is only when children are in the formal operational period (approximately 12 years and older) that they are generally capable of the type of hypothetico-deductive reasoning we believe is a necessary prerequisite for the disputational examination of irrational beliefs when they are presented in therapy as abstract propositions (e.g., "Does it make sense to demand that your fallible parent act fairly all the time?"). Bernard and Joyce (1984) have written:

> Many children do not have the cognitive capacity to (a) recognize *their general* irrational beliefs (e.g.,"The world should be fair and bad people should be punished") *when they are presented as a hypothetical proposition,* (b) rationally restate irrational as rational beliefs (e.g., "The world is not a fair place to live and people who act unfairly can be helped to correct their ways"), and (c) utilize and generalize their rationally restated belief as rational self-statements in all situations (where they are treated unfairly).

We know from Piaget and others (e.g., Flavell, 1977) that children between the approximate ages of 7 and 11 structure their world in an empirical and inductive manner. As a consequence, basic RET attitudes, insights, concepts, and beliefs are taught to children *through intensive analyses of specific situations*. Concrete examples and teaching illustrations are the rule. Bernard and Joyce (1984) illustrated this developmental orientation as follows:

> For example, in working with aggressive and conduct disordered young boys (7–11 years of age), we find they frequently believe that people whom they perceive "doing them in" deserve to be "done in" themselves. We have achieved good success in getting this population to change their beliefs by (a) discussing a specific situation (e.g., being unfairly treated in a math class by a teacher), (b) defining the concept of "fairness" and having them empirically analyze whether the current situation is unfair or not; this step frequently involves using puppets so that the child can view

the situation from another's perspective, (c) discussing the concept of "mistake making" and explaining the different reasons why a math teacher may act unfairly and make mistakes, (d) providing a set of rational self-instructions (e.g., "It's okay to make mistakes; no one's perfect; I can handle this situation; I don't have to get upset") which are modeled and role-played, (e) discussing the concepts of "fairness" and "mistake making" in the context of other problematic situations (e.g., other teachers, parents, siblings, in-class, at play, at home), (f) giving practice in applying the rational self-statements to novel situations, and (g) reinforcing the child (and getting him to self-reinforce) for using rational self-talk with the practitioner and in "real life situations."

In a section of this chapter, we illustrate how disputational strategies can be modified for use with younger populations taking into account their developmental characteristics. When we work with very young children (under 7 years old) we are especially cognizant of their difficulty in readily taking into account the perspective of others (egocentrism) as well as considering more than one relevant dimension at a time. As children during this period rely heavily on perceptual analysis rather than conceptual inference (Morris and Cohen, 1982), we deemphasize extensive discussion and analysis of irrational beliefs and, instead, rely on the child's more advanced capacity for dealing with iconic representation, and employ a great many concrete and simple materials (pictures, diagrams, stories) that young children can readily learn from. Developmental work in verbal mediation (e.g., Flavell *et al.,* 1966) indicates that children between the ages of 6 and 9 who fail to spontaneously produce functional self-guiding verbal mediators may learn to do so from instruction. Therefore, we spend a great deal of time with younger children teaching them through a variety of different techniques what to think and how to spontaneously use rational self-talk in problem situations.

REBT practitioners are also aware that children, especially at the earlier developmental levels, are active learners and that knowledge acquisition is facilitated by "doing" and "seeing" as much as by "hearing." We again recommend the use of pictures and stories, which may serve as imaginal mnemonic aids and may also to enhance the experiential aspect of the learning episode.

Relationship Building

While REBT practice with children views a positive working relationship as an essential condition for progress to be made, REBT practitioners assume that the relationship will develop as therapy progresses. That is, REBTers do not wait for the relationship to develop before commencing therapy; rather starting in the first session with children, REBT practice combines relationship building practices (e.g., warmth, unconditional acceptance, empathy) with data-gathering that initiates the change process including the identification of negative events and the assessment of rational and irrational thoughts, appropriate and inappropriate negative emotions, and adaptive and dysfunctional behaviors (see Table 1 for suggestions for beginning the first session with children). The exception to this rule is when children arrive at therapy with limited understanding of why they are there or have limited self-awareness of the need to change.

TABLE 1. Suggestions for REBT child session number one.

1	Define role of therapist/counselor (problem solver: "I am good at helping you if you have hassles with others, worries about the future, hurt feelings.") Reassure young clients that they are not crazy and that having a problem is not "bad"—everyone has problems—especially when growing up. Explain that just as they go to a medical doctor when they have a cold, break a leg, etc., they go to someone when they have a social, behavioral or emotional problem. Explain that counseling is a safe place to explore feelings and thoughts.
2	Establish confidentiality limits with parents, teachers and young client. Ask whether there is anything they have shared with you that they do not want someone else to know.
3	Share reason for referral.
4	If you sense a young client's reluctance/resistance to being referred, normalize feelings ("It seems that you don't want to be here and that's all right. However, someone who cares about you thinks there is something wrong, maybe I can help.")
5	Share information about the counseling/therapy process you are using. Explain that the two of you will be working together helping the young person deal with particular problems. Indicate that for most sessions, you will be asking them to talk about their thoughts, feelings, behaviors and you will be showing them different ways to manage their feelings so that when something bad happens, they do not feel so upset and will know how to feel better. Indicate you will be asking them to perform various "experiments" during the week that can provide them with additional ways to solve problems. Stress that it is very important that the young client carry through with the practice involved in conducting the experiments. Indicate the number of sessions.
6	Normalize problem and communicate hope ("Lots of kids lose their temper a lot, have big worries, get very down." And lots of kids learn how to feel better and not be so upset. We can come up with some ideas to deal with this.") (With adolescents, share information about typical adolescent development).
7	Start off by finding out about interests/hobbies/skills/talents of young client including pets/family members ("teach me about you"). Ways to do this: write a story; draw a picture of family, an acrostic poem. Consider using a "get acquainted" structured activity (share something personal).
8	Ask one question about the presenting problem ("I heard you are being treated badly by a classmate?") and then paraphrase/summarize the answer. Gain agreement. Do not minimize the problem nor dramatize.
9	Indicate that you would like to be able to talk with the young client about ways to make things better.
10	Review what young clients can to say to their classmates in response to the question: "Where were you?" during time client was with you (possible answer: "I was getting extra help with my homework"). Have clients select what they feel comfortable saying.
11	Inform the child how you will be communicating with parents.
12	Work on developing their self-awareness and readiness to change as a prerequisite to REBT.

Expectations

Few children understand what psychotherapy is about. They have some notion that a psychologist is a person who "helps" people, but outside of this, most of their notions are negative. Many children believe that our profession treats "crazy people" and therefore that being at our office is a stigma. The other model that children have for us is the school psychologist. Often, they perceive this role as a disciplinary one.

Young clients present with different degrees of willingness to change. Some may be so caught up in their personal issues (e.g., abuse) they may be unaware of the need for therapy and the need for them to work on changing themselves. Said another way, you may be ready to do REBT, but they might not. In these cases, be patient.

Besides not knowing about the process of psychotherapy, many children arrive at our offices with no awareness of why they have come. Their parents have not discussed it with them. Children are unlikely to become collaborators in a process they do not understand. Therefore, a first job is to explain to them what a psychologist is, who we help, how we help people, and what we help people with. After such an explanation, the child should have a problem-solving set and hopefully a positive schema for the profession, as well as no negative stereotypes. The following transcript shows how this topic can be introduced to children (from DiGiuseppe, 1981, p. 54):

THERAPIST: Johnny, I'm a psychologist. Do you know what that is?

JOHNNY: Oh! No. Well a kind of doctor for crazy people?

THERAPIST: Well, that's not totally true. Psychologists are doctors who study how people learn things. And psychologists help people learn things they have been unable to learn. For example, some children have trouble learning to read. And psychologists help them learn to read better. Other children are sad or scared. They haven't learned not to be unhappy or afraid. Psychologists help them learn not to feel that way. We help children with other problems, too, like anger, bed-wetting, making friends, and lots of things they don't know how to do. Do you understand that?

JOHNNY: Yes.

THERAPIST: Well, what problem do you think I can help you with?

Self-Disclosure and Rapport

Self-disclosure is a prerequisite for any verbal psychotherapy. Children are less likely than adults to self-disclose to therapists because they desire help. For most children a warm, accepting relationship is probably a necessity before they will honestly tell how they feel or think. We do not mean to imply that rapport is curative in and of itself with children, but that it is more desirable to attain self-disclosure and to convince them to listen so that the therapist's interventions can have an effect. Although reflection has been the primary strategy by which therapists develop rapport, reflection is not the only way to accomplish this end. Another strategy is honest, direct questions that communicate a commitment to help. Children are quite sensitive to dishonesty, and they generally respond well to people who are open and who trust them. Many therapists ask children questions when they already know the answer (e.g., after the mother has called to inform the therapist that $20 is missing from her pocketbook, the therapist's first inquiry is "Were there any problems at home this week?" or "Did you do anything wrong?"). Children are not stupid and are not likely to bring about rejection willingly. Therefore, they may be reluctant to disclose their misdemeanors. So they usually respond to inquiries about their misdeeds with "No, I didn't do anything," or "No there are no problems." Here the therapist has set up a situation in which the child is most likely to lie. Once the child has lied, the therapist is placed in the difficult situation of revealing a lie before it can be discussed. Exposing the child's lie impacts negatively on rapport. To avoid such situations, we think it better to confront children honestly with the facts as you know them, and then to ask for their opinion or interpretation of the events.

Another strategy to help foster rapport is to discuss with the child how therapy can achieve ends that the *child* desires, rather than focusing on the goals of the parents and teachers. Because children are not self-referred and they may not always have the goals of the significant others in their lives, it may be particularly important to show children how they can benefit from therapy before they will be willing to participate. Some goals of therapy that children desire may be (1) to lessen the degree of their parents' anger at them; (2) to develop more predictable rules within the family so that life does not seem as arbitrary; or (3) to attain some major rewards they are seeking, such as a larger allowance, staying out later, or a home video game. The therapist may then act as the child's agent in negotiating for these items when contracting for appropriate behaviors.

An additional strategy is to help shift some of the responsibility for the problem and referral away from the child. A child may feel outnumbered if there is a group of adults trying to induce change. By focusing on how the parents' behavior may contribute to the child's problems or how the parents' upset exaggerates the problem, one diffuses responsibility away from the child and may form an alliance with the child.

We have already alluded to the necessity of building a relationship with a young client to maximize the likelihood that the child will be open about thoughts and actions. To facilitate self-disclosure, three strategies have been recommended:

1. *Do not be all business.* If your initial expectations are too high, the child may find the sessions aversive and then just not talk to you. Allow the child some time to get acquainted with you through play and off-task conversation. Shaping can be used to develop the self-disclosure and on-task conversation required in therapy.

2. *Always be honest with the child.* Children are more cautious than adults, probably because they are more vulnerable. They appear to be sensitive to deception, which they use as a measure of a person's trustworthiness.
3. Go *easily and carefully on the questions.* Children do not trust those who try to give them "the third degree." (DiGiuseppe, 1981, p. 56)

Waters (1982) indicated that self-disclosure can be learned quite effectively if the practitioner: (1) is a good model for self-disclosure; (2) accepts whatever the child says without putting her or him down; and (3) reinforces the child for disclosing.

Consequences and Alternatives

Disputing is the process whereby a client's irrational beliefs are challenged and attempts are made to substitute more rational alternative ways of thinking. Disputing makes sense to rational therapists because they have some prerequisite assumptions about the client and about the nature or emotional disturbance. The first assumption seems somewhat obvious. It is the idea that the client's affect or behavior is negative, disturbed, self-destructive, and better changed. The second assumption is that negative, disturbed emotions can be replaced with alternative non-disturbing, non-self-destructive, albeit unpleasant, affective states. A third is that irrational beliefs create the disturbed affect in the first place. Given these prerequisite assumptions, it logically follows that disputing one's irrational cognitions would be helpful. If these assumptions are not made, however, a client might find disputing a critical, unpleasant process and either drop out of therapy or become extremely uncooperative.

Many children do not recognize that their behaviors or emotional states have a negative impact on their lives. Nor are they necessarily aware that there are alternative ways to act or feel. Most adult clients have a head start on children in this way. Because adults are usually self-referred, they usually recognize that their actions and emotions are self-defeating and that the therapist is there to help them develop alternative ways of responding. If they did not believe this, they probably would not have come in the first place. Children are almost never self-referred. The initial stages of treatment may be exclusively devoted to an evaluation of children's affect and action potential and to convincing them that these bring about negative consequences that are avoidable. Focusing on the consequences of the child's present modus operandi is the first treatment step. Children may have limited schemata for emotional reactions. They may conceptualize feelings as bipolar dichotomous constructs (i.e., happy-mad or glad-sad). It would be quite unlikely for a child to work with a therapist to change being extremely mad to only annoyed when her brother pulls her hair if she has no schema to incorporate the latter emotion.

In many cases, children say that they have no options and that their disturbed emotions are the way they should or must feel. Children may have developed these beliefs concerning their emotional responses by either modeling or direct reinforcement from their parents or families. In many families, the parents respond in the same exaggerated ways as their children do, so that the child has never seen an alternative response. The parents may show a wider range of emotional reactions, but they may never expect this range of their children and fail to directly teach them alternatives.

In summary, before one can proceed to identifying and disputing irrational beliefs, one must first agree on a goal. Before one can agree on a goal, it might be necessary to expand the child's schema concerning emotional reactions so that the goal is within his or her frame of reference. This expansion can be accomplished through modeling, imagery, stories, parables, and discussions of TV characters that play out different emotional reactions. Evaluating the consequences of the child's emotional reactions, and developing a wider range of perceived, possible emotional reactions is likely to be an important and lengthy step in therapy. Once children perceive that their affect and action tendencies are self-defeating and conceptualize alternative ways of responding both emotionally and behaviorally, they will be more willing to enter into a discussion of how their thinking causes their emotions, and they will be more likely to participate in the disputing and not to see it as an attempt to be critical of them.

The therapist is advised not to assume that these two initial steps in therapy will be achieved instantaneously. It may take a number of sessions to explore these issues before the child becomes convinced of them.

Language

A common error among novice rational-emotive behavior therapists who work with children is to use the jargon of REBT (e.g., awfulizing, terrible, should, shithood, self-acceptance). Children are likely to express their irrational ideas in vocabularies different from adults' or rational-emotive behavior therapists'. Pay close attention to the child's words that represent the irrational concept. Many children express the concept of demandingness by referring to "unfairness." The concept of self-downing or self-worth may be expressed by phrases such as "He is a jerk" or a "jerk-off," or whatever word is currently in vogue in the child's subculture. It is best to avoid translating the child's vocabulary to REBT jargon and, rather, to attempt to use the child's own lexicon. Children may also lack a vocabulary for expressing emotions. Even if they do possess a schema for a wide degree of emotional reactions to problems, they might not have the words to express these differences. If they do not have the wide range of alternative emotional reactions mentioned in the above sections, along with teaching the emotions themselves it is desirable to provide children with a vocabulary for easily expressing the emotions.

The lack of a vocabulary for expressing subtleties in emotional reaction may partly be a result of the structure of the English language. The common use of words to define emotion is rather vague and imprecise. People frequently use affective words in idiosyncratic ways. One child's "fear" may be another's "panic" or a third's "concern." It is also helpful to check out what the child means by emotional words behaviorally, physiologically, and phenomenologically. Setting definitions of emotional words helps to prevent confusion as the sessions progress. One helpful suggestion is to use Wolpe's (1973) SUD scale (subjective units of discomfort) to describe the child's present emotional state and to provide a numerical rating that indicates the intensity of an emotion. In this way, children learn that affects can be named along a continuum and that their own emotional states can be compared with the desired goal of the treatment. Thus, a child may talk about becoming angry at an SUD 4. If this numerical system appears undesirable to the therapist, she or he can set a specific vocabulary to try to describe the different intensities of emotional states.

The following are suggestions culled from the REBT child literature on how to work at developing a therapeutic alliance with children while at the same time initiating REBT assessment and intervention.

1. Be empathic no matter how trivial child's concern/problem appears to be ("That must be hard"). Do not be too quick to move into problem analysis/solving.
2. Be non-judgmental (unconditional acceptance) of client when you hear about problem even when you disapprove of their behavior (if client broke law, engaged in sexual behavior). Do not feel you are judging them.
3. Respect resistance and move forward to build trust. When experienced, move slower and back off from interpretation. Use more indirect methods (e.g., puppets; reference to problems of a friend).
4. Be patient as trust can be a slow process.
5. Show genuine interest in them. Ask them to share personal stories. Ask them to bring in work and other prize possessions to show you (e.g., CDs, books, yearbooks, artwork).
6. Do not act like a teacher or parent. do not communicate a negative tone about their behavioral infractions (e.g., Do not try to coerce change).
7. Build trust through mutual self-disclosure.
8. In early sessions, listen, listen and reflect back feelings and information.
9. Do not become over-involved emotionally; maintain objectivity.
10. As a rule, do not give treats.

Assessment Guidelines and Practices

The REBT approach to the assessment of childhood disorders consists of two identifiable stages (Bernard and Joyce, 1984).

Problem identification involves the use of both formal and informal tests and methods to determine whether a problem does exist or whether it is solely in the mind of the parent or teacher who has referred the child. During the initial phase of assessment, the dynamics of the referral are untangled. It is not infrequently the case that parents and teachers refer a child who is exhibiting perfectly normal behavior. They may misdiagnose a problem because of ignorance of the normal patterns of child behavior, because of conflicts that they may be experiencing with the child, or as a sole consequence of their own psychological difficulties. During this phase, it is recommended that the practitioner collect information from a variety of sources to determine whether a problem exists and, if it does, whether it belongs to the child, the parents, or the teachers. A review of a child's cumulative school report, as well as interviews with a variety of people who know the referred child and the circumstances that surround the referral, is advisable. The identification of a problem as well as whether it seems to be a child problem or someone else's is a prerequisite to more thorough problem exploration and definition. The importance of determining problem ownership is revealed in the following excerpt from a case report:

Mr. and Mrs. S. sought help about their children's behavior. Mrs. S. had been married twice before and the three children were the product of these previous unions. Mr. S. had no previous marriage and had no children. During the two years of their marriage Mr. and Mrs. S. fought frequently about the children. Mr. S. viewed them as "destructive, unkempt barbarians." He complained they talked too much, ate too much, played too roughly, and spoke too loudly. Mrs. S. felt angry at her husband and enforced rigid rules and harsh penalties to avoid his wrath.

A total assessment involving behavior analysis, psychological testing, and family and individual interviews was conducted. It revealed that the older daughter had a mild learning disability and considerable social anxiety, and that one of the sons was encopretic and had some minor school difficulties; the other son displayed no behavioral problems at all. The children's behavior at home which Mr. S. complained about most vehemently appeared to be quite normal. The problem seemed more to lie in Mr. S.'s low frustration tolerance and low anger threshold and Mrs. S.'s unassertiveness with her husband. The therapist made attempts to change some of the children's behavior (i.e., the encopretic behavior); however, most of the interventions were aimed at the parents. (DiGiuseppe, 1981, p. 54).

Once the practitioner has established that a problem does exist and who owns it, the *problem analysis* phase of assessment is conducted. Problem analysis results in a determination of the client's dysfunctional cognitions, emotion, and behavior of concern, which then become integrated into an overall treatment plan.

It is important to emphasize that *problem analysis is an ongoing part of therapy*. That is to say, although it is possible to arrive at insights into behavioral problems and their cognitive and emotive concomitants during initial interview sessions, it is often not until more advanced levels of rapport have been achieved between the practitioner and the child that the central concerns of the client and their internal and external activating events are revealed. As new information is disclosed over the course of therapy, it is repeatedly analyzed into cognitive, emotive, and behavioral components as a prerequisite to problem solving.

As the practitioner analyzes the presenting problem, he or she is also tuned into the cognitive strengths and weaknesses of the child. Although the age of the client provides a very rough index to abstract reasoning capacities, the manner in which the young client describes problems is a direct guide to how the client arrives at knowledge, the degree to which behavior is under the control of language, and the capacity of the client to distance himself or herself from the problem.

Prerequisities

As indicated, many children have a limited cognitive schema for representing emotions at different levels of intensity as we as often present with a limited vocabulary to describe different emotional states. As such, it is recommended that before commencing a cognitive-emotional-behavioral assessment that young clients are taught two prerequisite skills.

1. An *emotional schema* for conceptualizing their feelings. Many young people have an "all or none" view of their emotions. For example, they believe they can either be angry or happy. You can use a 10-point scale from "Feeling nothing at all" to "Could not be anymore upset" to illustrate to young people they have options in terms of how upset they become when faced with negative events. Help them see that moderate levels of anger, anxiety and feeling down are not only normal but also helpful in solving problems but extreme levels are harmful and can lead to self-defeating behavior on their part. An Emotional Thermometer can be used for this purpose (see Figure 1).
2. Help develop in young clients an *emotional vocabulary* for describing and differentiating their feelings. Many young people are aware that they are upset but may lack the linguistic tools for analyzing their different emotional states.

When assessing emotions in children, it is important to normalize and validate their feelings. It is important for you to explain that everyone gets angry, worried and sad from time to time and that there is nothing wrong with them or bad about them if they get extremely upset. Later on, you will, of course, discuss the negative aspects of getting extremely upset as a way to motivate the child to work on emotional change.

In assessing emotions, the REBT approach is to help children not use the word "upset" to describe their feelings but to use their emotional vocabulary. It is essential for the practitioners to know whether the child is feeling angry, down, and/or worried in order for appropriate goals of treatment to be discussed and shared, but also to help guide the practitioner's cognitive

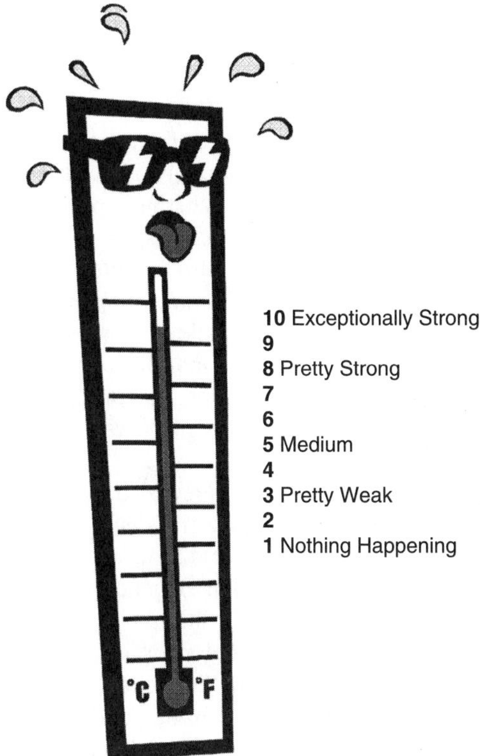

FIGURE 1. The Emotional Thermometer

assessment. For example, to know a child is down rather than angry alerts the practitioner to assess the child's degree of self-downing.

Different Targets for Cognitive Assessment

After the practitioner ascertains maladaptive emotions (including degree of upset) and behavior, the analysis of dysfunctional cognition begins. A variety of different types of cognitions are of concern. The REBT-oriented cognitive assessment is directed at identifying *faulty inferences* (incorrect predictions, conclusions), *absolutes* (shoulds, oughts, needs, musts) and *evaluations* (awfulizing, I can't stand it-it is, global rating of self, others, world) that are expressed in the child's irrational self-talk and beliefs. The REBT practitioner is also on the look out for *cognitive/thinking errors* that lead to reality distortion (e.g., arbitrary inference, selective abstraction, over generalization).

Another area assessed is the client's *causal attributions*. If a young client tends to believe falsely that negative events in his or her life are caused by internal and stable personal characteristics (i.e., ability), whereas positive events and success experiences derive from external forces (i.e., luck), then a variety of self-defeating emotional and behavioral consequences are likely to manifest themselves.

When emotionally overwrought, children not only upset themselves by their own negative self-talk but also suffer from an absence of coping *self-statements*. It is important for the practitioner to be able to tap into the young client's self-talk in order to determine whether appropriate cognitions are available to combat anger, anxiety, and depression.

It is often apparent that young clients who are referred for behavioral problems lack *practical-problem-solving skills and solutions*. Behavioral repertoire deficits stem from the client's being unable to conceptualize other ways of reaching a goal or resolving an interpersonal difficulty. Through a variety of direct and indirect elicitational techniques, the practitioner determines the extent to which the client is to think his or her way out of situations (alternative and consequential thinking).

An example of a cognitive assessment is revealed in the case of John, age 11, referred to the second author for fighting and disruptive classroom behavior. As is not uncommon, John's school reports indicated that he had a moderate reading difficulty. A group-administered intelligence test (OTIS) revealed a test score of 106. When John's parents were initially interviewed, they indicated that he had a history of noncompliant behavior at home. When he was asked to do something, he would often get extremely angry and sometimes break something. John frequently fought both verbally and physically with his older brother, Andrew, though the intensity of the fights appeared to be moderate and the duration short-lived. John's father would become extremely angry with John when he refused to do what he was asked to do. His father would frequently slap John or use a strap on him. John's mother would attempt to get John to help around the house by being excessively nice to him. As a consequence, John appeared to have things pretty much his way—though at some cost. The therapy with parents, which was successful, involved the father's learning to control his temper largely by changing his belief that "My son must always obey me when I ask him to do something" and by teaching him to accept his son with all his imperfections. Both parents were taught to be more firm and assertive with John, and the use of logical and natural consequences as a punishment procedure proved effective in increasing compliant behavior.

John was seen for 16 sessions. A problem analysis revealed a complex set of cognitive deficiencies. John appeared to break rules and get into fights (consequent behavior) when he interpreted a situation as being "unfair" (antecedent events). At these times, his emotions were generally of anger and frequently registered above 8 on a 1-10 scale of intensity. John was quite open in discussing his thoughts and feelings. His expressive language was somewhat restricted, leading to an inference of an inadequate self-control inner-language system. Primary among his dysfunctional beliefs were (1) "Everyone should be fair to me at all times"; (2) "I should always get what I want"; (3) "I'm no good if I break a rule or make a mistake"; and

(4) "I must be comfortable at all times and I can't stand the discomfort I have when I have to work hard." This last belief resulted in undesirable levels of frustration tolerance and discomfort anxiety, which, because of John's pattern of work avoidance, led to a low level of educational achievement. When John was confronted with situations with his peers in which he believed they wanted to "take the 'mickey' out of me," he could not think of any alternatives to fighting. When he believed that a teacher was saying something or requesting something that he felt was unfair, his only response was simply to refuse to comply with the teacher's instruction. Moreover, when he became aroused, he failed to consider at that moment the range of negative consequences that would result from his misdeeds. At times when he became angry, his self-talk was highly provoking, and he lacked appropriate self-statements for keeping his anger in check. Therapy was partially successful in helping John to give up his "demandingness" and was very successful in improving his self-esteem. He acquired the ability to control his temper by the use of coping self-statements and was "caught" only once for fighting during the remainder of the school year. During treatment, he became more aware of the perspective of others, began to recognize when situations were fair and when they were not, and began to realize that the world did not always have to revolve around him. He began to accept the behavior of others, understood the notion that it is unfair to get angry with people who make mistakes, and was seen by both parents and teachers as being more cooperative.

It is very important for the REBT practitioners to be thoroughly familiar with the different types of cognitions (inferences, absolutes, evaluations) that REBT hypothesizes as leading to different emotional disorders as this will assist in helping young clients become more self-aware of the specific cognitions leading to their specific emotional reactions (see review in Chapter One). While REBT's cognitive assessment questions are never meant to put words in a young client's mouth nor is it the goal of the practitioner to have the child agree with what the practitioner intimates the young client is likely to be thinking, REBT theory of emotional disorders does help the practitioner formulate questions used in cognitive assessment.

When the REBT practitioner is faced with a child who cannot report on his/her thinking in situations where she/he became extremely upset, the REBT employs the theory in the form of hypothesis-driven questioning (e.g., "Many children when they are very angry with a classmate think they really cannot stand it when they are called a name. When you get very angry with Richard when he calls you names first thing in the morning do you think something like that?").

Different Methods of Assessment

In both the assessment and the treatment phases, it is most important that the practitioner be able, when necessary, to tap into the self-talk of the young client. Many children have probably never been asked to report their thoughts to someone else. Most do not have a sufficient vocabulary to describe the thoughts they experience when they are upset. Moreover, children who manifest a variety of different conduct disorders appear to very quickly subvocalize anger-producing ideas in problem situations and, as a consequence, are unaware that they are thinking anything at all. In both assessing dysfunctional cognitions and preparing the young client for the teaching of emotional-problem-solving skills, the practitioner has the tasks of (1) helping children to be more aware of their feelings and (2) enabling them to tune into and report their self-talk.

There are a number of *informal methods* that you can use to assess how upset a child was when confronted with adverse, negative events. The REBT practitioners is on the lookout for both healthy and unhealthy emotions. Healthy negative emotions are generally those that are moderate in intensity and that do not lead to problematic behaviors. Examples include a child being annoyed but not furious with a sibling for perceived unfair treatment on the part of a parent or a child who felt sad but did not get extremely down when not being invited to sit with classmates at lunch.

The REBT practitioners asks targeted questions to locate extreme degrees of anger, feeling down or anxious. "At its worst, how angry where you were with your brother?" "At other times, do you ever get extremely down about not being invited to be with your classmates?" *A crucial aspect of REBT assessment is knowing that it is only when children experience inordinately extreme negative emotions that they are likely to be harboring irrational beliefs.*

In assessing anger, REBT practitioners always make sure they identify the dysfunctional behavior of children at the time when they were extremely angry. They then make a point of identifying with children the negative consequences of their anger in terms of the environmental response (what people say or do) when they behave in a very aggressive fashion. Negative consequences are the prime factors for angry young clients to be motivated to change their emotions, behaviors and anger-creating beliefs. The Anger Thermometer is often used to represent these relationships to children (see Figure 2).

Assessing Cognitions

REBT practitioners use the REBT model of an emotional episode (see Chapter One) to guide their cognitive assessment. That is, REBT assessment is designed to identify three distinct types of cognitions: faulty inferences (predictions, conclusions), absolutes (shoulds, oughts, musts, needs) and evaluations (awfulizing, I can't-stand-it-it is, self rating, other rating, global rating of world).

Once you have identified a specific Activating event and Consequence (emotional) to work on, assess client's thinking. You will want to "gather" as many examples of client's faulty inferences (conclusions, predictions), absolutes (shoulds, oughts, musts, needs) and evaluations (e.g., awfulizing, I-can't-stand-it-it is, global rating of self, another, world).

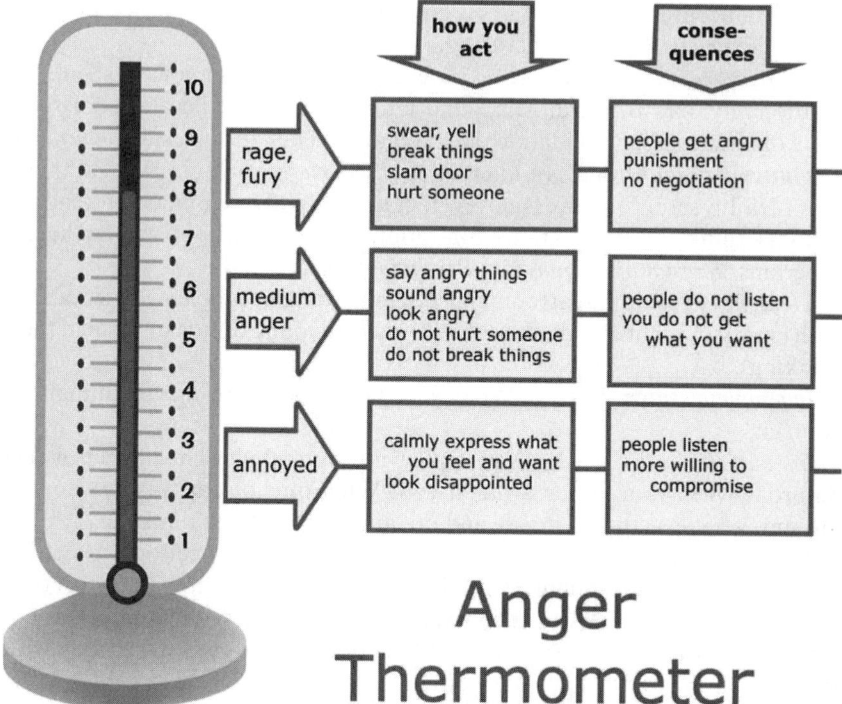

FIGURE 2. The Anger Thermometer

Irrational beliefs—especially the absolutes—are frequently out of conscious awareness of young clients as well as other irrational evaluations. For young clients who have difficulty reporting on their thinking, you will need to use directive questioning and probing to get at these core irrationalities. Do not expect your clients to always provide them for you when you ask: "What else were you thinking?"

When children are unaware of their irrational beliefs, you can use a hypothesis-testing form of questioning sometimes called *deductive interpretation* as can be seen in the following. "When people get angry, they often think to themselves that people really *should* act respectfully and fairly. Did you have this idea when your father refused to listen to your point of view?" If the client agrees, use client's verbal and non-verbal language to validate whether client is merely agreeing to agree and please you or whether client really had the irrational thought during the time he/she was upset. If the young client gives you negative feedback, start over again to formulate a new hypothesis.

A number of assessment methods, described below, have been developed to elicit feelings and thoughts from young clients; to enable them to describe their thoughts orally in a manner that will facilitate and further their self-understanding; and to provide the practitioner with the young client's conceptual outlook and verbal-linguistic repertoire, which provides the basis for cognitive restructuring.

Standardized self-report surveys: The Child and Adolescent Scale of Irrationality, (see Bernard, M.E., and Cronan, F. The child and adolescent scale of irrationality: Validation data and mental health correlates. *Journal of Cognitive Psychotherapy: An International Quarterly,* 1999, *13*, 121–132) and The Idea Inventory (see Kassinove, H. et al., 1977,) Developmental trends in rational thinking: Implications for rational-emotive school mental health programs. *Journal of Community Psychology, 5,* 266–274).

Thought clouds (e.g., cartoon characters in various problematic situations with empty thought clouds above their head for young clients to write in their thinking).

Incomplete sentences (e.g., "When your father swore at you, you thought to yourself, __________").

Instant Reply (e.g., "Can you replay in your mind what happened last Saturday when your father swore at you? What time of day was it, who was around, what exactly did he say and do, and what did you think?").

Inference chaining is a common strategy for assessing irrational beliefs of children. Assume the young client's inferences (e.g., predictions, conclusions) are true and ask the young client what would it mean to him/her if his/her inference were true. An example of inference chaining used with a boy with learning disabilities who was depressed:

CLIENT: "I know I'll fail today's test."

THERAPIST: "And what do you think would happen if you did fail it?"

CLIENT: "Well, I might fail all the tests."

THERAPIST: "Well, let's suppose that would happen. What might you think then?"

CLIENT: "I guess I would think that I'd be stupid or dumb."

THERAPIST: "Well, what would it mean to you if you were not as smart as you would like to be?"

CLIENT: "I'd be no good."

ASK: "When __________ happened, you felt __________ because...?" When client provides answer (e.g., "I was angry because he acted so unfairly") elicit additional cognitions by asking "and" and "because" questions.

Thought bubbles can be employed to convey the general idea that thoughts create feelings; it can also be used to elicit responses from the unforthcoming child. For example, in a series of cartoons, it is possible to illustrate different temporally related scenes that illustrate a problem that the child may be having. Empty bubbles then can appear over the child in the next scene. The emotional expressions on the faces of the characters help to dramatize the scenes, and the child is asked to fill in the bubble with what he or she thinks the child in the scene is thinking.

The sentence completion technique is employed to elicit a variety of cognitions including copying self-statements, irrational beliefs, and practical-problem-solving and emotional-problem-solving skills. The practitioner develops a number of incomplete sentences that tap into the relevant content area (e.g., "When I find my math homework hard, I generally think . . .").

Think-aloud approaches (Genest and Turk, 1981) involve the practitioner's assigning the child a task to complete and requesting the child to think out loud at the same time. For example, a child who is having difficulty with his mathematics could be asked to work for fifteen minutes on some difficult problems. Aside from being able to examine the child's mathematical algorithms, the practitioner can also get an idea of the affective quality of the child's self-talk, such as "This is hopeless; I'm dumb; I'll never get this done."

The TAT-like approach (Meichenbaum, 1977) is an elicitational method that may be helpful when more direct techniques are not successful. This method uses pictures of ambiguous social situations selected for their relevance to the target behaviors. The child is asked to make up a story, including the thoughts and feelings of the characters and what they can do about the situation.

Expansion-contraction (Bernard, 1981) is a procedure that attempts to expand the abbreviated and elliptical self-talk of young clients through the use of verbal prompts. The youngster is directed to describe in his or her own words the thoughts that he or she has during a problem situation. As the youngster begins to describe these thoughts, (the practitioner provides verbal instructions and questions such as "What do you mean when you say 'you thought that . . .'?" "Why do you think that . . . ?" "What did you think after that?" "Describe to me the first thing that comes into your mind when you think about . . . ?" Contraction refers to the need to be sure that therapeutic instructions and ideas are expressed in a linguistic-conceptual form that can be meaningfully and non-arbitrarily incorporated by the young person.

Peeling the onion (Bernard, 1981) can almost be viewed as a component of expansion-contraction and can be described as involving the peeling away of the layers of thought until one reaches the level that is activating emotional upset. Often, hidden behind a facade of rational thought statements are layers of thought not immediately accessible to the client. It is recommended that the practitioner not be dissuaded, fooled, or discouraged in searching for irrational thoughts and that she or he keep focusing the youngster's attention on thoughts through the use of verbal prompts.

"And," "but," and "because" (Hauck, 1980) are extremely useful words that practitioners can use to help young clients to tune into and report automatic self-talk. If the child pauses at the end of what seems to be an incomplete sentence about what he or she is thinking, the practitioner coaxes and prods the client along with words such as *but, and,* and *because*.

Instant replay (Bedford, 1974) is a therapeutic technique developed for use with parents and children. Bedford requests that each member of the family keep track of situations and events during the week that result in unpleasant emotions ("rough spots"). During the next meeting, each member of the family is requested to do a "rerun" or "instant replay" of the rough spot.

Children and parents are asked to describe the feelings and thoughts that they had in relation to the problem.

Guided imagery (Meichenbaum, 1977) involves the practitioner's asking the youngster to relax and then to imagine as vividly as possible a problem situation and to focus on feelings and self-talk. The client is asked to describe the scene and is encouraged to experience and communicate the feelings and thoughts associated with the setting.

Methods of Treatment

We will now detail special consideration in using REBT treatment methods with children. We have included several illustrative case studies on using REBT with children.

Goal Setting

Once you have identified different emotional-behavioral problems of a child, determine which shall be the first problem to work on. Indicate that problems will be worked on one at a time. Help client to set a goal for emotional-behavioral change. Ask: "The next time __________ occurs, rather than feeling extremely (down/anxious/angry) how would you rather feel and behave?" Seek agreement from client that rather than feeling extremely down/anxious/angry (8-10 on the Emotional thermometer), it would be better to feel only moderately down/anxious/angry and for his/her behavior to change from negative to positive.

The Importance of Teaching Prerequisite Critical Thinking Skills

REBT is concerned primarily with epistemology, the philosophical study of knowledge. In therapy, we are constantly asking clients, "How do you know that what you are thinking is accurate?" Disputing assumes that the client and the therapist share criteria for determining the truth or falsity of a statement. Many children have failed to develop critical thinking skills. Even if they have developed critical thinking skills and logic about the objective world, they may not have transferred these logical manipulations to the intrapersonal or interpersonal realm. As a result, they may have separate epistemologies for judging objective data and psychologically interpersonal statements. Children often have quite simple personal epistemologies. They may believe that things are true, so that they think they are true. Or just because they think them. Or because Mommy or Daddy says that they are true. Or because some other people think they are true, and, for adolescents, because their peers think they are true. All of these philosophical positions can get one into trouble.

Before attempting to dispute a child's irrational beliefs, it is a good idea to check out whether he or she can tell the differences among facts, opinions, and hypotheses and to ascertain if he or she can follow logical arguments in verifying statements or in discovering illogic. If they are like most adults, children may find it easier to be logical about external matters and may find it easy to believe that all automatic negative thoughts are true because they have thought them. The idea of examining and questioning one's thoughts about private, personal issues may be new to many young clients. It may be best to start teaching these skills by modeling and parable rather than by first challenging their irrational creations.

One strategy is to present the irrational ideas of other clients when one has helped and to talk about how their errors were spotted and how they learned to challenge them. It may also help to talk about the therapist's own irrationalities and how he or she tested these out and discovered that they were false.

A common REBT technique for teaching children that what they are thinking may or may not be true and the difference between assumptions and facts is to discuss how people from ancient times used to think the world was flat and as a result did not sail very far away from home for fear of falling off the side of the world. However, through evidence such as some provided by intrepid or reckless explorers of the day sailing around the world and returning safely, people realized their assumption that the world was flat was incorrect and they changed their way of thinking to accommodate reality. We also sometimes play a game with a young child called "Thought Detective" with the aim of discovering which thoughts of the child are true and which are false.

Cognitive Methods

REBT therapists try to help clients of all ages reach the elegant solution of changing broad, pervasive beliefs and to realize that even if life's events are bad, they need not upset themselves and that they appraise these events less negatively. In working with children, this is still our goal; however, it is less often accomplished. Ellis has commented many times in supervision that not all clients reach the elegant solution, and some appear particularly resistant no matter how hard they try. Children are less likely to reach this goal because of their inability to handle the degree of abstraction necessary. When the elegant solution appears unreachable with a child, there are three alternative solutions:

1. To change the child's appraisal of the one particular activating event about which she or he is upset.
2. To change the child's inferences when distortions of reality precede negative appraisals and disturbed effect. This approach is easier than elegant disputing because the empirical solution is more concrete.

3. To settle for verbal self-instruction that guides the child toward non-upsetting emotional responses and more adaptive behavior. This approach requires no disputing of the child's cognitions, but it does require an overriding cognition that directs the child to react differently. It is likely to be successful for a single stimulus or a narrow set of stimuli.

The main REBT treatment methods (described in Chapter One) used with young children include: a) teaching rational self-statements, b) empirical disputing (and empirical problem solving) of faulty inferences (predictions, conclusions), c)semantic disputing of absolutes and evaluations, d) logical and empirical disputing of absolutes and evaluations in concrete situations, e) rational role play/rehearsal, f) practical problem-solving skills including interpersonal cognitive problem-solving skills and g) homework assignments.

Some case studies may help demonstrate the use of these methods with children.

Sara was a 9-year-old who was particularly depressed because of the infrequency with which she saw her father. Her parents had been divorced for six years, and her mother and father still continued to argue. Sara had a large number of siblings, all of whom were much older than she and who felt a great deal of animosity toward the father. The father reacted by avoiding them. Our discussions revealed that Sara believed that as her father did not love or care for her mother or her siblings, he could not really care for her. Empirical disputing of this inference revealed quite the opposite. While the father made little attempt to see the siblings and continued to argue with the mother whenever he came to visit Sara, he came to visit Sara quite regularly. Although he was not the most demonstrative person, he was much more dedicated to this child than to any of his other children and spent a considerable amount of time visiting her, calling her, and taking her places. Sara's upset was caused, first, by her inference that her father's behavior toward other members of the family indicated that he felt the same way toward her and, second, by her appraisal that, if he did not care for her, that would be catastrophic. Sara was quite unwilling even to discuss this last possibility. Challenging the idea that it would not be terrible if her father did not care for her led to silence and withdrawal. However, the empirical solution here interested her in collecting data to verify her inferences. She was pleased with the results. This strategy was acceptable because of the therapist's inference that the father really did care for Sara. If the empirical disputing had not led in the direction that it did, a more elegant approach would have been necessary. However here, it was acceptable to limit ourselves to the empirical solution.

Greg was a 9-year-old who was referred by his parents for temper tantrums, pouting, and noncooperative behavior. Greg had a family history of extreme noncontingent reward. During most of his life, his parents had pampered him and he had been allowed to do what he pleased. Although this behavior had been cute when he was younger, with maturity it became more unacceptable. Greg's parents attempted to have him follow rules and to behave appropriately. They punished him whenever he did not complete chores or show age-appropriate behaviors. Greg believed that this meant that they no longer cared for him. He also thought that it was terribly unfair that he should have to do such mundane things as clean his room and put his dirty clothes in the hamper. These things were just too difficult. Greg was a nonverbal child with low average intelligence, and he had difficulty following many of the disputing strategies. However, he was able to role-play these situations with the therapist. During these role plays, the therapist modeled verbal self-instructions such as "My parents care for me, they are only trying to do their job and help me grow up," and "I don't have to feel upset about these things because I can do them." Through practicing these self-statements and through reinforcement for appropriate behavior, Greg slowly learned to stop pouting, and this reaction provided the impetus for more mature, independent behaviors.

Thomas was a 13-year-old student with a history of behavioral and academic problems. Thomas reported that his teacher had a great dislike of him, and she *had* become quite disgusted with him. As therapy progressed, Thomas made changes and behaved more appropriately in school. He became less angry and less disruptive. However, empirical disputing of his thoughts that the teacher did not like him showed them to be accurate. Given the way he had been behaving, it was hard to blame her. When Thomas made some improvements or behaved well, she frequently did not acknowledge the change or still accused him of behaving inappropriately. Thomas became angry at this point and had the action potential of giving up and acting badly again. His irrational beliefs leading to this anger were somewhat along the lines that "people should be fair." My attempts to dispute this idea with Thomas got nowhere. He believed that people should be fair. After all, how would the world survive if people couldn't be trusted. Fairness was necessary for social life, so he said. Rather than trying to convince him that unfairness was a fact of life, which it is, and that there were probably millions of unfair people out there, we focused on a more narrow set of beliefs, that is, that this particular teacher had to be fair. We discussed the particular reasons that she should be unfair; the fact that we could not change her even though we thought most people should be fair; to have an ordered world, we could not demand that she be fair and, that there was no way we could force her to be so. Although Thomas was not willing to accept the fact that unfairness would survive in the universe, he was willing to concede that this particular individual would remain unfair and that he could tolerate that little degree of unfairness. Thus, although we did not reach an elegant solution in changing his appraisal to a wide span of stimuli, we did teach him to appraise this particular stimulus in a very different way. His anger was reduced, and he continued to make behavioral gains throughout the school year.

Disputing Inferences: A Cautionary Note

Focusing on changing children's misperceptions of reality including their conclusions and predictions through empirical testing and disputing is often the easiest for children to grasp. Because of this ease, it is the strategy taken for many cognitive-behavior child therapists. A caveat is in order. A serious problem can arise in using this approach when the child gets upset about the behavior of significant other adults, as children so frequently do. Children are apt to become upset when they believe that important adults in their lives do not love them, behave unfairly, or display serious personality disturbances. We have noticed a disturbing tendency on the part of child therapists to assume that the child incorrectly perceives such events. Rather than assuming that the child may be correct ("Let's suppose you're right that your mother doesn't love you, but why is that so awful?" as Albert Ellis so often says) and pursuing the elegant solution, the therapist sticks to the disputing of the inference even though the data may indicate that the child is correct. Many therapists do this because *they believe* that the realization that their parents are uncaring, unfair, or disturbed may be too much for the child to bear. Such a realization, they believe, would present an insurmountable obstacle to the child's emotional health.

Suppose children do confront situations in which a parent really does not care for them, or in which a parent does love another sibling more than the identified client, or in which a teacher or parent is grossly unfair toward the child, or in which a parent is severely disturbed. When such situations are reality, the empirical disputing the inference could cause iatrogenic damage. If a child is not cared for by a parent and we try to reduce that child's depression by (1) relabeling the parent's behavior as caring, (2) attempting to find good in this parent and to deny the uncaring behaviors, or (3) convincing the child that the parent really does care, are we not creating a disturbed perception of love and caring in that child? If a parent does behave unfairly and we pursue an empirical strategy to reduce the child's upset by presenting the parent as possibly fair, are we not also creating a distorted idea of fairness if we succeed? In the above two situations, the therapist may choose to avoid the issue and may choose not to corroborate the child's perceptions one way or the other. If this strategy is pursued, are we sending the child a nonverbal message that this is a topic not to be talked about and that one cannot criticize parents or recognize their faults? Who knows what other solutions or conclusions the child may draw and how healthy they may be? Thus, not to comment on the child's perceptions may lead to unknown conclusions on the part of the child and unknown iatrogenic side effects.

Some children correctly perceive that they have verifiable adversity in their lives. Uncaring, capricious, and disturbed parents exist. They are not only characters in Grimm's fairy tales. Therapists are often unwilling to pursue the elegant solution in such cases because they believe that it must be awful to live in such a situation. Empirical solutions for the children of these parents are unlikely to help and are likely at best to lead to reduced rapport because the child will know that the therapist cannot or will not help. At the worst, the therapist may succeed and leave the child feeling temporarily better, but with some distortions about love, fairness, and authority. Another therapeutic intervention often tried in such cases is to provide the child with a supportive relationship, again, temporarily making the child feel better. According to rational-emotive therapy, this strategy is merely palliative and leads to no permanent resolution. When children's adversity is verified by the therapist, it may be best largely to seek the elegant solution. Children may be more resilient than we believe, and at least, we may do them no harm. A case summary (RD) illustrates this point:

Jack, a 9-year-old, was also depressed. His father worked long hours at a very successful practice. Jack believed that his father did not love him. My initial intervention was to help Jack to make an operational definition of loving behaviors and then to see how many of these behaviors his father performed and how frequently. After a few sessions of defining the list and empirically verifying his father's responses, we unfortunately came to the conclusion that Jack's father did not fare too well on this empirical test. Although he performed most of the behaviors on the caring list, he did so at a very low frequency.

Did the father love Jack? That was the next question that Jack struggled with. How many loving behaviors does one have to perform toward another to demonstrate love? How frequently does one have to perform loving behaviors toward a person to receive that person's love? I tried to convince Jack that any decision we made about a cutoff score of frequency of loving behaviors and types of loving behaviors was arbitrary. My cutoff score might be different from his. Someone else's might be different altogether. Love is what one person defines it to be. Any definition that we made of love would be just that, our definition, and might not represent a universal reality. We could not define whether or not Jack's father loved him, and we also did not know how Jack's father *felt*. Although we could infer his affective state toward Jack from his behavior, the result would be just that, an inference. I used lots of examples to show how Jack very often felt quite differently from the way he acted. Jack was still left with one real adversity. He experienced fewer loving behaviors from his father than he wanted. It was evident that Jack's father demonstrated caring behaviors much less frequently than the fathers of Jack's peers. So Jack's lack of received affection was real. The important issue I pointed out to Jack was not whether his father loved him, but how miserable he was going to make himself over the way his father reacted. I challenged the ultimate irrational belief that one has to experience love and loving behaviors from one's parents in order to be worthwhile and even to be happy. Jack's father might never change; he might always prefer work to family involvement, but Jack learned to be less upset about this fact and to enjoy other things in his life.

In this case, several aspects seem clinically important. Children often have negative perceptions about their parents that are emotionally charged. Unless the therapist shows a willingness to entertain these ideas and acceptance of the child for thinking them and speaking about them, it is unlikely that the child will be open with the therapist. Some therapists may feel frightened about confirming the child's ideas. Other therapists have often told me that the discussion of such situations would be too traumatic for a child to face. We maintain that an openness and willingness to discuss such issues will get to the true irrational beliefs that are often upsetting children and to the true evaluations that they make.

Homework

The final phase of REBT treatment, practice and application, involves the practitioner's helping the young client to practice his or her newly acquired skills in problem situations at home and in school. In seeking to foster generalization, the child is given a variety of homework assignments (e.g., Waters, 1982).

You will want to explain to all your young clients that as a part of your work with them in helping them solve problems and to overcome difficulties as well as to feel better, it is vital that they put into practice the ideas you will be discussing with them during your sessions. These "homework activities" are crucial in helping them move from cognitive insight to active practice and application of new ways of thinking, feeling and behaving.

Assign homework that you are reasonably sure your young client can perform. Do not assign too many tasks and activities for your client to accomplish. If your client fails to perform homework, identify the excuse(s) and help eliminate the reasons your client offers for not doing homework before assigning new homework. Be prepared for your young clients to "forget" or otherwise fail to perform weekly homework assignments. This is especially likely for young clients with low frustration tolerance who routinely procrastinate doing chores and/or homework.

Below are examples of REBT child-oriented homework exercises culled from the literature.

Examples of Cognitive Homework Assignments

Each day, rehearse rational self-statements (write rational statements on card for young client to remember and practice).

For young clients who get angry, have them rehearse rational self-talk when they do not get their way (e.g., "Nobody can do everything they want whenever they want." "It is disappointing when I can't do what I want, but it isn't terrible and awful." "Talking back only makes things worse." "I still love them anyway even though I do not like the way they are acting."

Assign stories to read that illustrate rational thinking of the protagonist.

Present clients with thought clouds above illustrations of characters that are experiencing problems similar to theirs. Have them write in examples of irrational, and also, rational self-talk that will help the character deal with a difficult situation.

Present young clients with a blank Happening→Thinking→Feeling→Behaving chart and have them complete one that illustrates how they dealt with a problematic situation during the week.

Invite young clients to teach their parents what they have been learning about rational thinking.

Make a list of personal demands.

Examples of Emotive Homework Assignments

Provide child a simple chart for recording their feelings during the week

Have child practice changing feelings and thoughts in a real situation

Suggest that the client gather data about his anger by keeping track of its frequency, location, outcome, as well as who else was involved (self-monitoring).

Have child use rational-emotive imagery during the week. (The client is asked to vividly imagine a situation where they experience a hurtful feeling. While they are imagining the scene they are asked to change the feeling to a more appropriate one and to become aware of the changes in their self-talk).

Have clients practice rational self-statements using evocative and forceful language ("I *can* stand it when my brother teases me!!").

Have young clients agree to working on getting only moderately upset (angry, anxious, worried) during the forthcoming week.

Examples of Behavioral Homework Assignments

Take a responsible risk.

Design an experiment where young clients agree to do something during the week they do not believe they can stand doing (e.g., working 10 minutes on their math homework).

For clients subjected to peer group pressure, provide them with a list of phrases dealing with how to say "No" and have the client practice their use during the week (e.g., "No thanks, I don't want to, if you want to, go ahead. I don't." "I don't think we should be doing this." "Please don't touch me like that!").

For perfectionists, gain agreement on something they will do during the week where they have a high likelihood of failing (risk taking exercise).

For approval seekers, design a shame attacking exercise where they agree to engage in a behavior that will, with high likelihood, invite negative comments and laughs from peers/family members. The fact that they survive the episode will provide evidence to dispute their belief that they need people's approval and it would be awful to be criticized or thought badly of.

Design an experiment where the client agrees to gather evidence to support or contradict a belief they have that is more than likely irrational. For example, if a child believes as a result of repeated criticism from his mother "My mother doesn't love me," help the child agree upon a list of maternal loving behaviors (e.g., cooks for me, picks me up from school, asks me about my date, gives me a hug/kiss, buys me something I need). Then, provide the child with a chart that lists these behaviors and have the child record the number of times each day he observes his mother engaging in the behavior. Once the child can see that despite his mother's criticism, she still engages in different loving behaviors, the child will have concrete evidence to dispute his belief about his mother not loving him (not to be used in cases where you believe that the child will not observe any loving behaviors).

Have clients practice assertive behavior while employing rational self-talk to manage anger and/or anxiety.

Behavior Management Training for Parents

REBT has always been a cognitive-behavior therapy. Even though Ellis (1979, 1994) stressed the role of cognitions in pathology, he has frequently acknowledged that for change to be lasting, one had better get clients to start acting differently. Because children are not self-referred, are likely to be less motivated for change, and are less responsible, it is incorrect to assume that they will carry out their behavioral assignments alone. However, their parents are usually willing to cooperate and can be enlisted to help structure the behavioral components of therapy. In almost all cases, except where the parents are uncooperative, one can use a behavioral modification program to reinforce the desired target behaviors while doing REBT. Whether the emotional problem is anxiety, depression, or anger, the parents can provide structured, systematic rewards for the nonoccurrence of the target behaviors and for behaviors that are incompatible with the target behavior, or they can provide response costs when the target behavior does occur. Behavioral programs that reward or penalize behavior may not only help children to behave better but may also help them to become more motivated to cooperate with the therapist and learn cognitive strategies to control their emotions and to internalize behavioral gains—now there will be some payoff for overcoming their fear, depression, or anger.

The case of Karen, a school phobic, is a good illustration. She experienced extreme panic whenever called on in class to give an answer. As a result, she did not wish to attend school. She developed stomach pains and had a few days off, and the illness seemed to linger. Her mother, realizing that the ailment was more than an upset stomach, kept Karen home and felt sorry for her daughter when she realized the extent of Karen's emotional reaction to school. Karen was allowed to stay home and experienced no response cost for this behavior. During school hours, Karen watched TV, played alone, or listened to her records. After school, she met friends and joined in their activities. Not a bad life! Karen felt no desire to attend school and was not interested in any of the rewards that this institution dispensed. Why should she want to change? She listened carefully to a discussion of how thoughts caused feelings and how her catastrophizing about making mistakes caused her to feel frightened. She agreed. However, this is as far as we got. There was no negative consequence for her staying home and plenty of secondary gains; therefore, she had little motivation for her to overcome her fear. Disputing was out of the question. After a few sessions with Karen's mother, we succeeded in lessening her sympathy for Karen's fear. We then set out the following rules. Karen was denied access to her TV and stereo whenever absent from school. She was not allowed to join her peers unless she attended class that day. Once these rules were in effect, Karen was more willing to start disputing those irrational beliefs that she had identified earlier and was now willing to attend school and control her anxiety with the procedures we had used. Once she was inside school, there was really no reason for Karen to attempt to raise her hand and answer questions, and she continued to make excuses to avoid answering questions when called on. We had made some progress, but the lack of any continued motivation stalled treatment. At this point, a reinforcement system was provided for answering in class. The teacher sent home daily feedback on the number of questions Karen attempted to answer. For each question, she was allotted a certain degree of money. Although this reinforcement did not help Karen to overcome her problems completely and she still experienced fear, again she was more interested in discussing her irrational beliefs and in attempting to overcome them because she wanted the money.

Behavioral incentives may provide the motivation for children to attempt to search for alternative strategies to overcome their emotional reactions. Although behavioral approaches to fear have achieved some success, it has not been the total improvement that one would expect. A cognitive-behavioral program, though, may be more successful. The behavioral incentives provide the motivation to change, and the cognitive interventions help to foster that change and to reduce the fear.

References

Bedford, S. (1974). *Instant replay: A method of counseling and talking to little (and other) people*. New York: Institute for Rational Living.

Bern, S. (1971). The role of comprehension in children's problem solving. *Developmental Psychology, 2*, 351–359.

Bernard, M. E. (1981). Private thought in rational-emotive psychotherapy. *Cognitive Therapy and Research, 5*, 125–142.

Bernard, M. E. (2001a, b, c). *Program Achieve: A curriculum of lessons for teaching students how to achieve and develop social-emotional-behavioral Well-Being*, Vol. 1. Oakleigh, VIC (AUS): Australian Scholarships Group; Laguna Beach, CA (USA): You Can Do It! Education, Priorslee, Telford (ENG): Time Marque.

Bernard, M. E. (2004). *The REBT therapist's pocket companion for working with children and adolescents*. New York: Albert Ellis Institute.

Bernard, M. E., and Cronan, F. (1999). The child and adolescent scale of irrationality: Validation data and mental health correlates. *Journal of Cognitive Psychotherapy: An International Quarterly, 13*, 121–132.

Bernard, M. E., and Joyce, M. R. (1984). *Rational-emotive therapy with children and adolescents*. New York: Wiley.

Cohen, R., and Meyers, A. W. (1983). Cognitive development and self-instruction interventions. In B. Gholson and T. L. Rosenthal (eds.), *Applications of cognitive development theory*. New York: Academic Press.

DiGiuseppe, R. A. (1981). Cognitive therapy with children. In G. Emery, S. D. Hollon, and R. C. Bedrosian (eds.), *New directions in cognitive therapy*. New York: Guilford Press.

Dollard, J., and Miller, N. E. (1950). *Personality and psychotherapy*. New York: McGraw-Hill.

Ellis, A. (1979). The theory of rational-emotive therapy. In A. Ellis and J. M. Whiteley (eds.),*Theoretical and empirical foundations of rational-emotive therapy*. Monterey, CA.: Brooks/Cole.

Ellis, A. (1994). *Reason and emotion in psychotherapy, 2nd Ed.* New York: Lyle Stuart.

Flavel, J. H. (1977). *Cognitive development*. Englewood-Cliffs, N.J.: Prentice-Hall.

Flavell, J., Beach, D., and Chinsky, J. (1966). Spontaneous verbal rehearsal in a memory task as a function of age. *Child Development, 37,* 283–299.

Genest, M., and Turk, D. C. (1981). Think-aloud approaches to cognitive assessment. In.Merluzzi, T. V . . . Glass, C. R., and . Genest, M., (eds.), *Cognitive assessment*. New York: Guilford Press.

Hauck, P. (1980). *Brief counseling with RET*, Philadelphia: Westminster Press.

Kendall, P. C. (2000). *Child and adolescent therapy: Cognitive-behavioral procedures*. New York: Guilford Press.

Meichenbaum, D. (1977). *Cognitive behavior modification*. New York: Plenum Press.

Morris, C. W., and Cohen, R. (1982). Cognitive considerations in cognitive behavior modification. *School Psychological Review, 12,* 14–20.

Vernon, A. (1989). *Thinking, feeling, behaving: An emotional education program for children*. Champaign, IL: Research Press.

Vernon, A. (1998). *The passport program: A journey through emotional, social, cognitive, and self-development, grades 1-5*. Champaign, IL: Research Press.

Vernon, A., and Clemente, R. (2006). *Assessment and intervention with children and adolescents: Developmental and cultural considerations*. Alexandria, VA: American Counseling Association.

Waters, V. (1982). Therapies for children: Rational-emotive therapy. In C. R. Reynolds and T. B. Gutkin (Eds.), *Handbook of school psychology*. New York: Wiley.

Wolpe, J. (1973). *The practice of behavior therapy*. New York: Pergamon Press.

3

REBT Assessment and Treatment with Adolescents

HOWARD YOUNG

Historical and clinical evidence is replete with innumerable instances in which adolescents have habitually, rather than merely occasionally or sporadically, acted in the most maladaptive and self-defeating ways imaginable (Ellis, 1971). Various explanations have been offered for this phenomenon, ranging from the hormonal changes of puberty to the psychosocial pressures of growing up. My observations, however, suggest that the self-defeating behavior so common to adolescence is primarily the result of the young person's evaluation and appraisal of his or her life experiences rather than being the result of any particular set of biological, social, or environmental circumstances. This conclusion flows from an ongoing exposure to the beliefs and value systems of countless teenagers, who consistently reveal thinking patterns grounded in ignorance, misconception, and, quite often, utter nonsense.

Let me point out that practically every adolescent client I have worked with has managed to distort, exaggerate, and misinterpret, reality and to suffer accordingly. Adolescents seem to find it incredibly easy to turn disappointments into disasters; desires into demands; wants into necessities; difficulties into impossibilities; and failure and criticism into proof that they are subhuman creatures. Although they do so unwittingly, adolescents *think* themselves into their social and emotional problems.

When faced with the teenager as a client, therefore, the counselor would ideally direct therapeutic endeavors at changing attitudes—persuading the young person to think in logical, sensible, and scientific ways. Unfortunately, this is not an easy task. Not only do adolescents possess the normal human inclination to resist change, but they are frequently rebellious and contrary, sometimes to the point of sabotaging their own best interests. Add these attitudes to what appears to be a universal distrust of adults and adult values, and the resulting situation is one that is hardly conducive to a therapeutic exchange.

In spite of their well-earned status as difficult clients, however, adolescents can be helped to overcome their emotional and behavioral conflicts through psychotherapy. The approach I have found most effective is based on the theoretical principles of rational-emotive, behavior psychotherapy (REBT) (Bard, 1980; Ellis, 1962, 1974; Ellis and Harper, 1975; Walen et al., 1980; Wessler and Wessler, 1980). This approach structures the counseling process according to the following considerations:

- Relationship building
- Problem defining
- Problem intervention
- Problem solving

Although each area usually requires attention, one need not hold to this particular order, and it is understood that there is overlapping. For instance, one could be developing a relationship while defining a problem, and vice versa. The therapist might also want to concentrate more on one area than on another. Regardless of how it is managed, I have found reliance on this framework is productive in maintaining a therapeutic direction with the adolescent client.

Relationship Building

The purpose of relationship development in REBT is to create an atmosphere in which the client can feel free to talk about personal problems and difficulties. This usually involves the sharing of one's thoughts, fantasies, feelings, and the like. Unfortunately, the average adolescent is usually unaccustomed to discussing such private concerns with an adult. Because this kind of disclosure is essential to cognitive analysis and intervention and is best encouraged by the well-known virtues of empathy, warmth, nonjudgmental regard, and the like, relationship building is a primary consideration when attempting to counsel young people. I do emphasize, however, that the relationship is not the therapy. It is, rather, the means by which a problem-facing and problem-solving format can be established on behalf of the client. Some of the approaches I have found helpful in fostering a trusting and accepting alliance with the adolescent are the following:

1. *Allowing long periods of uninterrupted listening*. This is, perhaps, a departure from the more active, interventional approach usually employed in REBT. However, I have found that many adolescents have not had the opportunity to "tell their story" without some kind of admonishment or interruption. As a result, I tend sometimes to allow chatting or rapping in the interest of encouraging ease and comfort in the therapeutic situation.

   I also try to avoid silences with teenagers. With the exception of a client who is pausing to collect his or her thoughts or to frame an answer to a question, every attempt is made to keep the conversation going without breaks. I find that most teenagers feel very uncomfortable and self-conscious when silences are deliberately allowed to last.

2. *Accepting the client's reality perspective regardless of how distorted or limited it may be.* If, for example, a young client decides that his parents are always on his back or that a probation officer is out to get him, I usually accept such convictions at face value, even though I may know that they are untrue. Often, this acceptance indicates that I am an ally rather than an opponent and accordingly decreases the client's defensiveness. This is an especially useful technique with adolescents considered delinquent or anti-establishment.
3. *Discussing openly my own opinions and attitudes.* I try to answer all personal questions casually and directly, including questions about my marriage, my political preferences, religious issues, and personal problems. I have found that I tend to be asked questions of a more personal nature by teenagers; this is understandable, because many of them are trying to find out what adulthood is really all about. They usually do not have such an opportunity to question other adults—parents or teachers, for example, who often hide in moral or idealistic roles.
4. *Allowing a companion to sit in on a session.* Quite often, permitting a young person to bring along a friend seems to ease the situation and pave the way for future progress. In fact, I sometimes use the companion to make a point or two. On more than one occasion, I have found that the companion has perceived a message quite clearly and has been able to repeat it to the primary client, thus facilitating the therapy. I have also used this approach with good results by allowing a pet to join us for a session or two. Encounters have been shared with dogs, hamsters, cats, mice, turtles, and birds, although I did turn down a pony.
5. *Giving the adolescent priority.* When a teenager is brought in by parents who are registering a complaint and asking for therapy, I very frequently see the teenager first. Thus, I can sometimes give the impression that I am willing to listen to her or him and to respect her or his point of view, and it can help lessen her or his concern that I am in collaboration with the parents.
6. *Extracting from the parents an initial concession.* I sometimes try to have especially strict or overprotective parents give in on some of their demands or restrictions. Increasing the amount of an allowance, extending a curfew, or reducing a yard-work commitment are good examples, This approach sometimes gives the teenager the idea that I have influence over the parents, a concept not previously considered, and it often paves the way to a more responsive relationship.

Problem Defining

The purpose of problem defining in REBT is to obtain a diagnostic assessment of the client's reality-based and psychologically induced complaints. Although this might seem an obvious step with any client, it deserves special attention with the adolescent. It is not unusual for young people to be vague, general, and downright hostile when asked why they have come in for counseling. Furthermore, adolescents seem to wander into tangents easily, to get wrapped up in the details of their volatile life experiences, or to get lost in meaningless philosophy-of-life excursions. Sometimes, I permit such meanderings in the interest of relationship building, but usually, I make an effort to encourage the young person to be problem-focused. Some of the tactics I have used to introduce a problem-facing format are:

1. *Defining the problem for the adolescent.* In many cases, young people who come to my attention are initially referred by parents, schools, or police. Usually, I have some knowledge of their difficulties beforehand; a simple statement like "I understand you are here because you ran away from home" leads to a lively problem-focused discussion.

   Sometimes, however, the client denies the problem suggested by the referral agent. For instance, a probation officer might see dropping out of school as the reason for counseling, whereas the client might see difficulties with a boy or girl friend as the problem area. Faced with this kind of dilemma, I usually offer help on the problem identified by the adolescent with the hope that I can get to other concerns later.

   On other occasions, the client flatly denies problems. Often, this denial is best handled by suggesting that the referral agent is the problem. If, for example, a teenager is referred by her parents for school underachievement and the young person vehemently insists that neither this nor anything else is troubling her, I try to gain her cooperation by suggesting that I can help her deal with her parents who are trying to run her life. In other words, I suggest that she has problem parents who could be the subjects of counseling endeavors. This tactic is sometimes useful with teenagers who come to therapy against their wishes.
2. *Simplifying the definition of a problem.* Many times a young client is afraid to reveal a problem because he thinks he has to tell his innermost secrets or that anyone with a problem is crazy. In order to overcome this obstacle, I will sometimes oversimplify, describing a problem that deserves counseling as hurt feelings, hassles with others, or doubts about the future. A problem-facing discussion often ensues, because most adolescents usually admit to concerns in one of these areas.
3. *Using a representative example from the life of another young person.* By discussing another teenager's problem, I am sometimes able to illustrate what I am looking for. This approach not only provides the client with a sense of "At least I'm not the only one with problems," but it also offers a concrete example of the kind of subject matter discussed in counseling.
4. *Offering a problem example out of my own life.* This tactic is especially effective if it deals with criticism, rejection, and failure—all areas about which adolescents are frequently overly concerned. Not only do such

admissions humanize the therapist, but they also help the young person to discover that such problems are inherent in life, no matter what the person's age.

5. *Using visual aids*. I have found the most effective approach with the evasive or "problem-free" client is to use wall posters illustrating irrational ideas and their corollaries. I ask the young person to look at this list and see if she or he holds any of the ideas. This is a quick way to get a diagnostic impression of the client's thinking, and it can serve as a stepping-stone to identifying a specific problem area.
6. *Unraveling the problem from a rambling dialogue*. Some teenagers come in for counseling and admit that they have problems but remain unable to pinpoint an issue. With this group, I merely ask questions about school, family, friends, love life, and so on. Before long, I usually perceive a problem that could use counseling assistance. I then suggest this area to the client with a brief explanation of how I could help. For example, one teenager, referred by her mother, admitted that she wanted counseling but was unable to identify with any of the problem examples I suggested. I let her give me a rundown of her life experiences on a typical day. After a few minutes, it was evident that she was extremely upset with a younger sister who was always borrowing her clothes. I asked if she wanted to know how to feel less angry about the situation and perhaps learn how to stand up to her sister without getting in trouble with her mother. She agreed and we were in business.

Problem Intervention

Problem intervention in REBT is the place in which the so-called work of therapy occurs. Ideally, this involves helping clients learn to recognize, challenge, and correct the irrational attitudes that cause emotional distress and generate self-defeating behavior. Even when I have his or her undivided attention, this is often an arduous task with the average teenaged client. Perhaps, this difficulty might be explained by the likelihood that adolescents are only beginners when it comes to manipulating thought and understanding abstract concepts (Piaget and Inhelder, 1969). Most likely, too, they have had scant training in or encouragement of the capacity for logical or sensible thinking. I have therefore found it best to keep things *simple, visual,* and *brief*. The following suggestions follow this framework and have been generally effective in imparting rational insights to adolescent clients:

1. *Teaching or not teaching the relationship between thinking, feelings, and actions*. Usually, I make an initial effort to teach the role of cognitions in causing emotions and behavior. I rely on the ABC model, sometimes introducing it verbally and other times using cartoon drawings or some other kind of illustrations. I explain the ABCs to adolescents as a formula that

can be used for understanding their problems more clearly, and I rarely devote more than five minutes to the task.

Most of the time, however, I avoid teaching this principle as such. Experience has shown that many teenagers do not want to learn "psychology"or have too much difficulty fitting their problems into an ABC format to make this approach feasible. In most cases, I am lucky if they remember my name, so I figure it is unlikely that they are going to spend much time learning a process. With this group, probably the majority of my adolescent clients, I discuss problems in terms of their thinking, but I am not concerned with their understanding or with applying the theory behind what we are doing.

2. *Confronting and confuting "awfuls," "terribles," and "horribles."* According to RET theory (Wessler and Wessler, 1980), irrational thinking is most often characterized by "catastrophizing": mentally converting hassles into outright horrors. Once this ideational pattern is detected, every effort is expended to make the adolescent client aware that he or she is "awfulizing," why such thinking is unrealistic, and what a more sensible outlook might be. This goal is usually achieved in the following way:

    a. Substituting the words *disaster, catastrophe,* or *tragedy or awful, terrible,* or *horrible*. The words *awful, terrible,* or *horrible* are so much a part of the average adolescent's working vocabulary that I have found it difficult to convince the adolescent that the meaning behind such words is the cause of his or her suffering. The emotionally distressed adolescent who insists that his or her problem is awful is asked, "Was it a disaster?" or "Was it really a tragedy?" These words have a more precise meaning and can be subjected to question and reason more easily than *awful*.
    b. Using the phrase "end of the world" to show the client that he or she is awfulizing. Again, I find that asking, "Would it be the end of the world?" usually elicits an eye-rolling "Of course not" from most adolescents and permits the next question, "Then exactly what would it be?" The answer, almost always in the realm of realistic disadvantage, begins to persuade the client to correct his or her exaggerated evaluation of the problem.
    c. Using the phrase "a fate worse than death." Once more the use of a familiar but obviously magnified term sometimes helps adolescents to begin to understand that their excessive, disturbing feelings come from exagger-ated, unrealistic ideas in their minds.
    d. Asking, "Could it be any worse?" Often young clients exaggerate, considering a situation totally bad. Encouraging them to conjure something that could make their problem even worse sometimes enables them to see that it is highly unlikely that any disadvantage (especially their own) is 100 % bad. This tactic can sometimes be used in a humorous way by adding all kinds of ridiculous dimensions to the problem

situation. I find that this approach helps clients to realize that problems are not always as bad as they think they are; by viewing situations in less exaggerated and more realistic terms, they learn to feel much less distressed.

e. Asking, "What's the worst that could actually happen?" I show anxiety-ridden teenagers they are catastrophizing their complaints by encouraging them to focus on the most realistic but worst outcome they can imagine. This forces them to stay away from possibilities and to concentrate on actualities. In essence, they are learning to deal with the hassle and not with the horror of their problem.

3. *Confronting and confuting "shoulds" "oughts," and "musts."* Another, equally significant aspect of irrational thinking is the tendency of clients to treat their wants and desires as if they were Jehovah's commandments. Adolescents typically believe that they must have their way simply because it is deserved, earned, right, fair, just, or whatever. A good many of my efforts, therefore, go to sensitizing teenagers to their personal imperatives and helping them to understand why absolutistic thinking usually results in emotional and social conflict. The most useful tactics for accomplishing this end include:

   a. Using *must* in place of *should.* Teenagers use the word *should* so frequently and indiscriminately that sometimes just getting them to change the word to *must* gets the imperative quality across. Once this is established, they can begin to learn how to live without absolutes.
   b. Using *gotta* in place of *should.* "I should get an A" makes sense to a lot of teenagers, but "I gotta get an A" often encourages them to see the error of their ways.
   c. Changing *should* to *no right.* Another method of getting across the absolutistic meaning of *should,* especially with angry teenagers, is to exchange "He shouldn't do that" for "He's got no right to do that." The irrationality of "He's got no right" is often easy for teenagers to understand.
   d. Using the want-need concept. Another way of getting teenagers to recognize and challenge absolutes is to teach them the difference between wanting and needing. I have found that some of the most resistant and stubborn young people, especially those involved in behavioral excesses, are capable of understanding the critical distinction between desires and necessities and of using this insight productively.
   e. Teaching *should* equals "unbreakable law." I sometimes get somewhere with young clients who have difficulty understanding the absolutistic meaning of *should's* and *must's* by suggesting that they are upset because their self-proclaimed laws have been broken. "Debbie's Commandments have been violated"or "It was Tom's turn to be God, and he got upset because someone broke one of His rules" are examples of this approach. Once the adolescents understand what it means to be

unrealistically demanding, I proceed to show them that they do not run the universe, so they had better expect things to go wrong.

4. *Challenging the "can't stand" philosophy*. Probably the main source of teenagers' low frustration tolerance is their persistent conviction that they can withstand no inconvenience or discomfort. This kind of irrational thinking, which seems endemic to this age group, generates a variety of neurotic behaviors, ranging from school underachievement to drug abuse. My experience shows that adolescents seem able to grasp the irrationality of "can't stand" thinking more easily than other REBT concepts. If I do run into problems, though, I find the following usually get results:

    a. Substituting "unbearable" for "can't stand." Often, I can help a young client realize how pernicious the "can't stand" concept is by equating it with the term *unbearable*. Hearing things put this way, many teenagers conclude, "Well, it's not *that* bad. I mean I can *bear* it."
    b. Explaining *difficult* versus *impossible*. Often, the "can't stand" concept can be better understood by investigating whether a particular problem situation is impossible or is merely difficult to tolerate. Even some of the most resistant teenagers, grasping this point, can realize that just because something is a pain in the neck does not mean that it cannot be lived with.
    c. Substituting *won't* for *can't*. Frequently, when I hear the word *can't*, I quickly substitute *won't*. This is an effective way of showing that the situation is governed by one's attitude, which is under the individual's control. It is the attitude, not the situation, that is overwhelming.
    d. Suggesting to the client that he or she is tolerating the conflict in question. Despite complaints and protests, I remind the client, he or she is enduring the problem. This tactic is especially useful with clients experiencing long-running problems with parents, teachers, or siblings. For example, the teenager who threatens to quit school in his senior year because he claims he can no longer stomach the bullshit is advised that he is, in fact, stomaching things. He may be miserable, but he has nevertheless been putting up with school for twelve years, and this qualifies him as an outstanding stomacher of bullshit!
    e. Explaining that a genuine "can't stand" situation would either end the client's life or render her unconscious. I frequently suggest that if her problem were truly impossible to bear, it would either cost her life or she would very likely pass out from the overwhelming agony involved. Up to that point, I suggest, the client is standing the adversity or discomfort; she may not like it, but she is standing it.

5. *Teaching the principle of self-acceptance*. When low self-esteem is responsible for adolescent distress, I make every effort to show the client how to avoid global ratings of oneself (or others). I find that self-acceptance is one of the most difficult REBT principles to get across to teenagers, perhaps because comprehension requires a sophisticated level of understanding;

what's more, teenagers are geared to judging their self-image solely on the basis of peer opinion. Usually, however, I get somewhere with the following maneuvers:

a. Using a visual aid. I draw a circle and label it *self*. Next I draw a series of smaller circles inside the "self" circle. These represent the various traits, characteristics, and performances of the individual client. I try to demonstrate that rating one trait or feature as bad does not make all the other circles bad. In essence, I try to show adolescents that they are a collection of qualities, some good and some bad, none of which equal the whole self.
b. Using an analogy. Although many examples can illustrate the illogicality of overgeneralizing from act to personhood, I have found that the flat tire example works best with teenagers. I ask if they would junk a whole car because it had a flat tire. The key word is *junk*. Once clients pick up on this word image, I use it thereafter when they overgeneralize about mistakes or criticism. There you go again, I tell them, junking yourself because you did such and such.
c. Helping the client understand that although one is responsible for what one does, one is not the *same* as one does. This is sometimes tricky for adolescents to understand. They frequently argue that if they do something bad, they, too, are bad. I counter by suggesting, "If you went around mooing like a cow, would that make you a cow?" I usually receive a negative answer. Then I say, "But you are the one doing it. How come it doesn't turn you into a cow?" A few more examples like this one, and clients usually begin to separate what they do from who they are.
d. Explaining the difference between a person-with-less and less-of-a-person. Young clients suffering from feelings of shame, embarrassment, or inferiority have usually fallen victim to downing or degrading themselves. To the client who gets criticized or makes mistakes, I point out that such problems only prove that he is a person with less of what he wants (success or approval), rather than being less of a person. Sometimes I illustrate this principle by taking something from him (a shoe, a watch, etc.) and then asking, "What are you now? Are you less of a person or just a person with less of what you want?"
e. Showing that blaming oneself is like being punished twice for the same crime. With those adolescents who damn themselves and feel excessively guilty, I usually try to illustrate that mistakes and failings have built-in penalties. Whenever we err, I point out, we not only disappoint ourselves and fail to live up to our own standards, but we very likely endure some kind of adverse consequence. Through examples, I help clients to see that just living with the disappointments or consequences of their actions is punishment enough. Adding to these by damning oneself only adds insult to injury and makes matters worse than they need be.

6. *Correcting misperceptions of reality*. In addition to the disputation of irrational thinking, another area of cognitive intervention with teenagers involves reality misperception. Teenagers are especially prone to inaccurate descriptions and conclusions about their reality experiences, particularly those involving peer relationships. Such errors in thinking, identified and discussed in detail by Beck (1976) and Beck et al., (1979), sometimes lend themselves to more understandable analysis and effective remedy with adolescents than do the dialectics involved in correcting irrational thinking.

For example, a teenager reported feeling quite upset because a boyfriend had ignored her flirtations in history class that day. She had decided that he hated her and would never speak to her again, even though earlier in the day he had arranged a date with her for the weekend. Encouraged to offer proof of her conclusions, she eventually decided that the young man hadn't really rejected her and that it was highly unlikely that he hated her and would never speak to her again.

No attempt was made to get at the irrational ideas behind the client's upset, because she was able to correct her misperceptions and come to the conclusion that she really was not facing the loss of a boyfriend. If, however, her observations had actually been correct (or had she demonstrated a chronic overconcern about rejection), efforts would have been made to help her realize that her distress was the result not of poor reality testing but of a grossly distorted evaluation of that reality.

I will note that the correction of misperceptions and the disputation of irrational thinking in the problem intervention phase of counseling adolescents is not an either- or proposition; in actual practice, the two approaches are often used together. RET, however, places primary emphasis on the disputation of irrational beliefs because the highly evaluative, absolutistic quality of such thinking is considered the controlling dynamic in emotional and psychological disorders.

Problem Solving

Problem solving, the basic goal of REBT, is usually accomplished by persuading clients to put the knowledge gained in therapy into practice in concrete and specific life situations. This usually requires conscious effort and hard work, traits that unfortunately are not high on the list of adolescent virtues. Young people are notoriously reluctant to apply themselves to any task that does not promise immediate results.

It is important, therefore, not to harbor unrealistic expectations about counseling adolescents. Clinical experience has shown that teenagers usually do not undergo sweeping or dramatic personality changes, living happily ever after as a result of their therapy endeavors. Most come in for relatively few interviews; if these clients are handled skillfully along the lines I have suggested, they generally make moderate improvement. The following tactics usually encourage rational problem-solving by helping teenagers understand what therapy is about, what to expect from their efforts, and how to put insight into action:

1. *Explaining psychological and emotional problems as habits.* Sometimes I can encourage effort by adolescents through labeling their problems as habits. This labeling often takes the mystery out of how psychotherapy is supposed to work and puts the clients' roles in the change process in a framework that they can understand and accept. What I usually do is ask in each session about progress. When a reported lack of improvement can be traced to a client's failure to put into practice what we have been discussing, I suggest that the clients problem, no matter how complicated or painful, is merely a habit. After some explaining and clarifying, I point out that the client can expect improvement if she or he puts in the necessary work to change that habit.
2. *Checking out the client's expectations about therapy.* Often adolescents have the wrong idea about what to expect from counseling. They usually believe that therapy will leave them either carefree and happy or uncaring and unemotional about their problems. Unless these misconceptions are corrected, clients will very likely lose faith in therapy because it will not give them what they want.

   To those who expect to feel good all the time in spite of their problems, I point out that I follow the principles I am trying to teach them and that I have yet to enjoy disappointments. If I can't feel cheerful about disappointments, how do they expect to do so? I also note that those who smile or feel cheerful in the face of adversity or hardship are usually not termed well adjusted or normal. They are usually called crazy!

   To those who believe that rational thinking will rob them of their emotions, I suggest that our goal is to make them feel unhappy instead of miserable. Sometimes, I use a continuum illustration to get the concept across, showing the client that he or she belongs somewhere in the middle of the continuum between "calm" and "upset." At other times, I suggest that rational thinking about disappointments will only help him or her to feel *less* upset—less angry, less anxious, less embarrassed, and so on. The point that I try to emphasize is that our efforts will not eliminate emotions; they will only lessen the intensity, frequency, and duration of their distress.
3. *Writing out an ABC homework for them.* Although I am frequently successful in helping adolescents to understand why their thinking is irrational, I find it difficult to get them to practice challenging and correcting their irrational ideas outside of therapy sessions. With this group, the hard work involved in changing cognitions begins and ends in the office. For this reason, I try to outline their problems on a blackboard or a sheet of paper,

using the ABC model. At each session, I try to take the client through the model, and I also suggest that she or he take my writing efforts home and look at them if the problem comes up during the week.

4. *Sticking to accepted insights.* Once a particular insight has been presented, understood, and accepted by a teenager, I strongly suggest that this information be repeated without significant change. In other words, stick to what seems to impress the client as the cognitive source of his or her distress and use the same words, analogies, visual examples, and the like to reinforce the message. Putting clarifications and interpretations into different words or using other but similar analogies may prove stimulating and creative to the therapist but confusing and bewildering to most adolescents. Although such repetition may be monotonous at times, it usually proves effective in helping young clients to understand and accept rational concepts.
5. *Telling the adolescent what to think.* I have found that, despite heroic efforts, some adolescents are not going to learn how to reason things out according to prescribed REBT dogma. In such cases, I simply give them the correct sentences to think. I am not concerned with whether they understand the logic behind the statements, just so they will repeat the ideas during a time of distress. This kind of approach is usually recommended for young children, but I have found that it works equally well with certain teenagers. For instance, I might tell a client, "Next time someone calls you an asshole, tell yourself, 'If they called me a finger, it wouldn't make me a finger, so why get so upset over being called an asshole?' "
6. *Arranging homework assignments.* I usually try to design some kind of appropriate homework assignment for the client between sessions. This is probably the most efficacious way to encourage the client to put therapeutic insights to the test. It is also the best way for the therapist to check on the client. For instance, I might help a shy adolescent understand the cognitive source of his shyness, but I also want to get him to do something assertive, such as going to a party, asking a girl out, or maybe saying no to someone he usually accommodates with a yes. I have found that young people are more likely to accept the ideas of rational thinking after they have tried them out in emotionally provoking situations.

For the most part, these homework tasks are activity-oriented as opposed to being reading or writing assignments. I have not been particularly successful in persuading adolescents to read the REBT literature or to write out ABC forms or their equivalent. No doubt, reading and writing chores are too closely associated with unpleasant school duties; although I sometimes suggest such assignments, I do not become concerned about lack of interest in these areas. I usually figure it's unlikely that adolescents will extend themselves much beyond appearing for their sessions. For this reason, I frequently put more effort into those sessions than I would with adult clients.

Other Methods

Finally, I would like to mention some problem-solving tactics that do not necessarily rely on direct cognitive intervention. Although I usually make a determined effort to help adolescent clients through philosophical methods, experience has shown that this approach is not always feasible. Sometimes, less elegant and more practical methods are better used. With some adolescents, it is advisable to take what we can get as long as it relieves suffering and does not create further difficulties. This approach can be put into practice in the following way:

1. *Telling clients what to do*. Some adolescents do not respond to direct efforts to change their thinking, no matter what method I use or how simple I make things. In cases like this, I concentrate on telling them how to do things in such a way as to still enjoy themselves and yet keep out of trouble. For instance, I advised a teenaged girl on parole to cry in front of her parole officer. She was the type who consistently broke the rules of parole and was on the verge of returning to a correctional school. Her parole officer did not like the girl, because she was defiant and did not respect his authority. The girl did cry, and although she continued to break the rules, she was not incarcerated because she had gained the good graces of her parole officer, who now thought he had "broken" her.
2. *Teaching verbal assertiveness techniques*. Many teenagers believe themselves to be trapped in oppressive relationships. Those viewed as holding them in bondage include parents, teachers, or other adults charged with their keeping. In some cases the adolescents' complaints are valid, but often these clients have created oppressive situations through their own defiance or rebellion. Although I make an effort to get at the cognitive source of the problem ("I must have what I want" or "I can't stand being deprived"), I usually find that adolescents in this category are best helped by teaching them verbal assertiveness behaviors such as fogging and negative assertion. Those teenagers who learn such methods usually report good results.
3. *Getting a reduction rather than an elimination*. Sometimes, I am able to modify the behavior of certain adolescents by getting them to cut down rather than cut out. In other words, I try to convince them to pass just one of four subjects they are failing or to smoke only outside their homes. Sometimes, such a minor alteration in behavior alleviates parental or school pressures. I emphasize that this tactic will not work with the abuse of drugs or alcohol.
4. *Making use of the relationship to encourage change*. I find that, at least initially, some young people change because they want to please me. This motivation may keep them working until they can experience the rewards of their own efforts, rewards that thereafter can replace the relationship as a motivating factor. As I mentioned earlier, relationship development with adolescents is an integral part of REBT and is often a significant factor

influencing positive outcome. Although I could list a number of ways to use "friendship power" to encourage problem solving, 1 am not above telling some clients, "Do it for me!" Others I sometimes advise, "My job depends on your changing." I do this half kiddingly but still I try to get the message across that their lack of progress could have serious implications for me.

5. *Making use of parental involvement.* Often, adolescent problems are best resolved by including the parents in the counseling process. This inclusion could be in the form of family interviews or sessions with one or both parents. Sometimes, especially in those cases in which the adolescent refuses to participate in the counseling, the parents become the clients and are helped to cope more rationally with the situation. The same could be said for those occasions when the teenager is discovered to have fairly normal problems to which the parents are overreacting and thereby putting unnecessary pressure on the adolescent. On the other hand, there are times, as with issues involving subjects such as sex and drugs, when it is wise to leave parents out of the therapy. There are no hard-and-fast rules governing when to involve parents in counseling teenagers. It depends on the teenager, the problem, the parents, the laws governing the treatment of adolescents in one's community, and the skill and judgment of the counselor.
6. *Referring to a more appropriate resource.* With some adolescents, the most effective tactic is referral to a more appropriate service. Some teenagers, in spite of what appears to be an obvious need for counseling, do not respond no matter how ingenious the approach. For example, a teacher referred a bright 14-year-old boy with extremely low self-esteem. The client was overcompensating for feelings of inferiority by acting out and casting himself in the role of class clown. He possessed a number of well-entrenched irrational ideas about self-worth and a need for the approval of others. Unfortunately, after a few sessions, it was apparent he would be unable to benefit from therapy no matter how I put things. I suggested to the school that he be referred to a Big Brother program. It was my hope that a friendship-oriented experience with an adult would bolster his self-image and reduce his attention-getting behavior in school. Although hardly an elegant solution, it was, under the circumstances, the only viable alternative if the young man was to receive any help at all.

Case Illustration

The following condensed and edited interview illustrates some of the techniques suggested in this chapter. Dave, a 17-year-old, was referred by his parents in a telephone conversation. Their main concern was school truancy, but they mentioned, rather casually, that Dave's "horrible temper" had frequently got him into trouble. Dave showed up for his first interview alone, insulted the receptionist, and announced to the office staff that this was his first and last interview with a shrink.

THERAPIST (T): What brings you to see a counselor?
CLIENT (C) *(sarcastically):* My car!

T: Clever! You mean you have a car problem? If so, you're in the wrong place. You need a mechanic, not a head shrinker. I help people with mental and emotional problems.
C: *(even more sarcastically):* Then I don't belong here, because I'm not mental. I'm not crazy.
T: I agree. You certainly don't seem crazy to me. Who told you to come here for help?
C: My asshole parents!
T: What reason did they give you for sending you to a counselor?
C: I don't know. Why don't you ask them?
T: I can't. They're not here now. But I think I know what your problem is.
C: (very defiantly): What?
T: You've got problem parents. You've got parents that think they know everything. They plan your life for you, and if you don't like it, they figure there's something wrong with *you,* not them!
C: You're goddamned right! My parents are all f___ed up! They're all over my case.
T: Then you're in the right place.
C: What do you mean?
T: I specialize in problem parents. I can help you learn to manage your parents better.
C: I don't need your help!
T: Sure you do! You're getting nowhere doing things your way. In fact, that's what got you in here, isn't it? Do you like being here?
C: No!
T: I'll bet coming here isn't the only hassle you've had to endure because of your parents.
C: Yeah. They won't allow me to drive the car, and no one's allowed to come over to the house.
T: The more you fight them, the worse it gets. And you're telling me you don't need help with your parents.
C: What kind of help?
T: First, help in controlling your temper. I've talked to you just a little while, but it seems that your temper is a problem. Second, I can show you how to talk to your parents so you don't always end up in trouble.
C: Yeah, I got a temper. My friends are all afraid of me when I get mad. They think I'm crazy.
T: Okay, then, let's start with your temper. Give me an example of the last time you got really mad and lost your cool.
C: That's easy. An hour ago, when they told me I had to see you.
T: Okay, now let me ask this: What do you think made you so mad?
C: I told you: my parents' making me see you.

T: I'd like you to consider another possibility: maybe *you're* the one who made you feel angry.

C: Me? I didn't make myself come in here! *They* did!

T: No, no, Dave. I'm suggesting it's your attitude about your parents' making you come in that did the damage and got you so upset. Sure, they told you what to do, but it was your brain that turned a pain in the ass into a major crime! Here, let me show you what I mean. Take this. *(I hand him a rubber hammer.)* Now, suppose you were to hit yourself over the head with it. Whose fault would that be? Whom would you blame?

C: Me!

T: Even if I was the one who gave the hammer to you?

C: You just handed it to me. It would be my fault if I hit mysel over the head with it.

T: Dave, it's the same with your parents' making you come in here. *(Dave looks inquisitive.)* They hand you the crap and you hit yourself over the head with it. They tell you what to do, and you make a big deal, a major crime out of it. *(Dave nods attentively.)* So, it's not what they do, but what you do in your mind that's probably causing your anger. You're blaming your parents for something you're doing to yourself. They keep handing you the hammer, and you keep hitting yourself over the head with it. You put all your energy into blaming them instead of working on a way to stop giving yourself a hard time.

C: You mean my parents have nothing to do with it? I make it all up?

T: That's a good question, Dave, because that's not what I mean. Your parents contribute—they dish it out. But it's the way you take it, the way you blow it up in your mind, that's the real cause of your anger. Your parents play a part—they're not innocent bystanders—but you're the one that's mentally making a big deal out of things. *(There's a pause of a few minutes while Dave considers what I've been saying.)*

C: It makes sense, I guess. I never thought about it that way.

T: Would you like to learn what kind of thinking makes you so angry? *(Dave shrugs his shoulders in resigned agreement.)* Okay, let's use an illustration. I'm not an artist, but maybe this cartoon will help you understand better. *(7 draw a face that looks angry and put a thought bubble next to it. I leave the bubble blank.)* You notice I left the idea part blank, because I want you to help me fill it in. What went through your mind right after your parents told you that you had to come in and see me?

C: Oh, shit! Here we go again! I'm fed up with all this shit! Enough's enough! *(I write in the thought bubble, "I can't stand it anymore!")*

T: Anything else?

C: Who do they think they are? Why can't they get off my back. They're f___ing up my life! *(I add to the thought bubble, "They've got no right telling me what to do!"and hold it up for Dave to see.)* Is this it? Is this what went through your mind when your parents told you that you had to see me?

C: *(showing surprise):* That's what I was trying to say. Especially that last one. I think that all the time.
T: These two ideas not only get *you* angry, but they probably would get anyone just as upset. In fact, these are two of the nuttiest ideas people think. Would you like to learn how to change these ideas, feel less angry, stop blaming your parents, and get a grip on your temper? Or maybe you want to keep having temper tantrums.
C: No, the anger gets me into trouble. I got kicked out of school one time because of a stupid fight.
T: Okay. Here's how we do it. First, we see if the ideas make any sense or if they're just bullshit. We'll tackle that "I can't stand it anymore" idea. Do you really believe that you can't stand it when your parents tell you what to do and try to run your life?
C: It seems as though I can't, as though it's too much. Sometimes it's . . .
T: It's what you make of it. "It" doesn't have any power over you at all. For example, is your parents' interference in your life difficult to handle or is it impossible to handle? Which is it? Difficult or impossible?
C: Well, difficult, I guess.
T: Why isn't it impossible? *(A blank look crosses Dave's face.)* If it were impossible to put up with your parents, you would've been killed off by now, but you're still alive. In other words, no matter how much of a pain in the ass your parents give you, you've survived, haven't you?
C: Yeah.
T: Suppose that the next time your parents tell you to do something stupid, such as coming in to see me, you tell yourself, "Here we go again. Sure, it's the same old bullshit, but it won't kill me. I can stand it, even though I don't like it." How do you think you'd feel?
C: If I could think like that? *(1 nod.)* A lot less angry.
T: Okay, let's take a look at that other anger-producing idea. (I point to the cartoon and to "They've got no right telling me what to do!")
C: Well, they don't have a right. I've got my rights ...
T: Okay, wait a minute. Let me agree with you on one thing. It's wrong for your parents to order you around and tell you what to do. Your parents are wrong, okay?
C: You're goddamned right!
T: Are your parents human? Be serious.
C: Yeah.
T: Do humans make mistakes?
C: Yeah.
T: Do your parents have a right to make mistakes, such as bossing you around?
C: Not when it comes to me. They ought to know . . .
T: Are your parents human? Do humans make mistakes? Isn't it human nature to do wrong things?
C: Yeah.

T: Do your parents have a right to be wrong? Even when they're bossing you around and trying to run your life?
C: Yeah, I guess so, when you put it that way.
T: Suppose the next time they tell you what to do, the next time they make you do something you don't like, you say to yourself, "It's wrong, but they have a right to be wrong. After all they're just f___ed-up humans like everyone else!" How angry do you think you'd feel if you thought things out like that?
C: If I could think that way, it wouldn't bother me so much.

In addition to cognitive intervention, I suggested some verbal assertiveness techniques that Dave could use when he felt pressured by his parents. Subsequent sessions revealed that Dave's anger with his friends was the result of low self-esteem; this issue was handled in much the same style. After the third session, I encouraged Dave to have his girlfriend join us. She exercised a profound influence over him, made sure he kept appointments, and assisted my efforts by repeating rational insights to Dave between sessions. He proved quite receptive to REBT philosophy, showed marked improvement, and was able to work on a number of issues in addition to his temper, including his school attendance.

References

Bard, J. (1980). *Rational emotive therapy in practice*. Champaign: Research Press. p. 111.

Beck, A. (1976). *Cognitive therapy and the emotional disorders*. New York: International Universities Press.

Beck, A., Rush, A., Shaw, B., and Emery, G. (1979). *Cognitive therapy of depression*. New York: Guilford Press.

Ellis, A. (1962). *Reason and emotion in psychotherapy*. Secaucus, N.J.: Lyle Stuart.

Ellis, A. (1971). Sexual problems of the young adult. *Rational Living, 5*, 2–11.

Ellis, A. (1974). *Humanistic psychotherapy*. New York: McGraw-Hill.

Ellis, A. and Harper, R. A. (1975). *A new guide to rational living*. Englewood Cliffs, N.J.: Prentice-Hall.

Piaget, J., and Inhelder, B. (1969). *The psychology of the child*. New York: Basic Books.

Walen, S., DiGiuseppe, R., and Wessler, R. (1980). *A practitioner's guide to rational-emotive therapy*. New York: Oxford University Press.

Wessler, R., and Wessler, R. (1980). *The principles and practice of rational-emotive therapy*. San Francisco: Jossey-Bass.

4

Frustration Tolerance Training for Children

WILLIAM J. KNAUS

When fatigued, lacking sleep, and suffering a mild "cold," most adults will find that they are more easily distracted, and more susceptible to overreacting to frustrating conditions. Their tolerance for frustration can drop further when they run behind schedule.

From time to time, practically everybody will have multiple frustrations that relate to a physical vulnerability and undesired condition(s), and will magnify the situation. These transitory, frustration-related, everyday events, come and go. Among stable and mature adults, they are short-lived and rarely interfere with long-term goals, plans, and the quality of life.

Imagine for a moment the experience of a child who frustrates more often, easily, and intensely than his or her peers. Children who frustrate easily and often, are likely to blame, rationalize, make excuses, and maintain poor self-concepts compared to their more highly frustration tolerant peers. For such children, normal impediments tend to evoke an unpleasant visceral reaction and negative thinking. Such reaction patterns can serve as a barrier to many socially desired performances and achievements. Achievement gaps are normally visible to the child who looks at peers who can better tolerate and cope with frustration.

What can be done? Admonishing an easily frustrated child, can exacerbate an already negative situation. Preaching rarely promotes a positive outcome. Expedient statements, such as "Stop getting yourself so upset," normally promote more friction than the words relieve. If the child could automatically stop overreacting, the child would likely do so. Positive changes in boosting frustration tolerance are partially developmental, and partially achieved through learning to interpret frustrating circumstances in ways that would give the child a sense of inner control.

Since frustrations are so much a part of daily life, a prime challenge is to provide frustration tolerance training so that children can progressively acquire effective frustration mastery skills, and build upon these competencies throughout childhood, adolescence, and their adult lives. Guided frustration mastery efforts can lead to high frustration tolerance, which is the ability to accept the sensations of frustration, the conditions that evoke it, and, whenever possible, to actively and responsibly address the frustration-related problem(s). Helping children develop higher levels of frustration tolerance can aid in the prevention of the projected 50 % increase in childhood mental disability predicted by the World Health Organization (Murray and Lopez, 1996). The technology to do this is here, and getting better. What we need is a large-scale positive prevention program. Perhaps the most critical element in this program is to boost children's tolerance for frustration through promoting evidence-based psychological education programs to increase reasoning and psychological problem-solving competencies. I will later describe an evidence-based rational-emotive psychological education program designed for this purpose.

In this chapter I will discuss frustration, low frustration tolerance, and frustration disturbances before describing techniques for helping children progressively master frustration and progressively increase personal, social, and academic performances.

Frustration: A Complex Process

Psychologists John Dollard, Norman Miller, O. Hobart Mower, and Robert Sears (1938) define frustration as a condition that exists when a goal "suffers interference." Frustration involves goal blockage or thwarting, followed by dissatisfaction Few can avoid feeling frustrated over events such as walking to one's motor vehicle and seeing an unexpected flat tire. Learning can involve frustration when we go over the same territory, and progress seems stalled.

Frustration is a natural, primary, affective response to a perceived barrier. This reaction can occur in the twinkle of an eye.

- Frustration can have many causes and complications (Bull, 1955, 1957; Bull and Strongin, 1956; Knaus, 2000; Kretch et al., 1991).
- This reaction to a barrier is often colored and shaped by the language we use to describe experience. Frustrations can erupt when we face a disparity between what we tell ourselves *what we wanted,* and *what is* (Knaus 1983).
- Frustration resides on a continuum. The process involves sensations of discomfort that can range from barely perceptible to powerful. If sufficiently intense, frustration can disrupt memory functions and result in disorganized thinking and behaving.

In studying the relationship between frustrating conditions and children's responses, some early researchers thought that frustration led to aggression. A classic frustration-aggression study was conducted by Barker, Dembo, and

Lewin (1941). In the experiment, kindergarten children initially played with a mixture of toys with missing pieces: the ironing board had no iron, the water toys had no water. At first, the children disregarded the missing pieces and made imaginative use of the toys. Later, the experimenters exposed the children to superior and complete toys, and blocked the children from using them. When the children returned to play with the old toys, they squabbled among themselves, behaved poorly toward the experimenters, and destroyed some toys. With raised expectations, the children found little satisfaction with the inferior toys. (Aggression will sometimes occur in the context of a frustrating situation, but not necessarily.)

Psychologist Leonard Berkowitz (1969) saw the frustration-aggression model as both too sweeping and too simple. He proposed that we need to focus on other considerations to understand the relationship between frustration and aggression. These include:

- Motives the aggressor ascribes toward others
- The child's attitude toward the problem area
- Past learning
- The child's interpretation of his or her own reaction to the frustration conditions

Berowitz's contextual dimension for frustration and aggression, is consistent the rational-emotive position that we feel the way we think (Ellis, 1994, 2001; Ellis and Greiger, 1977; Ellis and Knaus, 1979). According to the rational-emotive theory of emotion, we can self-induce frustration because of how we view and experience impediments in the context of our moods, and other physical states.

Once we develop language and expectations, frustration can result from perceived negative gaps between our personal demands, rules, and reality. This process is normally accompanied by an urgency to gain immediate satisfaction. Urgent, demand-driven frustration is among the more intense, persistent, and maladaptive kind.

Low Frustration Tolerance

Low frustration tolerance is a strong urge to throw off discomfort without much forethought. This reaction tendency is normally a maladaptive response to frustration. The low frustration tolerance response typically includes adding negative surplus meanings to the situation, such as telling oneself that one cannot stand it.

Low frustration tolerance is implicated as a prime distress factor in psychologist Albert Ellis' rational-emotive behavior therapy approach (Ellis, 1982, 1994; Ellis and Dryden, 1987; Ellis and Knaus, 1979; Knaus, 2002). Different views and elements of this process have been described by clinicians of various theoretical orientations such as Ainslie (1975)., Cattell

(1962), Freud (1955), Hybl and Stagner (1952), Low (1950), Overstreet (1925) and Payot (1909). Although each theorist employs a different label, (i.e., laziness, primary process thinking, comfort cult, specious reward), they describe an active, primitive, gratification-seeking frustration-avoidance process.

Practically everybody will periodically experience low frustration tolerance, sometimes from imaginary problems. When low frustration tolerance patterns interfere with social and personal goals, this process is maladaptive and a viable target for a positive intervention.

Low frustration tolerance takes many forms among school children: importunity; daydreaming; refusing to discharge responsibilities, procrastinating, whining and complaining, arguing and fussing, fabricating to cover minor mistakes, focusing on "unfairnesses" and demanding that they cease, quivering in terror at the thought of talking in front of the class, shyness; compulsive eating; violence; copying other children's homework, poor spelling due to failure to look up words, inattentiveness, disrupting the class, blaming others, impatience, and withdrawal.

Here is a sample low frustration tolerance process:

- A child cannot get what is wanted or do what is wanted, and exaggerates and acts like the situation is *too* uncomfortable or intolerable.
- The child's impression of a frustrating condition can include various combinations of low-frustration tolerance language: (1) avoidance phrases ("I don't want to."), (2) extropunitive phrases (Blaming others or events for the frustration), (3) distress or catastrophic phrases ("It's overwhelming." It's too much." "I can't take it." "I can't do it."), (4) demands ("It is unfair" [the world should be fair], "I shouldn't have to."), (5) intolerance phrases ("I can't stand it"), (6) self-reference phrases ("I hate myself.").
- The child behaves in a predictable maladaptive way through withdrawal, whining, lashing out, or other similar behavior.

The low frustration tolerance language system develops in daily living, and can reflect "familial" or "cultural" cliché thinking such as "I can't stand it." But what is the *it*? Is *it* the frustration, the situation, a reactive habit, or combination?

Low frustration tolerance self-talk intensifies stress sensations that can interfere with normal routes of reason. This process is often circular. The frustration stress sensations can trigger distress thinking. Negatively elaborated interpretations about not getting what one wants, can evoke frustration stress sensations.

Low frustration tolerance is likely to co-occur with a self-concept disturbance and have maladaptive consequences. A child with a poor self-concept is likely to avoid age-related challenges, and to overreact to normal daily hassles. This can result in another vicious circle of frustration and negative self-attributions.

Low Frustration Tolerance Disturbances

Like an over-practiced script, low frustration tolerance can flow into a seamless automatic frustration disturbance habit process. What distinguishes low frustration tolerance from a frustration disturbance is in the persistent, predictable maladaptive quality of low frustration tolerance reactions. Cultural ways of describing this process include, "short-fuse," and "raw-nerved" at one end of the continuum. At the other end of this distress continuum we find words such as tense, inhibited or fearful.

Various negative coexisting processes commonly accompany frustration disturbances. These conditions can include perfectionism, magnifications, lying, an unhealthy inhibition, a negative self-concept, anxiety, depression, or substance abuse. Low frustration tolerance disturbances often underlay distinguishable symptom clusters that include eating problems, impulse disorders, compulsive disorders, avoidant disorders, anxiety disorders, depression, conduct disorders, and so forth. For example, children with conduct disorders, such as fighting, stealing, or truancy, predictably and persistently react to frustrating situations with low frustration tolerance and poor impulse control.

A low frustration tolerance disturbance pattern can both reflect and exacerbate attention deficit disorders. For example, when frustration disturbances correlate with deficiencies in attention and impulse control, this elevates the risk of poor academic performance, family problems, needless fears and inhibitions, and trouble with authorities and the law.

The following factors can contribute to the development of a low frustration tolerance disturbance pattern and poor behavioral coping competencies. General frustration management strategies follow each hypothesized factor.

- *Temperament predisposition*. Some children are genetically equipped with advantageous tendencies such as athletic prowess, musical ability, and frustration tolerance. Others are predisposed toward low frustration tolerance, perceptual distortions, anxiety, or depression. Tendencies, of course, need not be actualized. The person with musical talent need not learn to play music. The person primed for intolerance toward frustration can learn and apply tolerance techniques.
- *Social conditioning*. There are conditionable and conflicting ideas common to Western Society: Get ahead and achieve if you can; avoid tension if you can. If a child comes to believe that achievement should be tension free, that person is likely to feel especially frustrated when excellence fails to follow a lack of meaningful effort. We can help the child alter this dysfunctional viewpoint through exercises in developing a perspective on the relationship between planning, effort, and results.
- *Inadequate emotional expressive language skills*. Children with restricted vocabularies may not have the words to accurately define or express their desires or discontents (Bernstein, 1961). This can add a layer of frustration

to situational frustrating circumstances. We can help children build expressive vocabularies through educational methods.

- *Imitating models who show weak self-control.* A child reared in an environment where significant people display low frustration tolerance, may imitate this response. To alter this trend, expose the child to effective models and provide opportunities to practice the observed effective new behaviors.
- *Misreading the signal.* The child misinterprets the meaning of frustration. Instead of using the feeling as an impetus for purposeful action, the child interprets the feeling as a signal to avoid the frustrating stimulus. By helping the child learn to view the frustrating condition as a challenge, the frustration avoidance bias can be changed to a problem-solving bias.
- *Reward for delay.* The child discovers that when he or she puts something off, makes up excuses, lies, or engages in other expedient actions, he or she is intermittently rewarded for this behavior. We can help to reverse this trend by helping the child examine the consequences of delaying actions on his or her emotional security and accomplishments.

Low frustration tolerance prone children are likely to increase their frustration tolerance as they get older (Marcotte, 1996). Nevertheless, children prone to low frustration tolerance tend to grow into adults prone to low frustration tolerance. They risk going through life avoiding long-term challenges, demonstrating impatience, giving up easily, procrastinating, and agitating themselves about their frustrations. This is a formula that can have career, social, and health consequences. It can be a link to depression. Low frustration tolerance patterns are highly desirable to nip in the bud.

Action Strategies

Children are surprisingly weak in their ability to detect errors of omissions and to detect cognitive distortions. They do little monitoring of their memory and other cognitive processes (Flavell 1979). However, when prompted, even 3-year-olds show ability to separate thoughts that are factual from those that are false. (Woolley and Bruell 1996).

Children can and do learn to tolerate frustrations and master frustration evoking problems; (Kagan 1971; Knaus, 1977; Knaus and Haberstroh 1993; Meichenbaum and Goodman 1971; Pollack 1968; Schaefer and Milman 1977). Children with age-related low frustration tolerance can learn to think about their thinking, and apply a metacognitive self-management approach that involves recognizing and correcting false frustration eliciting beliefs, goal setting, planning, executing, and evaluating.

Metacognitive procedures appear useful for promoting personal effectiveness and positive mental health (Dollard, 1943; Flavell, 1978; Kuhn et al., 1995; Vygotsky, 1934\1988; Wallen, 1935). These approaches appear instrumental to developing what Stanford University professor Albert Bandura describes as positive self-efficacy, or the ability to purposefully organize, regulate, and direct one's actions toward a productive outcome. (Bandura, 1986, 1989, 1997, 2000.)

Children's irrational beliefs are major contributors to emotional distress that include low frustration tolerance disorders (Bernard, 2004; Ellis and Bernard, 2005). A prime challenge is to create conditions for children to strengthen their critical thinking competencies to challenge and to reduce the negative effects of irrational low frustration tolerance self-talk, accept discomfort as a fact of life, and act to gain long-term benefits.

Frustration tolerance training includes providing opportunities for children to recognize low frustration tolerance self-talk, think about and challenge this thinking, and to develop behavioral coping and mastery competencies. These competencies include deciding when it is appropriate and beneficial to delay gratification, and where it is normally wiser to face and solve personal problems than to avoid them. This is an evolutionary process that can continue over a lifetime. We start *frustration tolerance training* with Rational-Emotive Education.

Rational-Emotive Education

In an Aesop fable of two frogs, the reptiles' marsh dried during the summer heat. They went on a search for a wet area. Eventually, they came upon a well filled with water. One excitedly leaped to the brim and said, "We have found a new home." The second paused and said, "Suppose this well dried up like our marsh. Then, how would we get out?" A certain amount of reflecting and reasoning can save the day.

Rational-emotive education (REE) is an approach I developed to help children improve their reasoning and psychological problem-solving competencies to prevent, or to identify, clarify, and cope with repetitive social, emotional and behavioral problems (Knaus, 1974). The REE system is philosophically similar to rational-emotive therapy (REBT) as described by Ellis (1979, 2004). Originally designed for use in schools, REE is also used in individual and group counseling with children and adolescents.

REE is an evidence-based mental health program that can be used with classes of "normal" children or adolescents. The REE approach can be effectively used in both group and individual psychotherapy with emotionally and behaviorally disturbed children with low frustration tolerance and self-concept disturbances.

REE: An Evidence-based System

Since 1970, researchers have tested the REE curriculum in different settings and with populations ranging from learning disabled kindergarten children to the elderly. The REE research was summarized in three large-scale literature surveys (DiGiuseppe and Bernard, 1990; Hajzler and Bernard 1991; Watter, 1988). The data support the REE model as an effective system.

Researchers empirically tested the REE curriculum with children (Albert, 1972; Bokor, 1975; Brody, 1974; Buckley, 1983; Casper, 1983; DeStefano, 1988; DiGiuseppe, 1976; Grassi, 1984; Greenwald, 1985; Harris, 1976; Hooper and Layne1985; Katz, 1974; Knaus and; Miller, 1977; Miller and Kassinove, 1978; Leibowitz, 1979; Ritchie, 1978; Rose, 1983; Rosenbaum, 1991; Streeter, 1999 Wilde, 1996). The REE program shows effectiveness in areas such as increasing rational thinking, boosting self-concept, and reducing neuroticism. Encouraging preliminary longitudinal data suggest that children taught rational concepts through an REE program, maintained their gains between the fourth and eight grades (Wilde, 1999). These results support the efficacy of the REE program.

We can use REE with diverse populations (Knaus, 1977, 1977a, 1980, 1983, 1985). The program shows efficacy with learning disabled students (Gruenke, 2000;Knaus, McKeever, 1977; Lo 1986; Meyer, 1981; and Omizo et al., 1985, 1986). REE has effectively been carried out with a "special needs" population (Eluto, 1980). The curriculum was researched and found effective in middle and high school settings (Block, 1976; Dye, 1980; Geizhals, 1981; Handleman, 1982; Hernaez et al., 2000; Kachman, 1988; Kachman and Mazer, 1990; Sandilos, 1986; Voelm, 1984; Wu, 1986).When used with college students, the REE curriculum promoted improvement in social skills (Wu, 1987). REE has been effective in the reduction of stress among test-anxious college freshman (Balther and Godsey 1979). At the end of the life cycle, REE has been effectively used with elderly populations (Keller et al., 1975; Krenitsky 1978). This research suggests that REE can appeal to a broad range of groups at different ages, and has efficacy with diverse populations.

We have promising research that suggests that using the REE curriculum, correlates with increases in academic achievement (Katchman and Mazer 1989; Streeter, 1999). Teachers challenged by violent student behavior and disruptive classroom behavior, find that they can use REE to support the teaching process through reducing behavioral incidents (Zionts, 1983; Vernon, 1990).

The REE Program

The REE program (Knaus, 1974), consists of a series of *rational-emotive education lessons* developed to aid children in identifying and understanding their feelings; to understand from where those feelings came; to develop an objective perspective; to problem-solve; to build self confidence; and to develop tolerance for frustration. The program includes multiple experiential exercises including a *Mr. Head Game* that can be used to identify rational and irrational ideas, and their accompanying emotions (Knaus, 2004).

At its most basic level, REE involves the introduction of a rational concept, a simulation where the child tests the concept, and an application where the child uses the concept as it applies in daily life. Children can then be prompted to apply the acquired and practiced REE concepts.

Calling upon a child to use what has already been learned is easier than to have a child learn a problem-solving skill set in the middle of an agitated state of frustration or distress. As a child increasingly uses REE techniques to solve problems, the results are likely to feel rewarding, promote confidence, and boost tolerance for frustration.

I designed the REE program as a "cookbook" method where teachers can teach brief but powerful lessons using this preventive mental health program. The program aids children to develop coping competencies while providing teachers with a tested method to reduce classroom behavioral problems. REE can be integrated into the classroom curriculum, and can be supported by related parts of the curriculum (Knaus, 1977a, 1977b, 2004; Knaus and Haberstroh, 1993).

A related principle underlying the REE program is that the positive mental health concepts can effectively be employed in a psychotherapeutic setting where the therapist helps the child apply REE concepts he or she has been taught. In that environment, the child can learn new problem solving concepts tailored to his or her special needs. The REE approach can be clinically deployed by school counselors working in tandem with classroom teachers and parents. This joint approach provides an economy of scale.

I nested frustration tolerance training throughout the REE program. In this psychological educational process, children learn about emotions, separate erroneous from sensible beliefs, and recognize and challenge negative thinking such as low frustration tolerance self-talk. Through this guided-discovery experiential-learning approach, children learn, test, acquire, and apply rational reasoning and problem-solving competencies.

Students who complete REE training, have an array of experientially tested life-skills to use to meet challenging circumstances including those that can elicit low frustration tolerance reactions. The REE lessons may also help support student resilience (Bernard, 2004). The following section describes low frustration tolerance and negative self-concept factors that can be addressed through the REE approach.

The Self-doubt and Discomfort-Dodging Model

Frustration disturbances are self-generated. For example, some youngsters (and adults) act like they were afraid of almost any negative sensation. When frustrated, these sensation-sensitive youngsters tend to overreact. As the poet Marcel Proust has said, it is, "that fear of suffering in the immediate present which condemns us to perpetual suffering" (Painter, 1965).

The Self-Doubt and Discomfort-Dodging model describes the relationships between self-concept disturbances, intolerance for frustration, and self-defeating behaviors such as procrastination (Knaus, 1982a, 1982b). According to this reciprocal model, both children and adults disturb themselves when engaged in a negative self-concept and low frustration tolerance process. They tend to be free of frustration disturbance once outside this process.

The self-doubt dimension of the model describes what happens when a child comes to doubt herself or himself (see Figure 1). For example, if the child doubts her or his capabilities, the child is likely to second-guess and hesitate. Engaged in this cycle, a child will tend toward various forms of self-downing (stupid, bad, weird). Self-downing will tend to elicit more self-doubts.

The second phase of the model describes low frustration tolerance. In a low frustration tolerance mode, the child will tend to be sensation-sensitive and will likely focus on tensions, magnify them, and try to escape.

A child entangled in this whirlpool of mental-physical enervation is primed to get emotionally drenched in a "cognitive storm" where self-doubts fuel frustration-tensions which disrupt reasoning, discharge short term memory, and add more self-doubt fuel to the affective fires.

The third phase of the model describes the defensive escape hatch. The individual diverts himself from this vicious cycle through various self-protective avenues, such as procrastination, withdrawal and\or lashing out. In the process, the child fails to cope adaptively with the precipitating conditions, loses opportunity to gain practice in developing problem-solving competencies, and tends to maintain a distorted view toward self and circumstances.

The model provides a conceptual map for treatment planning. It describes intervention points where elements of the low frustration tolerance disturbance processes can be disrupted and replaced with a beneficial and realistic style of thinking, emoting, and responding. For example, a counselor can help the child build self-confidence by teaching him or her to challenge erroneous self-doubts and self-downing self-talk.

Constructive changes in one phase of the Self-Doubt and Discomfort-Dodging process predictably weaken the other links. For example, a child who engages in self-downing, can learn to build self-efficacy through recognizing and successfully challenging erroneous beliefs, and by working toward a meaningful long-term goal(s). Targeted psychological homework assignments prompt the child to act on the basis of alternative methods that demonstrate the benefits of orderly actions. For example, the child might try to think of three alternative actions to take when frustrated, and implement the one that predicts the best long-term result.

Applying Procrastination Technology to Low Frustration Tolerance Disturbances

Procrastination is an automatic habit process involving a needless delay of a timely and relevant activity (Knaus and Haber Stroh, 1993; Knaus, 1982, 2002). Although this complex habit process has multiple mechanisms and takes multiple forms, frustration and discomfort avoidance is a prime mechanism underlying most forms of procrastination.

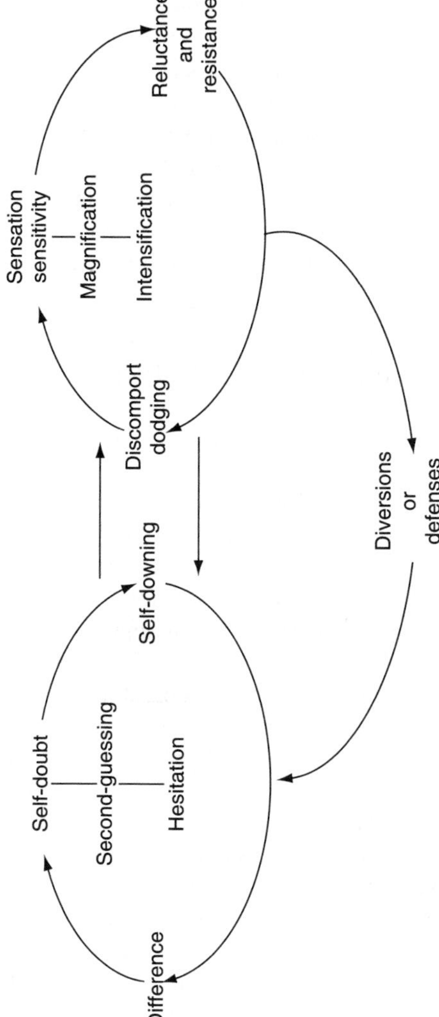

FIGURE 1. The self-doubt tension-intolerance model

In addressing low frustration tolerance, here is a sampling of counter-procrastination techniques that apply:

- *Metacognitive training*. Through guided discovery, the child sets goals and outlines plans to boost frustration tolerance. The plans typically involve breaking a challenge down to manageable parts (bits and pieces approach).
- *Check-off list technique*. The child has a list of attainable, hierarchically ordered challenges, and follows this stepping stone approach to develop self-regulation skills.
- *The five-minute system*. The child agrees to work for five-minutes on a normally frustrating task, then decides at the end of the five minutes to continue or quit. Normally, when a negative inertial is broken, the child will tend to continue beyond the five-minute "agreement." This approach has the additional value of allowing the child to gain exposure to frustration under controlled conditions, to learn that tension is tolerable, and to learn that frustration can be countered through purposeful action.

If low frustration tolerance disturbances represent an automatic habit process, rationally interrupting the process can help disrupt and reduce its intensity, frequency, and duration. The PURRRRS system is a method to counteract the automatic procrastination process (Knaus, 2002). The system applies to aiding children build competencies and resilience against low frustration tolerance reactions.

In using PURRRRS, the child learns to *pause* when recognizing the onset of a frustration situation, and take time to get composed. Next, the child *utilizes* cognitive resources to intentionally slow thinking and to note the thoughts and beliefs associated with the frustration. Following that, the child shifts focus to *reflect* on what is happening. This includes mapping the relationships between low-frustration self-talk, emotions, reactions, and potential outcomes. Thereafter, the child *reasons* things out by separating emotional low-frustration tolerance language from fact-based beliefs, and impulse from reflective thought. Rational self-questioning techniques are applied to correct the irrational ideas. This step pits reason against low frustration tolerance thinking and impulsive reactions. The child devises a new action script for rationally responding to the frustrating situation. The next phase is to *respond* by following the "new" script for addressing the frustration problem. Since plans are rarely perfect, *revision* normally follows responding. The process is repeated until this approach becomes a *stable* and repeatable part of managing frustration.

The REE approach involves teaching preliminary cognitive and behavioral competencies. The PURRRRS system would be introduced following the application of the basic REE program.

REE, counter-procrastination, and PURRRRS problem solving processes are designed to provide children with opportunities to develop reflective competencies and to delay gratification. A slight shift in the direction of reflective reasoning and psychological problem-solving can make a significant difference.

Delays in Gratification and Acceptance: A Prime Outcome

In one degree or other, children can choose to avoid specious gratification that comes from impulsively trying to satisfy low frustration tolerance urges, and to accept normal hassle and discomfort. Children progressing in these areas, are more likely to demonstrate self-regulatory behavior associated with adaptive functioning. In contrast, self-regulation failures are associated with violence, substance abuse, poor school and social performances, eating disorders, and a compliment of related destructive outcomes.

Constructive self-regulation is a basic competency related to emotional stability and what is called will power (Peake et al., 2002; Goleman, 1995; Baumeister et al.,1994). Frustration tolerance training emphasizes the development of self-regulatory behaviors.

Acceptance can be a byproduct of developing rational self-regulatory competencies. Acceptance is not a passive process. The child chooses to live with unpleasant feelings of frustration without magnifying them. This comes about through a refocusing of attention from thinking about the onerousness of a frustrating situation, to taking it for what it is, and doing what can be done. Through this active, constructive, reflective process, the frustration tolerance process is put into a reasoned perspective.

Applying Rational-emotive Education to Individual Children with Low Frustration Tolerance

Childhood mental disturbances can be detected early and treated effectively (Weiss et al., 1987; Weissberg et al. 1983). A first step in ths process is to develop a comprehensive cognitive-behavioral assessment. The following outlines a sample assessment-prescriptive process:

Step 1: Identify determinants of behavior: what, how, where, when, and to what extent. Define exceptions to pattern. Determine what has previously proven helpful in alleviating the problem. Find out what has served to aggravate the problem.

Step 2: Determine the extent to which the described problem represents pathological deviancy through analysis of age-expectant behavior, cultural and sub-cultural norms, socioeconomic expectancies, problem intensity, and problem persistence. When called for, use psychometric evaluation, observation, and special problem simulation techniques to make the assessment.

Step 3: Make a conceptual assessment concerning beliefs the child holds about self, problem situation(s), and frustration sensations. This phase is designed to reveal the quality and extent of the child's emotive vocabulary, quality of self-expression, and low frustration tolerance language system.

It includes a description of the degree, and frequency of self-downing statements, and other self-defeating beliefs.

Step 4: Use appropriate aspects of the *Self-Doubt and Discomfort-Dodging* framework to help decide the interventions you will use and how, when, and where to apply them.

Step 5: Set the stage by guiding the child through a sequence of REE lessons designed to give him or her a problem solving frame of reference and basic psychological coping tools. This step can include: teaching an emotive vocabulary; showing that the way one thinks influences how one feels and behaves. Involve the child in this process so that he or she can learn directly from experience.

Step 6: In session problem simulation. The child has the opportunity apply what he has learned to solve the frustration problem(s) under simulated conditions such as role playing, acting out the problem solution, and so forth.

Step 7: Behavioral assignment. The child tests and practices the frustration management strategy(s) under *in vivo* problem conditions.

In REE-oriented therapy, assessment and skill building are part of the ongoing fluid process of positive change. The therapist's interventions ordinarily start with introducing basic REE lessons to give the child a set of rational understandings geared to help the child learn clear thinking and effective behavior competencies. This provides a platform for the child to engage in self-monitoring and self-regulating behavior. However, therapy is rarely a linear process. The therapist can weave in REE exercises as they apply to what is therapeutically relevant.

Therapy with children is as much an art filled with ingenuity, as it involves a structured set of therapeutic interventions. Ingenuity comes into play in response to the often changing issues that arise, and in finding ways to make rational ideas comprehensible to a child to promote understanding, reasoning, and psychological problem-solving competencies.

Some low frustration tolerance prone children will dramatize the frustration they experience, and habitually and irrationally externalize or internalize blame. Sometimes, a simple exercise, such as having the child look though a rolled up telescope-shaped paper, can help her or him realize what is meant by blowing problems out of proportion. The rolled paper provides an example of tunnel vision. The child can only see what is at the open end of the paper. If that was all the child believed was in the room, this would be like losing perspective by "making a mountain out of a molehill."

The *Chicken Little* story can augment the lesson. Chicken Little was a story character who, when hit with a twig from a tree, thought the sky was falling down. The chicken panicked, and got other barnyard animals involved in the commotion that followed. To use the story to teach coping competencies, the child can play detective. How would Detective Little deal with the falling sky problem? Through playing detective, a child can actively and experientially participate in developing the reflective thinking competencies important to changing problem-magnifying low frustration tolerance thought patterns.

The mountain and mole hill, and Chicken Little exercises, fit with the REE approach of providing an age-related concept, creating simulations to experientially teach the concept, and prompting direct applications in problem-related circumstances. Through multiple interventions like the molehill and Chicken Little scenarios, the child is exposed to a concept that is likely to be remembered. Following these experiences, it will be far easier for a child to understand how a person can make a lot out of a little, and what to do to change a low frustration tolerance disturbance pattern.

Case Application: Ree with a Battered Child

The following case example illustrates the use of the REE frustration tolerance training method with a child with low frustration tolerance.

Kathy was a 5-year-old child with five older siblings. At the time she entered therapy, she was temporarily living in a foster home and was scheduled to return to her natural mother within three months. Before her removal from her natural parents, she had been routinely battered by her mother. On occasion her mother burned her with a hot iron. Significantly, Kathy was the only one among her siblings who was battered.

From court records, the foster mother's description, and the child's own report, Kathy experienced considerable difficulty containing her impulses. If she had an impulse to do something, she would act on it. For example, she unraveled a sweater her foster mother was knitting. She pulled up the foster mother's prize flowers from the garden. She threw groceries from the shelves when she went shopping with her foster mother. She jumped up and down in a moving automobile yelling and laughing and directly disrupting the driver. She routinely broke glasses and dishes. She also had a habit of doing the opposite of what she was told to do. In addition, Kathy had a short attention span and was enuretic.

At least part of Kathy's problem was low frustration tolerance characterized by poor impulse control. Her poor impulse control also served as an expedient way of attracting negative attention.

I assumed that Kathy's natural mother was irrationally exasperated by the child's impulse behavior. Since the mother had not beaten her other children, it made sense to try to teach Kathy how to deal with her impulses and to get attention in a less destructive manner. Since part of the beatings were associated with her enuresis, this became the second behavior targeted for extinction.

To reduce Kathy's impulse control problem, two behaviors were initially targeted for extinction—jumping in the car and throwing groceries off shelves in grocery stores. To reduce these behaviors, it was important first to get Kathy to think before she acted. By developing reflective thinking competencies, many youngsters learn to manage low frustration tolerance urges.

A method I used to teach Kathy reflective thinking competencies was the "if you want something, you do something" method. The purpose of the method is to teach cause, effect, and accountability. The method breaks down to the basic REE framework of demonstrating the concept, simulated practice of the principle, and direct problem solving application. These three steps supported Kathy's frustration tolerance training program.

The first step was to demonstrate the principle. Initially, I discussed the grocery throwing problem with Kathy. I told her that if we were going to make a movie and I was going to play her part, I would need her to help me learn my part. Once I understood how to play the part, I asked her to watch me to see if I knew how she acted in the grocery store. Then I pretended to skip down a grocery store isle pushing a shopping cart, and feigned throwing groceries out of the cart and pushing them off the shelves. As I dramatized her role I shouted, "Oh boy, I'm having such fun! I'm going to get mommy mad at me so I can lose my privileges. What fun!" After acting this part with the child laughing at my antics, we got back to being serious again. It seemed I got the right idea except that Kathy was not looking forward to the outcome—losing privileges. Then we went back to the grocery throwing act but this time we had a new twist: She acted out her own part and as she did, we made up a song called the "If You Want to Lose Privileges, You Have to Throw the Groceries." She quickly caught onto the concept: If she wanted to get in trouble she had many ways to succeed.

Kathy liked to ride in the car and go shopping and watch her favorite television shows. These "privileges" had been regularly taken away from her. So it was clear that if she wanted to miss her television shows and get into trouble, then she could do something to make that happen. Yet, she could also "do something to get something" that she wanted.

In the following week, she made a 180 degree turn in her behavior. She stopped breaking dishes, she stopped jumping up and down in the automobile, and she went grocery shopping and helped put the groceries in the cart. Over the next few weeks, this new pattern dominated. Only a few lapses occurred. Kathy learned that even if you act well, you may not always get what you want but you can often avoid penalties that you do not want.

Next, we tackled her enuresis pattern. While she was still too young to be classified as an enuretic, the behavior was a conflict point. Thus, it was important to deal with this problem before her return home, as there was no guarantee that her natural mother would prove flexible in coping with daily bed sheet changes until the child gained night control.

Over the next several sessions, it became clear that she did have considerable control over her bed-wetting. It was also determined that she was very desirous of visiting a local amusement park. Her foster parents wanted her to stop bed-wetting. She thought she could succeed if she got to go to the amusement park. The procedure was that she would eat supper early and would not drink any liquids after supper. She would go to the bathroom just before she went to bed. She would get out of bed and go to the bathroom if she had to urinate during the night. If she succeeded for five nights (Kathy could count to five) she would go to the amusement park. If she wet her bed before the five days were up, she would have to start from scratch.

During the next three weeks, Kathy kept a dry bed for four successive nights and wet it on the fifth. She showed she could maintain constancy. She knew the "if you want something you have to do something" principle. She could count to five. Why would she not stay dry on the fifth night?

By this time it was clear that she did not want to return home. With a little prodding I found out that she believed that if she was too good, she would have to go home right away. She didn't want to do that. Staying where she was, was more important than the amusement park. If she misbehaved she could not do some things she liked to do: Go shopping, watch television, or go out to play. The solution was to be *almost* good enough. After this point, the tone of the session changed to one of great seriousness. I explained to her that whether she behaved or misbehaved she would have to return to her home at the end of summer. In this process I used analogies, stories, and descriptions of natural phenomenon to show that there are some things you can control and some things you cannot control. She cried but understood. Two weeks later she went to the amusement park because she succeeded in overcoming bed-wetting.

Following this accomplishment, she spent several weekends with her natural family before permanently returning home. During those visits she kept trying the "if you want something you have to do something" method. She succeeded in her attempts to maintain control. Fortunately, the state agency had worked with the mother teaching her new ways to deal with her low frustration tolerance reactions toward her child, and so the visits worked out for both mother and daughter.

In the remaining sessions, we worked on how she felt about herself and why she was not a bad person even if she acted poorly. In this phase of Kathy's therapy the REE Self-Concept Pinwheel Technique proved helpful (Knaus, 1974).

The *Self-Concept Pinwheel* method consisted of Kathy creating a pinwheel by cutting a square of text cover paper to create a pinwheel shape. Then she drew symbols and stick figures onto each of the pinwheel propellers. These attributes were feeling, doing, thinking, "quality" attributes. She used a straight pin to attach the wheel onto a stick so that she could spin it. She then spun the pinwheel and answered the question about the attributes that were on the propeller that aligned with a green mark the top of the stick. For example, "Are you only a person who washed dishes?" "Are you only a person who feels sad?" "Are you only a person who laughs at jokes?" Kathy soon got the idea that she could not be only one way at all times. Then we moved on to whether she could only be bad or good based on single qualities, ideas, feelings, or actions?

Believing that she could only be bad or good, she struggled with that idea that there are shades of gray, and that people can not only be one way. Eventually she decided that she could not be a person with many qualities, and still be only one way, bad or good. She could act badly or act well. Yet, she would not lose all else that she knew about herself. She also learned that if she had "bad" thoughts about herself she would feel badly, but she could match those thoughts against other thoughts she has about herself that were more positive. This awareness opened the door to another. She could question her "badness beliefs," and see herself in more than one way. She could change her behavior if she wanted different results. This process prompted her to develop a broader perspective, and that perspective was accompanied by a higher level of frustration tolerance.

Both the *want something–do something*, and *self-concept pinwheel* ideas proved versatile and valuable. Kathy left therapy with a few new coping tools and a whole life to practice them.

References

Ainslie, G. (1975). Specious reward: A behavioral theory of impulsiveness and impulse control. *Psychological Bulletin, 82,* 463–496.

Albert, S. (1972). *A study to determine the effectiveness of affective education with fifth grade students.* Unpublished master's thesis, Queens College.

Balther, R. C. and Godsey, R. (1979). Rational-emotive education and relaxation training in large group treatment of test anxiety. *Psychological Reports*, *45*(l), 326.

Bandura, A. (1986). *Social foundations of thought and action: A social-cognitive theory*. NJ: Prentice-Hall.

Bandura, A. (1989). Regulation of cognitive processes through perceived self-efficacy. *Developmental Psychology*, *25*(5), Sep 1989, 729–735.

Bandura, A. (1997). *Self-efficacy: The exercise of control.* NY: Freeman.

Bandura, A. (2000). Social cognitive theory: An agentic perspective. *Annual Review of Psychology*, *52*, 1–26.

Barker, R.G., Dembo, T., and Lewin, K. (1941). Frustration and regression: An experiment with young children. *University of Iowa Studies in Child Welfare*, *18* (Whole no. 386).

Berkowitz, L. (1969) Control of aggression.. In B.M. Caldwell and H. Ricciuti (eds.), *Review of Child Development Research*. Chicago: University of Chicago Press.

Bernard, M. E., (2004). *The REBT therapist's pocket companion for working with children and adolescents*. NY: Albert Ellis Institute.

Bernard, M. E., (2004). Emotional resilience in children: Implications for Rational Emotive Education. *Romanian Journal of Cognitive and Behavioral Psychotherapies*, *4*(1), 39–52.

Bernstein, B. (1961). Social structure, language, and learning. *Educational Research*, *3*, 163–176.

Block, J. (1978). Effects of a rational emotive mental health program on poorly achieving, disruptive, high school students. *Journal of Counseling Psychology*, *25*(1), 61–65.

Baumeister, R. F., Heatherton,T. F., and Tice,D. M.(1994).*Losing control: How and why people fail at self-regulation*.CA: Academic Press.

Brody, M. (1974). The effects of the rational-emotive affective education approach on anxiety, frustration tolerance, a-rid self-esteem with fifth grade students. (Doctorial dissertation, Temple University) *Dissertation Abstracts International. 35* (6-A), 3506.

Bull, N. (1955). The mechanism of goal orientation and the manner of its disruption. *Journal of Nervous & Mental Disease, 122*, 42–46.

Bull, N. and Strongin, E. (1956). The complex of frustration. *Journal of Nervous & Mental Disease, 123*, 531–535.

Bull, N. (1957). Emotion as frustrational behavior. *Journal of Nervous & Mental Disease, 125*, 622–626.

Buckley. P. C. (1983). Rational-emotive affective education with socially and emotionally disturbed children (Temple University) *Dissertation Abstracts International*. July *44* (1-A), 110–111.

Casper, E. F. (1983). A study to determine the effectiveness of rational-emotive affective education upon the academic achievement of sixth-grade children (Doctoral dissertation, University of Virginia). *Dissertation Abstracts International. 43* (10-B), 3353

Cattell, R. (1962). Advances in the measurement of neuroticism and anxiety in a conceptual framework of a unitary trait theory. *Annuals of the New York Academy of Sciences, 93*(20) 813–856.

De Stefano, C. A. (1988). Effects of rational-emotive education and emotion awareness training on self-concept, anxiety, school attitudes, and coping skills, (Doctoral dissertation, Fordham University). *Dissertation Abstracts International*. (4906-a), 1406

DiGiuseppe, R. A. (1976). A developmental study of the efficacy of rational-emotive education (Doctoral dissertation, Hofstra University). *Dissertation Abstracts International 36*(8-B), 4150.

DiGiuseppe, R. A, and Bernard, M. E. (1990). The application of rational-emotive theory and therapy to school-aged children. *School Psychology Review, 19* (3), 268–286.

DiGiuseppe, R. and Kassinove, H. (1976). Effects of rational-emotive school mental health Program on children's emotional adjustment. *Journal of Community Psychology, 4*(4), 382–387.

Dollard, J., W., L., Miller, N., Mower, O. H., and Sears, R. R. (1938). *Frustration and aggression*. CT: Yale University Press.

Dollard, J. (1943). *Victory Over Fear*. NY: Reynal and Hitchcock.

Dye, S. 0. (1980). The influence of rational-emotive education on the self-concept of adolescents living in a residential group home (Doctoral dissertation, University of Virginia). *Dissertation Abstracts International. 41*(9), 3881-A.

Ellis, A. (1994). *Reason and Emotion in Psychotherapy* (Rev. ed.). NY: Kensington.

Ellis. A. (2001). *Feeling better, getting better, and staying better*. Atascadero CA: Impact.

Ellis, A. (1979). *Theoretical and empirical foundations of rational-emotive psychotherapy*. CA: Brooks/Cole.

Ellis, A. (1982). Psychoneurosis and anxiety problems. In R. Greiger and I. Greiger (eds.). *Cognition and emotional disturbance*. NY: Human Sciences Press.

Ellis, A. (2004). How my theory and practice of psychotherapy has changed other psychotherapies. *Journal of rational emotive cognitive-behavior therapy, 22*(2),79–83.

Ellis, A., and Greiger, R. (1977). *Handbook of rational-emotive therapy*. NY: Springer.

Ellis, A., and Knaus, W. J. (1979). *Overcoming procrastination*. NY: New American Library.
Ellis, A. and Dryden, W. (1987). *The practice of rational emotive therapy*. NY: Springer.
Ellis A. and Bernard, M. E. (2005). Rational Emotive Behavior Approaches in Childhood Disorders. NY: Kluver Academic\Plenum Publishers.
Flavell, J. H. (1978). Metacognitive development. In J. M. Scandura and C. J. Brainerd (eds.), *Structural process theories of complex human behavior* (pp. 213–245). Ayphen and Rijn, The Netherlands: Sijtoff and Noordhoff.
Flavell, J. H. (1979). Metacognition and cognitive monitoring: A new area of cognitive-developmental inquiry. *American Psychologist*, *34*(10), 906–911.
Freud, S. (1955). *Beyond the pleasure principle* (Standard ed.). London: Hogarth,
Eluto, M. S. (1980). The effects of a rational-emotive education and problem-solving therapy on the adjustment of intermediate special education students (Doctoral dissertation, Hofstra University). *Dissertation Abstracts International. 41*(12-B, Pt. 1), 4657–4658.
Geizhals, J. S. (1981). The effects of rational-emotive education on a hearing impaired, high school population (Doctoral dissertation, Hofstra University). *Dissertation Abstracts International. 41*(12-B, Pt. 1), 4662.
Goleman, D. (1995). *Emotional intelligence*. New York: Bantam Books.
Grassi, R. (1984). Effects of self instructional training and rational-emotive education on emotional adjustment in elementary school children (Doctoral dissertation, Hofstra University). *Dissertation Abstracts International. 46*(5-B),1730–1731.
Greenwald, E. K. (1985). Effects of rational-emotive education, imagery and bibliotherapy on self concept, individual achievement responsibility, and anxiety in sixth grade children (Doctoral dissertation, Hofstra University). *Dissertation Abstracts International. 46*(3-B), 979.
Gruenke, M. (2000).Erziehung bei Schuelern mit Lernbehinderung. /Rational-emotive education with learning disabled students. *Psychologie in Erziehung und Unterricht*, *47*(4), 296–306. Abstract.
Hajzler, D. J., and Bernard, M. E. (1991). A review of rational-emotive education outcome studies. *School Psychology Quarterly*, *6*(l), 27–49.
Handelman, D. R. (1982). The effects of a rational-emotive educative course on the rational beliefs, frustration tolerance and self-acceptance of high school students (Doctoral dissertation, Temple University). *Dissertation Abstracts International. 42*(12-B, Pt. 1), 4931.
Harris, S. L. (1976). Rational-emotive education and the human development program: A comparative outcome study (Doctoral dissertation, University of Oregon). *Dissertation Abstracts International. 37* (06-a), 3419.
Hernaez, C., Morales, D. and Francisco, J. (2000). Self-esteem and anxiety modification by the application of different treatments (rational-emotive education and relaxation) in adolescents. *Ansiedad y Estres. 6*(2-3), 295–306. Abstract.
Hooper, S. R., and Layne, C. C. (1985). Rational-emotive education as a short-term primary prevention technique. *Techniques*, *1*(4), 264–269.
Hybl, A. R., and Stagner, R. (1952). Frustration tolerance in relation to diagnosis and therapy. *Journal of Consulting Psychology,16*(3), 163–170.
Kagan, J. (1971). *Understanding children: Behavior, motives, thought*. NY: Harcourt Brace Javanovich.
Kachman, D. J. (1988). The effects of rational-emotive education on the rationality, neuroticism and defense mechanisms of adolescents. (Doctorial dissertation,

Western Michigan University). *Dissertation Abstracts International. 48*(11-B), 3418

Kachman, D. J. and Mazer, G. E. (1990). Effects of rational-emotive education on the rationality, neuroticism and defense mechanisms of adolescents. *Adolescence, 25*(97), 131–144.

Katz, S. G. (1974). The effects of cognitive emotional education on locus of control and self concept (Doctoral dissertation, Hofstra University). *Dissertation Abstracts International. 35*(5-B), 2435

Keller, J. F., Croake, J. W. and Brooking, J. Y. (1975). Effects of a program in rational thinking on anxieties in older persons. *Journal of Counseling Psychology, 22*(l), 54–57.

Knaus, W. J. (1974). *Rational emotive education: A manual for elementary school teachers*. NY: Albert Ellis Institute.

Knaus, W. J. (1977). Rational-emotive education. In A. Ellis and R. Greiger (eds.), *Handbook of rational-emotive therapy*, pp. 398–408. NY: Springer.

Knaus, W. J. (1977a) Rational-emotive education. In A. Ellis and R. Grieger (eds.), *Handbook of rational emotive therapy*. New York: Springer.

Knaus, W. J. (1977b). Rational-emotive education. *Theory into Practice, 14*(4), 251–255.

Knaus, W. J. (1980). Psychological skills training for children and adolescents. *Ontario Psychological Association special symposium on exceptional children*. Ontario, Canada.

Knaus, W. J. (1982). The parameters of procrastination. In R. Greiger and I. Greiger (eds.), *Cognition and emotional disturbance* NY: Human Science Press.

Knaus, W. J. (1982). *How to get out of a rut*. NJ: Prentice-Hall\Spectrum Books.

Knaus, W. J. (1983). How to conquer your frustration. NJ: Prentice Hall\Spectrum Books.

Knaus, W. J. (1985) The prevention and treatment of school age burnout. In A. Ellis and M. E. Bernard (Eds.), *Clinical Applications of Rational Emotive Therapy*, pp.257–276 NY: Plenum.

Knaus, W. J. (2000). Take charge now: Powerful techniques for breaking the blame habit. NY: John Wiley.

Knaus, W. J. (2002). *The procrastination workbook*. CA: New Harbinger.

Knaus, W. J. (2004). Rational Emotive Education: Trends and Directions. *Romanian Journal of Cognitive and Behavioral Psychotherapies*, *4*(1), 9–22.

Knaus, W. J., and Bokor, S. (1975). The effects of rational-emotive education lessons on anxiety and self-concept in sixth grade students. *Rational Living, 11*(2), 25–28.

Knaus, W. J. and Haberstroh, N. B, (1993). A rational-emotive education program to help disruptive mentally retarded clients develop self-control. In W. Dryden (ed) *Innovations in rational-emotive therapy*, pp. 201-217. London: Sage Publications.

Knaus, W. J. and McKeever, C. (1977). Rational-emotive education with learning disabled children. *Journal of Learning Disabilities, 10*(1), 10–14.

Kuhn, D., Garcia-Mila, M., Zohar, A., and Andersen, C. (1995). Strategies of knowledge acquisition. *Monographs of the Society for Research in Child Development, 60*(4, Serial No. 245)

Krech, D., Crutchfield, R. and Livson, N. (1991). Constructive and destructive effects of frustration and conflict. *Voprosy*, *6*, 68–82.

Krenitsky, D. L. (1978). The relationship of age and verbal intelligence to the efficacy of rational-emotive education with older adults (Doctoral dissertation, Hofstra University). *Dissertation Abstracts International. 39*(5-b), 22506.

Leibowitz, A. L. (1979). Effects of "ABC" homework sheets, initial level of adjustment, and duration of treatment on the efficacy of rational -emotive education in elementary school children (Doctoral dissertation, Hofstra University). *Dissertation Abstracts International.*(4000-B), 5009.

Lo, F. G. (1986). The effects of a rational-emotive education program on self-concept and locus of control among learning disabled adolescents (Doctoral dissertation, University of Houston). *Dissertation Abstracts International. 46*(10-A), 2973.

Low, A. A. (1950). *Mental health through will training*. Boston: Christopher Publishing.

Marcotte D. (1996). Irrational beliefs and depression in adolescence. *Adolescence, 31*(124),935–54.

Meichenbaum, D., and Goodman, J. (1971) Training impulsive children to talk to themselves. *Journal of Experimental Psychology, 34*, 349–360.

Meyer, D. J. (1981). Effects of rational-emotive group therapy upon anxiety and self-esteem of learning disabled children (Doctoral dissertation, Andrews University). *Dissertation Abstracts International. 42*(10-b), 4201.

Miller, N. J. (1977). Effects of behavior rehearsal, written homework, and level of intelligence on the efficacy of rational-emotive education in elementary school children (Doctoral dissertation, Hofstra University). *Dissertation Abstracts International. 39*(08-b) 3899.

Miller, N. J. and Kassinove, H. (1978). Effects of lecture, rehearsal, written homework, and IQ on the efficacy of a rational emotive school mental health program. *Journal of Clinical Child and Adolescent Psychology, 6*(4), 366–373.

Murray, C.J.L. and Lopez, A.D. eds. (1996) *The global burden of disease: A comprehensive assessment of mortality and disability from diseases, injuries, and risk factors in 1990 and projected to 2020*. Cambridge: Harvard University Press.

Omizo, M. M., Lo, F. G. and Williams, R. E. (1986). Rational-emotive education, self-concept, and locus of control among learning-disabled students. *Journal of Humanistic Education and Development, 25*(2), 58–69.

Omizo, M. M., Cubberly, W. E., Omizo, S. A. (1985). The effects of rational-emotive education groups on self-concept and locus of control among learning disabled children. *Exceptional Child, 32*(1), 13–19.

Overstreet, O. H. (1925). *Influencing human behavior*. NY: Norton.

Painter, G.D. (1965). *Proust, the later years* (Vol. 2). Boston: Little Brown.

Payot, J. (1909). *The education of the will*. NY: Funk & Wagnalls

Peake, P. K., Hebl, M. and Mischel, W. A. (2002). Strategic attention deployment for delay of gratification in working and waiting ituations. *Developmental Psychology, 38*,(2),313–326

Pollack, C. (1968). A conditioning approach to frustration reaction in minimally brain injured children. Journal of Learning Disabilities, *1*, 688–691.

Ritchie, B. C. (1978). The effect of rational-emotive education on irrational beliefs, assertiveness, and/or locus of control in fifth grade students (Doctoral dissertation, Virginia Polytechnic Institute and State University). *Dissertation Abstracts International. 39* (04-a), 2069–2070.

Rose, N. (1983). Effects of rational-emotive education and rational-emotive education plus rational-emotive imagery on the adjustment of disturbed and normal elementary school children (Doctoral dissertation, Hofstra University). *Dissertation Abstracts International. 44*(3-B), 925–926.

Rosenbaum, T. (1991). The effects of rational-emotive education on locus of control, rationality and anxiety in primary school children. *Australian Journal of Education, 35*(2), 187–200.

Sandilos, E. P. (1986). The comparative effectiveness of rational-emotive education and youth effectiveness training on high school students' emotional adjustment (Doctoral dissertation, Temple University). *Dissertation Abstracts International. 46*(8-A), 2240–2241.

Schaefer, C. E., and Milman, H. L. 1977. *Therapies for children*. San Francisco: Jossey Bass.

Streeter, K. R. (1999).The effects of Rational-Emotive Education on academic performance and career perspectives of at-risk elementary students. *Dissertation Abstracts International*: Section B: The Sciences & Engineering. *59* (7-B), 3728.

Vernon, A. (1990). The school psychologist's role in preventative education: Applications of rational-emotive education. *School Psychology Review, 19*(3), 322–330.

Voelm, C. E. (1984). The efficacy of rational-emotive education for acting-out and socially withdrawn adolescents. Paper presented at the Annual Meeting of the American Educational Research Association (68th, New Orleans, LA, 23-27April).

Vygotsky, L. S. (1988). *Thought and language*. MA: MIT Press. (Original work published 1934).

Wallen, J. E.W. (1935). *Personality maladjustments and mental hygiene*. NY: McGraw-Hill.

Watter, D. N. (1988). Rational-emotive education: A review of the literature. *Journal of Rational-Emotive & Cognitive Behavior Therapy*, *6*(3), 139–145.

Weiss, J. R., Weiss, B., Alicke, M. D., Klotz, M. L. (1987). Effectiveness of psychotherapy with children and Adolescents: a meta-analysis for clinicians. *Journal of Consulting and Clinical Psychology 55*, (4), 542–549.

Weissberg, R. P., Cowen, E. I., Lotyczewski, B. S., and Gesten, E. I. (1983). The primary health project: Seven consecutive years of program outcome research. *Journal of Consulting and Clinical Psychology, 51*(1), 100–107.

Wilde, J. K. (1999). The efficacy of short-term rational-emotive education: A follow-up evaluation. *Journal of Cognitive Psychotherapy*, *3*(2), 133–143.

Wilde, J.K. (1996). The efficacy of short-term Rational-Emotive education with fourth-grade students. *Elementary School Guidance and Counseling Journal, 31* (2), 131–138.

Woolley, J. D. and Bruell, M. J. (1996). Young children's awareness of the origins of their mental representations. *Developmental Psychology, 32* (2), 335–346.

Wu, L. (1986). The effects of rational-emotive education on rational thinking, emotional stability and self-esteem of junior high school students. *Bulletin of Educational Psychology*, *19*, 177–218.

Wu, L. (1987). The effects of a rational-emotive group on rational thinking, social anxiety and self-acceptance of college students. *Bulletin of Educational Psychology*, *20*, 183–203.

Zionts, P. (1983). A strategy for understanding and correcting irrational beliefs in pupils: The rational-emotive approach. *Pointer*, *27*(3), 13–17.

5

Emotional Resilience in Children and Adolescence: Implications for Rational-Emotive Behavior Therapy

Michael E. Bernard, Ph.D. and Daniela Pires

That before coming here, everything went wrong. I used to blame it on myself. I used to say I was no good at anything and why don't I just kill myself. I didn't know the meaning of Rational or ERational thoughts-they have slowly changed the way I think, so I don't get upset as I used to. I used to think of my bad points but know I also think of my good points, so now I don't go off my rocker. I am lucky to be able to think Rational thoughts.

(words of a 14-year-old boy referred for to a REE-based group counseling for depression)

The above anecdotal description of an adolescent who attended 12 weekly rational-emotive education (REE) oriented group counseling sessions attests to the positive effects of rational-emotive behavior therapy (REBT) methods in bringing about emotional self-management in youth (e.g., Bernard and Keefauver, 1979). Since the 1970s, I (Bernard) have witnessed in my clinical practice the extraordinary empowerment that Ellis' ABC model, disputation and rational beliefs have on young people's ability to modify their intense negative emotions in response to adverse events. That being said, recent non-REBT theory and research into children's developing capacity for emotional regulation (termed in this chapter "emotional resilience") leads to the identification of new cognitive and behavioral emotional resilience skills (e.g., Brenner and Salovey, 1997) that can bring about emotional regulation and which, when incorporated within REBT, can enhance the combined effects of these new skills and REBT.

A reading of the literature on rational-emotive behavior therapy (REBT) and its applications with children and adolescents (e.g., Bernard and Joyce, 1984; Bernard, 2004a) as well as research investigating irrational beliefs in children (Bernard and Cronan, 1999) points to the role of children's irrational beliefs as being major contributors to their emotional distress.

In therapy, REBT-oriented practitioners assess the intensity of children's emotional reactions (anger, anxiety and down) to adverse activating events. When extreme levels of emotional upset are identified (e.g., rage, panic and/or very down/depressed), children's inferences (predictions, conclusions) and evaluations (absolutes, awfulizing, I can't stand it, it is, global rating) are examined including a focused assessment of Ellis' major categories of irrational beliefs:

1. I must do well and be approved of by significant others, and if not, then it's awful, I can't stand it, and I am a hopeless person, People should treat me fairly and considerately.
2. People should treat me fairly and well, it's awful and I can't stand it when they don't, and they (such people) are bad and deserve to be punished.
3. My life should be comfortable and easy and conditions must be the way I want and when they are not, it's awful and I cannot stand it.

Irrational beliefs are deemed a major catalyst for extreme anger, anxiety and depression whereas rational beliefs are associated with more moderate negative feelings of annoyance, concern and sadness. According to REBT theory, children and adolescents who manifest irrational beliefs are more likely to demonstrate poor emotional regulation and control in comparison with young people who evaluate adverse events from a more rational viewpoint.

Rational-emotive education (REE), the educational derivative of REBT (e.g., Knaus, 1974; Vernon, 1989) has been developed for use in classroom and clinical settings to teach young people emotional problem solving and resilience through helping them to recognize their emotions that they experience in the face of adverse events, how rational and irrational beliefs contribute to their emotions and behaviors, how to recognize, challenge/dispute irrational beliefs and restructure them as more rational beliefs. It is proposed that recent research investigating emotional regulation and resilience in children point to additional methods for helping children develop emotional resilience.

Conceptualizing Emotional Resilience

Emotional regulation is a construct that researchers have been interested in for many years. However, it has only been since the early 1960s, that cognitively oriented behavioral researchers began to examine the extent to which human behavior is moderated by thought processes and associated with emotional states (Landy, 2002). Child developmental research has begun to focus on the extent to which children are able to moderate their emotions and behaviors when faced with stressful events. The construct that has been studied, emotional resilience, sometimes called emotional regulation or affect regulation, has been found to contribute to children's ability to prevent stressful levels of negative emotions and maladaptive behavior from occurring (Landy, 2002). It has been argued that failure to develop sufficient emotional resilience is largely responsible for the development of behavior problems and can lead to a variety of serious psychopathologies.

Definition of Emotional Resilience

Saarni (1999) indicates that emotional regulation refers to one's ability to manage one's subjective experience of emotion, especially in terms of intensity and duration of the emotion, and how one manages the expression of emotions while communicating it to others. Landy (2002) refers to emotional resilience as the process by which people control or self-regulate internal reactions to emotions as well as their outward expression of the emotion in terms of behaviors. Emotional resilience or emotional regulation in children has been defined by Bernard (2004b) as children's developing capacities to use coping strategies (e.g., distraction, changing thinking, exercise, seeking support, etc.) that help them regulate the intensity of negative emotions they experience in the presence of adverse events. According to Bernard's view, children's differences in the level of coping capability they present are governed by many factors, including the biologically driven temperament of children, parenting practices, and the emerging belief system of each child.

According to emotional regulation theorists, when children experience intense negative emotions, they utilize three systems or processes to make sense of and react to the emotion (e.g., Brenner and Salovey, 1997). These processes are (1) the physiological reactions, which include nervous system activity, such as activity of the heart, stomach, brain and hormonal secretions, (2) cognitions or subjective experiences to the emotional response, which include the explanations one gives the self for the adverse events one experiences, and (3) action responses, which include the behaviors one presents in response to the emotions experienced.

Bernard (2004b) defines emotional resilience as the ability to stay calm when confronted with adverse events, maintain behavioral control, and to, when upset, calm down in a developmentally appropriate period of time. The following is a list of examples of emotional resilience:

- Not getting down when your friends seem to understand their schoolwork and do better on tests than you.
- Not getting overly frustrated and angry with yourself when you do not understand something.
- Not getting overly upset from mistakes in your work or when you have not been as successful as you would like to be.
- Avoiding getting extremely worried before an important test or event in which you have to perform in public.
- Avoiding excessive worry concerning your popularity with peers.
- Not getting overly angry when peers are mean to you.

- Remaining calm and in control when an adult treats you unfairly or disrespectfully.
- Not getting too down when being teased or ignored by friends.
- When meeting someone new, not getting extremely nervous and being calm.
- Stopping yourself from getting extremely worked up when you want to stand up and say "No" to someone who is putting pressure on you to do the wrong thing.
- Not losing your cool when you have lots of homework to do.
- Staying in control when your parents say "No" and the parents of your friends seem to be saying "Yes."

Emotional Resilience Strategies or Coping Skills

Over the first five years of life, a child gradually changes from relying primarily on caregivers or external support for coping with intense negative emotions to learning to control or manage emotions alone through the use of a variety of emotional resilience or coping skills (Landy, 2002). Coping skills in children have been described as (1) efforts by the child involving trying to alter external or behavioral factors such as the environment or the individual's behavior, by for example, deciding to study hard for a difficult test that is coming and doing physical exercise to alleviate tension, or as (2) efforts of the child trying to alter his or her cognitions or internal emotional experience, by for example, substituting positive thoughts for negative ones, learning to put things into perspective, using distraction and relaxation techniques (Brenner and Salovey, 1997; Landy, 2002). Strategies that exist in the middle of this continuum involve the child trying to alter both, external and internal factors (Brenner and Salovey 1997).

Researchers have used different dimensions to portray the different types of stressors that children face (Brenner and Salovey, 1997). The degree of controllability a child has over a stressor also becomes an important feature of the coping process as children mature and learn to distinguish between controllable and uncontrollable stressors. As further described in the next section, children learn to match coping strategy to stressor as they mature. At one end of the continuum are the stressors that are largely within the child's control (e.g., an upcoming test) and at the other end are stressors that are largely outside the child's control (e.g., the need for medical surgery).

Child Development Research on Children's Emotional Regulation

In order to deal with daily frustrations and other strong emotions, children develop a number of coping strategies to deal with stressors. Children who can effectively cope with stressors get along better and are more accepted by their peers. These children are friendlier in their interactions, have a greater ability to deal with conflicts without becoming overwhelmed by their emotions, and therefore are capable of accepting others' perspectives. Children who are successful at coping do not utilize aggression and venting and can focus away from an emotionally arousing stimulus in order to view the situation from a positive aspect (Landy, 2002).

When children continuously attempt to cope with stress by using maladaptive skills or when they constantly fail to cope, underachievement, violent behavior, daydreaming, and psychosomatic illnesses are some of the sequelae that can be left, as encountered in the literature in the area of coping. Children who are not successful at coping with adverse emotions become emotionally overwhelmed by stressful situations they experience are therefore are more likely to exhibit difficulties concentrating, problem solving, and difficulties with memory (Landy, 2002).

Understanding how typical children cope with life hassles and regulate their emotions provides us with a practical way of communicating with children about the things that they can do to manage their emotions when faced with unpleasant experiences and helps us understand developmental changes in the types of strategies that children in different developmental stages employ.

During the past twenty years the amount of research on children's regulation of emotion has increased. Much of what we know about the development of children' emotional regulation comes from studies in which children of different ages are asked to report what they would do to cope with a stressful situation. In this type of research, coping is seen as a process containing two main elements: stressor and strategy to cope with stressor. According to this line of thought, successful coping can be interpreted as having a diversified repertoire of coping strategies (e.g., use of positive self-talk, relaxation, and perspective taking), having the ability to select strategies that meet the demands of the particular stressor in question, and having the ability to implement the chosen strategy (Brenner and Salovey, 1997).

A review of literature in the area of development of emotional regulation and coping conducted by Brenner and Salovey (1997) yielded three age-related, developmental trends. The first developmental trend revealed that children's use of internal or cognitive strategies increases as they get older while their use of behavioral strategies remains relatively constant throughout development. This trend is illustrated in a study by Altshuler and Ruble (1989), in which 8 and 11 year-old children were more likely to identify cognitive strategies to cope with negative emotions than were 5-year-old children, while there were no significant age differences reported in respect to the usage of behavioral techniques by the three groups of children.

The second developmental trend is the children's ability to cope by using solitary strategies (e.g., coping without the assistance of another person) increases throughout development. This trend is illustrated in a study by Kliewer (1991) who found that 7-year-old-children relied more on support from others than did the 10-year-old children (see also Garber et al., 1991).

Brenner and Salovey (1997) suggested that there is an age related increase in children's use of cognitive coping strategies, while behavioral strategies were reported as being used relatively constantly throughout all stages of development. The researchers also discussed that as children develop, they start relying more upon cognitive, or emotion focused, strategies such as substituting positive thoughts for negative ones to reduce sadness. Research has also found some differences in girls' and boys' use of regulatory strategies. Some studies suggest that girls are more likely to seek and rely on social support and guidance to cope with negative emotions (e.g., Dise-Leiws, 1988). Other studies have found that girls are more likely to use emotion-focused strategies, such as distraction (e.g., Wierzbicki, 1989) and that boys are more likely than girls to use physical exercise to manage negative emotions (e.g., Kurdek, 1987).

The way parents socialize with their children and display emotions, such as being generally positive rather then displaying constant anger, anxiety, or depression has been related to the child's capacity to emotionally regulate. Children who experience high levels of negative affect, such as fear, anger, sadness, and anxiety from caregivers, have fewer coping strategies in comparison to those who experience more positive displays of affect. When family life is loaded with tension, negative moods, unpredictable parenting, and marital conflict, children's capabilities to cope may be hindered, leading children to have a strong propensity to tend to use externalizing and maladaptive coping (Saarni 1999).

Teaching Emotional Resilience to Young People: Integrating REBT with Emotional Resilience Skill Training

Based on the review of REBT methods and the child developmental literature of emotional, coping strategies that children naturally develop over time, the following methods can be taught to individual, small or large groups of children and adolescents to strengthen their emotional resilience.

1. Help young people construct a list of events that can occur at school or home that can be considered adverse, bad or negative. Leave off the list any events that are life threatening. Include examples of lack of achievement, including mistakes in class assignments, rejection including teasing, not being invited to play, being yelled at by parents, etc.
2. Introduce the idea that there are three negative emotions that people can have when they are confronted with these negative events. Ask for and acknowledge suggestions and list the following three on the board: anger, worry and down.Discuss differences in these three feelings in terms of things that can happen that lead to one or more of these feelings. Have students portray/role play how the different feelings look and how people sound when they experience a feeling. You can have students search for

illustrations of people who demonstrate these three feelings in magazines/newspaper and cut them out.

3. Introduce the Emotional Thermometer that represents a 10-point scale of emotions (1 = feeling a little bit upset . . . 10 = could not feel any more upset). Explain that it measures how strongly one feels. Explain that all feelings vary in intensity from strong to weak. Give students practice in evaluating how strong someone is feeling employing the Emotional Thermometer and using cut out pictures of people displaying different emotions (see Fig. 1).
4. Make the point that when something bad happens, people have options in how strongly they feel. Ask: Does everyone feel the same way about different things? Ask: Can people feel different degrees of the same feeling (e.g., when someone calls you a name, can you feel different degrees of anger or feeling down)? Illustrate using the events listed in Step 1 how people can feel different about the same negative events.

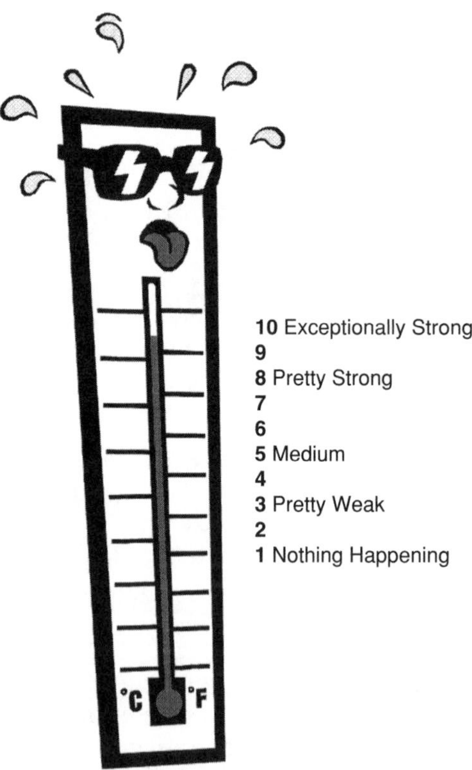

FIGURE 1. The Emotional Thermometer (Bernard, 2001)

5. Explain the relationship between how strongly one feels, their behavior, and different types of negative consequences that are associated with different levels of emotions and behaviors. Help young people see that, generally speaking, extremely high levels of anger, worry and feeling down are harmful to them because of the effects extremely high emotions have on their behaviors and ensuing consequences. Provide plentiful examples so that students appreciate that getting overly upset is not good and that they do have options in how strongly they feel when something bad happens.
6. Explain to young people that while it is very natural to feel upset when something bad happens, getting *extremely* upset (extremely angry, highly nervous, very down) is *not* generally good. Explain that very high degrees of negative emotions not only can feel bad, but also can lead people to behave in unhelpful ways. For example, when someone is extremely angry with someone who may have acted badly, s/he can say or do things in an aggressive fashion (e.g., yell, scream, swear) that can get him/her into trouble. Or too much worry about a test can lead to a loss of memory during the exam. Feeling very down can cause the child to withdraw from others and lose motivation to work. Use the Emotional Thermometer and Anger Thermometer (see Figs. 1 and 2) to illustrate these relationships

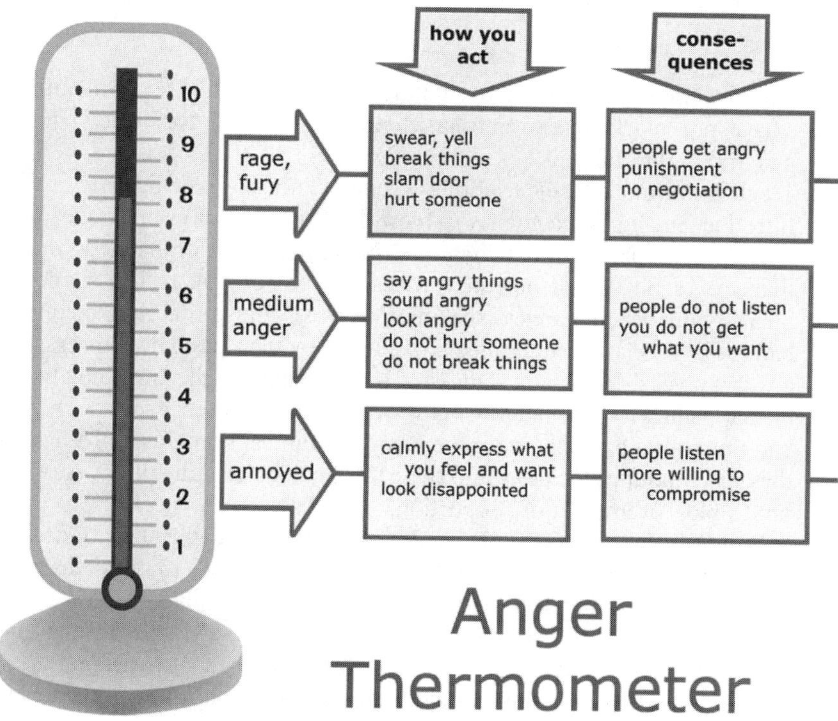

FIGURE 2. The Anger Thermometer (Bernard, 2004a)

7. Introduce the term "Emotional Resilience." Explain that Emotional Resilience means knowing how to stop yourself from getting extremely angry, down or worried when something "bad" happens—for example, by thinking positively rather than negatively and not thinking that the "bad" thing is the worst thing in the world that could happen if it is not really that bad. It means knowing what you can do when you are very upset to calm down including talking about what happened to a trusted friend or adult and learning to relax. Provide examples of Emotional Resilience as related to the adverse circumstances listed in Step 1.
8. Explain that people vary in their degree of Emotional Resilience and that over one's life; it is good to continue to develop Emotional Resilience as a way to help cope with adversity when it happens.
9. Provide young people with the following questions to survey their own Emotional Resilience:

- When someone treats me unfairly or is mean to me, I am good at controlling my temper.
- I have someone I can talk with when I get really upset.
- When I find myself getting very stressed, I know how to relax.
- I am good at thinking positive thoughts when bad stuff happens.
- I am someone who does not take mistakes or disappointments personally.

Discuss how some young people will have marked all the boxes, while others may have not marked any. Emphasize that Emotional Resilience can be learned and is very helpful.

10. Teach Emotional Resilience Skill: Keeping Things in Perspective.
    Introduce the human tendency to blow the "badness" of events out of proportion by explaining that there are different degrees of badness: things that are "a bit" bad (someone pushes in front of you in line, someone breaks your pencil, careless spelling mistakes), things that are "medium" bad (failing a class, being called a bad name by the class bully), things that are "very, very" bad (natural disaster, being terminally ill, something horrible happening to your parents). Give young people practice in categorizing bad things that happen during the school day and at home, as well as events they read about in the news into these three categories. Encourage students not to blow events out of proportion.

    Build/display a Catastrophe Scale that goes from 1 to 100 in your room that illustrates events that are 90–100 "catastrophic" (natural disaster, death, terminal illness), events that are 50–90 "very bad" (house burns down, car accident, losing lots of money, best friend moves away), and events that are 10–50 "bad" (making mistakes on a test, being teased, someone steals your lunch money). Refer to the Catastrophe Scale during the year to help students keep hassles and other adverse events listed in Step 1 in proportion.

11. Teach Emotional Resilience Skill: Positive vs. Negative Self-Talk. Introduce the concept of "self-talk" as the way we think about events and how our self-talk can be negative and positive. Provide illustrations of how when something adverse happens, it is easy to get into a negative mode of thinking using negative self-talk. Explain that Emotional Resilience and becoming calm can be achieved by countering negative self-talk with positive self-talk.
12. Teach Emotional Resilience Skill: Challenge/Dispute Irrational Beliefs and Replace with Rational Beliefs.

    You can have young people complete a survey to determine which irrational beliefs hold (see Table 1).

    - Self-Downing: thinking you're hopeless when something bad happens (replace with Self-Acceptance).
    - Needing to Be Perfect: thinking you must do everything perfectly and that it's horrible to make mistakes (replace with Responsible Risk Taking).
    - Seeking: believing you must have the approval of peers (or adults) for everything you do and being thought to be silly or stupid by others cannot be endured (replace with Non-Approval Seeking).

TABLE 1. Negative Ways of Thinking Checklist (Bernard, 2003).

Instructions: Place a mark to indicate how often a child tends to think in a particular negative way.

	Rarely	Sometimes	Often
1. *Self-Downing* – Does the child think that s/he is totally useless or a failure *when* she/he is has been rejected or has not achieved a good result?	☐	☐	☐
2. *Needing to Be Perfect* – Does the child think that she/he must be successful or perfect in everything important that I do and that it's horrible when s/he is not?	☐	☐	☐
3. *Needing Approval* – Does the child think that she/he needs people (peers, parents, teachers) to approve of him/her and that when they do not, it's the worst thing in the world?	☐	☐	☐
4. *Pessimism* – Does the child think when s/he has not been successful at something that s/he is no good at anything and never will be?	☐	☐	☐
5. *Low Frustration Tolerance* – Does the child think that life should always be fun and exciting and that s/he can't stand it when things are frustrating or boring?	☐	☐	☐
6. *Being Intolerant of Others* – Does the child think that people should always treat him/her fairly, considerately and the way s/he wants and when they do not, they are rotten and s/he has a right to get back at them?	☐	☐	☐

- Pessimism: thinking that when something is difficult, you'll be more likely to fail than to be successful (replace with Optimism).
- Low Frustration Tolerance: believing that everything in life should be fun and exciting and that you cannot stand to do things that are not fun or easy (replace with High Frustration Tolerance).
- Being Intolerant of Others: believing that people who are unfair, inconsiderate or different, or inferior or bad people who deserve punishment (replace with Unconditional Acceptance of Others).

13. Teach Emotional Resilience Skill: Explicit Teaching of Rational Beliefs
Discuss with young people in a variety of ways how the following beliefs can lead to less emotional misery and more emotional control.

    - Accepting Myself: knowing that I have many good qualities and a few that could be improved, and accepting myself warts and all.
    - Taking Risks: knowing that it is good to try new things even if I make mistakes.
    - Being Independent: knowing that it's good to speak up even if others think I'm silly or stupid.
    - I Can Do It!: trusting myself when I'm doing something hard that I will be more likely to be successful than to fail.
    - Working Tough: knowing that in order to be successful, I sometimes have to do things that are boring and not fun.
    - Being Tolerant of Others: accepting that people make mistakes and have differences from me and that while I might not like their behavior, they are not totally bad or deserving of punishment when they do the wrong thing.

14. Teach Emotional Resilience Skill: Relaxation.
Explain to young people that when they are faced with pressures or other adverse circumstances and notice they are getting uptight, they can learn to cut their stress down to size by learning to relax. There are a variety of relaxation skills that young people can be taught.
For example, you can teach the 5-3-5 Relaxation Technique. In using this deep breathing technique, young people can be taught to use the following instructions:

    "To begin with, rapidly exhale all the air from your lungs. Next, slowly to a count of five, inhale . . . one . . . two . . . three . . . four . . . five. Hold your breath of air for a slow count of three . . . one . . . two . . . three. Now slowly, very slowly, exhale the air to a slow count of five . . . one . . . two . . . three . . . four . . . five. You have just completed one repetition. To continue to relax, breathe in slowly to a count of five, hold for a count of three, and again exhale to a slow count of five."

15. Teach Emotional Resilience Skill: Assertive Behavior.
Explain that in the face of pressure by peers to do something they do not want to do (e.g., drink, smoke) or when faced with someone treating them

badly, it is common for emotions to run high. You can indicate that "assertiveness" can help all people reduce levels of negative emotions by helping to change the circumstances that helped create the emotions in the first place. Discuss how when you're assertive, you state clearly and directly your honest feelings and wishes. Rather than raising your voice or mumbling, you use a warm and yet firm tone of voice. You wear a relaxed expression and look directly at the person who is pressuring you or treated you with disrespect. Explain the differences between acting assertively to being too aggressive or passive/shy.

16. Teach Emotional Resilience Skill: Find Someone to Talk To. Discuss with students how when things are not going well and you've tried everything to remain positive and not blow things out of proportion, sometimes it is good to seek out someone you trust and who is a good listener. Make the point that trusted friends and adults are never too busy to not have time. Brainstorm types of people whom students would trust to talk to. Make sure that everyone has identified a source of support.

An Example of Rebt-based Emotional Resilience Group Counseling

What follows is a summary of a small group counseling program introduced to a group of primary age children attending regular, general education classes in two different public schools in Southern California who were identified through the use of a screening procedure as having social, emotional, behavioral and/or achievement problems. The schools where the study took place are mainly composed of students ranging from middle to low socioeconomic backgrounds. The effects of the program were evaluated as part of the second author's mater's thesis (Major Area: Educational Psychology).

Students attending the program were not randomly selected from the whole schools' population. All 4th, 5th and 6th graders of two elementary schools, approximately 547 students, were rated by their teachers on the Teacher Survey: Student Social Emotional Behavioral Functioning (TS-SSEBF) (Bernard, 2003), an eight-item screening instrument that measures teacher perceptions of four dimensions of student adjustment (two items for each dimension): educational under-achievement, social problems, behavioral problems, and emotional problems. On this 5 point Likert scale, a rating of 5 meant that the student is almost always displaying adaptive and well adjusted behaviors and emotions, and a rating of 1 meant that the student does not display adaptive and adjusted behaviors and emotions. Sixty-one of these 4th, 5th, and 6th grade students, ranging in age from 9 to 12 years, who were designated as having significantly low levels of social emotional well-being and/or significantly high levels of underachievement as measured by the TS-SSEBF—students who received a total rating of 15 or less from their respective teachers—were selected to receive services to be provided by school counselors.

All 61 children selected to receive counseling services from school counselors were then randomly assigned to experimental and control groups. Thirty students were invited to participate in 8 weeks of emotional resilience training while the other 31 students were invited to receive 8 weeks of counseling sessions that were delivered by licensed school counselors who adopt eclectic approaches to counseling. The experimental group consisted of 12 boys and 10 girls and the control groups consisted of 16 boys and 14 girls. Students were participating in general education classes only, had no diagnosed disability, and ranged from 9 to 11 years of age. The ethnic composition of the sample was 50% Hispanic or Latino, 41% Caucasian, 4.5% Asian and 4.5% Other.

The Cognitive Behavioral Emotional Resilience Lessons

During eight weeks, the investigator taught lessons on emotional resilience that were adapted from Bernard's (2002, 2003b) Program Achieve curriculum to students in the experimental group. The curriculum was designed for elementary school children and judged to be appropriate for the children in this sample. Once a week over a period of 50 minutes, students met the investigator in the counselor's office in groups of 5–7 children to participate in the group sessions. Each session covered a specific content. All sessions' content was presented in a continuous and logical format. The following is a list of the concepts that were taught in the sessions. A conceptual description of what the goals of every session were was included.

Session 1. Introducing Emotions

The content in this session is designed to help students become more familiar with each other, with rules and expectations that surround participating in group sessions and, above all, to help students build an emotional vocabulary and to become aware of their own emotions and emotions on others. Through activities and role-plays, students become acquainted with and explore the meanings of the words angry, sad/down, worried/anxious, the accompanying physiological feelings of tension that one might encounter when extremely angry, down, or worried, what a person looks like when feeling such emotions, and how one might react when experiencing different degrees of anger, sadness, or worry.

Session 2. Adversity: Bad Stuff that Happens

The content in this session is designed to help students identify the different degrees of anger, sadness and anxiety that different children can experience. Children help the facilitator name common adverse circumstances that can make a child very angry, down or worried. The concept that we all go through "tough times" is carefully explored and children are presented with the

"Emotional Thermometer" (see Fig. 1). The Emotional Thermometer is a picture of a thermometer that measures emotions. Children learn to rate the degree, ranging from 1 to 10, of emotion they think they would feel in the face of several adverse events. As the lesson progresses children understand that (a) there are different intensities of emotions that one might feel when faced with adversity, and (b) people display different behavioral and emotional reactions when experiencing different intensities of anger, sadness and worry (e.g., when feeling angry at a level ten a child may scream at and hit a friend but feeling angry at a level 5 a child might be assertive and express his negative experience of emotions in a more rational form).

Session 3. Introducing Emotional Resilience: Do Not Let Your Emotions Rule You

The content in this session is designed to help students understand that getting upset is a normal part of human existence, however, getting too upset works against one's and others' personal interests and well-being. The facilitator leads students in a discussion about the fact that when /one experiences high levels of emotion, one will find it very difficult to make responsible and wise choices and make good decisions. During this session students are referred back to the Emotional Thermometer and are guided to explore how different intensities of the same emotion can make a person react differently in the face of an adverse situation. The facilitator helps the students understand that high levels of anger, sadness, or worry hinder one's ability to successfully solve problems and can make the problem much more difficult to cope with. The students and the facilitator discuss the difference between being assertive and aggressive. Last, during this session, students are presented with the first emotional resilience coping skill covered in this curriculum: talking to someone you trust. Students participate in an activity that shows the importance of talking to someone you trust when experiencing strong negative feelings, and how talking to others can help one calm down and, perhaps help one discover solutions to his or her problems. Students role-play talking to each other about personal or made-up problems and the listener in each role play dyad is guided to carefully listen, validate the person's feelings, and offer comfort and "advice," if possible.

Session 4. Do Not Sweat the Small Stuff

The content in this session is designed to help students: (a) understand that not all thoughts that a person has are always and necessarily true, and (b) learn about the thought, feeling, and behaving connection, which is core to dealing with irrational thoughts according to Rational-Emotive Behavioral Therapy, and (c) not to blow adverse, bad events out of proportion. In this session students participate in an activity in which they learn to rate the level of "badness" of many different adverse circumstances and learn about putting things in perspective. They learn about the Catastrophe

Scale, in which students rate different adverse situations by their level of difficulty in terms of coping with the situation in question. Students learn to put things in perspective and realize that most bad situations encountered daily should not be viewed as terrible and impossible to cope with. Students realize that there are many adverse circumstances that they were currently rating as awful and terrible, that in reality do not appear so bad, once you put in perspective many other things that could happen in one's life. For example, students are asked to rate a situation as really bad, medium bad, or "bit" bad. When given scenarios such as, all my family but me died in a car accident (something really bad) and I tripped on the hall in front of many people this morning, students rate both situations in terms of how hard it would be for one to cope with it and how the situation should be categorized; really, medium or just "bit" bad. The facilitator models to the children coping with adverse situations by using many different rational thoughts, such as, "This is bad but it could be worse" and "I do not like it but I can deal with it." Last, the children are invited to choose a coping statement and are given scenarios to role-play successful coping by using the statements. They are asked to identify the intensity of emotions they felt when successfully coping and are directed to adopt this approach to their personal lives when facing difficult situations.

Session 5. Increase Your Tease Tolerance

The content in this session is designed to help students realize that after one learns to put things in perspective, one should not categorize teasing as the worst thing that could happen and as something impossible to cope with. During the session students review the Catastrophe Scale and appraise where teasing would fit in: really, medium, or "bit" bad stuff. The facilitator subsequently introduces the children to the Happening→Thinking→Feeling→Behaving Chart (HTFB). The children think of a typical situation where a child is being teased. Together, the children and the facilitator write down what is happening, what the person—who is having a hard time being teased—is feeling, how the person is behaving and what the person is likely to be thinking. The facilitator writes all this information down in the HTFB chart. The children are guided to evaluate the original thoughts experienced by the child, who is experiencing high intensities of emotions, and to decide if the thoughts are rational, positive and make sense. The children think of more rational and positive thoughts to substitute the original irrational ones and a new HTFB chart is created with the new, more effective and logic thoughts that better help in coping with teasing. The facilitator and the children explore the concept that one cannot control the teaser but one can control how one chooses to think about the teasing. Each child chooses a coping statement that can be used when facing teasing and the children and facilitator role play different teasing situations in which students are capable of coping by using rational and positive coping statements.

Session 6. More Coping Skills and Positive Habits of the Mind

The content in this session is designed to help students identify and practice the skills that they already have for coping with stressful situations, practice the new coping skills that they have learned, to learn to identify the negative habits of the mind they are currently engaging in, and to learn the positive habits of the mind that replace the negative ones. Emotional Resilience coping skills covered are: (a) use of positive vs. negative self-talk, (b) talking to someone you trust, (c) doing some type of physical activity, (d) using relaxation techniques such as breathing deeply and slowly repetitively, (e) putting things in perspective, (f) being assertive, (g) any other coping techniques already available to the children that they have been using and find it to be effective. After covering the emotional resilience skills, the facilitator engages the children in an activity that leads them to identify which negative habits of the mind they have been engaging in. The facilitator models to the children some of the negative habits of the mind, namely: self-downing, needing to be perfect, needing approval, I cannot do it, I cannot be bothered, being intolerant of limits, acting without thinking, giving up, and being intolerant of others inside several scenarios. While presenting the scenarios the facilitator asks the children to write down on a piece of paper the scenarios they identify with and the types of negative habits of the mind they have been engaging in. The children in the group identify the negative habits of the mind and the irrational thoughts that they have being engaging in and together with the facilitator they write down new positive habits of the mind and accompanying thoughts that can be used to substitute the negative habits of the mind. Last, the facilitator spends more time creating scenarios that go with the negative habits of the mind that the children identified and together the children and the facilitator role play using the positive habits of the mind and its accompanying rational thoughts when trying to cope with the hypothetical situations.

Session 7. Rethink

During the week prior to this session, the facilitator collects information from the children's teachers. The facilitator asks the teachers to share some real examples of situations that lead to students in the experimental group to become really angry, sad or worried. During the session the facilitator tells the students she knows about some bad things that have been happening to them, without revealing the children's identity or linking any child to a specific situation. The children and the facilitator choose a scenario from the examples collected from the teachers and together they build a Happening→Thinking→Feeling→Behaving (HTFB) chart. The children choose the Happening, among the options they have from the situations collected with the teachers' help, and then identify the Feelings the person in question might be experiencing, how the person is likely to be Behaving, and with help from the facilitator, the children hypothesize how the child in question is likely to be Thinking. The facilitator collects the hypothesized irrational thoughts that are making the child in question feel so bad and together the children and the facilitator create alternative thoughts that are more rational. Last, a role-play of the situation takes place by having the children practice the rational thoughts.

Session 8. Emotional Resilience at Work

The content in this session is designed to help students understand that they can use positive self-talk to do better at school. Students learn that by using positive self-talk they can acquire the attitude and thinking that can help motivate them to do work they find difficult or boring. Students and the facilitator create a list of homework and classroom activities that students find to be very difficult or boring and which might cause students to feel very angry, sad or worried. The facilitator models negative irrational thinking when faced with boring and difficult classroom tasks and asks students why it does not help to think this way. Students are shown the Emotional Thermometer and rate how the facilitator is likely feeling while thinking negatively and irrationally. The facilitator asks the students what could be done in order for the facilitator not to get so high in the Emotional Thermometer and for the facilitator to better solve the problem. Together, the children and the facilitator transform the irrational thoughts the facilitator had previously modeled into more rational ones. The facilitator then models having to do the same boring or difficult classroom tasks, but now using positive self-talk and the children rate the new level of emotion the facilitator is likely experiencing, now that the more rational thoughts are being used. During this final session students are given handouts that summarize and illustrate the coping skills that they have learned about and practiced in sessions. The techniques described in the handout are: (a) use of positive and rational self-talk (b) talking to someone you trust, (c) doing physical activities, (d) use of relaxation breathing techniques, and (e) putting things in perspective—the Catastrophe Scale. The students are then asked which techniques they could use when they do not understand something during a lecture, when they get a bad grade, and when they have to do boring or difficult school work. Last, students role-play talking to each other about what they can think and do when they have to do boring or difficult schoolwork, and when they get a bad grade.

As a matter of interest, results indicated a statistically significant increase in social competence and school adjustment of students who received both eclectic forms of group counseling as well as cognitive-behavioral resilience training as measured by pretest to posttest differences on the Walker-McConnell Scale of Social Competence and School Adjustment Elementary Version (1988).However, only students who participated in the resilience-training groups in comparison with students receiving eclectic forms of group counseling showed increases in emotional resilience (teacher rating and self-perception) as measured by a sub-scale of the Well-Being Surveys (Bernard, 2004d).

Conclusions

It is surely reassuring to know that children develop as a result of maturation a range of coping skills that enable then to manage their emotions that arise from different adverse circumstances. However, research into individual differences amongst children of the same age reveals a range of differences. Children with lower levels of development of emotional resilience have been found to at greater risk for poor educational achievement than children with higher levels of development (e.g., Bernard, 2004c). Intervention and prevention programs based on principles and practices of REBT that include a range of adaptive emotional regulation strategies hold the promise of influencing the developmental trajectories of "at risk" young people.

References

Altshuler, J., and Ruble, D. (1989). Developmental changes in children's awareness of strategies for coping with uncontrollable stress. *Child Development, 60,* 1337–1349.

Bernard, M.E. (2001). *Program achieve: A curriculum of lessons for teaching students how to achieve and develop social-emotional-behavioral well-being,* Vols. 1–6. Oakleigh, VIC (AUS): Australian Scholarships Group; Laguna Beach, CA (USA): You Can Do It! Education, Priorslee, Telford (ENG): Time Marque.

Bernard, M.E. (2002). *The You Can Do It! Education mentoring program.* Oakleigh, VIC (AUS): Australian Scholarships Group; Laguna Beach, CA (USA): You Can Do It! Education, Priorslee, Telford (ENG): Time Marque.

Bernard, M.E. (2002b). *Providing all children with the foundations for achievement and social-emotional-behavioral well-being,* 2nd ed. rev. Oakleigh, VIC (AUS): Australian Scholarships Group; Laguna Beach, CA (USA): You Can Do It! Education, Priorslee, Telford (ENG): Time Marque.

Bernard, M.E. (2003). *Developing the social-emotional-motivational competence of young people with achievement and behavior problems: A Guide for Working with Parents and Teachers.* Oakleigh, VIC (AUS): Australian Scholarships Group; Laguna Beach, CA (USA): You Can Do It! Education, Priorslee, Telford (ENG): Time Marque.

Bernard, M.E. (2004a). *The REBT therapist's pocket companion for working with children and adolescents.* New York: Albert Ellis Institute.

Bernard, M.E. (2004b). *The You Can Do It! early childhood education program: A social-emotional learning curriculum (ages 4–6).* Oakleigh, VIC (AUS): Australian Scholarships Group; Laguna Beach, CA (USA): You Can Do It! Education, Priorslee, Telford (ENG): Time Marque.

Bernard, M.E. (2004c). The relationship of young children's social-emotional-motivational competence to their achievement and social-emotional well-being. Paper to be presented at the annual conference of XXIV World Congress of OMEP (World Organization of Early Childhood), Melbourne, July.

Bernard, M. E. (2004d). The *Well-Being Surveys.* Camberwell, VIC: Australian Council for Educational Research.

Bernard, M.E., and Cronan, F. (1999). The child and adolescent scale of irrationality: Validation data and mental health correlates. *Journal of Cognitive Psychotherapy: An International Quarterly, 13*, 121–132.

Bernard, M. E., and Joyce, M. R. (1984). *Rational emotive therapy with children and adolescents*. New York: John Wiley.

Bernard, M.E. and Keefauver, L. Rational-emotive group counseling in a school setting. Paper presented at the American Educational Research Association's Annual Meeting, San Francisco, April 1979.

Brenner, E. and Salovey, P. (1997). Emotional regulation during childhood: Developmental, interpersonal and individual considerations. In Salovey, P. and Sluyter, D.J. (eds.), *Emotional development and emotional intelligence: Educational implications*. New York: Basic Books.

Dise-Lewis, J. E. (1988). The life events and coping inventory: An assessment of stress in Children. *Psychosomatic Medicine, 50*, 484–499.

Garber, J., Braafladt, N., and Zelman, J. (1991). The regulation of sad affect: An information processing perspective. In J. Garber and K. Dodge (eds.), *The development of emotional regulation and dysregulation*. New York: Cambridge University Press.

Kliewer, W. (1991). Coping in middle childhood: Relations to competence. *Developmental Psychology, 27,* 689–697.

Knaus, W. J. (1974). *Rational emotive education*. New York: Institute for Rational Living.

Kurdek, L. A. (1987). Gender differences in the psychological symptomalogy and copying strategies of young adolescents. *Journal of Early Adolescence, 7,* 395–410.

Landy, S. (2002). *Pathways to competence. Encouraging healthy social and emotional development in young children*. Baltimore, Maryland: Paul A. Brookes.

Pires, D. The effects of a cognitive behavioral emotional resilience program on the emotional resilience, social competence and school adjustment of elementary school students. Master of Education Thesis, California State University, Long Beach, August 2004.

Salovey, P. and Sluyter, D.J. (eds.) (1997). *Emotional development and emotional intelligence: Educational implications*. New York: Basic Books.

Saarni, C. (1999). *The development of emotional competence*. New York: Guilford Press.

Vernon, A. (1989). *The thinking, feeling, behaving curriculum*. Champaign, ILL: Research Press.

Walker, H. and McConnell, S. (1995). *Walker-McConnell scale of social competence and school adjustment*. Florence, KY: Wadsworth.

Wierzbicki, M. (1989). Children's perceptions in counter-depressive activities. *Psychological Reports, 65,* 1251–1258.

Section II

Disorders of Childhood

6

A Developmental, Rational-Emotive Behavioral Approach for Working with Parents

Marie R. Joyce

The work of Albert Ellis and other Rational-Emotive Behavior Therapy (REBT)-oriented practitioners summarized in this chapter represent some of the earliest work published in the 1960s of cognitive-behavioral theory applied to understanding the influence of parents and parenting style on children's adjustment including problems of childhood. This work has led to the incorporation within REBT child treatment and adolescent treatment of a focus not only on the child but on the parenting styles of the child's parents and, more broadly, on the effect that overall family functioning has on the child.

Ellis et al. (1966) wrote about the role of parental beliefs about their children and how their beliefs influence their children's view of the world in "How to Raise an Emotionally Healthy, Happy Child."

> The worst care parents can provide their children is that of blaming them for their mistake making and wrongdoing. Parents or other early teachers usually help a child plummet down the toboggan slide towards disturbed feelings and behaviors by doing two things when he (child) does something that displeases them: (a) they tell him that he is wrong for acting in this displeasing manner, and (b) they strongly indicate to him that he is a worthless individual for being wrong, and that he therefore deserves to be damned and severely punished for his wrongdoing.

As well as calling for parents to communicate rational messages to their children, included in this work is a range of practical advice for parents on how to overcome a variety of their children's common childhood problems.

Another example of REBT, cognitive-behavioral theory applied to parenting is the pioneering text authored by Paul Hauck in 1967, *The Rational Management of Children* (1967). In this book, Hauck identified different irrational beliefs of parents that lead to distinct positive and negative styles of parenting.

Unkind and firm patterns ("unquestioning obedience toward authority combined with a kick in the ego) involve parental behavior of setting rigid rules, never letting their child question their authority, focusing on the wrongdoing of their child, attacking the personality of their child, strictness and little praise ("Children must never disagree with their superiors").

Kind and not firm child-rearing practices involve parents who while showing love and affection make few demands and set few limits. Parents who demonstrate this pattern appear to do so out of either not wanting to frustrate their child ("Children must not be frustrated") or out of guilt ("I am responsible for all my child's problems and, therefore, I am hopeless.").

Kind and firm child-rearing practice is the preferred and skilled form of parenting. Parents who raise their children in this fashion talk and reason with them about objectionable behavior, focus on the behavior but do not blame the child, set limits with clear consequences for rule violations, set punishment that is related to rule learning, not blame, sometimes frustrate their child when necessary, apply reasonable pressure to teach self-discipline and delay of gratification, never punish out of anger and frequently praise and show love.

Today, in their practice, REBT-oriented practitioners spend time with the parents of children discussing and challenging irrational beliefs of parents with a view to developing a firm and kind, authoritative style of parenting. Further, parent psychoeducation provides parents with an understanding of how their children's emotions and behaviors are influenced by their children's beliefs and includes ways in which parents can challenge and change irrational beliefs and develop more rational ones.

Bernard and Joyce (1984) identified irrational beliefs of parents which are associated with ineffective parenting, for example, "I have little ability to control my feelings when things go wrong at home" (a belief underlying general parent upset) and "my child must always behave the way I demand" (a belief underlying parent anger). Alternative rational parent beliefs were presented which form the foundation for effective parenting.

Rational-Emotive Behavior Therapy consultation, an intervention which aims to help an individual or organization which has identified a problem, and is characterized by collaborative problem solving, has been described in detail elsewhere (Bernard and DiGiuseppe, 1994; Joyce, 1990; 1994; Meyers et al., 1979). Client-Centered Consultation between the practitioner and parent-consultee provides the parent with new ways to help their child who is the (absent) client. Consultee-Centered Consultation addresses aspects of the parent's functioning and practice to improve the parent's management of their own thinking and behavior in their parenting role.

Rational-Emotive Behavior Therapy continues to offer a unique contribution to understanding and intervening with parents who report problems in their relationship with their children or whose children have been identified as having problems. This chapter brings together REBT approaches with recent advances in theory and research on the role of parents in their children's mental health and well-being. It covers problems from the milder end of the spectrum, which may involve psychoeducation only, through to more complex dysfunctional family problems. It brings a focus on the emotional self-regulation of parents and its relationship to the child's emotional regulation. Not every psychological disorder of childhood can be covered in the chapter but disorders common at particular stages of development will be used to illustrate ways to work with parents in alleviating the problems of their children.

Recent Advances in Understanding Parent-child Problems

From the earliest days of psychology, the importance of parents in the emotional well-being of children has been emphasized. It has been conceptualized in different theoretical frameworks, from the psychoanalytic which proposed overriding unconscious influences, to strict behavior theories which stressed learning via precise reinforcement regimes. An influential theory concerning the primary importance of early parenting influences on children's socialization and adjustment is attachment theory (Bowlby, 1988). This theory evolved from ethology and identified children's inbuilt behavior systems which promote responsive care of the child from early infancy. According to attachment theory, the foundation of trust upon which all relationships depend are laid in the early years. Of particular interest to the current topic is that the central mechanism, which attachment theory proposes that moderates the development of the child's emotional life in the context of primary care, is a cognitive one, namely internal working models (IWMs). According to attachment theory, IWMs which evolve within the child's mind are internal representations of attachment figures and their likely responsiveness to the child's needs. Healthy experiences in infancy and early childhood lead to secure attachment mediated by positive IWMs. Attachment theory proposes that these IWMs can be modified over time by experience. Further, intergenerational studies have shown that adults' experiences as children (and hence their IWMs) influence their parenting behavior and, therefore, these cognitive patterns can be carried over into the next generation (Serbin and Karp, 2003).

The cognitive revolution of the eighties and nineties transformed the possibilities of understanding the role of parents and families. The cognitive-behavioral framework provided by REBT (Bernard and Joyce, 1984; Hauck, 1967, 1983; Woulff, 1983) allowed new methods of assessment and intervention with parents, especially regarding detailed beliefs about their parenting roles (Borcherdt, 1996). It emphasized rational parent beliefs and emotional self-management as a prior condition for children's emotional well-being. Woulff further demonstrated the problems that can arise when children are treated in isolation from their family context.

For many decades the history of interventions with parents, especially school-based interventions, was dominated by a behaviorist approach which emphasized teaching parents behavior management skills in an approach known as parent training (Patterson and Dishion, 1985). More recently, theory and research have focussed on parent cognition and parent emotion from a variety of perspectives. Gottman et al. (1996), Eisenberg et al. (2002), Dukes et al. (2003) and Flory (2004; 2005) have all linked cognitive factors in parents to emotional outcomes of their children through the concepts of emotional intelligence, emotional regulation and empathy.

Gottman and DeClaire (1997) in an approach linked to emotional intelligence, introduced the concept of parent meta-emotion. In their research studies, they identified a sub group of parents who engaged in meta-emotion, a reflective capacity which enabled them to regulate their own emotions in a conscious and deliberate way. These parents were aware of their own emotions and how they thought and acted to self regulate them, and were able to help their children to name and identify their emotions, as well as guide them to become more self-managing. Parents who were able to do this were conceptualised as "emotion coaches" to their children. The far-reaching positive outcomes associated with emotion coaching in a longitudinal study of preschool to early school years children included better emotional self-regulation, higher levels of academic success, better social competencies and better physical health (Gottman et al., 1996).

These diverse approaches contribute to the field's recognition of the importance of parent cognition and its influence on parent and child emotion. A systematic means of assessing and intervening with parents is provided by a REBT framework which focuses on beliefs and proposes rational and irrational (helpful and unhelpful) beliefs of parents and children as core constructs. REBT also recognises that beliefs of both kinds can be shared by parents and children to create a family culture. Thus, parents and extended families may induct their children into shared ways of thinking that perpetuate irrational patterns across generations. Little has appeared about this in the literature but clinical experience indicates this as a fertile ground for further exploration.

In assisting parents to reflect on their beliefs REBT focuses on both *inferences* and *evaluations* but emphasizes the dysfunctional effect of irrational evaluations which operate as unacknowledged, philosophical belief systems. It is a binary theory which uniquely includes both appropriate and inappropriate negative emotions (e.g., parental sadness versus depression; parental annoyance versus parental rage; parental concern versus parental anxiety) (David et al., 2005).

Common Underlying Difficulties of Parents

Before describing REBT-oriented parent interventions, some common experiences of parents that need to be addressed early on in therapy are considered. REBT theory alerts practitioners to be on the lookout for parental *guilt* and parental *low frustration tolerance (LFT)* as both are unhelpful states for parents and often contribute to the establishment and maintenance of the problems of their children.

Cultural values, family norms and individual personality characteristics may influence parents to hold perfectionist standards and, therefore, experience guilt about their level of perceived success as parents (and as human beings) especially when they rightly or wrongly perceive that their children are not turning out perfectly. Parents rarely volunteer feelings of guilt but easily acknowledge such feelings as part of their current and past experience. Such feelings are likely to be to the fore when their child has a serious problem that requires them to seek professional help. This secondary emotional problem of the parent needs to be acknowledged by the therapist in a supportive way that helps the parent to ease their anxiety about failure and criticism. It can provide an excellent opportunity to teach the ABCs of REBT which can then form the basis of the wider intervention, as illustrated below.

A	B	C
Antecedent Event	Beliefs (Helpful or Unhelpful?)	Consequences (Feelings and Behavior)
I think about my child's problem. (He is not settling well at bedtime and hasn't for years. He keeps running around until our bedtime).	I should be able to get him to settle down to sleep.	Anger
	What if he never improves?	Anxiety
	Other parents don't have this problem so there must be something wrong with me.	Guilt Behaviors: Yelling at the child. Blaming others.
	I am no good.	Crying, misusing alcohol.

A good first step to help the parent overcome their guilt is to acknowledge both their responsibility and its limits (they cannot control their child in every way), and to teach them to challenge their unhelpful beliefs and replace them with helpful beliefs such as:

My child's problem behaviour does not mean I am a totally bad parent or a worthless person.
My commitment to gaining assistance shows I am concerned and responsible.
Just about all parents feel guilty sometimes about their children. No parent can be 100% perfect in raising their children!
I can learn new ways to teach and help my child.

Low frustration tolerance (LFT) is a less recognised dynamic in parent-child relations. It can be particularly pernicious as parents with strong LFT frequently also project it onto their children, believing that their children "cannot stand" what is expected of them. Irrational beliefs associated with LFT in parents include:

My child can upset me.
I can't stand it when things go wrong at home.

I can't stand my child's behaviour.
I can't stand my child.
I don't need this!
It's awful to have to put up with this.

As with guilt, it is important to teach parents that their own beliefs rather than their child's behavior are at the heart of their upset. Teaching them that they are upsetting themselves about their child's behavior is a good way of introducing the ABC model. The next step in intervention to assist parents to overcome their LFT when they begin to work on their problems is to ask them to check on the evidence: how long have they in fact been "standing" the behaviours and difficulties they *tell themselves* that they cannot stand? Even if it is a short time (and often it is quite long) they can be helped to reframe their thoughts and beliefs about themselves and especially what they *think* they can stand. Injecting some humour into the disputation assists parents to laugh a little at their arbitrary thinking.

Steps in REBT Parent Interventions

The general goals of REBT interventions with parents involve teaching parents the cognitive-emotional–behavioral links in their own parenting role and in their child's emotional distress and problem behavior. Parents receive psychoeducation to understand their child's problem and they learn to use the ABCD model to improve their emotional self-management as parents. A REBT approach to parent interventions can be conceptualized in seven steps by which a parent, guided by a therapist, may help their child with emotional distress and behavioural difficulties.

1. Receive psychoeducation regarding parents' and children's emotions.
2. Learn the *kind and firm* rational parenting style. Practice observing their own levels of emotion and monitoring their emotional expression.
3. Practice observing their child's emotional states.
4. Practice communicating with their child about specific emotions.
5. Model emotional management for their child.
6. Guide their child through ongoing emotional and behavioral learning.
7. Reinforce their child's efforts.

This learning process will foster in the parent: awareness, empathy, proactive thinking and appropriate, authoritative leadership in their family. From the child's perspective, there is an experience of emotional validation and acceptance as well as a sense of safety and containment.

This chapter next highlights some developmental issues and then moves to problems in children of different age ranges and specific problems common in children and young people. Drawing on from developmental theory (Kegan, 1982) and from my clinical experience, I have formulated goals of parenting appropriate to different ages. These goals are presented and some case illustrations have been provided.

Developmental Issues

When children demonstrate problems in affect and behavior, these problems are often set in a context of age-stage asynchrony (Kegan, 1995). Such asynchrony occurs when the developmental tasks a child is yet to master are not the age-appropriate ones. An example would be a child of late elementary school age who cannot differentiate fantasy from reality. Another example would be a teenager who would not accept the rules of play in team games. Therefore, while the age-related goals presented below represent the contextual demands on the child at a given stage, it is important in helping parents to assess whether the child is in fact still struggling to master a previous stage. Most parents whose teenagers are experiencing problems are trying to achieve the parenting goals of previous stages. Helping parents to understand realistically where their child's development is along this path can bring them to a clearer understanding of why their child is not coping in their life context. However, it is important to clarify which goals they could most appropriately work towards given their child's current needs. For example, a child may be 16-years-old but may not have basic understanding of emotions or any skills in negotiation.

Working with Parents to Help Children of Different Ages

Before presenting a systematic account of specific REBT interventions with parents, it is important to review some general principles in relation to parent involvement or participation in therapy. Decisions about working with parents may vary according to the age of the child. Therefore, three sections are presented, one for each age range: young children (3–7), middle years (8–12) and young people (13–17). *A useful guiding principle is that the younger the child, the more important it is to involve the parents where possible.* In assisting older children, decisions can be guided by the severity of the problem, whether it is manifested at home as well as school, the willingness of the parents to be involved, and the wishes of the young person.

In this context it is important to help parents understand the goals of parenting as guiding principles in the implementation of interventions. Parents will vary in their ability to articulate their goals but some basic points which need attention are presented in Table 1 below. With psychological interventions, the primary need of the child for emotional security is paramount and it is clear that parents do not always know how to provide this for their child or how to communicate it to them in verbal and non-verbal ways. All interventions with children and young people should attend to this basic need and ensure that the proposed intervention meets this need.

TABLE 1. General Goals of Parenting.

(1) Providing a safe, healthy and loving environment for their child, leading to emotional security and increasing independence.
(2) Guiding the child's behavior towards socially acceptable standards
(3) Teaching the child values, especially moral values.
(4) Providing interest in and support for their child's education.
(5) Supporting the child through phases of change.

Considerations When Working with Parents of Young Children Three to Seven Years

With young children, parents are much more likely to want to be involved as they are often still very open to learning about child rearing and how to do the best for their child. There is also the advantage of explaining to them that if they learn new skills these can carry over across the years of the child's development.

Table 2 sets out these and other reasons in a manner that can help parents to understand the need to become involved and appreciate the benefits of doing so.

It is important to spell out these perspectives for parents because there is no reason to assume that a parent coming for assistance with their child, is expecting to be involved themselves, especially at a level of working on, and possibly changing their own emotional self management. Central goals of parenting young children are presented in Table 3 below. The following case history illustrates the experience of a single mother in learning to intervene with her child.

Case Illustration: Marion and her Daughter Kelly

Marion was a single mother in her twenties and Kelly was her only child aged 3 years 11 months. Kelly attended crèche three half days per week while her mother attended a university course in professional training. She had previously attended family day care at 2 years of age. Marion had stated very

TABLE 2. Reasons to be Involved in Your Child's Treatment.

(1) You will gain a greater understanding of your child and his/her individual needs.
(2) You will have the satisfaction of helping your child to overcome the current problem.
(3) The bonds between you and your child can be strengthened as your child will know you do not reject him/her for having a problem.
(4) The skills you learn can be applied in later years with new problems should they arise.
(5) The experience of problem solving together can help the child understand your ongoing commitment to him/her.
(6) In the process of learning how to help your child you may gain greater understanding of yourself and establish new skills for application in your own life

TABLE 3. Specific Age-Related Parenting Goals for Young Children.

(1) Placing external limits on the child's behaviour
(2) Helping the child establish the beginnings of impulse control.
(3) Helping the child distinguish between fantasy and reality.
(4) Helping the child name and acknowledge emotions.
(5) Helping the child begin to understand others and their needs

clearly in the process of making the referral that she did not want to bring Kelly in but rather she wanted to learn how to help her child.

Kelly's Problem: Marion reported that Kelly demonstrated anxiety and fears, specifically her distress at separation and obsessive questioning and checking prior to attending crèche. Her withdrawal in certain home situations also concerned her mother and we agreed to work on alleviating this behavior.

The two relevant levels of consultation were explained to Marion, namely direct consultation for herself in regard to her parenting (Consultee-Centered Consultation) and indirect consultation for Kelly's problems (Client-Centered Consultation). Marion identified her own problem as: "My parenting of Kelly at the moment". She was experiencing anxiety but wanted to give Kelly "the confidence I never had". She identified multiple problems including separation anxiety, fears, tension, sleep disturbance, toileting and tantrums. While I indicated to Marion that each of the identified areas deserved our attention, she was firm in her decision that only certain ones were to be addressed by us. For example, toileting was "off limits" as she had decided to wait to address toilet training difficulties until other problems were alleviated. Therefore, we agreed to work together to alleviate Kelly's emotions and behaviors of concern.

Consultee-Centered Consultation

Through Consultee-Centered Consultation Marion was taught emotional self-management. A functional analysis showed that Marion's behavior and expression of emotions were acting as discriminatory stimuli or "triggers" for Kelly's problem emotions and behaviors. Specifically, Marion's displays of anger in response to an accumulation of home responsibilities and restriction of her freedom appeared to lead to anxiety, fear and withdrawal in the child. She became aware that thinking about the extent of her responsibilities in parenting Kelly and evaluating them as unbearable, awful and unfair, were activating events for her angry feelings and behavior, which then in turn became activating events for Kelly's anxiety and withdrawal. The cycle continued with Kelly's reactions becoming activating events for Marion's guilt as she believed that her child "should not have" problem behavior and, as she did, it must be her fault as mother.

Marion had a hypothesis that Kelly had generalized her disturbed emotions, especially fear, to a staff member at crèche. According to Marion, fear of this person had led to an obsessive checking ritual in the evenings and mornings in which Kelly asked her mother a series of repetitious questions which she wanted Marion to ask on her behalf at crèche and "I have to be there when you ask them." Kelly appeared to experience severe anxiety when faced with her mother's outbursts of very loud yelling. These same reactions appeared to generalize to a teacher at crèche who had raised her voice (and probably looked angry) and now elicited in Kelly withdrawal responses and obsessive questioning.

Further **Client-Centered Consultation** involved psychoeducation about:

- Kelly's emotions: Marion learned that Kelly's behavior was a direct expression of Kelly's emotions and that there was a reason for the behavior.
- The relationship between the parent's emotional states and the child's disturbance: It was explained to Marion that children react to the emotional tone of what parents say to the child as much as to what the parent says to the child. It was clearly stated that seeing a parent upset and angry can threaten a child's emotional security.
- Kelly's developmental needs/problems (history and current): Marion reported on Kelly's relationship with her father who lived separately. She was helped to understand the developmental context of Kelly and her limited ability to understand adult behavior and interactions. Kelly, at three years of age, could not understand the reasons for adult behavior and, being unable to predict when her mother or teacher would erupt in anger, experienced increased anxiety and fear.

In summary the goals of the intervention with the mother involved:

- first, new emotional self-regulation by Marion;
- second, teaching emotional management for Kelly;
- third, teach developmentally appropriate behavior management skills to Marion

Following the psychoeducation phase Marion was helped to identify and acknowledge her emotions, with a particular focus on her LFT anger and guilt. Understanding that her anger was affecting her daughter motivated her to change her patterns of behavior very quickly. Her beliefs included "It is not fair I have to work so hard, bringing up Kelly all on my own", "If I'm angry it's OK to let it out. It won't hurt anyone." She learned to challenge these evaluations and inferences, building new high frustration tolerance. She challenged the inference of "all on my own" by reminding herself of supports in her life—her sister, the child's father. She also challenged the irrational "awful" and "unbearable" nature of her situation by reasoning about what she has managed by herself so far, and about her ability to be a good parent and to manage her life overall, including studying to become a teacher.

She recognized her angry outbursts as stimulus conditions for Kelly's withdrawal at home and changed her emotional expression. She began to tune in to her frustration levels and, using new emotional resilience skills, remove herself from the situation if she was becoming angry instead of yelling very loudly. She would then calm herself with new rational thinking and return to the situation. Her new self talk included: "It's very hard to parent on one's own, but I've been doing it up to now and I can continue. There are people I can turn to for help when I need them"; "letting my anger out can hurt my child's security, so I'll calm myself down and not yell around her". It was hoped over time she would do this while remaining in the situation but initially she needed to remove herself briefly to manage her emotions.

As the assessment of Marion also revealed that she was experiencing intense guilt, as she judged herself to blame for Kelly's problems, the intervention also included helping her to challenge her self rejection for her child's problems. She learned to evaluate her parenting but not her self in total, to accept that she, like all parents, did not know everything, and to appreciate her commitment as a loving parent seeking assistance for her daughter. A new self-acceptance emerged and her level of guilt was lowered.

Marion implemented her new emotional self-management (anger and guilt) as the first step with her child. This included monitoring her non-verbal behavior, (e.g. looking angry). She also talked with Kelly in a simple way about emotions, teaching her that she understood how Kelly was feeling, including both the thoughts that bothered Kelly and the tight sensations in her body; that everyone has strong feelings sometimes and although they can feel scary Kelly doesn't need to be very afraid of how she feels.

New emotional exchanges took place: Marion talked with Kelly more calmly about her fears at crèche and asked Kelly whether the teacher reminded Kelly of her mother. Kelly agreed that she was like her mother when she was angry and Marion needed to reassure her about the teacher's trustworthiness. Behavior management was implemented to reduce the frequency of the repetitious questioning: Marion explained to Kelly that she had a new plan to help Kelly with her worries. It was explained to Kelly that she could ask a few questions once per night but not keep repeating them. After that Marion ignored more than three questions.

Processes of Change and Outcome

As a result of change in the content and tone of communication between Marion and her daughter (empathic talks with Kelly, acknowledging her fears and worries and listening to Kelly's feelings without any "buts"), Kelly's protests at separation ceased. She no longer cried when her mother left her at crèche. Marion was firm in implementing the limits on questioning and the questioning was soon extinguished. This happened in conjunction with counter-conditioning regarding the feared teacher. Kelly was helped to observe that the teacher had never in fact expressed angry at Kelly or been threatening to her. This helped Kelly to modify the anxiety associated with attendance at crèche. An unexpected change also occurred with Kelly and her father. Marion reported that Kelly's (previously unreported) anxious protests when she left Kelly with her father every Sunday had stopped. The change in his daughter's behavior resulted in her father feeling relieved as he no longer believed that there was something wrong with him as a father.

Marion followed the consultation plan carefully and saw results for her efforts. She had been ambivalent about attending in the first place and only came because she was desperate. Three sessions were the most I could keep her coming and she cancelled the follow up session. However she said: "You have given me back my Kelly. She is playing, laughing and happy again". Marion's desire was to go it alone from there.

Considerations When Working with Parents of Children 8–12 Years

Problems of children in this age group may be occurring at home, at school or in other social situations such as sporting groups. It is helpful to parents if the practitioner demonstrates willingness to work with others involved in the care and education of the child, such as teachers or sporting coaches.

The timing of referral is often related to the parent's limits of frustration tolerance or to a particular event, sometimes at school, that prompts the recognition that professional help is needed for a child, even though the problem in one form or another may have been present previously for a long time. At other times the problem is in the nature of an adjustment difficulty which has arisen during a period of transition such as beginning school, moving from one school to another, or a significant change in home circumstances such as death, divorce or the arrival of a new baby. Therefore, assessment needs to evaluate carefully the context and duration of the problems. Listed in Table 4 are major goals of parenting for children in this age group which may help parents to understand important developmental needs of their child.

Case Illustration: Carmen and her Son Joel

Carmen and her son, Joel, aged 9, were referred by the school following episodes of Joel's verbal aggression towards peers in the playground and verbal clashes with his teachers. Both Carmen and Joel attended a university-based clinic and both recognized there were problems to address, although they understood them very differently.

Joel was impulsive in his reactions to frustration and extremely determined to have what he wanted. Once having made up his mind he wanted something, especially if it was to do with his football team, he was rigidly

TABLE 4. Specific Age-Related Parenting Goals for Children 8-12.

(1) Giving the child a simple understanding of their emotional experience and teaching simple strategies for calming themselves.
(2) Supporting the child's early logic of associative, rule governed thinking
(3) Teaching the child simple negotiation skills to manage external conflict.
(4) Teaching the child to take turns and to make efforts to acknowledge others' needs.
(5) Supporting the child's emerging individual interests and achievements

determined to obtain it at any costs. He reacted emotionally and with verbal aggression to those who frustrated him and as the school staff were not successfully managing the problems there was some risk that he would be excluded from school. Problems were also apparent at home, for example Joel would swear when frustrated and sometimes leave the situation (e.g., run out from home even though it was dark and refuse to come back in response to parental instructions).The intervention was carried out with the mother and son in separate sessions by two REBT-oriented practitioners who communicated with the school in consultation with the parent.

REBT Consultation with Carmen was at two levels:

(1) improve her mental health including emotional self-management and overall functioning/knowledge as to what it means to be a good parent and (2) assist her in developing management skills (including parent-child relationship skills) and in understanding and changing her son's ABCs.

Consultee-Centered Consultation

Goals of treatment were discussed with Carmen including the role of her emotions as contributing to Joel's problems. It was agreed that she would work on her anxiety and other relevant emotions and try to change how she reacted to Joel in problem situations as well as modifying her oftentimes overanxious communications on a broader everyday basis. She indicated she would try to bring her husband into this process as best she could.

Carmen learned about the importance of accepting Joel's emotional state even when his emotional state and behavior are problematic. She learned that she needed to and could communicate differently with him at these problematic times; for example, communicating positively with him to acknowledge what it is that he strongly wants and how frustrating it is that he is unable to have it right away. Importantly, she learned about the negative effects of global self-rating and rating of her son.

The work with Carmen focussed on her anxiety and guilt regarding Joel's problem behaviour. Using the ABC model, she identified her "As" as being Joel's misbehavior, or his teachers' or grandparents' upset and complaints about Joel. At C, she would become anxious and feel very guilty. Her beliefs at "B" included: "It is awful that my child has these problems", "I should be able to stop them", "What if he never gets over them?", "What if he never has any friends?", "What if he is expelled from school?", "That would be terrible", "My child's problems prove I'm no good".

The practitioner disputed these irrational beliefs and helped her with new self talk: "Just because I don't like Joel's problems doesn't mean they shouldn't exist", "his current problems don't mean he'll always have problems and even worse ones", "As his mother I can help him to overcome what ever problems he has", "His problems don't make me worthless".

Specific negative activating events were identified for her to practise her additional thinking skills to help her maintain emotional calmness. These occurred when Joel was noncompliant and when he became angry. She would say to herself "This is all he has learned so far", "To learn the next steps he needs me to be calm", "I'll remember our plan to not overreact but to speak to him calmly".

Joint session time between the two therapists and Carmen and Joel enabled the boy to understand that his mother wanted to help him solve his problem. A collaborative rather than antagonistic relationship was built. In his own sessions Joel was learning:

- To be less demanding and angry by thinking more rationally.
- To clarify what he wanted (to get to the High School his big brother attended, to make friends and stay out of trouble).
- To think before he acted: alternative solution thinking skills were taught in concrete detail and practised.

His efforts were reinforced by his therapist. This was good modelling for Carmen who also needed to refocus on his good behaviour (which was most of the time) and his achievements and not on his poor behaviour.

Client-Centered Consultation

Carmen planned to begin listening to Joel with an ear for his emotions, always being able to "side with him" in these in a validating way. She helped him to name his feelings appropriately and express his desires verbally as strong wishes rather than through demands and negative behavior. She also communicated to him positive expectations through an attitude of "I know you can do it". She reinforced his good behavior and his efforts. To achieve these changes Carmen had worked hard at changing her irrational beliefs that maintained her anxiety and guilt.

Processes of Change and Outcome

Joel appreciated the new approach by his mother, feeling validated and supported by her instead of receiving frequent disapproval and criticism. Over a period of twelve weeks, the incidents at school became less frequent—about one per month instead of several per week. Carmen expressed increased confidence in herself in her parenting role and new expectations that Joel could succeed at High School.

Considerations When Working with Parents of Young People 13–17 Years

The level of maturity as well as the severity and type of presenting problem of adolescents needs to be taken into account in deciding whether to work with the parents. Several factors will influence this decision directly, including who communicates first with the psychologist and in what context. In private practice it will certainly be the parents referring the young person. In some school settings a young person may approach the psychologist for assistance on their own initiative. There may be organisational policies in place to govern whether parents need to be brought in immediately to every case or not. This section of the chapter is relevant where parents have come for assistance either by themselves or jointly with their young person.

In my experience, difficulties coming to professional attention for the first time in adolescence are either adjustment difficulties which are generally best dealt with in direct intervention with the young person (e.g., emotional problems with transition, peer conflict, social anxieties) or symptoms of deep seated psychopathology, such as mood disorders, which require long term intervention with both parents and young person. Emerging personality disorders in young people fall into this category and may present initially in a variety of symptoms such as panic attacks, depression or eating problems. Multiple diagnoses frequently apply in these cases.

Case Illustration: Alma and Bill and their Son, Jeffrey

Alma and Bill sought assistance regarding their 15-year-old son, Jeffrey, who was refusing to go to school. Assessment of the young man led to a diagnosis of panic disorder and an emergent borderline personality disorder. There were also features of generalized anxiety and marked social immaturity. Narcissism and severe rigidity of thought were characteristic of this young man. He made incessant and unrelenting demands for consumer goods. Strengths of the family included strong friendship and support networks and a shared sense of humour.

Initial discussions required clear communication to the parents of the results of the assessment. It took time for them to realise the seriousness of the disorders their son was experiencing. Initial steps were planned to get him back to school as this was deemed a priority.

Consultee-Centered Consultation

As there was a culture of mutual blame in the family, the parents were taught the REBT model and given homework via reading and ABCD practice. Alma

TABLE 5. Specific Age Related Parenting Goals for Young People 13–17.

(1) Helping the adolescent adjust to the physiological and psychological changes of puberty.
(2) Supporting their adolescent's participation in groups outside the family.
(3) Supporting the young person in clarifying and testing values.
(4) Supporting the young person in widening their experience as a basis for vocational choice and linking them to the wider community.
(5) Allowing increasing autonomy as appropriate, while still setting limits
(6) Listening to the young person's emotional experience and guiding him/her in the management of internal conflict.
(7) Supporting the young person through mistakes.

blamed herself ("It's my fault our son has these problems. I'm no good") and Jeffrey's behavior was an activating event for Alma's self downing beliefs. Bill was unable to engage in reflection and focussed only on his demands towards Alma. The coming together and expectation for joint responsibility for their son's welfare led to increased stress in the marriage relationship. As the son resisted efforts to support his return to school, this steadily worsened and a marriage break-up ensued. Alma was keen to continue to help her son while Bill, his father, was unable to assume this responsibility. He was referred to another therapist for his own individual work.

Alma learned that her own anxiety and depression were an important part of the family dynamics but nevertheless that it was not helpful to blame herself for the problems. She learned that blaming herself would make things worse rather than better. She learned that there were strategies that both she and her son could learn in order to manage their anxiety and that these took practice to make a difference in their lives.

Part of Alma's difficulties lay in her own partial transition to adult maturity, her primary emotional ties to her mother still influencing her thinking and especially her self criticism and rejection as she continued to need her mother's affirmation to feel worthwhile. Her "need" for her mother's approval was disputed as a pre-requisite for her being able to assume a more mature adult role especially as it related to parenting and being more confident in her approach to her son. This was basic to enabling her to set limits on her son's behavior as her desire to please him and be liked by him was helping to maintain the problems at the beginning. Education about frustration tolerance (hers and his) as well as the goals of parenting for her son enabled her to adopt new attitudes and behaviors. It was agreed that the son be referred to another therapist for intensive individual work.

The intervention with Alma included personal therapy for her anxiety and depression. She worked hard in sessions on learning to dispute her irrational self downing beliefs and achieved some relief. Her anxiety levels were very high and hard for her to work on. She had aptitude for reflective thinking work and was successful in disputing her irrational beliefs; however, she had difficulty employing relaxation skills to combat her physiological arousal accompanying her anxiety. This was problematic in the intervention as physiological responding was a strong element in her anxiety.

Specific plans for minimizing her anxiety in the way she communicated with her son were put in place. She learned that her emotions and accompanying behaviors could be his triggers (As) and she worked to increase the calmness in her parenting. Her beliefs about her parenting leading to anxiety and depression included:

I should have been able to prevent my son's problems.
There must be something wrong with me.
It's terrible that he has these problems.
People (especially my family) will think I'm worthless.
I should be able to solve my son's problems.

She practised challenging her irrational beliefs and was able to lessen her distress and act more calmly in her parenting role.

Her new beliefs included:

In spite of my best efforts in the past my son does have serious problems.
My parenting in the past was the best I knew at the time.
My son's problems do not mean there is something wrong with me.
His problems are very serious and it will take a long time to help him but that's just a fact of life.
I like to have my family's approval but I don't absolutely have to have it. If they criticise me I can still think and act independently of them.
When people have major problems there are many resources in the community to assist and it is appropriate to call on them for support.

Client-Centered Consultation

Alma's plan for intervening with her son to support his individual therapy was to teach him to become aware of his emotions and understanding of the B-C (thinking–feeling) connection. She also learned about the principle of successive approximations and was careful to reward any improvements in his behaviors if they represented changes in the right direction. She kept as specific goals to remain calm in communicating with him and to stay firm in the face of his strong and persistent demands for purchases. She also planned to set limits on his behaviour in the home (verbal abuse).

Processes of Change and Outcome

The therapeutic work continued over a period of 5 years and Alma's tasks were extremely difficult as Jeffrey met her efforts with resistance and escalated aggression. Even with individual support and multiple attempts he would not return to school and eventually, in the face of physical abuse in the home he was excluded from the home and helped to set up independently in a small flat. His financial affairs were placed in the hands of a government body to avoid family conflict over consumer goods.

Jeffrey did not persist with his own therapy and the management of his difficulties was left to the mother, especially after the break-up of the marriage. Over a period of several years Alma persisted in her own therapeutic work, persisting in her disputation skills, and continued her regime of rewarding his approximations to appropriate social behaviour. She supported his interests and guided him to introductory courses which enabled him to "put a toe in the water" of education again.

Her major effort to develop high frustration tolerance, combined with firm limit setting, resulted in Jeffrey slowly learning where the limits of his behavior lay. He took positive steps towards his own career goals, joined a peer group in his post secondary education setting and began to learn from interpersonal relationships outside his immediate family. For Jeffrey each new step was like a mountain to be climbed and it was three steps forward, one step back, but gradually progress was made. It was essential for Alma to be able to take the long term view and not get overly caught up in the minutiae of each of Jeffrey's mini-crises. In the longer term, Jeffrey has been able to move interstate to attend university, having organised his applications and interviews himself and is nearing the end of his degree. Alma has continued to work on her anxiety and has worked through various adult developmental tasks, especially in relation to her primary emotional ties.

This chapter turns now to three major types of disturbance and distress, namely anxiety, anger and depression and considers ways REBT is used in work with parents whose children suffer these problems.

Working With Parents to Alleviate Children's Anxiety

Anxiety has two components, the mainly cognitive one of worry and the other of physiological responding. Individuals differ in the extent of involvement of each component in their anxiety problem. Recent clinical writings and research (Cox et al., 1999; Flett et al., 2004) have identified "anxiety sensitivity" as playing a part in how individuals manage their anxiety. REBT has consistently made the distinction between ego anxiety (performance and/or social anxiety) and discomfort anxiety (Ellis, 2003) reflecting similar processes of anxiety experience and reactions to this experience.

Children are known to experience both ego and discomfort anxiety. Many cognitive interventions address only the ego anxiety and omit the sensitivity or reactivity to the physiological experience. This section will address ways in which parents both contribute to and can moderate anxiety in their children.

It is very common to find an anxious parent (or grandparent) in the family of a child suffering from anxiety. This person may not be aware that they suffer from anxiety but through the assessment of their child it can become apparent to them they demonstrate symptoms of anxiety. In these cases, the child's symptoms appear to represent either shared temperament, or emotional learning, or both.

Psychoeducation of Parents Regarding Anxiety

The process of teaching a parent about their child's anxiety generally begins with an explanation of the two components of anxiety: worry about being rejected or about their achievement and worry about the physiological responding that accompanies worry such as "butterflies in the stomach", shakiness, sweaty hands, nausea, tightness and tension. The practitioner explains to parents that children experience these symptoms just as much as adults and may be quite frightened by them. For example, some children interpret their physiological arousal to mean exaggerated or extreme danger.

The parent needs to learn that anxiety may be of different kinds: performance or social anxiety which arises from the child's extreme reactions to external situations, and discomfort anxiety which arises from the child's disturbance about their feelings.

The therapist's explanation of anxiety needs to provide a model for the parent as to how to talk to their child about anxiety. Therefore, it needs to be kept simple and clear and the therapist should check that the parent understands what is being said. Parents are provided with simple words to use with their children, for example, they could talk with their children about "thoughts that bother them and won't go away", or "thoughts that go round and round in their heads". During this phase of psychoeducation, it is important for the therapist to elicit examples from the parents of their ability to communicate to their child about anxiety using simple language. Asking the parent to give back to you verbally what you have said is a good way to give practice to the parent in putting it into words, as well as an opportunity to check for any misunderstanding and also a chance to reinforce their new behaviors. Parents whose children demonstrate discomfort anxiety should be taught that their child is "sensation-sensitive", even perhaps extra sensitive, and therefore reacts to their feelings in an anxious way. Parents learn that children with performance or social anxiety react to new or uncertain situations and people in an anxious way. The parent can help their child to overcome the anxiety, not by urging that "there is nothing to be frightened about" but by *acknowledging and accepting* the child's reactions, both emotional and behavioural, and by teaching the child emotional self-management. The parent helps the child to dispute irrational beliefs underlying ego anxiety such as "I must not let people criticise me—better to avoid the situation". "I must always do well or I will be rejected". They can also help the child dispute irrational beliefs underlying discomfort anxiety for example "I must be able to stop feeling this way—it's horrible and dangerous".

In cases where the parent also experiences high levels of anxiety, anxiety will be observed in relation to the task of helping their child. This provides the opportunity to raise the parent's consciousness of their own thinking, feelings and reactions and to begin to understand their child in a new way, by gaining insight into their own experiences. Resistance is sometimes apparent in the parent in recognising their anxiety, so observable signs can be discussed: the parent speaking very fast, looking tense, showing over-concern about doing their new task perfectly. Sometimes one parent can be drawn in to assist the other by saying what they have noticed about the other's anxiety. Talking about the parent's reactions in the here-and-now is a useful teaching strategy. It is useful to ask the parent what strategies he or she has used in life to manage anxiety as the parent may be able to identify such methods as taking a deep breath, or reminding themselves they can manage. It is necessary to point out directly to the parents that these are examples of what their child needs to learn but does not yet know.

For young children, communication about their physiological responding is primary because it often is accompanied by withdrawal and avoidance behaviors, which are then negatively reinforced as the tension is relieved. The child who experiences discomfort anxiety, the fear about his/her anxious reactions, is a problem which needs addressing before the "danger" (rejection, poor performance) external to the child can be managed. In severe cases the child feels sabotaged inside and out, as the danger seems everywhere—within as well as in the world outside. REBT has always emphasized the importance of treating any secondary emotional problem before the primary emotion can be alleviated. So, this is the case in working with parents to help their child overcome anxiety, and fear or anxiety about their anxious feelings can be the first focus.

The communication with children, however young, should always begin with a focus on their body: where in their body do they feel the anxiety? Surprising answers are given by children: "it's my heart, it's going to burst" "my brain gets bigger—too big for my head" "it's my tummy" but they always, in my experience, have a clear answer and the knowledge of this body focus then is a crucial basis for the adult to help them communicate throughout the intervention.

Initially, what the parents need to learn to do is to teach their child to "normalize" the experience of feeling anxious. The therapist needs to help the parent put into child-friendly language that many children feel anxiety and that while such feelings are unpleasant and uncomfortable, they are not dangerous. Parents need to be coached in being able to communicate to their child the idea that there is nothing terrible about feeling anxious but that anxiety is a clue that they need to solve a problem. At this point in psychoeducation, parents are taught how to communicate to their anxious child that he or she can learn new ways to calm down when they feel anxious.

Steps for Parent to Help a Child with Anxiety Cope with Their Physiological Responding:

1. Invite child to tell someone (parent) about how they feel.
2. Listen to child.
3. Explain that it is an ordinary experience and he/she is OK.
4. Explain that others feel this way often.
5. Explain it is not terrible and will not hurt them even though it feels "bad".
6. Teach them directly some new strategies to calm down, especially relaxation, finding something funny to do and finding someone to talk to.

Steps for a Parent to Help a Child with Anxiety:

1. Explain the primary sources of anxiety in their child or adolescent; namely, worry about being laughed at/rejected and worry about not doing things perfectly or making mistakes.
2. Teach the child about the thinking-feeling-behaving connection.

3. Teach the child any relevant facts to help the child restructure their anticipation that they will be rejected or make mistakes, and that if the worst came to the worst something awful would happen if they were rejected or made mistakes (e.g., when teachers frown it does not mean they do not like you).
4. Teach them directly some new thoughts that will help them stay calm, for example "I can just try my best. It's OK to make mistakes sometimes. It's only human".
5. Together make plans to overcome the anxiety provoking situation by taking new small steps, a little at a time, gaining confidence gradually. If it is a school or kindergarten problem, bring the teacher in on the plan so that she/he will support the child's efforts at new behavior.

Case Illustration: Jenny, Sam and their twins, Lily and Georgina

This case study is one limited to client-centered consultation in which helping parents to work with their children's discomfort anxiety and sensation sensitivity moderated the children's social anxiety. Jenny and Sam were referred with their 4-year-old twins who were then diagnosed with selective mutism. The twins, Lily and Georgina, spoke normally at home but at kindergarten just stayed close to each other and did not speak to any other child or any teacher. The parents recognized that their daughters were shy by nature and had observed their withdrawal and hesitation in new social situations. Urging and encouragement by adults had not alleviated this problem.

Psychoeducation

The therapist explained to the parents that their children's temperament had combined with (unintended) learning that unpleasant feelings could be minimized if they avoided certain experiences, namely talking outside the home. The parents became aware that they did not know what their children were experiencing subjectively and were assisted to communicate with them about their feelings. As REBT predicts, the children were experiencing unpleasant physiological responses and were feeling overwhelmed and anxious about these feelings. The parents learned that establishing a problem solving framework with the children (even ones so young) can enable a change of emotional management and behavior patterns in the children.

Although neither parent demonstrated high anxiety, they were high achievers and expectations were certainly high for their children's success, educationally and socially. The main belief shared by both parents was that their child's failure to speak at kinder was a terrible and awful problem for them. They quickly overcame this thinking when they understood the nature of the problem and found there was a systematic way forward to alleviate the problem. No direct therapeutic intervention was necessary with the parents.

Client-Centered Consultation

The parents established communication with their daughters regarding their anxious feelings which were "normalized" and validated by acceptance in these discussions. They talked with their daughters about their own feelings on different occasions and told them how they managed them. They explained to the girls that there was a new plan "to help them join in at kindergarten and make more friends". The teacher was going to help with this plan too.

As functional analysis carried out during observation of the girls at kindergarten showed that they were not participating in group play activities, joining in/participation was added to the goals of the intervention, along with verbal interaction. The plan was a simple reinforcement one, with specific steps identified day by day and week by week, for example:

Say "Good Morning" to teacher at the beginning of the day, "Good-bye" at the end of the day.
Make eye contact with the teacher while giving greetings.
Pick up the paint brush and put it to the paper during painting time.

That is, behaviors were clearly identified for their children to practice and they knew that completing the behaviors on a given day would mean a gold star on their chart at home. The teacher recorded their relevant behaviors each day. At the same time, the parents would monitor the children's physiological responses before and after school and offer guidance in how to understand and manage them. They communicated positive expectations of their children but showed understanding and acceptance of their "failures" along the way. They also planned to invite the teacher to their home to bridge the two environments.

Processes of Change and Outcome

Lily and Georgina were happy with the new plan and indicated they would put it into effect. They made their first efforts at morning and afternoon greetings to their teacher and received their first gold stars and praise at home. They practised their new thinking that "It's all right to feel butterflies in my tummy. They don't mean I have to freeze and not talk" "Just because the teacher is looking straight at me doesn't mean she doesn't like me".

The kindergarten teacher's visit to their home was successful and this experience helped the girls to generalize their talking from home to kindergarten. They progressed rapidly until after a few weeks they were ahead of the plan—they had begun talking to the other children, had socialized with new children invited to their home and began to visit their school for the following year to make contact with their new teacher. Follow up at six months revealed they were in separate grades at school and were doing well.

Working With Parents to Help their Child Overcome Anger Problems

Problems with anger management generally arise in a context of twofold aetiology, similar to anxiety: there is a contribution of child temperament as well as a contribution of environmental influence (parenting style, parental emotional make-up, and family problems). When parents fail to teach their children delay of gratification and frustration tolerance skills (impulse control) and when they model strong negative emotions that they fail to self-regulate, a child born with a feisty temperament is likely to display problems of conduct and display developmentally inappropriate levels of anger. In the initial assessment of the children with anger management problems and disorders of conduct, it is important to identify which factors are operating so that the planned intervention can be appropriate and effective.

Psychoeducation of Parents About Anger

The REBT psychoeducational approach to parents serves the purpose of acquainting parents with the distinction between their own practical problem-solving skills needed to help their children behave in less impulsive, core developmentally appropriate ways and emotional problem solving where parents learn of the role of their own emotions and emotional reactions in their ability to implement an effective child management approach and in their child's learning through modelling of inappropriate ways to express emotions. Two REBT key ideas about anger for parents to learn are the role of their own beliefs regarding frustration and frustration tolerance in anger, and the relationship between their own feelings of anger and their child's unacceptable behavior.

The REBT therapist teaches that one important aspect of socialization of their children involves helping them to increase their ability to put up with frustration—from the beginning of infancy when they have no frustration tolerance (NFT), up to late adolescence when they are expected to have high frustration tolerance (HFT), to function satisfactorily in society.

Anger problems in children may or may not be accompanied by aggressive behavior such as swearing, hitting or destroying property. Sometimes children have trouble regulating their feelings of anger (due to LFT) and, recognizing this, want help in managing better. Other children are used to self-indulgent behavior and resist efforts to change. The former group of children will be willing participants in new emotional learning, and communication and joint problem solving will be the main types of intervention. Children with accompanying behavioural problems will benefit from the emotional learning but will need systematic consequences to be put in place as well for their undesirable behavior.

Parents are taught that their children's physiological reactivity is important to address in learning how to teach their child the regulation of anger. As in helping anxious children, parents help children to identify parts of their body where they feel the anger most. They can be helped to think about these perceived bodily experiences as cues to use their new strategies: these will most likely be a combination of cognitive and behavioral techniques.

Discussion of the parents' own anger will be a key part of psychoeducation. It is extremely common for children with anger problems to have a parental model for their anger outbursts. Often this is when parents are frustrated with their child's inappropriate behaviour and the parent is unaware that they are providing a poor model for the child. On the contrary, they think they are teaching the child good behavior. To clarify this I teach parents about the two simultaneous lessons a child is learning from them: *the behavior lesson* (what to do) and *the emotional lesson* (how to manage emotions, including anger). Often the parent's focus is on the behavior lesson, as they are telling the child what to do and not do. But, if they do this angrily, unfortunately the child also learns that when frustrated, the way to be is angry!

Parents are also provided with a list of irrational beliefs of children who get angry and are given practice in discussing with their children why the beliefs are unhelpful. Parents learn how to discuss, model and reinforce their children's rational beliefs that lead to better anger management.

Children's Irrational Beliefs Associated with Anger

Parents should always be fair.
Teachers should always be fair.
When they are unfair it is awful.
I should get what I want when I want it.
I can't stand waiting for things.
I have to win.
When others don't give me what I want they deserve what they get.

Steps for Parents to Help their Children with Anger Problems

1. Teach the child to name and recognize their frustration and anger.
2. Teach the child that anger varies in intensity and duration.
3. Teach the child that they have a choice in how angry they get.
4. Teach the child that it is OK to have feelings but acting to hurt others is not OK.
5. Teach them that the more intense their anger, the more likely that they will do something hurtful, and the more likely it will have bad consequences for them.

6. Teach the child that everyone feels angry sometimes and there are things we can do to overcome the anger.
7. Teach the child there are simple things (like counting to ten before responding, leaving the situation) that can help in the short term.
8. Teach the child that learning to think differently can be the best way to know how to put up with difficult people and things that happen in life and therefore to keep anger to a minimum.
9. Teach the child new rational beliefs about fairness, what "should" and "should not" happen.
10. Teach the child tolerance of other people's imperfections.
11. Teach the child that it is much easier to use their anger strategies if the anger is not too intense and therefore it is important to use them as soon as they notice the beginnings of angry feelings.

Case Illustration: Dora and Her Daughter, Susan

This case illustration goes beyond the scenarios painted in the psychoeducation section as it occurred in a deeply dysfunctional context. The child's anger was part of a wider set of problems and I have included the case as one that draws attention to the need to address the child's basic emotional security as well as the more obvious problems.

Dora brought her daughter, Susan, aged 13, to a university clinic for help. She reported that Susan was frequently angry and aggressive, would not do her homework and was sulky and unpleasant around the home. Her husband, Susan's father, had died unexpectedly as the result of a workplace accident a few months ago. Neither Dora nor Susan could speak about his death or their loss.

Attempts to help Susan in individual therapy were not successful as she was barely verbal with her therapist. Attempts at cognitive assessment using drawing techniques revealed that her angry episodes at home were triggered by her brother's bullying which was not being contained by the mother. The only way Susan knew how to communicate her distress to her mother was to come near to her and explode with anger. She would often do this on the kitchen floor just out of sight behind the kitchen table. Dora reacted very negatively to this behavior and these emotions, becoming punitive in her attitude to her daughter. This led to Susan feeling even more isolated and threatened—and more angry. She was unable to express her desire for protection and reassurance in an appropriate way as she was of low verbal ability and had poor emotional expression skills.

Consultee-Centered Consultation

The focus of intervention became Dora and her relationship with Susan. Dora learned that her "bottling up" of her feelings of normal grief and loss on the death of her husband was having a negative effect on herself and her family. She was helped to express these feelings safely. She learned that things would not go well at home if any of her children were lacking in basic emotional security and that, though this was hard to provide on her own without her husband, it was necessary for her to face this challenge if her problems were to lessen and her daughter was to improve.

She learned that Susan had very little insight into her own needs or how to get what she wanted and needed, and that she often used inappropriate means to try to get relief from her own frustrations. Angry outbursts were one such way. Also, Susan was sleeping with her mother which her mother tolerated (and perhaps relied on), a pattern which was not appropriate at her age.

She was helped to reflect on her own irrational beliefs and how these were hindering her. They included: "It's not fair that I have to manage the family alone", "I can't stand it when my daughter is angry all the time—in fact I can't stand her!", "They should all just leave me alone!" "It shouldn't be this hard to bring up a family!"

Dora needed help to challenge her irrational beliefs that were underlying her rejecting attitude to Susan. Expression of her feelings of grief and understanding that Susan also was experiencing grief helped her to begin to have empathy for her daughter. Her LFT in relation to the level of difficulty in helping Susan was a major challenge in therapy. Dora needed to learn the arbitrary nature of frustration tolerance levels. A certain level of frustration is arbitrarily selected by the individual in an implicit way so that anything beyond this is deemed "unbearable". So, if a parent believes they can "stand" complaining and mild temper tantrums but not yelling and screaming, then their threshold will be crossed and their own distress come into play. Dora needed to challenge her arbitrary threshold and think differently about her ability to deal with difficult situations.

She needed time and support to find new ways in which she could provide emotional security for her daughter, for example by setting limits on the brother's threatening behavior and giving comfort and love when Susan was distressed, at the same time teaching her appropriate ways to seek this comfort instead of through expressed anger. The issue of her family culture was addressed, with tolerance of others being an important ingredient to foster for all members' well-being.

Client-Centered Consultation

Building on her own changes, Dora implemented the following steps with Susan:

1. Communicated clearly to her that she was available to comfort and reassure her when Susan felt insecure.
2. Taught Susan awareness of her emotions, helped her to name them and communicated the acceptability of emotions, though acknowledged some are distressing.

3. Taught Susan the thoughts that lead to anger and alternative thoughts she could think in her frustrating situations.
4. Taught Susan that she could learn to feel less distressed if she learned from her mother calming thoughts to help her both in a crisis and in everyday situations.
5. Taught Susan that she herself was learning and practising new ways of managing emotions.
6. Discuss with Susan her school difficulties and what kind of help Susan would like to try for her schoolwork.
7. Support new age-appropriate activities for Susan including peer group activities.

Processes and Outcome

Over a period of months Dora managed to make some changes in her own functioning which formed the basis for her intervention with her daughter. Susan began to experience acceptance and love from her mother instead of rejection. Although she was not a verbal child she was reassured by the changes and gradually learned to let her mother know what she needed in a direct and appropriate way. The anger episodes reduced and the mother's frustration experiences also lessened, easing the stress in the family.

Working with Parents to Overcome Children's Depression

Depression in children and young people, like anxiety, may be related to both constitutional predispositions and to experience. It is extremely important for a child who is experiencing depression to be assisted by adults to overcome this mood so that it does not become a destructive force in the child's life, even to the point of being life threatening.

Children and young people form simple philosophies of life and where this includes strongly held negative beliefs about themselves and those around them, they are vulnerable to depression and other disturbances. While children more often demonstrate symptoms of action rather than thought prior to adolescence, it is nevertheless possible for younger children to experience depression and even suicidal thoughts. This mood can be expressed by children through irritability, withdrawal, silence, loss of interest in activity, decrease in pleasurable activity, sleeping and eating problems. Unless parents recognize the emotional distress accompanying these behavioral signs they may react to the child in ways that increase rather than relieve the distress. It is important therefore to assess the immediate history of parental attempts to overcome the problem(s) when they come for assistance.

Psychoeducation of Parents Regarding the Treatment of Depression in Children

Events that commonly precede depression in children include family conflict, divorce, death of a family member, loss of a friend and death of a pet. The child believes that they "must have" what they have lost and that it is terrible for life to be this way. The parent will need to learn to help their child to moderate their response to loss or disappointment and to know that they can still be happy about other things in their life.

Where severe depression is apparent in a child or adolescent, individual therapy is recommended. Parents can nevertheless play a significant adjunct role in the first stages of the child receiving help and an increasingly important role in maintaining the gains of therapy over time. Where suicidal ideation or self harm is part of the child's or young person's presenting problems, individual therapy is always recommended as well as parent involvement.

Parents often need to learn that the depressed mood of their child can be expressed in a variety of ways. The particular behaviors which they may wish their child to change need to be considered in conjunction with the emotions accompanying them. Concepts of emotional expression and emotional regulation can be taught. The need for their child to receive validation, (i.e. acceptance of their emotions), is a basic concept as the foundation for teaching or learning self-regulation.

Sometimes, the precipitating events that lead to the child's depression may not be objective "events" that can be known directly by the parents. They may be "events" that occur in the mind of the child, especially for young children. Examples of this I have experienced are fantasies of a child about the implications of the death of a loved pet, and ideas a child formed about parental conflict and the child's role in and responsibility for that.

These examples underline the central role of cognitions in children's depression and the importance of correcting faulty inferences as well as modifying irrational evaluations that according to Ellis give rise to emotional distress. As with other parent interventions, as well as depression-specific learning, parents will need to learn basic knowledge regarding emotions and the importance of validating their children's emotions.

As a part of their REBT psychoeducation, parents are provided instruction regarding the process of self-downing and how to talk to their child about this negative habit. Parents learn about global self-rating, are shown how such rating often operates in a child's world and are provided with examples of how to dispute their child's self-downing and to teach, model and reinforce self-acceptance. Thoughts such as "I'm no good", "I'll never be any good", "I'm totally ugly", "I'm stupid", "I'm a failure" are all examples of such evaluative beliefs. Parents can learn ways to talk to their child about mistake making in a way that teaches the child to accept him/herself *with* mistakes and not to demand perfection of themselves. Parents are shown ways to talk with their child about the difference between needing the approval of others and preferring positive affirmations. Additionally, in the case where a child is depressed about family break-up or being abandoned by one parent, a parent can learn about the dysfunctional nature of a depressed child's beliefs ("It's my fault. My parent doesn't love me. I'm a loser") and how the parent can help change a child's depressed pattern of thinking.

Steps for Parent to Help their Child with Depression

1. Acknowledge with the child significant changes the parent has noticed (e.g., eating, mood) and express concern about these.
2. Ask the child about his/her feelings and assist the child in naming the feelings of depression.
3. Teach the child that many people experience these unpleasant feelings but that it is possible to alleviate them (feel better).
4. Establish trust with the child to allow expression of inner thoughts that may seem weird, extreme or otherwise difficult to share.
5. Listen to the child uncritically (no "buts").
6. Teach the child that they have a choice in how depressed they get.
7. Teach the child in a simple way the connection between thoughts and feelings.
8. Ask the child about other feelings which may be present along with the depression such as anxiety and anger.
9. Help the child express their self downing and other negative thoughts.
10. Suggest new helpful thoughts to the child and encourage practice of them.
11. Remember to smile at the child when appropriate to communicate a positive mood on your part. (It is sometimes easy to "enter into" and reinforce another person's gloomy world without intending to do so).
12. Encourage age-appropriate activity for the child to counter withdrawal and disconnection.
13. Encourage positive social interaction for the child (e.g., encourage them to invite friends over).

Children's Irrational Beliefs Associated with Depression

1. When something bad happens it means I am to blame and I am no good.
2. No parents could love me.
3. If my parents are angry it means they don't love me because I am no good.
4. I should be different (a boy, a girl, more beautiful, cleverer).
5. I'll never be different.
6. There's no hope for me to be happy.
7. The world is a bad place.
8. If I have lost something or someone important to me I can never get over it.

9. I'll never.....get my parents' love.....have friends,... succeed in school.
10. No-one can help me.
11. No-one could understand how I feel.
12. I shouldn't live / have been born.

Case Illustration: Gina and Her son, Paul

Gina referred her son, Paul, aged 9 to a university clinic for depressed moods. According to his mother, he cried very easily, seemed to be "in his own world" and got into trouble at school for not attending and completing work. Paul's father had separated from his mother following a violent relationship and had left the country to return to his country of origin.

Assessment showed that Paul had an extremely vivid imagination and had not yet achieved the ability to distinguish between imagined and real occurrences. He reacted with great anxiety to his experience of imagined threats and dangers. This imaginary world was very elaborate and sustained but he had communicated it to no-one.

Consultee-Centered Consultation

Gina was helped to understand that, although her son was 9-years-old, he was still thinking like a 4 or 5-year-old in some respects and that he was also a very deeply feeling child who was not managing well the events surrounding his father's departure. Paul had irrational thoughts about his father "He comes in the night to hurt me" "I see him in the dark" "He left so I know he doesn't love me". Gina struggled to understand these matters but had an attitude of respect for the professional and an intense desire for her son to be helped. She believed she could not help him herself. She was prepared to attend sessions, in parallel to her son's individual work by another therapist and to try to implement changes.

Client-Centered Consultation

Prior to coming to the sessions she had reacted to Paul's behavior with anxiety, frustration and negativity. She fussed about his crying and distress which she perceived as dependency and which she tried to inhibit by scolding. Her homework was to firmly communicate to her son her expectations of his behavior. She was also to employ active listening when her son appeared upset "tuning in" to his feelings. At these times, she was to ask him about his bad feelings and listen if he wished to share them. She was to avoid any communications that modelled irrational thinking (e.g., any sentences such as "You are a...." or I am a....)"

As the therapist was working with Paul to empower him in the face of his depression-creating thoughts and ideas Gina was encouraged to support his self-efficacy at home and school. If small frustrations (such as falling over or missing out on something) were experienced by Paul, she would not rush to his aid and express anxiety for him but would watch surreptitiously from afar to see if he could cope by himself in the first instance. A crucial part of the intervention was her learning to overcome her anxieties, especially in relation to her parenting.

Process and Outcome

Several months of individual weekly work was provided for Paul. His mother attended weekly for the first six weeks and then fortnightly. Her first achievement was to understand that her anxiety was getting in the way of effective parenting. Next, she tried new ways of communication with Paul based on her new understanding of his development and thinking. She had strong relationships with friends who had children and discussed her new ideas with them, so that a support group emerged and increased opportunity for Paul to develop new interests and social skills with peers.

Paul's therapist helped him to make reality checks in his thinking, by seeing how his thinking matched with hers and, in his homework, asking his mother whether she agreed with his beliefs. His need to express fantasies of exaggerated control and power lessened as his reality testing improved. He understood himself and his world in a new way, enabling him to enjoy the everyday experiences in his life.

Conclusion

REBT provides a useful framework for working with parents to help their children and it also allows integration of other techniques that may be appropriate to particular families (Ellis, 2002). This chapter has shown that developmental factors including the child's degree of maturity in relation to goals of parenting across different ages can be incorporated sensitively into treatment plans. The importance of parents understanding the child's emotions and keeping a focus on a child's underlying need for emotional security is emphasized throughout.

TABLE 6. Beliefs of parents and their emotional consequences (Bernard, 2004a) (Location in chapter 6 TBD).

Beliefs that Underlie General Parent Emotional Upset

1. My child can upset me.
2. I have little ability to control my feelings and unhappiness.
3. One has to get upset when things go wrong.
4. My children cause all my unhappiness. They must change first before I can feel better.

Rational Alternatives

1. My emotional stress is self-created.
2. I decide how upset I am about my child.

(Continued)

TABLE 6. Beliefs of parents and their emotional consequences (Bernard, 2004a) (Location in chapter 6 TBD). *(Cont'd)*

3. Getting too upset makes matters worse.
4. Before my child will change, I will have to make some changes.

Beliefs which Underlie Parental Anxiety

1. I must be a perfect parent. If I am not always calm, competent and correct in handling my children, they will turn out badly.
2. I must see to it that my child is never uncomfortable, hurt or in any danger.
3. It would be awful if my children didn't love me all the time.
4. It's awful if others disapprove of the way I parent.
5. If I'm not consistently anxious and fearful about the welfare of my children, I'm a bad parent.

Rational Alternatives

1. I will try my best in caring for my child but I know I cannot be perfect.
2. It is not the end of world when my child is angry with me.
3. While it is preferable to try my best as a parent, there is no law of the universe that says I must be.
4. There is no such thing as a perfect parent.
5. When something bad happens to my child, it is rarely awful and terrible.

Beliefs that Underlie Parental Anger

1. Children should always and unequivocally do well (e.g., be motivated, achieve) and behave correctly (e.g., be kind, considerate, interested).
2. It is *horrible*, *terrible* and *awful* when children do not do well, misbehave or question or disobey their parents.
3. My child must always behave the way I demand.
4. My child must do what I say.
5. A child and his/her behavior are the same and thus children who act badly or err are bad.
6. My child must be fair to me at all times.
7. My child shouldn't be so difficult to help.

Rational Alternatives

1. Anger can be compared to a child having a temper tantrum.
2. When parents get angry, it brings them down to the level of a 4-year-old.
3. Do not discipline with anger because anger puts your children down and, as a consequence, your child may develop a spiteful reaction.
4. Getting angry will not help parents or their children; anger is only temporary at best.
5. No law of the universe says that what parents wish to happen, must happen; children are children, ignorant, mischievous.
6. Anger frequently generates more anger and resentment in others.
7. Never hate the child, only disapprove of his/her actions.

Beliefs that Underlie Parental Low Frustration Tolerance

1. Parenting shouldn't be so hard.
2. I must have fun in my life and I cannot stand having frustrations.
3. It is far easier to give in to my child's demands and whines.
4. I cannot stand the stress of following through on everything I say I am going to do for my child.
5. Things should always go my way and people should do my bidding.
6. I shouldn't have to put up with frustration.

TABLE 6. *(Cont'd)*

Rational Alternatives

1. It is easier to face a task than to avoid it.
2. Short-term tolerance of frustration may well lead to long-term gains.
3. Parenting is often very hard.
4. In order to parent successfully, I sometimes have to do things I do not feel like doing.
5. I can tolerate high amounts of frustration associated with my child and his/her behavior.

Beliefs that Underlie Parental Depression

1. When I don't perform as I think a good parent should (e.g., worry all the time, solve all my child's problems), I am a complete failure as a person.
2. If my child misbehaves frequently, it is awful and I am a failure as a parent.
3. If my children think I'm a poor parent, I'm worthless.
4. My worth as a person depends on the performance of my child.
5. My self-worth as a person is tied up to how I do as a parent, so I had better not make mistakes.
6. I am worthless because my child has so many problems.
7. I am a terrible parent for being so annoyed with my child who cannot completely help his/her problems.

Rational Alternatives

1. Never blame yourself as a person or others for anything.
2. Parents make themselves miserable, not their children.
3. Children's hardships are never as bad as parents make them out to be; parents shouldn't blow them out of proportion.
4. A person's performance as a parent does not determine his/her self-worth.
5. The performance of a child does not determine the value of a parent as a person.

Beliefs that Underlie Parental Guilt

1. Past or present adversity is so unpleasant and awful that my child cannot be expected to live normally; restitution for this adversity needs to follow.
2. It is awful for my child to suffer and I *must* prevent it at all costs.
3. I am the sole cause of my child's problems.
4. If I make a mistake, it will always affect my child.
5. I could have and should have done something to prevent my child's disability.
6. I am totally responsible for virtually everything that happens to my child.
7. My child is being punished for my own personal inadequacy.
8. I *must* always do right by my child.

Rational Alternatives

1. Parents are not the sole cause of their child's problems.
2. Parents can never be so omnipotent to prevent bad things from happening.
3. Children can overcome many of their adversities.
4. Children can tolerate frustration.
5. If parents should have known better, they would have done better.
6. While its preferable to be a perfect parent, there is no law of the universe that says you must be. Parents are fallible and make mistakes in raising children. They do not deserve to be condemned and punished for their fallibilities.

References

Bernard, M.E., and DiGiuseppe, R. (eds.) (1994). *Rational-emotive consultation in applied settings*. Hillsdale, New Jersey: Lawrence Erlbaum.

Bernard, M.E., and Joyce, M.R., (1984). *Rational Emotive Therapy with children and adolescents: Theory, treatment strategies, preventive methods*. New York: Wiley and Sons.

Borcherdt, B. (1996). *Making families work and what to do when they don't. Thirty guides for imperfect parents of imperfect children*. New York: The Haworth Press.

Bowlby, J. (1988). *A secure base: Parent-child attachment and healthy human development*. New York: Basic Books.

Cox, B.T., Borger, S.C., Taylor, S., Fuentes, K., and Ross, L.M. (1999). Anxiety sensitivity and the five factor model of personality. *Behavior Research and Therapy, 37,* 633–641.

David, D., Montgomery, G.H., Macavei, B., Bovbjerg, D.H. (2005). An empirical investigation of Albert Ellis's binary model of distress. *Journal of Clinical Psychology, 61*(4), 499–516.

Dukes, A., Mellor, D., Flory, V., Moore, K. (2003). A preliminary investigation of the relationship between parental empathy and social anxiety and children's social anxiety. *Proceedings of the 3*rd *Australasian Psychology of Relationships Conference,* 33–39.

Eisenberg, N., Zhou, Q., Losoya, S.H., Fabes, R.A., Shepard, S.A., Murphy, B.C., Reiser, M., Guthrie, I.K., and Cumberland, A. (2002). The relationships of parenting, effortful control, and ego control to children's emotional expressivity. *Child Development, 74*(3), 875–95.

Ellis, A. (2002). *Integrating other psychotherapies with REBT*. New York: Albert Ellis Institute Newsletter.

Ellis, A. (2003). A new cognitive-behavioral construct Part II. *Journal of Rational-Emotive and Cognitive Behavior Therapy. 21*(3–4), 193–202.

Ellis, A., Wolfe, J. H., and Moseley, S. (1966). *How to raise an emotionally healthy, happy child.* New York: Crown; and Hollywood: Wilshire Books.

Flett, G.L., Greene, A., and Hewitt, P.L. (2004). Dimensions of perfectionism and anxiety sensitivity. *Journal of Rational-Emotive and Cognitive Behavior Therapy, 22*(1), 39–57.

Flory, V. (2004). A novel intervention for severe childhood depression and anxiety. *Clinical Child Psychology and Psychiatry, 9*(1), 9–23.

Flory, V. (2005). *Your child's emotional needs. What they are and how to meet them.* Sydney: Finch Publishing.

Gottman, J. and DeClaire, J. (1997). *The heart of parenting. How to raise an emotionally intelligent child.* London: Bloomsbury.

Gottman, J., Katz, L., and Hooven, C. (1996). *Meta-emotion: How families communicate emotionally, links to child peer relations and other developmental outcomes.* Mahwah, N.J.: Lawrence Erlbaum.

Hauck, P. (1967). *The rational management of children.* New York: Libra Publishers.

Hauck, P. (1983) Working with parents. In A. Ellis and M.E. Bernard (eds.), *Rational-Emotive approaches to the problems of childhood.* New York: Plenum Press, pp. 333–366.

Joyce, M.R. (1994). Rational-emotive parent consultation. In M.E. Bernard and R. DiGiuseppe (eds.), *Rational-emotive consultation in applied settings.* Hillsdale, New Jersey: Lawrence Erlbaum.

Joyce, M.R. (1990). Rational-emotive parent consultation. *School Psychology Review, 19*(3), 304–314.

Kegan, R. (1982). *The evolving self. Problem and process in human development.* Cambridge, Mass.: Harvard University Press.

Kegan, R. (1995). *In over our heads. The mental demands of modern life*. Cambridge, Mass: Harvard University Press.

Meyers, J, Parsons, R.D. and Martin, R. (1979). *Mental health consultation in the schools*. San Francisco: Jossey Bass.

Patterson, G.R. and Dishion, T.J. (1985). Contributions of families and peers to delinquency. *Criminology, 23*, 63–79.

Serbin, L., and Karp, J. (2003). Intergenerational studies of parenting and the transfer of risk from parent to child. *Current Directions in Psychological Science, 12*(4), 138–142.

Woulff, N. (1983). Involving the family in the treatment of the child. A model for Rational-Emotive therapists. In A. Ellis and M.E. Bernard (eds.) *Rational-Emotive approaches to the problems of childhood.* New York: Plenum Press, pp. 367–385.

7

Depression in Children and Adolescents: REBT Approaches to Assessment and Treatment

ANN VERNON

University of Northern Iowa, Cedar Falls, IA 50614

It comes out of the blue, this insidious feeling that envelops me, scares me, and changes me from an outgoing, upbeat teenager to a sullen, withdrawn stranger whose fleeting thoughts of suicide as a way to deal with the hopelessness accompany apathy and confusion. Why me? Why do I have to struggle like this? It's so hard, but I try my best to hide the pain because I'm ashamed...and afraid that people will think I'm crazy. Am I? I don't know; I just understand what's going on with me.

These words describe how many depressed young clients feel as they struggle with depression, which has become increasingly prevalent with this population, especially among adolescents (Koplewicz, 2002; Lambert and Davis, 2002; Stark et al., 2000). Recent statistics indicate that anywhere from 10 to 15% of the child and adolescent populations have some signs of depression (Koplewicz, 2002). According to Koplewicz, it is still relatively rare among children and preteens, but Stark and his colleagues noted that the age of onset is earlier than previously thought, with prevalence progressively increasing until early adolescence, when the rate rapidly escalates and continues through late adolescence. Reinecke et al. (1998) stressed that depression is a serious condition that necessitates timely intervention, and Evans et al (2002) posited that "Depression may be one of the most overlooked and under-treated psychological disorders of adolescence" (p. 211).

Although currently there is general agreement that childhood depression exits, until the late 1960s, there was controversy regarding its existence prior to late adolescence or early adulthood (Evans et al., 2002; Parry-Jones, 2001; Shaffer and Waslick, 2002). In fact, Merrell (2001) pointed out that there was "widespread denial that certain types of internalizing disorders, such as depression, could even exist in children" (p. 1). A common belief was that children and adolescents were basically immune from depression because after all, childhood is a happy, carefree time, so what is there to be depressed about? And everyone knows that adolescents are moody, but isn't that just part of growing up? These beliefs reflect several major misconceptions: one, that depression is caused by something, so if there are no disturbing events in children's lives they won't be depressed; two, that disturbing events themselves cause depression; and three, that adolescent depression is just normal moodiness. In responding to the first two misconceptions, it is true that situations can be trigger events for depression, but there are also biological, (Thase and Howland, 1995), neurochemical (Ingram and Malcarne, 1995; Koplewicz, 2002), and genetic factors (Ingram and Malcarne). In addition, there are cognitive components to depression that cannot be ignored (Engel and DeRubeis, 1993; Stark et al., 2000). In fact, "cognitive theory suggests that negative thinking plays a pivotal role in the development and/or maintenance of depression" (Rush and Nowels, 1994, p. 3). With regard to the third misconception, there is a significant difference between "normal" adolescent moodiness and depression, which is more severe, atypical, and must be taken seriously (Koplewicz, 2002). It is the most common mental illness among teenagers and is more than "just teenagers with 'growing pains' or in a moody stage" (Evans et al., 2002, p. 211).

The purpose of this chapter is to describe what depression is and who is most vulnerable, how depression is manifested in children and adolescents, a rational-emotive behavioral perspective regarding the etiology and assessment of depression, and developmentally appropriate interventions. The chapter concludes with a case study illustrating the assessment and intervention process with a depressed adolescent.

What is Depression and Who is Most Vulnerable?

Children and adolescents experiencing depression exhibit various symptoms, including the following: affective symptoms (sad or depressed mood, also expressed as irritability in children and adolescents); negative cognitive styles and attributions (pessimism, overgeneralization, and prediction of negative outcomes); anhedonia (decreased interest and pleasure in usual activities), which may result in apathy and social withdrawal; loss of attention and concentration, as well as difficulty making decisions; problems with eating or sleeping, which could include significant weight loss or gain and insomnia or hypersomnia; somantic complaints (unfounded headaches, stomachaches, muscle aches); behavioral problems such as acting out or aggressive behavior; restlessness, psychomotor agitation, listlessness or lethargy; diminished self-esteem or feelings of worthlessness or guilt; outbursts of shouting, increased anger and irritability; tearfulness; hopelessness and helplessness; and suicide ideation, recurrent thoughts or preoccupation with death, or suicide attempts (American Psychiatric Association, 2000; Evans et al., 2002; Friedberg and McClure, 2002; Merrell, 2001; Koplewicz, 2002; Wilkes et al., 1994).

It is important to note that a hallmark characteristic for this population is loss of interest in usual activities and that depression in children and youth may be differentiated from adult depression by irritability, physical complaints, and lack of achieving expected weight gains (Merrell, 2001). Evans et al. (2002) pointed out that as compared with adults, adolescents exhibit more interpersonal difficulties, are more prone to demonstrate suicide ideation, and may exhibit peer problems, substance abuse, and nervousness rather than depressed mood. Common co-occurring problems include academic underachievement, school attendance problems, and school failure, which can be a consequence of depression or precede the onset of it (King and Bernstein, 2001).

Types of Depression

Depression is a broad term at includes four types of disorders. The first is major depressive disorder, which is a serious form of depression that lasts 7–9 months in adolescents (Koplewicz, 2002). It is similar to adult depression regarding the presence of major symptoms such as sadness or irritable mood, sleep and appetite disturbance, decreased concentration, loss of pleasure in activities, and repetitive thoughts of death or suicide attempts (Curry and Reinecke, 2003). However, according to Koplewicz, adolescents have an atypical form of this disorder because they are overly sensitive to their environment and respond in opposite ways, such as eating and sleeping too much.

Dysthymic disorder is a chronic, low-level form of depression that in adolescents, usually lasts four years (Koplewicz, 2002). Clients with dysthymia are usually melancholy, have little energy, experience few positive feelings and have a bleak outlook on life. They have trouble concentrating and experience problems with sleep and appetite. Stark et al. (2000) noted that dysthymia "may be more insidious than major depression relative to its long-term impact on the psychosocial adjustment of youth, and it appears to be more resistant to treatment" (p. 174).

Bipolar disorder, characterized by unusual mood and energy shifts, is another type of depression, but there is not a clear consensus on how prevalent it is with this population (Koplewicz, 2002). However, Koplewicz reported that 20–40 % of adolescents with major depression develop bipolar disorder within five years.

Reactive depression is the most common and least serious mood disorder in children and adolescents, and is brought on by difficulty adjusting to something serious, such as death of a parent, or by something far less significant, such as being rejected by a friend (Koplewicz, 2002). This form of depression is the most amenable to prevention and treatment through cognitive behavioral techniques which teach children and adolescents how to identify and dispute their distorted thinking patterns that perpetuate their depression about events they consider disturbing.

Who Is Most Vulnerable?

Several authors (Friedberg and McClure, 2002; Merrell, 2001; Shaffer and Waslick, 2002; Stark et al., 2000) reported that prior to puberty, the prevalence rate for depression is similar in girls and boys, but between ages 12 and 15, and on into adulthood, about twice as many girls as boys experience depressive symptoms. According to Koplewicz (2002), there are several explanations for this. First, females are more social, place greater value on relationships, and are therefore more vulnerable when things go wrong in social relationships. Furthermore, girls tend to view themselves more negatively than boys, and this predicts a higher risk for depression. They also are more likely than boys to blame themselves when things go wrong, which increases their vulnerability to depression. Biological factors also play a role. Before puberty, the rate of depression among boys and girls is about the same, but the female sex hormones that kick in at puberty may have a special effect on the mood regulators in the brain (Waslick et al., 2002). In fact, Koplewicz reported on research indicating that rising levels of estrogens and testosterone were significantly associated with increased rates of depression in females.

Other factors that contribute to increased vulnerability to depression include cultural and gender biases in early adolescence. According to Koplewicz (2002), males generally have more independence than females, which impacts their self-image and sense of competence. Sexual abuse is also a factor. Since girls are more likely to be victims at this age, they have more fear, helplessness, and social stigma that can contribute to depression.

Genetics must also be considered (Ingram and Malcarne, 1995; Klein et al., 2001; Shaffer and Waslick, 2002). Koplewicz (2002) reported that children of depressed parents are three times more likely to become depressed as compared with children who do not have a family history of depression. However, Koplewicz warned that because adolescent depression is so common, most teenagers who have it do not have an immediate relative who is depressed. In addition to genetics, other family influences such as strained family relationships, extensive conflict, and poor conflict resolution and communication skills increase the risk of depression in children and adolescents, according to Merrell (2001).

Anxiety is also a good predictor of vulnerability for depression. Koplewicz (2002) reported on a study that showed that among children with anxiety disorders, 30% developed depression later, and that half of all teens who become depressed also have anxiety disorders.

The REBT/CBT Perspective on the Etiology of Depression

REBT and CBT practitioners acknowledge the biological, neurochemical, and genetic predisposition to depression, but maintain that distorted, irrational thinking plays a pivotal role in the development, progression, and alleviation of depression (DiGiuseppe et al., 2002; Reinecke, 2002; Stark et al., 2000; Walen et al., 1992). Merrell (2001) stated that REBT is "based on the assumption that many emotional problems such as depression and anxiety are caused by irrational thinking and mistaken assumptions, which in turn lead to low self-esteem, unnecessary guilt and shame, psychological stress, and maladaptive problem solving" (p. 103). DiGiuseppe et al. (2002) postulated that "negative thoughts about oneself, one's environment, and one's future result in feelings of sadness and disappointment. However, . . . only when absolutistic demands that bad traits, an unpleasant environment, and a negative future must not exist will clinical depression ensue" (p. 223). Bernard (1998), as well as McDermut et al. (1997), noted a relationship between the endorsement of irrational beliefs and severity of depression.

A basic premise of cognitive models is that depressive symptoms can be moderated by changing the cognitions that in depressed clients are marked by distortions in attributions, self-evaluations, and information processing such as catastrophizing, predicting negative outcomes, and selectively attending to the negative as opposed to positive aspects of events (Evans et al., 2002). If children are successful in changing their distorted thinking, they will experience behavioral and emotional improvement (Reinecke, 2002).

According to this theory, depression is related to a belief about one's personal inadequacy, how awful and hopeless things are, and how terrible it is not to have what one "needs" (Walen et al., 1992). Depressed clients have a negative self-perception, believing that they are defective, unworthy, and inadequate, and attribute unpleasant experiences to their own defects. Not only do they interpret events negatively, but they also have a bleak view of the future (Evans et al., 2002; Wilkes et al., 1994). According to DiGiuseppe et al. (2002), depression impedes clients from achieving long-term goals.

Seligman (1995) cautioned that depression is at epidemic proportions among children and adolescents, citing pessimistic thinking as a major contributor to this problem. He identified the following three cognitive errors associated with depression: permanence, pervasiveness, and personalization. He explained that children and adolescents who are most at risk for depression believe that the causes of bad events that happen to them are *permanent* as opposed to temporary. Therefore, they are more likely to think about their failures, rejections, or challenges as always this way, or *never* getting better. Depressed children also incorrectly assume that the cause of something negative is generalizable across all situations, or *pervasive,* as opposed to situationally specific. For example, if two students are in a contest and work hard, but neither is selected as the winner, the pervasive thinker would consider him or herself a total loser who never does anything right. On the other hand, the non-pervasive thinker would understand that although he or she did not win the contest, it has nothing to do with being a failure or never doing anything right again. *Personalizing* refers to the idea that when bad things happen, children must blame themselves or others. When this occurs, they feel depressed, ashamed, and guilty, in contrast to children who realistically evaluate each situation and do not internalize blame consistently because they are able to separate themselves from their performance.

Merrell (2001) also agreed that the way in which children think has a strong influence in the development of depression. He identified three models: attributions children make about their world, cognitive distortions, and the self-control model. According to Merrell, if children believe that they are helpless to influence or change events in their life, they may become depressed. Since they feel as if they have no power to make any changes, they see no use in trying. Second, children who have a negative view of themselves, the world, and the future and interpret their experiences in dysfunctional ways tend to become depressed. Third, the self-control model relates to the idea that depressed children have a dysfunctional way of monitoring events in their lives. They pay more attention to immediate as opposed to future consequences of behavior, they evaluate themselves unrealistically, they pay more attention to negative events than to positive events, and they criticize rather than reward themselves. All of these thinking patterns, according to Merrell, contribute to a young person's susceptibility to depression.

Cognitions of Young Depressed Clients

Developmentally, young clients are more predisposed to irrational thinking because formal abstract thinking does not begin to develop until early adolescence, and this process is very gradual (Kaplan, 2000; Vernon, 2004). As a result of their distorted, illogical thinking, they may experience a number of significantly serious consequences. For one, children's failure to distinguish between facts and assumptions can result in multiple errors in judgment. Furthermore, children's sense of time is immediate (Vernon and Clemente, 2005), and when they feel depressed and hopeless, it is not uncommon for them to assume that they will be this way forever. It is this type of thinking that results in a variety of self-defeating behaviors such as self-mutilation, substance abuse, eating disorders, and suicide as a way to end their pain (Vernon, 2002). Kendall (1993) also noted that because their self-perceptions and self-evaluations reflect these distortions they also have deficiencies in problem solving which can affect all aspects of their lives.

According to Evans and Murphy (1997), depressed adolescents evaluate themselves more negatively, set more rigid standards for their performance, and are more likely to reinforce themselves negatively as compared to non-depressed peers. Depressed young people are also more likely to interpret negative events as their fault and positive events as something over which they have no control (Wilde, 1996).

Hauck (2003) identified three causes of depression: self-blame (constantly cutting yourself down, thinking you are the worst, and blaming yourself for everything), self-pity (feeling sorry for yourself when you are not treated fairly), and other-pity (feeling sorry for others when they have troubles). According to DiGiuseppe et al. (2002), clinical depression results when individuals have one or more of the following beliefs: a negative view of self (believing that they must not have negative attributes and because they do, they are inadequate), a negative view of their environment (thinking that it must be better and it is horrible because it is not), a bleak view of the future (believing it should be better and they cannot stand it if it is not), the prediction that negative things will happen to them and that they can do little to improve them (thinking that they should be able to improve things and believing they are incompetent because they can not), a belief that they must do better and receive approval from significant others (and if they do not, they deserve self-punishment), and the belief that they should be treated better in life and it is horrible when this doesn't happen.

Wilde (1996) also enumerated several irrational beliefs that contribute to depression in children and adolescents:

I'm no good and will never amount to anything.
No matter what I do, I will never succeed.
Nobody could love me because I am worthless.
I can't do anything right.
I deserve the rotten treatment I get.
What's the point of going on? I'll never get over this.
I can't change the horrible things that have happened to me, so I'm doomed forever.
Life sucks now and always will.

Cognitive models of depression focus on changing distorted, negative thinking patterns in order to achieve emotional and behavioral change. In applying REBT to the treatment of depression, the first step is identifying the signs and symptoms of depression as well as the client's irrational beliefs.

Assessment

Diagnosing depression is not as clear-cut as it is for other disorders, especially for children and adolescents. Unlike depressed adults who may be more consistently depressed and feel sad, depression in adolescents in particular is unstable. According to Koplewicz (2002), teenagers often have the ability to "snap out of it, even if it's just for a few hours" (p. 17). Furthermore, depressed adults usually lose their appetites and sex drive and have trouble sleeping, but adolescents sleep and eat more and still have interest in sex (Koplewicz, 2002). It is also important to note that young clients are more likely to be angry, irritable, or to act out more, in part because they have difficulty verbalizing emotions. Unfortunately, this may lead to a misdiagnosis of conduct problems as opposed to depression.

When assessing depression in children, it is usually necessary to involve the parents since young clients may have limited cognitive and verbal skills (Merrell, 2001). It is also advisable to obtain parental input with adolescents, in addition to their self-report. According to Merrell (2001), self-report instruments are now considered the preferred method for assessing internalizing disorders, although the cognitive maturity of the child is an important consideration to take into account. Their verbal skills and emotional development will have an impact on whether or not they can express their symptoms and concerns or understand the emotional vocabulary or concepts.

The first step in assessment involves identifying the frequency, intensity, and duration of the symptoms. Practitioners can use a standardized self-report scale such as the *Reynolds Child Depression Scale* or the *Reynolds Adolescent Scale* (cited in Merrell, 2001), the *Children's Depression Inventory* (Kovacs, 1981, as cited in Stark et al., 2000), or for a less formal assessment, they can develop a checklist based on the symptoms outlined in the *DSM IV* or the characteristics identified previously in this chapter. Interviews such as the *Schedule for Affective Disorders and Schizophrenia for School-Age Children—K-SADS* (Orvaschel and Puig-Antich, 1987, as cited in Stark et al., 2000) and the *Child Behavior Checklist*, which is a parent report measure (Achenbach and Ekdlbrock, 1983, as cited in Stark et al., 2000) are also useful.

Other cognitive techniques that may prove useful in assessing the intensity and frequency of the depression include the following:

1. *Mood Chart* (Vernon, 2002, p. 133). Young clients are given a chart listing the days of the week across the top and times of the day down the side. They are asked to rate each time period numerically—1 being very depressed or sad and 5 being happy, not depressed. This measure helps the practitioner as well as the client understand more about the frequency and intensity of the depressed feelings.
2. *Emotional Pie* (Merrell, 2001, pp. 86–87). This is a pictorial way of helping clients evaluate their moods. The assessment is like a pie chart graph, and the child is asked to indicate for a specific period of time (day or week) how his or her mood states were divided, like pieces of a pie with different sizes. The child divides the pie and can either color the feelings, such as blue for sad, yellow for happy, or use labels, such as H = Happy, S = Sad, W = Worried, and so forth.

In REBT, the presumption is that how one thinks affects how one feels, so a critical aspect of the assessment process is the cognitive component. One paper and pencil measure that assesses cognitive variables is the *Automatic Thoughts Questionnaire for* Children (ATQ-C; Stark, et al, 1993, as cited in Stark et al., 2000). This scale consists of 30 self-statements that the child rates according to how frequently each thought occurs. The *Cognitive Triad Inventory for Children* (CTI-C) (Kaslow et al., 1992, as cited in Stark et al., 2000) assesses the child's sense of self, the world, and the future. The Child and Adolescent Scale of Irrationality (Bernard and Cronan, 1999) contains a distinct sub-scale assessing self-downing tendencies. Other cognitive assessment strategies for identifying distorted thinking include the following:

1. *The Down Arrow Technique* (Merrell, 2001, p. 90). This technique is adapted from Burns' vertical arrow technique and is more suitable for older children and adolescents than for younger children because the assessment technique requires that clients have more abstract thinking skills. The intent is to identify underlying beliefs that contribute to the depressed mood. The practitioner will ask questions such as "So what?" "Why" and "What does that mean?" to try and help the client identify core irrational beliefs that lead to depression. An adaptation of this technique could be to draw a series of arrows on a sheet of paper, and as the client describes an upsetting event that he or she thinks "makes him or her depressed," ask the probing questions and beside each arrow, write the client's responses that reflect their distorted beliefs.
2. *Identifying Cognitive Distortions or Thinking Errors* (Merrell, 2001, p. 92). This technique would also be more appropriate with older children or adolescents who are more cognitively mature. For this assessment, you would need examples of cognitive distortions such as the following:

Binocular vision: looking at things so that they seem bigger or smaller than they really are.
Black and white thinking: looking at things as extreme opposites: things are either all good or all bad, for example.
Dark glasses: Looking at everything from a negative point of view; only focusing on the bad.
Fortune telling: Making predictions about what will happen in the future without having facts to support it.
Making it personal: Blaming yourself for things that happen when you can not control it or are not responsible for it.
Overgeneralizing: Drawing a conclusion based on a single event; assuming that you will always fail a test just because you failed one, for example.
Labeling: Putting a simple label on something that is more complicated.
Discounting the positive: Refusing to accept compliments, ignoring positive aspects of a situation.
Beating up on yourself: Insisting that things have to be done in a certain way and having unreasonable standards for yourself or others.

Providing the client with a handout of these distortions can be an effective way to help the client identify the cognitive distortions that contribute to his or her depression.

A thorough assessment includes emotions, cognitions, and behaviors. This is particularly important with depression because of the correlation between depression and suicide. As de Wilde et al. (2001) stated, "Discussing the topic of suicidal behaviour without discussing the context of depression is probably as precarious as is discussing depression without the possible implication of suidicality" (p. 267). Although the majority of depressed adolescents do not attempt or commit suicide, which is a leading cause of death among older adolescents, there is an increased risk (Evans et al., 2002). There is also a relationship between depression and self-mutilation (Conterio and Lader, 1998) and other self-defeating behaviors such as substance abuse (Evans et al., 2002) and eating disorders (Merrell, 2001), so these must be assessed as well. It is very common for depressed adolescents to journal or write poetry when they are depressed, so if they are willing to share, their writings often provide insight into what they do or feel like doing when they are depressed. Other suggestions for assessing the behavioral component include:

1. *S-T-E-B* (Vernon, unpublished; adapted from Knaus, 1974). This technique involves giving the client a sheet of paper with S-T-E-B written across the top in four columns. S stands for a situation, or what the client perceived as upsetting or depressing; T stands for thoughts—their beliefs about the situation; E stands for emotions such as depression or other feelings; and B stands for behaviors—what did the client do when he or she had these emotions and thoughts. This technique generally elicits good information that helps both the client and the practitioner identify the behaviors, as well as thoughts and feelings.
2. *Checklist*. Because it is often difficult or embarrassing for young depressed clients to identify what they do when they feel depressed, a checklist such as the following can be developed (and adapted or expanded depending on the age of the client):

When I Feel Depressed or Very Sad, I:

a. Sleep a lot	Yes_____No_____Sometimes_____
b. Isolate myself/withdraw from others	Yes_____No_____Sometimes_____
c. Drink alcohol or use drugs	Yes_____No_____Sometimes_____
d. Hurt myself (cuts, burns)	Yes_____No_____Sometimes_____
e. Don't eat or eat too much	Yes_____No_____Sometimes_____
f. Cry a lot	Yes_____No_____Sometimes_____
g. Talk to friends	Yes_____No_____Sometimes_____
h. Journal, write, or play music	Yes_____No_____Sometimes_____
i. Try to kill myself	Yes_____No_____Sometimes_____
j. Other	_________________________

Assessing depression is an ongoing process, and multiple approaches should be used. Having clients monitor their affective state on a weekly basis with the Mood Chart or Emotional Pie is recommended.

Treatment

Treatment of depression in young clients primarily involves the child or adolescent, but it is also important to include the parents, family, and school personnel to help them understand the nature of the depression and how it is manifested in young clients. In addition, these significant adults need to know the basic principles of REBT so they can help the child develop new strategies for managing their depressed feelings, challenging their distorted thinking, and changing self-defeating behaviors. At times, environmental changes need to occur, which also necessitates others' involvement (Stark et al., 2000).

Given the prevalence and seriousness of depression in children and adolescents, Evans et al. (2002) recommended cognitive behavioral therapy as a rapid and effective treatment. Numerous studies (Clarke et al., 1999; Kahn et al., 1990; Lerner and Clum, 1990; Wood et al., 1996) have found cognitive approaches to be effective in treating depression among adolescents, although the research on younger children is lacking. While Rush and Nowels (1994) acknowledged the success of cognitive methods with the adolescent population, they cautioned that there are differences between the adult and child-adolescent population, and that it is essential to adapt techniques to take into account developmental issues relevant to teenagers. Vernon (2002) agreed, stressing that it is also critical to consider how the level of development impacts a young client's ability to express feelings, think logically, and develop effective coping strategies. Therefore, the degree to which they have developed formal operational thinking must be taken into account in the selection and application of assessment techniques as well as interventions.

Prior to identifying specific interventions that address the cognitive, emotive, and behavioral aspects of depression, it is important to briefly address the issue of medication and treatment.

Medication or Therapy?

The question of medication or therapy, or a combination of the two, has been a source of concern for a long time (Wagner, 2004). Macaskill and Macaskill (1996) explored the effectiveness of treating unipolar depressed adults using medication with and without REBT. The results indicated that the combined treatment was significantly more effective than medication alone. Wagner (2004) reported similar findings with adolescents with moderate to severe depression, citing a recent landmark study by the Treatment for Adolescents With Depression Study Team (TADS). Results of this study indicated that the combination of medication (Prozac) and a 12-week CBT treatment approach that included psychoeducation about depression and its causes, goal setting, mood monitoring, increasing pleasant activities, social problem solving, and cognitive restructuring was significantly superior (71%) to medication alone (60.6%) or to CBT alone (43.2%). Wagner (2004) maintained that this study provides important clinical information and stressed the need for a similar study with children in order to determine the efficacy of medication.

Although there have been major concerns raised by the media about the use of medication for treatment of depression in adolescents, the results of this study seem to point to the fact that a combination of medication and therapy promised the best results. Koplewicz (2002) noted that there is evidence that the SSRIs (Selective Serotonin Reuptake Inhibitor) are effective with teenagers and described that the mood regulation system is out of balance for depressed adolescents, so the SSRI triggers a series of neurochemical events that eventually put the system back in balance. Koplewicz stressed that "medication can have remarkable results in bringing a young person out of a major depressive episode" (p. 278), but also emphasized the importance of therapy for a comprehensive treatment approach.

Therapeutic Interventions

Helping young clients understand what depression is and where it comes from is a first step in treating depression. Next, it is important to teach them how to dispute irrational beliefs associated with depression. Oftentimes depressed youth think they will never get better, so asking the client to provide evidence that they will never get better is a helpful dispute: "where's the proof you will always be depressed? Do you know others who have been depressed and never got better? How does it help you to think that you will never be undepressed . . . doesn't this just make you feel more hopeless" are examples of disputing questions. Depressed adolescents often think that they are the only ones who are depressed and that because they are, they are crazy. Disputes such as "where did you get the idea that you are the only adolescent in the entire world who is depressed? And where is the evidence that if you are depressed you are crazy?" are helpful.

It is also important to assess and dispute secondary emotional problems such as being depressed or anxious about being depressed. Challenging their shoulds (I shouldn't be depressed by asking if there is a law that says kids shouldn't get depressed) and their discomfort anxiety (I can't stand being depressed by pointing out that they are standing it, even if it is difficult) usually help. It is very important when disputing to be sensitive and gentle, as opposed to being too rigorous, because depressed youth are often overwhelmed and frightened by the depression and do not understand why they feel this way.

As a complement to therapy, it is advisable to use a variety of homework assignments. Asking clients to keep a mood chart, record their dysfunctional thoughts and challenge them, write rational letters to themselves, read books about overcoming depression, watch humorous movies to make them smile, exercise, or establish self-reward systems for having happy as opposed to depressed days are all effective.

"Interventions for doing this include the following original ideas (unless noted) which can be adapted depending on the age and developmental level of the client

1. *Doom and Gloom Glasses*. Have two pair of glasses available, one with dark colored lenses and the other with yellow paper taped to the lenses. Explain to clients that when they are depressed, they tend to look at things with the

doom and gloom (dark) glasses. Give examples, using a situation they identify as depressing for them, such as getting a bad grade on a test. Have them put on the doom and gloom (dark) glasses and verbalize their thoughts about this event: that they are stupid and worthless, will never pass the class, that they will never learn the material, that they will be made fun of by others (and that would be horrible) and so forth. Explain concepts such as awfulizing, overgeneralizing, and equating self-worth with performance. Then have them put on the yellow (happier) glasses and verbalize what they might be thinking if they had these on as opposed to the doom and gloom glasses.
2. *When You Need A Helping Hand* (adapted from Vernon, 2002, p. 131). Invite the client to draw around his or her hand. At the base of the hand, have the client identify an event that is depressing for him or her, such as breaking up with a significant other. Then, between each of the fingers, have the client identify his or her irrational beliefs, such as nobody will ever date me again, this isn't fair, I'm a loser. Then help the client dispute these thoughts and have him or her write rational beliefs on each of the fingers to serve as a reminder of how to change thinking about a negative event. Rational coping self-statements can also be written around the hand to help the client identify ways to cope.
3. *Silly Songs* (Vernon, 2002, p. 129–130). This technique is appropriate for children with mild depression or sadness. Take familiar childhood tunes and help your client write his or her own lyrics and sing them often as a way to remember what to do to feel better. An example of a silly song (to the tune of "Three Blind Mice") is:

Three sad kids, three sad kids See how they cry, see how they cry. They all got tired of crying so much, they ran around and made faces and such. You've never seen these kids laughing so much, they three happy kids, the three happy kids.

An adaptation for older children and adolescents is to take songs that they listen to when they are sad and encourage them to rewrite less-depressing lyrics.

4. *Act as If.* When young clients are depressed, they often feel powerless and give in to their depression. It is sometimes helpful to have them act as if they are not depressed for a designated period of time each day, keeping a log of what they do so they can repeat these behaviors in the future. Doing this shows them that they can have periods of time in which they are not as depressed as other times.
5. *Away with the Blues* (adapted from Vernon, 2002, p. 126–127). This is an intervention that helps the client learn during the counseling session how to minimize depressed feelings. It can be repeated out of session as well as activity homework. First, have the client verbalize what it is that is depressing, such as parents getting a divorce. After some discussion about this, give the client a small glass pitcher of water and a bottle of blue food

coloring. Ask the client to pour an amount of food coloring into the pitcher that depicts how depressing this is (the darker the color, the more depressed he or she is). Next, help the client identify their irrational beliefs (I can't stand this, this is the worst thing that could ever happen to me, I will never be happy again). Then help the client identify what he or she could think that would not make him or her so depressed, such as "It's hard, but I can stand it; there are worse things that could happen, like my parents could die." As the client verbalizes each thought, ask him or her to pour some of the blue water down the drain (sink) as a visual reminder of how to decrease depressing feelings. Then, help the client identify some behaviors that he or she can do to keep him or her from being so depressed: associate with happy people, plan fun into every day, exercise and keep active, and so forth.

6. *Depression Tool Box*. When they are very low, it is often difficult for clients to remember happier times or think that they could ever be happy again. This simple technique involves having them identify artifacts that remind them of important people or events in their lives, inspirational sayings or songs that "give them hope," books or stories that have a moral or message for them, and so forth. Then they decorate a box with cheerful sayings, cartoons to make them laugh, or bright colored paper, and put their artifacts inside the depression tool box. When they are feeling depressed, they get out their tool box, which is a concrete way of helping them look at life from a more positive perspective. One adolescent who did this included the children's book, *The Little Engine That Could* (Piper, 1986) as a reminder that she just had to keep trying to feel better and say to herself "I think I can, I think I can," which was the message of the story, when she felt like giving up.
7. *Story Time*. Have clients write a story in which they pretend that they are not depressed: what would they be thinking, feeling, and doing? Then help them establish a plan to make the story come true.
8. *Pros and Cons Analysis* (adapted from Burns, 1990). Sometimes young clients think there are pay offs for staying depressed—parents might ease up on chores, let them do more things because they think this will help them feel better, or not expect good grades, for example. These practices may inadvertently reinforce clients to stay depressed. The pros and cons technique involves having clients make a list of the positives (pros) of staying depressed and the negatives (cons) involved in staying this way as a way. The counselor can vigorously challenge assumptions and irrational thinking to help clients see how practical and functional it truly is to remain depressed and help them set goals for changing depressing thoughts that lead to depressed feeling and behaving.
9. *Fortune Telling*. Oftentimes depressed clients think they can predict the future, and if they are depressed, they predict that they will stay this way, which in turn does not motivate them to work on overcoming the depression. To help them address this, make a "crystal ball" by covering a ball

with foil. Urge clients to look into this crystal ball and predict what is going to happen with a specific issue that is troubling them. Usually they say they can not, but the therapist can challenge this by giving examples of when they have in the past—such as "knowing they would fail a test" (but didn't), and so forth. Discuss the disadvantages of predicting the future if there isn't good evidence to support it.

10. *Concrete Objects*. Use concrete objects as metaphors: a sponge, which signifies not "soaking" up negative, irrational thoughts; binoculars, which serve as a reminder not to magnify things and make them bigger than they really are; and a kaleidoscope to remind them that there are always multiple ways of looking at things and that some ways are less depressing than others. The objects are good reminders about how to think more rationally to avoid becoming so depressed.

Case Study

Larissa, a 16-year-old, asked her school counselor to help her find a therapist because although she was very depressed, her parents did not think she really needed counseling. She appeared alone at the first session looking very lethargic, sad, and discouraged. She reported that she had been feeling this way for about a year and it was getting worse. During this first session she was very open about discussing her feelings and identified the following symptoms of depression on a checklist: withdrawal, lack of interest in activities, sleep disturbance, sense of hopelessness, apathy and lethargy, and depressed mood most of the time. Interestingly, her grades were still very good, but she admitted that she had to put forth a lot of effort to maintain concentration. She denied any suicidal attempts or other self-injurious behaviors, but admitted that occasionally it crossed her mind that it would be easier not to live because it was so difficult to fight the depression. She knew her parents would be opposed to medication because her older sister had been on it for a time and it had not really helped her, so Larissa wanted to try to overcome this without it.

During this first session, the counselor asked Larissa to complete the Emotional Pie assessment previously described so that she could more accurately determine how much of the time Larissa had been depressed during the past week. The visual representation indicated a significant amount of depression, as indicated by blue markings, as well as some anxiety and anger. At the end of the first session, the counselor asked Larissa to keep track of her moods on a daily basis using the Mood Chart (previously described).

Larissa appeared at the second session with her mood chart as well as a notebook of poems she had written over the past year that very clearly conveyed her intense sadness, powerlessness and hopelessness, and low frustration tolerance. In several of her poems she also made references to difficulties in relationships with her boyfriend, peers, and parents.

During the second session, she and the counselor identified the goals for therapy: to reduce her sense of powerless and hopelessness, to elevate her depressed mood, to increase her tolerance to deal with the frustration of being depressed, and to address relationship issues. The counselor shared with her client that while there is not "quick fix," there are things that will help Larissa gain better control over her emotions. She explained that depression in adolescence may be attributed to family history, as well as to a chemical imbalance that often occurs in females as their hormones change during puberty. In addition, she told Larissa that depression can also result from dysfunctional negative thoughts such: "I can't stand being depressed—it's unbearable; my life is awful and it always will be; nothing ever goes the way I think it should, and that is awful; I must be a loser since I have problems in relationships—why I am so worthless?" She also helped her client see that it is not the event itself that creates negative feelings—it is how she thinks about it. Therefore, if Larissa could learn to change her negative thoughts, she could reduce the intensity of her depression. The counselor shared a handout, *Identifying Cognitive Distortions or Thinking Errors* (Merrell, 2001) and together they discussed how these types of thoughts can lead to depression. As a homework assignment for the next session, the counselor asked her to keep a record of her own dysfunctional thoughts.

During the third session, Larissa shared her dysfunctional thought record and the counselor explained more about the connection between thoughts, feelings, and behaviors. She then asked Larissa to share an example of a recent event that Larissa thought caused her to be depressed so that she could help her understand how to reduce the intensity of her negative feelings. Larissa shared that she had been depressed when her boyfriend ignored her and was not supportive of her. With the counselor's help, she identified several irrational beliefs: he should always be there for me (and if he isn't, I can't stand it); because he is ignoring me, he must not love my anymore, and that would be horrible; because he is acting this way, it probably means he will break up with me and I will never have another relationship that was as good as this one had been.

The counselor acknowledged that Larissa would obviously feel sad and disappointed if her boyfriend was ignoring her, but she helped her client see that when Larissa thought she could not stand it, predicted that he would not love her anymore, and assumed that she would never have another relationship as good as this one had been that her feelings were more intense. She had Larissa use the *Identifying Cognitive Distortions and Thinking Errors* handout (Merrell, 2001) and check off the ones that corresponded to her irrational beliefs. She then introduced the concept of challenging these beliefs, asking her questions such as the following: has your boyfriend every ignored you before? Did it mean the end of the relationship? But suppose this time it will be the end...where is the proof that you absolutely will not be able to handle it? Have you ever had anything more difficult happen that you were able to cope with, and how did you do that? She also asked Larissa if she had ever had another boyfriend, which she had, so the counselor asked if it might be possible that even this relationship did not work, she might find someone else, just as she had after the last relationship ended. Other disputations addressed her demands: he should not ignore me; he should always be there for me. After acknowledging that it would be nice if he was always there for her, the counselor asked if there was there an explicit list of "shoulds" that boyfriends had to follow and how much control she actually had over him.

At the end of this session, Larissa understood more about how her negative thoughts were contributing to intense negative feelings, but she still struggled with the actual disputation process, so the counselor taught her how to use an REBT self-help form and requested that she complete one after each emotionally upsetting event. She also suggested that she read *Recovering from Depression: A Workbook for Teen*s (Copeland and Copans, 2002) as a homework assignment.

During the next several sessions Larissa and the counselor worked through the REBT self-help homework sheets, which seemed to help with some dimensions of the problem. However, she continued to struggle with the belief that her depression was unbearable, so the counselor had her read *The Little Engine That Could* (Piper, 1986) and suggested to Larissa that she read this book every day and make a list of things she could do and had already done to prove to herself that she could bear this. She also had her implement a self-reward system so that each day she managed to stand the depression she could do something nice for herself.

Over the course of therapy, the counselor continued to work with Larissa to show her that she could lessen the intensity of her depression by changing her thoughts. She used several other interventions: increasing the number of pleasant activities Larissa engaged in; using a continuum (client cut out newspaper clippings of "awful" events and placed them on a continuum from worst to least bad, including her own) to help her put her events in proper perspective (Vernon, 1998, pp. 153–154); and writing rational letters to herself, pretending to be an advice columnist offering help about how to overcome depression. In addition, because she still tended to think about a bleak future, especially if it was without a boyfriend, the counselor had her think about what she wanted out of life and asked her to take photos of these things and make a collage to help remind her to stay focused on the future and not predict doom and gloom.

Gradually Larissa was better and the counselor saw her less frequently. As a preventive measure, the counselor taught her how to use rational coping self-statements and encouraged her to continue using the REBT self-help forms to help prevent relapse.

Conclusion

From a REBT perspective, "individuals who can accept events and attributes, no matter now negative, will experience natural feelings of disappointment and frustration, but will rarely manifest clinical depression" (DiGiuseppe et al., 2002, p. 224). Given the increasing prevalence of depression in the child and adolescent population, practitioners would be well advised to consider this approach in the prevention and treatment of depression in young clients. Obviously more effort and research is needed to determine particular strategies that work best with this population, but a concerted effort to promote school-based prevention programs that teach the connection between thoughts, feelings, and behaviors, combined with a comprehensive intervention approach will hopefully empower young people to deal with this serious mental health problem.

References

American Psychiatric Association (2000). *Diagnostic and statistical manual of mental disorders* (4th ed., Text Revision). Washington, DC: Author.

Bernard, M.E. (1998). Validation of the General Attitude and Belief Scale. *Journal of Rational Emotive and Cognitive Behavior Therapy, 16*(3), 183–196.

Bernard, M.E., and Cronan, F. (1999). The Child and Adolescent Scale of Irrationality: Validation data and mental health correlates. *Journal of Cognitive Psychotherapy: An International Quarterly, 13*, 121–132.

Burns, D.D. (1990). *The feeling good handbook*. New York: Plume.

Cicchetti, D., and Toth, S.L. (1998). The development of depression in children and adolescents. *American Psychologist, 53,* 221–241.

Clarke, G.N., Rohde, P., Leweinsohn, H.H., and Seeley, J.R. (1999). Cognitive-behavioral treatment of adolescent depression: Efficacy of acute group treatment and booster sessions. *Journal of the American Academy of Children, 38,* 1–8.

Conterio, K. and Lader, W. (1998). *Bodily harm: The breakthrough healing program for self-injurers*. New York: Hyperion.

Copeland, M.E., and Copans, S. (2002). *Recovering from depression: A workbook for teens*. Baltimore, MD: Paul H. Brookes Publishing.

Curry, J.F., and Reinecke, M.A. (2003). Modular therapy for adolescents with major depression. In M.A. Reinecke, F.M. Dattilio, and A. Freeman (eds.), *Cognitive therapy with children and adolescents: A casebook for clinical practice* (2nd ed.). New York: The Guilford Press, pp. 95–127

de Wilde, E.J., Kienhorst, I.C.W.M., and Diekstra, R.F.W. (2001). Suicidal behaviour in adolescents. In I.M. Goodyer (ed.)., *the depressed child and adolescent* (2nd ed.), Cambridge, England: University Press, pp. 267–291

DiGiuseppe, R., Doyle, K.A., and Rose, R.D. (2002). Rational emotive behavior therapy for depression: Achieving unconditional self-acceptance. In M.A. Reinecke and M.R. Davison (eds.), *Comparative treatments of depression*. New York: Springer, pp. 220–248.

Ellis, A.E., and Dryden, W. (1997). *The practice of rational emotive behavior therapy* (2nd ed.). New York: Springer.

Engel, R., and DeRubeis, R. (1993). The role of cognition in depression. In K. Dobson and P. Kendall (eds.), *Psychopathology and cognition*, San Diego, CA: Academic Press. pp. 83–119).

Evans, N., and Murphy, A. (1997). CBT for depression in children and adolescents. In K.N. Dwivdei and V.P. Varma (eds.), *Depression in children and adolescents* (pp. 75–93). *London, England: Whurr.*

Evans, J.R., Van Velsor, P., and Schumacher, J.E. (2002). Addressing adolescent depression: A role for school counselors. *Professional School Counseling, 5,* 211–218.

Friedberg, R.D., and McClure, J.M. (2002). *Clinical practice of cognitive therapy with children and adolescents.* New York: Guilford Press.

Hauck, P.A. (2003). *Overcoming depression.* London: Westminster John Knox Press.

Ingram, R.E., and Malcarne, V.L. (1995). Cognition in depression and anxiety: Same, different, or a little of both? In K.D. Craig and K.S. Dobson (eds.), *Anxiety and depression in adults and children* (pp. 37–56). Thousand Oaks, CA: Sage.

Kahn, J., Kehle, T., Jensen, W., and Clark, E. (1990). Comparison of cognitive-behavioral, relaxation, and self-modeling interventions for depression among middle-school students. *School Psychology Review, 19,* 196–211.

Kaplan, P.S. (2000). *A child's odyssey: Child and adolescent development* (3rd ed.). Belmont, CA: Wadsworth.

Kendall, P.C. (1993). Cognitive-behavioral therapies with youth: Guiding theory, current status, and emerging developments. *Journal of Consulting and Clinical Psychology, 61,* 235–247.

King, N.J., and Bernstein, G.A. (2001). School refusal in children and adolescents: A review of the past 10 years. *Journal of the American Academy of Child and Adolescent Psychiatry, 40,* 197–205.

Klein, D.N., Lewinsohn, P.M., and Seeley, J.R. (2001). A family study of major depressive disorder in a community sample of adolescents. *Archives of General Psychiatry, 58,* 13–20.

Knaus, W. J. (1974). *Rational emotive education: A manual for elementary school teachers.* New York: Institute for Rational Living.

Koplewicz, H.S. (2002). *More than moody: Recognizing and treating adolescent depression.* New York: Berkley Publishing.

Lambert, M.J., and Davis, M.J. (2002). Treatment for depression: What the research says. In M.A. Reinecke and M.R. Davison, eds.), *Comparative treatments of depression.* New York: Springer.

Lerner, M. and Clum, G. (1990). Treatment of suicide ideators: A problem-solving approach. *Behavior Therapy, 21,* 403–411.

Macaskill, N.D., and Macaskill, A. (1996). Rational emotive therapy plus pharmacotherapy versus pharmacotherapy alone in the treatment of high cognitive dysfunction depression. *Cognitive Therapy and Research, 20,* 575–592.

McDermut, J.F., Haaga, D.A. F., and Bilek, K.A. (1997). Cognitive bias and irrational beliefs in major depression and dysphoria. *Cognitive Therapy and Research, 21,* 459–476.

Merrell, K.W. (2001). *Helping students overcome depression and anxiety: A practical guide.* New York: The Guilford Press.

Parry-Jones, W.Ll (2001). Historical aspects of mood and its disorders in young people. In I.M. Goodyer, *The depressed child and adolescent* (2nd ed., pp. 1–23). New York: Cambridge University Press.

Piper, W. (1986). *The little engine that could.* New York: Platt and Munk.

Reinecke, M.A. (2002). Cognitive therapies of depression: A modularized treatment approach. In M.A. Reinecke and M.R. Davison (eds.), *Comparative treatments of depression* (pp. 249–289). New York: Springer.

Reinecke, M.A., Ryan, M.S., and DuBois, D.L. (1998). Cognitive-behavioral therapy of depression and depressive symptoms during adolescence: A review and meta-analysis. *Journal of the American Academy of Child and Adolescent Psychiatry, 37,* 26-34.

Rush, A.J., and Nowels, A. (1994). Adaptation of cognitive therapy for depressed adolescents. In T.C.R. Wilkes, G. Belsher, A.J. Rush, and E. Frank (eds.), *Cognitive therapy for depressed adolescents,* pp. 3–21. New York: The Guildford Press.

Seligman, M.E.P. (1995). *The optimistic child: A proven program to safeguard children against depression and build lifelong resilience.* New York: Harper Perennial.

Shaffer, D. and Waslick, B.D. (2002). *The many faces of depression in children and adolescents.* Washington, D.C.: American Psychiatric Publishing.

Stark, K.D., Sander, J.B., Yancy, M.G., Bronik, M.D., and Hoke, J.A. (2000). Treatment of depression in childhood and adolescence: Cognitive-behavioral procedures for the individual and family. In PC. Kendall (Ed.), *Child and adolescent therapy,* New York: Guilford, pp. 173–234.

Thase, M.E. and Howland, R.H. (1995). Biological processes in depression: An updated review and integration. In E.E. Beckham and W.R. Leber (eds.), *Handbook of depression* (2nd ed.). New York: Guilford Press, pp. 213–279.

Vernon, A. (1998). *The passport program: A journey through emotional, social, cognitive, and self-development, grades 6–8.* Champaign, IL: Research Press.

Vernon, A. (2002). *What works when with children and adolescents: A handbook of individual counseling techniques.* Champaign, IL: Research Press.

Vernon, A., (2004). Working with children, adolescents, and their parents: Practical application of developmental theory. In A. Vernon (ed.), *Counseling children and adolescents* (3rd ed.). Denver, CO: Love Publishing, pp. 1–34.

Vernon, A., and Clemente, R. (2005). *Assessment and intervention with children and adolescents: Developmental and multicultural approaches.* Alexandria, VA: American Counseling Association.

Wagner, K.D. (2004). Depressed adolescents: Medication or therapy. *Psychiatric Times,* p. 20.

Walen, S.R., DiGiuseppe, R., and Dryden, W. (1992). *A practitioner's guide to rational-emotive therapy* (2nd ed.). New York: Oxford University Press.

Waslick, B.D., Kandel, R., and Kakouros, A. (2002). Depression in children and adolescents: An overview. In D. Shaffer and B.D. Waslick (eds.), *The many faces of depression in children and adolescents.* Washington, D.C.: American Psychiatric Publishing, pp. 1–36.

Wilde, J. (1996). *Treating anger, anxiety, and depression in children and adolescents: A cognitive-behavioral perspective.* New York: Taylor and Francis.

Wilkes, T.C.R., Belsher, G., Rush, A.J., and Frand, E. (1994). *Cognitive therapy for depressed adolescents.* New York: Guilford Press.

Wood, A., Harrington, R., and Moore, A. (1996). Controlled trial of brief cognitive-behavioural intervention in adolescent patients with depressive disorders. *Journal of Child Psychological Psychiatry, 37,* 737-746.

8

Childhood Anxieties, Fears, and Phobias: A Cognitive-Behavioral, Psychosituational Approach

RUSSELL M. GRIEGER[a], PH.D. AND JOHN D. BOYD[b], PH.D.

[a]*Clinical Psychologist in Private Practice, 818 E. High Street, Charlottsville, VA 22902;* [b]*Clinical Psychologist, in Private, 1924 Arlington Blvd, Charlottesville, VA 22903*

It is perhaps unfortunate that in the field of childhood psychopathology and psychotherapy the old treatment models are no longer sufficient. In some ways, it was easy to view the referred child as "owning" a problem and then simply go about "fixing" it for him or her. A good many recent developments, however, have shown this "child-oriented" approach to be woefully inadequate and, indeed, very often wrong. The development of systems models of family therapy, factor-analytic studies of aberrant childhood behavior in which the child's impact on the environment is integral to problem definition, the emergence of the behavioral and cognitive-behavioral movements in psychotherapy; and the legal advances vis-a-vis children's rights are just a few of the things that argue for a model of childhood pathology and therapy that incorporates the interplay between the child and his or her significant environment as co-perpetrators of childhood clinical problems and their solution (Bersoff and Grieger, 1971; Grieger and Abidin, 1972; Mischel, 1968, 1973, 1990; Peterson, 1968). The consensus of current models of child treatment is that children function in a context and that not only does the child need treatment, but also the context (Kazdin and Weisz, 2003; Lerner, 1991). Those who work clinically with children testify to the frustrations inherent in being limited only to direct work with a disturbed" child. Current-day cognitive-behavioral treatment models for the treatment of childhood anxiety focus both on treating the child and parents (e.g., Barrett and Shoett, 2003; Bernard, 2004; Bernard and Joyce, 1984; Kazdin et al., 1990; Kendall et al., 2002).

Reflecting on these developments, this chapter describes a cognitive-behavioral, psycho-situational model (Bersoff and Grieger, 1971; Grieger and

Abidin, 1972; Grieger and Boyd, 1980, 1983) for understanding and treating different anxiety problems in children. It focuses on both the child and his or her significant others as "causes" of these problems and their cures. It first distinguishes among fears, anxieties, and phobias. Then, after describing the psycho-situational model as it pertains to emotional and behavioral problems in general, it emphasizes the cognitive factors in creating children's anxiety problems in *both* the child *and* the child's significant others. The chapter then addresses methods and issues in cognitive-behavioral, psycho-situational assessment and treatment of these types of problems, with a particular emphasis on REBT for the treatment of childhood anxiety disorders (also see Vernon, 2002).

Overview of Anxieties, Fears and Phobias

Fears have traditionally been differentiated from anxieties and phobias on the basis of objectivity. That is, if something can be objectively proved to be dangerous, such as a physically abusive parent or a live electrical wire, then the aversion to that object is considered reasonable and the reaction would be labeled -a fear; on the other hand, if some object or situation is not objectively dangerous, and the person still responds fearfully, then the reaction is considered unreasonable and labeled an anxiety or a phobia.

Although this may be a reasonable distinction when applied to adults, it is a dubious one with children. Very simply, children often find it difficult to distinguish real from imaginary dangers because of their limited cognitive development, and, hence, they respond anxiously to safe or neutral objects. Their thinking is characterized by animism (e.g., giving life to inanimate objects), egocentrism (e.g., confusing their own motivations and feelings with those of others), concreteness (or giving literal interpretations to experiences), and limitations in concepts of size, time, and distance. It is little wonder, then, that all children develop a certain number of unreasonable fears, often at particular ages (Kessler, 1966). Indeed, research shows that precocious intelligence accelerates the emergence and decline of age-related fears.

One way out of the definitional dilemma rests with the concepts, of reactions and overreactions. The "normal" child reacts appropriately (i.e., within reasonable limits, although perhaps in a frightened manner) to both real and sometimes fictional dangers while the anxious or phobic child overreacts to real or fictional danger. That is, the child with an anxiety emotional disturbance more frequently, habitually, and intensely reacts with apprehension for longer durations, and with more debilitating behavioral, social, and physical side effects, than the "normal" youngster of the same age and intelligence.

Thus, we define fear, anxieties, and phobias as follows:

A *fear* is an apprehensive reaction to an external event or situation that is (1) objectively dangerous or (2) objectively safe but typically feared by a child of a given age and intelligence. The fear neither debilitates the child nor significantly interferes in his or her life. Therapeutic intervention in these instances, if necessary at all, would consist of reassuring the parents- and perhaps the child-that her or his fears are "normal."

A *phobia* is an apprehensive overreaction (including an obsessive avoidance) to some external event or situation that is neither developmentally appropriate nor objectively dangerous. It can also be an apprehensive overreaction to some external event that is truly aversive or dangerous. In both instances, there is a belief that because the event is dangerous, it is horrible to experience, and that one should be deathly afraid of it. With these beliefs, the response is marked by its abnormal intensity, duration, and frequency. Social phobias and phobias to specific objects like dogs are examples.

An *anxiety* is an apprehensive overreaction to the possible consequences of some external event rather than to the event itself. For example, the child dreading taking a test is usually anxious about what will happen to him or her if the test is failed, such as being rejected by peers, feeling depressed, or being scolded by parents. Most typically, the dreaded consequence includes a strong, aversive feeling state (e.g., anxiety, depression, or feelings of worthlessness) that the youngster believes to be too horrible to experience. More is said about this subject later. In any event, the intensity, duration, and frequency again signify the anxiety. We may indeed offer reassurances in cases of phobia or anxiety, but it is generally agreed that some form of psychotherapeutic intervention is called for.

A Cognitive-behavioral, Psychosituational Model of Childhood Psychopathology

Before focusing on the cognitive distortions in children's anxieties and phobias, we would like to describe a general model of childhood psychopathology that underpins the REBT approach to treatment. The psychosituational model contrasts with a view that sees human behavior as resulting predominantly from the "press of basic needs or cardinal personality structures" (Wallace, 1966, p. 123). In this view, behavior is seen to occur independently of the situations in which the person operates, so that the stimulus for action is primarily self-generated. Behavioral or emotional disorders develop and reside within the child, and the thrust is to "fix" him or her.

The psychosituational model is consistent with both social cognitive and social learning theory (Bandura, 1986; Mischel, 1968, 1973a, 1973b; Rotter, 1954), cognitive-behavioral therapy (Beck, 1976; Beck and Newman, 2004; Meichenbaum, 1977, 1985, 2001; Seligman, 1991) and rational-emotive behavior therapy (Bernard and Joyce, 1984; Ellis, 1971, 1978, 1982, 1994) in regarding "personality as sets of abilities . . . which, with regard to acquisition, maintenance, and modification share much in common with other abilities" (Wallace, 1966, p. 132). Rather than assuming that human behavior results solely from internal traits destined to emerge, this model believes that a person's response patterns develop and are maintained through the interplay of situational presses and developing internal capabilities. In agreement with the basic view of Bandura (1986) B = f(P, E), this viewpoint eschews a conception of human motivations as unidirectional and holds a basic premise taught to all beginning psychology students: Behavior (and deviant behavior) is a function of the interaction between personality and environment.

The model of childhood behavior is illustrated in Fig. 1. The center of the model is an act (or the C of rational-emotive behavior therapy's ABC theory). Act is broadly defined as referring both to a simple response to some internal or external stimuli (e.g., hitting another child or leaving one's desk) and to more complex behavioral strategies that are purposeful (i.e., motivated by personal values and by situational appraisals) and multifaceted (i.e., containing emotional, behavioral, and attitudinal components).

Within this model, acts are seen to be influenced by three variables, the first two of which recognize the power of the child's significant others, particularly the parents, in motivating actions. The first of these variables, the consequences following a child's behavior, acknowledges the empirical law of effect. As Carson (1969, p. 68) noted, "With few exceptions, behavior tends in the direction of maximizing pleasure and minimizing displeasure." So, what others do to encourage or discourage, teach or suppress, is exceptionally important in forming children's response and strategy patterns. We hasten to caution the reader; however, against a reductionistic conceptualization of consequences. Although it is true that youngsters' actions are shaped directly by immediate and single rewards and punishments, it is also true as Bandura has shown that children observe the consequences of their actions, come to value some and disvalue others, learn to make predictions about the probability of their delivery, and adopt attitudes about themselves and their parents through the process. They, therefore, come to instrumentally plan and strategize, based on their experiences, to obtain complex, global, hedonically relevant outcomes (e.g., love, power, and recognition) and to avoid other, more aversive ones (e.g., rejection and pain). Through both simple and

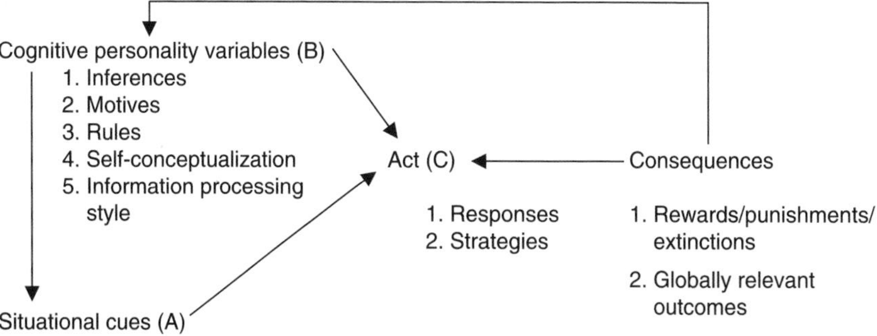

FIGURE 1. A schematic representation of a psychosituational model of behavior and psychopathology (derived from Peterson, 1968).

complex action-consequence sequences, both action patterns and various personality traits develop.

One more note about consequences. The consequences that parents provide are in part stimulated by the child's actions, but equally powerful are the various attitudes and feelings that the parents hold about themselves, their children, and child rearing in general. This subject is addressed more fully in the next section, where the irrational attitudes of parents that prompt anxiety problems in children are detailed.

The second parental ingredient influencing acts is the immediate *situational cue* (or the A in the ABC theory). Again, rather than taking a mechanistic view, the authors agree with Bandura (1986), Kelly (1955), Mischel (1968, 1973), Rotter (1954), and others in holding that the most relevant unit of study is the interaction of the child and his or her meaningful environment. That is, out of the array of situational cues, the individual will most likely select and attend to those that are most meaningful. In particular, the presence or absence of significant others, along with the personal and task rules they impose, and the child's inferences about their motivations, demands, and affections for the child, will be most relevant.

By far the most significant influence on children's actions are the *personality variables* learned over time through experience in the child's consequential world and carried from situation to situation. They are defined cognitively (the Bs of the ABC theory) and serve to flavor perceptions of and inferences about situational cues; they may also influence predictions about the consequences of actions and affect the child's personal experience of the consequences of her or his actions. They include at least the following:

1. *Inferences* are either some specific, situationally relevant perceptions or more habitual patterns of expectations, predictions, or conclusions (e.g., "No one likes me"). Inferences can be drawn about virtually anything, but they frequently fall into three categories: (a) stimulus-outcome inferences, in which a prediction is made about the likelihood of something's occurring if some other event occurs (Mischel, 1973); (b) behavior-outcome inferences, in which a prediction is made about the likelihood of some consequence if a particular action is taken (Mischel, 1973b); and (c) locus-of-control inferences, in which outcomes are consistently attributed to one's personal power or to chance (Rotter, 1954). The more stable the expectations, the more predictable is the youngster's behavior.
2. *Motives* in the broadest sense refer to "an internal stimulus which is effective in the initiation of behavior" (Peterson, 1968, p. 70). Rather than viewing motives as "senseless" drives, however, the psychosituational model interprets motives in terms of cognitively held values. That is, children learn to value positively certain outcomes or circumstances and to value negatively certain others; and, all things being equal, they tend to act to acquire the positive and to avoid the negative states of affairs, often after an *assessment* of the current situation and with a *prediction* of out-

come. Children often "awfulize" themselves into emotional distress by exaggerating the negative values during their assessment and prediction, and when this becomes characterological, it is called low *frustration tolerance*.

3. *Rules* are guidelines for correct behavior for oneself, for others, and for the correct ordering of the conditions of the world. Rules may be defined in terms of guidelines or preferences, and they lead the child to act reasonably in the appropriate direction; or they may be cast in absolute, all-or-none ways when held as absolutes (I should . . . ; you should . . .; the world should . . _.). Rational-emotive therapists refer to these latter rules as "irrational demands," which prompt the child to act desperately; they constitute the nucleus of most neurotic conditions.
4. *Self-conceptualizations* are the evaluative ideas that the child holds about herself or himself. Self-conceptualizations are learned and may be of a rating or an accepting kind. A self-rating view generally uses external criteria (usually success in some act or skill, or approval by another) to rate oneself as either good or bad; a self-acceptance view makes no generalization about the goodness or badness of the self at all and assumes either that the self is innately worthy or realizes that such a rating is simply an impossible chore. Most children are taught a self-rating view; that is, they learn to demand certain things of themselves and thereby act to succeed in those things; they then rate themselves as either good or bad, depending on their perception of their success in this endeavor. The criteria they hold to determine their self-rating is highly motivating, as is the general goal of viewing oneself as good.
5. The *information-processing style* is the child's typical manner of processing information. Distorted styles include selective attending to certain data while ignoring others; arbitrarily drawing conclusions without sufficient evidence; unjustifiably over-generalizing from one circumstance to another; magnifying the significance of something beyond its true importance; and thinking in all-or-none, black-and-white terms (Beck, 1976). Processing information via these styles leads the child to ignore relevant information from the environment, to draw false conclusions, to overreact falsely to events, and the like. The rub is that young children developmentally think in these ways.

Psychopathology

To sum up, the cognitive-behavioral, psychosituational model conceptualizes children's actions as resulting from the interplay of both situational variables (most notably the cues and consequences from significant others as generated in large part by their own attitudes and beliefs) *and* personality factors (particularly cognitive variables). With regard to reported or suspected child mental health problems, this model refuses to make an *a priori* judgment that a referred child is the sole owner or even the central figure in a problem. Instead, it takes the position that a child can be disturbed only in the context of a disturbed situation. It, therefore, advocates a systematic exploration of all elements of the problem situation. In the last analysis, the child may (a) "own" a behavioral or emotional problem, (b) have a problem that coexists with and may even result from problems that others in the situation "own," (c) the child may be totally free of problems whereas one or several other situational elements have a problem or (d) no problem may actually exist except for the referring adult's faulty perception that there is one.

Beyond these generalities, where might emotional and/or behavioral problems arise in the child or in his or her psychosituational world? For one thing, the child may act inappropriately because he or she is deficient in an ability to receive, perceive, organize, or appreciate the relevance of information and behavior in certain situations. Indeed, the abnormality of many children lies in the fact that they do not have the skills to comprehend, know, or do what is expected. For another, the child may act inappropriately (i.e., overreact emotionally and/or behaviorally) because he or she has learned from the consequential environment that such behavior will pay off. That is, the child's inappropriate actions may have been learned and maintained because of an accurate expectation that it will lead to some valued consequence or avoid some aversive consequence. And, finally, the child may act inappropriately (i.e., overreact) because of the acquisition of faulty inferences, rules, self-evaluations, and cognitive process styles that directly prompt the actions and that constitute a problem in and of themselves.

As for the situation itself, the significant others in the situation (e.g., the parents or teachers) may themselves act to provide cues and consequences for the child that directly "create" inappropriate actions in the child. These responses may be due to ignorance, to faulty expectations about what are appropriate child actions, or to irrational ideas about themselves and the child. Finally, the task demands and/or role demands of a particular situation (e.g., a third-grade class) may be so totally out of line in terms of what is reasonable or may be so conflicting and confusing that appropriate actions on the child's part may be impossible.

Cognitive Distortions in Children's Anxiety Problems

The relationship between anxiety problems and cognitions is basically the same in children and in adults. Like adults, children develop and maintain anxieties and phobias when they draw inferences and/or form irrational evaluations that logically lead to these emotional and related behavioral states.

Yet children, typically with limited logical thinking powers, are extremely vulnerable to faulty thinking in response to both the sensible and the not-so-sensible actions of their parents and other significant adults. Therefore, it behooves us to examine the cognitive distortions in children, or the personality variables of the psychosituational model, that constitute anxiety problems; but it is also important to examine those ideas and behaviors of parents that make it easy for children to adopt and maintain their anxiety-evoking ideation.

Cognitive Distortions in Parents

Faulty Inferences About Child Behavior

A growing body of literature indicates that children referred for psychological care are members of a highly select group (Kazdin et al., 1995). They are select in that what prompts their parents to seek treatment for them are behaviors that are often highly prevalent in unselected samples of children (Kazdin and Weisz, 2003). A number of interesting questions about the validity of the judgments, if not the motivations, of the significant people in the child's psychosituational world. Why are some children referred and others with the same behaviors not? When is a child's "problem" a problem? When is a problem attributed to the child really an adult's problem? In many cases, it is a powerful adult (a teacher or parent).who arbitrarily determines whether a child's actions are deemed a problem. The fact may be, however, that the actual problem may reside not in the child but in the adult's eyes.

Two major cognitive distortions often prompt parents (and sometimes teachers) to mistakenly view a child as having a problem. One is ignorance; that is, parents often mistake fairly appropriate child behavior for a problem. They do this because they know no better or have simply learned faulty expectations. They may then respond with some formal action (i.e., a referral) and/or react to the child as if there is indeed a problem, perhaps prompting the child to hold a similar idea.

A more serious psychosituational problem exists when parents hold cognitive distortions that constitute low frustration tolerance vis-a-vis their children (Bernard and Joyce, 1984). Low frustration tolerance is characterized by people's holding the irrational ideas that others or outside events can and do upset them; that it is horrible, awful, or terrible when things go wrong or hassles arise; and that it is catastrophic to be frustrated. Holding these attitudes, the parents then easily upset themselves about the disturbed and not-so-disturbed behavior of their child (DiGiuseppe, 1981; Ellis et al., 1966) they easily label their child's behavior as disturbed and act accordingly. If they are overreacting to fairly appropriate child behavior, then it is solely the parents who own a problem, one that would be best treated quickly and thoroughly before they become the source of a problem in their child. If they are overreacting to a problem that the child truly owns, then two problems exist, one of the child's and one of the parents. In either case, the danger is that the child will label himself or herself as having a problem and/or will develop anxiety problems or other emotional problems about all this.

Disturbed Parenting Styles

Probably the most important time to include parents in treatment is when they are themselves disturbed and behave in ways that create, maintain, or exacerbate emotional-behavioral problems in their children. It is when they hold inappropriate expectations for their child and/or hold irrational attitudes themselves that debilitating parental practices flourish.

Although there is a vast variety of parenting behavior, the following six faulty parenting styles seem to be most closely associated with the development of childhood anxiety problems.

The criticism trap (Becker, 1971) is the most frequently found pattern of poor parenting. Associated with fears of failure and disapproval, anxious withdrawal, low self-esteem, and a whole host of related childhood-anxiety difficulties, it is a style characterized by a high frequency of subtle and not-so-subtle criticizing behaviors: nagging, correcting, moralizing, reminding, blaming, and even ridiculing and directly putting down the child. The key to this style is that the parents, rather than noticing desirable behaviors and acknowledging them, catch the child being bad and then respond in one or more of the ways mentioned above. The parents who fall into this trap are usually fairly angry, demanding, and punitive people in general. They typically hold one or more of the following irrational attitudes: (1) children *should* always and unequivocally do well (e.g., be motivated and achieve) and behave correctly (e.g., be kind, considerate, and interested); (2) parents *are* always correct, or at least the authority in a situation, and therefore children *must* never question or disagree with them; (3) it is *horrible*, *terrible*, and *awful* when children do not do well, misbehave, or question or disobey their parents; (4) doing bad things *must* be punished because punishment, blame, and guilt are effective methods of child management; (5) because a child should do well, praise and rewards are unnecessary and spoil the child; and (6) a child and her or his behavior are the same, and thus children who act badly or err *are bad* (Grieger and Boyd, 1983; Hauck, 1967).

The perfectionism trap is also highly associated with childhood anxiety problems. Typically very demanding of themselves, parents who fall into this trap also act out their demandingness on their children. As with themselves, they take the attitude that the child *must* do well and succeed in most endeavors, and they hold that the child's value or worth, as well as their own, is dependent on superb performance. As a consequence, they habitually criticize and even reject the child for doing poorly, become angry at the child for less than sterling performance, and regularly let the child know that even good efforts could have been better. They are relentless in the pressure they place on the child, and they communicate that the child is valuable and loved only if she or he does well. Not surprisingly, it is easy for children who are exposed to the perfectionism trap to adopt the perfectionistic attitudes for themselves. In the process, they learn to fear disapproval and even abandonment if they do not do well; to become very anxious in the face of performance tasks like homework, tests, or athletic competition; and to illogically equate their self-worth with doing well and getting approval. As a dramatic example, the senior author once had a highly anxious sixth-grader, tell him that he most feared being "orphaned" by his dad if he did not do well in school. Emotionally and behaviorally, anxiously perfectionistic children either strive mightily to succeed (and are anxious all the time) or phobically tend to withdraw and avoid risks.

In *the scared-rabbit trap*, the parent is highly afraid of his or her own shadow. He or she chronically models both timid behaviors and fearful attitudes, including the attitudes that (1) dangers abound *everywhere*, and one *must* be constantly on the alert lest something harmful take one by surprise; (2) if something is painful or frustrating, it *must* be avoided at all costs; (3) bad things that happen are *awful*, *horrible*, and *terrible*; (4) one *cannot stand it* if something bad or painful happens; (5) one *has to get* upset when things go wrong; and (6) one *must* have a guarantee that things will go well or else one cannot survive. Clearly, the child who observes these attitudes and endorses them will likewise be fearful, timid, overcautious, and compulsively safety-seeking.

The false positive and *the guilt traps* most often lead to the egocentric, selfish, spoiled child with low frustration tolerance. Yet, these, parental styles sometimes contribute to anxiety problems in children as well. For when the child leaves the protective and indulgent world of the parent, she or he often encounters unexpected responses of others of which she or he has had little experience; other children reject, punish, and in general turn her or his expectations upside down. At these times, it is difficult for the child to predict how to act, and the child begins to awfulize about the consequences of wrong actions and to doubt her or his self-worth. In both these faulty parenting styles, the parents lavish a great deal of positive affection on the child, but excessively and indiscriminately. The youngster receives praise not only for appropriate behavior, but for inappropriate acts as well; and the parents attempt to remove all frustrations from his or her life. Although often couched in a great deal of love, these two parental styles are often motivated by rather neurotic attitudes: (1) "It is awful for my child to suffer, and *I must* therefore prevent it at all costs"; (2) "*I must* always do right by my child"; (3) "*I must* always be loved and approved of by my child"; and (4) "*My self-worth* is tied to how I do as a parent, so I had better riot make mistakes." The result is that the child has few if any limits and can easily conclude that anything and everything he or she does is OK.

A final disturbed parenting style might be called *the inconsistency trap*. In one variation of this style, parents essentially have no consistent way of dealing with the child, haphazardly rewarding and punishing the child by whim or mood. A second variation is strongly criticizing the child for errors while setting no rules or guidelines. Either way, the typical cognitive distortions include the following: (1) "Whatever feels right is right"; and (2) "I'm too weak and helpless to know what is the right thing to do, so I'll leave it up to the moment." The result is that the child has no predictability or certainty, not knowing how to act or exactly what the consequences of his or her actions will be Punishment, disapproval, and even catastrophe are ever-present possibilities.

Cognitive Distortions in Children

Clearly, parental attitudes and actions are significant in the genesis of childhood anxiety problems. Yet, children develop anxiety problems only when the cognitive dimensions of personality described earlier become illogical, distorted, or exaggerated. The cognitive-behavioral-psychosituational model, following Beck (1976) and Ellis (1994), recognizes that children, like adults, make two types of cognitive errors that cause themselves to be fearful, anxious, or phobic: (1) errors of inference about what has occurred or will occur and (2) errors of evaluation (i.e., irrational attitudes, ideas, or beliefs) about what has occurred or will occur. Although either type of error may occur alone and cause anxiety problems, it is probable that a child who has anxiety problems has both in his or her thinking.

Errors of Inference

Inferential errors are predictions or conclusions that falsely represent reality (DiGiuseppe, 1981). A child who consistently distorts reality probably does so through one or more of several illogical processes such as making arbitrary inferences, overgeneralizing, selectively abstracting, minimizing, and maximizing about what they experience (Beck, 1976).

A case in point is the highly school-anxious sixth-grader mentioned above. He found it virtually impossible to remain calm when taking tests, sitting through classes in which there, was a chance he might be called on to respond, or even doing schoolwork at home. He gauged his anxiety as rising to an 8 or 9 on a scale of 1–10 at these times. When asked to tell what went through his head, he said he thought or predicted that, if he failed or did poorly, his parents would "orphan" him and his friends would reject him. Of course, he also engaged in evaluative errors (e.g., it would be *terrible* for his friends to reject him), but his inferences made his academic enterprises apocalyptic and fed into the evaluative errors (discussed below).

The important elements in most children's lives include the home, the school, friends and play, and their abilities and skills. The cognitive-behavioral-psychosituational clinician would do well to be alert for evidence of erroneous inferences that youngsters might draw about these arenas when it comes to anxiety problems, particularly predictions about loss of love and approval, abandonment, rejection, harm, and incompetence.

Errors of Evaluation

The cataloging of evaluative errors or irrational attitudes in children's anxiety disorders has, to date, been sparse and is limited to only two attempts. Years ago Ellis et al. (1966) distinguished between children's fears of external things and fear of their own inadequacy. Shortly thereafter, Hauck (1967) discussed separately fears of people, fears of failure, fears of injury, and fears of rejection and ridicule.

Ellis (1978, 1982) has outlined two kinds of anxieties, each of which is prompted by its own set of cognitive distortions. In our experience, they are both relevant to understanding children's anxiety disorders. *Ego anxiety*, as its name implies, is "anxiety about one's self, one's being, and one's essence" (Ellis, 1982, p. 25). It results from a child's holding the belief that she or he must do well and be approved for doing well, or else she or he is a bad and unworthy person whom no one could ever care for again. With so much at stake (i.e., one's value and lovability), anxiety is a highly predictable outcome.

A good many typical childhood emotional and behavioral problems can be easily understood as manifestations of ego anxiety. Most of the more prominent ones are presented in Table 1.

In *discomfort anxiety*, the child may or may not begin a cognitive distortion with a faulty inference, such as, "Because the neighbor kid was pushed down on the school playground, I'll be hurt if I go to school." Regardless, discomfort anxiety always has a number of irrational evaluations at its core. The philosophical set is that it is *horrible*, *terrible*, and *awful* when things go wrong or when something difficult or dangerous is confronted (Grieger and Boyd, 1983). The child who makes a faulty inference but does not have discomfort anxiety will be afraid; the child with only discomfort anxiety will be highly fearful; and children with both are usually terrified of many things, and their terror prompts them to continually create more faulty inferences and irrational evaluations.

The catastrophizing of discomfort anxiety comes from the following kinds of attitudes: "I *cannot stand* troublesome events or emotional and physical pain; I *must* be certain that nothing bad will ever happen to me; I *must* be able to protect myself totally from dangerous or obnoxious conditions; I *cannot stand* to feel distress; if something is difficult, I must be terribly upset by it." In a nutshell, children with discomfort anxiety feel that their comfort is threatened and that it's *awful* to feel discomfort. Moreover, they grandiosely and demandingly believe that they *should* always get what they want, easily and quickly, and *should* never get what they don't want (Ellis, 1982).

The diagnosis of discomfort anxiety is difficult because the disorder is so easily disguised and overshadowed by other forms of irrational distortion (e.g., ego anxiety); likewise, other disturbing emotions may underlie discomfort anxiety. Four diagnostic guidelines are therefore offered here to help the clinician identify discomfort anxiety:

1. Children often make a faulty inference or receive incorrect information that leads them to expect discomfort in an upcoming situation; then they awfulize about the anticipated discomfort and create discomfort anxiety. Look for these inferences and faulty premises.
2. Unwanted and discomforting situations and tasks are a realistic part of life, but youngsters (particularly pampered and sheltered children) are

TABLE 1. Ego Anxiety Problems of Childhood.

	Accompanying Manifestations		
Anxiety problem	Behavioral	Emotional	Typical irrational ideas
Avoidance/ withdrawal from people	Shrinking from peers and strangers Dependency on family Labored communication Timidity Lack of assertion	Generalized anxiety Self-doubt Feelings of inferiority Depression (secondarily)	"I must do well and be lovable in all respects or I will be rejected." "Others not liking me makes me nothing." "If I do not do well and/or if I am not lovable, then I will be worthless. I must therefore avoid trying and getting noticed at all costs." "As long as I can be left alone, and nothing is demanded of me, my worthlessness will not be obvious, and I won't feel worthless."
Attention seeking	Model child-cute, charming Class clown-show-off, pest Apparently shy, helpless child	Anxiety Self-doubt Feelings of insecurity Sense of pleasure when efforts pay off	"I must be noticed at all costs or else I am lost and worthless." "I must be loved and approved at all times or else I am worthless."
Avoidance/ withdrawal from tasks	Expressions of concern about competence and/or difficulty of task	Generalized anxiety	"I must do well and be approved for doing well or else I will be a terrible person whom no one could love."
	Complaints about physical ailments	Worries about impending deadlines	"Since I will be proved to be worthless for doing poorly, it is better to try nothing at all."
	Passive in classroom-never volunteers Homework undone or sloppily done Procrastination	Feelings of inferiority Self-doubt	"As long as I try nothing, my worthlessness will not be obvious and I won't feel worthless." "If others saw my inadequacies, they would reject me, and that would make me worthless.
Perfectionism	Compulsive	Sense of pleasure when succeeds	"I must do well or else I will be rejected, lost, and worthless."
	Overachieving Overdriven	Generalized anxiety Heightened anxiety before performance Depression, guilt, self-downing when fails Worries about deadlines Obsessional self-doubt	"I must always do my best." "My performance at school and everywhere else must always be competent." "If I don't totally and always do well, then I am totally and always a failure."

known for exaggerating the pain involved, thereby creating a primary problem of discomfort anxiety. It is well to remember that low frustration tolerance is endemic to children, and that a child can become very anxious about what seems to be an ordinary responsibility.

3. Through various irrational thought processes, children can create ego anxiety, anger, depression, and other forms of emotional distress, and these unpleasantries then become the antecedents of secondary discomfort anxiety. Children are frequently afraid of the pain of their own distressful emotions.
4. Discomfort anxiety easily leads to other forms of emotional disturbance. Children can angrily damn others and the world for causing their discomfort, can pity themselves into dysphoria, or can adopt a hopeless and helpless attitude of depression. These emotions can mask a primary problem of discomfort anxiety.

Many childhood anxiety disorders have discomfort anxiety as the primary or secondary dynamic, and in Table 2, some of these are presented. When reading this table, it is important to remember that the philosophy and attitudes of discomfort anxiety are rarely articulated in consciously, and that an infinite variety of derivatives are possible. Though covert, this kind of ideation is, however, a driving mediational force that produces phobias, obsessions, compulsions, and various forms of anxiety-induced symptoms.

Cognitive-Behavioral, Psychosituational Assessment

The cognitive-behavioral-psychosituational (CBP) model emphasizes the interactive nature of the person (child) and the environment (particularly the parents) in the genesis and maintenance of anxiety problems. That is, individuals bring their own phenomenological perspective (i.e., patterns of thinking and behaving) to other family members and thereby play the major role in their own emotional and behavioral dysfunctioning; yet, children are tremendously vulnerable to the actions of their significant others and thus highly susceptible to the irrational thinking and behaving of those significant others.

Within the framework of the CBP model, then, it is crucial to sort out problem ownership, determining to what extent the child's problems really belong to the child (i.e., come from his or her aberrant actions) and to what extent the child's problems really belong to or are caused by the behaviors, feelings, perceptions, and attitudes of the parents.

In dealing with children's anxiety problems, we strongly recommend starting with a cognitive-behavioral, psychosituational assessment strategy (Bersoff and Grieger, 1971; Grieger and Abidin, 1972). The overall structure of this strategy focuses the clinician on the total psychosituational picture, not just on the referred child, and pays special attention to the mutual influences of both the parents and the child. It includes a detailed analysis of the child's alleged

TABLE 2. Discomfort anxiety problems of childhood.

	Accompanying Manifestations		
Anxiety problem	Behavioral	Emotional	Typical irrational ideas
School phobia	Refusal to attend school Avoidance of children who attend school	Acute anxiety in the morning Nightmares and/or insomnia	"Because a neighbor child got hurt at school, it means I will get hurt if I go. I might even be killed!" and/or "Bad things might happen at school and I couldn't stand that. I must have protection."
	Clinging to mother.	Psychosomatic symptoms Secondary ego anxiety, anger, depression	"I must never leave Mother and the comfort and security of home; it would be horrible to give them up even for a few hours; I couldn't survive." "Because I'm nervous, I'll make mistakes and the other children will not like me; this will show that I'm no good." "My feelings of anxiety are horrible, and they will increase if I go to school; I'll completely fall apart and look foolish." "They shouldn't make me do what I don't want to; they deserve to be punished."
Procrastination on schoolwork and home chores	Forgetfulness Avoids contact with/ requesting adults	Diffuse anxiety Insecurity, inferiority Tiredness, laziness	"Life should be easy and comfortable, and I should get everything I want and nothing I don't want."
	Feigns ignorance, ineptitude Dawdles, daydreams, incomplete work	Psychosomatic symptoms Secondary anger Guilt about procrastination Anxiety about adults' disapproval	"When life is not this way, it's horrible, awful. I can't stand the pain and fatigue of doing what I don't want to do." "Because doing what I can't stand is so horrible, I must find ways to put it off. Somehow, maybe it will go away if I avoid it." "Difficult tasks are impossible; work should be easy." "I can't do difficult things. I'll fail if I try and show how inept and worthless I am." "They should not make me do these painful things. They are awful people." "I am a bad person for not doing what I was told to do."

Obsessive worrying about an event or activity	Preoccupied with preparations Lack of spontaneity, too serious Intrusive thoughts Irritable behavior	Continual tension and anxiety Nausea and other psy-chosomatic symptoms Absence of laughter, controlled affect Acute anxiety before target event Secondary anger	"This event may be terribly horrible and aversive, so painful it's beyond description." "I can't stand aversion and pain; it's more than I can bear." "I shouldn't have to bear discomfort; I am en titled to a happy life without discomfort." "I must be absolutely sure nothing will happen to cause me discomfort. I must use. all my energies to plan and avoid potential pain. I must not relax until the danger is over." "People who cause me discomfort are bad and I hate them." "The world is rotten because it put me in this spot."
Childhood obesity	Continuous eating Timid, nonassertive Overweight Lethargic Socially withdrawn Sedentary activities	Affectively constricted Insecure Low self-esteem Nervous most of the time Sometimes is irritable and has anger outbursts Shame over appearance Guilt about eating habits	"I must have the approval of others and do well in my performances; otherwise, I'm a worthless nothing" (ego anxiety problem). "I can't stand the discomfort of anxiety, loneliness, and boredom; it is too painful, and it reminds me of how worthless and miserable I am". "I must have food to make me feel better; I need it to be less miserable." "Because of my fatness and eating, I am a slob. I should be a better person than I am, but there's nothing I can do. I can't stop eating." "Others have it easy and that's not fair. They shouldn't be happy if I can't be, damn them."

problem behaviors, including his or her feelings and attitudes, as elicited and maintained by the behaviors and attitudes of the relevant people in his or her life. It is comprised of three steps.

1. *Step I: Cognitive-Behavioral, Psychosituational Parent Interview.* The goals of this initial step are several: (1) to gather relevant information about the child, his or her problem, and the parents' perception of his or her problem; (2) to gather information about the role that the parents play in creating and/or maintaining the "problem"; (3) to ferret out perceptual distortions, irrational attitudes, and maladaptive behaviors in the parents; and (4) to begin to educate the parents to a psychosituational and cognitive definition of the problem and its eventual alleviation. The parent interview includes the following aspects, all of which have a significant cognitive focus:

1. An explicit, behavioral detailing of the parents' concerns or complaints about the child, including their frequency, intensity, and duration. This serves to reconstruct vague, interpretive, and/or blaming perceptions with objective units that lend themselves to problem solving, to perception checking about their "awfulness," and to the diffusion of overt or covert anger and hostility.
2. An explication of the specific situations or circumstances in which the "problem" behavior occurs. Particularly open to inquiry here are the expectations or rules (i.e., "shoulds") that the parents have about the child's behavior in these situations.
3. An identification of the immediate consequences following the child's behavior, including specifically what the parents think, feel, and do when the child behaves as she or he does at these times. The interview is particularly attentive at this point to the attitudes and behaviors that may serve to promote inappropriate and inhibit appropriate child behavior; concurrently, the interviewer is on the alert for evidences of the faulty parenting styles described previously as they impact on the child in relation to the "problem" behavior and in a more general sense.
4. A definition of goals for the child, again stated as explicitly and behaviorally as possible. This helps the interviewer to set appropriate goals; equally important, it provides another opportunity for both the clinician and the parents to reflect on the appropriateness of the expectations for the child and the rules or demands in the parents' cognitive schema.
5. An exploration of the more general, ongoing patterns of interaction between the parents and the child, including the perceived ratio of positive to negative interactions, the kind and quality of both positive and negative interactions, the methods and frequency of punishments, and the kind and quality of communication.

Step 2: Cognitive-Behavioral, Psychosituational Child Interview. The theoretical framework for interviewing the child is the same as that for parents.

That is, acts are seen as resulting from the interaction of the child with his or her significant environment. Within the psychosituational framework, an attempt is therefore made to assess the child's personality variables, and also the elements of his or her perceived prior and consequential environment. As with the parents, this interview step has several components:

1. An explication of who the practitioner is (e.g., a psychologist), what she or he does (e.g., "My job is to teach people to get along better and be happy . . ."), and what information she or he already has. We cannot agree too much with DiGiuseppe (1981) in emphasizing how helpful such an open approach is in fostering communication that is honest, direct, and nondefensive. At the same time, it leads naturally to the rest of the interview content.
2. A detailing of the child's perception of the problems. The child may indeed perceive the problem exactly as the parents do; yet, she or he might see the parents as "owning" the problem. Nevertheless, the interviewer takes each concern of the parents in turn and determines how the child views it. Not to be overlooked are complaints that the child has about the parents as well.
3. An explication of the specific situations in which the "problem" behaviors take place. What we have found particularly helpful at this point is to ask the child what she or he thinks causes the problem behavior to occur. This question not only serves to elicit beliefs about problem ownership but also often serves to reveal blaming or angry attitudes in the child, as well as the child's perception of the motivations, feelings, and attitudes of the parents toward him or her. Such a question might be answered with something like "My dad just doesn't like me." Follow-up questions like "What does he do to lead you to think this?" give details about the consequences that the child receives from the parents and may indeed prompt some cognitive restructuring as well.
4. A determination of the situational consequences of his or her action as perceived by the child. What exactly do the parents do when he or she misbehaves? How does he or she think the parents feel when they respond in these ways? What are their attitudes? Again, the answers reveal significant information about what the child experiences as a consequence of his or her actions, and they also serve as a check on the accuracy of the parents' reports about what they do at these times.
5. A functional cognitive analysis of the thoughts, attitudes or evaluations, and logical processes that the child goes through when acting in the identified ways. What are his or her thoughts? Does he or she awfulize or catastrophize when the parents criticize? What are the opinions that he or she holds about the self- are they accepting or rating-oriented? Are there coping statements in stressful or provoking situations, or is there an absence of these? In general, an attempt is made to ascertain the Bs that the child has when confronted with stimulating situations, when acting, and when receiving parental consequences.

6. Finally, an articulation, by the child of her or his goals. As before, the interviewer notes whether the goals are realistic and whether they are aimed at the child, the parent, or both. The interviewer can often act directly as a change agent at this point by helping the child to formulate realistic goals for himself or herself and others.

Step 3: Psycho-diagnosis and Goal Setting. The verbal or written description of the results of the assessment procedure is called a proper *psycho-diagnosis*. It is a general statement of the role that each party plays in the situational dilemma and may be delivered individually or in a family setting. It is highly behavioral and cognitive in nature. The purpose is to help each family member to see the complexity of the problem, to accept responsibility for his or her own actions as contributions to the problem, and to see what he or she can do to contribute to individual and family well-being.

Cognitive-Behavioral, Psychosituational Therapy of Anxiety Disorders

Cognitive-behavioral, psychosituational therapy of children's anxiety disorders most appropriately includes both the parents and the child. Although it may be wise to assemble all family members together in. one room, we often find it more helpful to see the child and the parents separately, perhaps bringing them together at various times during the course of therapy as clinical needs dictate. Our reasons for seeing parents and child separately are several: (1) to remove the child from the parental pressures and to provide him or her a safe haven for change; (2)to communicate the pyschosituational nature of the problem to the parents; (3) to, give the parents a safe forum for acknowledging their respective roles in the child's problems; and (4) to give ourselves the "space" to make statements to the child without risking alienating the parents.

Even when separating the parents from the child in treatment, however, cognitive-behavioral-psychosituational intervention for both follows the orderly process described previously by us (Grieger and Boyd, 1980, 1983) in our skills-based model of rational-emotive behavior therapy. This model sees cognitive-behavioral therapy as flowing through three overlapping yet distinct stages, as follows.

Cognitive-Behavioral Insight

The first task of therapy proper is to facilitate in both the parents and the child the insights necessary to making change possible. For the parents, these insights entail an awareness that (1) their actions have significantly negative consequences for their child's adjustment in general and for his or her anxiety problem in particular; (2) their own attitudes, ideas, and beliefs, not the behaviors of the child, are in large measure responsible for their actions toward the child (note: this is the ABC theory of RET); (3) certain particular attitudes that they hold about themselves and/or their child (e.g., shoulds, awfuls) prompt them to behave toward the child as they do; (4) these attitudes may be conceptually illogical and empirically unsupportable, as well as consequentially untenable, and that they can be analyzed to determine whether this is so or not; (5) the adoption of more rational attitudes and behaviors on their part will have markedly positive effects on the child's performance and adjustment; and (6) they can indeed give up their child-defeating and self-defeating attitudes and adopt more constructive ones if they are willing to devote time and energy to doing so. To establish these insights, the therapist uses the typical techniques with adult clients in general (Grieger and Boyd, 1980, 1983).

In outlining these insights, we do not suggest that they can be taught in only one session. Indeed, several may be needed, and the clinicians had better take pains to convey these points persuasively and gently to many parents, lest they become resistant. For instance, it has been our experience that parents caught in the criticism and/or perfectionism traps can easily conclude that the therapist is too soft on their child, and they worry that changing their attitudes and behaviors will give the youngster license to misbehave or act in a lazy, goalless fashion. Because of these and other pitfalls, we generally take great pains to initially empathize with their concerns. We let them know that we share their goals for their child, but that we fear that their strategies (supported by evidence) actually thwart rather than facilitate what we all want.

Because children are not as intellectually and emotionally developed as adults, the establishment of basic insights is more difficult and more fundamental for them than for adults. Probably, the most basic insight for children is the awareness that there are alternative ways that they can act and feel about their typical problems of responding (DiGiuseppe, 1981). This insight helps them to know that other responses exist and that change is possible, a revelation to a good many youngsters. In teaching this insight, we have found it helpful to draw a "feeling/behaving" graph, or thermometer, in which different emotional levels of responses are marked at various points. For example, I (R.G.) drew a "mad thermometer" for 12-year-old Jeff showing cool (0°), warm (25°), hot (50°), very hot (75°), and boiling (100°) points. Then, through example, self-disclosure, and especially role playing, the child is asked to imagine or act out (i.e., experience) different responses along the continuum.

Once children see that different responses exist and are possible to acquire, they are ready to explore the negative consequences of their disturbed feelings and behaviors and the positives that alternative responses could provide. This insight is designed to motivate them to put energy into changing. Virtually any technique is acceptable within the cognitive-behavioral-psycho situational framework, including making lists, observing other children, playing with puppets, using games and stories, and role playing.

The key insight for children, of course, is that their own thoughts are the bad guys that cause their anxiety. For older children, a mini-lecture, backed by examples, often works to teach the ABCs. For younger ones, however, the use of role playing and drawings is advisable, so that they can both experience and see how their thoughts lead to their reactions, and how different thoughts can lead to different reactions. For instance, 8-year-old Bobby was taught to label as "nervous thoughts" certain of his thoughts that led to his tantrums and to label as "cool thoughts" the ones that led to certain appropriate and rewarding responses (see Fig. 2).

Cognitive-Behavioral-Psychosituational Working Through

Once family members gain the insights, they are ready for CBP working through. For parents, this involves the use of the cognitive, imaginal, emotive, and behavioral challenging or disputation techniques of REBT and other forms of cognitive-behavioral therapy (Bernard and Joyce, 1984; Ellis, 1962,

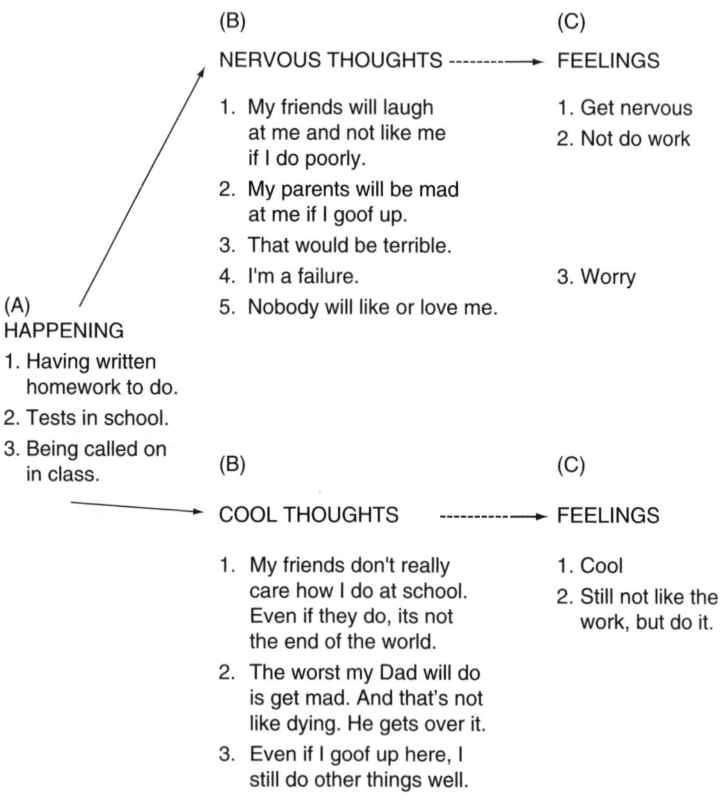

FIGURE 2. Bobby's Thought-Reaction drawing.

1993; Grieger and Boyd, 1983; Walen et al., 1980). The goal is a profound understanding of the illogic of, the lack of empirical support for, and the self-defeating and child-defeating nature of their basic beliefs, as well as an awareness of more plausible and constructive alternatives.

As opposed to adults,, however, children rarely appreciate the importance of logico-empirical disputation; most often have no idea how to do it; and, particularly in the , case of children below 7 or 8, often are incapable of doing it. For some older children, then, the therapist may find it more appropriate to teach critical thinking skills prior to a working-through process (DiGiuseppe, 1981). In this case, the therapist first instructs and then practices the youngster in empirical and conceptual disputations.

More typically, however, the therapist wants to construct a sequence of appropriate rational attitudes, positive emotional responses, and constructive behaviors with which to rehearse and train the child to think rationally (Grieger and Boyd, 1983). Central to this approach is the method of rational self-instruction and coping. It consists simply of constructing a rational self-talk dialogue that the child can practice at various times and can use when confronted with problem situations. The rational beliefs are put in the child's language and are practiced through imagery, role playing with the therapist, and rehearsal with adults, among other methods, with immediate and strong rewards for putting energy into this skill practice. This practice is most effective if it follows Meichenbaum's (1977, 1985) guidelines for teaching verbal self-instruction.

One final note here! We do not mean to imply that only cognitive strategies are used. On the contrary, this is the stage where the therapist attempts to "drown out" the child's habits of irrational thinking, feeling, and behaving through as many techniques as possible. They might include structured homework assignments (e.g., to tell a friend that you got a "D" on a test and see what happens), written homework, rational-emotive imagery, problem-solving training, and the like.

Generalized Learning and Skill Training

Success in the working-through stage means that the clients are doing well with those situation-specific problems on which therapy is focused. For older children and adults, an effort is made to generalize by helping them to adopt rational beliefs or philosophies that apply across situations. For these individuals, this stage of treatment is best focused on the learning of specific skills in effective living. There are two sets of skills that are the most relevant for parents whose child suffers from anxiety disorders: behavior modification techniques and empathetic listening techniques. The focus in both should be positive, supportive behaviors that help the child to feel accepted by the parents and acceptable to themselves as people.

For younger children, whose generalization ability is slim, a final stage is to generalize the therapeutic learning beyond the few specific situations in question to similar problems in other situations. This generalization would involve repeating the prior intervention steps in one or two new arenas at a time, until the child gradually chips away his or her irrational, anxiety-prompting cognitions across the board.

To sum up, the cognitive-behavioral, psychosituational therapy of children's anxiety disorders typically incorporates the treating of the family. This treatment can be given either in family sessions or, more likely, in separate sessions for the child and the parents. Regardless of the format, comprehensive REBT follows an orderly process, from a psycho-diagnosis through insight, working through, and generalized learning and skill training. At each stage, the emphasis is on the irrational cognitions that prompt the anxiety problems: on the parents' part, the ideas that cause them to behave in anxiety-inducing ways, and on the child's part, the irrational inferences and evaluations that directly cause her or his own anxiety reactions.

Conclusion

In this chapter, we have described and explained a comprehensive model for diagnosing and psychotherapeutically treating the anxieties, fears, and phobias of youngsters. The model considers those intrapersonal and ecological variables that theory and research have shown to be particularly keen influences on human behavior. We believe this approach to be the most clinically practical and effective schema that we have discovered in our years of study and practice.

References

Bandura, A. (1986). *Social foundations of thought and action: A social cognitive theory*. Englewood Cliffs, NJ: Prentice Hall.

Barrett, P. M., and Shoett, A. L. (2003). Parental involvement in the treatment of anxious children. In A. E. Kazdin and J. R. Weisz (eds.), *Evidence-based psychotherapies for children and adolescents*. New York: Guilford Press.

Beck, A. T. (1976). *Cognitive therapy and the emotional disorders*. New York: International Universities Press.

Beck, A. T., and Newman, C. F. (2004). Cognitive therapy. In R. M. Kaplan and B. J. Saddock (eds.), *Comprehensive textbook of psychiatry* (8th ed). Baltimore, MD: Lippincott, Williams, and Wilkins.

Becker, W. (1971). *Parents are teachers*. New York: Human Services Press, 1971.

Bernard, M. E. (2004). *The REBT therapist's pocket companion for working with children and adolescents*. New York: Albert Ellis Institute.

Bernard, M. E., and Joyce, M. R. (1984). *Rational emotive therapy with children and adolescents*. New York: Wiley.

Bernard, M.E., and Joyce, M.R. (1994). Rational-emotive therapy with children and adolescents. In T.R. Kratochwill and R. Morris (eds.), *Handbook of child and adolescent therapy*. Boston: Allyn and Bacon, pp. 221–246.

Bersoff, D. N., and Grieger, R. M. (1971). An interview model for the psychosituational assessment of children's behavior. *American Journal of Orthopsychiatry*, 41, 483–493.

Carson, R. C. (1969). *Interaction concepts of personality*. Chicago: Aldine.

DiGiuseppe, R. A. (1981). Cognitive therapy with children. In G. Emery, S. D. Hollon, and R. C. Bedrosian (eds.), *New directions in cognitive therapy*. New York: Guilford Press.

Ellis, A. (1962, 1994). *Reason and emotion in psychotherapy*. Secaucus, N.J.: Lyle Stuart/Carol Publishing.

Ellis, A. (1971). *Humanistic psychology: The rational-emotive approach*. New York: Crown, 1971.

Ellis, A. (1978). *Discomfort anxiety: A new cognitive-behavioral construct*. Invited address to the Association for Advancement of Behavior Therapy Annual Meeting, 17 November1978. New York, BMA Audio Cassettes.

Ellis, A. (1982). Psychoneurosis and anxiety problems. In R. Grieger and I. Grieger's (eds.), *Cognition and emotional disturbance*. New York: Human Sciences Press.

Ellis, A., Wolfe, J. L., and Moseley, S. (1966). *How to prevent your child from becoming a neurotic adult*. New York: Crown Publishers.

Grieger, R. M., and Abidin, R. (1972). Psychosocial assessment: A model for the school community psychologist. *Psychology in the Schools*, 9, 112–119.

Grieger, R., and Boyd, J. (1980). *Rational-emotive therapy: A skills-based approach*. New York: Van Nostrand Reinhold.

Grieger, R. M., and Boyd, J. D. (1983). Rational-emotive therapy. In H. T. Prout and D. T. Brown's (eds.), *Counseling and psychotherapy with children and adolescents: Theory and practice for school and clinic settings*. New York: Mariner Press.

Hauck, P. A. (1967). The rational management of children. New York: Libra Publishers.

Kazdin, A. E., Siegel, T. C., and Bass, D. (1990). Drawing upon clinical practice to inform research on child and adolescent psychotherapy: A survey of practitioners. *Professional Psychology: Research and Practice*, 21, 189–198.

Kazdin, A. E., Stolar, M. J., and Marciano, P. L. (1995). Risk factors for dropping out of treatment among White and Black families. *Journal of Family Psychology*, 9, 402–417.

Kazdin, A. E., and Weisz, J. R. (2003). Context and background evidence-based psychotherapies for children and adolescents. In A. E. Kazdin and J. R. Weisz (eds.), *Evidence-based psychotherapies for children and adolescents*. New York: Guilford Press.

Kelly, G. A. (1955). *The psychology of personal constructs* (2 vols.), New York: W. W. Norton.

Kendall, P. C., Choudhury, M., Hudson, J., and Webb, A. (2002). *The C.A.T. project workbook for the cognitive-behavioral treatment of anxious adolescents*. Ardmore, PA: Workbook Publishing.

Kessler, J. (1966). *Psychopathology of childhood*. Englewood Cliffs, N.J.: Prentice-Hall.

Lerner, R. M. (1991). Changing organism-context relations as the basic process of development: A developmental contextual perspective. *Developmental Psychology*, 27, 27–32.

Meichenbaum, D. (1977). *Cognitive-behavior modification: An integrative approach*. New York: Plenum Press.

Meichenbaum, D. (1985). *Stress inoculation training: A practitioner's guidebook*. New York: Allyn and Bacon.

Meichenbaum, D. (2001). *Treatment of individuals with anger control problems and aggressive behaviors: A clinical handbook*. Clearwater, Fl: Institute Press.

Mischel, W. (1968). *Personality and assessment*. New York: Wiley.

Mischel, W. (1973). Toward a cognitive social learning reconceptualization of personality. *Psychological Review, 80*, 252–283.

Mischel, W. (1990). Personality disposition revisited and revised: A review after three decades. In L. Pervin (ed.), *Handbook of personality: Theory and research*. New York: Guilford Press.

Peterson, D. (1968). *The clinical study of social behavior*. New York: Appleton-Century-Crofts.

Rotter, J. B. *Social learning and clinical psychology*. (1954). Englewood Cliffs, NJ: Prentice-Hall.

Seligman, M. E. P. (1991). *Learned optimism*. New York: Knopf.

Vernon, A. (2002). Philip: A third grader with anxiety. In A. Ellis and J. Wilde (eds.), *Case studies in rational emotive behavior therapy with children and adolescents*. Upper Saddle River, NJ: Prentice Hall.

Walen, S. R., DiGiuseppe, R., and Wessler, R. L. (1980). *A practitioner's guide to rational-emotive therapy*. New York: Oxford University Press.

Wallace, J. (1966). An abilities conception of personality: Some implications for personality measurement. *American Psychologist, 21,* 132–138.

9

Treating Aggressive Children: A Rational-Emotive Behavior Systems Approach

RAYMOND DIGIUSEPPE AND JILL KELTER

Description of the Problem of Aggression

Aggressive behavior remains stable from early childhood through adulthood and is one of the most invariable human traits. Aggressive children are likely to be aggressive as adults and to engage in physical abuse and criminal behavior (Huesmann et al., 1984; Loeber and Dishion, 1983). Effective early interventions may be necessary to change this trajectory. This chapter addresses the treatment of aggressive children with Rational-Emotive Behavior Therapy (REBT).

Professionals often confuse anger and aggression because they often occur together (DiGiuseppe et al., 1994). Distinguishing aggression from anger is important. Anger is an emotion, whereas aggression entails engaging in a physical or verbal action (Bernard and Joyce, 1984). One can be angry without exhibiting aggression, and one can behave aggressively without feeling angry. Aggression involves an external act, whereas angry emotions are private events. The distinction between aggression and anger is relevant in the clinical differentiation between emotionally reactive aggression versus instrumental or predatory aggression. Emotionally reactive aggression occurs when strong emotions of anger are elicited by some perceived threat to self. Thus anger and aggression coexist. Unlike emotionally reactive aggression, predatory aggression need not arise from any emotion. These aggressors simply take things from others by force or coerce others to maintain their own sense of power. Individuals engaging in predatory aggression may be categorized as psychopathic or as having an antisocial personality disorder.

Often children who are aggressive are classified as having either Oppositional Defiant Disorder (ODD) or Conduct Disorder (CD)

(American Psychiatric Association [APA], 1994). Children who are verbally aggressive and exhibit a pattern of hostile behavior particularly toward authority figures may be categorized as having (ODD). It is also possible, however, for children who are not aggressive to manifest signs of ODD. CD is a more severe problem occurring when the child violates major societal norms. Most of the CD criteria involve aggressive behavior toward people, animals, or property. CD is categorized further into subtypes of either childhood or adolescent onset. Children with CD who have childhood onset-type, where one criterion of CD is present before the age of ten, are more likely to demonstrate more pronounced aggression than those who manifest signs of CD in adolescence. Further, childhood onset CD is more likely than adolescent onset CD to develop into Antisocial Personality Disorder (APA, 1994). Therefore, we presume that children with childhood-onset CD are more likely than children with adolescent-onset CD to display predatory aggression.

Basic Approach

Rational-Emotive Behavior Therapy (REBT) provides an effective model for treating aggressive children. As its name implies, REBT is an integrative therapy that incorporates many interventions to accomplish its goals (Walen et al., 1992). Research suggests that disruptive and aggressive behaviors are often best treated behaviorally by changes in home or school contingencies. In fact, for children who display predatory aggression we recommend intervention based exclusively on concrete behavioral strategies. Based on our clinical experience, these children do not respond well to cognitive treatments. As an element of REBT, cognitive interventions may also be used and are often directed at the adults who need to implement the behavioral strategies.

REBT involves strategies for learning to control dysfunctional emotions. REBT can be used to treat aggressive children in two ways: by teaching children to control the underlying angry emotions that lead to aggression and by teaching parents to control their disruptive emotions that interfere with effective parenting skills.

The trademark of REBT is its emphasis on teaching people to learn the **"ABCs"** of emotional disturbance, identifying the **A**ctivating events, their **B**eliefs about those events, and the resulting **C**onsequences. REBT teaches that disturbed emotional and behavioral **c**onsequences result from irrational **b**eliefs individuals hold, rather than from **a**ctivating events. REBT works to alleviate emotional disturbance by helping people to identify their irrational **b**eliefs, recognize that the irrational **b**eliefs are maladaptive, and replace those dysfunctional cognitions with more adaptive, rational **b**eliefs. Rational cognitions express preferential, flexible desires, whereas irrational cognitions express absolutistic, rigid needs. Rational thinking leads to happiness and enables individuals to attain goals and strive toward their potential; irrational thinking causes people to be extremely disturbed, and thwarts individuals' ability to attain their goals, leading to unhappiness.

REBT also distinguishes between disturbed, dysfunctional emotions and normal, motivating, albeit negative emotions. Negative emotions do not reflect psychopathology. If an activating event occurs (**A**) and one thinks irrationally (**B**), one will experience a disturbed emotion such as anger or anxiety (**C**). If one then challenges one's irrational belief and replaces it with a rational belief (a new **B**), one will still experience a negative, nondisturbed, motivating emotion. Most psychotherapists understand therapeutic improvement as a quantitative shift in the emotion. However, Ellis (1962); Ellis and DiGiuseppe (1993) proposed that when people think rational thoughts they experience a qualitatively different emotion rather than a lower intensity of the disturbed emotion. The emotions generated by rational thoughts will be in the same family of emotions as the disturbed emotion, but they differ in many aspects. Ellis posits that although irrational thinking leads to anxiety, depression, or anger, rational thinking will lead to concern, sadness, and annoyance, respectively. These emotions are not necessarily less intense but they may lead to qualitatively different phenomenological experiences and they will elicit different behavioral reactions.

Intervention Procedures Based on Empirical Research

Several meta-analyses examining the effectiveness of psychotherapy with children and adolescents have concluded that behavioral and cognitive therapies are more effective than non-behavioral or traditional therapies (Casey and Berman, 1985; Weisz et al., 1987; 1995). However, these reviews failed to address which behavioral and cognitive treatments were most effective with which types of children. We have uncovered more than 30 cognitive and behavioral interventions used with children. Knowing that such interventions are generally more effective than non-behavioral interventions still leaves practitioners with the task of choosing from a variety of techniques. The results of two recent meta-analyses concerning cognitive and behavioral interventions with aggressive children can provide a basis for treatment planning.

Wellen (1997) conducted a meta-analysis of 20 single subject studies of cognitive and behavioral treatments with aggressive children. Studies of children presenting with aggression as the primary problem, and with no other major clinical syndromes such as psychoses or developmental disabilities, were selected from a comprehensive search of the research literature. The subjects in the studies ranged in age from 3 to 17 and exhibited verbal aggression, physical aggression, or both. Wellen coded the dependent variables as measures of prosocial behavior or antisocial behavior. The treatment variables that made the greatest impact on increasing prosocial behaviors sometimes had a small effect on reducing antisocial behaviors. Similarly, the treatments that had the largest effect sizes for reducing antisocial behaviors sometimes had minimal effect for increasing prosocial behaviors. Overall, treatments involving rehearsal (e.g., modeling, role-play, and social skills training) were the most effective.

Kendall's (1993) cognitive distortion and cognitive deficit model can explain Wellen's results. This model suggests that the cognitive processes of aggression involve both cognitive distortions and deficiencies. Aggressive children often engage in dysfunctional thinking and lack the skills to use environmental cues and process information accurately, especially regarding others' actions. Kendall suggested that practice involving techniques such as modeling and role-play leads to the development of more appropriate coping skills and social skills that were absent from the child's repertoire. None of the studies in Wellen's meta-analysis used rehearsal alone. Researchers combined rehearsal of new skills with other techniques. The combined treatments with the highest effect sizes were those that paired rehearsal with some form of contingency management such as contingent reinforcement, reprimands, response-cost, and time-out.

The type of contingency intervention employed had differential effects on the dependent variables. Positive behavioral interventions (positive rewards and praise) increased prosocial behaviors but did not reduce antisocial behavior. Negative behavioral interventions (reprimands, response-cost, and time-out) had larger effect sizes for reducing antisocial behavior but a much lesser effect on increasing prosocial behavior. Negative contingency management procedures yielded a larger effect size than the use of positive interventions.

DiGiuseppe et al. (1996) recently performed a meta-analysis on 20 between-groups outcome studies using cognitive and behavioral treatments for children and adolescents classified primarily as aggressive[1]. The findings suggested that the treatment components of modeling and behavior rehearsal (role-play) were most effective. This supports Wellen's (1997) finding with single case studies indicating that treatments involving rehearsal were most effective. As in Wellen's (1997) meta-analysis, use of negative contingency management techniques alone was more effective than use of positive treatments alone. Despite the greater acceptability of positive reinforcement, negative consequences might be more effective in reducing aggression. Surprisingly, negative techniques alone were also superior to the combination of negative and positive treatments. Further supporting Wellen's (1997) findings, positive techniques were most effective at increasing prosocial behaviors, whereas negative techniques were most effective in reducing undesirable behaviors. This suggests that therapists should choose different treatments depending on which types of behaviors are targeted for change.

---

[1] This meta-analysis is part of a larger ongoing meta-analysis of over 260 outcome studies involving a broader population of children with externalizing disorders.

DiGiuseppe et al. (1996) found that the combination of cognitive and behavioral therapies worked better with children than either one alone. Cognitive components included problem-solving, coping self-statements, and anger-management training, whereas behavioral components included positive and negative reinforcement techniques, relaxation training, and rehearsal techniques. Researchers often fail to operationalize their definitions of aggression and fail to distinguish between angry aggressive and predatory aggressive behavior. We believe that this distinction between types of aggression is important and that they may be responsive to different interventions.

Cognitive interventions may be more effective with children whose aggression is of the emotional type and less effective with the predatory type. Cognitive skills may help the child learn to reduce anger and thus limit impulsive aggression. Our clinical experience suggests that children with predatory aggression may respond better to contingency management and may be more resistant to treatment overall.

Wellen's (1997) meta-analysis of cognitive interventions consisted only of problem-solving strategies. However, the cognitive components of REBT involve more complex skills that require more motivation than problem-solving techniques alone. We recommend that instead of beginning with both behavioral and cognitive techniques, treatment should focus initially on behavioral techniques and then the cognitive component should be added as needed. At times it may be necessary to first use negative strategies so that the child's behavior can become more manageable. This may help the child to become more invested and motivated in treatment. A cognitive component can then be added while continuing the behavioral treatments. Also, at this time, one might include positive behavioral techniques with rehearsal. For instance, one might introduce a prosocial behavior one would like the child to increase. Besides positively reinforcing this behavior, the research indicates that giving the child an opportunity to practice the behavior through role-play or modeling, for example, is beneficial.

Results of these meta-analytic reviews suggest that therapists need to develop interventions that model and rehearse new cognitive and behavioral responses to emotionally laden eliciting stimuli. The effectiveness of these rehearsal interventions may be augmented by changes in the contingencies for aggressive behavior. Negative contingencies, such as response-cost and time-out, may be more effective than positive reinforcement. Also the negative interventions appear to eliminate antisocial behavior and positive contingencies help build new prosocial responses. However, the elimination of antisocial responses appears to need more attention initially when treating aggressive children. Finally, adding more interventions to the treatment does not necessarily lead to more effective treatment, and in fact, may reduce effectiveness. This presents a problem for clinicians treating angry children. Treatment usually entails teaching children to evaluate anger-provoking situations differently and to respond in new ways. Parents and teachers learn to control their own anger at the child, to consequate antisocial responses negatively without being punitive, and to reinforce new prosocial responses positively, which is a lot to cover in treatment. Developmentally appropriate treatment models need to be created that allow these new skills to be implemented effectively.

Major Mechanisms of Change

REBT theory posits four types of irrational thinking that lead to emotional disturbance: demandingness, awfulizing, global condemnation of human worth, and frustration intolerance. Two of these, demandingness and frustration intolerance, are most likely to be core schemas of children with emotionally reactive aggression.

Demandingness

Demandingness is represented in English by the words "must," "should," "ought to," and "have to." These words reflect demands on how the self, others, or the world must be. REBT makes the distinction between preferences and demands. Individuals' desires do not cause disturbance. However, when individuals demand that their preferences become reality, those individuals may become disturbed. Demandingness can be thought of as schema assimilation rather than schema accommodation. When disturbed individuals encounter a situation that is inconsistent with their desires, they assimilate and still construct the world as consistent with their desires. Failing to distinguish between the situation as it is and one's desire leads to poor coping. When adjusted people encounter a similar situation, they accommodate and restructure their schema to include the discrepancy between the way the world is and what they want. This construction of the situation as inconsistent with one's desires is more likely to lead to adaptive coping responses. For example, an adolescent might tell herself, "My parents must let me do what I want." Not only does she want her parents to allow her to do as she desires, but she believes that because she wants it, they will comply. She may be shocked when they punish her for transgressions of their rules and she may continue to behave against their rules despite their feedback indicating that they disapprove of her behavior and will initiate consequences for it. A different young woman, who recognizes that her parents will not behave as she wishes just because she wishes it, may try to win them over to her view or pursue other avenues of gratification.

Frustration Intolerance (FI)

Beliefs marked by FI imply that an individual cannot stand something he or she finds frustrating or that he or she does not have the endurance to survive in its presence. For example, someone who is addicted to caffeine might tell himself or herself, "I cannot stand feeling the slightest bit tired when I have all this work to do; I must have some coffee." Or, the adolescent mentioned above may say to herself, "I cannot stand it if my parents do not let me do what I want." These types of beliefs are illogical as well because, short of dying, one is tolerating whatever one claims one cannot stand.

Individual Psychotherapy with Children and Adolescents

Aggressive children often experience disapproval from many sources including parents, teachers, and peers. An important facet of aggressive behavior is that, like most externalized disorders, it is viewed as a problem primarily based on when and how others view it as a problem. However, those engaging in aggression are unlikely to view their behavior as a problem. As a result, most children attend therapy against their will. Aggressive children can be particularly difficult to treat because they are often not motivated to change their behaviors. Thus, when therapists encounter aggressive children, the initial goal of therapy is to motivate them for behavior change; that is, to ensure there is agreement on the goals and tasks of therapy.

Discussing the goals and tasks of therapy may be more critical to the establishment of a therapeutic alliance with children than with adults. Prochaska and DiClemente's (1981) constructs of stages and processes of change are particularly helpful in designing interventions for those unmotivated to change. They postulate that people pass through four stages of attitudes about change. These include the pre-contemplative stage (the person does not wish to change); the contemplative stage (the person is thinking about changing); the action stage (a person tries to change); and the maintenance stage (a person consolidates his or her gains and attempts to keep the new behaviors). Prochaska and DiClemente proposed that the type of therapy needs to match the clients' stage of change. REBT is an action-oriented therapy, designed for people in the action stage of change. Since most children and adolescents arrive in the pre-contemplative stage, the therapist must establish agreement on the goals and tasks of therapy to build the therapeutic alliance before using such an active approach.

DiGiuseppe and colleagues (DiGiuseppe, 1995; DiGiuseppe and Bernard, 1983; DiGiuseppe et al., 1996; Walen et al., 1992) presented a cognitive behavioral approach to establish the therapeutic alliance in children and adolescents who begin therapy in the pre-contemplative stage. A technique called the motivational syllogism may be used to reach agreement on the goals of therapy. The elements of this motivational syllogism are as follows and are described further in Table 1:

1. My present emotion is dysfunctional (for aggressive children, the dysfunctional emotion is primarily their anger).
2. An acceptable alternative emotional script exists for this type of activating event (e.g., annoyance).

TABLE 1. Steps of the Motivational Syllogism to Establish Agreement on the Goals and Tasks of Therapy.

Prerequisite Beliefs to Disputing Irrational Beliefs
Insight 1: My present emotion is dysfunctional. **Technique:** Through Socratic questioning, help the client understand how the present emotional reaction is dysfunctional.
Insight 2: There is an alternative acceptable emotional goal. **Technique:** Through teaching and reviewing acceptable models, help the client understand that there are alternative emotional scripts that are more adaptive.
Insight 3: It is better for me to give up my dysfunctional emotion and replace it with the alternative emotional script. **Technique:** Through Socratic questioning, have the client imagine feeling the new emotional script and review the consequences for the new emotions. This should accomplish agreement on the goals of therapy.
Insight 4: My beliefs influence my emotions, therefore, it is appropriate to examine and change my beliefs. **Techniques:** Teach the beliefs-consequences connection. This should accomplish agreement on the tasks of therapy.

3. Giving up the dysfunctional emotion and working toward feeling the alternative one is better for me.
4. My beliefs cause my emotions; therefore, I will work at changing my beliefs to change my emotions.

This model proscribes that the therapist ask clients in a Socratic fashion to assess the consequences of their emotional and behavioral responses. This helps clients identify the negative consequences for their maladaptive emotions and behaviors. Next, the therapist presents alternative emotional reactions that are culturally acceptable to each client. Because people learn emotional scripts from their families and some emotional scripts are culture-specific, it is possible that the disturbed child or adolescent has not changed because he or she cannot conceptualize and experience an acceptable emotional script in place of the disturbed emotion. REBT has adopted the script theories of emotions (DiGiuseppe, 1995) which proposes that clients need to learn adaptive emotional scripts, not just change the intensity of their feelings. As a result, it is helpful for therapists to be very careful with the words they use to describe emotions and to help clients to choose which emotions they will use to replace their disturbed emotion. They help clients formulate a vocabulary to describe adaptive, albeit negative, affective states that they could experience instead of the disturbed emotions. Therapists need to explore culturally acceptable alternative emotional reactions with the client. Next, therapists help clients connect the alternative script with an advantageous outcome.

Therapists then focus on helping the clients to change their dysfunctional cognitions and emotions. As mentioned earlier, with aggressive children and adolescents, the disturbed thoughts usually are centered around the irrational beliefs of demandingness or frustration intolerance, and the disturbed emotion is that of excessive anger. Therapists explain and demonstrate how thoughts can cause feelings and that certain thoughts, namely irrational beliefs (IBs) produce disturbed emotions, whereas other rational beliefs (RBs) lead to nondisturbed emotions. Some children may have difficulty distinguishing between disturbed and nondisturbed emotions, and therefore, the therapist may need to teach them to identify and label various emotions, and then to be able to distinguish between those that are helpful and those that are hurtful. Further, the therapist teaches that thoughts can be changed to produce nondisturbed feelings. The therapist helps the child practice how to distinguish between disturbed and nondisturbed cognitions and emotions. Additionally, the child practices disputing irrational beliefs and replacing them with more rational thoughts. Specific techniques used to help children practice these skills include modeling, role-playing, imagery, and homework involving the parents. Other REBT techniques used with children include assigning self-help books (i.e., bibliotherapy) and written homework assignments.

Children who have not yet reached the concrete operational phase (those who are younger than 8-years-old) will have difficulty with the logic of disputing and thinking about their thinking. For these children, therapists can use treatments that focus on concrete skills, such as problem-solving (Spivack and Shure, 1974; Spivack et al., 1976) and rehearsing rational coping statements (DiGiuseppe, 1977; Meichenbaum, 1971).

Adolescents are concerned with forming their own identities. They are often oppositional and refuse to heed the advice of people from a different generation. Therefore, with adolescents it is particularly important to ensure that the therapist and adolescent agree on the goals and tasks of therapy, and to explain how the tasks will improve his or her current situation. We recommend therapists go through the steps of the motivational syllogism before the discussion of each new problem and before the use of any intervention. Establishing these four beliefs will help motivate a child or adolescent to engage in the REBT process. This model facilitates agreement on the goals of therapy and moves clients to the action stage of change. Therapists need to assess each child's and adolescent's stage of change and agreement on the goals of therapy before proceeding with any interventions. If the child or adolescent has not reached the action stage and does not want to change, techniques outlined by DiGiuseppe et al. (1996) or other similar techniques like motivational interviewing (Miller and Rollnick, 2002) could be used to bring about a desire to change.

Parental Involvement in Treatment

Despite the context in which children are being treated, having parents involved in the treatment is crucial so that behavioral changes can generalize to the home setting. The problem is that although parents desperately want to see their child's behavior change, they often have difficulty carrying out behavioral interventions. Research has shown that the presence of parents' maladaptive emotions is the primary reason adults fail to engage in correct parenting practices (Dix, 1991) and fail to benefit from behavioral parent training programs (Dadds and McHugh, 1992). Although behavioral parent training may be the most successful intervention for children with externalized disorders (Kazdin, 1994), parents are unlikely to follow a therapist's recommendations if their emotional disturbance about their child's behavior interferes. The failure to address parents' emotional reactions to parenting may be the largest void in the extensive parent behavior training literature (Petersen et al., 1997). In fact, the failure to find combined interventions as more effective than singular interventions in our meta-analytic review may occur because parents are too upset while interacting with their children to follow the behavioral interventions taught to them.

DiGiuseppe (1988) devised a sequential family therapy model for the treatment of families of children with externalized disorders. In this model, changing the parents' irrational cognitions and emotional disturbance is the goal in order to get the parents to adopt more effective parenting skills. This is necessary to accomplish the primary goal of changing the child's symptomatic behavior. The parents' disturbance is a crucial target of the interventions; both the parents' and the child's disturbances are treated with REBT. It is also helpful to have the parents involved in treatment from the outset so that the therapy does not reinforce what the child is likely to feel at home—that he or she is the problem child and the cause of the family's problems. This REBT family therapy model focuses on the following steps: (1) Conduct a thorough assessment of the child's difficulties, including a behavioral analysis of the eliciting stimuli, consequences, reinforcers, and family functioning; (2) Form a therapeutic alliance with the parents; (3) Choose a target behavior and appropriate consequences collaboratively with the parents; (4) Assess parents' ability to carry out the interventions, including their emotional reactions and irrational beliefs; (5) Change parents' irrational beliefs and emotions that may interfere with performing the new parenting strategies; (6) Have parents predict what resistance they expect to occur to their new parenting strategies from the identified patient or other family members and generate solutions to confront these attempts at resistance; (7) Assess the parents' ability to follow the strategies they choose to handle the resistance, again focusing on their emotions and irrational beliefs; (8) Intervene with parents again to change irrational beliefs and schema that may prevent them from handling the resistance; (9) Continue to assess the child's progress and the parents' compliance with the behavioral skills and modify the behavior treatment plan as needed; (10) Begin individual therapy with the child to internalize gains made by the behavioral intervention. These steps are presented in Table 2.

Even when the child is treated individually, parents can still play a role in treatment. When individual therapy is employed, parents are often unaware of the issues discussed by the therapist and child. Parents often want to be involved in their child's therapy because of their natural concern for their child's well-being. If the child agrees, if the problem does not involve a family matter the child would be unable discuss in front of his or her parents, and if the parents

TABLE 2. Sequence of family therapy for treatment of externalized disorders.

Stages of Therapy
Stage 1: Conduct assessment: Assess (1) the nature of the psychopathology (2) the developmental level of functioning and the discriminative stimulus that elicit the problems and its reinforcers (3) the structure of the family (4) the roles of the individual members (5) who will resist? (6) the emotions, cognitions, and skills of each member.
Stage 2: Engage parents in the therapeutic alliance: If one parent is resistant to change, use motivational interviewing or problem-solving with the motivated parent to engage the resistant parent.
Stage 3: Plan behavioral intervention: Choose a target behavior and consequences. Depending on the needs of the child and the family, the intervention can aim to increase a positive behavior or to decrease a maladaptive behavior.
Stage 4: Assess parents' ability to carry out the agreed intervention: Assess the parents' emotions and the cognitions which will stop them from carrying out the agreed upon intervention. Some possible parental interfering emotions: guilt, anger, anxiety, and discomfort anxiety. Assess the parents' irrational beliefs. Some possible irrational beliefs: (1) demandingness (2) catastrophizing (3) frustration intolerance (4) projected frustration intolerance (5) condemnation of the child.
Stage 5: Conduct therapy with the parents: Cognitive restructuring of the parents' irrational beliefs. Use all of the appropriate techniques of adult REBT to focus on the emotions and the cognitions identified in the previous stage.
Stage 6: Predict resistance: What do the parents believe the child or others will do to sabotage their efforts? Problem-solve how they can respond to those attempts at sabotage. This will help them continue to deal with sabotage on their own after termination.
Stage 7: Assess the parents' ability to implement the intervention: Ask the parents to imagine themselves following through. What emotions and beliefs will they have about this new action? What do they believe their emotional reactions will be? Assess the emotions and the cognitions that will get in their way of following through on the intervention chosen to counteract the sabotage.
Stage 8: Conduct intervention with parents: Dispute the irrational beliefs that they will experience that may lead to resistance.
Stage 9: Assess how the child responds to the plan: (1) repeat the assessment (2) redesign the interventions through collaborative problem-solving, if necessary (3) continue to assess the parents' ability to carry out the new interventions (4) continue to use cognitive restructuring to help them follow through on the planned interventions.
Stage 10: Conduct individual therapy with the child or adolescent: At the beginning of each session, assess the progress the child and the parents have made. If parents have followed their interventions, remain in this stage. If they have not, return to stage 8. Use motivational syllogism to help the child internalize the desirability of change and cooperation with the therapists. Use all REBT and CBT methods to reduce the undesirable target behaviors and support the desired positive changes.

are willing, they can play a helpful role in the child's individual therapy. Bernard and DiGiuseppe (1990) recommend four different ways that parents can become involved to improve the effectiveness of individual therapy. First, children can be assigned the homework of describing important points of a session to their parents, such as the beliefs-consequences connection, disputes to irrational beliefs, or the rational coping statements they will use when they become upset.

This technique gives children opportunities to rehearse the principles therapists want to teach and allows the parents to feel involved in their child's treatment.

Second, parents can join the therapy session. When problematic activating events or emotional upset occurs between sessions, parents usually attempt to help their child and give advice. Sometimes parents' comments are inconsistent with the therapists' goals; they reinforce their child's irrational thinking, or they are just not helpful. If parents have been present during the sessions, they can remind their child of the rational coping statements provided in the session or they can use the principles of REBT that they learned in session to guide their responses to their child when the child experiences problems. Again, parents who participate in this way feel good about being part of the solution and learn how to talk to their child in ways that are helpful. Some parents even report that it has helped them with their own emotional problems.

Third, parents can provide information that children often forget. Weekly therapy sessions were designed for adults. Children often fail to remember significant events that happen between sessions, thus denying therapists important information about problems they have had since the last session. When parents are present, they often remind the children of their successful coping experiences which therapists can reinforce. The parents also report important activating events that children do not handle well which can be the focus of the session.

Fourth, therapists can often design homework assignments that include the parents. For example, children who react angrily when they are teased need to learn new rational coping statements in response to verbal attacks by peers. Often therapists can role-play the verbal attacks in the session and the children learn to rehearse their disputes and coping statements. Therapists can enlist the parents to role-play their children's tormentors between sessions. The parent can call out a barb to the child and the child will rehearse his or her new cognitions and new social skills. Here the parent prompts the rehearsal of a new response and can coach the child because of what the parent has learned in the session. Whenever and however possible, REBT involves parents in the child's treatment.

Case Study

Jamie, a 9-year-old girl, was referred for therapy by her mother, because her parents could not control her behavior and were concerned that soon her behavior would be entirely out of their control. Her parents' primary complaint was that Jamie did not follow their directions. When she did not get what she wanted, she became verbally and physically aggressive. Her parents explained that when they ask Jamie to do something (such as helping them set the table for dinner, or letting her father watch sports events on TV), she often ignores them. At first she pretends she does not hear them and when they persist, she says that she does not want to do whatever it is they have asked of her and that she should not have to do it. Further, often when Jamie asks something of her parents (such as if she can have a friend over) and they say, "No" to her, she whines and then becomes verbally aggressive, saying things such as "I hate you," or "You do not love me." If she still does not get what she wants she will, at times, begin to push and hit her parents. Jamie's parents reported that nothing they do helps. Socially, Jamie has few same-aged peers. Her friends are primarily younger children who let her control them. When they do not do what Jamie wants, she uses various verbal threats to scare them and when that does not work she will occasionally hit them. Academically, Jamie gets average grades and can be managed fairly easily in her classroom.

We can conceptualize this case from REBT, behavioral, and systemic perspectives. Because Jamie's parents had never established a pattern of firm limit setting with her, she learned that she could control the interactions with her parents and became used to getting her way. Her parents' attempts to enforce limits elicited IBs in Jamie that she *must* have her way and that she *cannot stand* failing to get what she wants. Feelings of extreme frustration and anger accompanied these IBs, which led Jamie to try even harder to get what she wanted, often by acting aggressively. Her parents' tendency to react to her by eventually giving in only served to reinforce the oppositional and aggressive behavior they wished to extinguish.

The first step in dealing with this case was to teach Jamie's parents to use more effective behavior management techniques. Before this could be accomplished, however, it was necessary to identify the core beliefs that were interfering with Jamie's parents' attempts at managing or disciplining their daughter. In working with her parents it was discovered that they felt guilty about punishing Jamie because they thought "It is awful if we cannot give her what she wants because then she might not love us. It must mean that we are not good parents if we make her upset." For Jamie's parents to be able to use behavioral techniques effectively, they first needed to work on challenging their IBs and replacing them with more rational beliefs. This helped them to change their dysfunctional feelings of guilt to more helpful feelings of concern.

Jamie's parents were then ready to choose a target behavior for Jamie. They wanted her to stop hitting her peers or parents. The therapist started with teaching her parents behavioral strategies of employing negative techniques through rehearsal, using strategies of time-out and punishment where natural consequences were established. In the therapy room, they role-played scenarios where Jamie pretended to hit her parents and her parents set consequences for her. Practice was accompanied by therapist feedback about how they could better carry out the techniques.

Once the initial negative behavioral strategies were in place, the next step was to begin having individual sessions with Jamie. Working on motivating her to want to change was crucial, making sure she agreed on the goals and tasks of therapy. This was accomplished through Socratic dialogue and the motivational syllogism. Jamie realized that becoming angry when things do not go her way is not helpful for various reasons. She said she did not like feeling upset and seeing her parents get upset. She recognized that sometimes her anger caused her to say or do things to others that she would rather not do. Further, Jamie began to realize that her anger and the aggressive behaviors she exhibited made it difficult for her to form and maintain friendships. Jamie was taught that she could feel other ways that would be more helpful to her. She worked on learning this new emotional script. Next, she was taught how her beliefs influence her behavior. At this point she was more motivated to change her behavior and specifically to think about what kind of beliefs she has that influence her behavior. As she approached the action stage of change she was willing to use rational self-statements and start challenging her own IBs saying things to herself such as, "I guess I do not have to have my parents do what I ask . . . though I prefer they do what I want. This way I won't feel so angry when they do not do what I want. Instead, I would feel a little mad and not really angry." At this point Jamie's parents were encouraged to begin using positive techniques with rehearsal in the therapy setting and at home. For example, one of Jamie's target behaviors was setting the table. The family, with the therapist, devised a reward system contingent upon Jamie's behavior. Jamie's parents continued to use negative strategies once they had successfully implemented the positive techniques.

Research Support of REBT

DiGiuseppe and Nevas (1997) discovered fourteen reviews of REBT (DiGiuseppe et al., 1977; Engels et al., 1993; Gossette and O'Brien, 1992; 1993; Haaga and Davison, 1989; Hajzler and Bernard, 1991; Jorm, 1989; Lyons and Woods, 1991; Mahoney, 1974; McGovern and Silverman, 1984; Oei et al., 1993; Polder, 1986; Silverman et al., 1992; Zettle, and Hayes, 1980). Most of these are narrative reviews. Three have been meta-analyses (i.e., Engels et al., 1993; Lyons and Woods, 1991; Polder, 1986). Most have included studies of adults and children. Others have focused only on adults (i.e., Gossette and O'Brien, 1992; Zettle and Hayes, 1980) and two have focused only on research with children and adolescents (i.e., Gossette and O'Brien, 1993; Hajzler and Bernard, 1991). Most reviews have been favorable, although some others have been critical. Table 3 lists the reviews alphabetically by author and includes the year published, the range of years included in the studies, the populations reviewed, and their general conclusions.

Each review employed a different selection criterion. More than 280 outcome studies are mentioned in these fourteen reviews. However, the reviews rarely included the same studies. Only 13 studies appeared in five reviews, and only 3 studies were included in six reviews. No study appeared in seven or more of the reviews. One hundred and twenty-four studies were mentioned in only one review. DiGiuseppe and Nevas (1997) point out that the reviews had

TABLE 3. Meta-analytic reviews of the REBT outcome literature.

Author(s)	Year Published	Range of Years Studied	Number of Studies	Population Reviewed	Conclusions
DiGiuseppe, Miller, and Trexler	1977	1970–1977	26	Published and unpublished studies of children and adults.	RET "... appear(s) generally positive and promising, but far from conclusive." p. 70
Engels, Garnefski, and Diekstra	1993	1970–1988	32	Published and unpublished studies of children and adults.	"RET on the whole was effective, compared with placebo and no treatment. Its effects were maintained over time, and it produced a delayed treatment effect with regard to behavioral outcome criteria." p. 1088
Gonzalez, Nelson, Gutkin, Saunders, Galloway, and Shwery	2004	1972–2002	19	Published studies of children and adolescents.	"The overall mean weighted effect of REBT was positive and significant...the longer the duration of REBT sessions, the greater the impact...children benefited more from REBT than adolescents" p. 222
Gossette and O'Brien	1992	1970–1990	85	Published and unpublished studis of adults.	"RET was effective in 25% of comparisons." p. 9 RET results in, "...a decreased score on scales of irrationality... a parallel decrease in self reported emotional distress. Other measures, noticeably behavior, were insensitive to RET...RET has little or no practical benefit " p. 20
Gossette and O'Brien	1993	1974–1992	36	Published and unpublished studies of children and adolescents.	RET has little or no practical benefit. "The most distinctive outcome of RET is a decrease in the endorsement of irrational beliefs." p. 21 "We can conclude that continued use of RET in the classroom is unjustified, in fact, contraindicated." p. 23

(Continued)

TABLE 3. Meta-analytic reviews of the REBT outcome literature. (*Cont'd*)

Author(s)	Year Published	Range of Years Studied	Number of Studies	Population Reviewed	Conclusions
Haaga and Davison	1989	1970–1987	69	Published and unpublished studies of children and adults.	Supported the effectiveness of REBT but pointed out limitations to the research designs used.
Hajzler and Bernard	1989	1970–1982	45	Published and unpublished studies of children and adolescents.	"...support for the notion of changes in irrationality and changes in other dimension of psychological functioning." ".....changes have been maintained at follow up periods." p. 31
Jorm	1989	1971–1986	16	Studies of any type of theory that included a measure of trait anxiety or neuroticism.	"While RET and related therapies proved superior in the present meta-analysis (to other therapies), this conclusion is limited by the breath of studies available." p. 25
Lyons and Woods	1991	1970–1988	70	Published and unpublished studies of children and adults.	"The results demonstrated that RET is an effective form of therapy. The efficacy was most clearly demonstrated when RET was compared to baseline or other forms of controls. Effect sizes were largest for dependent measures low in reactivity (i.e., low reactivity = behavioral or physiological measures; high reactivity = measures of irrational thinking)." p. 368
Mahoney	1974	1963–1974	10	Published and unpublished studies of cognitive restructuring and RET.	RET "... has yet to be adequately demonstrated" and "... may be viewed as tentatively promising." p. 182

McGovern and Silverman	1984	1977–1982	47	Published and unpublished studies of children and adults.	"...there were 31 studies favoring RET. In the remaining studies, the RET treatment groups all showed improvement and in no study was another treatment method significantly better than RET." p. 16
Oei, Hansen, and Miller	1993	1982–1988	9	Studies designed to assess whether irrational beliefs mediate change in other psychological constructs.	"This review demonstrates that while RET has been demonstrated to be an effective therapeutic intervention for a variety of target problems, there is no evidence to show that improvement in RET is due to changing irrational beliefs to rational beliefs." p. 199
Polder	1986	MI	53	Controlled studies of adults.	REBT yielded higher effect sizes than other forms of CBT.
Silverman, McCarthy, and McGovern	1992	1982–1989	89	Published and unpublished studies with children, adolescents, and adults.	"...49 studies resulted in positive findings for RET." When compared to other treatments, "...no other treatments were found to be significantly better than RET." p. 166
Zettle and Hayes	1980	1957–1979	20	Published and unpublished studies with college students and adults.	"... the clinical efficacy has yet to be adequately demonstrated." p. 161

*MI=Missing Information

very low agreement on which studies to include. Each of the fourteen reviews ignored, excluded, or failed to uncover many studies from the period from which the articles were selected. The most comprehensive reviews were the two by Silverman and colleagues (McGovern and Silverman, 1984; Silverman et al., 1992). More recently, Gonzalez et al. (2004) provided a meta-analysis in support of REBT for children and adolescents.

DiGiuseppe and Nevas (1997) found more than 70 REBT outcome studies not included in the reviews. More than 350 REBT outcome studies have been found. Many studies exist that compare REBT to no treatment, wait-list controls, or placebo controls, and support the efficacy of REBT across a wide range of problems including: social, testing, math, performance and public speaking anxiety, agoraphobia, neuroticism, stress, depression, anger, teacher burnout, personality disorder, obsessive compulsive disorder, marriage and relationship problems, alcohol abuse, poor dating skills, overweight/obesity, school discipline problems, unassertiveness, type A behavior, parenting problems, emotional reactions to learning disabilities, school underachievement, sexual fears and dysfunction, bulimia and anger. Few studies have specifically focused on the treatment of aggression but the outcome studies conducted on REBT with children who exhibited aggressive behavior displayed successful results (e.g., Block, 1978; Morris, 1993). A series of studies, not mentioned by any of the reviews, suggests that REBT can be useful for practitioners working in clinics or school settings. Sapp used an REBT program with African-American children to improve their academic performance (Sapp, 1994; 1996; Sapp and Farrell, 1994; Sapp et al., 1995).

Despite the large number of investigations of REBT, research has failed to advance our knowledge. The overwhelming majority of studies compared REBT with a no contact, wait-list, or placebo condition. Few studies compare REBT with a viable, alternative treatment. REBT is better than no treatment or placebo treatments for a wide variety of problems. However, no evidence exists that it is more efficacious than alternative treatments or that there is one condition for which it is the treatment of choice.

Also, the research has done little to advance our knowledge concerning the best way to practice REBT. For example, does the inclusion of imagery, written homework forms, bibliotherapy, or the style of disputation make a difference in the outcome? Or how many sessions of REBT are necessary for clinical improvement? Researchers have failed to examine the critical components of REBT. No studies have addressed the issue of whether the positive effects of REBT are obtained by changing clients' irrational beliefs before change occurs in other dependent measures (Oei et al., 1993). Lyons and Woods' (1991) meta-analysis suggested that more therapy sessions produced greater effect sizes and that more experienced therapists produced larger effect sizes than less experienced therapists. They concluded that dependent measures low in reactivity produced higher effect sizes than measures high in reactivity. These findings are the opposite of those reported by Gossette and O'Brien (1992, 1993).

Generally, psychotherapy research with children and adolescents has lagged behind research with adults (Kazdin, 1994). This has also been true of research in REBT. Sixty-nine studies mentioned in the 14 reviews of REBT treated children or adolescents. However, most of these studies could be considered analogue studies or tests of REBT as a preventive intervention because they focused on using REBT with normal children in groups or in classrooms. Studies of clinically diagnosed children and adolescents are lacking and fewer studies exist for externalizing disorders in children. No outcome study yet exists to test the Sequential REBT approach to family therapy advocated here. Research on modifying parents' irrational beliefs has found REBT to be successful in improving parents' emotional reactions to their children (Joyce, 1995). Greaves (1997) expanded on Joyce's program and showed that the program could reduce stress and improve parenting skills in parents of Downs Syndrome children. Although more research is needed, these studies suggest that psychologists may find REBT useful with children and parents.

Meta-analytic reviews of psychotherapy with children and adolescents have demonstrated that behavioral and cognitive therapies produce more change than non-behavioral, traditional non-directive, or play therapies (Weisz et al., 1987; see Kazdin, 1994 for a review). Since REBT shares many similarities with other behavioral and cognitive therapies, research on REBT with children and adolescents will continue to support its effectiveness.

Future Research

Researchers have failed to distinguish between predatory aggression and anger provoked aggression. We believe that such a distinction may be helpful in designing effective treatments. The relationship between anger and aggression is unclear for adults and unstudied with children (DiGiuseppe et al., 1994). Anger provoked, or emotionally reactive aggression may respond more to REBT or other individual cognitive interventions as compared to instrumental or predatory aggression. Children with predatory aggression may also need more time spent on interventions that reflect strategies such as the motivational syllogism so that they are invested in treatment. However, most of the efforts of this intervention would be focused on the negative consequences of their aggressive behavior. Children with angry aggression require a focus on alternative emotional reactions.

Further, many questions remain unanswered concerning the effectiveness of REBT with aggressive children and their parents. This is especially important in light of managed care demands. Is REBT more efficacious than other CBT or behavioral interventions? Addressing the effectiveness of specific techniques in REBT with children and adolescents is important for research. Do all children benefit from logical disputing, or would rehearsing rational coping skills without disputing be as effective? Although some evidence indicates that children can benefit from REBT written homework forms

(Miller and Kassinove, 1978), do all children benefit from the bibliotherapy and written homework sheets frequently used in REBT?

More research is also needed to examine the effects of modifying parents' irrational beliefs. Specifically, will this help to increase the parents' ability to benefit from parent training and will this directly be related to a decrease in their children's aggressive behavior? Further, research is needed to test the Sequential REBT approach to family therapy. These are only a few of the many research questions that need to be addressed in order to develop effective treatments for aggressive children.

Summary

In children with reactive aggression, feelings of anger drive their aggressive behavior. To treat these children most effectively, utilizing both behavioral and cognitive techniques is necessary. REBT is particularly well-suited for this purpose. The use of negative strategies and positive strategies combined with rehearsal are critical in decreasing inappropriate behaviors and increasing prosocial behaviors, respectively. One of the most important and challenging aspects of treating aggressive children is stimulating them to become motivated for treatment and helping them progress from the precontemplative to the action stage of change. The use of the motivational syllogism and obtaining agreement on the goals and tasks of therapy are critical to achieving this end. Further, helping children dispute and replace their IBs with RBs enables them to substitute feelings of anger with less disturbing feeling of annoyance. Besides working directly with the children, involving the parents in the treatment as much as possible is crucial. It is often necessary to work with the parents in disputing and replacing their IBs before they can manage their child's behavior effectively.

REBT focuses on the role of irrational, dogmatic, and rigid thinking in causing psychopathology. Irrational beliefs are tacit, pervasive, rigid schematic representations of the way the world is and ought to be. These beliefs are both factual and evaluative in nature. Beliefs are irrational when they are rigidly held in the face of evidence that they are logically inconsistent, anti-empirical, and self-defeating. The theory further discriminates between adaptive and maladaptive emotions. Its goal is not to eliminate negative emotions, but to replace maladaptive negative emotions with more adaptive negative emotions and to help individuals improve their lives and be free of emotional disturbance.

The primary techniques of REBT involve challenging and replacing dysfunctional irrational beliefs. Many logical, empirical, and functional strategies to challenge beliefs are recommended. In addition, REBT employs a wide range of behavioral, imaginal, and emotive exercises to cause change. The theory stresses the importance of rehearsing new ways of thinking and a variety of appropriate techniques that accomplish this.

Although REBT was originally designed for adults, it has been used with children and adolescents for more than 25 years. It follows a psychoeducational model that allows it to be used in groups, workshops, and classrooms as a preventative procedure. Because of its psychoeducational format, REBT can easily be integrated into educational settings. It can be used in an educational format to teach students, parents, and teachers how to reduce their emotional disturbance and improve their productivity. REBT provides a model for school mental health services including direct service and consultation.

REBT can be integrated with family systems theory to work with parents. The theory helps identify the clients' thinking that reinforces family dysfunction. The use of REBT techniques can eliminate parents' emotional disturbance so they are free to explore and follow more productive models of relating and parenting. Since REBT shares many similarities with other behavioral and cognitive therapies, there is reason to suspect that research in REBT with children and adolescents will continue to support its effectiveness.

There is a substantial body of research supporting the efficacy of REBT. However, this research has employed too few designs and has not compared REBT to alternate active treatments. Future research could focus on identifying the crucial techniques of REBT, the problems and populations for which it is best suited, and more efficient ways of achieving change in clients.

References

American Psychiatric Association (1994). *Diagnostic and Statistical Manual,* 4th ed. Washington, DC: American Psychiatric Association.

Bernard, M. (1990). *Taking the stress out of teaching*. North Blackburn, Victoria, Australia: Collins/Dove.

Bernard, M. E., and DiGiuseppe, R. (1990). The application of rational-emotive theory and therapy to school-aged children. *School Psychology Review*, *19*(3), 268–287.

Bernard, M. and Joyce, M. (1984). *Rational emotive therapy with children and adolescents*. New York: Wiley.

Block, J. (1978). Effects of rational-emotive therapy on overweight adults. *Psychotherapy: Therapy, Research, and Practice, 17*, 277–280.

Casey, R. J. and Berman, J. S. (1985). The outcome of psychotherapy with children. *Psychological Bulletin, 98,* 388–400.

Dadds, M. R. and McHugh, T. A. (1992). Social support and treatment outcome in behavioral family therapy for child conduct problems. *Journal of Consulting and Clinical Psychology, 60*, 252–259.

DiGiuseppe, R. (1977). Using behavior modification to teach rational self-statements to children, *Rational Living*. Reprinted in: A. Ellis and R. Grieger (eds.), *Rational Emotive Psychotherapy: A Handbook of Theory and Practice*. New York: Springer.

DiGiuseppe, R. (1988). A cognitive behavioral approach to the treatment of conduct disorder in children and adolescents. In N. Epstein, S. Schlesinger, and W. Dryden (eds.), *Cognitive behavioral therapy with families*. New York: Brunner/Mazel, pp. 183–214.

DiGiuseppe, R. (1995). Developing the therapeutic alliance with angry clients. In H. Kassinove (ed.), *Anger disorders*. Washington, DC: Taylor and Francis.

DiGiuseppe, R., and Bernard, M. E. (1983). Principles of assessment and methods of treatment with children: Special considerations. In. A. Ellis and M. E. Bernard (eds.), *Rational emotive approaches to the problems of childhood.* New York: Plenum.

DiGiuseppe, Goodman, and Nevas (1997). A review of research studies in REBT :Poseter Presented in the annual Convention of the Association for the Advancement of Behavior Therapy.

DiGiuseppe, R., Linscott, J., and Jilton, R. (1996). Developing the therapeutic alliance in child-adolescent psychotherapy. *Applied and Preventive Psychology, 5*(2), 85–100.

DiGiuseppe, R., Miller, N. J., and Trexler, T. D. (1977). A review of rational-emotive psychotherapy outcome studies. *The Counseling Psychologist, 7*, 64–72.

DiGiuseppe, R., Tafrate, R., and Eckhardt, C. (1994). Critical issues in the treatment of anger. *Cognitive and Behavioral Practice, 1*(1), 111–132.

DiGiuseppe, R., Turchiano, T., Li, C., Wellen, D., Anderson, T., and Jones, D. (1996). Childhood anger and aggression: A meta-analysis of behavioral and cognitive treatments. In E. Feindler (chair), *Anger in the schools: Diagnosis, assessment, treatment, and the costs to learning*. Symposium conducted at the meeting of the Association for Advancement of Behavior Therapy, Manhattan, New York.

Dix, T. (1991). The affective organization of parenting: Adaptive and maladaptive processes. *Psychological Bulletin, 110*(1), 3–25.

Ellis, A. (1962). *Reason and emotion in psychotherapy*. Seacacus: Lyle Stuart.

Ellis, A., and DiGiuseppe, R. (1993). Appropriate and Inappropriate emotions in rational emotive therapy: A response to Craemer and Fong. *Cognitive Therapy and Research, 17*(5), 471–477.

Engels, G. I., Garnefski, N., and Diekstra, R. F. W. (1993). Efficacy of rational-emotive therapy: A quantitative analysis. *Journal of Consulting and Clinical Psychology, 61*, 1083–1090.

Gonzalez, J. E., Nelson, J. R., Gutkin, T. B., Saunders, A., Galloway, A., and Shwery, C. S. (2004). Rational emotive therapy with children and adolescents: A meta-analysis. *Journal of Emotional and Behavioral Disorders, 12*(4), 222–235.

Gossette, R. L., and O'Brien, R. M. (1992). The efficacy of rational emotive therapy in adults: Clinical fact or psychometric artifact? *Journal of Behavior Therapy and Experimental Psychiatry, 23,* 9–24.

Gossette, R. L., and O'Brien, R. M. (1993). Efficacy of rational emotive therapy (RET) with children: A critical re-appraisal. *Journal of Behavior Therapy and Experimental* Greaves, D. (1997). The effect of rational-emotive parent education on the stress of mothers of young children with down's syndrome. *Journal of Rational Emotive and Cognitive Behavioral Therapy, 15*, 249–267.

Haaga, D. A., and Davison, G. C. (1989). Outcome studies of rational-emotive therapy. In Bernard, M. E., and DiGiuseppe, R. (eds.), *Inside rational-emotive therapy; A critical appraisal of the theory and therapy of Albert Ellis*. San Diego, CA: Academic Press, pp. 155–197.

Hajzler, D. J., and Bernard, M. E. (1991). A review of rational-emotive education outcome studies. *School Psychology Quarterly, 6*(1), 27–49.

Huesmann, L. R., Eron, L. D., Lefkowitz, M. M., and Walder, L. O. (1984). Stability of aggression over time and generations. *Developmental Psychology, 20*, 1120–1134.

Jorm, A. F. (1989). Modifiability of trait anxiety and neuroticism: A meta-analysis of the literature. *Australian and New Zealand Journal of Psychiatry, 23*, 21–29.

Joyce, M. (1995) Emotional relief for parent: Is rational-emotive parent education effective? *Journal of Rational Emotive and Cognitive Behavioral Therapy*, *13*, 55–75.

Kazdin, A. (1994). Psychotherapy for children and adolescents. In A.E. Bergin and S.L. Garfield (eds.), *Handbook of psychotherapy and behavior change,* 4th ed. New York: Wiley, pp. 543–594.

Kendall, P. C. (1993). Cognitive-behavioral therapies with youth: Guiding theory, current status and emerging developments. *Journal of Consulting and Clinical Psychology, 61*(2), 235–247.

Loeber, R., and Dishion, T. J. (1983). Early predictors of male delinquency: A review. *Psychological Bulletin, 94*, 68–99.

Lyons, L. C., and Woods, P. J. (1991). The efficacy of rational-emotive therapy: A quantitative review of the outcome research. *Clinical Psychology Review, 11*, 357–369.

Mahoney, M. J. (1974). *Cognition and behavior modification.* Cambridge, MA: Ballinger. McGovern, T. E., and Silverman, M. S. (1984). A review of outcome studies of rational-emotive therapy from 1977 to 1982. *Journal of Rational Emotive Therapy, 2*(1), 7–18.

Meichenbaum, D. (1971). *Cognitive-behavior modification*. New York: Plenum.

Miller, N. J., and Kassinove, H. (1978). Effects of lecture, rehearsal, written homework, and the IQ on the efficacy of a rational-emotive school mental health program. *Journal of Community Psychology, 6,* 366–373.

Miller, W., and Rollnick, S. (2002). *Motivational interviewing: Preparing people to change addictive behavior (second ed.)*. New York: Guilford Press.

Morris, G. B., (1993). A rational-emotive treatment program with conduct disorder and attention-deficit hyperactivity disorder adolescents. *Journal of Rational-Emotive and Cognitive Behavior Therapy, 11*(3), 123–134.

Oei, T. P. S., Hansen, J., and Miller, S. (1993). The empirical status of irrational beliefs in rational emotive therapy. *Australian Psychologist, 28*, 195–200.

Peterson, L., Gable, S., Doyle, C., and Ewigman, B. (1997). Beyond parenting skills: Battling barriers and building bonds to prevent child abuse and neglect. *Cognitive and Behavioral Practice, 4*(1), 53–74.

Polder, S. K. (1986). A meta-analysis of cognitive behavior therapy. *Dissertation Abstracts International, B4*, 1736.

Prochaska, J. and DiClemente, C. (1981). *The transtheoretical approach to therapy.* Chicago: Dorsey Press.

Sapp, M. (1996). Irrational beliefs that can lead to academic failure for African American middle school students who are at-risk. *Journal of Rational Emotive and Cognitive Behavior Therapy, 14*(2), 123–134.

Sapp, M. (1994). Cognitive behavioral counseling: Applications for African American middle school students who are academically at risk. *Journal of Instructional Psychology, 21*(2), 161–171.

Sapp, M. (1996). Irrational beliefs that can lead to academic failure for African American middle school students who are academically at risk. *Journal of Rational Emotive and Cognitive Behavior Therapy, 14*(2), 123–134.

Sapp, M. and Farrell, W. (1994). Cognitive behavioral interventions: Applications for academically at risk special education students. *Preventing School Failure, 38*(2), 19–24.

Sapp, M., Farrell, W. and Durand, H. (1995). Cognitive behavior therapy: Applications for African American middle school at risk students. *Journal of Instructional Psychology, 22*(2), 169–177.

Silverman, M. S., McCarthy, M., and McGovern, T. (1992). A review of outcome studies of rational-emotive therapy from 1982–1989. *Journal of Rational-Emotive and Cognitive-Behavior Therapy, 10*, 111–175.

Spivack, G. and Shure, M. (1974). *Social adjustment of young children; A cognitive approach to solving real-life problems*. San Francisco: Jossey-Bass.

Spivack, G., Platt, J., and Shure, M. (1976). *The social problem-solving approach to adjustment*. San Francisco: Jossey-Bass.

Walen, S., DiGiuseppe, R. and Dryden, W. (1992). *A practitioners' guide to rational emotive therapy* (2nd ed.), New York: Oxford University Press.

Weisz, J. R., Weiss, B., Alicke, M. D. and Klotz, M. L. (1987). Effectiveness of psychotherapy with children and adolescents; Meta-analytic findings for clinicians. *Journal of Consulting and Clinical Psychology, 55*, 542–549.

Weisz, J. R., Weiss, B., Han, S. S., Granger, D. A., and Morton, T. (1995). Effects of psychotherapy with children and adolescents revisited: A meta-analysis of treatment outcome studies. *Psychological Bulletin, 117*(3), 450–468.

Wellen, D. (1997). *A meta-analysis of single subject studies of therapies for children and adolescents with aggression*. Unpublished doctoral dissertation, St. John's University, Jamaica, NY.

Zettle, R., and Hayes, S. (1980). Conceptual and empirical status of rational emotive therapy. *Progress in Behavior Modification, 9*, 125–166.

10

Rational-Emotive Behavior Therapy and Attention Deficit Hyperactivity Disorder

KRISTENE A. DOYLE[a], PH.D. AND MARK D. TERJESEN[b], PH.D.

[a]*Albert Ellis Institute;* [b]*St. John's University*

Mailing address: Kristene A. Doyle at the Albert Ellis Institute, 45 East 65th Street, NYC, NY 10021 or Mark D. Terjesen at St. John's University, 8000 Utopia Parkway, Marillac Hall SB 36F Jamaica, NY, 11439

Attention-Deficit Hyperactivity Disorder (ADHD) is one of the most common disorders of childhood and adolescence, with current estimates being conservatively placed with 3 to 7% of the school-age children in the United States (American Psychiatric Association, 2000; Stevens, 2000). Researchers have reported that boys are six to eight times more likely to be affected by ADHD than girls, with about 20 to 30% of children with ADHD having siblings and parents who are also affected with the disorder (Sagvolden, 1999; Stevens, 2000).

The Diagnostic and Statistical Manual of Mental Disorders DSM-IV-TR (Text Revision) states that children with this disorder predominantly have difficulty in two major areas: inattention and hyperactivity/impulsivity (American Psychiatric Association, 2000). More specifically, students have difficulty sustaining attention, completing assigned work, remaining in their seat, adhering to rules in the classroom, and refraining from interrupting (Netherton et al., 1999).

The DSM-IV identifies and describes three types of ADHD: attention-deficit hyperactivity disorder, predominately inattentive type; attention-deficit hyperactivity disorder, predominately hyperactive-impulsive type; and attention-deficit hyperactivity disorder, combined type (American Psychiatric Association, 2000). Children who are diagnosed with the inattentive type of ADHD generally exhibit difficulty in organization, following directions, and in sustaining attention. The hyperactive-impulsive type of

ADHD lacks attentiveness difficulties but presents with more hyperactive and impulsive problems (e.g., impatience, acting without thought, excessive fidgetiness, impulsive responding, and difficulty speaking in turn) (Sagvolden, 1999). The combined type of ADHD contains a mixture of the other two categories, with the child exhibiting at least six symptoms that characterize inattention, hyperactivity and impulsivity (Reynolds and Gutkin, 1999). In addition, the DSM-IV also states that the symptoms which cause impairment should be present before age 7 and there must be clear evidence of impairment in social, academic, or occupational functioning (American Psychiatric Association, 2000).

This chapter provides on overview of children with ADHD with an eye on biological explanations of etiology as well as ways of making valid assessment of its behavioral manifestations. It will be proposed that a thorough assessment of a child with ADHD encompass not only secondary symptoms frequently found in children with ADHD (conduct, depression, underachievement) but the common irrational beliefs of children that give rise to these secondary symptoms. A variety of REBT and allied CBT and behavioral interventions will be reviewed that are commonly used in treatment. Finally, a case summary will then be presented that demonstrates the utility of REBT with a child with ADHD.

Biological Origin of the Disorder: Primary Symptoms

Unlike many of the other childhood disorders, ADHD is conceptualized as primarily a biological disorder. As such, we will spend a brief moment reviewing the literature on ADHD's origin. Following, we will describe how REBT/CBT attempts to elucidate the secondary symptoms of ADHD, which include, academic underachievement, low frustration tolerance, depression, anxiety, conduct problems and peer/interpersonal difficulties.

Rapport, Chung, Shore, and Isaacs (2001) provide a conceptual model of ADHD based on the extant literature. According to the authors, biological influences such as genetic composition, prenatal insults such as low birth weight, maternal ingestion of alcohol and tobacco, etc., give rise to idiosyncratic differences in the dopaminergic-noradrenergic neurotransmissions (i.e., dopamine, norepinephrine, and epinephrine) that are etiologically accountable for the central cognitive and behavioral features of ADHD (i.e., attention and motoric behavior). The catecholamine hypothesis for the etiology of ADHD is supported by the observation that medications that reduce the symptoms of ADHD increase the amount of catecholamines in the brain (Barkley, 1998). The secondary features of ADHD (academic underachievement; LFT; interpersonal difficulties; etc.) are seen as byproducts of the core features (Rapport et al., 2001). For a more extensive review of ADHD's etiology, please see Barkley (1997).

REBT Conceptualization of the Secondary Symptoms Associated with ADHD

While ADHD is viewed as more of a biological disorder than many of the other chapters in this book, the secondary symptoms, including low frustration tolerance (LFT), depression, anxiety, academic underachievement and interpersonal difficulties can be explained from a non-biological perspective. Let us take a look at each of the secondary symptoms.

Academic Underachievement

It has been well documented that children with ADHD tend to experience difficulties with their academic work including academic achievement, due to their deficits in attention, their disorganization as well as when present with co-morbid learning disabilities/difficulties. However, these estimates vary considerably, with some estimates being as high as 50–80% (Hinshaw, 2002). Hinshaw (1992) reports that when a strict IQ-achievement discrepancy is applied the co-morbidity between ADHD and a learning disability is approximately 15%. This is more consistent with the theory of Barkley (1998) who asserts that achievement is poor in ADHD students without a comorbid learning disability. Academic under-achievement is predictable in children with ADHD with or without LD as inattention and/or disorganization and/or impulsivity throws the learner off task. Barkley (1998) reports that greater than 50% of children with ADHD will require some form of academic remediation/tutoring, with approximately a third being placed in some form of special education and another third being retained a grade level in school.

There are two central aspects of the achievement of children with ADHD that we propose the REBT clinician address; namely self-downing and resultant feelings of depression and low frustration tolerance including patterns of work avoidance. As a result of repeated failure experiences perhaps due to their natural predisposition many children with ADHD globally rate themselves as "stupid" or view themselves as a "loser." With this type of self-schema, children with ADHD engage in a self-fulfilling prophecy, and may in fact perform worse in school than their normal ability would predict.

Furthermore, these same children have a general approach to learning characterized by low frustration tolerance, which manifests itself in many arenas including academic achievement. When young people approach their academic work believing, "I can't stand this. It's too hard for me. It should be easier", they are less likely to persevere. As a result, learning and grades suffer. A vicious cycle in children with ADHD occurs when low frustration tolerance leads to the avoidance of learning tasks and to poor academic performance and poor academic performance leads to self-downing and depression. The impact of self-downing and LFT equips the learner with a mindset that is not conducive to academic achievement.

Difficulties in Interpersonal Relationships

It has been extensively documented that children with ADHD often experience co-morbid social problems and aggressive behavior including, in extreme cases, conduct disorder (e.g., Lewinson et al., 2004). From an REBT perspective, an understanding of the anger and anti-social patterns of behavior can be gleaned from examining the irrational beliefs of those children with ADHD who also experience interpersonal difficulties. For example Dodge and Somberg (1987) have indicated that the thinking styles of children with conduct disorders can be characterized by often misreading ambiguous social cues, making irrational demands, and drawing hostile conclusions; for example, "I should be included in the game"; "They should treat me nicely," "This is terrible" (catastrophizing and awfulizing), "I can't stand to be excluded" (interpersonal LFT) and "Peers who treat me unfairly are very bad and deserve to be punished" (e.g., global rating of others).

Depression

As indicated previously, REBT concerns itself with the tendency of some young people with ADHD to experience depression as a result of repeated failures and rejections. REBT's theory suggests that when one holds rigid demands about oneself (e.g., "I must be liked/loved/competent...") and then self-depreciates (e.g.,". . . and if I'm not, then I'm unlovable/I'm nobody/I'm incompetent") (Hauck, 1973), depression is the result. Bernard and Cronan (1999) identified through the factor analysis of the Child and Adolescent Scale of Irrationality, a distinct, general irrational thinking involving young people putting themselves down when bad things happen to them. Given many of the attentional and behavioral difficulties inherent in ADHD, some children with this diagnosis engage in this type of demandingness and self-downing, leading to feelings of depression. Furthermore, additional cognitive distortions/errors identified by Beck accompany demandingness and self-downing including Black and White thinking, Overgeneralization, Negative Prediction, and Helplessness (DeRubeis et al., 2001).

Diagnosis of ADHD

Children who experience symptoms consistent with a diagnosis of ADHD are often regularly referred by parents and teachers, possibly even more than other childhood disorders. Primarily, this may be because students who present with these symptoms potentially pose more management problems that require additional help for the parent and the teacher. As such, an accurate diagnosis to develop treatment planning is integral to outcome, with diagnosis being derived from an empirically sound, multi-dimensional approach.

There are a number of pitfalls in a diagnosis of ADHD that the clinician would benefit from being aware of. Specifically, the DSM criteria can also describe "normal" children and as such, it is important for clinicians to be aware of age appropriate criteria especially in diagnosing young children (APA, 2000). That is, are the behaviors being demonstrated common in many children at this age, and if so, at what point does it become an area of clinical concern?

Another pitfall to be aware of is that the above mentioned problematic behaviors are only considered a disorder when they impair daily functioning in 2 or more settings (APA, 2000). The clinician may wish to look at the context in which the child is exhibiting the behaviors and how the environment (e.g., school adjustment) could be affecting the child (APA, 2000). Therefore, clinicians would benefit from collecting "data" regarding the potential diagnosis from multiple sources in multiple settings.

Another diagnostic pitfall to be aware of is the fact that although a diagnosis is made with a comprehensive evaluation, practitioners often may rely on behavior report forms which can be subjective in nature (Carey, 2002). The research examining biological differences as a function of diagnosis is still developing and, as a result, we are possibly over-relying on observation, clinical interviews, and rating checklists. While there may be some possible differences in EEG between ADHD and non-ADHD students, this has not been proven yet (Hermens et al., 2004; and Raz, 2004). Additionally, while children with ADHD have been found to have basal ganglia and cerebellum immersed with dopamine and, therefore, smaller than other structures (Neto et al., 2002), a full neurological examination may not be necessary if a comprehensive evaluation is conducted.

The accuracy of an ADHD diagnosis is further confounded by the fact that ADHD presents with significant overlap with other diagnoses. Kube et al. (2002) found that 40% of children referred for ADHD actually had other disorders, including mental retardation and learning disabilities. Lewinsohn et al. (2004) estimate that over half of students with ADHD have at least one subthreshold disorder, with more than 50% of children diagnosed with ADHD having Conduct Disorder (CD) or Oppositional Defiant Disorder (ODD) (APA, 2000). A number of other disorders (tic disorders, substance abuse, bipolar, antisocial personality disorder) warrant consideration in making an ADHD diagnosis. Additionally, clinicians may wish to look at family dysfunction/discord as having a child with ADHD predisposes families to have more conflicts, increased stress, and increased marital discord (Hinshaw, 2002)

Assessment and Diagnosis of ADHD

Unfortunately, the hallmark symptoms of ADHD described above may occur to some degree in many children. This may be a result of numerous factors/conditions and may make a differential diagnosis of ADHD very difficult for the clinician. Given the fact that, as mentioned previously, ADHD tends to have a high co-morbidity with externalizing as well as internalizing disorders (Barkley, 2002), accurate assessment is ever more important. Therefore, the clinician would be well served to select assessment devices that specifically address the symptoms that are specific to ADHD as well as assess those symptoms/disorders (i.e., depression, anxiety) that tend to be observed with, or perhaps be a consequence of, the diagnosis of ADHD. Much like with many childhood disorders, an accurate assessment of ADHD often requires data about the relative degree to which these behaviors deviate from age-appropriate levels (Anastopoulos and Shelton, 2001).

Miles (2000) reported that among school psychologists, behavior rating scales are the most widely used assessment devices. They have become a vital part of ADHD assessment because they supply normative data about the level of symptomatology in multiple settings (e.g., school, home). Currently, there are a number of nationally standardized, well-constructed behavior rating scales to aid in the assessment of ADHD. Several thorough reviews of the psychometric characteristics of these scales for the assessment of ADHD have been conducted (Anastopoulos and Shelton, 2001; Barkley, 1998; Hinshaw and Nigg, 1999). The most frequently reported scales used are the Connors instruments (Conners, 1997), the BASC (Reynolds and Kamphaus, 1994), ADDES (McCarney, 1995), and the CBCL (Achenbach, 1991).

Unfortunately, much of this literature focuses on the assessment of children above the age of five, which is problematic because the inception of ADHD symptoms typically occurs during the pre-school years (Anastopoulos and Shelton, 2001). Additionally, McGee et al. (1992) have proposed that an earlier symptom onset is linked with a greater likelihood of co-morbid conditions and subsequent functional impairment. Their suggestion is further supported by research that demonstrates the link between behavior problems present in early childhood and later problem behaviors (Campbell, 1995; Pierce et al., 1999).

As a result, early and accurate identification of ADHD symptoms may allow for the development of more clinically specific interventions geared to maximize the child's potential and prevent future difficulties. However, accurate assessment and diagnosis of ADHD in early childhood is often difficult, (McCarney, 1995) for at these ages it becomes more complicated to distinguish between normal and abnormal levels of hyperactivity, impulsivity and inattention (Shelton and Barkley, 1993). As a result, clinicians rely on these rating scales, as well as other assessment strategies, to help screen for ADHD.

Structured Diagnostic Interviews can be very helpful to the clinician in understanding the level of impairment and assisting in diagnosis. Given that ADHD is associated with significant impairment in 3 areas (Jensen and Cooper, 2002): social relationships, educational and occupational achievement, and unintentional injury, this information may also be helpful to gather. Structured diagnostic interviews are helpful in differential diagnosis of ADHD and have been shown to be a valid assessment tool, (Goldman et al., 1998; Schwab-Stone et al., 1996; Shaffer et al., 1996) as are behavioral observations in which the diagnosis is dependent on the observation of abnormal behaviors. It is important to be mindful that with behavioral observations, the greater the need for concentration and the less interesting the stimulus, the harder it is for the child with ADHD to concentrate (often this is what the school environment is like for the child), making teacher and parent observations crucial for diagnosis (Jensen and Cooper, 2002).

Given the biological etiological model of ADHD and the behavioral manifestation of this disorder, an area that is often overlooked is the cognitions that are frequently associated with it. An evaluation of these cognitions is important because if not successfully treated, the development of secondary emotional disturbances and possibly further exacerbation of symptoms that are part of the disorder may occur. As such, we will briefly outline the irrational and erroneous beliefs that clinicians may wish to assess and treat in the student with ADHD and their family.

Common Irrational Beliefs Seen in Attention Deficit Hyperactivity Disorder

A variety of irrational beliefs are held by individuals diagnosed with ADHD who present with secondary symptoms. The presence of low frustration tolerance, self-rating and other-rating, awfulizing, and demandingness of self or others and world conditions contribute to different secondary conditions that exacerbate the impact of ADHD on young people's achievement, well-being and social relationships. We will take each irrational belief individually and look at the impact of each on individuals with ADHD.

Low frustration tolerance (LFT)

Children and adolescents, whether or not they are diagnosed with ADHD, often demonstrate LFT, "I-can't-stand-it-itis" (Ellis and MacLaren, 1998), for events. Often defined in the REBT literature as a need for immediate gratification, or short-term hedonism, LFT is present in various degrees in all children, regardless of diagnosis. However, for children with ADHD, LFT often presents itself in extreme forms in both academic and social/interpersonal situations. When having difficulty in the classroom attending to important stimuli, many children will tell themselves, "This is too hard. I can't stand this. It should be easier for me." Bear in mind, that for other students without ADHD in the class, the work may in fact *be* easier for them, and this may be quite obvious to those with the diagnosis. The impact of LFT leads to work avoidance and lack of successful learning experiences which often contributes to subsequent self-downing and self-rating (discussed below). In the social/interpersonal arena, many children and adolescents with ADHD have difficulty interpreting and reacting to social cues. This deficit combined with LFT leads to negative social effects.

As an example of the impact of LFT, it is not uncommon when working with children with ADHD to hear that a fight broke out in the school yard. When you probe further, the following ABC framework becomes clear:

A-Kids playing dodgeball in the yard
B-I need to play right now!!!
C-Anger, pushing one's way into the game. (LFT emotions and behaviors)

Furthermore, because children with LFT tend to be overly focused on gratifying whatever need they have at the moment, they are less inclined to attend to other important stimuli, such as the verbal and non-verbal behaviors of the other children. As a result they may experience peer rejection which may trigger further emotional and behavioral difficulties. Below are some examples of the kinds of irrational beliefs that children in the above described example may experience and their accompanying affective and behavioral responses.

Self-Rating

As mentioned above, children and adolescents with ADHD because of the social skills deficits that lead to social rejection and academic difficulty may put themselves down as a result. Many of these children will tell you in session that "I'm a loser. Nobody likes me. I'm stupid." As a consequence, they experience chronic feelings of inferiority that interfere with their ability to adjust to and cope with ADHD. These children may experience depression or feelings of hopelessness, further withdraw and not experience any further opportunity to develop appropriate social skills.

Other-Rating

Alternatively (or on occasion simultaneously) in the face of rejection or school failure experiences they may globally rate others (e.g., "They're stupid") giving rise to extreme feelings of anger that also hinders their efforts to be successful in their schoolwork and relationships. In either case, it is crucial when working with the children to discuss the concept of rating oneself versus rating one's behavior. This is particularly important with ADHD because, at least during the academic years, such individuals may in fact struggle academically and socially. If they rate themselves as *totally stupid*, any academic and social difficulties may be exasperated by such a cognitive style. Unconditional Self-Acceptance and Other-Acceptance, although difficult concepts to teach adults, should be a focal point of treatment for children and adolescents with ADHD.

Demandingness of Self, Others, and the World

The REBT model proposes that demandingness of self, others and the world are three distinct sets of IBs oftentimes not present together in the same person. Each subset of beliefs may have specific emotive and behavioral responses that accompany them.

To be clear, such irrational beliefs may not be specific to children with ADHD. Different forms of demandingness are seen in children with and without diagnoses. Demands of self ("I should be a better student"; "I have to do well in the game") will often lead to feelings of depression. Demands of others ("I shouldn't be told what to do"; "They should listen to me"; "I should be able to do whatever I want"), often result in unhealthy negative emotions and behavior such as anger and aggression often seen in students with Conduct Disorder or Oppositional Defiant Disorder. Demands of the world: "Things shouldn't be this difficult"; "I should be able to do what I want" may lead to both anger and depression. This demandingness is seen by Ellis (1997) as the "musts" of emotional disturbance.

Awfulizing

Many children and adolescents with ADHD experience evaluative anxiety. We believe that it is important for the clinician to examine what the specific precipitates of this anxiety are, and if it is of a social nature or of an evaluative nature. While both involve the child believing the consequences to be "awful", the beliefs attached to them may be very distinct. For example, "What if I try and join in on the game and the others reject me? *That would be* ***awful, horrible, the end of the world***" leads to social anxiety while "What if I tried really hard and did poorly on my test? *That would be horrible and terrible*" leads to performance anxiety. Catastrophic thinking contributes to anxiety that is often seen in children with ADHD.

Parents of children with ADHD may also hold irrational beliefs regarding the child, themselves and the diagnosis. For example, parents who get depressed when first hearing of their child's diagnosis, may blame themselves, thinking they did something to "cause" this problem. You may often hear when talking to parents the irrational belief, *"I am an awful horrible parent for causing this. This is all of my fault."* Many parents with high anxiety about their child's future may catastrophize and awfulize about the diagnosis and its manifestations. *"This is the worst thing that could happen to a child, parent, family, etc. This is horrible."* are common irrational beliefs of many parentsOther parents of children with LFT get extremely angry about the effort required on their part to cater to their child's needs as a result of an LFT parenting philosophy (e.g., "Parenting shouldn't be so hard. I can't stand all that I have to do.").

An important point needs to be made when considering the issue of frustration tolerance in parents of children with ADHD. It is recognized that these parents require high amounts of frustration tolerance and that many parents who are already putting up with a great deal of frustration in raising a child with ADHD need to develop high frustration tolerance (HFT). Be careful when responding to parents' complaints and issues concerning their child's behavior not to make the mistake of assuming these parents have LFT. Given the nature of the diagnosis, the issue may not be that parents have LFT but rather in fact have insufficient HFT. Not realizing this issue and suggesting to parents that they are experiencing LFT may lead to a disruption in the therapeutic alliance. You will want to make the distinction between LFT, HFT, and a situation (such as a child with ADHD) that requires even more frustration tolerance.

Treatment of ADHD

Pharmacotherapy, cognitive-behavioral training, parent training, classroom behavior modification and contingency management, and the combination of psychostimulant medication and behavior modification are the most efficacious treatments currently used with children with ADHD (Abramowitz et al., 1992; Gage and Wilson, 2000; The MTA Cooperative Group, 1999; Pelham et al., 1998; Waschbusch et al., 1998).

The research indicates that carefully managed stimulant medication is effective in managing ADHD symptoms as reported by both parents and the teachers (The MTA Cooperative Group). Additionally, stimulants were shown to be more effective than behavioral interventions alone and the combination of the 2 were more effective than the behavioral interventions alone. Pelham (2002) concludes that while there have been many studies examining the effectiveness of cognitive behavioral approaches for treating ADHD, there is no established efficacy of cognitive treatment for ADHD. However, Pelham posits that perhaps cognitive interventions could have adjunctive treatment benefit for maintenance of behavioral and pharmacologic treatment as well as for treatment of other clinical issues associated with the disorder.

Individuals with a diagnosis of ADHD pose distinct challenges when it comes to treatment, compared to other disorders affecting children and adolescents. Cognitive-behavioral treatment procedures have not established beneficial effects for ADHD (Kendall, 2000). However, Hinshaw et al. (1998) have noted that psychosocial treatments with underpinnings in behavioral contingencies can have encouraging effects on ADHD-related symptomatology. Hinshaw (2000) emphasizes that any cognitive intervention with children diagnosed with ADHD should be linked with behavioral reinforcement strategies.

Research has shown that few treatment interventions for ADHD are effective in demonstrating long-term clinically meaningful gains in children diagnosed with the disorder. Pelham et al. (1998) describe the ineffective use of traditional one-to-one therapy, diets and allergy treatments, and play therapy. Additionally, psychostimulant medications do not appear to yield beneficial treatment for the child with ADHD long-term (Pelham, 2002). As such, Pelham contends that psychosocial treatments should be utilized as a first treatment option with medication as necessary. A more thorough review of outcome research in the treatment of ADHD is beyond the scope of this chapter; however we will briefly describe these interventions below.

Following this, we will talk specifically about REBT/CBT interventions to treat both the symptoms associated with the disorder of ADHD as well as many of the co-occurring disorders.

Pharmacological Treatments

The most common form of intervention for children with ADHD is pharmacological treatment (Abramowitz et al., 1992; Block, 1996; Findling and Dogin, 1998; Goldman et al., 1998; The MTA Cooperative Group, 1999; Pelham et al., 1993; Stevens, 2000). Two types of medications are predominantly used to treat the symptoms of ADHD—stimulants and antidepressants. Psychostimulant medications are the most frequently used of the two, because they increase the levels of dopamine in the brain and they are usually taken in the forms of methylphenidate (Ritalin), dextroamphetamine (Dexadrine), and pemoline (Cylert) (Waschbusch et al., 1998). These medications aid in the reduction of inattentiveness, overactivity, and impulsivity, and in the enhancement of pro-social behaviors in the classroom setting (American Academy of Pediatrics, 2001; Kolko et al., 1999; The MTA Cooperative Group, 1999;). Pelham, et al., (1998) state that 70–80% of children respond to stimulant medication. In terms of school functioning, methylphenidate has "been unequivocally shown (i.e., by double-blind, placebo-controlled studies) to reduce core symptoms of hyperactivity, impulsivity and inattentiveness... improve classroom behavior and academic performance [and] diminish oppositional and aggressive behaviors" (Goldman et al., 1998, p. 1103). There are side effects that are associated with medication, but they are generally mild. They include headache, sleep disturbances, decreased appetite, stomachache, and the possibility of becoming addicted or using Ritalin as a "gateway" drug to other narcotics use (Goldman et al., 1998).

Given that not all children respond to methylphenidate and other stimulants, low doses of tricyclic antidepressants, such as imipramine (Tofranil) and amitriptyline (Elavil), have been prescribed and are helpful in reducing impulsivity and disruptive behavior (Netherton et al., 1999). While found to be less effective than stimulants in improving the cognitive functioning of children with ADHD, they are typically used in situations where side effects (such as motor tics) are worsened by the use of stimulants (Waschbusch and Hill, 2001).

There are limitations in the use of stimulants. Despite evidence for short-term efficacy of results, psychostimulant medications have not demonstrated long-term lasting effects (The MTA Cooperative Group, 1999). There are no beneficial effects being maintained after discontinuing use of the drug with efficacy being limited to the time that children are actually taking the medication (Pelham et al., 1998; Reichenberg-Ullman and Ullman, 2000). This finding is important for the REBT practitioner as stimulants may only be useful in temporarily masking the symptoms of ADHD and cannot be considered curative of the disorder. The REBT clinician may work on decreasing any of the secondary disturbances that may accompany a diagnosis of ADHD as well as work with the family on accepting the limitations of pharmacologic treatments. Such work pays dividends for young people once medication has been suspended.

In addition, given that there is no evidence that stimulant medications improve the academic performance of children with ADHD symptoms (Pelham et al., 1998), the REBT clinician may assist the students with ADHD to develop emotional toughness to cope with the demands of the curriculum and issues related to peer relationships. In helping young people eliminate irrational beliefs that lead to depression, anxiety, anger, misbehavior and work avoidance and develop rational beliefs associated with a positive work and social orientation and emotional resilience, REBT is seen as a critical intervention to help improve a variety of outcomes for young people with ADHD.

The following section provides a review of REBT and allied cognitive-behavioral interventions that are available to practitioners in working with young people with ADHD who experience a range of secondary symptoms and co-morbid conditions.

REBT Based Interventions

Developing a therapeutic alliance can be particularly challenging for the clinician working with the child with ADHD and their family. It is important to consider that these children are oftentimes not here by their own volition but rather because their behavior has now become problematic to others (parent, teacher) in varied settings. Understanding and acknowledging that they may not want to be here we have found to be helpful as well as providing structure to the therapy session that integrates therapeutic goals with things that the child may enjoy. Clearly establishing session expectations and developing mechanisms to monitor therapy assignment completion also helps develop this relationship and allows the child to experience some success, something that may be missing from other aspects of his/her life. When working with a child who has ADHD, the therapy session can prove as challenging for the therapist as it is for the child. Additionally, we remind the clinician to be aware of his or her own beliefs about therapy progress and child behavior and to monitor our own expectations for performance of the child to make sure that they are consistent with something that the child is capable of doing.

Incorporating an in-session token economy to increase attention to the task at hand may prove advantageous to make the most out of the session. The use of a game to teach the concept of frustration tolerance has also been helpful for such children. For example, playing a board game, while at the same time modeling for the child High Frustration Tolerance self-statements such as "This is tough but I can get through it!" assists the ADHD child in seeing that there is another way of thinking about a problem. As previously mentioned, children with ADHD often have difficulty generating alternative behaviors to a problem. Rigidity in thinking may also be a problem for such children. This type of therapist modeling is especially helpful for children who are cognitively or developmentally not able to engage in more abstract thinking. Furthermore, playing a board game allows the therapist to observe whether or not the child has deficits in social skills, including an inability to take turns and impulsive play behaviors. Providing feedback for the child on how the therapist feels when he/she is interrupted or when the child does not allow turn-taking, can be an invaluable step in assisting the child to develop better social skills.

Pre-requites to Challenging/Disputing. Let us first begin by stating that children and adolescents (and often many adults!) often do not have the appropriate and necessary insight into the cognitive factors contributing to their emotional problems. Too often will you hear them say "He *made* me so angry I had to hit him", or "The situation *makes* me anxious." Before progressing to any disputation with children with ADHD, it is imperative that a cognitive model of emotions and behavior be taught and internalized. Teaching the concept that one's thinking/cognitions contribute to feelings/emotions is essential. The ABC framework (activating events, beliefs about those events, and subsequent healthy and unhealthy emotions and behaviors) preferably should be the cornerstone of your therapeutic interventions.

It often proves helpful to teach this ABC framework by incorporating a specific problem the child or adolescent brings into therapy. This makes what can be an abstract concept more concrete and relative to the child. Hence, emotional and behavioral responsibility on the part of the child becomes a primary therapy goal.

Additional prerequisites to successful challenging/disputing of children's irrational beliefs that are a cornerstone of REBT practice (see Bernard, 2004) include: teaching an *emotional vocabulary* and teaching an *emotional schema* (the same emotion varies in intensity and you have options in how upset you become when something negative occurs).

The age and developmental level of the child are important factors to consider before proceeding with disputation. Many children lack the cognitive ability to understand certain concepts you may present in therapy. Some children lack the verbal ability to express their thoughts and feelings. As a result, it is important to conduct a thorough assessment of where the child is cognitively and developmentally and for this the reader is referred to Vernon's handout on "Assessing a Child's Cognitive Level" (Bernard and

Wolfe, 2000). Disputation is difficult for children under the age of 11 to comprehend because they have not yet moved into the formal operational thinking stage (Bernard and Joyce, 1984) While not specific to the disorder of ADHD, we have found that students who frequently endorse LFT beliefs tend to be less mature and are also not as effective in disputation ("It's too difficult"). We believe that it is important for the clinician to consider both a child's chronological and developmental age when developing disputation strategies.

Disputing/Challenging. The different types of disputing described in the REBT literature (empirical, logical, semantic, heuristic/functional) (see Bernard, 2004) can be used to identify, challenge and change irrational to rational beliefs including low frustration tolerance, awfulizing, demandingness of self/others and the world, and self and other global ratings.

Disputing global self-ratings (i.e., I'm a loser) is a critical intervention for most young people with ADHD. The fruit bowl analogy (Walen et al., 1992) is very effective to teach the concept of Unconditional Self-Acceptance (and Other Acceptance). In this analogy, the therapist presents to the client the idea of a fruit dish, with all different types of fruits, including oranges, apples, pears and bananas, with one of the bananas having a brown spot on it. The therapist then poses to the client the following question: "What do you do with the fruit dish? Throw it away?" Typically, the client will look at you like you are crazy, and say, "Of course not. Eat around the brown spot, or pick off the brown spot." The therapist then draws the connection to accepting oneself with our brown spots. These disputes are more abstract in nature and may be more applicable to adolescents. With younger children, perhaps concrete disputations (empirical) with accompanying behavioral/experiential exercises are more appropriate.

Functional disputes ("How does thinking this way help me reach my goal"?) can be especially helpful with a child/adolescent with ADHD. Oftentimes, the empirical ("Where is the evidence for my belief?") and logical ("Does my demand logically follow from the preference?") disputes pose a challenge to children in terms of comprehension. Working with children to help them see that their current way of thinking, especially demandingness, is not working for them, and at the same time is *not* changing the reality, results in a more flexible style of thinking.

Disputing "catastrophic" thinking of children and adolescents with ADHD, whether it be around academic or social issues is important. Vernon (2002) has a number of techniques and interventions to use to dispute what is sometimes called "awfulizing." The goal is to have children see that they make themselves feel anxious about social situations, or academic situations, by telling themselves that it would be the end of the world if something happened or did not happen. Working with children to correctly evaluate the badness of a situation will reduce their level of anxiety.

Disputing low frustration tolerance is interesting when working with children with ADHD as their may be some validity to the fact that things may be more difficult for them due to their diagnosis as opposed to their peers. We recommend that the clinician acknowledge that certain tasks may be more difficult but that thinking it is *too* difficult will only further serve to have a negative impact upon their performance. We ask children to consider other times when they have thought things are "too difficult and unbearable" and have them discuss whether things were as difficult as they projected.

Use of Rational Self-Statements. Challenging faulty beliefs is only half of the battle in overcoming faulty thinking when working with children and adolescents with ADHD. The REBT model stresses the importance of developing rational self-statements that are theoretically and empirically opposite of the unhealthy beliefs that they have been endorsing that have led to behavioral and emotional difficulties. We think that the generation of these new beliefs is key when working with children, as they may not have a bank of alternative healthy beliefs and may instead just replace the unhealthy, irrational one with one that is equally (if not more) illogical and unhealthy. As an example, if a student believes that "They *can't stand* rejection", after utilizing a number of disputes we would work with the student on a healthy, rational alternative. We prefer to use the students own words, but if this does not occur initially we may provide them with a model: "While I may not like rejection, and really do not want to be rejected, *I can stand it*". We stress the tone and strength of the new belief at a level above and beyond the level of the irrational belief.

Cognitive Behavioral Rehearsal/Role Play. We have found that while children may agree with new beliefs in the therapy session, their ability to adopt this new philosophy in the real world is oftentimes limited. When confronted with similar situations that they have experienced in the past, children and adolescents may tend to go back to faulty patterns of thinking and not recall the new belief system. We actively test this system in the therapy session by engaging in role play activities. This allows us to challenge their "new philosophy" using some of their own words (prior faulty ideas) against them. We encourage children and adolescents to challenge back/disagree with their old unhealthy beliefs and in so doing they may internalize/believe their new philosophy. Role playing allows the clinician to see just how well they have internalized their new philosophy, provide feedback on more effective disputation strategies, and observe student behavior in session and provide feedback.

REBT is a very active approach, often having clients engage in various activities in between sessions to further help challenge their irrational beliefs and reinforce their new philosophy. Rather than calling it homework, we refer to these as "activities" or "experiments" that we will have the students work on between sessions. We like to generate these activities/experiments *with* the students as we have found that they are more likely to commit to working on one of these activities if they were equally responsible for choosing it. Activities may be assessment driven (e.g., "Write down your thoughts and feelings when you get upset this week"); behavioral/experiential in nature (e.g., "Start conversations with 3 peers this week"); risk-taking (e.g., "Raise your hand in class when you are not sure of the answer") or cognitive (e.g., "Practice disputing in front of a mirror 5 times this week."). We have found that varied activities lead to increased compliance as well. Upon activity generation, we look for any obstacles (i.e., practical or irrational) that the child or family may think would interfere with completion of the activity during the week. Depending on these potential blocks we may modify the assignment or work on disputing the beliefs that interfere with completion. Typically, we begin the next session by assessing their completion of the activity, reinforce completion, or examine what may have led to non-completion. Working on these activities may also be integrated into a token economy system as well.

Allied Behavioral Treatments

Children who exhibit behavior difficulties often present a challenge to the teacher who is trying to educate the class and to the parent who is trying to manage their children's behavior. Children with behavior problems are often disruptive and may have a negative impact upon the behavior of others (e.g., students, family) in their immediate environment. For those children with ADHD who are exhibiting chronic misbehavior, the literature has focused on behavior modification (The MTA Cooperative Group, 1999; Abramowitz et al., 1992; Hansen and Cohen, 1984; Miranda and Presentacion, 2000; Robinson et al., 1999)

Contingency management is the most common behavioral intervention that has been effective in the treatment of ADHD (Waschbusch et al., 1998) in which the child is rewarded for positive adaptive behaviors and punished for negative inappropriate behaviors. Techniques such as token economy reward systems, time out, response cost, removal of privileges, and maneuvering of attention are among the different forms of contingency management. Research indicates that contingency management programs have positive effects in classroom behavior (Rapport et al., 1982), and that in the case of children with ADHD (and conduct disorder for that matter), negative consequences such as consistent and immediate verbal reprimands with subsequent loss of privileges and time out, are effective and essential in classroom behavior management. Contingency management and positive consequences have not proven efficacious for the long-term (Pelham et al., 1993).

Despite the benefits of behavior modification therapy, this treatment has its limitations. Much like with medication, there is no evidence of consistent long-term efficacy (American Academy of Pediatrics, 2001; Goldman et al., 1998; Murphy and Hagerman, 1992; Pelham et al., 1993). That is, once behavioral interventions are removed, the short-term gains made by children are often lost (American Academy of Pediatrics, 2001; Pelham et al., 1998; Reichenberg-Ullman and Ullman, 2000). Secondly, behavior modification techniques require a lot of time and effort on the part of the teacher and parents. This is an area that the REBT practitioner could become involved in; namely, helping parents and teachers to remain calm in the face of children's difficult behavior in order to consistently apply the learned behavior management techniques.

Clinical behavior therapy is the most common application of behavioral procedures to children with disruptive and attentional problems (Hinshaw, 2000). This type of intervention involves working with the teacher (and parent) in a consultation model. Daily report cards that target specific individual problems for the child are developed in conjunction with teacher input. A procedure is designed for the teacher to monitor and provide feedback to the child regarding those specific problems. Teachers are instructed to give feedback to parents regarding the child's school performance, with a positive consequence delivered at home by the parent (Pelham et al., 1998). In addition, therapists also provide classroom management strategies (Kelley and McCain, 1995). Improvements in both home and school behavior have been reported using clinical behavior therapy.

Multimodal Treatments

Behavior modification and psychopharmacologic approaches each have their own benefits when used in treating ADHD children, but studies have found that it is most beneficial to the child when they are combined. Goldman et al. (1998) reports that "integrating pharmacotherapy with a number of environmental, educational, psychotherapeutic, and school-based approaches, is a tailored approach that seems intuitively powerful, matching the child's particular problems to selections from a menu of focused treatment interventions" (pp. 1104).

In what is probably the most exhaustive examination of medication and psycho-social treatments for ADHD, the MTA Cooperative Group ran a study in which 579 children aged 7 to 9 years of age were randomly assigned to one of four treatment groups: medication, medication and behavior management, behavior management, and control. Results indicated that school-aged children with ADHD symptoms showed a marked decrease in symptoms when they were treated with either medication alone or a combination of medication and behavior management. Regardless of which approach is used, the REBT practitioner would also benefit from examining prior exposure to a treatment intervention, child and parental compliance and perceived treatment acceptability. This will help guide your treatment selection as perhaps families who had a low level of adherence to a previous intervention may have done so out of a philosophical disagreement ("I don't believe in medicating children") or because of their own faulty beliefs ("It's too difficult to stick to the plan").

Other Cognitively Based Interventions

Cognitive behavioral treatments of ADHD include self-instructional training, self-monitoring, problem-solving strategies, self-evaluation, and self-reinforcement (Pelham et al., 1988). Cognitive behavioral interventions has as its goal to assist the child in acquiring mastery over his/her behavior via self-mediated strategies. It is important to note however, that research does not support the efficacy of cognitive treatments of ADHD alone without other forms of treatment, and therefore, cognitive treatments are advised as an adjunct to contingency management or clinical behavior therapy (Pelham et al., 1998).

Social-Problem Solving

As previously mentioned, poor impulse control is one of the manifestations of ADHD. As a result, children with ADHD do not pause to entertain alternative solutions to their problems. As a means of addressing this issue, problem-solving is suggested, in which the child is 1) taught to first identify a problem; 2) brainstorm as many alternative solutions as possible without evaluating them; 3) next take each alternative and identify the potential positive and negative consequences; 4) choose an alternative to try; and 5) then review/evaluate the outcome(s) of the chosen alternative. It should be noted that the research again does not support improved behavior when using problem-solving alone. Children with ADHD appear to have difficulty generalizing the problem-solving skills to different situations/scenarios (Ervin et al., 1996).

Self-Instructional Training

It is well-known that children with ADHD are less acquiescent to directions by parents and teachers than children without such a diagnosis. Self-instructional training, (SIT), developed by Meichenbaum and Goodman (1971), has been recommended as a means of teaching children with ADHD to talk to themselves in an effort to control their behavior. With SIT, the child is taught self-talk (i.e., verbal behavior) to eventually be internalized and therefore guide nonverbal behavior. SIT involves the therapist first modeling self-statements while performing a task. The child is then asked to perform the same task while instructing himself/herself aloud. The child gradually instructs himself/herself in a whispering tone. Ultimately, the use of covert speech to guide performance is achieved. The use of reinforcement is recommended to augment SIT's effects (Ervin et al., 1996). The use of games to teach SIT can be advantageous, as it increases the likelihood that the child will attend to the task.

Self-Monitoring

Self-monitoring is an intervention that is used across a variety of issues, including, depression, anger outbursts, binge-eating, and ADHD. Barkley (1990, as cited in Ervin et al.) has hypothesized that children with ADHD fail to focus on their own behaviors and their consequences. One of the goals of self-monitoring is to have children with ADHD increase their awareness. One way of doing so involves having the children make forced attempts to attend to and observe specific aspects of their behavior (e.g., calling out in class) and keep recordings of these events. By heightening awareness of specific behaviors, it is hoped that controlling such behaviors ensues. As with other interventions for this population, the addition of reinforcement may be necessary for improvement in behavior (Ervin et al., 1996).

Self-Reinforcement

An additional problem facing children with ADHD is their lack of evaluation following their performance. Children with ADHD may be more likely to disregard feedback provided by others, and furthermore, may not acknowledge or make positive proclamations about their performance, compared to children without such a diagnosis. Academic and social performance may be enhanced by teaching children with ADHD to learn to monitor (self-monitoring) and rate the quality of their work, followed by rewarding themselves when they obtain a targeted goal (Ervin et al., 1996).

Case Study

The case below was treated by the first author (KD).

Background

Chris is a 9-year-old only child who lives with his mother and father in a suburb just outside New York City. Both parents are college-educated and Chris' father is an attorney and his mother is a real estate agent. When Chris was in the fourth grade, his teacher noted concerns regarding his ability to pay attention, stay in his seat during group work, and his talking out behavior. As the year went on, Chris demonstrated more difficulty with concepts that were being taught. On the playground during recess, she noticed that altercations with other children would often ensue after Chris tried to join in the play. Chris' teacher investigated whether or not this was new behavior on the part of Chris, or whether he had displayed some of these behaviors in previous grades. His previous teachers indicated these behaviors were not new. Chris' teacher referred him for a psychological—evaluation at this time.

Assessment

Tests administered: WISC IV (Wechsler, 2003); Woodcock-Johnson Achievement Test (Woodcock et al., 2001); Thematic Apperception Test (Murray, 1943); Rational Sentence Completion Task (Wilde, 1992); Children's Personality Questionnaire (Porter and Cattell, 1975); Children's

Depression Inventory (Kovacs, 1992); Connor's Rating Form—Teacher and Parent (Connors, 1997); BASC—self-report, parent and teacher form (Reynolds and Kamphaus, 2004).

Chris' performance on the WISC-IV indicated a full scale IQ of 115, with no significant differences in verbal and nonverbal performance (although nonverbal was slightly below verbal scores). It was noted by the examiner that the evaluation was a difficult process, as Chris was "continually distracted by furniture in the testing room, aspects of the testing equipment, and anything else that came into his view." Woodcock Johnson Achievement Test results indicated academic achievement commensurate with his age

The Connors Rating Form—Teacher (CTRS—S)	T-Score	The Connors Rating Form—Parent (CPRS—S)	T-Score
Oppositional	61	Oppositional	61
Cognitive Problems/ Inattention	72	Cognitive Problems/ Inattention	61
Hyperactivity	70	Hyperactivity	74
Conners' ADHD Index	72	Conners' ADHD Index	62

Interestingly, there were some differences between Chris' mother's report and the teacher report. Teacher ratings were elevated and in the clinical range in all areas with the exception of oppositionality, which was slightly elevated. Results of the parent rating indicated slightly elevated scores with only one subscale (Hyperactivity) being classified in the clinically significant range.

The Rational Sentence Completion Task indicated that Chris has a tendency to globally rate himself as a failure or loser, has low frustration tolerance for tasks that are difficult for him, has a tendency to awfulize about social rejection, and overall, holds a number of demands about himself and others.

Results from the Children's Depression Inventory (Kovacs, 1992) indicated that responses were slightly elevated, suggesting that Chris is mildly depressed. This was consistent with scores on the BASC-self report form, in which he also demonstrated slightly elevated depression. Chris also reported he experiences anxiety.

Based on the results of the evaluation, Chris was diagnosed Attention-Deficit Hyperactivity Disorder, Combined Type.

Treatment Plan

Based on the results of the evaluation, as well as parent and child interview, the following treatment goals were established for Chris:

1. Teach Chris an REBT/CBT framework, including the ABCs to understand the interconnection of thoughts, feelings, and behaviors to help facilitate more effective emotive and behavioral responses.

2. Work with Chris to assume responsibility for his thoughts, feelings, and behaviors.
3. Teach Chris to identify helpful ways of thinking about things to replace the unhelpful ways he sometimes thinks about things. Specifically, work on his beliefs about:
   a. Rating himself globally as a failure or loser which may lead to his mild depression
   b. Tasks being too difficult for him (low frustration tolerance) which will serve to negatively impact upon his academic achievement
   c. Awfulizing about social rejection which may heighten his anxiety and impair his social performance
   d. Demands of others' behavior, which may lead to social altercations
4. Teach Chris' parents the ABC framework.
5. Work with Chris' parents on parenting and contingency management skills, including techniques such as time out, response cost, praise and other rewards, and token economies.
6. Challenge Chris' demandingness of himself and others while emphasizing the rational alternative. Challenging an irrational belief while working on a rational alternative will help Chris internalize a new set of rational beliefs and connect these beliefs with more positive emotions and behaviors.
7. In order to reduce anxiety, dispute Chris' awfulizing about peer rejection, while at the same time providing social skills training and feedback.
8. Develop an in-session token economy to improve attention and time on task.

Description of Therapy Case

In the initial therapy session, both Chris and his parents were asked to attend. The underlying philosophy of REBT/CBT was described to them, using a specific problem brought up by Chris' mother. The goal of this initial session was to have Chris and his parents leave with the idea that (1) they are responsible for their thoughts, feelings, and behaviors; and (2) it would be most helpful if they accept (not like) the current situation, rather than make themselves overly disturbed by it, thereby creating more problems. As a result of didactic discussion, a coping statement was devised with Chris and his parents that each could employ throughout the week when Chris engaged in some problematic behavior. For his parents, this was, "While I don't like what happened, getting overly upset about it will not help resolve the situation." For Chris, he used a mantra from a Star Wars movie character Yoda and his rational alternative was "I am not my behavior" said in the character's voice. He used this to make himself laugh while also reinforcing a healthy alternative.

For homework, which was presented as an "experiment" to Chris so as to reduce the aversive nature the term "homework" typically carries, I asked him to practice telling himself something helpful. Because Chris had a tendency to beat himself up after doing something that got him into trouble, we decided that he would tell himself "What I did was bad, but I am not a bad person. I am working on this problem." We put this statement on an index card for Chris to carry around with him through the week. In addition, I asked Chris to keep a Rational Thoughts Diary (see Appendix A) which we would review in the next session. We then came up with a statement his parents could tell themselves when a problematic behavior was demonstrated. Chris' parents agreed they would tell themselves, "We can get through this. It will not help matters to make myself angry over this."

Both Chris and his parents were seen for the first part of the second session. I followed up on the experiment given. Chris was able to tell himself the statement "most of the time, when I remembered to look at the card." When I asked him how he felt after telling himself the statement, he stated, "Pretty good. Much better than before." I reinforced the idea of helpful thinking. (This also served to reinforce the rB->C/iB->C connection). We then took a look at the Rational Thoughts Diary, and it was clear that Chris had a tendency to be impulsive during school, experienced a great deal of LFT beliefs, and then subsequent self-downing. Upon reviewing the form, Chris was surprised to see how often he beats himself up during the week. We agreed we would continue to make self-acceptance a priority for our initial sessions.

With respect to the experiment assigned to Chris' parents, they used each other as supports, reminding each other of the statement when things got a bit rough at home, particularly during homework time. They too seemed to buy into the B->C connection. The remainder of the session was spent with Chris alone. During this time, as we played a game of Monopoly, we talked about a fight Chris got into during recess. I asked him directly, "What was flashing through your mind right before you got into the fight"? Chris responded, "What? Nothing. You're crazy." I did not get discouraged, and pushed him to think about it. He still could not offer any possibilities. Because REBT is a hypothesis-driven theory, I offered to Chris that he *might have been thinking* "I should be allowed to play with them." This was a hypothesis based on Chris' report of getting into a fight (which I assumed included feeling some anger). REBT's theory of anger proposes that demandingness is at the core of this emotion (Ellis, 1977). As a result, I was able to hypothesize what Chris was telling himself. He looked at me like I was psychic. He nodded and said that was close, but it was more like *he wanted* to play with them. I then spent the rest of the session talking about "wants" versus "have tos". For homework (experiment), Chris was asked to keep a log (self-monitor) the times that he catches himself getting angry, and to see if he is "wanting" or "having to".

Sessions continued to address other irrational beliefs, including awfulizing about peer rejection and self-rating and other-rating. Through the use of board games, I was able to provide feedback and reinforcement to Chris regarding his social behaviors. The token economy we devised for session was also effective in helping Chris to attend to the topic being discussed during the session. I worked with Chris' parents to incorporate a token economy and contingency management program at home for specific targeted behaviors by Chris (See Appendices B and C).

Chris' teacher was contacted between the second and third session to get a better understanding of the problematic behaviors evidenced in the classroom. Specifically, Chris has difficulty staying on task during group work and he tends to call out when he knows the answer. We created a Daily Report Card for his teacher to complete and for Chris to bring home for his parents to see. Chris' teacher agreed to apply the contingency management techniques in the classroom. We agreed that I would follow-up with her once every two weeks, and that she should contact me in between with any questions or concerns. The contingency management plans in place at home, school, and in session all resulted in less frequent inappropriate behaviors.

Chris' ability to identify his irrational beliefs, challenge them, and replace them with more helpful thoughts all contributed to fewer difficulties at home and at school. He reported feeling better emotionally, and his peer relationships also improved. Chris' parents and teacher confirmed this report. While not perfect, Chris benefited from REBT and understands that he may have to continually work on his thinking and behaviors throughout his life. Chris' parents also reported less emotional disturbance in themselves, and often used each other as reminders of what they learned in therapy. Chris and his parents understand that they may need to return to therapy in the future, particularly around times of transition.

Conclusions and Summary

Research on REBT with ADHD is limited and we believe that this chapter provides a clinician with a solid integration of understanding of treatment strategies for ADHD and where REBT can play a role. The exact role of REBT in the treatment of ADHD is an area that still needs to be further examined empirically. Given that we have research which describes the efficacy of behavior management and psychopharmacologic interventions, REBT can be utilized to treat some of the secondary emotional disturbances often seen in children with ADHD and their accompanying cognitions. We have found REBT to be helpful in terms of these secondary emotional disturbances while also assisting in the impact of irrational beliefs that may further exacerbate the symptoms associated with ADHD. Too often children and families may "live the label" and believe because of the diagnosis that they are restricted in the things that they can do. REBT can be very helpful with increasing treatment compliance, managing many of the emotive and social difficulties that may accompany the disorder, preventing further difficulties, and assist the student and family in reducing difficulties and enhancing the quality of their lives and their relationship.

Appendix A: Attention Deficit Disorder (Inattentive Subtype) Keep a Rational Thoughts Diary

With regards to distractibility, irrational and unhelpful thoughts can contribute to emotional problems—and further increase your distractibility. Here is a way to show how your emotions are related to your thinking. Each time you find yourself distractible make an entry, rating your inattentiveness on a scale of 1–10. If possible do it at the time you are feeling badly. Also, write down a very brief description of the situation that you are in. Then write as many thoughts as you can "hear" in your head. Write them just as you think them, without "fixing them up."

Here is an example:

Date/Time	Inattentiveness	Emotions	Situation	Thoughts
Wed 11:40 a.m.	7	Anxious	Unable to follow through with morning goals	It's too difficult to do, I can't concentrate!

Appendix B: Reward/Consequence Contingency Assessment

List Five things that you find reinforcing/rewarding:

1. ________________________________

2. ________________________________

3. ________________________________

4. ________________________________

5. ________________________________

List Five things that you find negative/aversive:

1. ________________________________

2. ________________________________

3. ________________________________

4. ________________________________

5. ________________________________

Appendix C: Contingency Management Program

For this week, choose five tasks that you want to be able to accomplish that normally your distractibility/inattentiveness may interfere with.
Desired Tasks:

1. ________________________________
2. ________________________________
3. ________________________________
4. ________________________________
5. ________________________________

References

Abramowitz, A. J., Eckstrand, D., O'Leary, S. G., & Duncan, M. K. (1992). ADHD children's responses to stimulant medication and two intensities of a behavioral intervention. *Behavior Modification, 16(2)*, 193–203.

Achenbach, T.M. (1991). *Manual for the Child Behavior Checklist/4-18 and 1991 profile*. Burlington: University of Vermont, Department of Psychiatry.

American Academy of Pediatrics. (2001). Clinical Practice Guideline: Treatment of the school-aged child with Attention-Deficit/Hyperactivity Disorder. *Pediatrics, 108*(4), 1033–1044.

American Psychiatric Association. (2000). *Diagnostic and statistical manual of mental disorders (4th ed. Text revision)*. Washington, DC: Author.

Anastopoulos, A. D., & Shelton, T. L. (2001). *Assessing Attention-Deficit/Hyperactivity Disorder*. New York: Kluwer Academic/Plenum Publishers.

Barkley, R. A., Karlsson, J., & Pollard, S. (1985). Effects of age on the mother-child interactions of hyperactive children. *Journal of Abnormal Child Psychology, 13*. 631–638.

Barkley, R. A. (1990). *Attention-deficit hyperactivity disorder: A handbook for diagnosis and treatment*. New York: Guilford Press.

Barkley, R. A. (1997). *ADHD and the nature of self-control*. New York: Guilford Press.

Barkley, R. A. (1998). Attention-deficit hyperactivity disorder: A handbook for diagnosis and treatment (2nd ed). New York: Guilford Press.

Barkley, R. A. (2002). ADHD-Long Term Course, Adult Outcome, and Comorbid Disorders. In P. S. Jensen, and J. R. Cooper (eds.), *Attention Deficit Hyperactivity Disorder State of Science-Best Practices*, Kingston: Civic Research Institute, pp. 4-6–4-7.

Bernard, M.E., & Joyce, M. (1984). *Rational-emotive therapy with children and adolescents: Theory, treatment strategies, and preventative methods*. New York: Wiley.

Bernard, M.E., & Cronan, F. (1999). *The Child and Adolescent Scale of Irrationality: Validation data and mental health correlates*. Journal of Cognitive Psychotherapy, 13, 121–132.

Bernard, M. & Wolfe, J. (2002). *The REBT resource book for practitioners*. New York: Albert Ellis Institute.

Bernard, M. E. (2004). *The REBT therapist's pocket companion for working with children and adolescents.* New York: Albert Ellis Institute.

Block, M. A. (1996). *No more Ritalin: Treating ADHD without drugs*. New York: Kensington.

Campbell, S. B. (1995). Behavior problems in preschool children: A review of recent research. *Journal of Child Psychology & Psychiatry & Allied Disciplines, 36,* 113–149.

Carey, W. B. (2002). Is ADHD a Valid Disorder? In P. S. Jensen, and J. R. Cooper (eds.), *Attention Deficit Hyperactivity Disorder State of Science-Best Practices,* Kingston. Civic Research Institute, pp. 3-1–3-19.

Conners, C. K. (1997). *Conners' Rating Scales-Revised Technical Manual.* New York: Multi-Health Systems, Inc.

DeRubeis, R. J., Tang, T. Z., and Beck, A. T. (2001). Cognitive Therapy. In K. S. Dobson, (ed.), Handbook of Cognitive Behavioral therapies (2nd ed). New York: Guilford Press.

Dodge, K. A., and Somberg, D. R. (1987). Hostile attributional biases among aggressive boys are exacerbated under conditions of threats to self. *Child Development, 58,* 213–224.

Ellis, A. (1977). The basic clinical theory of rational-emotive therapy. In A. Ellis and R. Grieger (eds.), *Handbook of rational-emotive therapy.* New York: Springer Publishing

Ellis, A. (1997). *Anger-How to live with and without it.* New York: Kensington Publishing Corporation.

Ellis, A. & MacLaren, C. (1998). *Rational emotive behavior therapy: A therapist's guide.* California: Impact Publishing.

Ervin, R. A., Bankert, C. L., & DuPaul, G. J. (1996). Treatment of Attention-Deficit/Hyperactivity Disorder. In M. A. Reinecke, F. D. Dattilio, & A. Freeman (Eds.) *Cognitive Therapy with Children and Adolescents.* New York: Guilford Press.

Findling, R. L., & Dogin, J. W. (1998). Psychopharmacology of ADHD; children and adolescents. *Journal of Clinical Psychiatry, 59* (suppl 7), 42–49.

Gage, J.D. & Wilson, L.J. (2000). Acceptability to attention-Deficit/Hyperactivity Disorder interventions: A comparison of parents. *Journal of Attention Disorders, 4* (3), 174–182.

Goldman, L. S., Genel, M., Bezman, R. J., & Slanetz, P. J. (1998). Diagnosis and treatment of attention-deficit/hyperactivity disorder in children and adolescents. *JAMA – Journal of the American Medical Association, 279*(14), 1100–1107.

Goldman, L. S., Genel, M., Bezman, R. J., & Slanetz, P. J. (1998). Diagnosis and treatment of attention-deficit/hyperactivity disorder in children and adolescents. *JAMA – Journal of the American Medical Association, 279*, 1100–1107.

Hansen, C.R., Jr., & Cohen, D.J. (1984). Multimodality approaches in the treatment of attention deficit disorders. *Pediatric Clinics of North America, 31*(2), 499–513.

Hinshaw, S.P. (1992). Externalizing behavior Problems and academic achievement in childhood and adolescence: Causal relationships and underlying mechanisms. *Psychological Bulletin, 111,* 127–155.

Hinshaw, S. P., & Nigg, J. T. (1999). Behavior rating scales in the assessment of disruptive behavior problems in childhood. In D. Shaffer, C. P. Lucas, & Richters, J. E. (Eds.), *Diagnostic assessment in child and adolescent psychopathology* (pp. 91–126). New York: The Guilford Press.

Hinshaw, S. P. (2000). Attention-Deficit/Hyperactivity Disorder: The search for viable treatments. In P. C. Kendall (ed.) Child & Adolescent Therapy: Cognitive-behavioral procedures. New York: Guilford Press.

Hinshaw, S. P. (2002). Is ADHD an Impairing condition in childhood and adolescence? In P. S. Jensen, and J. R. Cooper (eds.), *Attention Deficit Hyperactivity Disorder State of Science-Best Practices.* Kingston: Civic Research Institute, pp. 5-2-5-21.

Hermans, D. F., Williams, L. M., Lazzaro, I., Whitmont, S., Melkonian, D., and Gordon E. (2004). Sex differences in adult ADHD: a double dissociation in brain activity and autonomic arousal. *Biological Psychology, 66*, 221–233.

Hudziak, J. J., Copeland, W., Stanger, C., and Wadsworth, M. (2004). Screening for DSM-IV externalizing disorders with the Child Behavior Checklist: a receiver-operating character analysis. *Journal of Child Psychology and Psychiatry, 45*, 1299–1307.

Jensen, P. S., & Cooper, J. R. (2002). *Attention deficit hyperactivity disorder: Sate of the science-best practices*. New Jersey: Civic Research Institute. xxiii, pp. 1–19.

Kelley, M. L., & McCain, A. P. (1995). Promoting academic performance in inattentive children: The relative efficacy of school-home notes with and without response-cost. *Behavior Modification, 19*, 357–375.

Kendall, P. C. (2000). Child & adolescent therapy: Cognitive-behavioral procedures (2nd ed.). NY: Guilford Press.

Kolko, D.J., Bukstein, O.G. & Barron, J. (1999). Methylphenidate and Behavior Modification in children with ADHD and comorbid ODD or CD: Main and incremental effects across settings. *Journal of the American Academy of Child and Adolescent Psychiatry, 38*, 578–586.

Kovacs M. (1992). *Children's depression inventory* (Manual). New York: Multi-Health Systems.

Kube, D. A., Peterson, M. C., and Palmer, F. B. (2002). Attention deficit hyperactivity disorder: Co morbidity and medication use. *Clinical Pediatrics, 47*, 461–470.

Lewsinson, P. M., Shankman, S. A., Gau, J. M., and Klein, D. (2004). The prevalence and co-morbidity of sub threshold psychiatric conditions. *Psychological Medicine, 34*, 613–622.

McCarney, S.B. (1995). *Early Childhood Attention Deficit Disorders Evaluation Scale (ECADDES)*. Columbia, MO: Hawthorne Educational Services.

McGee, R., Williams, S., & Feehan, M. (1992). Attention deficit disorder and age of onset of problem behaviors. *Journal of Abnormal Child Psychology, 20*, 487–502.

Meichenbaum, D. H., & Goodman, J. (1971). Training impulsive children to talk to themselves: A means of developing self-control. *Journal of Abnormal Psychology, 77*, 115–126.

Miles, D. (2000, March). Critical issues in assessing AD/HD: A survey of current practices. *NASP Comminique, 28*, 15.

Miranda, A. & Presentacion, M.J. (2000). Efficacy of cognitive-behavioral therapy in the treatment of children with ADHD, with and without aggressiveness. *Psychology in the Schools, 37*(2), 169–182.

MTA Cooperative Group. (1999). A 14-month randomized clinical trial of treatment strategies for attention-deficit hyperactivity disorder. *Archives of General Psychiatry, 56,* 1073–1086.

Murphy, M.A., & Hagerman, R.J. (1992). Attention deficit hyperactivity disorder in children: Diagnosis, treatment, and follow-up. *Journal of Pediatric Health Care, 6*, 2–11.

Murray, H.A. (1943). *Thematic Apperception Test Manual*. Cambridge, MA: Harvard University Press.

Netherton, S. D., Holmes, D., & Walker, C. E. (1999). *Child and Adolescent Psychological Disorders*. New York: Oxford University Press.

Neto, P. R., Lou, H., Cumming, P., Pryds, O., and Gjedde (2002). Methylphenidate-evoked potentiation of extracellular dopamine in the brain of adolescents with premature birth. *Annals of the New York Academy of Sciences, 965*, 434–439.

Pelham, W.E. (2002). Psychosocial Interventions for ADHD. In P. S. Jensen, and J. R. Cooper (eds.), *Attention Deficit Hyperactivity Disorder State of Science-Best Practices* Kingston: Civic Research Institute, pp. 12–4–12–7.

Pelham, W. E., Wheeler, T., and Chronis, A. (1998). Empirically supported psychosocial treatments for attention deficit hyperactivity disorder. *Journal of Clinical Child Psychology, 27*(2), 190–205.

Pelham, W.E., Carlson, C., Sams, S. E., Vallano, G., Dixon, M.J., and Hoza, B. (1993). Separate and combined effects of methylphenidate and behavior modification on boys with Attention-Deficit Hyperactivity Disorder in the classroom. *Journal of Consulting and Clinical Psychology, 61*(3), 506–515.

Pierce, E.W., Ewing, L. J., & Campbell, S. B. (1999). Diagnostic status and symptomatic behavior of hard-to-manage preschool children in middle childhood and early adolescence. *Journal of Clinical Child Psychology, 28*, 44–57.

Porter, R.B. and Cattell, R.B. (1975). *Children's Personality Questionnaire*. Institute for Personality and Ability Testing, Inc. (IPAT).

Rapport, M. D., Murphy, H. A., & Bailey, J. S. (1982). Ritalin vs. response cost in the control of hyperactive children: A within-subject comparison. *Journal of Applied Behavior Analysis, 15*, pp. 205–216.

Rapport, M. D., Chung, K., M., Shore, G., & Isaacs, P. (2001). A conceptual model of child psychopathology: Implications for understanding attention deficit hyperactivity disorder and treatment efficacy. *Journal of Clinical Child Psychology, 30(1)*, 48–64.

Raz, A. (2004). Brain imaging data of ADHD, 11, 1–9. *Adolescent Psychiatry, 34,* 987–1000.

Reichenberg-Ullman, J. & Ullman, R. (2000). *Ritalin free kids*. California: Prima.

Reynolds, C. R., & Gutkin, T. B. (1999), *The handbook of school psychology*. New York, NY: John Wiley & Sons, Inc.

Reynolds, C. and Kamphaus, R. (2004). *Behavior Assessment System for Children-2 (BASC-2)* (2nd ed.), Circle Pines, MN: American Guidance Service.

Robinson, L., Sclar, D., Skaer, T. L. & Galin, R. S. (1999). National trends in the prevalence of Attention Deficit/Hyperactivity Disorder and the prescribing of Methylphenidate among school aged children: 1990–1995. *Clinical Pediatrics, 38(4)*, 209–220.

Sagvolden, T. (1999). Attention Deficit/Hyperactivity Disorder. *European Psychologist*, *4*(2), 109–114.

Schwab-Stone, M. E., Shaffer, D., Dulcan, M. K., & Jensen, P.S.. (1996). Criterion validity of the NIMH Diagnostic Interview Schedule for Children Version 2.3 (DISC-2.3). *Journal of the American Academy of Child & Adolescent Psychiatry, 35*, pp. 878–888.

Shaffer, D., Fisher, P., Dulcan, M. K., & Davies, M. The NIMH Diagnostic Interview Schedule for Children Version 2.3 (DISC-2.3): Description, acceptability, prevalence rates, and performance in the MECA study (1996). *Journal of the American Academy of Child & Adolescent Psychiatry, 35*, pp. 865–877.

Shelton, T. L., & Barkley, R.A. (1993). Assessment of attention-deficit hyperactivity disorder in young Children. In J. L. Culbertson, & D. J. Willis, *Testing young children: a reference guide for developmental, psychoeducational, and psychosocial assessments* (pp. 290–318). Austin, TX: PRO-ED, Inc.

Stevens, L. J. (2000). *12 effective ways to help your ADD/ADHD child.* New York: Penguin.

Vernon, A. (2002). *What Works When*. Illinois: Research Press.

Walen, S. R., DiGiuseppe, R., and Dryden, W. (1992). *A Practitioner's Guide to Rational Emotive Therapy*. New York: Oxford University Press.

Waschbusch, D. A., Kipp, H. L., & Pelham, W. E. (1998). Generalization of behavioral and psychostimulant treatment of attention-deficit/hyperactivity disorder (ADHD): discussion and examples. *Behaviour Research and Therapy, 36*, 675–694.

Waschbusch, D. A., & Hill, G. P. (2001). Alternative treatments for children with attention-deficit/hyperactivity disorder: What does the research say? *Behavior Therapist, 24*, 161–171.

Wechsler, D. (2003). *Wechsler Intelligence Scale for Children-Fourth Edition*. San Antonio, TX: Psychological Corporation.

Wilde, J. (1992). *Rational Counseling with School-Aged Populations: A Practical Guide*. Bristol, PA: Accelerated Development.

Woodcock, R.W., McGrew, K.S., and Mather, N. (2001). *Woodcock-Johnson III Tests of Achievement*. Itasca, IL: Riverside Publishing.

11

Working with the Educational Underachiever: A Social and Emotional Developmental Approach

MICHAEL E. BERNARD, PH.D.

University of Melbourne

Internationally, educational underachievement continues to be of great concern for different reasons (e.g., Bernard, 1996, 1997a). Throughout the western world, politicians and educational policy advisors are concerned about data that shows that large percentages of young people who are capable of achieving academic standards are not doing so (e.g., NAEP, 2003). Specific concern surrounds underachievement in males (Lillico, 2001), on the substandard academic performance of students from different cultural groups (e.g., African-Caribbean; Latinos) (e.g., Ford, 1996) and students from economically disadvantaged backgrounds. Much research over the years has focused on underachievement in gifted students (e.g., McCall et al., 1992).

At the level individual students, teachers and parents are concerned when young people fail to live up to their academic potential. Students who demonstrate chronic under-achievement are oftentimes identified for further discussion by student study teams and, ultimately, in some cases, are referred for more intensive assessment to determine eligibility for special education as a result of learning disabilities or other health-related impairments (e.g., attention deficit/hyperactivity disorder).

Educational underachievement is frequently in evidence in children and adolescents who manifest social, emotional and behavioral difficulties (e.g., Woodward and Fergusson, 2001). Educational underachievement may also manifest itself without accompanying mental health problems and when chronic can be considered as a "problem" or "at risk" behavior much the same as use of illegal substances, truancy, school suspensions and precocious sex (Kazdin and Weisz, 2003). Developmentally, an increase in educational underachievement is associated with the onset of adolescence in some but not all teenagers (Bernard and Joyce, 1984).

This chapter presents a social and emotional developmental model that conceptualizes non-cognitive ability psychosocial factors which contribute to educational underachievement as well as promote achievement. The model identifies five *social and emotional disabilities* with accompanying irrational beliefs (negative Habits of the Mind) which when present act as barriers to student learning. Also identified are five *social and emotional capabilities* supported by rational beliefs (positive Habits of the Mind) that need to be well developed in order for students to achieve to the best of their ability. It is proposed that educational underachievement results from delays in social and emotional development as well as from different social and emotional disabilities with effects first appearing in the achievement of five 5-year-old children (e.g., Bernard, 2004a). The social and emotional learning approach advocated to treating underachievement involves a social and emotional learning program consisting of 1:1 counseling/therapy and, when possible, additional social and emotional learning support offered by parents and teachers. The social and emotional learning program combines rational-emotive behavior therapy (REBT) (Bernard and Joyce, 1984; Ellis and Bernard, 1983), rational-emotive education (REE) (Knaus, 1974; Vernon, 1983; Vernon, 2006a, 2006b) and methods found in a program called You Can Do It! Education (Bernard, 2001, 2002, 2005a). Three aspects of the social and emotional learning program are described: (a) methods to eliminating social and emotional disabilities including irrational beliefs, (b) methods for developing social and emotional capabilities including the strengthening of rational beliefs, and (c) methods which parents and teacher can employ in supporting the social and emotional development of the underachiever. A broad sweep of the field of educational underachievement including definitions of the syndrome and types of underachievers will initiate this discussion.

Defining Educational Underachievement

There are a variety of meanings of the term "underachievement." Schaefer and Millman (1981) describe underachievers as children who see little personal meaning in school or who have not developed achievement motivation and related goal setting and success behaviors. Brophy (1996) discusses underachievement as reflected in children who do a minimum to just "get buy" and who (a) are indifferent to school, (b) do minimum amounts of work, and (c) are not challenged by schoolwork and are poorly motivated. Bernard (1997b, p. 7) defined the construct as follows:

Educational underachievement means that a student's school performance as seen in grades or test results is lower than we would predict from a student's age, ability and potential . . . . Some signs of educational underachievement are when a student: (a) performs much better on a test of ability than in schoolwork, (b) performs well at one time and then does poorly at another, (c) performs well in some subjects, but does not do well in other subjects, (d) occasionally reveals in what they say or do good academic or creative ability relative to their usual performance, and (e) demonstrates one or more of the following characteristics: low self-esteem, fear of failure, discouragement, lack of confidence, lack of motivation and effort, goals which are too low or too high, poor time management, rebelliousness, and poor study techniques.

Underachievement is sometimes mistakenly operationalized as students not achieving minimum academic standards in one or more subjects at any grade level. Schools and school districts sometimes calculate the percentage of underachievers as the ratio of students not achieving standards in comparison with those that do. However, I believe there is considerable consensus in the field towards defining underachievement as a discrepancy between academic aptitude and achievement (classroom grades, standardized achievement test scores). So, for example, a student of high ability may underachieve even though she/he has achieved grade level expectations. Alternatively, a student with very low academic ability who works very hard but does not achieve grade level expectations would be considered an "achiever." Hard working students with low ability would be considered "low achievers" but not "underachievers" because they are performing to potential.

Different Types of Underachievers

Underachievers are a heterogeneous group with individual underachievers displaying unique patterns of symptoms and causal factors (Brophy, 1996). McCall et al. (1992) in their exhaustive study of high school underachievers described 23 characteristics that have been linked in the literature to underachievement, including low self-concept, low perception of abilities, unrealistic goal setting, lack of persistence, impulsive rather than reflective response to assignments, social immaturity and poor relationships with peers, oppositional defiance, excuse making, and absence of commitment to change. Of interest in the work of this research group is that they monitored high school underachievers into adulthood. Based on follow-up study, McCall et al., concluded that underachievement in school is part of a larger syndrome of underachievement dominated by a generalized tendency of the individual to avoid responsibilities and to lack persistence in response to expectations be they occupational, educational or interpersonal. The underachievers who were followed up were less likely to complete college and displayed less marital stability than a comparison group of high school students who obtained similar grades but less academic ability.

The literature identifies several distinct "types" of underachievers. It is useful when considering the particular circumstances surrounding the educational underachievement of an individual student to consider the extent to which she/he resembles one of the following types.

Rebellious/Aggressive Type (e.g., Whitmore, 1980). Typified by the "You can't make me do this," these young people believe they should be able to do what they want to do. This attitude may result from the way their parents raised them, their unique temperament (e.g., feisty) or a combination of both. They have lots of power struggles with their families and, in particular big battles over homework. These young people may use school non-performance as a way of punishing their parents for real or imagined injustices ("I'll fix their wagon!").

Immature/Dependent/Anxious Type (e.g., Bruns, 1982). These emotionally immature young people are very reluctant to do things on their own when they are young and tend to hover around their parents and teachers asking lots of questions. They are very concerned about what adults think of them if they make mistakes. In school, they rely too much on their teachers asking lots of questions and frequently showing their teacher their work. They have a high need for approval and they fail to develop the independence to try new or hard things.

Helpless-Discouraged-Depressed Type (Seligman, 1975). These students may have been a bit "immature" when starting school, have limited academic aptitude or a learning disability. They fall behind quickly and experience many fewer positive reinforcements for their school work. They begin to see a disconnect between their efforts and positive achievement outcomes and, as a consequence, develop a negative view of themselves and cannot see themselves accomplishing much at school in the future. Low academic self-concept and poor self-efficacy for most school subjects accompanies this type of underachiever throughout the years of schooling.

The Perfectionistic Type (e.g., Pacht, 1984). These students demand unrealistically high standards of themselves. They have the idea that to be successful and worthwhile, they must do things perfectly at school. When they anticipate not performing perfectly in an area, they can under-perform by not putting in the effort. Lack of effort provides them with a convenient rationalization for lack of perfection ("I simply didn't try very hard. If I did, I would have been perfect."). They can waste a lot of time getting started because they are afraid of not getting it right. They selectively achieve in areas where they have excellent talent and often under-perform in areas of perceived weakness. Perfectionists also tend to restrict their activities to only those where they have a better than average chance of achieving very high results.

Peer Conforming Type (e.g., Bernard, 1997b). The underachieving life style is becoming institutionalized as a sub-culture with many young people. Young people witness powerful and respected peer models with great prestige not valuing their schoolwork and who put pressure on students who appear to value their work. Bart Simpson, a very recognizable TV personality who is the prototypical underachieving student is still revered almost 20 years after being born on "The Simpsons." In many schools there can be great peer pressures beginning in middle primary grades on students not to do their work. While some who endorse this life style do so for reasons more associated with the culture of hedonism so prevalent in western society today, others conform to an anti-achieving life style for fear if they did not, they would be rejected by their peers.

Low Frustration Tolerance Type (e.g., Knaus, 1983). While a vast majority of underachievers have very little ability to tolerate normal levels of frustration, some have particularly abysmally low levels of frustration tolerance. Some of these young people whom we used to call "lazy" appear to have an allergy to hard or boring school work while carrying on successfully in other areas of their lives. Others display a social and emotional disability I refer to as *generalized avoidance of life's responsibilities*. Frequently these students are born with an easily frustratable temperament which they battle with for much of their lives. Combined with a smothering, over-protective or permissive style of parenting, these young people fail to develop the frustration tolerance and delay of gratification needed to meet the responsibilities of school and, in some cases, life. They frequently tell themselves: "Life should be fun and exciting all the time. I can't be bothered doing this. It's unfair that I have to do this. This is too hard, I cannot stand it."

Non-Achievement/Peter Pan Syndrome (e.g., Mandel and Marcus, 1988). These frequently good-natured students are motivated to do anything possible to avoid doing school work; that is, these students are strongly motivated to avoid success. They believe that doing school work successfully will reveal to others their true capabilities and will result in having to assume unwanted responsibilities and the sacrifice of fun.

A variety of techniques and strategies have been employed to combat underachievement. Some are comprehensive and involve teacher-parent collaboration in using behavior modification (e.g., behavioral contracting, daily/weekly school-home report card). Other approaches work directly with the student employing a variety of techniques (including study skills, goal setting, time management, self-monitoring, disputing irrational beliefs, use of positive self-statements, emotional self-management, coping skills). McCall et al. (1992) report that while many diverse treatments have met with success in ameliorating targeted symptoms (e.g., anxiety, self-esteem, poor study skills, social relationships), only comprehensive programs involving parents, teachers and the student and, which address the full array of symptoms observed in the student are effective in influencing student engagement in work and subsequent achievement. Different treatment protocols are typically employed in the treatment of the different types of underachievement outlined above.

Social Cognitive Learning Analysis of Underachievement

A variety of cognitive-behavioral and social learning theories and related research including shed light on the phenomena of underachievement.

REBT

The REBT literature dealing with educational under-achievement (e.g., Bard and Fisher, 1983; Bernard and Joyce, 1984) addresses parenting style and the belief system of children and adolescents as major contributors. On the one hand, according to existing REBT literature, young people whose parents parent with kindness and firmness achieve to their potential while parenting styles characterized by harshness and permissiveness are associated with children who under-perform in school (Hauck, 1967, 1983). On the other hand, there are irrational beliefs of young people associated with different types of underachievement that have been identified in the REBT literature as being associated with extreme negative feelings (e.g., anger, anxiety, depression) and dysfunctional patterns of behavior (e.g., work avoidance/procrastination) including: low frustration tolerance, self-depreciation, need for achievement and/or need for approval. Bernard (2004b) provided an in-depth ABC analysis of psychosocial problems of childhood that includes examples of typical irrational beliefs (inferences, absolutes, evaluations) (see Chapter One of this book).

Bernard (2002) employed the Happening→Thinking→Feeling→Behaving framework to represent how irrational beliefs (negative Habits of the Mind) and rational beliefs (positive Habits of the Mind) impact student motivation and achievement.

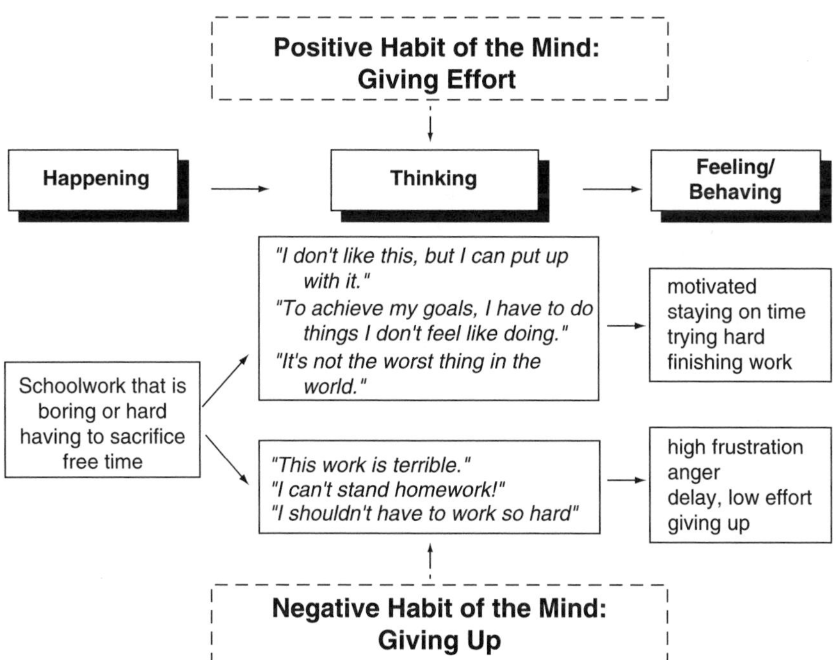

Perhaps, the most erudite discussion of the causes of under-achievement in children and adolescents in the REBT literature was provided by Bard and Fisher (1983). (Also see in this book the illuminating discussion by Bill Knaus on the dynamic interplay of low frustration tolerance and self-depreciation as a major catalyst for underachievement). Bard and Fisher define underachievement as poor academic performance resulting mainly from students' beliefs that are false and incompatible with the educational system. These authors identified five different irrational and/or erroneous beliefs that give rise to the problem and associated family characteristics that contribute to the dysfunctional belief systems of children.

"Everything Will Turn out OK Whether I Work or Not"

This unrealistic belief leads students to "dodge the bullet" when it comes to completing work on time and extended deadlines, negotiated homework assignments and makeup exams are the rule rather than the exception. The delay and avoidance tactics of these non-hostile happy-go-lucky students is justified by their naïve belief that they will be looked after.

According to Bard and Fisher (1983), this belief may results in some children from the experience of being overindulged and may originate in a parenting style where children are rewarded first rather than being rewarded after they have expended effort. "Instead of promising a reward after work has been completed, they deliver the reward first and then expect the task to be done thereafter" (p. 198). A key aspect of parents whose children cling onto these dysfunctional beliefs is that for different reasons, they do as much as they can to bail their children out of difficult situations so that things do not turn out badly for their children even if they have not done their work.

Three phases of therapy are advocated to change this dysfunctional belief. First, the establishment of a reliable school-home communication system where children's poor work performance and ensuing negative consequences are clear to all so that the child cannot pretend that things are improving. Second, serious work needs to occur so that the child can see through hard (and painful) evidence that the belief is very dubious and probably false. Here, parents and teachers alike refrain from bailing out the child with extending deadlines and the full brunt of failing grades are experienced by the child in the form of logical consequences (repeating a class/grade level, being grounded, and not receiving the latest video game). It is important for the therapist or counselor to have concrete evidence on hand to dispute the erroneous belief. Third, once the child sees that his/her philosophy will not work, a process of reconstruction of belief is initiated where the child is supported in coming up with what they really want in life (e.g., success, better self-concept, fewer hassles) and which new beliefs will enable them to achieve their goals.

"Everything Should Be Entertaining and/or Enjoyable and There Should Be No Unpleasantness Whatsoever"

According to Bard and Fisher, this belief may exist in combination with the first belief or can stand by itself. This belief which Ellis refers to as *low frustration tolerance* is one of the most difficult to modify. The performance of students who endorse this belief tends to be very uneven with strong achievement in evidence when the student is studying high interest material suited to his/her cognitive strengths and underachievement occurring when the student encounters someone or something that is not entertaining or enjoyable.

Features of parents associated with this belief include permissive and powerless parenting ("Children should not be frustrated," "It's too hard to be a strong parent"), inconsistent parenting (one parent setting very strict standards, the other who subverts the standards and subscribes to more permissive style), overindulgence and over-protectiveness (making excuses and covering up for the child) and lack of assertion in carrying through on standards.

"Talk" therapy for students with a *lft* philosophy often proves problematic. The regime is to meet with parents and have them clarify, communicate expectations (home rules) and to develop their emotional resilience in order to enforce consequences firmly but kindly. The therapeutic alliance is crucial in working with these difficult customers. If children with *lft* believe that their therapist is on their side and seek your approval, then it becomes possible to shift their *hedonic calculus* away from over-focusing on short-term pleasures and avoidance of short-term discomforts to one where they consider the long-term costs to their eventual success of avoiding short-term pain.

"To Do Well in School Would Betray Relationships I Have with My Friends"

Bard and Fisher (1983) propose that students who endorse this belief have been turned off and alienated by the policies and practices of their parents and turned on by a set of principles that diverge from their family tradition. There are notable instances of students who due to lack of effort fail academically in order to meet a peer group standard that does not exist (other students in peer group do not mind if the students gets good grades). An alternative or complimentary explanation is that some students who find themselves attracted to peers with non-conforming life styles as a way of rebelling against their parents and who believe they need the approval of their peers make conscious decisions not to do schoolwork despite an underlying desire to be successful in order to avoid rejection.

Oftentimes, parents of this group of under-achievers tend to have conservative values with an emphasis on "proper" customs including hard work and self-discipline. These parents communicate to their children a rigid set of "shoulds" concerning behavior with little discussion or rationale provided.

Children who endorse the values of what they perceive to be an anti-achieving peer group do so as a way of rejecting arbitrary, traditional values.

In therapy, it is important for the practitioner to establish him/herself as independent from representing the party line of the parents and as someone who is impartial and reasonable. This can be accomplished by questioning some of the more rigid standards for behavior held by the parents. Once credibility has been established, the therapist can discuss with the child the influence of the peer group. In particular, the therapist can employ *empirical disputation* to establish whether the peer group would, indeed, reject the young person who begins to demonstrate pro-academic work behavior. If the young person can see that the peer group will not reject him/her for doing schoolwork and if doing schoolwork does not represent in the young person's mind a victory for parents, then the young person may be motivated to start to engage in schoolwork. If the young person encounters evidence that she/he will be rejected by peers, then fruitful discussions can be held concerning wither peers in the group are really friends and whether an alternative peer group might be more suitable.

"It is Demeaning, Dishonorable, and Destructive of My Personal Integrity to Cooperate with Authority in Any Way"

Young people who endorse this anti-achieving philosophy tend to be very self-centered and reject in very hostile ways attempts of society to regulate their behavior. This type of anti-achiever may demonstrate their ability to resist authority and for others to do little about it through a variety of destructive and non-conforming behaviors.

According to Bard and Fisher, the common feature of parenting style associated with this belief system is powerless parenting that refers to parents' inability to enforce home rules or policies. The fact of parental helplessness serves to support the idea that "No one can make me do what I do not want to do." At a certain point in the power struggle between children and parents, the anti-achieving child makes up his/her mind that no matter how much his/her parents yell, scream and abuse, they cannot control his/her behavior. Frequently, such abuse is combined with unloving parental behavior.

It is difficult for us to get these difficult customers to agree to therapy as it is perceived as authority. Sometimes, if the young person is in trouble with the law, the student can be induced by an agent of the juvenile court to see a practitioner. Therapy involves the therapist using the full range of his/her persuasive powers to convince the young person that there is personal benefit in cooperating with others and doing schoolwork in particular.

"Nothing I Do at School Will Ever Benefit Me"

Oftentimes, students who hold to this philosophy enter school expecting little and are surprised that academic achievement is expected of them. These students are often hard to identify because they may do poorly from the very beginning of school. These students often are not noticed as teachers tend to hold low expectations for their school performance.

Bard and Fisher observe that families from lower socio-economic circumstances are more likely than other families to encourage this attitude towards school. High expectations for student achievement and the importance of student effort are not in evidence in parent-child communication.

In order for this belief to be challenged, it is vital that young people are provided with tangible benefits that the school offers to him/her and his/her family. That is, conventional psychotherapy will not be sufficient to change the mindset of young people coming out of home backgrounds where the value of education as cultural capital is not recognized.

Academic Procrastination

Many but certainly not all young people who underachieve engage in academic procrastination. While early research in the area of academic procrastination focussed on the absence of study skills in procrastinators, more recent work has examined the cognitive and emotional characteristics of high and low academic procrastinators. Solomon and Rothblum (1984) found two main psychological factors associated with procrastination:

1. Fear of failure, which includes anxiety about meeting others' expectations (evaluation anxiety), concerns about meeting one's own standards (perfectionism), lack of self-confidence, lack of assertion and low self-esteem.
2. Task aversiveness, which relates to the unpleasantness of the task and laziness.

Solomon and Rothblum found that there were two distinct groups of procrastinators. The first is a small homogeneous group who experience various symptoms surrounding fear of failure. The second group is larger and more heterogeneous; it includes those students who procrastinate due to the aversiveness of the task.

In another representative study, Rothblum et al. (1986) found that in comparison with low academic procrastinators, high academic procrastinators experience more anxiety, are more likely to attribute success on exams to external and fleeting circumstances (rather than their own ability and effort), have lower self-efficacy, and have less control over their emotional reactions.

In reviewing this area, Bernard (1991) identified four psychological characteristics associated with academic procrastination:

1. Depression/anxiety
2. General work avoidance/inability to delay gratification
3. Time disorganization
4. Hostility

Ellis and Knaus (1977) discussed the following common rationalizations of procrastinators in general that are often in evidence in clinical work with young people who underachieve:

- "I'll do it later."
- "I'll do later when I'm more in the mood."
- "I need to relax."
- "Make hay while the sun shines.
- "No one cares whether I do this or not."
- "I only work best under pressure so I'll wait until the last minute before beginning."
- "I achieved a good result before when I did my work at the last minute."

Over the years, a number of techniques have been shown to help academic procrastinators, including behavioural self-control in which students are taught to set goals, monitor their achievement and administer rewards and punishments (Ziesat et al., 1978) and cognitive restructuring to help students manage their anxiety and deal with issues related to self-esteem (Rothblum et al., 1986).

Social-Emotional Disabilities and Social-Emotional Disabilities

Bernard (2004a) is his writings concerning You Can Do It! Education has provided a new framework for conceptualizing diverse student positive and negative outcomes based on REBT and different social cognitive learning theories including attributional theory (Weiner, 1979), locus of control (e.g., Rotter, 1966), learned helplessness and optimism (e.g., Seligman, 1975), theories of internal motivation (e.g., Spaulding, 1983), self-efficacy (e.g., Bandura, 1986, 1997; Zimmerman, 1991), goal setting (e.g., Dweck and Elliott, 1983; Lange and Adler, 1997) and interpersonal cognitive problem solving (e.g., Shure, 1996; Spivack et al., 1976).

Briefly, based on existing REBT and CBT theories cited above and my own research, I have conceptualized factors that contribute to underachievement along two psychological dimensions: (1) Social and Emotional Capabilities and (2) Social and Emotional Disabilities (see Fig. 1). In my work, I have identified five social-emotional disabilities that contribute to negative outcomes in young people (educational underachievement, poor mental health, disaffection): poor emotion regulation, anxiety/depression, general disorganization (generalized LFT, avoidance of responsibilities, anger/chronic misbehavior. I have also delimited another five social-emotional capabilities that contribute to positive outcomes (educational achievement, well-being, positive relationships): confidence, persistence, organization, getting along, emotional resilience. These five social-emotional disabilities are dominated by different irrational beliefs (I use the term "Negative Habits of the Mind") while a range of rational beliefs (I use the term "Positive Habits of the

Mind") nourish and support the five social-emotional capabilities (Bernard, 2003a) (see the sections in this chapter "Eliminating Social and Emotional Disabilities" and "Developing Social and Emotional Capabilities" for more details).

Considerable research reported by Bernard (2006) indicates that regardless of the reasons for underachievement, the type of underachievement, and whether or not they display one or more social and emotional disabilities described in Fig. 1, as a group, underachievers show developmental delays in their academic confidence, work persistence, work organization, and teamwork skills and some also display one or more social and emotional disabilities.

A Social and Emotional Learning Approach for Combatting Educational Underachievement

The contributions to an individual young person's underachievement are varied and idiosyncratic. As such, a tool-box approach is often best to employ as one needs to be very flexible and creative in addressing the idiosyncratic needs of individual underachievers. That being said, I have developed a three-component approach to combating underachievement that involve engaging

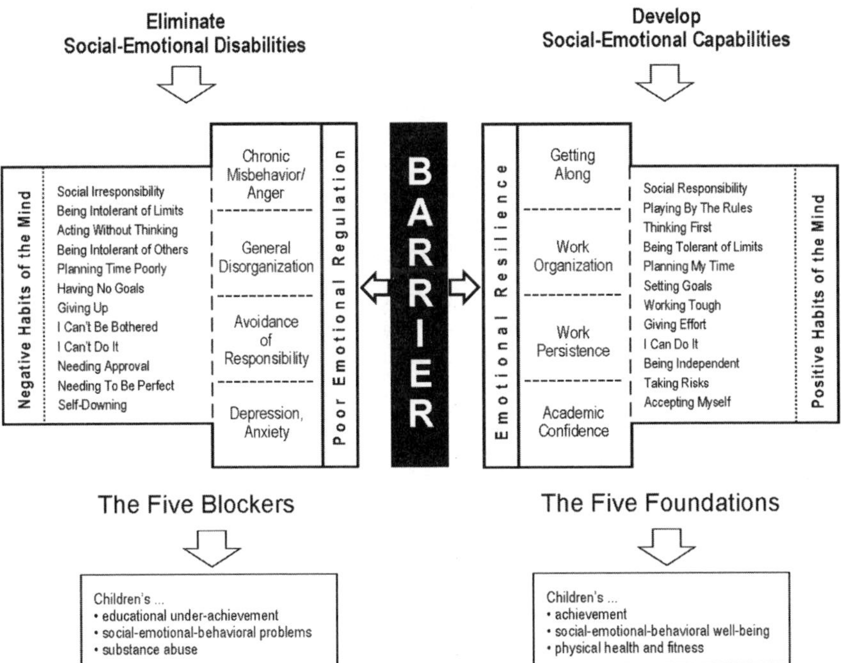

FIGURE 1. Social and emotional development and educational under-achievement (Bernard, 2004a).

the young person in a variety of social and emotional learning experiences based on REBT/REE/CBT practices.

Eliminate Social and Emotional Disabilities

This is the traditional REBT/CBT treatment approach. Here, the practitioner identifies which if any of the following social and emotional disabilities are contributing to underachievement: anxiety/depression, anger/chronic misbehavior, general avoidance of responsibilities (pervasive LFT), general disorganization and poor emotional regulation. For those social and emotional disabilities identified, the practitioner formulates an intervention plan to eliminate the targeted social and emotional disability that will be multisystemic and may call upon a variety of services and programs. Additionally, in 1:1 work, the practitioner will employ a variety of cognitive, emotive, behavioral and other practical methods to eliminate the targeted social and emotional disability. A major part of this work is helping the young person to see the connection among thoughts, feelings and behaviors, disputing and changing the young person's irrational belief/negative Habits of the Mind and using a variety of cognitive, emotional and behavioral methods and activities to eliminate the young person's negative mindset represented in his/her social and emotional disabilities (see Bernard, 2004a).

Develop Social and Emotional Capabilities

Here, the practitioner functions more as a teacher, mentor or mental skills coach than a therapist. The practitioner determines which of the social and emotional capabilities need further development and formulates a plan to strengthen: academic confidence, work persistence, work organization, work collaboration, and emotional resilience. In addition to methods and activities represented in REBT and REE-oriented resources, other resources specifically designed to strengthen rational beliefs/positive Habits of the Mind and social and emotional capabilities are utilized to being about a more positive mindset in the young person (e.g., Bernard, 2003b, Bernard, 2005a).

Work with Parents and Teachers

When appropriate as determined by the age of the young person, and extent of intervention deemed necessary to resolve underachievement and the willingness and availability of outside parties, work with parents and teachers to help them realize the importance of the young person's social and emotional development in achievement and to learn new methods to eliminate social and emotional disabilities anxiety/depression, anger/rebelliousness, general avoidance of responsibilities, general disorganization and poor emotional regulation and to develop young person's academic confidence, work persistence, work organization, work collaboration and emotional resilience including the explicit teaching of rational beliefs (e.g., Bernard, 2003b).

What follows now are suggestions for working with young people who underachieve.

Determine Existence of Under-Achievement

Before initiating an intervention of any sort, an initial assessment needs to substantiate the concerns of the referring parent or teacher that the young person is underachieving. That is, be sure to gather your own data before determining the existence of underachievement. During this process, you will want to note whether the young person underachieves in all subjects or in select classes. If not available, you may want to administer an individual intelligence test to get an objective gauge of academic aptitude. An examination of previous and current reports cards as well as standardized achievement test tests is the surest way to determine the existence and extent of underachievement. You will also be on the lookout for discrepancies in achievement in classes that call for similar abilities. For example, if a young person is achieving well in history but not in English, the underachievement alarm bell rings. Similarly, the bell can ring if you notice a dramatic drop in achievement in one or more classes from one year to the next.

It is not easy to detect underachievement in some young people. The ones that coast along achieving acceptable standards as well as the creative students sometimes show their teachers little to indicate that they are more capable. This is especially the case of the Nonachievement Syndrome young person described above who covers up underachievement with multiple excuses.

Therapeutic Alliance: Developing the Goals of Working Together

In the initial sessions in working with a child or adolescent who is underachieving, you will want to lay out the goals and purposes of your work together along with developing a working relationship where the young person respects you and believes you are on his/her side. You will want to be very clear that your goal is to help the young person achieve success in schoolwork and life. You will need to define "success" as doing the best you can in different classes rather than being the best.

Your goal for this discussion is for the young person to agree that she/he wants to be successful. You can review with the young person the advantages of success in school work and all endeavors (e.g., positive feelings, recognition from others, benefits in being able to choose classes, be with friends, attend a good university, earn better money, get a good job) and the disadvantages of not being successful (bad feelings, criticism from others, penalties such as being grounded, restrictions in classes and limitations in future classes, job, and universities). You can also have the young person "replay" moments of success in school work and other areas and moments of disappointment when goals where not met

You will want to obtain from the young person before beginning the intervention an agreement that she/he has the goal to be successful in school. This agreement may take some time to achieve and it is recommended that you do not speed ahead until it is reached. The shared goal should not be to eradicate underachievement; that is, avoid focusing in problems and their reduction.

Gaining "Buy In" on the Model

You will want to share with a student who underachieves a model that makes it clear as to the reasons why young people are not as successful in school as possible. You can say something like the following (I use illustrations I have developed to illustrate my argument, see Fig. 2).

We have discovered that for any person to be successful in life including students in school, they need to have five keys that unlock their potential. These keys are the most important things that determine whether students are successful in school. They are even more important than how smart you are, whether your parents are interested in your education and help you; they are as important as how good your teacher is; some think more important?

Now, you aren't born with these keys, you have to learn about them. Just listen while I talk about each one. See if you agree that they are the real keys for success.

Having the key of *confidence* means that you are not afraid to make mistakes or fail and that you trust that in time you will be more likely to be successful than to fail.

Having the key of *persistence* means that you keep trying even when things are hard or boring and that you know that to be successful you sometimes have to do things that are boring. You also know that the harder to try, the better you get.

The key of *organization* helps you to set goals to be successful, make good use of time, tackle big assignments by breaking them down into simpler steps and helps you locate needed things quickly.

The key of *getting along* helps you to work well with other students especially those who are different from you, solve conflicts and to follow important rules in school knowing that doing so makes school a safer and better place to learn.

Finally, the key of *resilience* helps a student to stay calm when bad stuff happens and when upset, to clam down quickly and return to doing school work and being with friends as quickly as possible.

You will want to gain agreement with the young person about the importance of the five keys to everyone's success. You can describe how they have helped you in your life.

The Five Keys to Success

FIGURE 2. The five keys to school success and happiness (Bernard, 2005b).

For older children and adolescents, you will want to bring to their attention those things that can block them from being successful and happy. You can discuss the "Five Blockers to School Success and Happiness" (see Fig. 3).

We have discovered that as young people grow up, they can develop one or more blockers that make it harder for them to be successful. You can see from this drawing that there are five blockers to success and happiness.

The Five Blockers to Success

FIGURE 3. The five blockers to school success and happiness (Bernard, 2005b).

Some young people worry so much about things or get so down on themselves when things are going badly for them that they find it hard to study.

Some young people seem to avoid responsibilities of any sort that are asked of them like chores, cleaning their room, or doing schoolwork.

Some young people are very disorganized. They have no goals in life, they are always running late, and they never can find what they need for school.

Some young people feel so angry towards teachers or parents or other classmates that they behave badly which means that they do not do their work.

Also, some young people get so easily upset by what goes on around them that they lose focus and the desire to learn.

You can ask the young person whether she/he agrees that each blocker can make it harder for young people to be successful.

At this stage, you will want to discuss with the young person that your role is to help the young person gain knowledge and skills in how to eliminate blockers and develop the keys that lead to achievement. You will also mention that the task of the young person is to learn as much as she/he can about how to eliminate blockers and about the keys during the time spent together and, then, to practice using this knowledge and skills during the week.

Assessment

It is important to decide the extent to which the young person's underachievement is due to a lack of social and emotional development with particular reference to academic confidence, work persistence, work organization, work collaboration and emotional resilience. That is, my own experience and research indicates that regardless of the type of underachievement displayed by a young person, all under-achievers demonstrate delays in one or more of these areas. I have found that the trifecta of social and emotional capabilities that when delayed most strongly effect the extent of a young person's underachievement are: academic confidence, work persistence, and work organization. That is, students for reasons having to do with their upbringing and/or temperament are "underdone" in the area of their social and emotional development. They have not developed strongly enough the academic confidence, work persistence, and work organization that is needed for them to achieve to the best of their ability; especially as they proceed into secondary school. A typical example would be children born to families where there is no history of anyone attending a college/university and where the "press for achievement" is not strong. Some but not all of these children have not developed a strong positive work orientation or what I have called a "positive mindset for achievement" represented by these social and emotional capabilities.

There are significant numbers of underachievers who are underperforming in classes they find difficult and/or boring due to a lack of a positive work orientation whereas in classes of interest and where they perceive sufficient capability, they perform up to potential. For these students, accelerating the development of these social and emotional capabilities including strengthening their endorsement of rational beliefs/positive Habits of the Mind in their weaker classes/subjects is the treatment goal. These methods are illustrated in a following section.

Other young people who underachieve do so not only because of delays in their positive work orientation (academic confidence, work persistence, work organization) as well as their resilience and work cooperation skills, they also have one or more contributing social and emotional disabilities represented in my model as blockers. It will be important to know which of the blockers may also be contributing to the under-achievement. A young person may be underachieving as a result of one or more of the following: anxiety, depression, anger/rebelliousness, general work avoidance/LFT general disorganization and/or poor emotional regulation. These students bring with them a number of irrational beliefs/negative Habits of the Mind that contribute to their social and emotional disability or blocker which need to be disputed.

The treatment plan for students whose underachievement is due to one or more social and emotional disabilities is generally *multisystemic* and can include a variety of interventions, programs and services for the young person and family (e.g., referral to anger management class). Students who present with ADHD symptoms of disorganization will need instructional modifications. Students who demonstrate internalizing problems often require more intensive forms or social support. Students with anger management or conduct problems will often need family interventions and stronger school-home links established. While the practitioner using REBT can offer valuable 1:1 assistance in helping to eliminate social and emotional disabilities through the use of rational-emotive education including challenging and changing irrational beliefs, it is recognized that for many of these young people, a more comprehensive program of services will be needed.

Once you have determined the existence of high levels of anxiety, depression, anger, generalized disorganization, avoidance of responsibilities (LFT), standard REBT assessment/elicitational techniques will yield a range of faulty inferences, absolutes and evaluations of the young person (see Chapter 1 of this book for typical irrational beliefs accompanying these psychosocial problems) as well as those described by Bard and Fisher (1983) presented in an earlier section of this chapter. Additionally, the Child and Adolescent Scale of Irrationality (Bernard and Cronan, 1999) may be used to assess irrational beliefs.

Eliminating Social and Emotional Disabilities

When one or more social and emotional disabilities are identified through assessment, your 1:1 work will be to employ cognitive, emotional and behavioral methods and activities that characterize REBT practice as described by Bernard (2004a) and in the chapters of this book. REBT's unique contribution is in the recognition of the unique irrational beliefs that are involved in the five dysfunctional clusters of cognitions-emotions-behaviors associated with social and emotional disabilities.

What follows are some illustrations of how comprehensive REBT that involves not only disputing and cognitive restructuring, but also emotive and behavioral methods (Bernard, 1986).

Explaining the ABCs and Disputing

When working to weaken and eliminate social and emotional disabilities, the basic Happening→Thinking→Feeling→Behaving framework is generally presented as a way to help underachievers understand their emotions and behaviors along with the teaching of an *emotional vocabulary* (anger, anxiety, down) and an *emotional schema* for understanding that feelings can vary from strong to weak and that extreme levels of emotions are generally unhealthy and unhelpful. The different between irrational beliefs/negative Habits of the Mind and rational beliefs/positive Habits of the Mind are discussed using illustrations and concrete examples along with the process of disputing (see Fig. 4). The power of negative, irrational self-talk and rational, positive self-talk is emphasized.

Underachievement Due to Anxiety/Depression

This social and emotional disability that blocks achievement means that young people worry a lot about what other people think of them and/or whether they

Challenging and Changing Your Negative Attitudes

The trick to changing attitudes is to look at them and challenge them by asking yourself these two questions:

- "Is what I'm thinking true and sensible or am I just kidding myself?"

  and

- "Is this attitude helping me or hurting me?"

If you find that what you are thinking is not true, not sensible, or not helping you, you can change it.

Keeping a negative attitude is like trying to high jump with a heavy weight on your back. Not only is there no point to it, you are only making it harder.

FIGURE 4. Illustrating the process of disputing/challenging (Bernard, 2005b).

will do as well in school work as they think they should. Young people get emotionally upset when others reject them and when they do not achieve at the level they expect of themselves. They get anxious in performance situations and some but not all students with anxiety get down when they perform poorly or are criticized or rejected. Common irrational, negative Habits of the Mind endorsed by young people depending on the type of anxiety include:

Self-Downing: Thinking that you are a total failure when you have been rejected and/or have not achieved a good result.

Needing to Be Perfect: Thinking that you need to be successful at everything important you do and that it is horrible when you are not.

Needing Approval: Thinking that you need people (parents, teachers or peers) to approve of what you do and that when they do not, it is the worst thing in the world.

I Can't Do It! (pessimism): Thinking that when I have not been successful at something, I am no good at doing that sort of work and I will never be.

What follows are some examples of the importance of identifying and challenging irrational beliefs that give rise to anxiety and/or depression-related underachievement (see chapter by Grieger and Boyd). (See Tables 1 and 2 for cognitive, emotive and behavioral methods your can use and share with parents and teachers).

Consider the case of Michael, a bright but anxious and moderately depressed 12-year-old who was underachieving in most of his classes in grade 6. In exploring issues surrounding his social and emotional disabilities of anxiety and depression, assessment data revealed that Michael was avoiding completing any school work because when he did, his teacher would write red comments on his work which his mother would view at home. At those times, his mother would become extremely angry with Michael who interpreted such behavior in terms of his mother not loving him; hence, his anxiety and avoidant behavior about handing in any new schoolwork likely to receive red comments and his depression about his mother's apparent rejecting behavior. You can see that Michael's irrational cognitions ("My mother doesn't love me. She'll never love me again. I need my mother's approval and recognition for everything that I do. I'm a loser.") that were challenged using REBT did not exist in a psychological vacuum but rather occurred simultaneously with unhealthy emotions (high anxiety, depression), and self-defeating behavior (avoiding schoolwork) which altogether constituted the social and emotional disability.

The intervention involved sharing with Michael's mother how Michael interpreted her angry behavior and the impact of her behavior on Michael's underachievement. In a combined meeting, his mother disputed Michael's irrational belief assuring him that even when she gets angry with him she still loves him very much. This turning point in the case led to Michael restructuring his irrational beliefs with concurrent changes occurring in his

TABLE 1. Cognitive, emotive and behavioral methods for working with underachieving students who are anxious and/or depressed (from Bernard, 1997).

1. Remind yourself that the student's lack of work engagement is motivated out of the fear of making mistakes, the fear of disapproval, and the need to manipulate you and others help with the work so that he/she doesn't make mistakes.
2. Teach non approval seeking distinguishing the desire to be approved of from the irrational need to be approved of.
3. Challenge the students self-downing tendencies and discuss self-acceptance as a more rational, helpful way to think.
4. Do not allow yourself to be manipulated into being overly supportive of the student.
5. Use the Praise, Prompt and Leave procedure (i.e., allow the student to struggle with difficult activities without rescuing him/her).
6. Develop a climate of encouragement of mistakes as a natural part of the learning process. React positively to the student when his/her work reveals mistakes.
7. Provide individual recognition of the student for independent work.
8. Give the student your vote of confidence.
9. Withdraw "nagging" attention.
10. Do not give the student too much attention when he/she expresses negative feelings about work.
11. Teach the student not to judge or evaluate his/her work until after a certain period of time.

TABLE 2. Cognitive, emotive and behavioral methods for working with underachieving students who feel helpless and discouraged (from Bernard, 1997).

1. Teach self-acceptance.
2. Encourage parents and classmates to see the student in a positive way.
3. Show enthusiasm and support for the learning efforts of the student.
4. Show interest in and excitement about non-curricular areas of the student's skills and talents.
5. Expose the student to a variety of extra-curricular activities and hobbies in which he/she is likely to be interested.
6. Ensure that parents do not prevent the student from engaging in extra-curricular activities as a penalty for poor performance in school. Explain to parents that the activity may help build the student's confidence.
7. Take special interest in the student.
8. Enlist the cooperation of the class in supporting the student's learning efforts.
9. Communicate your belief that the student will be successful.
10. Communicate the importance of effort in obtaining success.
11. Explain that a key to the student's success is his/her belief that the harder a person tries at something, the better they get. Provide real life examples of this concept.
12. Design assignments to ensure that the student achieves success with minimum effort.
13. Acknowledge and positively reinforce the student's efforts and successes.
14. Make sure that the student sees the connection between effort and achievement.
15. Make sure the student has time to develop and practice newly acquired skills before moving on to the next task.
16. Help the student make optimistic forecasts about his/her future success based on his/her past and present achievements.
17. Help the student set short-term, attainable goals for class assignments.
18. Graph the student's progress toward his/her goals.
19. Evaluate the student's progress based on the amount he/she has learned rather than comparisons with other students.
20. Have the student tutored in areas of weakness by a peer of his/her age or older.
21. Have the student tutor younger students in his/her areas of strength.

emotions and behaviors. As well, direct 1:1 interventions lead to an increase in his tolerance for the discomfort he felt when being criticized by his mother. A discussion with his teacher concerning the need to change the color of his ink when making comments on Michael's assignments and to provide more positive written feedback also helped allay his mother's anxieties about Michael and her own success or failure as a parent.

I was also referred Darren, a 17-year-old, in the second to the last year of secondary school, who was underachieving in physics, a subject needed as a prerequisite for his proposed university program that he very much wanted to attend. Data gathering revealed, in fact, that Darren had not turned in only 2 of 12 practicum assignments since the beginning of the year where he received an average grade. It was clear to everyone that Darren had enough ability to perform at a reasonable level on these assignments but to everyone's consternation and amazement given the physics assignment's importance to his future, he simply did not produce the goods. During the third session, Darren was asked about his physic teacher's perceptions concerning his lack of work completion. "Well," said Darren, "he probably thinks I'm lazy, but at least he doesn't think I'm stupid." It turned out that Darren had a high need for approval of his teacher and awfulized about his teacher thinking that he was unintelligent. Laziness was the excuse for lack of intelligence and this Darren could live with. Once again, irrational beliefs, unhealthy emotions (anxiety) and self-defeating behavior (lack of work completion), a social and emotional disability, were conspiring together to produce underachievement. The REBT intervention involved disputing his need for approval from his teacher and helping him reformulate his need into a preference or desire along with a series of anti-awfulizing exercises including the use of the catastrophe scale to help Darren not blow disapproval out of proportion. Darren was also given behavioral homework assignments to risk the displeasure of his teacher by asking his teacher for a plan to make up the missing assignments as well as emotive change skills of relaxation and rational-emotive imagery to help lessen his physiological arousal. These cognitive-behavioral elements together helped to dramatically lessen and for all intents and purposes eliminate anxiety as a social and emotional disability. Darren handed in enough of his missing assignments to achieve a credible grade at the end of the year.

A special form of anxiety is represented in the type of underachievement referred to previously as the Non-Achieving Syndrome. This type of underachiever is generally an adolescent who is afraid to grow up. I have found that this type of young person frequently displays irrational beliefs involving the need for comfort which need to be disputed as being counter-productive to the young person's expressed desire to be successful established earlier on in the therapeutic sequence. Cognitive, emotive and behavioral methods for working with this type of anxious, underachiever can be found in Table 3.

Some anxious students underachieve because they fear their peers will reject them if they display dedication to their school work and as a result, underachievement (need for peer approval + high anxiety + work avoidance = social and emotional disability leading to underachievement). Other anxious students as described earlier are perfectionists who underachieve by not putting enough effort in subjects where they anticipate a poor result (need for perfection + high anxiety + reduced effort = social and emotional disability leading to underachievement). The lack of effort is used as a rationalization for not being perfect ("I could have done a lot better but I didn't really try".). Cognitive-behavioral methods for working with both types of underachieving students are included in Tables 4 and 5.

Underachievement Due to Anger/Chronic Misbehavior

This social and emotional disability involves young people breaking important home and school rules including destroying property and hurting others. They act defiantly towards people in authority and may get very angry when faced with people blocking them from getting what they want. Irrational,

TABLE 3. Cognitive, emotive and behavioral methods for working with underachieving students who display the non-achievement syndrome (adapted from Mandel, Marcus and Mandel, 1992).

1. Do not become discouraged when the student doesn't follow through with what he/she promised to do.
2. Do not provide the student with solutions for solving problems. Give the problem-solving responsibility to the student.
3. Hold a private conference with the student.
4. Make an agreement with the student concerning the goal of getting better grades.
5. Offer the student assistance in achieving the goal of doing better in school.
6. Obtain from the student's other teachers information about the specific work requirements, which assignments the student has completed and which the student hasn't completed. Record this information without evaluative comments and discuss it with the student privately. Record the specific problems and excuses that the student offers as his/her reasons for each incomplete assignment.
7. Select a class in which the student has an incomplete assignment and the excuse that he/she uses to explain his/her failure to finish it. Record the exact details of the problem that hinders the student's achievement of better grades, including how often the problem has occurred in the past.
8. Inform the student of the consequences that will ensue if the problem continues. Confirm whether the student still has the goal of getting better grades.
9. Ask the student to generate different solutions to the problem that is blocking his/her path to better grades. Discuss things that could interfere with each solution, and have the student come up with counter measures for these interferences. Give the student the responsibility for thinking through the steps necessary to solve the problem.
10. Ask the student what he/she proposes to do now in light of the discussion about specific solutions. Once the student selects a solution, discuss the specifics of when, how, and how long the student will implement it.
11. Do not expect the student to have done everything in the proposed solution. Continue the above process of confrontation and having the student identify solutions and make plans to implement them until progress is evident.
12. As the student takes on more responsibility, use less confrontation and more supportive gestures. Help the student answer questions about himself/herself and the future.

negative Habits of the Mind typically held by these sorts of underachieving students include:

Being Intolerant of Others: Thinking that people should always treat me fairly and considerately and in the way I treat them, and when they do not, I cannot stand it, and that I have a perfect right to punish such despicable people.

Acting without Thinking (cognitive impulsivity): The young person when faced with demands, threats or something she/he wants fails to reflect upon the problem, different courses of action, different consequences and does not formulate an action plan.

Being Intolerant of Limits: Thinking that you should be able to do what you want, that nobody has the right to tell you what to do, that you cannot stand following rules, and that people who follow rules are stupid.

Social Irresponsibility: Thinking that you only have to be concerned about yourself and that it is not important to be a good citizen or to be sensitive to

TABLE 4. Cognitive, emotive and behavioral methods for working with underachieving students who are peer conforming/socially anxious (from Bernard, 1997).

1. Discuss with the student his/her long-term occupational goals and the importance of successful school accomplishment in achieving these goals.
2. Offer the student an opportunity to express a desire to do well in school and to please his or her parents or other significant people.
3. Point out the negative consequences on the student's efforts and success in school that will ensue if the student continues to hang out with his/her current peers.
4. Ask the student what would happen if he/she started to work harder and do better in school. Establish that in the student's mind, his or her peers would reject him or her.
5. Explain that the student's belief that his/her friends would reject him/her for doing schoolwork is probably erroneous, even though he or she might be hassled.
6. Ask the student if he/she would be willing to put this belief to the test by working harder and monitoring the effect that this has on friends.
7. Ask the student what it would say about his/her peers if they did reject him/her simply because he/she chose to work toward goals. Would they be "real" friends?
8. Point out to the student that either friends probably won't reject him/her for working toward goals, or state that if they do, it might be time for the student to look for friends who will accept his/her right to decide how he/she approaches schoolwork.
9. Explore the possibility of alternative friendships and peer groups with the student.

the feelings of others including treating others from different backgrounds with respect.

The preferred treatment approach for young people of any age who display chronic misbehavior is to work with their parents and teachers to set up contingency arrangements whereby the young person become explicitly aware of extreme penalties associated with rule breaking especially harmful behavior to others or the environment as well as the beneficial effects of compliant behavior (see chapter by DiGiuseppe and Kelter) (also see Table 6 for cognitive, emotive and behavioral methods you can use and share with teachers and parents). When working with young people whose underachievement is due to anger management issues, direct 1:1 intervention that addresses their irrational beliefs/negative Habits of the Mind and employs cognitive, emotive, and behavioral strategies is recommended.

What follows is a running commentary provided by a practitioner-in-training who successfully disputed the irrational beliefs of a 14-year-old boy, Aaron, who was refusing to work in science due to problems he was having with his teacher. Aaron would become furious with his teacher when he perceived he was being unfairly picked in and refused to do his work. Here, the practitioner focuses on the disputing of key irrational beliefs of Aaron but rather than confronting the adolescent with a forceful argument, humor was used to make the point and to avoid putting the adolescent on the defensive.

In order to dispute Aaron's irrational thoughts regarding Ms. H., I stressed the concept of human fallibility by disputing Aaron's global rating of others (Ms. H.). I used both logical and semantic disputation to dispute irrational thoughts regarding Ms.

H. I presented a Happening→Thinking→Feeling→Behaving→Consequences chart, on which I had summarized some of Aaron's irrational thoughts he had communicated to me regarding Ms. H. His thoughts were as follows: Ms. H. is unfair so I should not have to follow class rules or do class work. He also clearly stated that he cannot stand it when Ms. H. acts unfairly and that Ms. H. was a total bitch. Aaron confirmed that these statements accurately captured his thoughts about Ms. H. I then discussed with Aaron and the difference between irrational and rational thoughts. I then restated the following irrational thought with Aaron to see if he agreed with it: My teacher acts unfairly towards me all the time. He should act fairly all the time in order for me to do my work and follow rules. Aaron stated he agreed with this statement as well. I then discussed with Aaron whether this statement was true, logical, or helpful and if not maybe we needed to change it. Aaron stated that Ms. H. treats him unfairly all the time. I then used semantic disputation to correct his incorrect inference. I stated if that were true then the minute he hit the door, she would begin to accuse him of doing things he did not do. I began to imitate how Ms. H. would have to behave if she acted that way all the time. Aaron thought this was funny. I then asked Aaron if this was how Ms. H. acted all the time, to which he laughed and said "yes." I then disputed this empirically by saying if she treated him this way all the time she would not have time to teach. He then acknowledged that she did not act like that all the time but sometimes. I then asked Aaron when he first learned a new skateboarding trick, did he do it perfectly the first time. He responded negatively to this. I then drew the pie chart so we could list both Ms. H.'s positive and negative characteristics (I only put four spaces in case Aaron could not come up with any positive comments about Ms. H.). I told Aaron that Ms. H. always spoke very highly of him when I spoke to her and that was a positive characteristic. I then stated that the one negative characteristic I could state about Ms. H. was that as a new teacher who is still learning, she makes mistakes along the way like we all do when we are learning something new. I then asked him if he got a brand new skateboard and noticed that it had a small scratch on the wheel, would he throw it in the trash? He responded negatively to this. I then stated that is how we are as human beings. We all have our little scratches but we still have value as human beings. I then asked him to give me a positive characteristic about Ms. H. and to my surprise he was able to produce one fairly easily. We then came up with the following rational statement: Ms. H. is a new teacher and while I would prefer she not act unfairly, that's sometimes how teachers act. I then still need to pass this class so I can deal with it. I asked Aaron if he repeated this to himself when he felt Ms. H. was being unfair, would it at least allow him to decrease his anger so he would be able to do his work. He stated that he would still be angry, but thinking this thought might help him reduce his anger.

Underachievement Due to Avoidance of Responsibilities/Pervasive Low Frustration Tolerance

Some underachieving students not only have not developed high frustration tolerance associated with work persistence and effort, they have extremely low levels of frustration tolerance and have limited abilities to delay gratification. As a consequence, they avoid many developmentally appropriate responsibilities in all areas of their lives including school. They put off doing tasks and chores because they are frustrating, boring or hard and give up

TABLE 5. Cognitive, emotive and behavioral methods for working with underachieving students who are perfectionists (from Bernard, 1997).

1. Help the student become more aware of his or her perfectionism and the negative costs of this Habit of the Mind on his/her emotions (e.g., anxiety) and behavior (e.g., avoidance of activities that he/she anticipates not doing perfectly).
2. Teach the student about famous people or role models who stumbled and fumbled their way to success. Point out that these individuals needed to make mistakes and take risks in order to succeed (e.g., Edison).
3. Have the student list the things he/she has always wanted to do but has been afraid of not doing perfectly. Have the student agree to try one of these activities.
4. Encourage the student to identify his/her areas of weakness. Have them agree to try activities in these areas. When the student has attempted such an activity, point out that the student now has evidence that he/she can tolerate doing things imperfectly.
5. Encourage the student to stop ruminating about his/her grades. Encourage him/her to get involved in activities unrelated to school.
6. Teach the student that there is a continuum of achievement; achievement isn't an all (perfection) or nothing (complete failure). Help the student set goals at a place on the achievement continuum where he/she doesn't have to be the best in order to learn something and have fun.
7. Constantly challenge the student's Perfectionist Habit of the Mind (i.e., "I must do everything perfectly all the time"). Encourage the student to give him/herself permission to make mistakes.
8. Help the student to accept and become comfortable with doing things that are ambiguous and about which is uncertainty about how to proceed.
9. For long-term projects and assignments, require the student to hand in the beginning portion (e.g., introductory paragraph, outline) well in advance. Explain that what's important is that he/she does some work, not that the work be done perfectly.
10. Help the student to see tasks as a series of parts that have to be completed one after another rather than as a whole chunk that must be completed perfectly. Teach Time Management as a Habit of the Mind.
11. Teach the student the importance of having all materials necessary, for completing that portion of the assignment to be done, on hand.
12. Encourage the student to get organized by laying out or outlining the different parts of the work that have to be done.
13. Provide rewards for the student as he/she completes each portion of an assignment.
14. Reward the student for attempting things and not doing them perfectly.
15. Help the student enjoy the pleasure of doing new activities. Encourage him/her to reward him/herself for trying new things.
16. Reduce competition in class.
17. Establish classroom expectations that aren't too rigid.

easily after starting to do something because they find it hard or boring. They spend a lot of time having fun and enjoying themselves especially when there is work to be done. A variety of cognitive, emotive and behavioral methods have been described in the REBT/CBT literature to work with these types of underachievers (see Table 7).

I have identified two negative, irrational Habits of the Mind associated with this social and emotional disability:

I Can't Be Bothered (LFT): thinking that life should always be fun and exciting, and that they cannot stand it when things are frustrating and boring.

Table 6. Cognitive, emotive and behavioral methods for working with underachieving students who chronically misbehave (from Bernard, 1997).

1. Maintain your emotional control by focusing on the student's misbehavior and not the student.
2. Do not engage in a power struggle with the student (i.e., "take your wind out of his/her sails").
3. Discipline with dignity (i.e., do not say things that contribute to the student feeling bad about him/herself).
4. Encourage classmates to support the student so that he/she doesn't feel alienated from the group.
5. Offer the student opportunities to demonstrate what he/she knows and does well in front of the class.
6. Use humor to diffuse potential conflict situations.
7. Hold private rather than public conferences with the student; invite parents to attend a meeting.
8. Establish an agreement or goal that the student will do better in school by discussing the positive consequences of good grades and the negative consequences of bad grades with the student.
9. Draw up a behavioral contract in which the student agrees to work on his/her assignments for a specific amount of time each week. Be sure the contract outlines the rewards for achieving the goal and the penalties for not achieving goal. Enlist parental support, if available, in providing rewards or penalties. Ensure that the rewards and penalties are sufficiently powerful (i.e., pleasant or aversive) to act as motivators of the student's behavior.
10. Employ a daily report card in which teachers rate the student's behavior and the quality of his/her class work and homework. Have the student take the card home to show his parents every night. Require the student to have a parent sign the card and return it to you the next day.
11. Explain to the student that he/she has the choice and responsibility to make decisions concerning his/her own work-related behavior.
12. Encourage the student to work with peers who have an achievement orientation.
13. Identify an older student or adult mentor who can take an active interest in the student's progress and to whom the student can report on a regular basis.

Giving Up (external locus of control): Thinking that I have no control over what happens to be good or bad and that there is little point in trying because I will never be successful.

When seeking to challenge the beliefs of underachievers who avoid responsibility and display symptoms of distractibility and low frustration tolerance as well as who appear to lose interest in even the briefest of discussions, I recommend against pushing their limits of attention. I employ more interactive, engaging and practical cognitive, emotive and behavioral methods for challenging their irrational beliefs/Negative Habits of the Mind.

Here is an example of how a practitioner-in-training followed this advice is designing an activity to dispute the irrational beliefs of a sixth grade underachieving student, Winston. Winston appeared to have undiagnosed ADHD. In this excerpt, the practitioner describes her approach to tackling Winston's beliefs that science is boring and it should not be so.

TABLE 7. Cognitive, emotive and behavioral methods for working with underachieving students who aavoid responsibilities and display low frustration tolerance (from Bernard, 1997).

1. Help to organize the students' home and school study environment by making a checklist of materials that need to be taken to school and home each day.
2. Check the student's notebooks on a regular basis to ensure that papers and work are correctly organized.
3. Incorporate the student's interests in the content of assignments.
4. Design short-term and long-term assignments with success built in for the student.
5. Help the student break-down long-term assignments and projects into easier, short-term steps.
6. Help the student schedule assignment steps on weekly and semester/term calendars.
7. Be sure the student understands the directions before beginning his/her work.
8. Communicate high, realistic expectations for work to the student.
9. Do not accept poor work from the student.
10. Help the student set daily and short-term goals.
11. Discover the type of tangible reinforcements that the student prefers.
12. Provide strong, immediate reinforcement for effort the student puts toward work that he/she finds hard or boring.
13. Provide prompt and immediate feedback on the student's progress toward daily and short-term goals.
14. Give the student a free-day on Friday if he/she has worked hard during the week.
15. Negotiate with the student and establish a behavioral contract.
16. Provide positive reinforcements when the student edits or proofs his/her work.
17. Structure appropriate competition in the classroom.
18. Encourage the student to join an existing, work-oriented, peer study group.
19. Encourage the student to join a study skills group.

In order to dispute Winston's belief (inference) that science is boring I performed two simple science experiments with him. Both illustrated static electricity through the use of a balloon. In the first experiment we used a balloon and water from a faucet. In the second one we used a balloon and a piece of Fruit loop cereal on a string. The static electricity on the balloon made the water from the faucet and the cereal move toward the balloon. I then asked Winston if he thought the experiments were cool or boring. In both instances, he replied he thought both experiments were cool. I then told him that we had just conducted a science experiment and, therefore, we had just disproved his previously stated belief that science was boring. I also stated that his favorite hobby, skateboarding, was just applied scientific concepts so he could not possibly really think science was all that boring.

Winston also was found to hold the belief that all class work *should* be fun and if it was not, he *should not* have to do it. Once, again, a disputing strategy was devised that did not involve simple didactic or Socratic "talk" therapy.

Winston stated that he found his class work boring and that he should not have to do it so I thought it might be good try something different with him. I told the school counselor, Mr. K. that I wanted to bring Winston into his office during the session and just ask him if his job was fun and exciting all the time. Of course, when we did this Mr. K. stated that it was not and that even as a counselor he had to do things at times that he did not want to do. He also reiterated to Winston that he gets a report card just like Winston does and his goal was to do well on his report card. I asked Mr. K. if the principal asked him to do something that he felt was boring and not fun, could he tell the principal he was not going to do it since it was boring and he should not have to do it? Of course he stated he could not. When we got back to the counseling room, I asked Winston why we went to see Mr. K. and he said to show that school is not fun all the time but you have to do your work. I told him that not matter how old you are, you will always have to do things that are not considered fun, but in order to achieve your goals you have to do them. I told him that Im sure his mom has to do things everyday at work that she thinks are not fun, but because she has to take care of him, she does them. I then focused attention on disputing Winston's irrational statement that he could not stand doing boring school work. I asked him if he had completed boring work before to which he replied affirmatively. I asked him did his eyeballs fall out? Did he pass out or faint when he did boring work? He laughed and said, "Yes". I reiterated to him that he was able to complete boring work just like he had done before. I also stated that if he had different, rational thoughts about boring schoolwork he may have a different attitude about schoolwork. I reminded him about what Mr. K. stated about having to completing boring work even when he did not desire to do so. I re-iterated that boring work is part of life, but we can do things to make boring work more tolerable. I asked Winston what are some of things we talked about in the past that can help us complete boring work? He stated we can do it right away. I then asked him "What if the principal asked Mr. K. do a report on all the kids in the school and he did not want to do it, what are some things he could do to make it easier to do? Winston's homework for this week was to talk to one adult and one classmate and ask them if they thought school/work is fun and exciting all the time and what they do when it is not.

Underachievement Due to General Disorganization

I believe that research indicates that general disorganization is one of the most destructive of all social and emotional disabilities in young people. These young people do not have a general direction and goal towards which they self-regulate their behavior. They do not plan their time, do not keep track of time including when important things have to be done, do not set priorities. They also have no system for locating materials and resources for meeting the demands of school and home. Typical irrational beliefs/negative Habits of the Mind underpinning general disorganization include:

Having No Goals: Thinking that it is pointless to have any goals including areas involving schoolwork and relationships.

Planning Time Poorly. Thinking that it is pointless to plan your time, thinking that things will somehow get done as well as thinking, "When is the latest I can start?" when approaching schoolwork or chores that are not fun.

In treating this social and emotional disability, in addition for practitioners to have lots of cognitive, emotive and behavioral methods (see Table 8), she/he will, when possible, work with family members and teachers to help modify the young person's negative mindset towards the need to be organized as well as to model, communicate and reinforce routines and expectations for setting and achieving goals and for being on time.

What follows is an illustration of cognitive, emotive and behavioral methods for working with an underachiever who is chronically disorganized (see description of Winston above).

I asked Winston if breaking the assignment into smaller parts might make a boring assignment easier to do? He responded that it would. In my example I stated maybe if Mr. K. broke up the reports he was doing by doing the sixth grade girls first, than the sixth grade boys, than the seventh grade girls etc. that it may make doing a boring assignment easier to complete. I asked Winston if breaking an assignment into smaller pieces may make a boring assignment more manageable to him? He stated that it would. Prior to our meeting, I asked

TABLE 8. Cognitive, emotive and behavioral methods for working with underachieving students who are generally disorganized (from Bernard, 2003b).

1. Provide the young person with a checklist and instructions regarding how to organize his/her room, backpack, and notebooks.
2. Provide the young person with a checklist to complete of things to do each day and time when things need to be done (daily checklist: beginning 6:30 a.m., 7:00 a.m., 7:30 a.m. . . . 9:00 p.m. lights out).
3. Establish a homework routine and schedule, including a daily/weekly planner and homework folder.
4. Help the young person schedule steps of assignments on weekly and semester/term calendars.
5. Establish a routine of filing important school papers in a notebook/school binder.
6. Establish a set routine at home for wake-up, being dressed and ready for school, homework time, dinner, ready for bedtime, and sleep.
7. Establish with the young person times of the day when important things have to be done (out of bed, dressed, ready for school, homework, ready for bed).
8. Seat a disorganized young person next to well-organized and understanding peers.
9. Only provide materials the young person needs for current work.
10. Help the young person to break down tasks into smaller steps.
11. Ensure that the young person is ready for instruction (e.g., eye contact, sitting still).
12. Teach the young person strategies to record and remember directions and instructions (e.g., note taking, mnemonics).
13. Call a family meeting for what is expected of each child to do in the morning before school, in the afternoon after school, before/after dinner, and before bedtime. Post routines for each child.
14. Establish rules for putting things away in their proper place and for doing things on time and positive/negative consequences for following/breaking this rule.

Winston's science teacher for a science textbook and the page they were working on. I then had Winston turn to the page in the science textbook that they were on and told him when his science teacher told him to read 5 pages, he could break it up into smaller parts and that may make it easier to do. I then had him read the first two paragraphs on the first page and told him to stop for one minute, and then read the next two paragraphs. He was able to do this easily. He said doing work this way might help him to complete his work instead of thinking about having to do the whole assignment at once. I then asked Winston that during our science experience, if we did not put the balloon near the water or near the piece of cereal, would we have seen the effects of static electricity? He stated no. I then told him that sometimes after we start an assignment, it becomes more interesting than we thought. I stressed that in order to find this out though, we have to be willing to participate in our class work. I did this because Winston's science teacher stated that he sometimes does not even try in class, even when they are doing group projects. I told Winston that even when we think things are boring, if we try to participate in them anyway, we may discover they are not so boring after all. We then compiled the following list of strategies Winston can employ when undertaking boring class work: Do it right away, break the assignment into smaller parts, do the easiest parts first, and participate more often, even if the work is boring. I asked Winston if the following rational thought would help him complete boring school work: While I would prefer this schoolwork not be boring, I have to do it to pass this class. He said he liked the statement we had come up in a previous session that stated: When it's done, I can have some fun. I asked him if repeating this statement helped him complete his work in the past, to which he replied that it had. We then role played Winston first repeating this statement to himself then reading two paragraphs of his science textbook.

Underachievement Due to Poor Emotional Regulation

There are young people who have get easily agitated, frustrated and emotionally upset, find it difficult to calm down within a developmentally appropriate period of time, and find it very difficult to inhibit withdrawal and/or aggressive behavior when upset Sometimes the activating events in the lives of these young people are severe involving neglect or abuse. However, at other times, poor emotional regulation is displayed in the face of developmentally appropriate tasks and activities as well as in response to interpersonal problems and disagreements that are common in growing up. For these young people, underachievement is extremely common. Many children with diagnosable emotional disorders display poor emotional regulation (Bernard, 2004d). Examples of emotional regulation skills that are delayed include:

- Changing negative to positive self talk
- Relaxation
- Exercise

- Finding something fun to do
- Finding someone to talk to
- Exploring ways to solve presenting problem

Young people with poor emotional regulation also endorse a range of irrational beliefs/Negative Habits of the Mind that include inferences and evaluations associated with strong emotional arousal including (see Table 11 in following section):

- Self-Downing—thinking you are hopeless when something bad happens
- Needing to Be Perfect—thinking you must do everything perfectly and that it is horrible to make mistakes
- Need for Approval (approval seeking—believing you must have the approval of peers (or adults) for everything you do and being thought to be silly or stupid by others cannot be endured
- I Cannot Do It (pessimism)—thinking that when something is difficult, you will be more likely to fail than to be successful
- I cannot Be Bothered (low frustration tolerance)—believing that everything in life should be fun and exciting and that you cannot stand to do things that are not fun or easy
- Being Intolerant of Others—believing that people who are unfair, inconsiderate or different, or inferior or bad people who deserve punishment

In working with these young people, it will be important assess their irrational beliefs (e.g., CASI, Bernard and Cronan, 1999) as well as assess the developmental stage of their emotional regulation skills.

Young people with poor emotional regulation are likely to have diagnosable mental health problems requiring full ecological programming. While REBT/CBT can play a part in treatment, a full discussion is beyond the scope of this chapter. I will address emotional resilience development in the next section.

Developing Social and Emotional Capabilities

As I have indicated, young people can underachieve as a result of having underdeveloped social and emotional capabilities as a result of a combination of cultural, parenting and biological-temperament factors. They may not present with any psychosocial or mental health problems. These young people, as well as the young people with social and emotional disabilities described in the previous section, will greatly profit from a variety of social and emotional learning experiences designed to accelerate their social and emotional development.

Developing a Positive Work Orientation

The types of social and emotional capabilities including rational beliefs/positive Habits of the Mind that need to be taught to and developed by most underachievers are represented in Table 9 and are referred to as "Positive Work Orientation." These social and emotional capabilities include: academic confidence, work persistence, work organization, and work cooperation skills.

I have developed over the years a number of resources that REBT/CBT and other school practitioners including teachers, mentors and student welfare officers are using to teach these social and emotional capabilities. Chief amongst these are the *You Can Do It! Mentoring Program* (Bernard, 2003a) and *Program Achieve. A Curriculum of Lessons for Teaching Students How to Achieve Success and Develop Social-Emotional-Behavioral Well-Being* (Bernard, 2005a). Practitioners employ other activities and cognitive, behavioral and emotive methods for developing these qualities.

The psycho-educational principles to teach these social and emotional capabilities are relatively straight forward.

1. Assess young person's academic confidence, work persistence, work organization, and work cooperation skills and identify those that need further development. This can be accomplished available surveys (see Table 14).
2. Set goal for improvement working on one social and emotional capability at a time. Select one that is easiest to improve first.
3. Help young person identify and rip up any rationalizations she/he may hold that that block motivation to apply social and emotional capabilities (keys for success). Examples of these rationalizations include:
   - I'll do it later.
   - I will only get a low mark so what's the point in trying.
   - I'm too tired.
   - No one else is doing it. Why should I?
   - I need to relax.
   - I don't know how to do this.
4. Clearly define the capability for the young person, providing examples and review/discuss positive Habits of the Mind (including rational beliefs) that help the young person develop the area (see Appendix A. The Five Keys for Success and Happiness).
5. Discuss the "ins and outs" of using the targeted key in subjects/classes where young person is underachieving.
6. Use cognitive, emotive and behavioral activities to deepen young person's knowledge and skill of the targeted social and emotional capability.
7. Complete a weekly goal setting homework form where young person agrees to practice two or three examples of behavior that represent examples of the targeted social and emotional capability (see Table 10).
8. Review progress at the beginning of next session in achieving goals, Provide young person with feedback for using the targeted key (e.g., "You really showed persistence this week") as well as feedback for use of positive Habits of the Mind and self-talk (e.g., "You really seem to be getting the idea that success comes through effort. Giving Effort is becoming part of your approach to school work.").

TABLE 9. Social and emotional learning cluster: positive work orientation.

Description: Demonstrate a positive work orientation through being organized including setting goals and managing time, being confident and persistent in tackling difficult, frustrating work to achieve success in school and life.

1. Demonstrate organization as shown in a positive goal orientation towards achievement, time management with respect to developmentally appropriate activities and expectations, and self-management (storage, locating) and care of materials (work, play).
   A. Describes what it means to be organized in work including thinking, feeling and behaving.
   B. Develops positive attitudes and apply positive thoughts that help one to be organized.
   C. Identifies and sets academic and personal goals.
   D. Monitors progress toward achieving academic and personal goals.
   E. Listens to teachers for important details about what to do.
   F. Completes tasks in allotted time.
   G. Begins a task without having to be reminded by teacher.
   H. Readily finds own materials during the day.
   I. Arrives and leaves school prepared with materials in order.
   J. Describes aspects of organization needed to develop and implement a plan to build organization.

2. Demonstrate confidence when faced with new or difficult developmentally appropriate tasks or schoolwork.
   A. Describe what it means to be confident in work including thinking, feeling and behaving.
   B. Develop positive attitudes and apply positive thoughts that help one be confident.
   C. Stay on task even when task becomes difficult.
   D. Keep trying when mistakes are made.
   E. Ask for help when having to work on a difficult task, then independently complete task.
   F. Use appropriate voice (loudness) during whole group, small group and peer interactions.
   G. Sit and stand up straight with appropriate posture.
   H. Engage in eye-contact within a variety of verbal interactions that is appropriate for cultural context.
   I. Describe aspects of confidence needed to develop and implement a plan to build confidence.

3. Demonstrate persistence and high effort when faced with frustrating, time-consuming or low interest developmentally appropriate tasks, situations or school work.
   A. Describe what it means to be persistent including thinking, feeling and behaving.
   B. Develop positive attitudes and apply positive thoughts that help one to be persistent.
   C. Persevere in completing tasks.
   D. When frustrated in learning something new, stay engaged in task without giving up.
   E. Participate in learning activities that require skills not as yet mastered with or without teacher request.
   F. Show good concentration when learning skills not yet mastered.
   G. Describe aspects of persistence needed to develop and implement a plan to build persistence.

4. Demonstrate teamwork and cooperative learning skills when working on different learning tasks and activities.
   A. Identify and demonstrate ways to work well with others and in a variety of contexts.
   B. Demonstrate good teamwork skills with people who are different.

TABLE 10. Example of a weekly, goal-setting homework form.

Name of Student **Linda Suarez** Date **March 3**
Name of Counselor **Laura Thompson**

1. Which of the Foundations do you want to learn or practice (circle one)?
   confidence persistence organization getting along emotional resilience
2. My goal this week is (be specific):

   -write down complete details of homework assignments-
   remember to bring all books I need for class

3. List obstacles that might
   stop you from achieving your goal and how you will deal with them.
   -rushing
   -lazy
4. Write down any positive self-talk that will help you achieve your goal.
   "Being organized feels good!"
5. Date by which you want to achieve goal
   March 10
6. Your Signature Linda Suarez
   Signature of Mentor Laura Thompson

Result a week later:

Did you achieve your goal?

T yes no almost

Talk about what you learned, including the positives that happened when you achieved the goal or the negatives that occurred by not achieving your goal.

Developing Resilience

You will find that some young people who do not have emotional or behavioral disorders are somewhat delayed in being able to self-manage their own emotions and behaviors. For these young people, you will follow a similar series of steps as you would for developing social and emotional capabilities associated with a Positive Work Orientation. You will begin discuss what emotional resilience means and gain agreement from the young person that they wish to be more emotionally in charge of themselves.

Here the goal will be for you identify irrational beliefs/negative Habits of the Mind endorsed by the young person (see Table 11). Once identified you will want to discuss to contrast the irrational belief/negative Habit of the Mind with the contrasting rational belief/Habit of the Mind discussing how each affects emotions and behavior.

You will also help the young person strengthen and or learn basic emotional resilience skills (e.g., relaxation, positive self-talk, finding someone to talk to, finding something fun to do) using a variety of activities and methods (see Tables 12 and 13). (See chapter in this book on "Emotional Resilience Training in Children and Adolescents.")

TABLE 11. Negative types of thinking checklist (from Bernard, 2003a).

Negative Types of Thinking Checklist

Purpose: Present each of the following negative "Types of Thinking" to the teacher or parent to identify those Negative Types of Thinking that the young person is most likely to hold. Place a mark to indicate *how often* the young person tends to think in a particular negative way.

	Rarely	Some-times	Often
1. **Self-Downing**—Does the young person think that he/she is *totally* useless or a failure when he/she has been rejected or has not achieved a good result?	❑	❑	❑
2. **Needing to Be Perfect**—Does the young person think that he/she *must* be successful or perfect in everything important that he/she does and that it's horrible when he/she is not?	❑	❑	❑
3. **Needing Approval**—Does the young person think that he/she needs people (peers, parents, teachers) to approve of him/her and that when they do not, it's the worst thing in the world?	❑	❑	❑
4. **I Can't Do It**—Does the young person think when he/she has not been successful at something that he/she is no good at anything and never will be?	❑	❑	❑
5. **I Can't Be Bothered**—Does the young person think that life should always be fun and exciting and that he/she can't stand it when things are frustrating or boring?	❑	❑	❑
6. **Being Intolerant of Others**—Does the young person think that people should always treat him/her fairly, considerately, and the way he/she wants and when they do not, they are rotten and he/she has a right to get back at them?	❑	❑	❑

Working with Parents

A variety of styles of parenting some of which apply to teachers have been identified that contribute to underachievement (see Bernard, 2003c): over-protective style, permissive style, powerless style, authoritarian style, overly emotional style, excessive expectations style, lack of expectations style, and unsupportive of school style. In working with parents (and teachers) of underachievers, practitioners provide advice on the impact of these styles on a child's underachievement and provide information to parents on styles of parenting associated with achievement (firm/kind-authoritative). Behavior management strategies are also provided when deemed lacking in parents and/or teachers of children who due to chronic misbehavior and avoiding responsibilities, underachieve.

An additional element of parent and teacher involvement when working with young people who underachieve is with those who are willing and able to play a supportive role in developing the young person's social and emotional competence including their confidence, persistence, organization, get-

TABLE 12. An activity to teach an emotional resilience skill (from Bernard, 2003b).

Diversions

Place a circle around those diversions that can help you calm down when you notice yourself having a hard time relaxing and calming down after something unpleasant has happened (e.g., having a reasonable request refused by someone) or is about to happen (e.g., going for an important job interview tomorrow).

Listening to music	Going for a run
Reading a book	Talking to a friend on the telephone
Taking a bath	Reading magazines
Going to the movies	Going out with a friend
Having a special meal	Doing something involving my religion
Playing sport	Dancing
Swimming	Working on my hobby
Remembering fun times	Spending time on the internet
Playing computer games	Going to a youth group
Doing something for someone else	

List other "healthy life style" diversions you use to calm down and bounce back:

____
____
____

List the most powerful activities that you can engage in the next time you feel very "uptight" to help yourself calm down:

____
____
____

ting along and emotional resilience. Using a consultation approach as outlined in Bernard (2003b), the practitioner invites the parent(s) and/or teacher(s) without the young person being present to attend a number of sessions where the principles and methods of social and emotional development are explained and taught.

Initially, participating parents and teachers are asked to accept the following proposition (from Bernard, 2003b):

It has been discovered that every person, no matter their age, needs to have 5 Foundations to be successful and happy. The 5 Foundations everyone needs are: Confidence, Persistence, Organization, Getting Along, and Emotional Resilience.

"Confidence" means not being afraid to make a mistake or try something new, and not worrying too much what others think of you if you do or say something silly or stupid.

"Persistence" means trying hard and not giving up on doing things that are boring, frustrating, and not fun.

"Organization" means having goals to do your best to be successful, managing your time so that you are not rushing around at the last minute to get things done, and having all materials and resources you need at school and home to do your work and other activities (music, sport).

"Getting Along" means working well with others, helping others who have problems, solving conflicts peacefully, and contributing to make your school, home and community a better place to live and learn.

TABLE 13. Cognitive, emotive and behavioral methods for developing emotional resilience (Bernard, 2003a).

1. Accept that it is normal and healthy for young people to experience negative emotions. (It is good to show and talk about different negative feelings you have, as long as they are not too extreme.)
2. Explain to the young person that it is normal to have negative feelings and that there is nothing wrong with him/her if he/she goes through periods of time or reacts to events with high amounts of anger, anxiety, or feeling down.
3. Provide the young person with words to describe his/her own feelings (e.g., "You are feeling angry or worried or have hurt feelings and feel down.") as well as your own feelings (e.g., "I am worried about you staying out late.").
4. Help the young person become aware that when something bad happens to him/her (e.g., teasing, bad mark in school, no one to play with), he/she has options in how upset he/she gets (extremely upset, medium upset, a "bit" upset).
5. Help the young person put together a list of negative things that can happen to him/her at school, at home, or with friends and discuss with him/her the common negative feelings when these things occur.
6. Discuss with the young person how getting extremely upset (furious, panicked, very down) when negative events have occurred or are about to occur is not so good and that it is better to try to be only medium upset (The exception to this is when young people experience life threatening or catastrophic events).
7. Teach the young person that one way to control how upset he/she gets when something bad happens is to learn not to blow the "badness" of what happened out of proportion. Help the young person see that while some events are truly the worst things that could happen (e.g., death of a loved one, natural disasters), other things (e.g., difficult/boring homework; being teased) are bad but not the worst things that could happen. Help the young person to discriminate among things that are terrible/horrible/awful, things that are bad, and things that are "a bit" bad.
8. Teach the young person that one way not to get overly down is not to think negatively about himself/herself when he/she is not as successful in his/her schoolwork as he/she would like or someone is mean to him/her. Help the young person to identify all their positive qualities (e.g., good athlete, good friend, good reader) and help them see that doing something wrong, failing at something, or rejection doesn't take away their good qualities and doesn't show they are totally hopeless (see previous discussion on eliminating Self-Downing).
9. Help the young person understand that he/she will not always be treated fairly and considerately by others and that, when that happens, he/she can handle it.

Finally, "Emotional Resilience" (sometimes called "Emotional Toughness") means not getting extremely down, angry, or anxious when something "bad" happens or is about to happen (e.g., receiving a poor mark in school or on a school report, being hassled or teased by classmate, being treated unfairly by an adult, having too much work to do and not enough time to do it). It means being able to calm down quickly when your emotions get overheated.

Gain agreement from participants that these 5 Foundations are very important in helping everyone be successful and happy. Reinforce this message as follows:

If a stool had one or more of its legs that were weak, would it be very easy for someone to try to sit on the stool but fall off (gain agreement)? In a similar way, the 5 Foundations are like the legs of a stool. If one or more are weak, it is hard for us to stand up and be all that we can be. Also, with weak legs, we tend not to be as happy and are more stressed than we would otherwise be with stronger legs.

TABLE 14. Survey of young person's social and emotional capabilities (Bernard, 2003b).

Your Name	Today's Date
Young Person's Name	Grade/Year

Directions: As best as you can, please indicate *how often* the young person generally engages in the following behaviors *(circle a number)*.

	almost never	**rarely**	**sometimes**	**often**	**almost always**
1. Seems to have good friendship-making skills.	1	2	3	4	5
2. Demonstrates good conversation skills.	1	2	3	4	5
3. Is confident in social situations.	1	2	3	4	5
4. Looks people in the eye and uses firm tone of voice.	1	2	3	4	5
_____ **Total Score for Confidence (Social)**					
5. Volunteers to participate in a new activity.	1	2	3	4	5
6. Does hard homework without asking for help or giving up.	1	2	3	4	5
7. Shares a new idea—that might be wrong—with you and the family.	1	2	3	4	5
8. Is confident when doing schoolwork.	1	2	3	4	5
_____ **Total Score for Confidence (Work)**					
9. Continues to try, even when homework is hard.	1	2	3	4	5
10. Concentrates well when working.	1	2	3	4	5
11. Checks work when finished to make sure it's correct.	1	2	3	4	5
12. Puts in the effort necessary to complete difficult homework assignments.	1	2	3	4	5
_____ **Total Score for Persistence**					
13. Makes sure he/she understands the teacher's instructions before beginning to work.	1	2	3	4	5
14. Has all of his/her school supplies ready and maintains a neat school bag and desk.	1	2	3	4	5
15. Writes down assignments and when they have to be completed.	1	2	3	4	5
16. Plans when he/she will do homework so he/she has enough time.	1	2	3	4	5
_____ **Total Score for Organization**					
17. Works cooperatively with classmates.	1	2	3	4	5
18. Listens and does not interrupt when someone else is speaking.	1	2	3	4	5

(Continued)

TABLE 14. Survey of young person's social and emotional capabilities (Bernard, 2003b) *(Cont'd)*

Your Name		Today's Date			
Young Person's Name		Grade/Year			
19. Volunteers to help others.	1	2	3	4	5
20. Seems to understand that it is important to follow important home rules.	1	2	3	4	5
_____ **Total Score for Getting Along**					
21. Seems good at controlling how down he/she gets and how hopeless he/she feels when something bad happens, like getting a bad grade or when someone is mean to him/her.	1	2	3	4	5
22. Is good at controlling his/her temper.	1	2	3	4	5
23. Seems good at controlling his/her nerves, especially when he/she has to take a test, perform in front of a group, or meet someone new.	1	2	3	4	5
24. When he/she gets upset about something, is good at calming down quickly.	1	2	3	4	5
_____ **Total Score for Emotional Resilience**					

Place an asterisk (*) next to the specific behaviors that need improving.
Additional comments: ____

____

____

____

Once participants express agreement with this view of the needs of young people, the practitioner discusses those social and emotional capabilities of the referred underachieving student that appear to need further development. Surveys such as the one presented in Table 14 can be completed by all participants to assist in determining areas for development.

Once an area for development has been identified, participants are introduced to three ways to introduce social and emotional learning experiences geared to the development of social and emotional capabilities into the life of the young person (See Table 15).

So, by way of example, if the targeted social and emotional capability (called a "Foundation") is confidence, participants would be provided with a range on information to help them teach confidence (see Appendix B) including a definition, examples of confident behavior, and positive Habits of the Mind that help a young person be confident (see Table 16). Then, time is spent discussing, modeling and having participants role play the use of behavior-specific feedback ("Things to Say") and teaching positive Habits of

TABLE 15. Basic equation for introducing social and emotional learning (Bernard, 2003b).

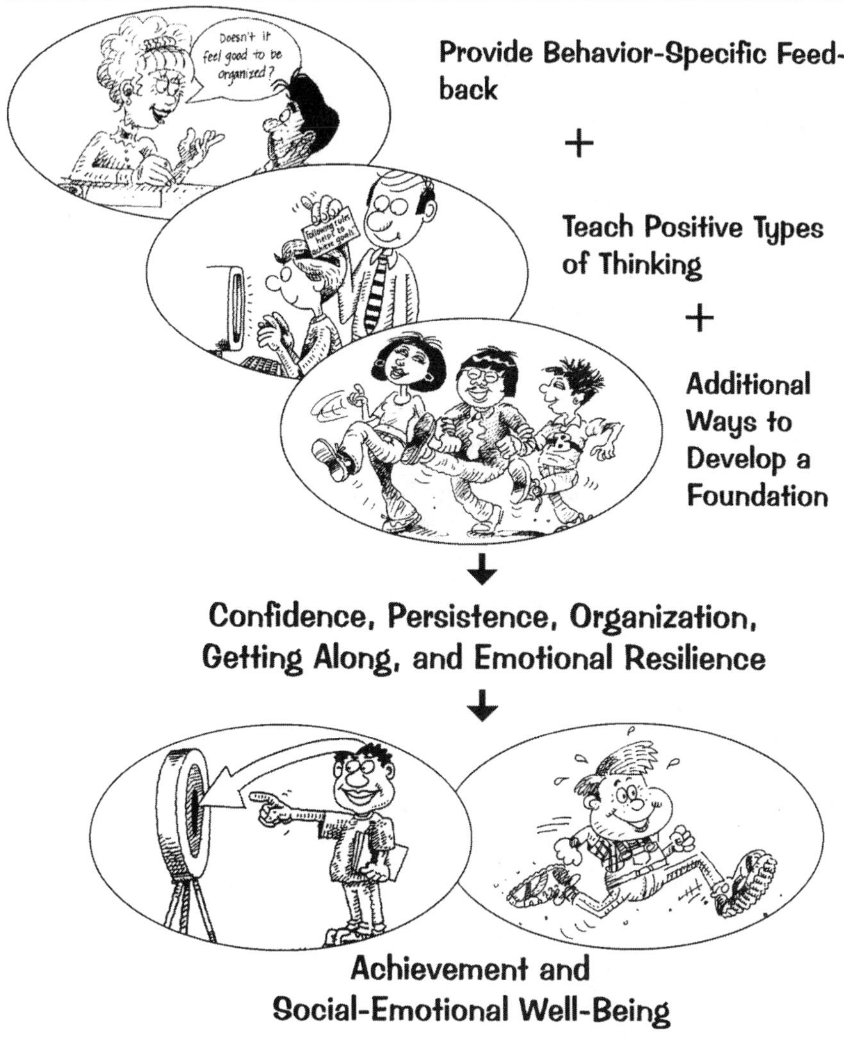

the Mind. Finally, participants select additional ways they can develop the young person's confidence at home and/or in the classroom.

Over the course of several weeks, parent(s) and or teacher(s) implement the social and emotional learning program and with the help of the practitioner monitor its success. Follow-up sessions reinforce ways to teach the targeted area, make improvements to the plan and introduce new social and emotional capabilities that includes material similar to those found in Appendix B.

TABLE 16. Parent/teaching handout introducing confidence.

What Is Confidence?

Definition of "Confidence"

Confidence means believing you can do it. It means not being afraid to make mistakes, to try something new, or to express an opinion.

Examples of Confident Behavior

- Raising your hand in class to answer a hard question
- Doing hard work without asking for help
- Sharing a new idea with your teacher and class
- Saying "hello" to someone new
- Asking to play with others
- Talking in a strong voice
- Greeting adults with good eye contact and using their names
- Sharing your ideas with the family
- Offering to take responsibility for organizing a family event (e.g., preparing a dish for a meal)
- Volunteering to participate in a new activity or experience
- Saying "no" when being pressured to do something wrong

Types of Thinking That Build Confidence

Accepting Myself—means not thinking badly about yourself when you make a mistake or are not as successful as you want to be, or when someone is critical of you.
Taking Risks—means thinking that it's good to try something new, even though you might make mistakes or you might not be the best at doing it.
Being Independent—means thinking that it's important for you to try new activities and to speak up even if other people think you are silly or stupid.
I Can Do It—means thinking that even when your work is hard, you are more likely to be successful than to fail.

Conclusions

In addressing the needs of young people who have academic problems including those who underachieve, the view expressed in this chapter that while cognizance needs to be placed on eradicating psychosocial barriers to learning (e.g., social and emotional disabilities), a more productive focus is in developing the social and emotional strengths of students who underachieve (e.g., Epstein et al., 2003). REBT clearly illuminates the irrational beliefs/negative Habits of the Mind and concomitant unhealthy emotions and unhelpful behaviors that need to be identified, challenged and changed in order to help remove the barriers to learning. However, as Albert Ellis has said, there is also the need to develop rational beliefs/positive Habits of the Mind and attendant positive emotion and behaviors that support motivation and school success.

References

Bandura, A. (1986). *Social foundations of thought and action: A social cognitive theory*. Englewoood Cliffs, NJ: Prentice-Hall.

Bandura, A. (1997). *Self-efficacy: The exercise of control*. New York: W.H. Freeman.

Bard, J., and Fisher, H. R. (1983). A rational emotive approach to academic underachievement. In A. Ellis and M. E. Bernard (eds.), *Rational-emotive approaches to the problems of childhood*. New York: Plenum Press.

Bernard, M. E. (1991). *Procrastinate later! How to motivate yourself to do it now*. Melbourne: Information Australia.

Bernard, M. E. (1996). Educational under-achievement: International epidemic in search of solutions. *Score: The National Periodical for Teachers, 3,* 6–7.

Bernard, M. E. (1997a). *Improving student motivation and school achievement: A professional development program for teachers, special educators, school administrators and pupil service personnel*. Oakleigh, VIC: Australian Scholarships Group.

Bernard, M. E. (1997b). *Teacher guide for boosting student motivation, self-esteem and school achievement,* 2nd ed. Oakleigh, VIC (AUS): Australian Scholarships Group.

Bernard, M. E. (1986). *Staying rational in an irrational world. Albert Ellis and rational-emotive therapy*. New York: Carol.

Bernard, M. E. (2001). Program achieve: A curriculum of lessons for teaching students how to achieve success and develop social-emotional-behavioral well-being, (Vols. 1–6, 3rd ed.), Laguna Beach, CA: You Can Do It! Education.

Bernard, M. E. (2002). *Providing all children with the foundations for Achievement and social-emotional-behavioral well-being*. Oakleigh, VIC (AUS): Australian Scholarships Group; Laguna Beach, CA (USA): You Can Do It! Education, Priorslee, Telford (ENG): Time Marque.

Bernard, M. E. (2003a). *Developing the social-emotional-motivational competence of young people with achievement and behavior problems: A guide for working with teachers and parents*. Oakleigh, VIC: Australian Scholarships Group.

Bernard, M. E. (2003b). *The You Can Do It! education mentoring program*, 2nd ed. Oakleigh, VIC (AUS): Australian Scholarships Group.

Bernard, M. E. (2003c). *Investing in parents: What parents need to know and do to support their children's achievement and social-emotional well-being*. Oakleigh, VIC (AUS): Australian Scholarships Group; Laguna Beach, CA (USA): You Can Do It! Education, Priorslee, Telford (ENG): Time Marque.

Bernard, M. E. (2004a). The relationship of young children's social-emotional-motivational competence to their achievement and social-emotional well-being. Invited presentation, Annual Research Conference of the Australian Council for Educational Research, Adelaide, October.

Bernard, M. E. (2004b). *The REBT therapist's pocket companion for working with children and adolescents*. New York: Albert Ellis Institute, p. 245.

Bernard, M. E. (2004d). Emotional resilience in children: Implications for Rational Emotive Education. *Romanian Journal of Cognitive and Behavioral Psychotherapies, 4,* 39–52.

Bernard, M. E. (2005a). *Program achieve: A curriculum of lessons for teaching students to achieve and develop social-emotional-behavioral well being,* (Vols. 1–6., 3rd ed.), Oakleigh, VIC (AUS): Australian Scholarships Group; Laguna Beach, CA (USA): You Can Do It! Education, Priorslee, Telford (ENG): Time Marque.

Bernard, M. E. (2005b). *The You Can Do It! Education images resource CD program.* Oakleigh, VIC (AUS): Australian Scholarships Group.

Bernard, M. E. (2006). Its time we teach social and emotional competence as well as we teach academic competence. *Reading and Writing Quarterly,* in press.

Bernard, M. E., and Cronan, F. (1999). The Child and Adolescent Scale of Irrationality: Validation data and mental health correlates. *Journal of Cognitive Psychotherapy: An International Quarterly, 13*, 121–132.

Bernard, M. E., and Joyce, M. R. (1984). *Rational emotive therapy with children and adolescents: Theory, treatment strategies, preventative methods.* New York: John Wiley.

Brophy, J. (1996). *Teaching problem students.* New York: Guilford Press.

Bruns, J. (1992). *They can but they don't: Helping students overcome work inhibition.* New York: Viking.

Dweck, C. S. and Elliott, E. S. (1983). Achievement motivation. In P.H. Mussen (ed.), *Handbook of child psychology* (Vol. 4, 3rd ed.), New York: John Wiley, pp. 643–691.

Ellis, A., and Bernard, M. E. (1983). *Rational-emotive approaches to the problems of childhood.* New York: Plenum Press.

Ellis, A., and Knaus, W. J. (1977). *Overcoming procrastination.* New York: New American Library.

Epstein, M. H., Harniss, M. K., Robbins, V., Wheeler, L., Cyrulik, S., Kriz, M., and Nelson, J. R. (2003). Strength-based approaches to assessment in schools. In M. D. Weist, S. W. Evans and N. A. Lever (eds.), *School mental health.* New York: Kluwer.

Ford, D. Y. (1996). *Reversing underachievement among gifted black students: Promising practices and programs.* New York: Teachers College Press.

Hauck, P. (1967). The rational management of children. New York: Libra Publishers.

Hauck, P. (1983). Working with parents. In A. Ellis and M. E. Bernard (eds.), *Rational emotive approaches to the problems of childhood.* New York: Plenum Press.

Kazdin, A. E., and Weisz, J. R. (2003). Context and background evidence-based psychotherapies for children and adolescents. In A. E. Kazdin and J. R. Weisz (eds.), *Evidence-based psychotherapies for children and adolescents.* New York: Guilford Press.

Knaus, W. J. (1974). *Rational emotive education. A manual for elementary school teachers.* New York: Albert Ellis Institute.

Knaus, W. J. (1983). Children and low frustration tolerance. In A. Ellis and M. E. Bernard (eds.), *Rational-emotive approaches to the problems of childhood.* New York: Plenum Press.

Lange, G. W. and Adler, F. (April 1997). Motivation and achievement in elementary children. Paper presented at the Biennial Meeting of the Society for Research in Child Development, Washington, DC (ERIC Document Reproduction Service No. ED 413 059).

Lillico, I. (2001). *Australian issues in boys' education.* Perth, WA: Tranton Enterprises.

Mandel, H. P., and Marcus, S. I. (1988). *The psychology of underachievement: Differential diagnosis and differential treatment.* New York: Wiley.

Mandel, H., Marcus, S. I., and Mandel, D. (1992). *Helping the non-achievement syndrome student: A clinical training manual.* Toronto: Institute on Achievement and Motivation Publication, York University.

McCall, R., Evahn, C., and Kratzer, L. (1992). *High school underachievers*. Newbury Park, CA: Sage.

Pacht, A. (1984). Reflection on perfection. *American Psychologist, 39,* 386–390.

NAEP (2003). Statement on NAEP 2003 mathematics and reading results. Washington, DC: National Center for Education Statistics, U.S. Department of Education.

Rothblum, E. D., Solomon, L. J. and Murakami, J. (1986). Affective, cognitive and behavioural differences between low and high procrastinators. *Journal of Counselling Psychology, 33,* 388–394.

Rotter, J. B. (1966). Generalized expectations for internal versus external control of reinforcement. *Psychological monographs, 80,* (Whole No. 609).

Schaeffer, C., and Millman, (1981). *How to help children with common problems*. New York: Van Nostrand Reinhold.

Seligman, M. E. P. (1975). *Learned helplessness*. San Francisco, CA: Freeman.

Shure, M. (1996). *I can problem solve: An interpersonal cognitive problem-solving program*. Champaign, Ill: Research Press.

Spivack, G., Platt, J. and Shure, M. (1976). *The problem solving approach to adjustment*. San Francisco: Jossey Bass.

Solomon, L. J. and Rothblum. E. D. (1984). Academic procrastination: Frequency and cognitive-behavioural correlated. *Journal of Counselling Psychology, 31,* 503–509.

Spaulding, C. L. (1992). *Motivation in the classroom*. New York: McGraw-Hill.

Vernon, A. (1983). Rational-emotive education. In A. Ellis and M. E. Bernard (eds.), *Rational-emotive approaches to the problems of childhood*. New York: Plenum Press.

Vernon, A. (2006a). *Thinking, feeling, behaving: An emotional education curriculum for children,* 2nd ed. (Rev.), Champaign, IL: Research Press.

Vernon, A. (2006b). *Thinking, feeling, behaving: An emotional education curriculum for adolescents,* 2nd ed. (rev.), Champaign, IL: Research Press.

Welner, B. (1979). A theory of Motivation for some classroom experiences. *Journal of Educational Psychology*, *71*, 3–25.

Ziestat, H. A., Rosenthal, T.L., and White, G. M. (1978). Behavioral Self-control in treating procrastination of studying. *Psychological Reports*, *42*, 59–69.

Zimmerman, B. J. (1991). A social cognitive view of self-regulated academic learning. *Journal of Educational Psychology*, *81*, 329–339.

Appendix A: The Five Keys for Success and Happiness

The Key of Confidence

Definition:

Having the belief that I will be successful in many areas of my schoolwork, social relationships and extracurricular activities (sports, music, art); trying new activities that I might not be perfect at; not being afraid to make mistakes; not being overly concerned with what others think if I try hard in my schoolwork, and expressing my opinion and standing up for what I believe without fear.

Examples of Confident Behavior...

- Continuing to work on a difficult assignment when you have trouble knowing what to do next.
- Standing up in the front of class and giving a speech.
- Raising your hand in class to answer a question.
- Working independently without asking the teacher for help.
- Speaking loudly and clearly when speaking.

Confidence-Building Habits of the Mind

Accepting Myself ... not thinking badly of myself when bad things happen.
Taking Risks ... thinking that I will try to be the best I can without needing everything to be perfect and that I am not afraid to make mistakes.
Being Independent ... knowing that, while it is important to be liked and approved of, I cannot please all people all the time. It is important to stand up for what I believe even if others disagree.
I Can Do It ... believing that I am more likely to be successful than I am to fail.

The Key of Persistence

Definition:

To try hard and not give up easily when doing schoolwork you find frustrating and do not feel like doing; to keep trying to complete an assignment rather than becoming distracted; to choose to play after you have done your work; when having a lot of work to do in different subjects, to not give up but make the additional effort required to complete it.

Persistent Behavior

- Trying and completing work found to be "boring."
- Listening when tired.
- Staying on task.
- Keeping track of progress on accomplishing different steps of doing an assignment.
- Staying up-to-date on writing in a journal.
- Completing homework on time.
- Asking necessary questions.
- Not being distracted by classmates.
- Finishing work instead of playing.
- Asking for help rather than giving up.
- Editing/checking completed work for mistakes.

Persistence Habits of the Mind

1. **I Can Do It**—thinking that I will be successful in doing my work, especially when working on difficult and time consuming material; taking credit for when I have been successful and not thinking when I do poorly that I am not good at doing anything nor will I ever be.
2. **Giving Effort**—thinking that the harder I try, the better my achievement and the more skilled I will become; knowing that it is not the case that I was either born to be good at my studies or not and believing that with persistence I will become more skillful.
3. **Working Tough**—thinking that in order to achieve pleasant results in the long-term, I will sometimes have to do unpleasant things in the short-term; believing I can stand things that are frustrating and that I do not like to do and not blowing the unpleasantness of events out of proportion.

The Key of Organization

Definition:

To value the importance of education and doing well at school; to set goals for how well you want to do in specific areas of your schoolwork and in school; to keep track of your assignments; to break down long-term projects into smaller/simpler steps; to schedule your time effectively; to bring needed resources to class and home.

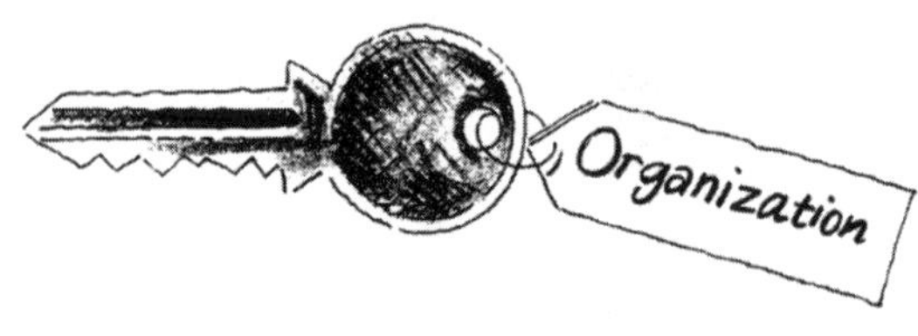

Organized Behavior:

- Making sure you understand the directions to assignments.
- Having a study schedule or weekly timetable.
- Writing down class assignments, including when they are due.
- Breaking down a large assignment into smaller parts or steps.
- Scheduling the various steps of an assignment far enough in advance to avoid rushing work.
- Following the information/directions written down on the board.
- Keeping class notes and handouts in an organized notebook with dividers.
- Handing in homework on time.
- Studying high priority material before working on less important material.
- Setting a goal.

Organizational Habits of the Mind:

1. **Setting Goals**—knowing that setting goals can help you do your personal best. It means making your long-term goals big, your short-term goals realistic, and your daily goals specific.
2. **Planning My Time**—thinking about how to plan your time so that you get everything done on time to the best of your ability. It means thinking about how you can break down long-term assignments, projects, and tasks into simpler steps and scheduling these steps on a calendar.

The Key of Getting Along

Definition:

To work cooperatively with other people, to resolve conflicts by discussion rather than fights, to manage anger, to show tolerance of other people's characteristics, to react to difficult people and pressure situations in a positive way, and to follow important school and home rules.

Getting Along Behavior:

- Not interrupting; waiting until someone has finished speaking.
- Waiting your turn..another.
- Not getting too angry with someone who behaves unfairly or inconsiderately.
- Ignoring others' rude comments.
- Including all classmates in a group activity or game.
- Making sure certain students are not left out or picked last for games.
- Sincerely complimenting another student.
- Sharing materials.
- Helping each other clean up.

Getting Along Habits of the Mind:

1. **Being Tolerant of Others**—thinking that all people are made up of many differences – some good, some not to your liking – and that it does not make sense to judge people on the basis of their differences. Knowing not to judge or condemn others as bad people on the basis of their differences or actions.
2. **Thinking First**—when faced with difficult problems, before taking actions, thinking about the different things you can do, the possible consequences of your proposed actions, and anticipating the impact of your actions on the feelings of others.
3. **Playing by the Rules**—knowing that following important rules by acting responsibly helps protect everyone's rights.
4. **Social Responsibility**—means thinking that it is important to be a good citizen and to help build a world with fairness and justice for all and where everyone feels safe and secure. It means being sensitive to the feelings of others, acting honestly, treating others—especially those who come from different backgrounds—with respect, caring and reaching out to people in need, and working towards protecting the environment.

The Key of Emotional Resilience

Definition:

Emotional Resilience means knowing how to stop yourself from getting extremely angry, down or worried when something "bad" happens. It means controlling your behavior when very upset Emotional Resilience also means being able to calm down and feel better when you get overly upset

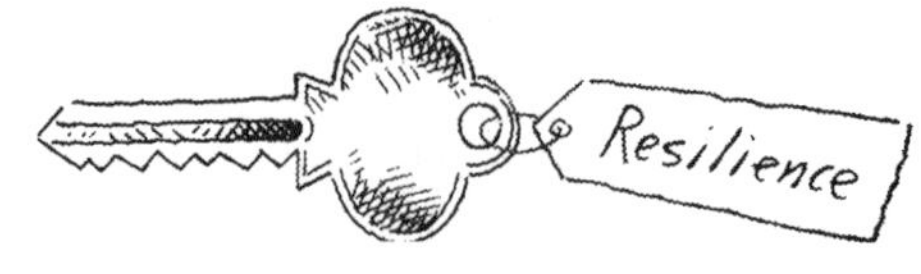

Examples of Emotional Resilience:

- Not getting overly upset from mistakes in your work or when you have not been as successful as you would like to be
- Not getting overly frustrated and angry with yourself when you do not understand something
- Not getting down when your friends seem to understand their schoolwork and do better on tests than you
- Not getting extremely worried before an important test or event in which you have to perform in public
- Avoiding excessive worry concerning your popularity with peers
- Not getting overly angry when peers are mean to you
- Remaining calm and in control when an adult treats you unfairly or disrespectfully
- Not getting too down when being teased or ignored by friends
- Being calm when meeting someone new, and not getting extremely nervous
- Stopping yourself from getting extremely worked up when you want to stand up and say "No" to someone who is putting pressure on you to do the wrong thing
- Not losing your cool when you have lots of homework to do
- Staying in control when your parents say "No" and the parents of your friends seem to be saying "Yes"

Negative Types of Thinking to Eliminate to Help Build Emotional Resilience

- **Self-Downing**—thinking that you are useless or a total failure when you have been rejected or have not achieved a good result (replace with **Accepting Myself**).
- **Needing To Be Perfect**—thinking that you have to be successful or perfect in everything important that you do and that it's horrible when you are not (replace with **Taking Risks**).
- **Needing Approval**—means thinking that you need people (peers, parents, teachers) to approve of what you do and that when they do not, it's the worst thing in the world (replace with **Being Independent**).

- **I Can't Do It**—thinking that when you have not been successful at something important, you are no good at anything and that you never will (replace with **I Can Do It**).
- **I Can't Be Bothered**—thinking that life should always be fun and exciting and that you can't stand it when things are frustrating or boring (replace with **Working Tough**).
- **Being Intolerant of Others**—thinking that people should always treat you fairly and considerately (and be the way you want) and when they do not, they are rotten people and you have a right to get back at them (replace with **Being Tolerant of Others**).

Skills to Help you be Resilient

- **Finding something fun to do**
- **Finding someone to talk to**
- **Relaxing**
- **Exercise**
- **Using positive self-talk**
- **Not blowing things out of proportion**
- **Solving the problem**

Appendix B: Material that Explains to Parents and Teachers How to Teach Confidence

How to Teach Confidence

Things to Say to Encourage Confident Behavior

When you catch the young person behaving confidently, say:

- "That took confidence."
- "You really stood up for what you believed."
- "That wasn't easy to do, but you did it."
- "Look at how far you have come."
- "Wow, I can't believe you did that."
- "Look at what you have learned."
- "You are not afraid to do things differently."
- "You can do it!"
- "All along, I knew you could do it."
- "I know that was challenging or difficult for you, but you did it."
- "You really had a confident voice when you spoke in class."
- "You tried and were not afraid of making a mistake."

Teach Types of Thinking That Develop Confidence

Teach Accepting Myself

- Have a discussion with the young person and help him/her come up with a list of many positive qualities he/she possesses in different areas of life (different school subjects, sports, music, art, hobbies, personality traits), as well as areas that need to be improved (negative qualities).
- Discuss with the young person how he/she has great value because of his/her many positive qualities and that it is important for the young person to always remember that he/she is valuable when bad things happen (not doing well in a class at school, being "picked on" by one or more classmates).

- Explain that people do not lose their good qualities when something bad happens.
- Indicate that when the young person does something wrong or gets a bad grade, or when one or more classmates treat him/her badly, he/she is never totally hopeless or a failure.
- Teach the young person never to put him/herself down and think of him/herself as a failure or hopeless when bad things happen (e.g., bad grade in school, someone treats them badly).
- Ask, "If one of your friends thought he was hopeless because he couldn't spell very well, would he be right?" Explain that it never makes sense to rate yourself as a person on the basis of your behavior, as everyone is made up of a wide variety of good and not-so-good characteristics. Who is to say what basis we use to judge the worth of a person?
- Encourage the young person to accept himself/herself and work hard at changing aspects of his/her behavior that may be leading to problems.

Things to Say to Communicate "Accepting Myself"

- "You are not a bad person because you received a bad mark."
- "One mistake does not a bad person make! We all make mistakes."
- "I'm glad you didn't seem to put yourself down when you made that mistake in class."
- "A slump in form, or a poor test result doesn't change the person you are."
- "Isn't it interesting? Fred just made a few mistakes in math, but he's a terrific book monitor, football player, friend, and son! What does that say about Fred?"

- "You can get a poor result, you can come to school with old socks on. You can fall over in assembly. You're still likable and capable. Remember, everyone makes mistakes."
- "You are you, warts and all. Be confident in knowing that when you make a mistake, it doesn't take away your good points."

Teach Taking Risks

- Encourage the young person to try new activities where he/she has a good chance of not being successful or the best. Discuss the phenomena of making mistakes and explain that mistakes are an important part of learning.
- After a span of time when the young person has tried and not been successful at a new activity, ask if doing poorly (or not achieving a top grade) is the end of the world. Explain that while it sometimes is bad not to be successful, it is never a catastrophe.
- Do not be too severe with the young person when he/she makes mistakes.
- Point out famous people who stumbled and fumbled their way to success.
- Constantly challenge the young person's thinking that everything he/she does must be done perfectly. Explain that, while it is preferable to do as well as one can, it only stresses you out to expect to be perfect or totally achieving all the time.

Things to Say to Communicate "Taking Risks"

- "You weren't afraid to make a mistake."
- "That took courage. How do you feel?"
- "Was it as bad as you thought it would be? You didn't know quite what to do, but you tried anyway."
- "You see, making mistakes is not the end of the world."
- "You were not afraid to try, even though you knew it might not turn out OK the first time."
- "A mistake can move you one more step towards success."
- "You're pretty brave. You tried and made some mistakes, but you didn't give up!"

Teach Being Independent

- Concretely explain that while it is nice to be liked, no one needs to be liked all the time by everyone. Discuss the idea that while there are some things we really need for survival (food, clothing, shelter), being liked is not a necessity. Discuss the difference between a "need" and a "want". Explain that being liked is a "want".
- Encourage the young person to speak his/her own opinions and to try new activities and not worry too much what others will think.
- Ask the young person to evaluate on a scale of catastrophes how bad being laughed at or thought badly of by peers is in comparison with war, divorce, terminal illness, house burning down, or best friend moving away. Encourage the young person not to blow bad events—like being laughed at—out of proportion.

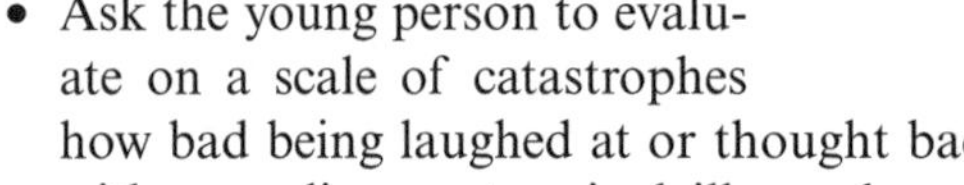

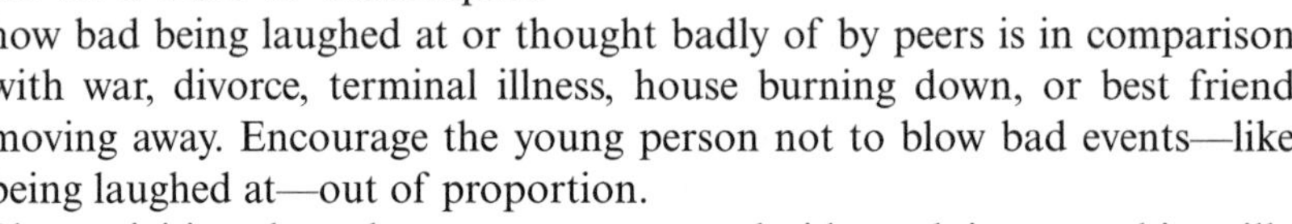

- Plan activities where the young person can decide on doing something silly in front of others and then, after they have done so, discuss how it wasn't so bad after all.
- Ask the young person to explain the motto, "Sticks and stones can break my bones but words can never hurt me."
- For dependent children who are overly concerned about making mistakes and constantly ask questions, use the "Praise, Prompt, and Leave Method." When they have a question, praise them for knowing anything about the problem at hand, provide the next step, and then leave their work area, reassuring them that they can do the rest.

Things to Say to Communicate "Being Independent"

- "You stuck to your guns even when others disagreed with you. Great!"
- "You were not afraid to put up your hand and answer a difficult question."
- "It isn't easy to maintain a point of view that isn't very popular."
- "You can see that even though other classmates disagreed with you, it's not the end of the world."

- "I think you can see now that while it's nice to be liked, you don't need it all the time."
- "You see, you don't have to do what others want.
- The world doesn't end."

Teach I Can Do It

- Discuss with the young person the difference between an "I Can Do It" optimistic type of thinking and an "I Can't Do It" pessimistic type of thinking. Explain that when schoolwork or another activity seems too hard, thinking that you are more likely to be successful than fail can help you continue to be confident and try hard.
- Explain that when "I Can Do It" thinkers are not successful at a task, they remind themselves of other work where they have been successful. "I Can't Do It" thinkers tend to think they are totally bad at everything when they have difficulty with their work, and that they might as well stop trying.
- Encourage the young person to stretch, struggle, and succeed. He/she needs to know that, although teachers and parents will help if they have to, completing schoolwork independently is the young person's responsibility. Do not protect him/her from work that is hard.
- Teach the young person to think of the last time he/she was successful at doing something he/she didn't think he/she could do. He/she can use this experience when approaching something new that is hard and think, "I did it before, I can do it again."

Things to Say to Communicate "I Can Do It"

- "You think 'I can', you can! You think 'I can't', you can't!"
- "You seem very positive."
- "Your body language tells me that you expect to do well."
- "You don't expect to fail. You project optimism."
- "Your optimistic approach helps everyone stay confident."
- "I can tell your thoughts aren't being helpful to you. What kind of optimistic thinking will help you be more confident?"
- "I'm amazed at how you don't say 'I can't' so much these days. Your attitude is great!"

Additional Ways to Develop Confidence in a Young Person

Instruction: Place a ✓ in the box to indicate activities that can help a young person develop Confidence.

- ❑ Give the young person a special responsibility (e.g., special role or job).
- ❑ Have the young person work with or tutor younger students.
- ❑ Ask the young person questions you know he/she can answer. Prompt the young person before asking question so he/she is prepared and experiences success.
- ❑ Set aside time each day for the young person to demonstrate what he/she has learned at school.
- ❑ Provide the young person with opportunities for leadership (e.g., tutoring younger students, classroom jobs or roles, organizing a family picnic).
- ❑ Help the young person to set short-term and long-term goals. Help the young person develop a concrete plan for achieving goals.
- ❑ Help the young person identify and develop individual interests and talents by showing interest in and excitement about non-curricular areas of the young person's skills and talents.
- ❑ Explain to the class/family members that they may only comment on positive things the young person does; negative comments must be written down and put in a box. Allow time for the class/family members to acknowledge positive things that the young person did.
- ❑ Do not give the young person too much attention when he/she expresses negative feelings about work.
- ❑ Teach the young person not to judge or evaluate his/her work until after a certain period of time.
- ❑ Teach the young person not to blow negative events out of proportion. Help the young person to construct three mental categories of badness:

  – A little bad (sniffles, broken pencil);
  – Moderately bad (bad report card, fight); and
  – Extremely bad (car accident, house burns down).

Then, when the young person makes a mistake or is teased, have him/her mentally categorize the event as moderately bad but not extremely bad.

- ❑ Do not prevent the young person from engaging in extracurricular activities as a penalty for poor performance in school. Participation in these interesting and fun activities may help build the young person's confidence.

Section III

Applications

12

Working with the Parents and Teachers of Exceptional Children

JOHN F. MCINERNEY[a] AND BRIDGET C.M. MCINERNEY[b]

[a]*Cape Behavioral Health Group L.L.C, Cape May Court House, NJ;*
[b]*Widener University, Chester, PA*

Since the advent of the Individuals with Disabilities Education Act (IDEA) in 1990, with subsequent revisions in 1997 and 2005, parents and teachers of specially challenged children have been called to face new demands. IDEA emphasizes, among other things, the importance of early intervention for the development of full potential in exceptional children and requires parental participation in all aspects of special education. This increases the need for collaboration between parents and schools to new and, at times, even more stressful levels.

The literature on early intervention (Cunningham and Slopper, 1980; Hayden and McGinnis, 1977) stresses the role of change agent played by the parent of the specially challenged child. Most early intervention programs include supportive parent-counseling services in recognition of the emotional demands of this role. It is the central contention of this chapter that the basic techniques and philosophy of cognitive-behavioral therapy, generically and specifically Rational Emotive Behavior Therapy (REBT), can assist those working with these parents to better address their emotional demands. REBT provides a rationale for the development of parent counseling programs based on an empirically derived theory of emotional distress, assessment constructs that allow a clear conceptualization of parents practical and emotional problems, and a variety of specific therapeutic techniques of demonstrated utility with similar problems in other populations.

Parents of specially challenged children face many demands in their daily efforts to meet the needs of their child. The supportive counseling so often advocated for such parents, although of some value, usually makes no specific attempt to teach parents the relationship among rational thinking, reasonable emotions and purposive behaviors. Although some parents may temporarily feel better with support, they frequently do not necessarily cope better or work more effectively with their exceptional child. Parents' distressing negative emotions can result in patterns of behavior that defeat their expressed purposes. These goals are to stimulate their child for maximum development and to effectively play their part in their child's educational planning. As pointed out by Ellis and Greiger (1977) cognitive behavioral approaches, best exemplified by REBT, have considerable potential in teaching parents and others working with specially challenged children as it demonstrates ways to manage emotions so that they may better meet the child's many requirements for care and stimulation.

Special education and related services are provided within a service delivery system whose critical components include not only parents and children, but also special educators and a variety of related service professionals. Current legislation mandates parent participation in team planning as well as teacher accountability for educational services that most effectively meet the child's needs. REBT informed parent counseling as suggested here will also reciprocally create new challenges for special educators in the given system. Despite this teachers, no less than the parents, experience a variety of distressing negative emotions that can interfere with the effective completion of their critical responsibilities. Angry, frequently anxious or "burned out" teachers and related services professionals may behave in self-defeating ways that adversely affect their students, students' families and themselves. Teachers, like parents, can be taught to manage their excessive negative emotions and self-defeating behaviors through individualized consultation, group counseling and/or training experiences based on the principals of REBT. It is the contention of this chapter that such training has a practical utility for special educators, is resource efficient as in-service education and takes advantage of the demonstrated clinical effectiveness of the REBT approach with other similar populations.

Parents of Specially Challenged Children

In his critical review of literature on parent training, Henry (1981) noted that there is an increasing emphasis on efforts to intervene in the problems of children by working with their parents. A variety of systematic training programs, as well as theoretical guidelines, have been advanced for helping parents help their children (Arnold, 1978). The literature on Rational-Emotive Consultation (REC) as described by Bernard and DiGuiseppe (1994) focuses on specific techniques for assisting children, both directly and indirectly to improve the management of their own thoughts, feelings and behaviors so that they may function more effectively. McInerney (1994) has described an REC informed approach to helping with emotional and behavioral problems through helping their parents apply basic REBT principals in their own lives and in child management. While there is now substantial literature on parent counseling with REBT, there are few specific programs for the parents of specially challenged children (Joyce, 1995). However Greaves (1996) describes such an application for parents of Down's syndrome children that provides an excellent example of the potential of this approach.

Basic Therapeutic Considerations

Rapport and Relationship Issues

An important initial step in working with all parents of specially challenged children involves establishing a relationship in which the parent will openly share their thoughts and feelings as well as accurately report their behavior. Although REBT practitioners do not believe that there is therapeutic magic in "empathetic understanding" few would argue that the quality of the therapeutic relationship or alliance is of no importance. Many parents of specially challenged children have had rather negative experiences with professionals and may be understandably defensive initially. Further some parents may have misconceptions about the therapeutic process, perhaps viewing therapy as a treatment imposed on the "sick" and therefore not appropriate for them. Some resent what they see as the implication that they, not their child, require help. It is useful then for the therapist to address these issues from the outset by clearly and simply stating what the parents can reasonably expect from their participation. Below is an example of such as statement:

> Psychologists over the years have found that people do not do difficult jobs very well when they are upset, angry, or depressed. Your job, as a parent of an exceptional child, is certainly a difficult one. Like anyone in your situation, you probably do your job better at times if you learned some proven ways to manage your own fears, resentments and guilty feelings in addition to learning how to stimulate and work with your child. In our work together, I am going to help you learn to manage your emotions better so that you can do a better job working with your child.

Statements like this help to establish a self-help atmosphere. Parents will more readily expect to help themselves by openly discussing their thoughts, feelings and actions in relation to their child and by sharing ideas on how to change these if they see a purpose to it. If parents at least tentatively agree to this effort, then a therapeutic contract can be established which gives the therapist permission to proceed with action-oriented, directive therapy towards this goal. In future work this contract can be reviewed as indicated. Furthermore the author has found group counseling to be particularly effective because discussion among parents with similar practical and emotional difficulties encourages a supportive and non-judgmental atmosphere while maintaining the basic contract. It has also been found that voluntary parent participation is most appropriate and effective. Practical considerations that encourage voluntary participation such as convenient scheduling and transportation may need to be addressed. However while one might find it necessary to try to strongly persuade a given parent to participate in the interest of the child, it may be ultimately self-defeating to require parent participation.

In the interest of initial rapport, it is often useful to reinforce verbal disclosure. This can be done in a variety of ways, including direct encouragement through specific topics of discussions, personally modeling self-disclosure and re-enforcing self-statements by active listening or an empathetic restatement of the parent's thoughts or feelings (Walen et al., 1980). A respect for the parent is communicated through statements accepting their thoughts and feelings as unconditional facts, although one may later suggest how these might be changed. Verbalizations that promote the parent's positive view of the therapist also help to establish a rapport (Wessler and Wessler, 1980). For example, the therapist may demonstrate knowledge and expertise relevant to the parent's concerns. It is also important to express genuine concern about the progress of both the parent and the child, although one should not be dependent on this progress. This trustworthiness is further aided when the therapist plays other roles in the child's total program; the parent then views the therapist as an expert with training and experience in work with children similar to their own. As in other applications of REBT, the therapist can be most persuasive when seen as a specialist with pertinent training and experience who shares a genuine interest in the child and the family's overall progress.

Disputation

Teaching individuals to recognize and dispute their irrational self-statements, as well as persuading them to do so vigorously and often, lies at the core of REBT. As pointed out by Wessler and Wessler (1980) disputation or "dissuasion" is a matter of both technique and therapeutic philosophy. The stereotype of the "argumentative" REBT practitioner is inaccurate; the main focus of REBT with the parents of exceptional children is to persuade them to effectively think and feel differently about the facts of their lives so that they can be less distressed and more effective. It is clear that trying to simply argue parents out of their feelings is short-sighted. Given appropriate attention to relationship issues and the establishment of a contract to proceed, REBT with these parents is not significantly different from work with other clients. In many ways the philosophy and technique of disputation are the same. Given the often traumatic facts involved in the lives of these families, philosophically there is even more reason to use all of one's persuasive skills, and the most proven methods available, to help parents learn to minimize their own distress and thus better cope with the experience of daily living.

Many parents of specially challenged appear especially sensitive to what they view as criticism of themselves or of their child. Disputation, therefore, must be done bearing this in mind, with attention to both the content and the timing of therapeutic disputes. Directed, Socratic dialogue is ideal for this purpose. Parents may misperceive disputation as (1) an attempt to get them to deny their strong emotions (2) a dismissal or trivialization of their thoughts/feelings (3) disapproval of their distress in the first place. These misconceptions need to be listened for, particularly when disputation fails. They must be corrected either directly or through further dialogue. Sometimes these reactions, once confirmed, may indicate that some of the relationship issues previously mentioned require reexamination and remediation. In other cases, it may indicate not that disputation has not worked, but that it has not worked yet. Persistence is required. Disputations can be varied in type and content to maintain interest.

The following are some practical suggestions for disputations often found to be effective with the parents of specially challenged children:

1. Use rational self-disclosure to model concrete examples of the disputation process, particularly at the initial stage.
2. When presenting the disputation process didactically (e.g., the ABC-D model), use relevant examples of practical value to the parents themselves.
3. Use pragmatic, relevant, although somewhat inelegant cognitive disputations instead of more abstract, philosophical ones.
4. Build in the generalization by providing the connection between the disputation process and the content from various practical problems. Use questions to encourage conclusions about generalizations and new applications.
5. Ask for feedback and listen for misconceptions. Be flexible and use all types of disputation, particularly when one approach is unsuccessful.
6. Do not hesitate to use the dissonance between expressed parental values ("it is important to stimulate my child") and self-defeating ones ("it should be easy") in disputation.
7. Be persistent, although a "hard sell" approach may be easily dismissed by parents.
8. Use homework assignments as well as reading oriented toward self-help to augment disputation.

Assessment

Bernard and Joyce (1984) and DiGiuseppe (1981) both noted the importance proper assessment in cognitive-behavioral therapy with children and their parents. It seems no less important in individual and group work with the parents of exceptional children. One can begin assessment by asking open-ended questions like, "What are your major concerns about your child?" Given a modicum of rapport and a supportive atmosphere, most parents will volunteer things such as, "I worry about his health" or "I am concerned about her lack of speech." Further guided discussion will help define the dimensions of the parents concerns. The second question to pose is whether these concerns are reasonable as defined by their efforts or whether they are excessive and self-defeating. Considerable judgment on the therapist's part must be exercised here in order to avoid work on "non-problems" as defined by the parents frame of reference. A hypothesis-testing approach is recommended to define operationally the cognitive, emotional, and behavioral meaning of the parents' concern and to allow for its subsequent exploration. For example, parents may worry about their child's "health", having a realistic concern about a sick child's many physical problems and requirements for medical care. On the other hand, a parent may mean by "worry" an excessive preoccupation with relatively minor health problems, to the point of creating excessive, dysfunctional fear that prevents the parents from handling and stimulating that child. This type of "worry", more correctly defined as anxiety, creates distress that is self-defeating of the more general goal of helping the child develop as fully as possible.

Assessment should also address the parents motivation for change as well as the resources available to assist them to do so in order that intervention can be planned appropriately and with realistic expectations. Initially many parents are relatively unwilling to give up feelings, even negative ones, which they feel they "should" have under their given, often objectively difficult, circumstances. They often say something like, "you would worry too, if your child had brain damage" or " I have to worry all the time because if I don't no one will care". An important determination here is to assess whether the parents are content with their feelings or not. One can ask in a variety of ways, "what are these feelings costing you?" Can the parent, at least intellectually, accept the idea that there are other ways or degrees of feeling possible and desirable for practical reasons? If not, intervention may need to begin with very concrete, experiential disputes of the parents belief in the inevitability of their negative emotions. Often this can be accomplished by introducing the parent to other, more experienced parents of children with similar children whose feelings are less self-defeating. Also a realistic inventory must be taken of the resources available for change. For instance, is one parent in the couple more open to change than the other? In single-parent situations, are others involved (such as grandparents)? These others may be involved productively in the counseling process. In other cases, arrangements can be made for supportive services, or practical problems can be solved so that the parents can participate more actively.

Issues of Program Development

Program planning requires an assessment of the service delivery system characteristics and resources in addition to an assessment of both parent and therapist variables. Clearly the context of service delivery may limit the professional time and resources allocated to a given therapeutic program. Although the approach presented here is applicable within an individual consultation or group discussion format, practical considerations often determine which format is selected. The author's preference for structured, time-limited group counseling in combination with brief individual consultation was initially established to accommodate both parent need and a specific system resource priorities (McInerney, 1983). A realistic appraisal of the limits of services provided will help parents, other staff and therapists to develop and set realistic goals and expectations. In addition, it can be used to develop guidelines for referral to other therapeutic resources (i.e., mental health resources) where appropriate. None of us can do everything for everyone; this is especially true of those employed within public settings, such as schools or treatment centers where funding can be limited.

Common Themes in Work with Parents of Exceptional Children

Experience using REBT, both with individuals and in groups, with the parents of specially challenged children and adolescents indicates that there are several common problem themes, or cognitive road blocks, causing difficulty for these parents. These themes are not unique to parents of special children, but they do seem to occur with more frequency and around certain practical issues common to this group. These common themes include self-defeating cognitions surrounding the following issues: denial versus acceptance, fear versus active concern, anger versus rational assertion and guilt versus self-acceptance.

Denial Versus Acceptance

Many authorities suggest that the most common initial response of a parent to having a specially challenged child is denial (Cunningham and Slopper, 1980). The psychoanalytic concept of grief and mourning (Solnit andStark, 1961) is often used descriptively in this context. This view postulates that there are stages of grief that a parent must work through before being able to accept the child. Many parents of exceptional children describe initial shock and disbelief as a reaction to their child, but in most cases this seems to dissipate with time and experience (Featherstone, 1980). It seems unwarranted for the therapist to assume that all or even most parents have difficulty accepting their child after this initial shock. In the author's experience, the concept of "acceptance" is misused to explain a family's lack of progress. Overwhelmed, uncooperative or simply less-able parents are sometimes blamed for this lack of progress by being labeled as being "unaccepting" of their child. Misuse of this concept is untherapeutic and self-defeating; it should be avoided as parents understandably resent it.

Careful assessment is required to determine if a problem in this area does, in fact, exist. For example, although some minimization of the child's condition may be natural in the initial stages, it is not necessarily a self-defeating defense.

However, a prolonged disregard of the extent of the child's problem may lead to ineffective intervention. It is important to assist the parents in looking at the logical consequences of their behavior and help them to clarify their thoughts, both rational and irrational, about their child's problem. Denial does produce self-defeating distress for some parents but rarely are these problems the result of simple denial of the facts. Often there are secondary emotional dimensions (anger, guilt, depression) that require identification and treatment.

If the therapist does find that the family is struggling with acceptance of the child's condition, it is necessary to dispute some of the irrational misconceptions and attitudes held by parents. Providing parents with guided experiences in interacting with their own child, as well as with parents of other exceptional children can help to counter both basic misconceptions and the "awfulizing" of the condition. Other parents and specially challenged adults can present models of acceptance in a way that didactic presentation and cognitive disputes presented by the therapist cannot. Both their words and their actions can demonstrate that disability does not mean disaster or an inevitably worthless existence.

Fear Versus Active Concern

Featherstone (1981) pointed out various types of fear experienced by the parents and families of specially challenged children. She points out that though these fears may be at times debilitating, they are not necessarily "neurotic". Many parents are quite sensitive to this issue as they see their fears surrounding their child as based on reality. They also, at times, see their fears as a necessary motivator for action in their child's interests. Hara (1975) expressed the outrage felt by many parents when they are told by professionals to "stop worrying." Parents view this as the dismissing of their fears as neurotic maladjustment rather than an important element of a parent's active concern. The cognitive-behavioral approach presented here can make a clear distinction between fear that is excessive (often debilitating) and concern, which is appropriate and motivating. This approach can help parents learn techniques to manage self-defeating fears and a philosophy of assertive, active concern.

The REBT perspective on fear has been well described by Hauck (1975) and others. It is most important to encourage an open discussion of fears and to ascertain the parent's perspective. Then a didactic but practical presentation can be made regarding the nature of fear and the role of "awfulizing" thoughts in its genesis. It is then worthwhile to have the parents re-examine their fears in the light of this perspective and to begin to make judgments about their fear's utility, perhaps questioning the ways in which these fears are helping them in their everyday lives. While reassuring them that overconcern is human and not "crazy", it is imperative to point out that it is neither always necessary nor useful.

REBT informed intervention helps parents to learn how to confront and actively dispute the irrational self-statements behind their fears. A most practical dispute involves variations of the idea that fear, in itself, rarely prevents a feared event from happening (McInerney, 1995). A good example to use is that of a parent who is so afraid that their child will be hurt while playing with other children and therefore deny the child the play experience. However, it is this socially inexperienced, overprotected child who is most likely to be hurt in play with other children. In this way, that parent's irrational fear is actually contributing to the likelihood of the feared event's occurrence. This issue of "overprotection" must be dealt with sensitively though because, in many cases, a degree of protection is warranted by the objective reality of the child's disability. The concept of *normalization* with regard to maximizing the child's social development and independence can be a helpful context within which to present to problem of overprotection. Most parents are in complete agreement with normalization and the cognitive dissonance between it and fearful overprotection can be therapeutically utilized.

A related misconception about fear held by some parents is that fear is a necessary motivator for behavior. Some appear to believe that, without fear, they would not be motivated to care for their child. It is important to point out that this is not the case; few parents would stop caring for their child if fear were reduced. Also there is sometimes a misconception surrounding the word "fear"; it is used throughout REBT work to teach ways of discriminating degrees of emotional experience. Teaching parents a simple "1 to 10" rating scale for their emotional experiences can be helpful in illustrating the difference between "concern" and "fear". Although this scale is individual for each parent, generally 7 to 10 can be labeled "excessive fears", 4 through 6 "realistic concerns" and 1 through 3 may be denoted "small concerns". Parents can be asked to place a variety of fears in each category and should be encouraged to identify the thoughts precipitating their "excessive fears". It can be demonstrated that the relationship between anxiety and performance dictates that performance tacks are most successful when aligned with realistic concern. However, pervasive or excessive fears do not yield the best performance. In this way therapy may be utilized to help parents scale down their "excessive fears" (fears that they have awfulized) to "realistic concerns".

While fearful thoughts are being extinguished, care should be taken that more rational thinking and problem solving are reinforced. A variety of related cognitive-behavioral techniques such as systematic desensitization, thought stopping, and implosion and paradoxical intention can be demonstrated and practiced. Rational assertiveness trainiing is also useful in providing the behavioral component for expressing realistic concern as an alternative to debilitating fear.

Anger Versus Rational Assertiveness

Anger is a major issue for many of the parents of exceptional children. The enormity of the "injustice" visited on the parents by the birth of the child can activate considerable rage. Parents may cry out for someone or something to blame for the circumstance. Although this anger may be a common stage in the grieving process mentioned above, it can nonetheless be troubling for families.

Many parents, while not perpetually angry, find themselves most distressed when other people are not as they "should be" and therefore merit punishment. They mistakenly think that anger works when, in reality, it most often only generates anger and resentment in others. Parents of exceptional children are not, as a group, less tolerant of frustration than others. They are simply confronted with many more frustrating circumstances. As in other areas, dealing successfully with anger issues requires a careful assessment so that the intervention may be appropriately directed.

Initial work with such parents must begin by creating conditions in which parents can express anger and resentment openly. The central message to convey at this point is that anger is a natural human response to frustration, but that it is not inevitable and is often self-defeating. It is important to explore the costs of anger lest some parents incorrectly confuse anger with standing up for your rights and see it as desirable. Anger is extreme and pervasive when it has psychosomatic consequences, interfere with problem solving or communication, interfere with personal relationships or leads to undesirable secondary emotions like guilt or depression (Ellis 1977, Waters, 1980). All of these costs can be concretely illustrated by discussion, personal example and directed role-playing of concrete situations common to the parents experience.

Once parents see a practical reason for addressing their anger, the rational-emotive psychology of anger can be presented (Hauck, 1974; Ellis 1977, Ellis and Tafrate, 1997). This is best done with practical examples of how we upset ourselves. Rational-emotive imagery can also be used to demonstrate both that it is not events that upset us but that it is our irrational thoughts about the events that are largely responsible for our anger. It is critical to discuss real-life anger issues whenever possible. If parents are encouraged to make explicit their self-talk in anger situations, they can become further aware of the relationship between one's "shoulds" for people/things and anger. As noted earlier, role playing can be particularly useful in this context. These can be played out with instructions for both angry and non-angry self-talk. Discussion can focus on the self-talk that leads to anger, the likely logical consequences of the anger and alternative thoughts and behaviors.

In disputing the angry self-talk of parent of exceptional children, it is often most useful to stay with the concrete facts of a given situation. Self-talk such as "this is awful! I can't stand it!", which gives rise to anger is simply not consistent with the facts. The fact that these parents do "stand it", as well as successfully cope with such circumstances, on a daily basis can be persistently pointed out. Coping with frustrations by giving up demanding that they not exist, rather than eliminating the frustration or anger, is the more appropriate focus. It is often important to point out to parents that acceptance of an unjust reality does not mean approval of it. Ultimately philosophical acceptance of the reality is the goal.

Therapeutic treatment of anger is not complete without providing experience and practice in rational assertion as an alternative to anger. Rational, assertive behavior can be encouraged through the well-established techniques of rational assertiveness training described in detail in several sources (Hauck, 1979, Jakubowski and Lange, 1978; Lange and Jakubowski, 1976). The situations used in this training can easily be tailored by the therapist to reflect the experiences common to the parents of exceptional children. It should be emphasized that annoyance, not rage, most often results in assertive behavior. Assertiveness is no guarantee of getting what one wants, but it generally works better than angry demands.

Guilt Versus Self-Acceptance

Many parents of specially challenged children report feelings of guilt about their child difficulties, particularly early in the child's life. Some parents believe that they could have or should have done something to prevent the child's disability. Despite the uncertain etiology of many conditions, some parents believe that their child is being punished because of their own inadequacies. The initial guilt may be a time-dependent part of the natural grieving process, but in some cases, the problem generalizes to other areas. In these cases the guilt may generalize in one or both parents to symptoms of clinical depression. Because of this, a frank discussion of the problem of guilt should be included in virtually all therapeutic work with the parents from the REBT perspective. More than the other negative emotions, the irrational self-talk at the root of guilt seems to respond only to vigorous, persistent and pragmatic disputation (Ellis and Harper, 1975).

Rational thinking about responsibility can be reinforced in a variety of ways. Didactic exposition of REBT perspective on depression (Ellis and Harper, 1975; Hauck 1973) and the psychological difference between guilt and responsibility is useful to discuss in detail. Responsibility can be explained as a concept of the relationship between identifiable actions and their probable consequence. Further, responsibility also implies that the consequences are usually identifiable before hand and that the actions in question are a result of some choice. When people fail to live up to these types of responsibilities, the logical consequence is irresponsibility and negative events. Guilt, on the other hand, implies much more than irresponsibility. Guilt implies that human beings should omnipotently know the right thing to do in every situation and invariably do it. When they do not, they have done something so awful that they lose all worth or value as a person and should be "damned" for all time.

Much of the guilt experienced by parents of exceptional children results from misinformation surrounding the child's disability. More often this guilt is a result of an impossibly broad definition of the parent's responsibilities. Through therapeutic dialogue, misconceptions can be factually corrected and a more realistic concept on responsibility can be developed. For example a parent might say, "I feel guilty because I'm not doing enough for my child". It is useful then to question concretely what they mean by "enough". Often "enough" in the parent's mind means "everything". In a variety of concrete ways, the impossibility of doing "everything" should be pointed out. Further the self-defeating nature of obsessing about doing "everything" can be made readily apparent to most people. "Do you want to spend all of your time and energy thinking about everything that should be done but hasn't or in doing the things that are important and *can* be done?". Even when the inevitable mistakes are made, there is no utility in making a bad situation worse by feeling guilty about it. An attitude of self-acceptance whereby the parent learns to evaluate his or her behavior only in terms of usefulness rather than for what it is incorrectly assumed to demonstrate about their personal worth ought to be reinforced.

Many parents are not aware of all that they are doing to cope. An assignment may be to keep a "coping log" in which they are instructed to record in simple behavioral terms all their daily accomplishments for the child, the family or themselves. This and other variations of Beck's pleasure and mastery techniques (Beck et al., 1979) can be most useful because, in many cases, the daily accomplishments of the family are quite remarkable, even though they are often devalued by the family itself. The coping log provides concrete evidence that contradicts their belief that they are failures Why are the other accomplishments, ones not related to the child in need, any less important than the ones that are? Clearly it all depends on the way one views them. That is the major point to get across: it all depends on the way one views his or her own accomplishments.

It should also be pointed out that a parent's guilt-driven obsession with doing "everything" for the exceptional child may lead to a relative neglect of other family members. This self-defeating imbalance in the family system can best be addressed by focusing on both the reduction of guilt-driven, over-involvement in the exceptional child and by providing behavioral assignments to help parents redistribute attention. Although resistance can be expected, the likely reduction in distressing guilt and family tension provides its own reinforcement once the process begins.

Parents troubled by problems of guilt in relation to their children have often lost perspective on their own value as a person. They no longer see themselves as being of any worth except in relationship to their child. Such a view may be accompanied by clinical symptoms of depression. Sexual, marital and family adjustment problems are significantly related considerations. In such cases, the cognitive-behavioral approached used in the treatment of depression are most appropriate and referral for comprehensive treatment may be indicated. The nature of depression and helplessness often need to be concretely pointed out. The contradiction involved in devaluing oneself to the point of dysfunction, which prevents the accomplishment of one's original goal (to help one's child develop fully) should be vigorously made explicit. Suggested homework assignments could include direction to be good to yourself while exploring the importance difference between "selfishness" and "self-interest". There is value in exploring this difference with all parents of exceptional children.

Teachers of Exceptional Children

Special educators, though competent in their area of expertise, have most often received very little training to help them cope with the emotional demands of their complex role. They are expected to plan and implement individualized classroom instruction, coordinate related services and participate with parents, administrators and various specialists in programatic decision making for the child. This is not a simple task. At times the ultimate goal of the process is obscured by the irrational demands of individual participants and excessive negative emotions may be generated. Special educators have been committed to in-service training for some time but the issues of emotional survival skills are rarely addressed. As Bernard (1990) has shown, teachers who are better at managing their own emotional stress are better at teaching.

Experience as a consultant to both teachers and parents of special children has suggested that they share several emotional and practical problems. Teachers, like some parents, find it difficult to motivate themselves to consistently follow through on simple, often commonsense, behavioral recommendations. When one talks frankly with special educators about their feelings about themselves and their jobs, they describe feelings not unlike those described by the children parents. Teachers report feelings of self-criticism, anxiety about failing the child, guilt over not doing "enough", anger at the "injustice" of the child's condition and anger at others who are not doing what they should be doing to help. Like the parents and other helping professionals, they run a higher than average risk of burnout, along with its deteriorating job performance and symptoms of depression. The burnout issue alone justifies providing therapeutic experiences like those discussed above for parents. REBT has been proven to be both relevant and powerfully therapeutic for stress management; such should be true for special educators.

Common Themes Expressed by Teachers

Special education teachers often experience self-defeating anxiety when they feel that they are being evaluated negatively. They appear to fear criticism because of three distinct and irrational self-statements: (1) "I must be approved of all the time; I've earned it by my care of this child" (2) "criticism is so devastating that I can't stand it" and (3) "I must fear criticism in order to prevent it". These statements can be disputed by directed dialogue, including questions concerning the absolute need for approval, the presumed catastrophic consequences of criticism and the value of worry in presenting it.

These self-statements can be disputed experientially by role-playing common situations in which criticism occurs (i.e., supervisory conferences, parent interactions etc) with irrational instructions as well as more rational coping strategies. Cognitive-behavioral strategies for rebutting criticism may also be practiced. Specific homework assignments may include doing an ABC analysis of several criticism situations paired with later discussion.

Anger is a frequently discussed issue. Teachers often anger themselves at colleagues, administrators, parents and their students in a variety of contexts. Suffice it to say that special educators, no less than the rest of us, often need to be vigorously persuaded that anger is self-defeating. Teachers may need to be inelegantly asked, "is your anger changing his behavior?" and/or "did she ever criticize you again?" until the logical consequences of anger are appreciated. This is important because, as we all know, anger does sometimes work in the short run. However, attention must be paid to the long-range personal consequences of frequent, excessive anger in terms of psychosomatic distress, fatigue, impaired interpersonal relationships and guilt feelings i.e., burnout. It has also been found that concrete discussion of alternatives to anger in terms of both rational thinking and assertive behavior may be useful. Given the host of frustrations involved in the job of a special educator, coping with frustration philosophically and behaviorally is an all important skill.

Related to anger is the problem of blame, both of self and of others. The rational alternative to blame is acceptance of reality as what it "is", instead of what it should be, while trying to change what can be changed. The essential point here is that human beings largely create their own emotions, an idea that can be demonstrated effectively through rational-emotive imagery and other methods. The point that one is responsible for one own emotions allows for a more complete consideration of the anger-guilt cycle as experienced by many special educators. This is particularly true when one gets angry at people who they "should" not get angry at, most especially their specially challenged students. Unacknowledged anger at the child is then often misdirected at the child parents. The guilt stemming from this self-defined unacceptable anger leads to a variety of self-defeating compensations that may have consequences on the child's behavior and adjustment. Unconditional self-acceptance is the elegant solution to the problem; more immediately one might be less self-damning in order to break up the anger-guilt cycle. This includes recognizing that, "I'm angry and I should calm down," instead of berating oneself as, "a rotten teacher and person for being angry at this poor kid".

A final area of importance for special educators involves strategies for rational problem solving. These can be presented in a structured way, with emphasis on removing the largely emotional element of the problem through rational thinking prior to tackling the practical issue. For example, a teacher who is facing a very difficult parent conference becomes anxious and defensive. This reaction clearly has the potential for making an already difficult situation far worse. Instruction and practice in dealing with this and other similar situations can be provided.

Special educators, not unlike the parents of educationally challenged children, appear to benefit from therapeutic experiences grounded in REBT. This approach has the advantages of efficiency, flexibility and practical value as seen by the participants as well as demonstrated efficacy with other populations. It is amenable to use in the satisfaction of existing professional development requirements and provides a clear methodology for addressing staff concerns regarding stress management and burnout.

Conclusion

REBT as it is, and as it continues to develop, is as applicable today to the experiences of those working with specially challenged children as it was when then original version of this chapter was written (McInerney, 1983). Parents, educators and professional support personnel can benefit from the interventions described above. Furthermore, the basic principles and techniques described in the present work can be integrated into school-based programs to support parental involvement in special education programs, as a supportive intervention for the parents of emotionally and behaviorally disturbed students as well as more generally disaffected or substance misusing adolescents not typically part of a school's special education population. In the future, the authors hope to see school-based programs grounded in the priciples of REBT implemented in both regular education and special education settings.

References

Arnold, L. E. (ed.). (1978) *Helping parents help their children*. New York: Brunner/Mazel.

Beck, A. T., Rush, A. J., Shaw, B. F. and Emery, G. (1979). *Cognitive therapy with depression*. New York: Guilford Press.

Bernard, M. E and Digiuseppe, R. (eds). (1994) *Rational-emotive consultation in applied settings*. Hillsdale, NJ: Erlbaum.

Bernard, M. E. and Joyce, M. J. (1984). *Rational-emotive therapy with children and adolescents: Theory, treatment strategies, proventitive methods*. New York: John Wiley and Sons.

Bernard, M. E. (1990). *Taking the stress out of teaching*. New York: Institute for Rational Emotive Therapy.

Cunningham, C. and Sloper, P. (1980) *Helping your exceptional baby: A practical and honest approach to raising a mentally handicapped child*. New York: Pantheon.

DiGiuseppe, R. (1981). Cognitive therapy with children. In G. Emery, S. Holton, and R. Bedrosian (eds.), *New directions in cognitive therapy*. New York: Guilford, pp. 50–67.

Ellis, A. (1977). How to live with and without anger. New York: Reader's Digest Press.

Ellis, A. and Grieger, R. (1977). The present and future of RET. In A. Ellis and R. Grieger (eds.) *Handbook of rational-emotive therapy*. New York: Springer.

Ellis, A. and Harper, R. (1975). *A new guide to rational living*. Englewood Cliffs, NJ: Prentice Hall.

Ellis, A. and Tafrate, R. C. (1997). *How to control your anger before it controls you.* Secaucus, NJ: Birch Lane Press.

Featherstone, H. (1980) *A difference in the family: Life with a disabled child.* New York: Basic Books.

Greaves, D. (1996). The effect of rational-emotive parent education on the stress of mothers of young children with down's syndrome. *Journal of Rational Emotive and Cognitive Behavioral Therapy, 15*, 249–267.

Greenfield, J (1978). *A place for Noah.* New York: Holt, Rinehart and Winston.

Hauck, P. A. (1973). *Overcoming depression.* Philadelphia: Westminster Press.

Hauck, P. A. (1974). *Overcoming frustration and anger.* Philadelphia: Westminster Press.

Hauck, P. A. (1975). *Overcoming worry and fear.* Philadelphia: Westminster Press.

Hauck, P. A. (1977). Irrational parenting styles. In A. Ellis and R. Grieger (eds.), *Handbook of rational-emotive therapy.* New York: Springer.

Hauck, P. A. (1979). *How to stand up for yourself.* Philadelphia: Westminster Press.

Hauck, P. A. (1980). *Brief counseling with RET.* Philadelphia: Westminster Press.

Hara, V. (1975) Stop worrying? Nonsense! *The exceptional parent.* Jan–Feb., *5*, 12–15.

Hayden, A. H. and McGinness, G. D. (1977) *Educational programming for the severely retarded.* Reston, VA: Council for Exceptional Children.

Henry, S. A.(1981). Current dimensions of parent training. *School Psychology Review,10*(1), 4–14.

Jakubowski, P. and Lange, A. J. (1976). *The assertive option: Your rights and responsibilities.* Champaign, Ill: Research Press.

Joyce, M. (1995) Emotional relief for parent: Is rational-emotive parent education effective? *Journal of Rational Emotive and Cognitive Behavioral Therapy*, *13*, 55–75.

Lange, A. J. and Jakubowski, P (1976). *Responsible assertive behavior: Cognitive behavioral procedures for trainers.* Champaign, Ill: Research Press.

McInerney, J.F. (1994). Rational-emotive parent consultation. In Bernard, M.E. and DiGiuseppe, R. (eds.), *Rational-emotive consultation in applied settings.* Hillsdale, NJ: Erlbaum.

Solnit, A. J. and Startk, M. H. (1961). Mourning and the birth of a defective child. *Psychoanalytic Study of the Child, 16,* 523–537.

Walen, S. R., DiGuiseppe, R. and Wessler, R. L. (1980). *A practioner's guide to rational emotive therapy.* New York: Oxford University Press.

Waters, V. (1980). *Rational stories for children: Rational parenting series.* New York: Institute for Rational Living.

Wessler, R. A. and Wessler, R. L. (1980). *The principles and practice of rational-emotive therapy.* San Francisco: Jossey-Bass.

13

Rational-Emotive Behavior Group Therapy with Children and Adolescents

Mark D. Terjesen, Ph.D. and Maria A. Esposito

St. John's University

Mailing address:
Mark D. Terjesen or Maria A. Esposito at St. John's University, 8000 Utopia Parkway, Marillac Hall SB 36F Jamaica, NY, 11439

Humans are social creatures and we begin functioning as members of groups the moment we are born. We continue to work, play, and live in groups for the entire span of our lives. Therefore, it is not surprising that group therapy has been a common and popular treatment option for over half a century. There are a number of key considerations about the application of group therapy when working with children and adolescents, and, more specifically, about the application of REBT and cognitive change methods in these groups.

According to Ellis (1997), Rational-Emotive Behavior Therapy (REBT) and Cognitive Behavior Therapy (CBT) lend themselves particularly well to use in group settings. Ellis (2002) stated that:

> Rational-Emotive Behavior Therapy (REBT) and Cognitive-Behavior Therapy (CBT) are efficient kinds of group therapy, because they involve people who regularly meet together with a leader in order to work on their psychological problems, they focus on the members' thoughts, feelings and behaviors, and they encourage all the participants to help each other change their cognitions, emotions and actions. (p. 51)

Ellis has been successfully using REBT in groups since 1959 (Ellis, 2002) and claims that it is usually more effective than individual REBT. Its use in child and adolescent groups has been described in the literature over the past three decades (e.g., Elkin, 1983).

Initially, we will present an overview of group therapy, followed by a discussion of some of the specific applications of it when working with children, specific discussion of REBT when working with children and adolescents, a brief discussion of the research regarding the effectiveness of group therapy in comparison to individual therapy as well as control groups, along with the effectiveness of REBT group therapy.

General Considerations in Group Therapy with Children and Adolescents

The advantages of and disadvantages of group therapy with children and adolescents will now be briefly reviewed

Advantages

Group therapy is a common method used with children and adolescents due to its numerous advantages over individual therapy. Several authors, most notably Yalom (1994), have identified specific therapeutic factors that exist in groups. Corey and Corey (1997) refer to these factors as "the special forces within groups that produce constructive changes" (p. 239). "Universality" is one such powerful factor and it can be used in group therapy, as when students recognize that other members of the group share in some of the same afflictions as they do and, as a consequence, it may help them to feel less isolated in their struggle. In this and other ways, students in group therapy can serve as excellent support for each other. Children and adolescents who have already made progress toward overcoming universal hardships (such as divorce of parents or death of a loved one) can also provide hope and inspiration for those who are still struggling.

An additional advantage of group therapy is that children and adolescents receive feedback from a number of people as opposed to only receiving feedback from the clinician in individual therapy. Giving and receiving feedback helps members to understand "the impact they have on others and decide what, if anything, they want to change about their interpersonal style" (Corey and Corey, 1997, p. 243). We have found that students are very frank in their giving of feedback to their peers and are readily comfortable in "calling out their friends" when they are not being forthright, something that as clinicians we may not always be able to pick up upon.

An example of where feedback can be helpful may be seen in an REBT-based study group, in which homework is discussed as well as beliefs that interfere with completion. Students in group therapy may receive several critiques of their homework and actively participate in reviewing the work of others, which can facilitate increased awareness and improved critical thinking. The mild competition that exists in groups with children and adolescents can also be beneficial, especially in its ability to motivate members to work harder toward completing their homework, as well as toward reaching personal goals. At the same time, students may receive feedback from multiple sources on how to better challenge their faulty logic that interferes with their homework completion. See Appendix A for an example of a REBT group format utilized by Forte et al. (2004).

It is our experience that some group members tend to learn therapeutic techniques better than those in individual therapy may, which may be particularly true for children and adolescents. This also holds true for problem solving aspects and REBT techniques.

Students in groups observe modeling not only by the therapist but also by other peers. Such modeling by other members of the group can be especially advantageous as children are more likely to identify with other children than with the therapist. Modeling can also increase the amount of sharing and disclosure that occurs in groups. When one group member opens up to the group, for example, other members often open up as well. Modeling of effective challenging of unhealthy thinking and the development of logical, rational thoughts may help individual students in the group setting develop more healthy approaches to handling potential adversity.

Another benefit of groups is that they can be educational beyond the structured intent of the group. For example, in a task oriented group (test anxiety) having a mixed gender group may allow students an opportunity to learn about members of the opposite gender. In addition, groups can be a source of school environmental knowledge, where members learn about various aspects of the school (classroom, teachers, etc) that different group members have experienced. Furthermore, groups provide a safe environment for members to share and grow. This environment allows students who are trying to alter some aspect of their behavior an opportunity to test new behaviors and receive constructive feedback from the group leader and their peers.

Specifically, when working with children and adolescents, group therapy has a further important advantage over individual therapy in that it allows the therapist to observe the group members in action interacting with one another. This provides the therapist with important information on members interpersonal skills and styles, which can be more accurate and helpful than the child's self-reports of behavior provided in individual therapy. Direct observation also enables the group leader to report on any discrepancies between what the person is reporting and what they actually carry out.

Disadvantages

Despite its popularity, group therapy is not for everyone, and it certainly has its limitations in working with both children and adults. Perhaps, the most obvious disadvantage of group therapy is that, by its nature, it reduces the amount of time spent addressing the individual needs of each student. Thus, this reduction in time for direct intervention leads many to consider group therapy to be an inefficient method. While this may be true in some cases, it is important to recognize that many if not most groups are comprised of clients with similar needs or complaints. Consequently, it is often the case that though only one group member's specific needs are addressed at a time, the majority of the members can benefit from the general information supplied. Later in this chapter we will discuss the differences between having homogeneous and heterogeneous groups for children and adolescents in terms of content, membership, and presenting problem.

Another possible concern about group therapy is that the idea of therapy in a group format may intimidate a student who could benefit from the approach. The limited degree of confidentiality that can be guaranteed is one of the reasons some children are wary of the group setting for therapy. Students in individual therapy are reassured that for the most part everything they reveal (excepting child abuse and the intention to harm oneself or others) will remain confidential by the fact that the therapist is bound to legal and ethical codes and can face severe consequences for breaking confidentiality. However, it is far more difficult to secure complete confidentiality when therapy is conducted in a group. This may be even more true when considering children and adolescents in groups. One way to address the issue of confidentiality in groups is to create written contracts that all members must sign at the start of the group (see Appendix B). This can help ease the minds of those who may be hesitant to enter the group due to fears about confidentiality.

Compulsive talkers or interrupters can also be a potential problem in groups. Therapists can reduce the risk of constant interruption by certain group members by setting up specific "ground rules" for the group in the first session. These rules should stress the importance of being respectful when each member has the floor and should specify appropriate and inappropriate times for members to make comments. We have found that students sometimes do a good job of policing other group members and providing feedback when they think that other members may be monopolizing the group therapy. This may be particularly true for adolescents, and we use this feedback as part of the therapy process. In addition, group leaders may wish to pull a student aside at a later time and point out that they may be monopolizing the group process and encourage them to self-monitor their own behavior.

Other areas of caution in group therapy have to do with the potential high level of suggestibility of some members. It is important to recognize the specific needs and persona of individual group members and anticipate how they may be affected by group participation. For example, some students may only do their group assignment (we eschew the word homework, as do students) because, "they MUST have approval of the group leader and/or group members." While this serves the purpose of getting the group assignment completed, it is important to address the motive, or potential irrationality, behind the behavior. In addition, group members may give bad advice or provide the wrong solution. This can be detrimental to highly suggestible members.

Another obstacle that can hinder the progress of some groups is the existence of narcissistic members, which does occur with some regularity in working with adolescents. Narcissistic group members, members who only care about themselves and their problems, and members who are simply uncaring can hamper other members ability to improve and can be destructive to the entire group process. However, appropriate pre-group screening (to be discussed later in this chapter) should eliminate this potential problem by preventing these individuals from entering the group.

Overall, we have found that groups can be an important resource in working with children and adolescents. Additionally, the structure of the approach of REBT lends itself nicely to the format of group therapy. We will briefly discuss the theory of REBT and its core assumptions as they relate to groups and then present some general guidelines for running groups with children and adolescents.

REBT Applied to Child and Adolescent Groups

At this point in the book, readers will be fairly familiar with the REBT model and how it is applied when working with children, adolescents, and parents. However, we would like to provide a brief review of the model as it pertains to group therapy when working with these populations.

REBT in Child and Adolescent Groups

REBT operates under the premise that individuals possess disruptive, dysfunctional/irrational cognitions about events that negatively impact their behavior and affect. That is, cognitions mediate emotions and behaviors. This is different from a cognitive deficit model, which implies that typical normal development involves the acquisition of certain cognitive processes that have failed to develop in these children who experience difficulty. To illustrate the difference between the two, we will consider the case of a child who is socially anxious from that of a child who is diagnosed with Asperger's disorder.

In order to meet their criteria for Asperger's disorder, a child needed to have impairment in reciprocal social interaction (Gillberg and Gillberg, 1989). According to the DSM-IV-TR (APA, 2000), the diagnostic criteria include a "severe and sustained impairment in social interaction" (p. 80). The ability to engage in appropriate social interaction with others is a skill that failed to develop in the student with Asperger's. This is different from socially anxious students. These students may in fact know what the correct behavior to engage in is, but fail to do so. The dysfunctional cognitions model would propose that this may be because the student is thinking: "If I say something and mess up and others think poorly of me . . . it would be terrible" or "I *have to/must* have approval of others, because not to would be intolerable." These cognitions are irrational in nature and would interfere with the students' ability to engage in a socially appropriate behavior.

The reason that this distinction is important for group therapy is that the kind of therapy group that students might be assigned to may vary dependent upon whether they never acquired/learned the appropriate cognitive, social, and behavioral processes or if they engage in distorted interpretations and perceptions of reality. If a students' primary disorder stems from cognitive deficits, the therapy group may be more skill focused, with rehearsal of behavioral and cognitive coping strategies; that is, teaching students what they failed to develop. The groups may be staggered in terms of skill acquisition level, to allow other students who have demonstrated some level of competency in skill acquisition to provide a model for their peers. These deficit driven groups appear to be more often focused on behaviors that are externalizing in nature as they are the ones that can receive direct feedback from others, whereas the internal cognitions are based upon insight and ability to report one's own cognitions. For example, if they have not formed cognitions and appropriate strategies to effectively manage anger, these deficits will be remediated in this group.

In group therapy, the clinician is able to see the interaction of the students' cognitions, their behaviors, and the environment (their peers) that these behaviors actually occur in. This opportunity allows for a greater understanding of the dynamic interaction of these variables and for an opportunity to practice/rehearse effective cognitions and behaviors in more natural contexts than present in 1:1 therapy.

Some Distinctive Features of REBT Groups

REBT group therapy with children and adolescents, like individual therapy, is more psychoeducational than motivational. The group leader is not just there to inspire the group members but rather to provide them with knowledge and information to help in achieving goals. That is, the goal is to inform and educate members of the group on the dysfunctionality of their present cognitive schemas, teach them strategies to actively challenge them, and work with them on developing more appropriate affective and behavioral responses to go along with these more healthy cognitions.

REBT proposes that regardless of the origin of emotional disturbances we focus in the group on the irrational beliefs and cognitive processing underlying these emotions. Through a group format, peers may help group members readily identify the cognitive schemas/irrational beliefs that maintain the disturbance. This is one particular benefit of the group format, as peers may be better at understanding what some of the underlying cognitions are that lead to the unhealthy emotions experienced by their peers than an adult clinician. In REBT groups, students go through a number of exercises, which will be detailed later, that assist to direct change of cognitions that will help facilitate emotional and behavioral change.

As mentioned previously, REBT groups are psychoeducational and seek to increase students' knowledge about the cause of destructive emotions and behaviors. That being said, early on in REBT groups with children we focus on the REBT theory of emotions, and assist students in understanding the differences between functional and dysfunctional emotions. This is where we suggest the clinician think about the level of functioning of the group members and cater their language in therapy to a level that the student will understand. While words like "functional", "dispute", and "irrational" may be appropriate for older students, their use may really serve to hinder the understanding of some of the core principals of REBT with younger children. We suggest more user friendly terms that, while not consistent with the actual terminology used in REBT-speak, do share the same content/message. As such, we use "helpful", "challenge", and "healthy thinking" in place of the terms above.

Developing an emotional vocabulary is an important aspect of REBT psychoeducation. The group leader, especially with younger children, may spend some time helping foster their emotional vocabulary. We have found many students, when asked what they feel, offer "bad" as a response. The group leader, through didactic instruction as well as experiential exercises, will help students see a range of feelings (anger, sadness, frustration, anxiety). At the same time, the group leader and group members assist students in understanding the four aspects of every emotion:

1. Phenomenological—how the emotion feels.
2. Social Expression—how we communicate our goals and upset to others.
3. Physiological Arousal—biological response.
4. Behavioral Predisposition—emotions are often important cues that we must act on problems. They may lead to behavior coping strategies that may be adaptive or dysfunctional in nature.

In addition to helping students become aware of their emotional experiences and develop an emotional vocabulary, REBT groups also focus on teaching students that irrational beliefs are what lead to these dysfunctional, disturbed emotions. Using the Happening-Thinking-Feeling-Reaction/Behavior framework, students are taught the differences between irrational beliefs and the more rational, healthy cognitions that may lead to negative emotions, but ones that are more functional in nature. However, before one begins a REBT group, or any group for that matter, there are a few things that we believe warrant consideration.

General Guidelines for Forming REBT Groups

The screening and selection of individuals to participate in the group is a very important aspect of group therapy, especially in REBT, which utilizes focal groups with very specific goals. Elkin (1983) provides some important guidelines for group formation that we have expanded upon below. We suggest that the group leader hold a preliminary session with potential members either prior to the start of the group (in the case of a closed group) or before a new person joins the group (in the case of an open group). The main goal of this preliminary session is to determine whether the goals of the potential member are consistent with group goals. This preliminary meeting also provides an opportunity for the potential student to interview the group leader. At this time, potential group members can ask questions that may help them decide if they want to join the group. When screening for a group of children or adolescents, it is important to involve both parents and children in the initial meeting. As with adults, this preliminary meeting with parents and children should discuss confidentiality, the goals of both the child or adolescent and the group, and answer any questions that may arise.

Prior to holding a preliminary session, leaders should be sure that potential members do not meet the exclusionary criteria of the group. The exclusionary criteria of any group are entirely dependent upon the group, its leaders, and its goals. REBT groups often have exclusionary criteria that may be more stringent than other groups. First, leaders may wish to rule out potential members who are psychotic, suicidal, brain damaged, or sociopathic. In addition, students who are uncommunicative or silent may be excluded from groups, as neither they, nor other students will benefit from their participation (or the lack thereof). At the same time, students with some of the more extreme external disorders (conduct disorder, oppositional defiant disorder) may be excluded as well. An important exclusionary criterion specific to REBT groups is unwillingness to do group assignments or therapy homework. Group assignments are a central aspect of REBT groups and individuals who are not willing to participate in this aspect of the group would generally benefit more from an alternate approach.

Potential group members must also meet the inclusionary criteria, which, like the exclusionary criteria, are dependent on the specific goals of the group. In order to be included in an REBT group, potential members are informed of the general REBT framework, to ensure that this is something in which they wish to participate. Since these are essential components of REBT, potential members agree to work on assignments and actively participate in all aspects of the group, especially disputing their own and other members' irrational beliefs. What's more, it is essential that students have very specific goals they want to work on during the group. We find that the ability to set goals is easier done with adolescents than with younger children. Younger children are often told what their goals are by others and may expect that to continue to be the case in therapy.

Inclusionary criteria can become extremely specific for some groups. In a closed group, for example, it is important that members agree to attend all sessions. Furthermore, a group addressing social anxiety will screen for students with some level of fear toward interacting with others and would probably exclude a person who is very comfortable socially and the next candidate for Mr. Popular in the yearbook.

In a REBT group, the initial meeting also provides an opportunity for the leader to familiarize potential group members with the REBT model. Leaders should provide a brief history of REBT and a synopsis of the REBT techniques that will be used in the group. This helps to ensure that members come to the initial group session informed, prepared and ready to work. In addition, the preliminary session is an optimal time to inform potential students of any ground rules that may exist in the group. For example, the group leader may have specific rules about attendance, socializing outside the group, etc. All potential members are to agree to abide by these rules prior to joining the group. It may also be helpful to provide students with a written list of the rules, or even have them sign a contract in which they agree to abide by the rules. See Appendix B for an example of a group contract.

The preliminary meeting also provides the group leader with the opportunity to discuss and reinforce the important issue of confidentiality. Leaders are to inform potential group members of their rights regarding confidentiality as well as the limits of confidentiality, including the circumstances in which clinicians become mandated reporters. In addition, it is important that all potential members be reminded that they are responsible for assuring that all information revealed by fellow students remains confidential. Unfortunately, given the social nature of a school, our impression is that confidential issues are not always kept secure with students when groups are run in a school setting. Given that the group members regularly see and interact with one another throughout the school day affords more opportunities for confidential issues to be expressed. When this occurs, we recommend that it is addressed both with the student individually and in the group, and we suggest that it provides an additional opportunity for review of the rules of confidentiality. It is also at this time that the decision to allow a student to remain in the group following this breach of confidentiality is discussed.

Some other issues that must be decided before beginning the group include the time, dates, and location of group meetings and the group size. While these decisions will vary dependent upon setting, typically we have found that groups of younger students (up to age seven) should have no more than 4 to 5 members, while groups of older students (over age eight) should have a 7 to 8 member maximum. Groups held in school should not be during major academic areas nor should they compete with other school related activities that students find desirable (i.e., gym class). Creative ideas are also helpful, for example, Flanagan et al. (1998) held their group during a lunch period and provided popcorn. It is also important that the leader determines in advance what methods will be used for data collection to evaluate change and administers all pre-test measures.

In addition, the group leader must determine the group type: open or closed. In an open group, students can join anytime there is space in the group. An open group can run for as long as the leader is willing to hold it and there are sufficient members. This method has the advantage of allowing students to stay until they have attained their goals. However, this potentially never-ending group can become expensive when not done in a school setting which may deter some potential members (Corey et al., 1992). Another disadvantage of this method is what Corey, et al., (1992) refer to as the, "cozy-nest syndrome," in which students are, "always 'working' and perhaps never changing." (p. 35). Closed groups have a set number of sessions and all members begin and finish together. The obvious disadvantage of a closed group is that the group will end whether or not the student has reached his or her goals. However, this can also act as an advantage in that the knowledge that the group will end at a set time may be a source of motivation to begin actively making changes (Corey et al., 1992). Another advantage of closed groups is that they are more cost effective than groups lasting for over a year.

Types of REBT Groups for Children and Adolescents

REBT has been applied to many different types of groups, both short-term as well as long-term (e.g., Elkin, 1983). Where REBT groups with children and adolescents may differ from REBT groups with adults is the fact that with adult REBT groups, the goal may be to provide individual therapy within a group setting with several members talking to one member, disputing, etc. While this can and does occur in child and adolescent groups, they appear to involve more group tasks with less boundaries/structure than those that exist in the adult groups. That is, we tend to do more group experiential exercises focusing on interaction and development of healthy thinking and appropriate behaviors in child groups as compared to adults groups.

REBT groups for children and adolescents may be viewed as both content and process focused. That is, group leaders are concerned with the content in order to successfully teach students more effective means of thinking, feeling and behaving. However, REBT groups are also process-oriented in that many of the in-group exercises will ask students to address how they are feeling and thinking at that moment. Identification of these thoughts will also assist in generating alternative views and accompanying adaptive emotions and behaviors.

Smead (1995) discussed three different types of groups for children and adolescents. Even though they were not formally designed as groups through which to run REBT, we believe that REBT can potentially play an important role in these group typologies in facilitating emotional and behavioral change. As such, we will briefly discuss these below.

Counseling/Therapy Groups

Here, the focus is on behavioral and emotional change. Groups can deal with general, wide-range problems or can be geared towards specific issues: divorce, relationship issues, grief. These are the groups that we believe REBT is most closely associated with and they may assist students in developing better coping strategies and a healthier way of looking at the world. The more general groups may be for students who are just having a difficult time on a fairly regular basis, while in the issue driven groups, students are aware of the content focus of the groups. General groups are often helpful, as students get to hear peers work through an area of difficulty (e.g., college selection) that may not currently be an issue for them, but may become one in the future, at which point they will hopefully be able to recall the effective solutions of their peers. Content specific groups are helpful because students hear and help others who are at varying stages of distress when exposed to similar environmental stressors. They help students see that they are not alone, they are not the only ones experiencing difficulty, and it normalizes their affective experiences and may provide a resource for support outside the structure of the group.

Task Groups

Task work groups strive towards a specific goal that is not necessarily emotional in nature, but may be more of the academic/achievement sort. These tasks may be specific group tasks (e.g., create a violence prevention program), or all members of the group may be working towards the same task (e.g., SAT preparation). While this type of group is more practical in nature, we also focus on the emotional components that may interfere with working towards the task. REBT may assist in helping clarify which goal(s) to work on (e.g., college selection) and identifying potential practical and cognitive/emotive blocks ("it's too difficult") to goal attainment. We have found that these groups work better if they have a clear objective and a limited time frame in which to achieve that objective. At the beginning of these groups, group leaders may serve as a facilitator in helping the group clearly identify and define the goal, identify the irrational beliefs that lead to self-defeating, goal impeding extreme negative emotions and behaviors, restructure irrational to rational beliefs, and brainstorm effective strategies to meet this goal. At times, students may wish to select strategies that are impractical in nature and the REBT group leader may help them examine all potential solutions and evaluate which ones have the highest degree of success, are practical, and are acceptable to the group philosophically. This last point we believe is important as the REBT group leader will work to make sure the tasks chosen have a high degree of acceptability on the part of the group members, as low acceptability will lead to low effort towards goal attainment. After selecting an intervention, task groups will assign specific tasks to individual members of the group.

Much REBT group work has students engage in "risk taking" or "shame attacking" exercises, often done to help socially anxious students overcome their need for approval. In task oriented groups, we encourage students to go "out of their comfort zone." While not necessarily the goal of the task oriented groups, this is consistent with other aspects of REBT. Students are encouraged to select a task they are not necessarily comfortable with, which helps promote risk-taking. At the same time, we do not have group members select tasks that have a low probability for success. Given that these may be a group task (i.e., one task for all members to achieve), we try to assist students in achieving the task. If groups, either as a whole or individually, fail to achieve the selected goal, the REBT clinician will use this as an opportunity to discuss feelings and cognitions, differentiating between healthy and unhealthy responses to the lack of goal attainment. That is, working towards more self-acceptance and avoiding self-defeating beliefs. If an individual is allowed to select a task that they may not be particularly well suited for, this may lead them or the group to blame the individual for the failure to achieve the goal. While this may be true and could be used for further discussion about managing disappointment, if the goal of the group is to successfully complete a task (e.g., develop a conflict resolution forum), the group leader will help the group work towards that goal, while continuing to educate group members about the core concepts of REBT.

Psycho-education/Guidance Groups

These groups work with "at-risk" populations. This may involve students who are at risk for a number of potential disorders and may take on less of an academic focus as Task Groups. This could include dealing with students who are at risk for eating disorders, drug and alcohol abuse, or may possibly involve AIDS education. In some settings, these may be students who have shown some of the early warning signs of developing a disorder but may not be eligible for formal services at this point. In these groups, REBT assists students in overcoming faulty thinking that may put these students at risk, developing frustration tolerance, and in increasing their ability to engage in consequential thinking. Education is a major part of these groups and the REBT clinician can better serve these groups if they have a good balance of knowledge of the theory of REBT along with knowledge about the specific area that students need guidance in. Additional work can be done with families to reduce the exposure to factors that may elicit risk-taking behavior. As an example, for students who are at risk for drug and alcohol abuse, these groups may focus on helping students learn how to express their feelings, develop effective coping skills to resist peer pressure and learn strategies on how to interact more effectively with others. At the same time, children and families will also receive comprehensive information on drugs and alcohol and learn about the dangers associated with them. In family based sessions, these programs may involve parent training, family skills training, and family self-help groups to learn how to reinforce the lessons at home.

Developing a Therapeutic/Working Relationship with Children and Adolescents in Groups

We have found that the greatest challenge facing clinicians working with children and adolescents in groups is to establish the therapeutic alliance. The three main components of the therapeutic alliance are: (1) agreement on the goals of therapy; (2) agreement on the tasks of therapy; and (3) the relationship bond. Despite the importance paid to the topic of the therapeutic alliance (also referred to as the working relationship) with children, very few empirical studies on the topic exist. Unfortunately, while we have a rich, voluminous literature on the therapeutic alliance with adults, we currently know much less about this topic with children.

What is exceedingly clear about developing the therapeutic alliance is that it is a far more difficult task when attempted with children and adolescents than when done with adults, and may be even more difficult in a group setting. DiGiuseppe, Linscott, and Jilton (1996) have identified the two main barriers to forming the therapeutic alliance with children and adolescents: (1) most children and adolescents are mandated to therapy; and (2) children and adolescents usually enter therapy in a pre-contemplative stage.

Elkin (1983) describes how difficult it may be for the clinician to keep members interested in the group. The level of motivation for change of children and adolescent in REBT group therapy is seen as an important moderator of treatment effectiveness. Most children and adolescents entering therapy do so against their own will as they are usually brought into therapy because they present with externalizing problems that are disturbing others (peers, teachers, family). For this reason, they generally do not believe they have a problem, do not wish to change, and may be completely unmotivated for treatment. This presents a major obstacle to the process of establishing therapeutic goals with children and adolescents, which is the first aspect of developing the therapeutic alliance (DiGiuseppe et al., 1996).

DiGiuseppe et al. (1996) have developed a cognitive-behavioral approach towards motivating children/adolescents to change based on the work of Prochaska and DiClemente (1988; as cited in DiGiuseppe et al., 1996). We believe that their approach has important implications when working with children and adolescents in group therapy as well. The approach utilizes a Stages of Change Model, which lists the five stages of change a person goes through as (1) pre-contemplative; (2) contemplative; (3) preparation; (4) action; and (5) maintenance. Students in the pre-contemplative stage have no intention of changing and usually do not recognize the issue at hand as problematic. Once the student reaches the contemplative stage, he or she is beginning to perceive a problem and may be seeking help. Then, during the preparation stage, the student intends to make some immediate steps toward change and has often already begun to do so. By the time the student reaches the action stage, change has occurred. Finally, in the maintenance stage the student is working toward sustaining the changes that have been attained. In an on-going group format, you will have students at varying stages of change who may be able to provide insight for their peers as to how change will benefit them.

Most people entering therapy have reached at least the contemplative stage, while, as was mentioned earlier, children and adolescents, like other mandated patients, enter the group at the pre-contemplative stage and, therefore, do not perceive any problems. This is especially problematic in a group setting, as groups rely on active participation of members.

Although most approaches to establishing the therapeutic alliance focus on the development of the relationship bond between the therapist and client, cognitive-behavior approaches stress the importance of discussing goals with young clients in an open and frank manner. It is important that therapists seek to understand how the children and adolescents feel about these goals and target behaviors. This is a crucial step when working with children especially considering that these goals are almost always set by others and are likely to be different from, or even completely contradictory to, the child or adolescent's own internal goals. According to DiGiuseppe, et al. (1996) Jilton, "helping the children to explore the consequences of their behaviors and emotions and alternative ways of feeling and behaving, can help formulate the goals of therapy," (1996, p. 90). This can be an important step toward bringing children and adolescents from the pre-contemplative stage into the contemplative stage. In a group setting, this provides a unique interactive opportunity for other group members, as they may be able to point out consequences that the child or the therapist may not have been able to identify.

When working with children and adolescents, it is also important to recognize that age and developmental level can affect which aspects of the therapeutic alliance will be most important (DiGiuseppe et al., 1996). Agreement on the goals is likely to be most important with adolescents. However, establishing the therapeutic bond is more important in groups of young children (DiGiuseppe et al., 1996). Therefore, when working in groups of children it is often helpful to begin and end the group with an engaging task or game. Wilde (1992) suggests trying the following techniques: (1) each child writes something describing himself/herself, then the leader reads the descriptions and the children have to guess which belongs with whom; (2) play Simon Says with the group leader as Simon; (3) each child names his/her favorite song, movie, sport, etc., and explains why they like it; and (4) the child describes his/her feeling metaphorically like the weather. These are just some of the techniques that can be used to help establish the bond between the child and both other children in the group and the group leader.

Assessment in REBT Child and Adolescent Groups

We propose that assessment should be an on-going part of the group therapy experience; that is, before, during, and after treatment. Involvement of data collection at multiple data points increases the responsiveness of the intervention to meet the needs of the students, assesses effectiveness of intervention, and examines the stability over time and situations. As the group leader may alter the course of the group content to meet the focus of the group, we recommend that assessment should also be catered in consideration of the developmental level of the child to be able to assist in treatment modifications as well as to allow the clinician to evaluate therapeutic change. We will briefly discuss some recommendations for standardized mental health batteries that we have found useful in working with children and adolescents, followed by more specific recommendations for REBT groups.

Standardized Batteries for Assessment

A review of all evaluation measures that may be beneficial for children and adolescents in group therapy is beyond the scope of this chapter. However, we would suggest that for general problem groups, the group leader consider a broad based measure, like the BASC-2 (Reynolds and Kamphaus, 2004) or the CBCL (Achenbach and Rescorla, 2001), while for more of the content specific groups, the group leader consider a measure that addresses the content of that group (e.g., the CDI [Kovacs, 1992] for Depression or the Revised Fear Survey Schedule for Children [Ollendick, 1983] for childhood anxiety).

Given that group therapy takes place with and fosters interactions with peers, we believe that it is important to know how a child understands the social expectations for their behavior as well as others. Literature on children's social goals has demonstrated that children who are "liked" report prosocial, effective, relationship-enhancing strategies and friendly goals, while rejected children have a tendency towards more aggressive and unfriendly strategies (Crick and Ladd, 1990). As such, we recommend a measure that assesses social perspective taking, such as the Self-Perceptions Inventory (SPI) (Soares and Soares, 1999), which describes the current affective dimension of children and adults primarily in regard to themselves and their relationships with others (Plake et al., 2003).

An area of recent exploration with regards to children and adolescents is the concept of emotional intelligence (EQ), as children with high EQ are believed to be better able to regulate their emotional distress and handle adversity more effectively. This is a concept that we believe is key to REBT work with children and adolescents and may be something that a clinician wishes to assess in an REBT group. The Bar-On Emotional Quotient Inventory: Youth Version (EQ-I:YV) (Bar-On and Parker, 2000) has a long version (60 items) and short version (30 items) self-report instrument that measures EQ in ages 7 through 18, yielding an overall EQ score which is subdivided into scores on four domains: Intrapersonal, Interpersonal, Stress Management, and Adaptability.

Finally, it is very important to assess students' irrational thinking. More specifically, this allows us to evaluate how effective the REBT component is with regards to changing unhelpful thinking, while also serving to assist in group treatment direction. With regards to irrational thinking in children and adolescents we recommend the Child and Adolescent Scale of Irrationality (CASI) (Bernard and Cronan, 1999). The CASI is a self-report measure of irrational beliefs of children and adolescents, which yields scores on six scales, including self-downing, dependence, conformity, demandingness, low frustration tolerance, and discomfort anxiety, in addition to a total irrationality score. The sample utilized in the standardization of the CASI consisted of 567 children and adolescents grades 4–11 and ages 10 through 17, and the authors report good internal reliability for the revised edition of the CASI.

General Cognitive Behavioral Assessment Guidelines

Developmentally younger children may have difficulty in problem identification, emotional labeling, and introspection and require a slower pace, experiential exercises, and games to enhance assessment. That is why assessment in groups with children and adolescents is on-going in nature, allowing the clinician to gear assessment towards a student's current emotive, cognitive, and behavioral functioning. Asking students to recall events that occurred subsequent to the last session may be difficult. A relatively simple approach to collecting data about events occurred that has a greater likelihood of being accurate, is to have students complete an "emotion log" (see Appendix C). Another factor to consider in assessment is whether or not the students' behavior is manipulative in nature. That is, do students engage in these behaviors to change something in their environment (parent/teacher behavior) or do they perform these behaviors for endogenous reasons, be they biological or cognitive in nature? These logs (and the consequences received for behavior) may help in understanding this.

Prior to intervention, we have found that assessing problem-solving skills and deficiencies is important given that the solutions often selected by children and adolescents are poor. The REBT group therapist may want to determine whether the student knows effective ways of behaving but due to their irrationality they do not behave appropriately, or have they not learned alternative problem solving options. The direction you take clinically may vary dependent upon whether or not you need to teach emotional along with practical problem skills.

Later on in the group process, the group leader may utilize group exercises (discussed below) to assess whether or not a student has learned more effective, healthy ways of thinking and behaving. A rational role play in the group setting may be a way to assess the students' overt behavior as well as to determine whether they are able to think and therefore behave more rationally in this role play.

Core Content in REBT Groups with Children and Adolescents

As indicated earlier, the focus of the REBT group when working with children and adolescents may vary as a function of the developmental level of the students that comprise the group, the objectives of the group, and the presenting problems of the group members. What follows below are some general areas that we have found are helpful for a group leader to consider when running groups as well as some group exercises and strategies that the group leader may wish to incorporate.

Obviously, the group leader would benefit from having a strong conceptual understanding of REBT and its techniques utilized as a mechanism of change. With student beliefs at the core of this group change process, the group leader may wish to distinguish between irrational evaluations and appraisals of misinterpretations (inferences, absolutes, evaluations). Depending upon the developmental level of the child, REBT practitioners could target for change: the distorted interpretations of reality ("They'll never like me"), the absolute ("I need friends to like me all the time") or evaluative beliefs ("It's awful that they don't like me"). Conceptually, these three cognitions are very different and the group process allows for the leader and the group members to effectively target one or all types of beliefs systems.

The distorted interpretations of reality (incorrect conclusions/predictions) are an example of a point in the therapeutic process where group therapy may be more effective in treating these beliefs than individual treatment. Peers are a great source of data collection and feedback and may help provide evidence that contradicts the belief. With regards to the challenging of absolutes and derivative evaluative assumptions, group therapy can be very helpful in that peers who share common absolutes and irrational evaluations can be helped by their peers to see that they are not alone in this experience. Often, hearing these evaluative beliefs come out of the mouth of peers may help them see how faulty/unhelpful that way of thinking truly is. In addition, the group therapy approach may expose children to peers who have successfully changed different types of cognitions and as such they may be able to benefit from this model.

We encourage the group leader to discuss the relationship of emotions, cognitions, and behavior early on in the group therapy process. We believe this is a key to facilitating change, as we have yet to encounter a child who enters group looking to "change their faulty thinking." They come, as stated earlier, because they have a problem (emotional or behavioral) or are perceived as having a problem by another, not to change cognitions. Therefore, we believe it is key for the group leader to demonstrate the role of cognition in emotion and that other options are available to students in terms of how we feel and behave.

Early on in the group, we present the idea that extreme negative emotions (such as high degrees of anger, anxiety, depression) interfere with overall healthy functioning and can transform reasonable students into those who say and do things they would rather not and develop problems at school, at home, or with friends. We might facilitate this conversation by asking group members to recall the last time they made a bad decision. We then will ask them what they were thinking and feeling when they made that decision and whether they ever let what they felt, emotionally, make the decision for them. We have found that students are pretty good at recalling bad decisions and once one student is able to identify the role their affect played in this decision it opens the doors for their peers. We have also used video examples ("The Simpsons", "Spiderman") to help show how people may make bad decisions when they are extremely upset. We emphasize that stress, anxiety, anger, and depression interfere with their ability to make smart choices and may cloud some options, making their capacity to choose the best option unlikely. We help students see that while extreme negative emotions are normal, they are undesirable.

Early on in the group process, we point out the distinction between non-hurtful and hurtful emotions. Non-hurtful emotions involve students dealing with difficult situations when they are annoyed, irritated, or aggravated. These students are able to problem solve and manage things effectively in difficult situations. Whereas hurtful emotions involve escalating conflict, name calling, and a number of emotional (anger, depression, anxiety) and behavioral (avoidance, aggression) manifestations. As most children are aware of it, we will often use the television show "Star Trek" as an example of the continuum of emotions that one may experience. On the one hand you have Captain Kirk who makes very impulsive, emotionally charged decisions, while at the other end of the continuum, you have Mr. Spock, whose species (Vulcans), are highly logical and do not experience or express emotions. We make sure to highlight that neither approach is better, as it is expected that students will "feel" something when adversity occurs, we just work on helping them experience more of the healthy, appropriate negative emotions. We try never to give the impression that feeling bad is abnormal nor bad.

Doyle (2003) offers some suggested exercises for group settings that we think are excellent in general and that have specific applications to the REBT group therapy process with children and adolescents. We have highlighted a few below.

- **Introduction Exercises:** Have students finish the sentence, "One thing I'm hoping to gain from this group is . . . ." We have found that this is helpful in terms of goal setting and it also allows children and adolescents to hear what their peers are looking to work towards and may serve to further allow other group members to help them in the group process.
- **Comprehensive Self-Inventory:** Have each student use paper and pencil to assess their strengths and weaknesses; have them start on the weaknesses which they think might be remediable. With younger students you may have them draw pictures. This approach again helps with increasing insight into their problem as well as helping with goal selection.
- **Expectations/Fears:** Each student is asked to report his/her expectations and fears about participating in the group. We find this to be particularly helpful when working with children and adolescents, as it helps normalize cognitions they may be experiencing and may also allow for clarification of misperceptions of the group process that they may have. We also see this as

a way of further clarifying specific rules of the group therapy process that are often concerns of students (e.g., confidentiality).

- **Best and Worst Day:** Here, group members are asked to draw a composite of their best and worst day in the past month or so and share these with the group. The group leader facilitates a conversation about what kinds of experiences make a "good" day and what are the common ingredients in a "bad" day. The group leader may help in looking for patterns of thinking that may differentiate between the two.
- **Learning from Mistakes:** Students are asked to think of a situation that they believe they did not handle particularly well. More specifically they are asked to close their eyes and try and recall the feelings and thoughts that they had at the time. They are then asked to write them down and share them with the group and allow the group to help them identify any thought distortions. The group leader may have them discuss what they would have liked to have happened and have the group develop a list of rational beliefs and coping statements that might have been helpful.
- **Strongest Hour:** This we usually try to do right after the Learning from Mistakes exercise. In this exercise, students are asked to recall a time when they relied primarily on themselves to deal with a difficult situation. We ask them to bring the situation clearly to mind by recalling the details (the setting, the people involved, the time and place, the things said, etc.,). We help them experience both satisfaction and pride about their successful handling of themselves in the situation. This may work particularly well for students with Low Frustration Tolerance, as they may see that they can handle adversity and things are not too difficult. We ask them to recall what they told themselves during that situation and discuss how they can increase the likelihood of thinking and behaving that way again in the future. This is a very powerful exercise for child and adolescent groups as peers hear of the success of their colleagues, which may serve to motivate them.
- **Dear Dr. Rational:** Each student writes a brief letter about one of their problems, as though they were writing to Oprah or Dr. Phil (the Dear Abby reference gets lost on the youth of today). These letters are then passed around the room and each person answers someone else's letter in writing. We encourage that they help each other come up with a practical solution as well as a solution that utilizes the rational thinking they have been developing.
- **Evidence Against IBs:** In this exercise for older students, on one side of an index card we have students write down their irrational beliefs, while on the other side, they write five negative things that have happened to them because they think this way. Students are then encouraged to read the card several times a week to remind them of how that belief is not working for them.
- **Anonymous Disputing:** This exercise occurs with students who possess a good understanding of the REBT framework, and most specifically of disputation. Students are asked to write down their irrational beliefs and pass them forward on a piece of paper to the group leader. The group leader

reads them aloud and the group as a whole provides challenges or disputes for them. We have modified this at points to use a small ball as a "hot potato" exercise, in which group members throw the ball to their peers to try and involve all in the art of disputation.

- **Shame-Attacking:** This is one of the more well known of the REBT techniques and involves having individuals do something or tell the group to do something which they would normally never do (typically for fear of others' negative reactions). We have found the group format to be an excellent forum for this in that peers support one another and also do not let each other "off the hook" for non-completion of the exercise.
- **Round of Applause:** Have students applaud something or someone they are grateful for. We have used this exercise at the beginning and the end of the group, around holidays (Thanksgiving or New Year's resolution) and have found this to be a very fun and enjoyable exercise. The group leader leads standing ovations, whistles, cheering for positive things/people, and helps refocus the group members on positive things in their lives, which is contrary to what the focus is of many therapy groups. We actively reinforce group participants.
- **Positive Talk:** Usually done in conjunction with the round of applause and it often serves the same purpose. Each student is asked to talk positively about themselves for a full 2 minutes. (If they qualify or modify what they say, they get a penalty of an additional 30 seconds).
- **Role-Play:** Group members are asked to think of upcoming situations that they are apprehensive about (e.g., exam, social event) and act them out with other group members. Students can use this opportunity to provide feedback on behavior of their peers as well as offer hypotheses as to what they are experiencing cognitively.
- **Reverse Role-Play:** This exercise is usually done after group members are familiar with one another. In this exercise, one group member takes another's irrational beliefs and holds onto them rigidly and forcefully. The student who's IB it is has to try and talk the role-player out of the firmly held belief. This reinforces vigorous disputing for the individual and may further provide a model for their peers.
- **Hotseat:** One at a time, group members take the "seat" and as many participants as want to give feedback (both positive and negative), while the student remains silent. This helps students to learn to accept feedback from others and then as a group we process how the student felt and the validity of some of this feedback.

Parenting and REBT Groups

Although two other chapters in this book deal with parents, we thought that it would be appropriate to address a few specific aspects of REBT parenting groups. REBT practitioners appear to recognize that "disturbed" parenting styles can produce problems in relatively "normal" children (Bernard, 1986; Bernard and Joyce, 1991). Often, an effective means of parent training can take place in a group format. Group sessions are used for more didactic teaching of the rationale and components of specific child-management skills, to be practiced at home between sessions.

The rationale for REBT based parent training group interventions includes: giving parents a source of support and a reference group through which they may see that they are not alone; providing knowledge and information regarding parental management strategies; and having parents become familiar with the REBT model and the role that cognitions and affect can play in parenting. We have found that training techniques that are mainly behavioral in nature, while they do have an impact upon behavior and disciplinary problems in parent-child interaction, do not change parenting attitudes, beliefs, and emotions. The REBT parent training groups emphasize both affective/cognitive and behavioral/disciplinary domains.

Beavers and Hampson (1990) report that group parent training may have led to a significant enrollment of people who would probably not be seen in clinics or in individual therapy. Although parents may become defensive if weaknesses are pointed out in front of others, the goal of a parent training group is education not embarrassment. For many of these clients, "education" and training" become acceptable descriptors of skill enhancement, since they do not "need" counseling or therapy. Wright, Stroud, and Keenan (1993) reported that group parent-training is more cost effective than individual and described essentially equal gains with both group and individual parent training (Brightman et al., 1982).

Furthermore, Bernard (1986) proposed that overly permissive child-rearing practices are based on a number of unfounded assumptions ("children should never be frustrated"; "I must always be loved and approved of by my child") and that they may lead to self-centered, demanding, easily frustrated children, with low self-esteem. Additionally, parents who are overly rigid, accusing, and unaffectionate hold a collection of faulty ideas ("Children should not disagree with their parents"; "Praise spoils a child"; "Children must do well and behave correctly all the time") which can lead to their children becoming anxious, tense, guilty, and depressed (Bernard, 1986).

REBT theorists (e.g., Ellis et al., 1966) have for many years described how certain parenting styles, along with parental emotions, hinder the children's development. Bernard and Joyce (1991) argued that child psychopathology results from an interaction of child temperament with parenting style and, in particular, that adaptive development occurs because of a good match between the parents' child raising approach and the child's temperament.

We would like to highlight two examples of research performed in a group format regarding parenting. Greaves (1996) investigated the effect of Rational-Emotive Parent Education on the stress of mothers of young children with Down syndrome. Greaves compared an REBT methodology with an Applied

Behavioral Analysis group and a control condition. The REBT condition reported a significant reduction in level of stress in comparison with the control and with the Applied Behavior Analysis condition in the Greaves (1996) study.

Terjesen (1998) compared the efficacy of a combined Rational-Emotive Behavior Therapy (REBT) and Behavior Management (BM) approach (REBT/BM) with a BM approach in reducing parent stress and increasing child compliance with thirty parents of children receiving special education services. Parental stress, parental emotional functioning, and child behavior were evaluated at onset and completion of 4 weekly group treatment sessions of 90 minutes each, and again at a 4-week follow-up for all three groups. Support was generated for the usefulness of REBT in a comparison with no treatment on all dependent measures at posttest and on all measures with the exception of child compliance at follow-up. While the results did not provide support for the REBT group intervention being more effective than the BM intervention in terms of child compliance and parent emotional functioning, the combined group (REBT/BM) reported higher life satisfaction at follow-up than BM. Given that behavior management groups are the highest standard or barometer for group parent training that we currently have, the fact that REBT stood up to this standard provides some support for its further use and investigation. For an example of the REBT group format used by Terjesen (1998), see Appendix D.

REBT Group Research with Children and Adolescents

Ford (2005) conducted a meta-analysis of 25 studies using group REBT with children and adolescents. The studies analyzed used REBT in the treatment of various disorders including anxiety, adjustment disorder, and learning disabilities, as well as in the normal population to help improve areas including self-esteem, study skills, and school discipline. Preliminary results of this meta-analysis found a moderate effect size of 0.59 in REBT group treatment of children and adolescents with anxiety. Furthermore, an effect size of 0.63 revealed that REBT group treatment was significantly more effective than a control group in treating anxiety. However, these effects are lower than those observed in adults (Ford, 2004).

A meta-analysis of REBT group therapy studies with children and adolescents conducted by Ford (2004) revealed a mean effect size of 1.12 across the REBT group therapy treatments as compared to a mean effect size of 0.81 across the REBT individual therapy treatments, indicating that although both methods were effective, group therapy led to greater gains.

In addition, it has been demonstrated that REBT and CBT approaches are effective methods when used in groups of children and adolescents. For example, Kachman and Mazer (1990) studied the use of a group Rational-Emotive Education (REE) program in a sample of normal eleventh and twelfth grade students. The results of this study indicated that the REE group experienced greater increases in academic effort, grades, and use of constructive defense mechanisms than the control group.

In a study of group CBT with African-American seventh and eighth grade students, Sapp et al. (1995) demonstrated that CBT effectively reduced the number of days tardy, and number of absences, and increased grade point average in students identified as being academically at risk.

Furthermore, a study by Shannon and Allen (1998) indicated that group CBT is more effective than attention control at improving the math grades of African-American high school students enrolled in Upward Bound, a program aimed at increasing college enrollment of high-school students from low-income families.

Together these results provide significant evidence in support of the use of REBT and CBT in group treatment of children and adolescents across multiple disorders and presenting problems. Further research is needed to allow group leaders to understand specifically what it is about the REBT group therapy process that leads to change in working with children and adolescents. Clearly, written treatment manuals that lend themselves to research replicability and that have high practical utility with group leaders are further warranted. As a whole, REBT as a therapeutic approach works well with children and adolescents, and it is hopeful that we will continue to see further applications of REBT group therapy techniques with varied populations of children and adolescents.

Appendix A: REBT Study Group

Lecture One Outline

- Introduction of self and *goals of workshop series*
- Have students complete attached questionnaire. Discuss what they wrote. This should take up the most time.
- Explain rationale behind surveys. INSURE CONFIDENTIALITY!
- Go around the room, have students introduce themselves and discuss areas in which they are **experiencing difficulty** in school work, write these on a board/flip chart and try to categorize them.

Didactic/Interactive Discussion

Using the lecture notes below, lecturer is to discuss the importance of studying. Brainstorm this with them:

WHY SHOULD I STUDY?

Because studying can help you achieve your goals. The more you know the more you can do. Good study skills can help you succeed:

In School. Learning how to study can make you a better student.

In the Future: Many skills that make you a success in school can also help you succeed on the job.

The goal of the first lecture is not to get students into some of the specifics of REBT, but more to demonstrate the role of attitude towards studying and how these attitudes can and do affect how we prepare and how we perform.

- **Negative emotions** (such as stress, anger, anxiety) interfere with studying behavior. Brainstorm examples that they can think of when they get frustrated while preparing for an exam/paper or while taking a test.
- **Additional Stressors:** Sometimes we may experience emotions from a multitude of other stressors in daily life-family, friends, etc and regrettably, these can spill over into the other role of student.

Bad Thoughts Can Interfere with Overall Study behavior:

- Discuss thoughts that they may have and how these can and do interfere with their study preparation.

EXAMPLES:

1. I **MUST** do well or very well, at all times!
2. "Stupid is as Stupid does."When I act weakly or stupidly that makes me a bad, worthless, stupid person.
3. **I CAN'T STAND IT** when people are not fair.
4. **I CAN'T STAND** really tough tests.
5. **It's TERRIBLE and AWFUL** if I fail a test or do poorly.

Nonhurtful vs. Hurtful Thinking

- Nonhurtful thoughts involve approaching tests and studying in a healthy manner that helps students prepare EVEN IF THEY DON'T LIKE STUDYING.
- Hurtful thoughts lead to avoidance, procrastination, failure, etc. This often can cause long-term difficulty to the student.

Discuss Benefits of Working On Your Own Thoughts.

Appendix B: Pre-Group Contract for an REBT Group with Students

- I agree to attend all group sessions. If I will miss a group session, I will discuss this with the group leader in advance.
- I agree to actively participate in all group sessions and activities.

- I agree to actively work toward reaching my goals.
- I agree to complete all group assignments.
- I agree to be honest at all times in the group, both with myself and with other group members.
- I promise that I will not be physically or verbally abusive to either the group leader or other students in this group.
- *Confidentiality*: I agree to respect the privacy of all other students in this group. I promise not to discuss anything said or done in this group, except during group sessions. I understand that this applies even to talking to other group members when outside the group. The rules of confidentiality have been explained to me, and I understand and accept these rules.

I ______ (Print Name) have carefully read all the above rules about joining this group. I understand these rules, including confidentiality; I promise to follow them, and I accept that there will be serious consequences if I break any of these rules.

____

Signature

Appendix C

Emotion Log

Student Name: ______________________ Date: ______

Date	Time	Activating Event	Beliefs	Emotion	Intensity (1–10)	Duration	Action
June 12	12:00	Parents said "no" to sleep-over	"It's Not fair"; "I should be allowed to go"	Angry	8	45 minutes	After yelling, I went and watched TV, did e-mail, and played with my older brother

Appendix D

REBT Parenting Lecture One Outline

- Introduction of self and *goals of workshop series*
- Have parents honestly **complete questionnaires** and answer questions individually
- Go around room, have parents introduce themselves and discuss the areas in which they are **experiencing difficulty** as parents. Write these on a board and try to categorize them into internal stressors, external stressors, and child behavioral difficulties
- Have parents **complete goal-setting sheet (Handout 1)**

Didactic/Interactive Discussion

Using the lecture notes below, lecturer is to discuss the relationship of emotions to behavior management and is to regularly be a facilitator in involving parents in the discussion. The goal of the first lecture is not to get parents into some of the specifics of REBT, but more to demonstrate the role of cognition in emotion and how there are other options in how we feel and behave.

- **Negative parental emotions** (such as anger, anxiety, depression) interfere with any type of behavioral strategies and can transform the most reasonable caring parent among us into harsh parents whom may say things they would rather they didn't, and develop gaps between us and our children.
- **Preparation for parenthood** is often poor, and especially for parental emotions. More so, we typically will get feedback in feeding, dressing, and behavioral issues but never much training in working on our emotions.
- **Additional Stressors:** Sometimes we may experience emotions from a multitude of other stressors in daily life-work, marital concerns, financial concerns, and regrettably, these can spill over into our parenting role.
- **Developing Rules for Children:** Imparting personal, familial and societal rules onto our children is crucial to parenting, almost as crucial as understanding that no matter how explicit and clear our rules may be, children will march to their own tune. This breaking of rules should be understood, yet oftentimes this can lead to a build-up of stress and emotions within ourselves. Catch you child following the rules and reward them justly, much like parents try to immediately punish the rule-breaking behaviors.
- **Admission of Emotions:** You make me so . . . . This is a lot of power to give children or others and may place us in a "permanent victim" type of role. Before we engage in any stress management training, we need to acknowledge that the responsibility of anxiety is within ourselves. Once we do that we see that anxiety is within our control and we can learn to manage our anxiety and improve our parenting ability and relationship with children. Children's misbehavior does not cause stress, rather it is the way that we perceive the misbehavior.

Stress Interferes with Successful parenting:

Stress, anxiety, anger, and depression interfere with your ability to make intelligent choices and may cloud some options and make your capacity to choose the best option unlikely.

- What happens when you direct your parental anger or stress at the children instead of at the inappropriate behavior?
- Child who withdraws, removes self from parents, or may put self down "I'm a bad person"
- May also get a parent who feels bad about expressing the anger, no one likes being the "Bad guy"

"My children only listen when I'm angry" or "I have no other choice but to get angry"

- These are frequent statements by parents, but these have faulty logic. Most of the time there are other choices, but those may be clouded or we may not be aware of the other options. We may have had poor role models ourselves growing up re: parenting skills and anger management.

Nonhurtful vs. Hurtful Emotions

- Nonhurtful emotions involve dealing with children when you are annoyed, irritated, or aggravated. These parents are able to problem solve and be assertive in focusing on their children's behaviors. Additionally, children are more likely to "hear" their parents when they approach them at this level as there is no need to be defensive.
- Hurtful Emotions involve escalating familial conflict, name calling, emotional and physical abuse. This often comes from reactively responding to the child as a person rather than to the child's behavior. This impulsive response can lead to a lowering of the self-esteem of the child and experiences of guilt and anxiety.
- Work on having parents understand the concepts **that: All children misbehave and My children will misbehave.** Oftentimes parents have difficulty understanding this in the sense that they think that they should accept these misbehavior and not try to correct them. That is not true! We would rather have parents accept the children but not the misbehavior. Firm consistent rules must be implemented unangrily to change the misbehavior.

Not taking your children's behaviors personally:

- Sometimes we tend to think that when our children behave this way, they are doing it **TO** me, when we think this way we are setting ourselves up for anger.

Summarize workshop

- Develop individually based **homework assignments** based upon what parents have reported during the discussion. Homework should involve

writing and tracking one's thoughts and emotions during the week and the circumstances involved around them.
- Present the REBT library and encourage parents to borrow REBT books or audiotapes.

References

Achenbach, T. M., and Rescorla, L. A. (2001). *Manual for ASEBA School-Age Forms and Profiles*. Burlington, VT: University of Vermont, Research Center for Children, Youth, and Families.

American Psychiatric Association (2000). *Diagnostic and statistical manual of mental disorders* (4th ed., text revision). Washington, DC: Author

Bar-On, R., and Parker, J. D. A. (2000). *Emotional Quotient Inventory: Youth Version (EQ-i: YV): Technical manual*. Toronto, Canada: Multi-Health Systems.

Beavers, W. R., and Hampson, R. B. (1990). *Successful families: Assessment and Intervention*. New York: W. W. Norton and Company.

Bernard, M. (1986). Enhancing the Psychological Adjustment of School-Age Children: A Rational-Emotive Perspective. In W. Dryden and P. Trower (eds.). *Rational-Emotive Therapy: Recent Developments in Theory and Practice*. UK: Institute for RET, pp. 188–211.

Bernard, M. E., Cronan, F. (1999). The child and adolescent scale of irrationality: Validation data and mental health correlates. *Journal of Cognitive Psychotherapy, 13*, 121–132.

Bernard, M. E., and Joyce, M. R. (1991). RET with children and adolescents. In M. E. Bernard (ed.), *Using Rational-Emotive Therapy effectively: A practitioner's guide*. New York: Plenum Press.

Brightman, R. P., Baker, B. L., Clark, D. B., and Ambrose, S. A. (1982). Effectiveness of alternative parent training formats. *Journal of Behavior Therapy and Experimental Psychiatry, 13,* 113–117.

Corey, M. S., and Corey, G. (1997) *Groups: Process and practice*. Pacific Grove, CA: Brooks/Cole Publishing Company.

Corey, G., Corey, M. S., Callanan, P., and Russell, J. M. (1992). *Group techniques: Second edition*. Pacific Grove, California: Brooks/Cole Publishing Company.

Crick, N. R. and Ladd, G. W. (1990). Children's perceptions of the outcomes of social strategies: Do the ends justify being mean? *Developmental Psychology, 26,* 612–620.

DiGiuseppe, R., Linscott, J., and Jilton, R. (1996). Developing the therapeutic alliance in child-adolescent psychotherapy. *Applied and Preventative Psychology, 5,* 85–100.

Doyle, K. (2003). (personal communication, 14 February 2005).

Elkin, A. (1983). Working with children in groups. In A. Ellis and M. E. Bernard (eds.), *Rational-emotive approaches to the problems of childhood*. New York: Plenum Press, pp. 485–507.

Ellis, A. (1997). REBT and its application to group therapy. In J. Yankura and W. Dryden (eds.), *Special applications of REBT: A therapist's casebook*. New York: Springer Publishing Company, pp. 131–161.

Ellis, A. (2002). REBT and its application to group therapy. In W. Dryden and M. Neenan (eds.), *Rational-emotive behaviour group therapy*. Philadelphia: Whurr Publishers, pp. 30–54.

Ellis, A., Moseley, S., and Wolfe, J. (1966). *How to raise an emotionally healthy, happy, child.* Hollywood, CA: Wilshire.

Flanagan, R., Povall, L., Dellino, M. J., and Byrne, L. (1998). A comparison of problem solving with and without rational-emotive behavior therapy to improve children's social skills. *Journal of Rational-Emotive and Cognitive-Behavior Therapy, 16*, 125–134.

Ford, P. W. (2004, November). *Evaluating the efficacy and process of REBT group psychotherapy: Implications for practice and research.* Discussion presented at the 38th annual convention of the Association for Advancement of Behavior Therapy (AABT), New Orleans, LA.

Ford, P. W. (2005). [A meta-analysis of REBT studies]. Unpublished raw data.

Forte, J., Terjesen, M., and Matovic, M. (2004). *Making the Difference: Cognitive Behavioral Interventions for Academic Underachievers.* Paper presented as part of the symposium: Rational Emotive Behavior Therapy Group Psychotherapy: What Do we Know and Where We Going? at the 38th Association for Advancement of Behavior Therapy Annual Convention, New Orleans, LA.

Gillberg, I. and Gillberg, C. (1989). Asperger syndrome—some epidemiological considerations: A research note. *Journal of Child Psychology and Psychiatry, 30*(4), 631–638.

Greaves, D. (1996). *The Effect of Rational Emotive Parent Education on the Stress of Mothers of Young Children with Down Syndrome.* Doctoral Dissertation, University of Melbourne.

Kachman, D. J. and Mazer, G. E. (1990). Effects of rational-emotive education on the defense mechanisms of adolescents. *Adolescence, 25*, 131–144.

Kovacs M. (1992). Children's depression inventory (Manual). New York: Multi-Health Systems.

McRoberts, C., Burlingame, G. M., and Hoag, M. J. (1998). Comparative efficacy of individual and group psychotherapy: A meta-analytic perspective. *Group Dynamics: Theory, Research, and Practice, 2*, 101–117.

Ollendick, T. H. (1983). Reliability and validity of the Revised Fear Survey Schedule for Children. *Behaviour Research and Therapy, 21*, 685–692.

Plake, B. S., Impara, J. C., and Spies, R. A. (eds.) (2003). *Mental Measurements Yearbook: Fifteenth Edition.* Nebraska: Buros Institute.

Price, J. R., Hescheles, D. R., Price, A. R. (1999b). Selecting clients for group psychotherapy. In J. R. Price, D. R. Hescheles, and A. R. Price (eds.), *A guide to starting psychotherapy groups.* California: Harcourt, Inc, pp. 15–19.

Reynolds, C. and Kamphaus, R. (2004). *Behavior Assessment System for children-2 (BASC-2).* Circle Pines,MN: American Guidance Service.

Sapp, M., Farrell, W. and Durand, H. (1995). Cognitive behavior therapy: Applications for African American middle school at risk students. *Journal of Instructional Psychology, 22*, 169–177.

Shannon, H. D., Allen, T. W. (1998). The effectiveness of a REBT training program in increasing the performance of high school students in mathematics. *Journal of Rational-Emotive and Cognitive Behavior Therapy, 16*, 197–209.

Smead, R. (1995). *Skills and techniques for group work with children and adolescents.* Champaign, IL: Research Press.

Soares, L. M. and Soares, A. T. (1999). *Self-Perception Inventory.* Trumbull, CT: Castle Consultants.

Terjesen, M. D. (1998). *Comparison of REBT and parent training with parents of special education preschoolers*, Unpublished doctoral dissertation, Hofstra University, New York.

Wilde, J. (1992). *Rational counseling with school-aged populations: A practical guide*. Bristol, PA: Accelerated Development Inc.

Wright, L., Stroud, R., and Keenan, M. (1993). Indirect treatment of children via parent raining: A burgeoning form of secondary prevention. *Applied and Preventive Psychology, 2,* 191–200.

Yalom, I. D. (1994). *The theory and practice of group psychotherapy,* 4th ed. New York: Basic Books.

14

Applications of REBT in Schools: Prevention, Promotion, Intervention

ANN VERNON AND MICHAEL E. BERNARD

More than ever before there is a need in schools today for evidence-based, comprehensive, developmentally-based school-wide programs designed to promote social and emotional competence as well as to prevent and or reduce behavior and emotional problems including educational under-achievement. Fortunately, there now exists an increasing number of "promising" school-based programs being implemented that focus on the social and emotional learning of children and adolescents that are designed to equip young people with an array of social and emotional capabilities seen as intrinsic to academic success, emotional well-being and positive relationships (see review in Zins et al., 2004) including the PATHS curriculum (e.g., Greenberg et al., 2004), the Child Development Project (e.g., Schaps et al., 2005), the Resolving Conflict Creatively Program (e.g., Brown et al., 2004), the I Can Problem Solve Program (e.g., Shure, 1996) and Think First (e.g., Larson, 2005).

It is now recognized that teaching children social and emotional competence is central not only to their social and emotional well-being but also their academic achievement (e.g., Bernard, 2006; Zins et al., 2004). As well, the promotion of emotional intelligence of young people is becoming more accepted (Goleman, 1995; Mayer and Salovey, 1997). Bernard (2005a) has delimited a range of social and emotional learning standards (what students are expected to know and do in the area of social and emotional learning) that are seen as crucial for student emotional well-being, success in school and life and to their positive relationships including social responsibility.

Recent reviews indicate that successful school-based social and emotional learning programs share common characteristics. Good practice has teachers with the support of psychologists and counselors teaching social and emotional skills in formal lessons as an integrated component of the curriculum. However, it is recognized that in order for students to general these skills,

TABLE 1. Summary of social and emotional learning standards (Bernard, 2005a).

Goal I: Emotional Well-Being
Social and Emotional Learning Standards Cluster: Resilience

1. Identify and correctly label emotions and how they are linked to thinking and behavior.
2. Describe and apply emotional resilience skills and positive attitudes in being able to stay calm and independently calm down within a developmentally-appropriate period of time in the face of troubling or negative events without needing the guidance and support of someone else.
3. Demonstrate a realistic self-perception of one's personal strengths and challenges (e.g., interests, abilities, skills, behavior), develop accepting attitudes towards oneself, and a desire to build on strengths and to work on challenges.
4. Demonstrate self-control of aggressive, withdrawal or irresponsible behavior when emotionally upset and "bounce back" to normal routine.
5. Identify, locate and interact with peers and adults in school, home, and community who offer support and assistance in handling stress and achieving goals of building strengths and addressing challenges.

Goal II: Success in School and Life
Social and Emotional Learning Standards Cluster: Positive Work Orientation

1. Demonstrate organization as shown in a positive goal orientation towards achievement, time management with respect to developmentally appropriate activities and expectations, and self-management (storage, locating) and care of materials (work, play).
2. Demonstrate confidence when faced with new or difficult developmentally appropriate tasks or schoolwork.
3. Demonstrate persistence and high effort when faced with frustrating, time-consuming or low interest developmentally appropriate tasks, situations or school work.
4. Demonstrate teamwork and cooperative learning skills when working on different learning tasks and activities.

Goal III: Positive Relationships and Social Responsibility
Social and Emotional Learning Standards Cluster: Positive Social Orientation

1. Recognize, value and respect the feelings of others and how others see the world.
2. Recognize and value similarities and differences among people.
3. Demonstrate social confidence, friendship-making, assertive and leadership skills when interacting with peers and adults in work, play, and social situations.
4. Demonstrate conflict resolution skills in different contexts with different people including listening, problem identification and analysis, conflict solution generation and evaluation and negotiation skills.
5. Demonstrate decision-making skills leading to pro-social and health-related, low risk behaviors.
6. Demonstrates social responsibility by displaying the values of honesty, fairness, respect, caring and citizenship thereby making their classroom, school, home, and community a better place to live and learn.
7. Demonstrates social responsibility by actively contributing in making their classroom, school, home and community a better place to live and learn.

social and emotional learning experiences need to be present throughout the school day including during academic instruction and throughout the school year. Other characteristics include: (a) are of longer duration, (b) synthesize a number of successful approaches, (c) incorporate a developmental model, (d) provide greater focus on the role of emotions and emotional development, (e) provide increased emphasis on generalization techniques, (f) provide ongoing training and support for implementation, and (g) utilize multiple measures and follow-ups for assessing program effectiveness (Greenberg et al., 2004; Zins et al., 2004).

Albert Ellis pioneered the application of rational-emotive behavior therapy (REBT) to the treatment of children and adolescents in the mid 1950s and from its inception REBT and its educational derivative, Rational Emotive Education, has always been a social-emotional learning program. A long-time proponent of the use of REBT in schools, Ellis has always stressed the importance of a prevention curriculum designed to help young people help themselves by learning positive social-emotional learning concepts (Ellis, 1971, 1972). From 1971 to 1975, Ellis and his staff taught rational thinking as a preventive social-emotional learning program in addition to regular subjects at The Living School, a small private grade school housed in the Institute for Advanced Study in Rational Psychotherapy (now called the Albert Ellis Institute). The school prospered for several years, during which time the staff discovered that not only therapists but teachers, could teach REBT principles in the classroom to improve children's emotional well-being.

Based on the effective thinking, feeling, and behaving strategies that were taught at The Living School, Knaus (1974) developed a curriculum that would educate children in the ABCs of REBT. Bedford (1974) wrote a short story emphasizing the connection between thinking, feeling, and behaving, and Waters (1979) created a coloring book that incorporated rational principles. Since that time, other curricula (Bernard, 2001, 2005; Gerald and Eyman, 1981; Vernon, 1989a, 1989b, 1998a, 1998b, 1998c) have been developed that teach children to develop critical thinking skills, differentiate between facts and assumptions, distinguish between thoughts and feelings, link thoughts and feelings, identify what leads to emotional upset, distinguish between rational and irrational beliefs, and learn to challenge irrational beliefs.

Rational-Emotive Education (REE) has a long-standing presence in the field of school-based mental health programs and has always been used as a form of prevention, promotion and intervention focused on young people and their problems (e.g., Knaus, 1974). Its focus has been on the elimination of the irrational beliefs of children and adolescents associated with emotional, behavioral and achievement problems and the promotion of rational beliefs associated with social, emotional, and work competence. The research across four decades indicates that when REBT is used in schools with both clinical and non-clinical populations it has a positive effect (e.g., DiGiuseppe et al., 1979; Gonzalez et al., 2004; Hajzler and Bernard, 1991).

As prevention, REE programs are employed in classrooms to help prevent the development of irrational beliefs and associated unhealthy emotions and behaviors (e.g., Vernon, 2006a, 2006b). It helps children of all ages recognize the self-defeating effects of irrational beliefs and the beneficial outcomes of rational beliefs. More recently, as represented in a REBT-oriented program, You Can Do It! Education (e.g., Bernard, 2001, 2003, 2004, 2005), children as young as 4 and as old as 18 are being taught positive Habits of the Mind (rational beliefs) and associated emotion and behavioral action tendencies that Bernard has found leads not only to emotional well-being and positive relations, but which contribute greatly to academic achievement; these *social and emotional capabilities* include academic confidence, work persistence, organization, work cooperation, and emotional resilience). As well, when young people are equipped with emotional problem solving skills including rational self-statements and disputing skills, they are able to diffuse potential problem situations that potentially can lead to more harmful outcomes.

As promotion, REBT-based programs are, again, being used with groups of young people with an eye to the strengthening of rational beliefs and self-management skills that help young people make the very most of their innate potential by helping them minimize unhealthy emotions, irrational beliefs and to maximize their effort and well-being.

As intervention, REBT has a long track record and supportive research (e.g., Hajzler and Bernard, 1991) as a form of 1:1 and group interventions for young people with psychosocial and mental health problems (anxiety, low self-esteem, behavior problems). Apparently, REBT is being used more frequently with young people with internalizing than externalizing problems (Terjesen et al., 1999). When working with children who manifest internal or externalizing disorders, REBT practitioners recognize the need for multisystemic solutions encompassing the child's full ecology.

The purpose of this chapter is to provide a rationale for emotional education and to discuss why REBT principles inherently form the basis for a comprehensive form of emotional education that serves the multiple functions of prevention, promotion and intervention. Examples of core concepts and implementation approaches are also addressed, along with specific lessons to illustrate the process. The chapter will review the theory and practice of Rational-Emotive Education (REE) and, then, a REBT- and CBT-based program, You Can Do It! Education.

Rationale for Emotional Education Programs

Growing up is increasingly more challenging, and young people have to deal with the complexities of a contemporary society in addition to the normal developmental challenges they all face in varying degrees. Today's youth are growing up too fast, too soon, and while they may be young chronologically, they are exposed to adult issues through the media and the Internet, as well as from their day-to-day experiences. Despite this exposure, many are not developmentally equipped to deal with many of the issues they are confronted with. A compounding factor is that children and many adolescents function in their emotional lives in the pre-concrete stage of cognitive development, which has significant ramifications for how they perceive events and predisposes them to irrational thinking in the form of overgeneralizations, low-frustration tolerance, demandingness, and self-downing.

For increasing numbers of young people, the combination of dealing with day-to-day developmental issues, as well as more serious situational problems such as varying forms of family dysfunction, abuse, loss, poverty, or homelessness, is too much to handle. As a result of this helplessness, depression, suicide, eating disorders, teen pregnancy, and substance abuse are all on the rise as young people try unsuccessfully to deal with their problems (McWhirter et al., 2004; Vernon and Clemente, in press).

The reality is that many youngsters will not receive mental health services, and even for those who do, the effectiveness of the "cure" approach is somewhat questionable. These factors, coupled with the recognition that young people need more effective coping mechanisms than ever before, necessitates a more proactive approach.

Over 25 years ago, Pothier (1976) advocated problem prevention, noting that we are in danger of wasting one of our major resources unless we initiate and support preventive as well as remedial mental health programs. Pothier strongly suggested that preventive mental-health programs be implemented in the schools as a way of ensuring that all children are provided with a learning environment that promotes positive cognitive, social, and emotional growth. Unfortunately, this has not occurred to the extent that it should or we would see a decrease, not an increase, in self-destructive behaviors such as suicide, self-mutilation, eating disorders, and the like.

Rational-Emotive Education

Rational-emotive education (REE) is uniquely suited for a prevention curriculum for several reasons: (a) the principles can be readily transferred into lessons that teach children the core REBT concepts; (b) it is a comprehensive approach in that by identifying irrational beliefs that perpetuate the problem, children gain a better understanding of how to change their negative feelings and self-defeating behaviors; (c) a wide variety of cognitive behavioral methods are employed in delivering the lessons; (d) the concepts can be adapted to different age levels, ethnicities, and intelligence levels; (e) the principles emphasize helping children "get better" not just "feel better"; (f) it is a skills-oriented approach that equips children with cognitive, emotive, and behavioral strategies to apply to problems of daily living, both in the present and future.

Rational-emotive education (REE) is based on the assumption that it is possible and desirable to teach children how to help themselves cope with life more effectively. Specifically, the importance of preventing emotional disturbances by providing children with "tools" with which to cope is the basis of rational-emotive education. The core principles of REBT—that emotional problems result from faulty thinking about events rather than from the event itself and that these faulty, irrational thoughts can be disputed, resulting in more moderate, healthy feelings and productive behaviors—forms the basis of an REE program, along with the A-B-C-D-E-F paradigm and an understanding of the core irrational beliefs: self-downing, demandingness, and low-frustration tolerance.

Unlike other emotional education programs, REE empowers recipients to take charge of their lives, first by understanding the connection between what they think, feel, and do, and then by learning that while they may not be able to change other people or the events in their lives, they can exercise control over themselves. Given the realities that many young people have to contend with, this pragmatic approach enables them to make changes that are within their control, which at the same time, will enhance the quality of their lives.

In the following sections, a several ways of implementing REE will be described, followed by examples of REE lessons and further applications.

Implementing REE

There are four basic approaches to implementing an REE program: the informal approach (teachable moment), structured emotional education lessons, learning centers, and integration into the curriculum. Each has its merits. Optimally, all four approaches will be used, in addition to REBT concepts being practiced and modeled in the environment.

The Informal Approach

The basic assumption of this approach is that teachers and parents will seize "teachable moments" to introduce and reinforce rational thinking concepts. There are numerous ways in which this can be done: with the entire class, individually, or with small groups of children.

As an example, suppose that a teacher returns a test and it is obvious that almost all the children are upset with their low scores. At this point, the teacher could introduce rational thinking in the classroom setting by asking children what the score says about them: does it make them a better or worse person? Does this bad score mean that they will always do poorly on exams? Just because they did not do well on this test, does it necessarily mean they will not do well in the course? Is getting a bad score the worst possible thing that could ever happen to them? Raising disputations of this sort helps children avoid self-downing, awfulizing, and overgeneralizing. A next step could be to ask them what they could have done, if anything, to improve their score, which could result in appropriate goal setting for the next exam.

Similarly, this approach can be used with an individual. Selina, a fourth-grader, frequently got upset when learning something new. She would throw down her pencil and tear up her paper and simply not finish the task. When the teacher approached her and asked her to explain what was wrong, Selina replied, "It's too hard—I'll never learn this." The teacher introduced some disputations: had she ever tried to learn anything before and succeeded? Just because something was hard, did it mean she should give up? Although Selina responded appropriately to these questions, she remained frustrated, so the teacher drew two talking heads. On the first one, she listed Selina's irrational beliefs: "This is too hard—I'll never learn this." On the second one, she helped Selina identify rational self-talk, such as: "This is hard, but I just have to work harder to learn it; I don't like learning hard things, but I can stand it if I do a little at a time." The teacher instructed Selina to keep this visual inside her desk to use as a reminder when she felt frustrated and wanted to give up. As a homework assignment, she asked Selina to read *The Little Engine That Could*, a book that described how a little train chanted "I think I can, I think I can" as he tried to make it up a mountain, and think about how this story applied to her situation.

The informal approach can also be used with small groups. For instance, as the teacher was walking through the hall, he noticed a group of young adolescents arguing with each other. As he approached the group, he heard all sorts of accusations being directed at one individual: "You're a horrible, selfish friend . . . you stole Katinka's boyfriend and we will never forgive you for it. We know you are the one who started all the rumors about us, and we are going to turn all the other girls against you so that no one in this class will ever speak to you again." The teacher wanted to diffuse the situation, so he pulled the group into an empty classroom and asked them to tell him more about the situation. As they talked, he began to challenge some of their assumptions: where was the evidence that this girl had started all the rumors? Did they know for a fact that she "stole" another's boyfriend? Did they have so much power that they could turn *everyone* against her? Forever is a long, long time—do they really believe that they will *never* speak to her again, or is it possible that they will eventually get over being so upset? These disputations seemed to help de-escalate their emotions and put the problem in better perspective, and eventually they reached a point where they could communicate more effectively about how they felt and listen to the other side of the story.

In each of these situations, if the teacher had not intervened, the problems would have compounded themselves and interfered with children's ability to concentrate in school. Furthermore, until the underlying beliefs are addressed, the problems would have perpetuated themselves. Nipping problems in the bud through this informal approach helps prevent this from occurring.

To use this approach, it is necessary to have a thorough understanding of the basic REBT principles and the disputation process. In addition, it is important to realize that while it might be easier to tell children how to feel or what to do to solve a problem, it is advisable that they be allowed to work things out for themselves, with proper guidance. Once they are able to dispute their irrational beliefs that will result in more moderate, healthy feelings, they are in a better position to look at alternatives and develop a plan to resolve the problem.

Structured REE Lessons

The second approach, the most structured of all, is a series of emotional education lessons that can be presented to a small group or to a total class of children. In contrast to subject-matter lessons, these lessons are typically not graded because the emphasis is on personal application of concepts. However, in this age of accountability, teachers can develop effective ways to measure whether or not the concepts have been attained, since skill acquisition is also an inherent part of the lessons.

Rational-emotive education lessons are typically experiential, with a good deal of student involvement and group interaction, which increases the likelihood that children will be engaged in the activity. Understandings are deduced from the use of such methods as simulations, games, role-playing, art activities, bibliotherapy, guided discussions, and music and writing activities. In addition, time is spent debriefing the lesson so that, through guided questions, children master the content.

REE Concepts

REE lessons are developed around the following basic concepts: self-acceptance, feelings, beliefs, and disputing beliefs (Vernon, 2004).

1. *Self-acceptance*. REE emphasizes the importance of developing a realistic self-concept, including accepting the notion of personal weaknesses as well as strengths. Learning that who a person is should not be equated with what he or she does is also a key component, as well as understanding that people are fallible human beings who make mistakes and must accept the fact that they are not perfect.
2. *Feelings*. A critical component of REE lessons is learning the connection between thoughts, feelings, and behaviors. Developing a feeling vocabulary, learning to deal with emotional overreactions, assessing the intensity of feelings, and distinguishing between healthy and unhealthy ways to express feelings are also important. Understanding that feelings can change, that the same event can result in different feelings depending on how the event is perceived, and that it is natural to have feelings, are significant concepts.
3. *Beliefs*. A key component of REE is that there are two types of beliefs, rational and irrational. Irrational beliefs result in negative feelings that can lead to self-defeating behaviors. These irrational beliefs manifest themselves in the form of a basic "must" that falls into three main categories: self-demandingness, other-demandingness, and world-demandingness. Self-demandingness refers to the idea that you must always perform well and win others' approval; and if you do not, you are incompetent, unworthy, and deserve to suffer. Other-demandingness implies that people with whom you associate must always treat you kindly, considerately, and fairly; and if they do not, they are unworthy, bad, rotten, and deserve to be punished. World-demandingness means that the conditions in which you live must be enjoyable, hassle free, safe, and favorable; and if they are not, it is awful and horrible and unbearable. Rational beliefs are self-enhancing and result in moderate feelings that help people achieve their goals; they are

realistic preferences that typically result in constructive behaviors (Dryden, 1999). The goal of the disputation process is to replace irrational beliefs with rational beliefs.

4. *Facts versus Assumptions*. It is also important that children understand the difference between facts and assumptions. As concrete thinkers, children and many adolescents readily misconstrue events by failing to distinguish between a fact (she didn't sit by me) from assumptions (she's mad at me and doesn't want to be my friend). Because of their impulsive nature, it is all too common for young people to act on their assumptions and create more problems when others react to their overreaction.
5. *Disputing Beliefs*. The concept of disputing, a cornerstone of this theory, entails replacing irrational beliefs with rational beliefs in order to achieve a more sensible way of thinking, which in turn results in more moderate emotions and more self-enhancing behavior. The disputational process can take several forms: functional disputes, or questioning the practicality of the irrational beliefs (Bernard, 2004b; Ellis and MacClaren, 1998); the Socratic approach, in which questioning gives clients insight into the irrationality of their thinking (Dawson, 1991); the didactic approach, where the differences between rational and irrational beliefs are explained (Ellis and MacClaren, 1998); empirical disputes, which help people evaluate the factual aspects of their beliefs; logical disputes, which enables people to see how illogical it is to escalate desires into demands and use of exaggeration or humor. These types of disputes can be taught directly to children in REE lessons or the concepts can be incorporated into lessons that teach children to apply the various types of disputations.

These basic concepts form the essence of the REE lessons, but it is critical that they be presented in accordance with the developmental level of the child. For example, it is appropriate to use the terms *rational* and *irrational* with older adolescents, but with younger children, the terms *sensible* and *insensible* would be easier for them to grasp. Likewise, younger children will not understand the concept of disputing unless it is presented in a very concrete manner, such as with the use of puppets in a dialogue, with one puppet being insensible and the other being sensible. Similarly, whereas adolescents can more readily understand the how irrational beliefs result in negative feelings and unproductive behaviors, younger children need to have these concepts presented in a very concrete method, such as making a paper chain to visually illustrate how insensible thoughts create negative feelings which result in poor behavioral choices.

It is also important to present the concepts in a sequential manner to assure greater mastery of the concepts. It is best to introduce these concepts in units. For example, the first unit might be self-acceptance, and all concepts pertaining to that would be introduced, followed by those relating to beliefs, and so forth. It is also advisable to have a sequential progression of lessons within the specific units so that concepts can be introduced and expanded on.

For example, in a feelings unit, the distinction between healthy and unhealthy feelings precedes the more difficult concept that feelings come from thoughts. Likewise, when introducing beliefs, a first level would be to distinguish facts from beliefs before moving on the notion of rational and irrational beliefs. In addition, the lessons should follow a similar structure, as subsequently described.

REE Lesson Plan Format

Having a well-developed lesson is essential, as is the notion of presenting the activities in developmentally-appropriate formats to help children master the concepts. For example, rather than explain in a short lecture the difference between facts and assumptions, it is much more effective to engage students in identifying facts and assumptions in a game format similar to tic-tac-toe (Vernon, 1980), or to learn that everyone makes mistakes by attempting to juggle tennis balls (Vernon, 1989a). As previously mentioned, a wide variety of methods can be incorporated into REE lessons: games, simulations, role-playing, puppetry, music and art activities, writing and worksheet activities, drama, experiments, bibliotherapy, and rational-emotive imagery, for example (Bernard, 2001, 2005; Vernon, 1980, 1989b, 1998a, 1998b, 1998c).

A lesson should contain the following:

1. *Learning objectives.* It is important to have one or two learning objectives for each lesson. For example, in a unit on beliefs for second graders, a specific objective would be to identify the negative effects of demandingness. For a sixth grader, a specific objective would be to identify the connection between thoughts and actions. The objectives should be stated in behavioral terms so that they can be measured, and they should be developmentally appropriate for the age level. It is preferable, in delivering a sequential curriculum, that there be separate objectives for each grade level.
2. *Stimulus activity.* This is the heart and soul of the lesson, where the concepts are introduced. The stimulus activity should be engaging and can assume a variety of formats as previously described. For example, an REE lesson on tease tolerance can be developed using art—children make a radio out of a cardboard box and write rational thoughts they can use to tune out teasing around a dial on the radio (Vernon, 2002, pp. 222–224). Art can also be used to help adolescents deal with depressed feelings. They can draw around their hand and in the palm, write down the things they are depressed about, and then identify rational coping self-statements on each finger to serve as a reminder about how to cope with depression (Vernon, 2002, pp. 131–132). Experiential activities can also be very engaging. Elementary children can be divided into two groups, procrastinators and non-procrastinators. They are to pretend that they are recruiting "members" to their club, so the procrastinators make a poster of all the good things about being a procrastinator, and the non-procrastinators do the same. Discussion follows about the advantages and disadvantages of procrastination (Vernon, 2002, p. 184).

Adolescents can learn how to use rational thoughts to de-escalate anger by making a paper accordion, identifying thoughts about an anger-provoking incident on one level of the accordion sheet, and then writing a rational thought to counteract the irrational thought contributing to the anger on the next level of the accordion (Vernon, 2002, p. 167).

It is advisable to use more concrete activities with younger children and gradually introduce more abstract lessons with adolescents. However, it is also important to be experiential and to use wide array of activities to maintain interest. The stimulus activity should take no more than half of the allotted time for the lesson, leaving time for discussion.

3. *Content and personalization questions*. Because a critical part of the lesson is the personal application of concepts, it is very important to allow sufficient time for discussion. Two types of questions provide the most effective debriefing: content questions, which focus on the cognitive concepts presented in the lesson, and personalization questions, which involve applying the concepts to the child's own life. For example, in a lesson on rational thinking, the objective was to learn how to distinguish between rational and irrational thinking. The activity, for high school students, involved a short lecturette on the difference between rational and irrational thinking, followed by a worksheet, where students were asked to identify irrational beliefs in statements such as: "My parents never let me do anything—everyone else has more freedom than I do"; "I can't stand it if my boyfriend breaks up with me—I'll never find anyone like him again." The content questions asked students to describe the difference between rational and irrational thinking and examples of key irrational beliefs. The personalization questions asked students if they were generally rational or irrational thinkers, what they would need to do to change the way they think in order to handle situations more effectively, and how they can apply what they learned to their own lives (Vernon, 1998c).
4. Using this lesson plan format provides a basic structure, but at the same time, allows for flexibility and creativity in the actual design of the activity. The inclusion of both content and personalization questions achieves the objectives of emotional education programs: to present mental health concepts and to help students personally apply these to their own lives. The primary focus is prevention, with the hope that these concepts will reduce the frequency and intensity of future problems.

Considerations in Implementing Lessons

In conducting emotional education lessons, it is vital to establish an atmosphere of trust and group cohesion because children are encouraged to look at themselves, to share with others, to apply concepts to their own lives, and to learn from classmates with regard to emotional and behavioral adjustment. Sensitivity should be exercised, listening carefully to children's responses, supporting their struggles to gain new insights, and encouraging their attempts to acquire REE concepts.

It is also important to create an atmosphere where students respect each other's expression. The facilitator of the lesson has the responsibility for seeing that this minimal rule is respected so that children will feel comfortable in sharing. At the elementary level, this may not be a problem, but as adolescence approaches, students become more self-conscious and hesitant. A non-threatening classroom atmosphere helps to assure the success of the emotional education experiences.

As previously mentioned, assigning a grade to an REE lesson is not recommended because it is difficult to evaluate personal application of concepts, which is one of the significant components of an REE lesson. However, since the objectives are measurable, quizzes or other types of evaluation can be used to determine cognitive acquisition of concepts. For example, after presenting a lesson on the difference between facts and assumptions, the teacher could have students complete a short True/False quiz, identifying which statements were facts and which were assumptions.

It is very appropriate to ask students what they learned following a lesson or to assign homework as a follow up to the lesson to help reinforce the concepts. After the lesson on facts and assumptions, a homework assignment for younger children could involve having them be "fact detectives," where they attempt to identify facts versus assumptions in their interactions with peers or siblings. Or, after a lesson on developing high frustration tolerance, middle school students were asked to try something that had previously proven to be frustrating, and to practice the examples of self-talk they had learned in the lesson to help them deal more effectively with their frustration.

Sample REE Lessons

There are numerous ways to introduce REE concepts. The following two lessons illustrate the lesson plan procedure. The first lesson is for elementary students to help them learn that people can feel differently about the same event based on what they think, and the second is a self-acceptance activity for adolescents.

Face Your Feelings

Objective: To learn that people can feel differently about the same event.
Materials: Four paper plates per student; markers or crayons

Stimulus Activity:

1. Ask students to draw faces on their paper plates to represent the following emotions: happy, sad, angry (mad), worried.
2. Explain that you will be reading some situations and that they are to think about how they feel when they experience a situation similar to the ones they are hearing about.

3. Read aloud each of the following situations, one at time, instructing students to respond by flipping up the face that illustrates how they would feel. Before reading another situation, note the different feelings that were portrayed and make a tally on the board.

Situations:

It is going to snow tonight.
Your younger cousins are coming to visit.
Your parents are taking you shopping after school.
Your teacher is keeping you in for recess.
You did not get picked for the kickball game.
You are moving to a new reading group.
You might move to a different town and go to a different school.

Discussion:
Content Questions:

1. Did everyone respond to a given situation with the same feeling? If not, why do you think this happened?
2. Do you think that there is any situation in which all people would feel exactly the same? If so, what would be some examples?
3. Why do you think two people can feel differently about the same situation?

Personalization Questions:

1. Can you think of a time when you felt one way about something and your friend felt another way? (Encourage sharing of examples).
2. How do you think you should act if someone feels differently about a situation than you do?
3. What did you learn about feelings from this activity?

To the Leader:

In the discussion, emphasize that feelings vary based on what the person is thinking. Use examples to illustrate this process so that it is clear to the children.

Don't Soak It Up

Objective: To identify how to deal with criticism and put-downs which contribute to self-downing.
Materials: One sponge and a bucket of water, paper and pencil for each student

Stimulus Activity:

1. Introduce the activity by stating the objective of the lesson and asking for a volunteer.
2. Ask the volunteer to dip the sponge into the bucket and pull it back out. Discuss with the class what has happened to the sponge (it soaked up lots of water).

3. Next, explain that when people say negative things about us that often we "soak up" the negative words, just as in the demonstration, without examining the content of the message to see if in fact it is true. For example, if someone says that you are ugly and stupid, you need to look at the evidence, asking yourself if that is really true. If not, you do not have to "soak it up." Instead, you need to think about wringing out the sponge, getting rid of the put-downs or criticisms that are not true.
4. Invite students to write down three recent examples of times they were absorbed by criticism or put-downs. Have them identify things they could say to themselves to avoid "soaking up" the negatives that lead to self-downing.
5. Invite students to share examples.

Discussion:
Content Questions:

1. What does the concept of "soaking it up" mean?
2. What can you do to avoid "soaking it up?"

Personalization Questions:

1. Are you someone who "soaks up the negative" often? If so, how do you feel when you do that? If not, how do you avoid soaking it up?
2. Suppose that some of the things others say about you are true—does that make you a bad person?
3. What did you learn from this lesson that you can apply to your life?

To the Leader:

Emphasize the importance of examining criticism to avoid excessive self-downing. Also stress that if some it is true, it does not make you a bad person.

REE Learning Centers

Oftentimes elementary and middle school teachers establish learning centers, where students work independently on activities to reinforce concepts presented in class or to introduce new ideas. REE activities can easily be incorporated into this type of format through worksheets, writing, or games. For example, Waters (1979) *Color Us Rational* stories lend themselves to a learning center activity. A copy of several of the stories can placed at the center, along with paper and pencil. After reading one or more of the stories, students are instructed to write a rational story based on one of their own experiences. Other good center activities involve having students write rational limericks or make rational bumper stickers or posters for their rooms, making up silly songs to help them deal with sad feelings, putting on rational puppet plays, or playing a game of hop scotch, where children have to identify rational self-talk to help them deal with anger or anxiety before jumping to the next space.

The teacher is limited only by his or her creativity in designing center activities. They should be engaging and able to be completed independently.

Integration into the Curriculum

Yet another approach to REE is to integrate the concepts into an existing subject-matter curriculum. When teaching literature, teachers could select and discuss stories that present characters solving problems rationally or expressing feelings in a healthy manner. Topics for themes could be related to self-awareness such as making mistakes, identifying strengths and weaknesses, and the prices and payoffs for perfection. Vocabulary and spelling lessons could include feeling-word vocabularies and definitions.

Social studies lessons could focus on personal and societal values and on a rational understanding of the concept of fairness as it applies to societal groups or to law and order, for example. Students could examine the rational and irrational practices of politicians, the difference between facts and assumptions in political campaigns, or the concept of high-frustration tolerance as it applies to political leaders.

Integration into the curriculum is less direct than a structured lesson, but it is a viable way of reinforcing rational concepts and making them an integral part of the school structure. Although it may seem awkward and forced initially, once teachers become more familiar with the REE concepts, they will find that integration becomes more natural.

You Can Do It! Education

You Can Do It! Education (YCDI) (e.g., Bernard, 1995, 2001, 2002, 2003a, 2003b, 2004a, 2004c, 2005a) derives from diverse psychological and educational theory as well as REBT and cognitive-behavior therapy that identifies distinct social-emotional capabilities and disabilities associated with students' well-being, achievement and relationships. The goals of YCDI as presented in Fig. 1 are twofold: (a) to eliminate the *social and emotional disabilities* that lead to a variety of psychosocial and mental health problems and (b) to develop the social and emotional capabilities that research indicates as leading to success in emotional well-being, school and life, positive relationships (see Fig. 1).

A close examination of this model will reveal 12 negative Habits of the Mind that are associated with different social and emotional disabilities such as anger, anxiety, depression and work avoidance. Additionally, there are 12 positive Habits of the Mind supporting social and emotional capabilities. Many of these Habits of the Mind are simple re-labelling of Ellis' core set of rational and irrational beliefs to more child-friendly language. Other negative and positive Habits of the Mind are distillations of different dysfunctional and functional cognitions that other CBT theories have identified including attributional theory (e.g., Dweck and Elliott, 1983; Weiner, 2000), locus of control (e.g., Bar-tal and

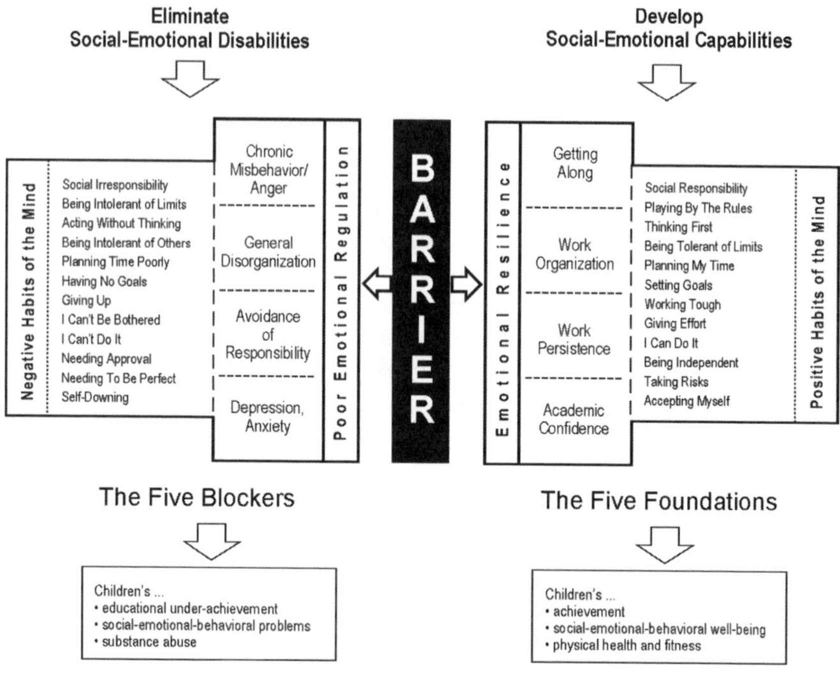

FIGURE 1. You Can Do It! Education Model (Bernard, 2005a).

Bar-Zohar, 1977; Rotter, 1966), learned helplessness and optimism (e.g., Seligman, 1975, 1991), self-efficacy e.g., Bandura, 1986, 1997; Zimmerman, 1991), goal setting (e.g., Ames, 1992; Lange and Adler, 1997; Schunk, 1996), internal motivation (e.g., Spaulding, 1993) and interpersonal cognitive problem solving (e.g., Spivack and Shure, 1974; Spivack et al., 1976). A more detailed representation of the relationships of positive and negative Habits of the Mind to different social and emotional capabilities and disabilities are presented in Tables 2 and 3.

Research supporting YCDI's central propositions are reported in the literature (see Bernard, 2006, for a complete review). Findings indicate that young people who have achievement and/or behavior problems are delayed in the development of social and emotional capabilities and manifest many more social and emotional disabilities in comparison with young people with no psychosocial disorders.

Teaching You Can Do It! Education

There are a number of school entry points for YCDI. These will be briefly reviewed including personal development programs (whole class, individual/small group mentoring), integration in classroom teaching-learning, whole school culture, and parent education).

TABLE 2. 12 Positive habits of the mind (rational beliefs) and the five social and emotional capabilities they support (Bernard, 2003a).

Confidence means knowing that you will likely be successful at many things you study. It means not being afraid to make mistakes or to try something new. Examples of confident behavior are raising your hand in class to answer a hard question, doing hard work without asking for help, or sharing a new idea with a teacher or the class. Positive HOMs that help develop a young person's Confidence include:

- Accepting Myself—not thinking badly about myself when I make a mistake.
- Taking Risks—thinking that it's good to try something new even though I might not be able to do it.
- Being Independent—thinking that it's important to try new activities and to speak up even if my classmates think I'm silly or stupid.

Persistence means trying hard and not giving up when schoolwork feels like it's too difficult or boring. Examples of persistent behavior are continuing to try even when school work is hard, not being distracted by others, and checking work when it's finished to make sure it's correct. Positive HOMs that help develop a young person's Persistence include:

- I Can Do It–thinking that I'm more likely to be successful than I am to fail.
- Giving Effort–thinking that the harder I try, the more successful I will be, and knowing that success is not caused by external factors (luck, ease of task), but by internal factors (effort).
- Working Tough–thinking that in order to be successful in the future, I sometimes have to do things that are not easy or fun in the present.

Organization means setting a goal to do your best in your school work, planning your time so that you are not rushed, having all your supplies ready, and keeping track of your assignments' due dates. Examples of organized behavior include making sure you understand the teacher's instructions before you begin work, having all your school supplies ready at a neat desk, recording your assignments and their due dates, and planning when you're going to do your homework so that you have enough time. Positive HOMs that help develop a young person's Organization include:

- Setting Goals—thinking that setting a goal can help me be more successful at a task.
- Planning My Time—thinking about how long it will take me to do my schoolwork and planning enough time to get it done.

Getting Along means working well with teachers and classmates, solving problems without getting too angry, and following the rules of the classroom. Examples of getting along behavior are being helpful when working in a group, listening and not interrupting when someone else is speaking, talking rather than fighting when someone acts unfairly, and not breaking classroom rules. Positive HOMs that help develop Getting Along behavior in a young person include:

- Being Tolerant of Others—accepting that everyone acts unfairly towards others some of the time, and not making overall judgments of people's character ("good person," "bad person") based on their differences or behavior.
- Thinking First—thinking that when someone treats me badly I need to think about different ways I can react, the consequences of each, and the impact of my actions on the other person's feelings.
- Playing by the Rules—thinking that by following important school and home rules, I will live in a better world where everyone's rights are protected.
- Social Responsibility—thinking that it is important to be a good citizen and to help build a world with fairness and justice for all and where everyone feels safe and secure. Examples of social responsibility include being sensitive to the feelings of others, acting honestly, treating others (especially those who come from different backgrounds) with respect, caring about and reaching out to people in need, and working towards protecting the environment.

(Continued)

TABLE 2. 12 Positive habits of the mind (rational beliefs) and the five social and emotional capabilities they support (Bernard, 2003a) *(Cont'd)*

Emotional Resilience means knowing how to stop yourself from getting extremely angry, down, or worried when something "bad" happens. It means being able to calm down and feel better when you get very upset. It also means being able to control your behavior when you are very upset.

Examples of Emotional Resilience

- When someone treats you unfairly, inconsiderately, or disrespectfully, you can stop yourself from getting too angry and lashing out.
- When you make mistakes, do not understand something, get a bad school report, or are teased or ignored, you can stop yourself from getting very down.
- When you have an important test or activity to perform, you can stop yourself from getting extremely worried.
- When you want to meet someone new, you can stop yourself from getting extremely worried.
- When someone is putting pressure on you to do the wrong thing, you can stop yourself from getting extremely worried about what that person will think if you stand up and say "no."

Positive Habits of the Mind that Help Your Emotional Resilience

- Accepting Myself—not thinking badly about myself when I make a mistake.
- Taking Risks—thinking that it's good to try something new even though I might not be able to do it.
- Being Independent—thinking that it's important to try new activities and to speak up even if my classmates think I'm silly or stupid.
- I Can Do It—hinking that I'm more likely to be successful than I am to fail.
- Working Tough—thinking that in order to be successful in the future, I sometimes have to do things that are not easy or fun in the present
- Being Tolerant of Others—accepting that everyone acts unfairly towards others some of the time, and not making overall judgments of people's character ("good person," "bad person") based on their differences or behavior.

Emotional Resilience Skills include:

- Finding something fun to do
- Finding someone to talk to
- Relaxation
- Exercise
- Solving the problem
- Changing negative to positive self-talk
- Not blowing things out of proportion

TABLE 3. Negative habits of the mind (irrational beliefs) that lead to problems (Bernard, 2003a).

Depression/Anxiety means that you worry a lot about whether other people like you and/or whether you will do as well at your school work as you think you should; you get emotionally upset when others reject (e.g., tease) you or when you do not achieve at the level you think you should (e.g., receive a low grade); you get extremely down when you are rejected and/or do not do well on a school assignment; you may delay starting homework, saying that you do not know what to do or how to do it (characterizes the "perfectionist"). Negative HOMs that lead to Low Self-Esteem/Anxiety include:

- **Self-Downing**—thinking that I am a total failure or useless when I have been rejected or have not achieved a good result.
- **Needing to be Perfect**—thinking that I have to be successful in everything important I do and that it's horrible when I'm not.
- **Needing Approval**—thinking that I need people (parents, teachers, peers) to approve of what I do and that, when they don't, it's the worst thing in the world.
- **I Can't Do It** (also called Pessimism)—thinking that, when I have not been successful at something, I am no good at anything, that I will never be good at anything, and that I'm a hopeless person.

General Work Avoidance means that you put off doing tasks and chores because they are frustrating, boring or hard; you give up easily after having started something that is difficult or boring to do; you rush to finish your work so that you can do fun things; you spend a lot of time having fun and enjoying yourself even when there is work to be done. Negative HOMs associated with General Work Avoidance include:

- **I Can't Be Bothered**—thinking that life should always be fun and exciting, and that I can't stand it when things are frustrating or boring.
- **Giving Up** (also called External Locus of Control for Learning)—thinking that I have no control over what happens to me (good or bad) and that there is little point in trying anything because I'll never be successful

General Disorganization means that you do not have a definite direction for how you use your time; you do not have goals to do well in any area of your life; you do not keep track of when important things have to be done and the steps you have to take to get them done; you do not decide ahead of time what are the most important things to be doing (e.g., not good at setting priorities). Negative HOMs associated with General Disorganization include:

- **Having No Goals**—thinking that it's pointless to have any goals associated with being successful for anything I do.
- **Planning Time Poorly**—thinking that it's pointless to plan my time; thinking that things will somehow get done; thinking, "When is the latest I can start?" when approaching some chore or task that isn't fun.

Anger/Chronic Misbehavior means that you break important rules at home and school even if property is destroyed or people get hurt; you act defiantly towards people in authority; you may lose your temper easily when faced with people who block you from getting what you want. Negative Habits of the Mind associated with Rebelliousness/Anger include:

- **Being Intolerant of Others**—thinking that people should always treat me fairly and considerately and in the way I treat them, and when they do not, I can't stand it and they are totally bad.
- **Acting Without Thinking** *(this Habit of the Mind can be defined by the absence of reflection about different ways to handle interpersonal conflict, the consequences of different course of action, and how someone else will feel after you have chosen to act in a certain way)* - thinking that if you treat me badly, I have no other choice but to treat you badly.

(Continued)

TABLE 3. Negative habits of the mind (irrational beliefs) that lead to five social and emotional disabilities (Bernard, 2003a) *(Cont'd)*

- **Being Intolerant of Limits**—thinking that I should be able to do what I want, that nobody should be able to tell me what to do, and that I can't stand having to follow rules.
- **Social Irresponsibility**—thinking that I only have to be concerned about me and that it is not important to be a good citizen and to help make contributions to my community. It also means that I do not need to concern myself with others who are less fortunate, nor do I need to be sensitive to the feelings of others, act honestly, and to treat others—especially those from different backgrounds—with respect.

Poor Emotion Regulation means that you get quickly upset and stay upset when things around you are unsettling or difficult such as when someone teases you or you do not understand something the teacher is saying. It means that you have a lot of trouble controlling your behavior when you get upset and you take a long time to bounce back to playing or working without the help of someone else to calm you down.

Negative Habits of the Mind that that lead to poor emotion regulation include:

- Self-Downing—means thinking that you are useless or a total failure when you have been rejected or have not achieved a good result.
- Needing To Be Perfect—means thinking that you have to be successful or perfect in everything important you do.
- Needing Approval—means thinking that you need people (peers, parents, teachers) to approve of you and that, when they do not, it's the worst thing in the world.
- I Can't Do It—means thinking that, when you have not been successful at something important, you are not good at anything and never will be.
- I Can't Be Bothered—means thinking that life should always be fun and exciting and that you can't stand it when things are frustrating or boring.
- Being Intolerant of Others—means thinking that people should always treat you fairly, considerately, and the way you want and that, when they do not, they are rotten people and you have a right to get back at them.

People who have a hard time controlling their emotions seem not to have learned coping skills for calming themselves down when upset or in the face of frustrating or challenging situations.

Personal Development Programs

Program Achieve (Bernard, 2001, 2005a) is a six volume curriculum of structured lessons designed for teachers and others to use in a whole group classroom setting that are designed to eliminate negative Habits of the Mind and associated social and emotional disabilities and to develop the five social emotional capabilities of confidence, persistence, organization, getting along and emotional resilience including strengthening positive Habits of the Mind (including rational beliefs). All lessons contain objectives, a scripted lesson plan, handouts, overheads and homework activities. Program Achieve is currently being used in over 6,000 schools in Australia, New Zealand, England, and North America. The *You Can Do It! Education Mentoring Program* (Bernard, 2003b) consists of individual activities that a mentor can employ with individual or small groups of young people (ages 12 +) who are identified as having achievement and/or behavior problems and are felt to be likely to profit from intensive social and emotional learning experiences (see sample activity in Table 4). Bernard (2004a) published the YCDI! Early Childhood

TABLE 4. Sample personal development mentoring activity (Bernard, 2003b).

Inventory of Hard Yakka

Directions: Indicate which of the tasks or activities below you find or would find to be hard yakka (e.g., tiresome, dull, boring) and which you often do not feel like doing.

Activity	Hard Yakka? (Y) Yes	No
1. knowing what is important to study when preparing for an exam		
2. reading required books		
3. writing in-class essays		
4. putting up with a boring teacher		
5. regular attendance at after-school extra-curricular activities (e.g., sporting practice, drama rehearsals)		
6. being required to study in class or library		
7. saving money		
8. having to do "compulsory" classes to graduate		
9. having to give a public "thank you" to a coach or other teacher		
10. having to run errands for parents		
11. doing community service		
12. other		
13. other		

You can indicate to students that this activity will help them identify activities they find to be "hard yakka." You will need to ask students whether they have ever heard the expression "hard yakka." Unless they are Australian, it is unlikely that they will know the meaning.

You can indicate that Hard Yakka is an Australian expression that has come to mean "hard work." The expression is used in conversation in Australia when people discuss tasks or activities that they have to do but are not fun to do because they are tedious, hard, or both.

Ask your students to say out loud: "Hard Yakka!"

You will want to explain to your students that it will come as no surprise to them that some parts of their school work and homework they have been assigned and completed over the years have not been fun or exciting to do and, therefore, could be called hard yakka.

Indicate that from your experience, you have noticed that successful learners in school have developed the ability to do hard yakka.

You can discuss the hard yakka you have done in the past and present that helps you to be successful.

Discussion Questions and Sample Answers

You will want to ask students the following two questions:

1. Does school have its fair share of things that are hard yakka?

   Sample answer: Yes.
2. To be successful at things you are learning at school, do you sometimes have to do hard yakka?

   Sample answer: Yes. The Habit of the Mind is called "Working Tough."

"Real Life" Application

1. Have students to agree to spend more time doing specific hard yakka in the coming week.
2. Have students to identify and then remove any obstacles (telephone, television, computer, friends) that might prevent them from doing hard yakka.
3. Discuss with students any successes in doing hard yakka at the beginning of the following mentoring session.

program for 4 to 7-years-olds that consists of structured curriculum activities, songs, puppets and posters geared to teach young people social and emotional capabilities including positive Habits of the Mind (rational beliefs). A teacher guide for working with parents is also included.

The You Can Do It! Classroom: Integration of Social and Emotional Learning

It has long been recognized that it is important to reinforce the ideas and skills learned in life-skills type classes throughout the school day; otherwise, many of the ideas and skills do not generalize. In YCDI, there are a wide variety of practices that teachers use for integrating confidence, persistence, organization, getting along, and emotional resilience along with the positive Habits of the Mind (including rational beliefs) into the school day. Many You Can Do It! classrooms are in existence today. Their purpose is to help all students develop their academic, emotional and interpersonal potential through the learning and application of the 5 Foundations and the supporting 12 positive Habits of the Mind.

One of the biggest lessons learned from many years of experience is that for personal development curricula like Program Achieve to have a maximum impact on young people's achievement and emotional well-being, the Foundations and Habits of the Mind need to be taught and reinforced in the classroom (and school) throughout the school year. While Program Achieve has definite benefits when it is taught, it has more benefit when students' regular classroom teachers are as passionate about and determined to teach and reinforce the material taught in Program Achieve as they approach teaching the academic curriculum.

Just as teachers introduce to their students "classroom rules" and the academic standards that constitute the objectives of the curriculum early on in the school year, it is recommend that the 5 Foundations and 12 Habits of the Mind become part of the overall purpose of the class. It is recommended that teachers integrate the 5 Foundations into the classroom ethos so that their students know that it is important for them to learn the 5 Foundations and 12 Habits of the Mind and apply them in their doing schoolwork, in their interpersonal relationships, and in managing their own emotions. One of the best practices for doing this is to display on the walls on a permanent basis examples of positive Habits of the Mind and negative Habits of the Mind and how they impact their emotions and behaviors in the classroom and refer to them on a regular basis (see Table 5).

The following practices are ways in which teachers can incorporate You Can Do It! Education into the ethos and practices of their classroom.

Practice 1. Establish Student Understanding of the Goals of You Can Do It! Education

TABLE 5. Positive and negative habits of the mind (Bernard, 2005b)

Accepting Myself
. . . leads to confidence

Self-Downing
. . . leads to feeling down

Taking Risks
. . . leads to confidence and not feeling worried

Needing To Be Perfect
. . . leads to feeling worried and not doing or saying things

Being Independent
. . . leads to confidence and not feeling worried

Needing Approval
. . . leads to feeling worried and not doing or saying things

(Continued)

TABLE 5. Positive and negative habits of the mind (Bernard, 2005b) *(Cont'd)*

I Can Do It!
. . . leads to confidence to try new things and persistence

I Can't Do It
. . . leads to feeling down and not trying

Giving Effort
. . . leads to persistence and effort

Giving Up
. . . leads to feeling down and not trying

Working Tough
. . . leads to persistence and effort

I Can't Be Bothered
. . . leads to feeling angry and avoiding responsibility

(Continued)

TABLE 5. Positive and negative habits of the mind (Bernard, 2005b). *(cont'd)*

Setting Goals
. . . leads to organization and trying hard to be successful

Having No Goals
. . . leads to being disorganized and avoiding responsibility

Planning My Time
. . . leads to organization and trying hard to be successful

Planning Time Poorly
. . . leads to being disorganized and avoiding responsibility

Being Tolerant of Others
. . . leads to getting along with people

Being Intolerant of Others
. . . leads to feeling angry and behaving badly

(Continued)

TABLE 5. Positive and negative habits of the mind (Bernard, 2005b) *(Cont'd)*

Thinking First
. . . leads to solving conflicts peacefully and getting along

Acting Without Thinking
. . . leads to behaving badly and getting into trouble

Playing By The Rules
. . . leads to behaving in ways that help everyone get along

Being Intolerant of Rules
. . . leads to behaving badly and getting into trouble

Social Responsibility
. . . leads to behaving in ways that help everyone get along

Social Irresponsibility
. . . leads to behaving in ways that do not help everyone get along

In order for students to be motivated to participate in learning about YCDI, it is important that they clearly understand the purpose of the program. To develop student "buy in," teachers will want to begin by describing the keys for success and happiness and the characteristics of achieving students who are relating well to others and who are managing their feelings successfully. Students will be more likely to be motivated to become interested in YCDI if they see that they will learn tools that can help them be successful; that is, the program is of benefit to them. Another point teachers will want to communicate is that all students in their class have great potential and that a teacher cannot really predict or know how successful they will be at mastering the many things they will be learning during the school year in their classes. It all depends on whether they use the 5 keys for success (see Fig. 2).

Practice 2. Present/Display Images and Explicit Statements of the 5 Foundations Including the 12 Habits of the Mind

It is vital that students clearly understand what specific behaviors go along with each of the 5 Foundations. Teachers should not take for granted that

The Five Keys to Success

FIGURE 2. The Five Keys to School Success and Happiness (Bernard, 2005b).

TABLE 6. Example of in class display of "persistence" (Bernard, 2003a).

The Key of Persistence

Definition:

To try hard and not give up easily when doing schoolwork you find frustrating and do not feel like doing; to keep trying to complete an assignment rather than becoming distracted; to choose to play after you have done your work; when having a lot of work to do in different subjects, to not give up but make the additional effort required to complete it.

Persistent Behavior

- Trying and completing work found to be "boring."
- Listening when tired.
- Staying on task.
- Keeping track of progress on accomplishing different steps of doing an assignment.
- Staying up-to-date on writing in a journal.
- Completing homework on time.
- Asking necessary questions.
- Not being distracted by classmates.
- Finishing work instead of playing.
- Asking for help rather than giving up.
- Editing/checking completed work for mistakes.

Persistence Habits of the Mind

1. **I Can Do It** – thinking that I will be successful in doing my work, especially when working on difficult and time consuming material; taking credit for when I have been successful and not thinking when I do poorly that I am not good at doing anything nor will I ever be.
2. **Giving Effort** – thinking that the harder I try, the better my achievement and the more skilled I will become; knowing that it is not the case that I was either born to be good at my studies or not and believing that with persistence I will become more skillful.
3. **Working Tough** – thinking that in order to achieve pleasant results in the long-term, I will sometimes have to unpleasant things in the short-term; believing I can stand things that are frustrating and that I do not like to do and not blowing the unpleasantness of events out of proportion.

their students know what it means to be persistent or confident. When it comes time to formally teach each of the 5 Foundations, teachers will want to review what each Foundation means. A classroom teacher will want to display a statement that describes the Foundation, including examples of behavior that reflect the Foundations, in a prominent position in the classroom (as they probably have done with their classroom rules). Teachers may also choose to design a handout for students that summarizes in very simple language what each Foundation means, and provides examples of behaviour that reflects the Foundation and the specific Habits of the Mind (ideas) that help support the Foundation (see Table 6).

Practice 3. Communicate Behavior-Specific Feedback When You Notice That A Student is Engaging in or Has Engaged in Behaviour That Reflects the 5 Foundations

For the most part, teachers tend to focus on the product of students' efforts rather than on the processes employed in producing the product. Finished products include the English essay, the math test, the science project, and the musical score played. Genuine praise for the end product sounds like: "Good job." "Excellent work." "Well done." "High standard." Constructive criticism of the end product sounds like: "You could have done better." "You rushed your work." "You didn't answer the question." While there is nothing wrong with this focus, it needs to be balanced with behavior-specific feedback that focuses on the process of learning. When teachers use the behavior-specific feedback technique, they "are not allowed" to refer to the outcome or final result of a student's efforts. Rather, they will want to have their eye on a student, looking for instances of confident behaviour, persistent behaviour, organised behaviour, getting along and resilient behaviour. At those times, they will want to communicate both verbally and non-verbally their recognition of the behavior (e.g., "Great effort." "You did that confidently." "Didn't it feel good to have organized your time?" "You worked cooperatively on that project" "You didn't lose your cool.").

In using behavior-specific feedback, teachers communicate to the student immediately following the occurrence of a behavior they are teaching or hoping the student is using (confident behavior, persistent behavior, organized behavior, getting along behavior, resilient behavior). For example, if the student they are teaching is really trying hard on a piece of work, and they are working with him to develop persistent behavior, they could say, "Great effort. You are can see now that there is a pay off to your hard work." Notice that there is little attention placed on the end product of the student's labors; rather, attention is focused on the *process*.

Practice 4. Regularly Assess Students' Use of the 5 Foundations

Some teachers have formalized their assessment of students' progress in learning the 5 Foundations. A report form that is a part of the regular assessment of students' academic progress can be used as a basis of discussions at parent-teacher-student conferences (see Table 7).

Practice 5. Teach Students about the Important Role of Their Thinking (Habits of the Mind) in Their Success and Social-Emotional-Behavioral Well-Being

One of the important ideas for teachers to impart to students is that it is not what happens to them that determines how successful and happy they are. You can mention that this idea has been around for some time. Epictetus, a stoic-Roman philosopher, wrote in the second century A.D. that "People are

TABLE 7. Sample student report card assessing social and emotional capabilities (Bernard, 2002).

Student Progress Report

Our goal at our school is for all students to realize their potential and to achieve to the best of their ability. Using the proven and effective You Can Do It! approach, we endeavor to instill in our students the attitudes and values that are vital for academic achievement, sound interpersonal relationships, and healthy psychological development. We actively teach the 5 Foundations and the 12 Habits of the Mind which are the characteristics of successful learners. This report reflects your child's progress in these areas. Please read this report, in conjunction with your child's learning journal, for discussion at mid-year interviews. (We have not included as assessment of your child's Emotional Resilience)

Student ____

Confidence ...	**Persistence ...**
is the ability to believe in yourself, to work independently, have an optimistic outlook and recognise mistake making as part of authentic learning.	is the ability to stick to a job until it is completed, even if it is difficult or "boring." It is the ability to work hard to achieve results.
sometimes usually	sometimes usually consistently
Organisation ...	**Getting Along ...**
is the ability to set goals and manage time effectively. It means being responsible for personal items and belongings in the classroom and playground.	is the ability to mix well with others, to be tolerant and non-judgmental, to be able to think through problems independently and to work within accepted rules of the school and the classroom.
sometimes usually	sometimes usually consistently

Comments:____

____

____

Principal ____

Classroom Teacher ____

____

not affected by events, but by their view of events." Shakespeare wrote that "Things are neither good nor bad but thinking makes them so." The step teachers need to take is to introduce this notion to students. They can do this in a number of ways. A favorite parable gets this point across. It is called "The Mule Story."

The Mule Story

A parable is told of a farmer who owned an old mule. The mule fell into the farmer's well. The farmer heard the mule "braying" or whatever mules do when they fall into wells. After carefully assessing the situation, the farmer sympathized with the mule, but decided that neither the mule nor the well was worth the trouble of saving. Instead, he called his neighbors together and told them what had happened and enlisted them to help haul dirt to bury the old mule in the well and put him out of his misery. Initially, the old mule was hysterical! But as the farmer and his neighbours continued shovelling and the dirt hit the mule's back, a thought struck him. It suddenly dawned on him that every time a shovel load of dirt landed on his back, he should shake it off and step up! This he did, blow after blow. 'Shake it off and step up . . . shake it off and step up . . . shake it off and step up!' he repeated to himself. No matter how painful the blows, or distressing the situation seemed, the old mule fought "panic" and just kept right on shaking it off and stepping up! You're right! It wasn't long before the old mule, battered and exhausted, stepped triumphantly over the wall of that well! What seemed like it would bury him, actually blessed him. All because of the manner in which he handled his adversity.

Whether teachers use examples from literature (e.g., "The Little Train that Could"), from movies that are well known, or from their own experience, they will want to discuss and illustrate how a positive, optimistic, tolerant mind can make the critical difference between success and failure. One idea that they can introduce to students is "self-talk." Teachers can explain to students that positive or rational self-talk can encourage them to do things they do not feel like doing ("This maths homework isn't the worst thing in the world. Even if I don't understand it at first, I can still be successful by trying hard. I'm not stupid or hopeless because it's hard. That's the way homework is sometimes – hard."). Negative self-talk can discourage them from doing things that are hard or boring ("I can't stand doing this. School should be more fun. I'll do it later when I'm in the mood."). One of the goals of YCDI is to help students recognise their negative self-talk and replace it with positive self-talk (see Fig. 3).

Practice 6. Take Opportunities to Teach the 12 Habits of the Mind (Rational Beliefs)

The different Habits of the Mind that students have already learned in their short lives determine how Confident, Persistent, and Organised they are, how well they Get Along and their Emotional Resilience. It is important for teachers as they learn more about these Habits of the Mind from reading, using Program Achieve and from discussions with colleagues in professional development to take opportunities to teach them to your students.

It is suggested that they identify a five-minute period during the school week and on a routine basis discuss a Habit of the Mind and how it influences how we feel and what we do. They can relate the Habit of the Mind to an existing person who is in the news, to their own lives, or to something they observed in one of your students. They may choose to formalise this five-minute period in name (e.g., "A You Can Do It! Moment," "A Self-Reflective Moment.").

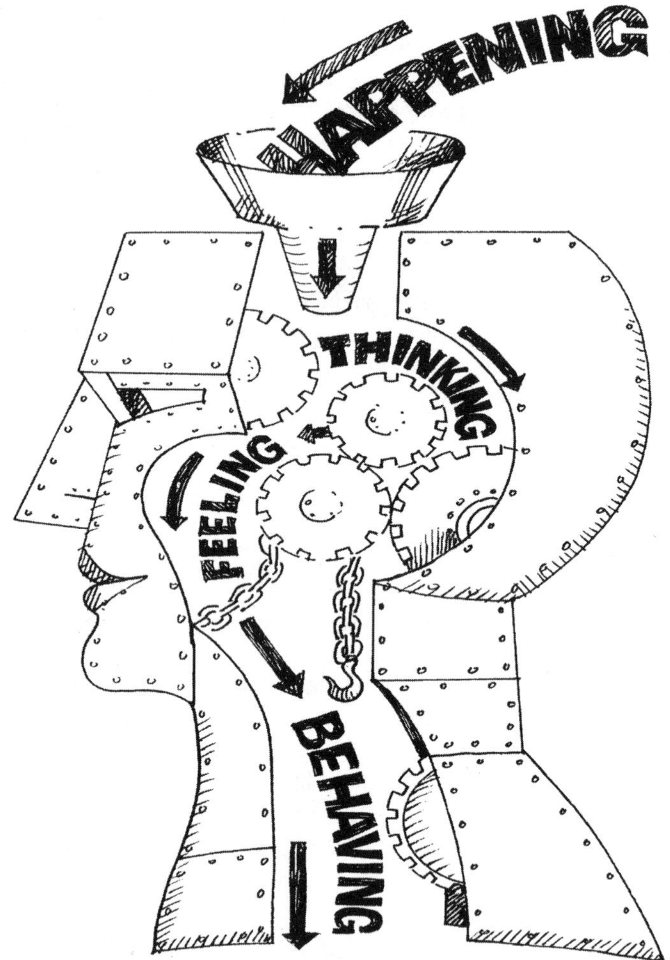

FIGURE 3. Classroom Image: Your Thinking about Things That Happen Causes Your Feelings and Behaviors (from Bernard, 2005b).

Other suggestions for teaching HOMs include: (a) when writing letters home to parents, have students include what Habits of the Mind they used that week; (b) when sharing books they have read, ask students to find examples of when main characters used different Habits of the Mind.

Practice 7. Provide Written (And Oral) Feedback to Students on Homework Assignments That Communicate the 5 Foundations and the 12 Habits of the Mind

Sometimes teachers can be too "product-oriented" in our feedback to students (e.g., "Good job."). It is recommend that teacher feedback also focus on the process of achieving the product by highlighting aspects of students' work that reflects their application of Confidence (e.g., "You had a confident tone of voice in your oral presentation."), Persistence (e.g., "You really tried hard."), Organisation (e.g., "You set a big goal and achieved it."), Getting Along (e.g., "This good grade reflects how well you worked with your partner.") and Emotional Resilience (e.g., "You really were calm!").

Practice 8. Employ Academic Goal/Target Setting on a Regular Basis and Teach Students How the Foundations Can Help Them Achieve Their Goals

It has been found that a good route for helping students apply the 5 Foundations to their school work is through academic goal setting. Academic goal setting can be effectively employed when teachers are assigning students a piece of work (e.g., research report, science project, book report) that is due in a week to two weeks and that requires students to work on the assignment for homework. General guidelines for doing this are as follows.

1. Present students with the assignment. Indicate the purpose of the assignment, important elements to be included (including questions to be answered), style/format of final product, and date due.
2. Present learning/curriculum objectives the assignment is designed to accomplish (knowledge/skills to be taught in the lesson). Review with students the skills and knowledge the assignment is designed to teach. For example, a writing assignment may be designed to provide students with practice in writing paragraphs (topic sentences, supporting sentences, etc.), using varied vocabulary, and employing correct punctuation.
3. Share with students the criteria for success/grading rubric. Using the grading scheme that is employed for the assignment (e.g., 1, 2, 3, 4, 5; A, B, C, D, F; below grade level, grade level, above grade level) the teacher should discuss with students and, if possible, provide examples from previous students' work of what they need to demonstrate in their finished product to achieve the different grades. For example, they could indicate to their students, to receive a grade of A, your assignment will need to include the following; to receive a grade of B, you will need to include the following, etc.
4. In light of the learning objectives for the assignment and the criteria for success, the teacher should have students set one or more academic targets they wish to achieve and the mark they want to obtain. These academic targets can be recorded by each student on a goal setting form and can be handed into the teacher. You will want to explain the purpose of setting a goal (to help motivate you, to help you plan your time). You will also want to discuss those elements that constitute a "good" goal. Good goals are realistic for students to achieve, challenging (not too easy or hard), specific, and proximal (capable of being achieved in a short period of time).

5. Discuss how the one or more of the 5 Foundations (and specific Habits of the Mind) can assist students in managing the process of achieving their goal. For example, teachers can:
   - Have students discuss what activities they will need to accomplish and when they will accomplish them before they get started with their assignment.
   - Have students discuss the aspects of the assignment they may find hard or boring (Hard Yakka) and ways of thinking and studying that can help them do the work anyway.
   - Help students identify aspects of the assignment that involve creative applications or areas where they might make mistakes and encourage them to discuss how they can be confident (Habits of the Mind: Taking Risks, Being Independent).
   - Help students identify any aspects of the assignment that can involve working together with each other or a parent at home. Have students discuss aspects of getting along.
6. Encourage students to self-observe their progress along the way as they accomplish those activities necessary to achieve their goal and complete the assignment. Teachers may elect to have students use a checklist to record their successes in accomplishing different aspects of the assignment.
7. Once assignments have been turned in and graded, have students reflect on the goal they initially set and whether it was achieved. Teachers can discuss with students whether the initial goal they set was appropriate and, if it was not achieved, how they could achieve their goal the next time. Also, discuss how setting goals can help them be more successful. Teachers can help students react to negative feedback (e.g., not achieving goal) by discussing the Habit of the Mind of self-acceptance (e.g., "Don't think badly about yourself when you don't achieve your goals. Work out a plan to do better next time.").
8. Have students discuss how any of the 5 Foundations and/or the 12 Habits of the Mind helped them achieve their goal.

Practice 9. Especially for Students Who Are Under-Achieving or Experiencing Poor Social-Emotional-Behavioural Adjustment, Employ YCDI Weekly Goal Setting with Feedback and Follow-Up Targeting Increases in the Use of the 4 Foundations

One of the best ways a teacher can help students take responsibility for learning each of the 5 Foundations is involving them in weekly goal setting. Using the accompanying form (see Table 8), teachers can discuss with a student in private conference which specific Foundations they would like to work on during the following week. They can work through the form with the student. It is a good idea to help students identify goals that are in their area of academic weakness (e.g., "I need to be more persistent in reviewing my spelling

TABLE 8. Weekly goal setting form (Bernard, 2002).

YCDI Weekly Goal Setting Sheet

Your Name ______________________________ Date ______________

Name of Teacher ______________________________

1. Which of the Foundations do you want to learn or practise (circle one)? confidence persistence (trying hard) organisation getting along resilience

2. My goal this week is (be specific):

   ____

   ____

   ____

3. List obstacles that might stop you from achieving your goal and how you will deal with them.

   ____

   ____

   ____

4. Write down any positive thinking that will help you achieve your goal.

   ____

   ____

   ____

5. Date by which you want to achieve goal _____

6. Your Signature

   Signature of Teacher/Tutor

Result a week later:

Did you achieve your goal? yes no almost

Talk about what you learned, including the positives that happened when you achieved the goal or the negatives that occurred by not achieving your goal.

words."). Using this form on a weekly basis provides students with visible means of improvement.

Practice 10. Use Supplementary Activities to Teach the Foundations and the Habits of the Mind

The more teachers can incorporate the Foundations and the Habits of the Mind in other activities of their class or in one-to-one mentoring discussions, the more rapidly students will internalise them. Teachers can be encouraged to utilize their creative ideas and activities to help develop the themes of Confidence, Persistence, Organization, Getting Along and

TABLE 9. Character analysis using different social and emotional capabilities as tools (Bernard, 2002).

Foundations for Achievement Habits of the Mind

Report on Rat Compiled by Ashleigh

–	0	+		
Organization				
Planning My Time		Y		Comment: Rat, your organisation is brilliant. You set your goals and achieve them. You make sure everything is in the right place.
Setting Goals			Y	
Getting Along				
Playing by the Rules		Y		Comment: Your level of tolerance is high. You solve your problems quickly and theoretically. You tolerate others who annoy you.
Thinking First			Y	
Being Tolerant of Others			Y	
Persistence				
Working Tough		Y		Comment: Rat, you can persist very well. You never give up and you tell others to keep on going. When you make mistakes, you learn from them.
Giving Effort		Y		
I Can Do It			Y	
Confidence				
Taking Risks	Y			Comment: You have confidence, but you never take risks. You are independent and optimistic.
Being Independent			Y	
Accepting Myself		Y		
General Comment: **Rat, you were born to lead. You are wise, kind, persistent, organised and helpful.**				

Emotional Resilience. Successful teachers utilize creative stories, posters, and plays to illustrate, dramatize and bring to life these critical keys to success.

One common technique that teachers can be taught to use with students is "role play" where volunteers from the class practice thinking out loud both positive, rational and negative, irrational self-talk when confronted with difficult circumstances (e.g., being teased, not understanding a piece of homework). Role play helps students recognise the role of their thinking in their own lives and that, by changing their thinking, they can change how they feel about what has happened or what they are doing.

A popular activity is for students to identify a character from a book they are reading or a movie they have seen and conduct a character analysis using key YCDI concepts (see Table 9 for an example of a student's character analysis of Rat, a major character in *Wind in the Willows*. Note that Emotional Resilience was not included in the analysis).

Embedding Social and Emotional Learning in School-Wide Culture

It is clear that when social and emotional learning including the 12 positive Habits of the Mind and the 5 Foundations become embedded within school-wide culture and common language, more students take them seriously and are more influenced by them. Some suggestions for school-wide infusion of social and emotional learning include:

School Assemblies

School assemblies are excellent forums for principals/head teachers and others to address the school community on one or more of the Foundations and Positive Habits of the Mind that are being stressed in your school. Guest speakers, plays and other discussion groups can address the meaning and

TABLE 10. Student recognition awards (Bernard, 2002).

You Can Do It!
Student Achievement Awards

This ACHIEVING STUDENT
has been recognised for demonstrating:

CONFIDENCE · PERSISTENCE
ORGANISATION · GETTING ALONG
RESILIENCE

(in the following way) ______________________________

YOU CAN DO IT!

______________________ ______________________
Student *Teacher*

importance of the 5 Foundations and positive Habits of the Mind to student well-being, success and relationships.

Student Recognition Awards

An excellent vehicle for bringing all students in a class/grade/year level of school "on board" is to award students recognition certificates for employing one or more of the 5 Foundations on a regular basis. Many schools present awards for achievement, citizenship, or "Student of the Month." It is recommended that awards for demonstrating characteristics consistent with the goals of YCDI be employed (see Table 10).

It's Worth a Re-Think

(This practice has been developed by Rob Steventon, Principal of Madison Park Primary School, to address problems of misbehaviour by employing ideas taught in Program Achieve. Description provided by Rob)

"Re-Think" is an important element of our school's general You Can Do It! Education support for students. "Re-Think" is a 20-minute portion of the lunch period in which particular students meet with the principal. The meeting addresses the reasons for any particular student's referral by a teacher for Behaviour Code infringements. In a group of five to eight students, each student discusses why he/she is in referral, and a joint-decision is made on the particular referral to be discussed. Sometimes the selection is based on the severity of the reason for the referral. At other times, the selection is based on a request from a teacher. The selection might be related to a pattern of infringement that might be emerging. For whatever reason, a particular student's reason is selected for discussion.

The student outlines the circumstances in which the behaviour of concern occurred. The student discusses the incident in sufficient detail for everyone to identify the key players. In most cases, the incident involves non-compliance and/or harassment, which might be physical or psychological.

On most occasions, the familiar model of:

Happenings → Thoughts → Feelings → Behaviors

is written on the white board, and the incident from the particular student's perspective is reconstructed in this framework. Consistent with Program Achieve's process for "New Thinking," the students work together to identify how new behavior outcomes can be achieved. Students are helped to see their behavior (and feelings) as a result of their thinking. Commonly, the student is not sufficiently self-aware to recall the particular thought pattern that might have influenced his/her behaviour during the incident. This is where group work is particularly helpful. In response to the student's common response of "I don't know" to the question "What were you thinking at the time?" the group is able to suggest/hypothesise a range of reasonable alternatives. More sensible or rational alternative thought-patterns are suggested by the group. The new feelings and behavior likely to flow from the new, alternative, rational thought patterns are listed.

Role playing is often an important component of "Re-Think." For example, it is common for us to be helping the students who respond angrily to teasing. We identify that the key Foundation for these students is Getting Along. Further, we identify Being Tolerant of Others and Thinking First as important positive Habits of the Mind to have in order to cope with feelings of anger about being teased. We reiterate what we have learned from Programme Achieve—that there is no requirement for others to see us as we see ourselves. Teasing by others is simply an indication that others do not accept us. There is no rule that they must. We might prefer them to like us, but we can easily survive without their approval. Through the role play, we rehearse new ways of thinking (e.g., "You can say what you like about me. Just don't expect me to get upset about it.").

This approach is consistent with the school's broad teaching of You Can Do It! Education. Children coming to "Re-Think" are already familiar with the language and the concepts. The few recidivists benefit from repeated practice.

Over the years since YCDI! took hold in our school, the old detention numbers have crashed. Helpers even volunteer to come to Re-Think to support their friends! The emphasis is on reeducation. Students do not walk out chastened or with their tails between their legs. They are aware of the school's position about their behaviour and that failure to stick to the school's behaviour code has its consequences. Yet the students know "why" they do what they do, they do not blame others, and they know "how" to make a change.

You may create a running record on each student's use of the 4 Foundations. A note home can acknowledge students for having demonstrated use of one or more of the Foundations or one or more of the Habits of the Mind. Alternatively, weekly summaries can be discussed at parent conferences.

School-Wide Behavior Management

Many schools have incorporated social and emotional learning represented by the 5 Foundations and supporting 12 habits of the Mind. They have done this in two distinct ways.

Schools are incorporating within individual behavior management plans social and emotional capabilities that need to be developed in the individual student who demonstrates chronic misbehavior. Research indicates that children with problem behaviors display developmental delays in their social and emotional capabilities.

Some schools award students cards or stickers when they demonstrate behavior reflecting one or more of 5 Foundations. Sometimes, students are issued "Good behavior" cards or booklets that enable them to collect points for displaying all 5 Foundations. When certain thresholds are achieved, some schools award students with a pencil that displays the name of Confidence, Persistence, Organization, Getting Along or Resilience.

Integration of Social and Emotional Learning in School Excursions and Special Events

TABLE 11. Social and emotional learning parent education material: teacher guide (Bernard, 2004a).

How to Extend YCDI Education into the Home

You can say to parents that there are three main things they can do to help their children at home develop each of the 5 Foundations.

1. Use the five words that describe each of the 5 Foundations in everyday conversation with your child.
   You can illustrate to parents how to talk about the 5 Foundations:[S1]
   4. **It really took a lot of confidence for your brother to pet the dog even though he's scared of dogs.**
   5. **Gee, that athlete really shows persistence in his training even though his leg is bandaged.**
   6. **Putting things away where they belong helps your father get organized.**
   7. **It is good to see your two friends getting along so well together and sharing their toys.**
   8. **Even though I was angry, I calmed down quickly. It's good to calm down.**
2. Acknowledge your children when they demonstrate behavior that reflects the 5 Foundations.
   You can discuss with parents how children who are praised when they display the 5 Foundations in their behavior are more likely to do so. (You may elect to offer a parent education session devoted to teaching parents how they can employ praise to strengthen their children's Foundations). Examples of praise that parents can use at home to acknowledge their children's behavior that reflects the 5 Foundations include:
   9. **When your child does an activity independently without first asking for help, say: That took confidence.**
   10. **When your child completes a difficult puzzle without giving up, say: Wow! You found that hard, but you kept on trying. You are persistent.**
   11. **When your child puts away any toys that are left lying around in their proper place, say: You put things away were they belong. You are very organized.**
   12. **When your child takes turns when playing with others, say: Taking turns really shows how well you are learning to get along.**
   13. **When your child calms down quickly after having been upset without yelling or screaming or withdrawing from the situation, say: I can see you have calmed down and did not yell or scream. You're a lot like Ricky Resilience!**
3. Read books to your children and discuss characters who display Confidence, Persistence, Organization, Getting Along, and Emotional Resilience.

   Say to parents:

   Story books that you will be reading with your child offer your child a great opportunity to see how each of the 5 Foundations is applied in characters they will be learning about in different stories.

   Discuss with parents some of the titles of books that cover themes associated with each of the 5 Foundations (see list of Recommended Literature for Children that appears in this Guide).

TABLE 11. Social and emotional learning parent education material: teacher guide (Bernard, 2004a) *(Cont'd)*

Share with parents some of the questions they can ask their children during and after the story has been read aloud. The questions below are illustrated for a story that focuses on the trait of Confidence. (See Parent Information Session 3 for similar questions that can be posed when parents have read a story dealing with different traits such as Persistence, Organization, Getting Along, and Emotional Resilience):

14. **What did the character do that showed that he/she was/was not confident?**
15. **What happened to the character because he/she was/was not confident?**
16. **Did the character believe that he/she was good at many things?**
17. **Did the character believe that he/she was likeable and could make new friends?**
18. **Was the character afraid to make mistakes when he/she was learning something new?**
19. **Did the character keep trying, even when things were hard?**
20. **Did the character look and sound confident?**

YCDI School-Home Notes

Explain to the parents:

At the beginning of each unit of the YCDI Early Childhood Education Program, I will be sending home an YCDI Home-School Note that will explain the Foundation that is being taught at school. This will provide you with the opportunity to discuss, practice, and extend your child's learning of each Foundation at home.

(Optional: show an overhead example of a School-Home Note found in a subsequent session.)

Indicate to parents that in the note, they will be provided with some things to say and do with their child to help support what their child is learning. Explain that at the bottom of each of the YCDI School-Home Notes there is a tear-away slip that they can sign and return to you after they have discussed the idea with their child.

It is good practice for those in charge of special events at schools (e.g., building a radio studio; going on a camping expedition; visiting a museum) to remind and acknowledge students about how the 5 Foundations can help everyone make the event a success.

Parent Education

Involving parents in supporting social and emotional learning at home including the 5 Foundations and Habits of the Mind is good practice. In YCDI, a variety of material is available for teachers and parent educators to use with parents of children of different ages (e.g., Bernard, 2003a, 2003c, 2004a).

At home, teachers and parent educators can encourage to discuss positive Habits of the Mind (rational beliefs) with their children. They can also be encouraged to provide behavior-specific feedback to their children when they catch them in the act of being confident, persistent, organized, getting along and emotionally resilient. Depending on the age of the child, parents can be instructed in how to select and discuss books and movie videos with characters displaying varying degrees of these qualities. Teachers can inform

TABLE 12. Social and emotional learning material for parents: school-home note (Bernard, 2004a).

Dear Parent,

We are teaching children all about the Foundation of Persistence. The character "Pete Persistence" will be introduced this week to help your child learn that persistence means:

- Trying hard and keep trying when something feels like it is too hard to do

Some ideas that we would like for you to discuss this week with your child that help develop persistence are: (1) When work is hard, I can do it, (2) The harder I try, the better I get, and (3) To do the best I can, I sometimes have to do things that are not easy or fun.

When you catch your child being persistent, give lots of praise ("You did that even though it was not easy or fun, "You see, the harder you try, the better you get!" and "You are becoming persistent.")

✂ -

Return to Teacher Slip

Name of the Child ______________________ Date ______________

We have discussed the ideas: ❑ Yes ❑ No

My child understands the ideas: ❑ Yes ❑ No

Signature of Parent ______________________________________

Your comments ____

____

parents when in their class they begin to introduce a social and emotional capabilities and indicate in a school-home note what parents should know and do (see Tables 11 and 12).

Conclusions

In the ideal world, approaches such as rational-emotive education and You can Do It! Education would be routinely implemented in schools throughout the world in a systematic effort to enhance the emotional health of children. The major assumption of emotional education programs is that prevention is more effective than remediation, and that if we can teach children how to think rationally, they will approach both developmental and situational challenges in a healthier manner, which in turn will decrease the proliferation of self-defeating behaviors that far too many young people succumb to.

In order to effectively implement REE and YCDI, teachers and other school personnel must learn the theory and model it. Professionals need to continually challenge their own irrational thinking, getting rid of their demands that their job should always be easy, that their students should always behave perfectly, or that they will always be treated fairly. They must stop making overgeneralizations about student behavior or performance, avoid awfulizing about their work conditions, refrain from equating their own self-worth with their performance as a teacher; and force themselves to give up their demandingness that everything should come easily to their students. Until teachers themselves "walk the talk" and believe in the REBT principles, implementing REE and YCDI will not be as effective.

Although REE lessons appear to be an effective way to help children and adolescents approach life more successfully, rational thinking principles need to be an inherent part of every young person's experience. Adults are important models, and although it is difficult to develop a rational stance toward life when surrounded by irrationality in the world, every effort to teach rational principles, directly or indirectly, will help facilitate healthy emotional development.

References

Ames, C. (1992). Classrooms: Goals, structures and student motivation. *Journal of Educational Psychology, 84,* 261–271.

Bandura, A. (1986). *Social foundations of thought and action: A social cognitive theory*. Englewoood Cliffs, NJ: Prentice-Hall.

Bandura, A. (1997). *Self-efficacy: The Exercise of control*. New York: W.H. Freeman.

Bar-Tal, D. and Bar-Zohar, Y. (1977). The relationship between perception of locus of control and academic achievement. *Contemporary Educational Psychology, 61,* 181–199.

Bedford, S. (1974). *Instant replay*. New York: Institute for Rational Living.

Bernard, M. E. (1995). *Improving student motivation and school achievement: A professional development program for teachers, special educators, school administrators and pupil service personnel*. ONT, CA: Hindle and Associates, p. 320.

Bernard, M. E. (2001). *Program achieve: A curriculum of lessons for teaching students how to achieve success and develop social-emotional-behavioral well-being,* 2nd ed., Vols. 1–6. Oakleigh, VIC (AUS): Australian Scholarships Group.

Bernard, M. E. (2002). *Providing all children with the foundation for achievement and social-emotional-behavioral well-being,* 2nd ed. Priorslee, Telford (UK): Time Marque.

Bernard, M .E. (2003a). *Developing the social-emotional-motivational competence of young people with achievement and behavior problems: A guide for working with teachers and parents*. Oakleigh, VIC: Australian Scholarships Group.

Bernard, M. E. (2003b). *The You Can Do It! education mentoring program*, 2nd ed. Oakleigh, VIC (AUS): Australian Scholarships Group.

Bernard, M. E. (2003c). Investing in parents: What parents need to know and do to support their children's achievement and social-emotional well-being. Oakleigh, VIC (AUS): Australian Scholarships Group; Laguna Beach, CA (USA): You Can Do It! Education, Priorslee, Telford (ENG): Time Marque.

Bernard, M. E. (2004a). *The You Can Do It! early childhood education program: Developing social-emotional-motivational competencies (4–6 Year-Olds)*. Oakleigh, VIC (AUS): Australian Scholarships Group; Laguna Beach, CA (USA): You Can Do It! Education, Priorslee, Telford (ENG): Time Marque.

Bernard, M. E. (2004b). *The REBT therapist's pocket companion for working with children and adolescents*. New York: Albert Ellis Institute, p. 245.

Bernard, M. E. (2004c). Emotional resilience in children: Implications for Rational-emotive Education. *Romanian Journal of Cognitive and Behavioral Psychotherapies, 4,* 39–52.

Bernard, M. E. (2005a). *Program achieve: A curriculum of lessons for teaching students to achieve and develop social-emotional-behavioral well being,* Vols. 1–6., 3rd ed. Oakleigh, VIC (AUS): Australian Scholarships Group; Laguna Beach, CA (USA): You Can Do It! Education, Priorslee, Telford (ENG): Time Marque.

Bernard, M. E. (2005b). *The You Can Do It! Education images resource CD program*. Oakleigh, VIC (AUS): Australian Scholarships Group.

Bernard, M. E. (2006). It's time we teach social and emotional competence as well as we teach academic competence. *Reading and Writing Quarterly,* in press.

Brown, J. L., Roderick, T., Lantieri, L., and Aber, J. L. (2004). The Resolving Conflict Creatively program: A school based social and emotional learning program. In J. E. Zins, R. P., Weissberg, M. C. Wang, and R. P. Walberg, (eds.), *Building academic success on social and emotional learning: What does the research say?* New York: Teachers College Press.

Dawson, R. W. (1991). REGIME: A counseling and educational model for using RET effectively. In M.E. Bernard (ed.), *Using rational-emotive therapy effectively: A practitioner's guide*. New York: Plenum Press, pp. 112–132.

DiGiuseppe, R., Miller N. J., and Trexler, L. D. (1979). A review of rational-emotive psychotherapy outcome studies. In A. Ellis and J. M. Whiteley (eds.), *Theoretical and empirical foundations of rational-emotive therapy*. Monterey, Calif.: Brooks/Cole.

Dryden, W. (1999). Rational-emotive behavioral counseling in action (2nd ed.). London: Sage.

Dweck, C. S. and Elliott, E. S. (1983). Achievement motivation. In P.H. Mussen (Ed.), Handbook *of child psychology* (Vol. 4, 3rd ed.), New York: John Wiley, pp. 643–691.

Ellis, A. (1971). An experiment in emotional education. *Educational Technology, 11,* 61–64.

Ellis, A. (1972). Emotional education in the classroom: The living school. *Journal of Child Psychology*, *1*, 19–22.

Ellis, A. and MacClaren, C. (1998). *Rational-emotive behavior therapy: A therapist's guide*. Atascadero, CA: Impact.

Gerald, M., and Eyman, W. (1981). Thinking straight and talking sense. New York: Institute for Rational-Emotive Therapy.

Goleman, D. (1995). *Emotional intelligence*. New York: Bantam Books.

Gonzalez, J. E., Nelson, J. R., Gutkin, T. B., Saunders, A., Galloway, A., and Shwery, C. S. (2004). Rational-emotive therapy with children and adolescents: A meta-analysis. *Journal of Emotional and behavioral Disorders, 12,* 222–235.

Greenberg, M. T., Kusche, C. A., and Riggs, N. (2004). The PATHS Curriculum: Theory and research on neurocognitive development and school success. In J. E. Zins, R. P., Weissberg, M. C. Wang, and R. P. Walberg, (eds.), *Building academic success on social and emotional learning: What does the research say?* New York: Teachers College Press.

Hajzler, D. J., and Bernard, M. E. (1991). A review of rational-emotive outcome studies. *School Psychology Quarterly, 6,* 27–49.

Knaus, W. (1974). *Rational-emotive education: A manual for elementary school teachers.* New York: Institute for Rational Living.

Lange, G.W. and Adler, F. (April 1997). Motivation and achievement in elementary children. Paper presented at the Biennial Meeting of the Society for Research in Child Development, Washington, DC (ERIC Document Reproduction Service No. ED 413 059).

Larson, J. (2005). Think first: Addressing aggressive behavior in secondary schools. New York: Guilford Press.

Mayer, J. D., and Salovey, P. (1997). What is emotional intelligence. In P. Salovey and J. D. Sluyter (eds.), *Emotional development and emotional intelligence: Educational implications.* New York: Basic Books.

McWhirter, E., Shepard, R.E., and Hung-Morse, M.C. (2004). *Counseling at-risk children and adolescents.* In A. Vernon (Ed.), *Counseling children and adolescents* (3rd ed.), Denver, CO: Love Publishing, pp. 311–354.

Pothier, P.C. (1976). *Mental health counseling with children.* Boston, MA: Little, Brown.

Rotter, J.B. (1966). Generalized expectations for internal versus external control of reinforcement. *Psychological monographs, 80,* (Whole No. 609).

Schaps, E., Battish, V., and Solomon, D. (2004). Community in school as key to student growth: Findings from the Child Development Project. In J. E. Zins, R. P., Weissberg, M. C. Wang, and R. P. Walberg (eds.), *Building academic success on social and emotional learning: What does the research say?* New York: Teachers College Press.

Schunk, D. H. (1996). Goal and self-evaluative influences during children's cognitive skill learning. *American Educational Research Journal, 33,* 359–382.

Shure, M. (1966). I Can problem Solve: An interpersonal cognitive problem-solving program. Champaign, Ill: Research Press.

Seligman, M.E.P. (1975). *Learned helplessness.* San Francisco, CA: Freeman.

Seligman, M.E.P. (1991). *Learned optimism.* New York: Knopf.

Spaulding, C.L. (1993). *Motivation in the classroom.* New York: McGraw-Hill.

Spivack, G., Platt, J. and Shure, M. (1976). *The problem solving approach to adjustment.* San Francisco: Jossey Bass.

Spivack, G., and Shure, M. (1974). *The social adjustment of young children: A cognitive approach to solving real problems.* San Francisco: Jossey Bass.

Terjesen, M., Doyle, K., Rose, R., Sciutto, M., Iovine-Calabro, E. and Zampano, G. (1999). *REBT in the schools: A review and implications for school psychologists.* Poster presented at the 107th annual convention of the American Psychological Association (APA; Division 16). Boston, MA.

Tur-Kaspa, H., and Bryan, T. (1995). Teacher ratings of the social competence and school adjustment of students with learning disabilities. *Journal of Learning Disabilities, 28,* 44–50.

Vernon, A. (1980). *Help yourself to a healthier you*. Washington, DC: University Press of America.

Vernon, A. (1989a). *Thinking, feeling, behaving: An emotional education program for children*. Champaign, IL: Research Press.

Vernon, A. (1989b). *Thinking, feeling, behaving: An emotional education program for adolescents*. Champaign, IL: Research Press.

Vernon, A. (1998a). *The passport program: A journey through emotional, social, cognitive, and self-development, grades 1–5*. Champaign, IL: Research Press.

Vernon, A. (1998b). The passport program: A journey through emotional, social, cognitive, and self-development, grades 6–8. Champaign, IL: Research Press.

Vernon, A. (1998c). *The passport program: A journey through emotional, social, cognitive, and self-development, grades 9–12*. Champaign, IL: Research Press.

Vernon, A. (2002). *What works when with children and adolescents: A handbook of individual counseling techniques*. Champaign, IL: Research Press.

Vernon, A. (2004). *Counseling children and adolescents* (3rd ed.), Denver, CO: Love Publishing.

Vernon, A. (2006a). Thinking, feeling, behaving: An emotional education curriculum for children (2nd ed.; Grades 1–6). Champaign, IL: Research Press.

Vernon, A. (2006b). Thinking, feeling, behaving: An emotional education curriculum for adolescents (2nd ed.; Grades 7–12). Champaign, IL: Research Press.

Vernon, A., and Clemente, R. (in press). *Assessment and intervention with children and adolescents: Developmental and cultural considerations*. Alexandria, VA: American Counseling Association.

Waters, V. (1979). *Color us rational*. New York: Institute for Rational Living.

Weiner, B. (2000). Intrapersonal and interpersonal theories of motivation from an attributional perspective. *Educational Psychology Review, 12,* 1–14.

Zimmerman, B.J. (1991). A social cognitive view of self-regulated academic learning. *Journal of Educational Psychology*, *81*, 329–339.

Zins, J. E., Weissberg, R. P., Wang, M. C., and Walberg, R. P. (2004). *Building academic success on social and emotional learning: What does the research say?* New York: Teachers College Press.

Index

Page numbers with *t* and *f* represent table and figures, respectively

A

ABC (DE) theory of emotional disturbance, 15
ABC framework of ADHD, 288
ABC model, 182, 189
ABCs of REBT, 181*t*
Absolutism, 9
Academic goal setting, 447–448
Academic procrastination
  common rationalizations, 320
  different groups of, 319
  psychological characteristics associated with, 319
  psychological factors associated with, 319
Action strategies for combating frustration tolerance, 138
ADDES, 286
ADHD symptoms of disorganization, 327, 337
ADHD, biological influences of, 282
Adolescent therapy, 3
Age and developmental level of child, importance of, 293
Age-stage asynchrony, 183
Allied cognitive-behavioral
  approaches, 45
  theories, 20
Alternative thinking, 48
Ambiguous social cues, 284
Amitriptyline, 291
Anger provoked aggression, 275
Anger thermometer, 100, 101*f*
Anger, 377
Antisocial behavior, 260
Antisocial personality disorder, 257–258
Anxieties in children, types of
  discomfort anxiety, 243, 246*t*–247*t*
  ego anxiety, 243, 244*t*
Arbitrary inferences, 10
Asperger's disorder, 389
Assessment guideline and practices in REBT treatment
  assessment of anger, 100
  assessing cognitions, 100–104
  crucial aspect of, 100
  different methods of assessment, *see* Assessment, different methods of
  different targets for cognitive assessment, 97–99
  prerequisites, 96–97
Assessment in REBT children and adolescent groups
  general guidelines for, 400
  standardized batteries for, 399–400
Assessment of behavioral component
  checklist, 221
  S-T-E-B, 221
Assessment, different methods of
  "and," "but," and "because", 103
  expansion-contraction, 103
  guided imagery, 104
  incomplete sentences, 102
  inference chaining, 102
  instant reply, 103–104

Assessment, different methods of *(Continued)*
peeling the onion, 103
sentence completion technique, 102
standardized self report surveys, 102
TAT-like approach, 103
think-aloud, 103
thought bubbles, 102
thought clouds, 102
At risk population, 396
Attachment theory, 179
Attention-deficit hyperactivity disorder (ADHD)
assessment of, 285–287
case illustration, 299–303
diagnosis of, 284–285
irrational beliefs with, 287–290
symptoms associated with, 282
treatment of, 290
types of, 281
Attention-deficit hyperactivity disorder (ADHD), symptoms of
primary, 282
secondary, 283
Attention-deficit hyperactivity disorder (ADHD), types of
combined type, 281
predominately hyperactive-impulsive type, 281
predominately inattentive type, 281
Attributional retraining, 49
Automatic thoughts questionnaire for children (ATQ-C), 219
Automatic thoughts, 18
Awfulizing, *see* Irrational beliefs associated with ADHD

B

Bar-On Emotional Quotient Inventory: Youth Version (EQ-I:YV), 399
BASC, 286, 399
Basic concepts of REF development of REF lessons
beliefs, 422
disputing beliefs, 423
facts versus assumptions, 423
feelings, 422
self-acceptance, 422
Behavior management (BM) approach, 406
Behavior modification therapy, 296
Behavior of children with conduct disorders, 100
Behavioral homework assignments, examples of, 111–112
Behavioral problems, 10
Behavioral techniques, 261
Belief and belief system, 15
Beliefs of parents and their emotional consequences, 207*t*–209*t*
Blame, 382
Burnout, risk of, 381

C

"Coping log", 380
"Cozy-nest syndrome,"393
Catastrophe scale, 164, 169, 172
Catastrophic thinking, 289
Causal
attributions, 97
thinking, 48
CBCL, 286, 399
CDI, 399
Challenging of children's irrational beliefs, 292, 294
Change, willingness to, degrees of, 90
Check-off list technique, *see* Sampling of counter-procrastination techniques
Child and adolescent
certificate in rational-emotive-behavior therapy, 6
scale of irrationality, 20, 219, 284, 399
Child behavior checklist, 219
Child depression, case illustration of, 226–228
Child development project, 415
Child therapy, 3
Child's schema, expansion of, 93
Childhood
disorders, stages to the assessment of, 94–95
maladjustment, 7
problems, ABCS of common, 74
Child-oriented practitioners, 85–87
Children with chronic misbehavior, treatment approach for, 334
case illustration, 334

Children's actions, influence on
  inferences, 236
  information-processing style, 237
  motives, 236
  parental feelings, 236
  personality variables, 236
  rules, 237
  self-conceptualizations, 237
  situational cue, 236
Children's depression inventory, 219
Children's irrational beliefs associated with
  anger, 200
  depression, 205
Children's use of internal or cognitive strategies, developmental trend of, 160
  age related differences, 161
  experiences with high levels of negative affect, 161
  first trend, 160
  gender differences, 161
  second trend, 160
Client's emotional disturbance, assumptions about, 92
Clinical behavior therapy, 296
Clinical depression, causes of, 217–218
Closed group type, 394
Cognitions
  of young depressed clients, 217–218
  role of, 85
Cognitive behavior
  rehearsal, 41
  therapists, 85
Cognitive behavioral emotional resilience lessons
  adversity, 168
  coping skills and positive habits of the mind, 171
  emotional resilience at work, 172
  increasing tease tolerance, 170
  introducing emotional resilience, 169
  introducing emotions, 168
  putting things in perspective, 169–170
  rethink strategy, 171–172
Cognitive behavioral treatments
  problem-solving strategies, 297
  self-evaluation, 297
  self-instructional training, 297
  self-monitoring, 297
  self reinforcement, 297
Cognitive behavioral
  interventions, 292
  role play, 295
Cognitive distortions
  examples of, 220
  in children, 238, 242
  in parents, 239
Cognitive distortions, causes of
  ignorance, 239
  irrational ideas, 239
Cognitive processing, 9
  errors, 20
Cognitive triad inventory for children (CTI-C), 219
Cognitive
  case of, 98–99
  components, 261
  deficit model, 260
  development influences, 87
  distortion model, 260
  emotive and behavioral methods for developing emotional resilience, 348*t*
  errors, 85
  homework assignments, examples of, 110
  interventions, 261
  limitations, 9
  models, basic premise of, 216
  processes of aggression, 260
  restructuring, 3
  role play, 41
  skills, 261
  strategies, 23
  techniques, 261
Cognitive, emotive and behavioral methods for working with underachievers
  who are anxious and/or depressed, 330*t*
  who avoid responsibilities and display low frustration tolerance, 338*t*
  who chronically misbehave, 337*t*
  who are generally disorganized, 340*t*
  who are peer conforming/socially anxious, 334*t*
  who are perfectionists, 336*t*
  who display the non-achievement syndrome, 333*t*
  who feel helpless and discouraged, 331*t*

Cognitive/thinking errors, 97
Cognitive-behavioral assessment, process of
  behavioral assignment, 146
  determine, 145
  identify, 145
  in session problem simulation, 146
  make a conceptual assessment, 145
  self-doubt and discomfort-dodging, 146
  set the stage, 146
Cognitive-behavioral therapy
  basic techniques, 369
  philosophy, 369
Cognitive-behavioral therapy, stages of
  cognitive-behavioral insight, 250
  cognitive-behavioral-psychosituational working through, 252
  generalized learning and skill training, 253
Cognitive-behavioral
  child treatment, 6
  solutions, 22
  treatment models, 232, 234
Cognitive-behavioral-psychosituational (CBP) model, 245
Common irrational beliefs, 18
Conduct disorder (CD), 257–258, 285, 289
Confidentiality, 393
Connors instruments, 286
Consequential thinking, 48
Constructivism, 8
Consultee-Centered Consultation, 178
Contents of REE lessons
  content and personalization questions, 425
  learning objectives, 424
  lesson plan format, 425
  stimulus activity, 424
Contingency intervention, 260
Contingency management, different forms of
  economy reward systems, 296
  maneuvering of attention, 296
  removal of privileges, 296
  response cost, 296
  time out, 296
Coping behavior of children, factors governing, 158
Coping skills in children
  definition of, 159
  successful with adverse emotions, 160
Counter procrastination techniques,
  check-off list technique, 144
  metacognitive training, 144
  the five-minute system, 144
Critical components of service delivery system, 370

D

Deductive interpretation, 101
Degree of confidentiality, 388
Degree of controllability, importance of, 159
Demandingness, 262
Demands for fairness, 19
Depression
  causes of, 217
  definition of, 213
  diagnosis of, 218–221
  people vulnerable to, 215
  types of, 214
Developing a therapeutic alliance, strategies for, 94
Developing social and emotional capabilities
  developing positive work orientation, 342–343, 344*t*
  developing resilience, 345
Developmental work in verbal mediation, 88
Developmentally-appropriate formats, 424
Dextroamphetamine (Dexadrine), 291
Diagnosis of ADHD
  dopamine concentration, 285
  pitfalls associated with, 285
Diagnostic and statistical manual of mental disorders DSM-IV-TR, 281
Diagnostic guidelines, 243–244
Dichotomous thinking, 10
Didactic style, 35
Different irrational and/or erroneous beliefs, 316–319
Diffusing responsibility, strategies for, 91
Direct cognitive intervention, 127

Disputation
  process, 421
  strategies, use of, 88
Disputing, different types of
  catastrophic thinking, 295
  empirical, 294
  functional, 294
  global self-ratings, 294
  heuristic, 294
  logical, 294
  low frustration tolerance, 295
  semantic, 294
Disruptive behaviors, 57
Distillations of different dysfunctional cognitions, 429
Distillations of different functional cognitions, 429
Distinguishing aggression from anger, importance of, 257
Dopaminergic-noradrenergic neurotransmissions, 282
Down arrow technique, 220
Down's syndrome, 371, 405
Drawing hostile conclusions, 284
DSM IV, 219
Dysfunctional cognitions model, 389

E
Educational underachievement, 310
  definition of, 311–312
  different types of underachievers, *see* Educational underachievers, different types of
  psychological factors contributing, 320, 327
Educational underachievement, social and emotional learning approaches
  assessment, 326–328
  determine existence of under-achievement, 323
  develop social and emotional capabilities, 322
  work with parents and teachers, 322–323
  eliminate social and emotional disabilities, 322
  gaining "buy in" on the model assessment, 324–326
  therapeutic alliance to develop goals of working together, 323–324
Educational underachievers, different types of
  helpless-discouraged-depressed type, 313
  immature/dependent/anxious type, 313
  low frustration tolerance type, 314
  non-achievement/peter pan syndrome, 314
  peer conforming type, 313
  perfectionistic type, 313
  rebellious/aggressive type, 313
Effect of fatigue on adults, 133
Egocentrism, 10
Elements of the emotional episode, 14
Eliminating social and emotional disabilities, case illustration of, 330–332
Ellis' ABC model, 156
Ellis' major categories of irrational beliefs, 157
Emotion log, 400, 409
Emotion, aspects of
  behavioral predisposition, 391
  phenomenological, 391
  physiological arousal, 391
  social expression, 391
Emotional
  development, 9
  disorders, 345
  distress, 156
  education lessons, 421
Emotional disturbance, learning of
  activating events, 258
  beliefs about those events, 258
  consequences, 258
Emotional intelligence (EQ), 399
Emotional
  pie, 219
  problems, 10
  reactions, effect of, 93
  resilience, 359
Emotional regulation, 157, 159
  skills that are delayed, 341–342
Emotional resilience skill training with REBT, 161–167
Emotional resilience skill, teaching
  assertive behavior, 166–167
  explicit teaching of rational beliefs, 166
  find someone to talk to, 167
  keeping things in perspective, 164
  relaxation, 166

Emotional resilience, conceptualization of
  definition of emotional resilience, 158–159
  development research on children's emotional regulation, 159–161
  emotional resilience strategies or coping skills, 159
Emotional
  resilience, definition of, 164
  responses of children, 91–92
  schema, 96, 293, 328
  self-management skills, 8
  thermometer, 162, 169
  upset, characteristics of, 157
  vocabulary, 96, 293 , 328
Emotional vocabulary, importance of, 391
  emotional well-being, school and life, positive relationships, 429, 430*f*
  to eliminate the social and emotional disabilities, 429, 430*f*
Emotive homework assignments, examples of, 111
Empirical disputation, 33, 318
  use of, 86
Errors
  of evaluation, 242
  of inference, 242
Exclusionary criteria of any group, 392
Exercises for group settings
  anonymous disputing, 403
  best and worst day, 403
  comprehensive self-inventory, 402
  dear Dr. rational, 403
  evidence against IBs, 403
  expectations/fears, 402
  hotseat, 404
  introduction exercises, 402
  learning from mistakes, 403
  positive talk, 404
  reverse role-play, 404
  role-play, 404
  round of applause, 404
  shame-attacking, 404
  strongest hour, 403
Experiences in infancy and early childhood, 179

F

Faulty inferences, 97, 100
Five blockers to school success and happiness, 326*f*
Five keys to school success and happiness, 441*f*
Five keys to success, 325*f*, 441*f*
Five-minute system, *see* Sampling of counter-procrastination techniques
"Foundation", 350
Frustrated children, behavior of, 133
Frustration
  disturbances, 134, 137
  mastering techniques, 134–136
Frustration intolerance (FI), 262
Frustration tolerance, 292
  training, 134, 141
Frustration-aggression study, 134–135

G

General frustration management strategies
  inadequate emotional expressive language skills, 137
  imitating models who show weak self-control, 138
  misreading the signal, 138
  reward for delay, 138
  social conditioning, 137
  temperament predisposition, 137
Getting along behavior, 359
Getting along habits of the mind, 359
Goals of therapy children desires, 91
Group assignments, 392
Group therapy with children and adolescents
  advantages, 386–387
  disadvantages, 387–389
Guilt, 379–380

H

Hahnemann medical college and hospital, 47
Handout introducing confidence, 352*t*
Happy-go-lucky students, 316
High frustration tolerance (HFT), 4, 25, 199, 290, 292
How to live with a neurotic, 4

HTFB chart, 170–171, 315, 328, 335, 391
Human cognition, 15
Human fallibility, 36
Hurtful emotions, 402
Hyperactivity/impulsivity, 281
Hypothetico-deductive reasoning, 87

I

I can problem solve program, 415
I-can't-stand-it-it-is", 287
Identifying cognitive distortions or thinking errors technique, 220
Imipramine, 291
Imperfections, 11
Implementation of REE
 considerations in implementing lessons, 425–426
 important REE concepts, 422–424
 informal approach, 420–421
 integration into the curriculum, 429
 REE lesson format, 424–425
 sample REE lessons, 426
 structured REE lessons, 421–422
Implementing REE applying informal approach, case illustration of, 420
Impulsive aggression, 261
Impulsivity and disruptive behavior, 291
Inattention, 281
Inclusionary criteria of any group, 392
Individual psychotherapy with children, 263
Individuals with disabilities education act (IDEA), 369
Initial stages of treatment, strategies at, 92
Institute for rational-emotive therapy, 4
Integration of social and emotional learning, 436
 in school excursions, 454
Interactionism, perspective of, 7
Internal working models (IWMs), 179
Interpersonal cognitive problem solving (ICPS), 47, 49
Intolerance
 of frustrating rules, 19
 of work frustration, 19
Irrational beliefs (IBs), 264, 276
 and distortions of reality, effect of, 85
Irrational beliefs associated with ADHD
 awfulizing, 289–290
 demandingness of self, others, and the world, 289
 low frustration tolerance (LFT), 287–288
 other-rating, 288
 self-rating, 288
Irrational beliefs
 contributing to depression in children and adolescents, 218
 role of, in children, 85, 92, 101, 156–157
 role of, in parents, 178
Irrational beliefs/negative habits of the mind with general disorganization
 having no goals, 339
 planning time poorly, 340
Irrational demands, 284

K

Kind and firm child-rearing practice, 178
Kind and not firm child-rearing practices, 178
Knowledge acquisition, 88

L

Labeling of thought, 252*f*
Learning disability, 283
Logical disputation, 34
Low frustration tolerance disturbances, 137, 139
 behavior of children with, 146
 importance of, pattern, 137
Low frustration tolerance level, 141, 134, 283, 290, 317
 forms of, 136

M

Magnification/minimization, 10
Maladaptive
 behavior, 11
 emotions of parents, 265
Means-ends thinking, 48
Meditations, 3

Mental development, 9
Metacognitive
  development, 87
  strategies, 23
  training, *see* Sampling of counter-procrastination techniques
Method of treatment using REBT with children
  behavior management training for parents, 112–113
  cognitive methods, 105–107
  critical thinking skills, 104–105
  disputing inferences, 108–110
  goal setting, 104
  home work, 110–112
Methylphenidate (Ritalin), 291
Model of childhood behavior, 235*f*
Mood chart, 219
Motivational syllogism, 265
  elements of, 264*t*
MTA Cooperative Group, 296
Multisystemic treatment, 327, 418

N
Narcissistic group members, 388–389
Negative behavioral interventions, 260
Negative contingency management procedures, 260–261
Negative emotions
  healthy negative emotions, 100
  systems or processes to react to, 158
Negative habits of mind of young anxious people
  I can't do it, 329
  needing approval, 329
  needing to be perfect, 329
  self-downing, 329
Negative habits of mind, 322, 328; *see also* Social-emotional disabilities
Negative habits of the mind that lead to problems
  anger, 433
  anxiety, 433
  chronic misbehavior, 433
  depression, 433
  general disorganization, 433
  general work avoidance, 433
  poor emotion regulation, 434
Negative habits of the mind, 429
Negative types of thinking checklist, 346*t*
Negative ways of thinking checklist, 165*t*
No frustration tolerance (NFT), 199
Non-achieving syndrome, 332
Non-constructive disciplinary action, 11
Non-disturbed emotions, 265
Non-hurtful emotions, 402
Normalization, concept of, 377

O
Open group type, 393
Operational thinking stage, 294
Oppositional defiant disorder (ODD), 257–258; *see also* Conduct disorder
Organizational habits of the mind, 358
Organized behavior, 358
Other methods in problem solving in REBT with adolescents
  getting a reduction rather than an elimination, 127
  making use of parental involvement, 128
  making use of the relationship to encourage change, 127
  referring to a more appropriate resource, 128
  telling clients what to do, 127
  teaching verbal assertiveness techniques, 127
Other-acceptance, 36
Other-pity, *see* Depression, causes of
Overgeneralization, 10, 420

P
Parent behavior, factors influencing, 181
Parent interventions to help children of different age groups
  children eight to twelve years, 188–190
  children thirteen to seventeen years, 191–194
  children three to seven years, 184–188
Parent meta-emotion, 180
Parent psychoeducation, 178–179
Parental
  beliefs, role of, 177
  guilt, 180–181

Parental involvement in child's treatment, 265
case illustration, 268–270
different ways of, 267–268
Parental low frustration tolerance (LFT), 181
Parent-child relationship, 12
importance of, 179–180
Parenting styles contributing to underachievement
authoritarian style, 346
excessive expectations style, 346
lack of expectations style, 346
overly emotional style, 346
overprotective style, 346
permissive style, 346
powerless style, 346
unsupportive of school style, 346
Parenting styles,
criticism trap, 240
false positive, 241
guilt traps, 241
inconsistency trap, 241
perfectionism trap, 240
scared-rabbit trap, 241
Parents of children with ADHD, beliefs of, 289
Parents of specially challenged children
common themes in work, 375–381
disputations, suggestions for, 373
working with, 370–371
Parents of specially challenged children, common themes in work with
anger versus rational assertiveness, 377–379
denial versus acceptance, 375–376
fear versus active concern, 376–377
guilt versus self-acceptance, 379–381
PATHS curriculum, 415
Pemoline (Cylert), 291
Persistence habits of the mind, 357, 442
Pessimism, 166
Phases of self-doubt dimension model, 142
Phases of therapy to change dysfunctional beliefs, 316
Piaget's stages, 8
Pictures and stories, use of, 88
Positive and negative habits of the mind, 436*t*–440*t*
Positive behavioral interventions, 260
Positive habits of mind, 328, 429; *see also* Social-emotional disabilities
Positive work orientation, 327
Positive working relationship, 88
Powerless parenting, 318
Preconcrete operational levels of thinking, 10
Predatory aggression, 275
Prerequisite skills for REBT assessment and treatment of children, 96
Primary caregivers of young people, 6
Problem assessment, 44
Problem behaviors of children, analysis of
cognitive-behavioral, psychosituational child interview, 248
cognitive-behavioral, psychosituational parent interview, 248
psycho-diagnosis and goal setting, 250
Problem defining in REBT with adolescents
defining the problem for the adolescent, 118
offering a problem example, 118
simplifying the problem, 118
unraveling the problem, 119
using a representative example, 118
using visual aids, 119
Problem identification, *see* Childhood, disorders, stages to the assessment of
Problem intervention in REBT with adolescents
challenging the "can't stand" philosophy, 122
confronting and confuting "awfuls," "terribles," and "horribles", 120
confronting and confuting "shoulds" "oughts," and "musts", 121
correcting misperceptions of reality, 124
teaching or not teaching the relationship between thinking, feelings, and actions, 120
teaching the principle of self-acceptance, 122

Problem solving in REBT with adolescents
arranging homework assignments, 126
checking out the client's expectations about therapy, 125
explaining psychological and emotional problems as habits, 125
other methods, *see* Other methods in problem solving in REBT with adolescents
sticking to accepted insights, 126
telling the adolescent what to think, 126
writing out an ABC homework, 125
Procrastination technology, 142
Program achieve, 86, 434, 453
Prosocial behaviors, 260
Psychoeducation of parents of young children aged eight to twelve years
case illustration, 188–189
client centered consultation, 189–190
consultee-centered consultation, 190
process of change and outcome, 190
Psychoeducation of parents of young children aged thirteen to seventeen years
case illustration, 191
client centered consultation, 191–193
consultee-centered consultation, 193
process of change and outcome, 193–194
Psychoeducation of parents of young children aged three to seven years
case illustration, 184–185
client centered consultation, 185–186
consultee-centered consultation, 185–186
process of change and outcome, 187–188
Psycho-educational principles, different, 343
Psychological maladjustment, 10
Psychopathic, 257
Psychopathology, 237
Psychopharmacologic approaches, 296
Psycho-situational approach, overview of
anxiety, 234
fear, 233
phobia, 234
Psycho-situational model, 232–234
Psychostimulant medications, 291
Psychotherapy, 51
PURRRRS system, 144

R

Rational assertive behavior, 379
Rational assertiveness training, 377
Rational beliefs (RBs), 265, 276
Rational Emotive Education: A Manual for Elementary School Teachers, 85
Rational self-statements, 40
use of, 86, 295
Rational-emotive approaches to the problems of childhood, 5
Rational-emotive consultation in applied settings, 6
Rational-emotive education (REE), 6, 56, 138–139, 141, 146, 311, 417, 422
assumptions related to, 419
implementing REE, 420
importance of, 419
learning centres, 428–429
oriented group counseling sessions, 156
use of, 157
Rational-emotive imagery (REI), 41, 378
Rational-emotive therapy (RET), 4–5, 15, 49
Reasons to be involved in child's treatment, 184*t*
REBT applied to child and adolescent groups, 5
assessment in, 398–400
conceptuals in, 400–404
development of therapeutic alliance, 396–398
features of REBT groups, 390–391
group format, 407
guidelines for forming groups, 391–394
parenting in, 404–406
pre-group contract, 408–409
types of REBT groups, 394–396
REBT assessment and treatment with children, relationship building in
consequences and alternatives, 92–93
expectations, 90
language, 93–94

REBT assessment and treatment with children, relationship building in *(Continued)*
prerequisite skills, 96
self disclosure and rapport, 90–92
assessment and treatment with adolescents, case illustration of, 128–132
child session, suggestions for, 89*t*
conceptualization of an emotional episode, 13
developmental model of childhood disorders, 7
family therapy model, focus of, 266, 267*t*
REBT, first stage in, 90
therapeutic methods, 8
REBT groups, types of
counseling/therapy groups, 394–395
psycho-education/guidance groups, 396
task groups, 395–396
REBT outcome literature, meta-analytic reviews of, 270, 271*t*–273*t*, 274
effect of behavioral and cognitive therapies, 275
lapses in REBT studies, 274
REBT outcome studies, 274
REBT parent interventions
developmental issues, 183
steps in, 182–183
REBT, approach structures in
problem defining, 117–119
problem intervention, 119–124
problem solving, 124–126
relationship building, 116–117
REBT-based emotional resilience group counseling, example of, 167–168
Reflections, 90–91
Relation between emotions and thoughts, 304
Relationship between frustration and aggression, 134
Relationship development in REBT with adolescents
accepting client's reality perspective, 117
allowing a companion to attend a session, 117
Relationship development in REBT with adolescents *(Continued)*
allowing long periods of uninterrupted listening, 116
discussing openly own opinions and attitudes, 117
extracting from the parents an initial concession, 117
giving the adolescent priority, 117
Relationships of positive and negative habits of the mind, 431*t*–432*t*
Resolving conflict creatively program, 415
Re-think, 452
Reynolds adolescent scale, 219
Reynolds child depression scale, 219
Role playing, 453

S
Sample personal development mentoring activity, 435*t*
Sample REE Lessons, 426–428
Sample student report card assessing social and emotional capabilities, 444*t*
Sampling of counter-procrastination techniques
check-off list technique, 144
five-minute system, 144
metacognitive training, 144
SAT preparation, 395
Schedule for affective disorders and schizophrenia for school-age children, 219
School counselors, *see* Child-oriented practitioners
School psychologists, 90; *see also* Child-oriented practitioners
School Psychology Handbook, 86
School-wide behavior management, 453
Secondary symptoms of ADHD
academic underachievement, 283
difficulties in interpersonal relationships, 284
depression, 284
Selective abstraction, 10
Selective serotonin reuptake inhibitor, 223

Self disclosure, strategies for, 91–92
Self-acceptance, 24, 379
Self-blame, *see* Depression, causes of
Self-concept pinwheel method, 149
Self-control model, 217
Self-depreciation, 19
Self-doubt and discomfort-dodging model, 141
Self-downing, 19, 97, 165, 204, 283, 288, 420
Self-esteem, 320, 405
Self-instructional training (SIT), 46-47
Self-management skills, 12
Self-perceptions inventory (SPI), 399
Self-pity, *see* Depression, causes of
Self-rating, 288
Self-statements, 98
Semantic disputation, 34
Sensitivity or perspective thinking, 48
Sequential family therapy model, 266
Social cognitive learning analysis of underachievement
  academic procrastination, 319–320
  REBT, 315–319
  social-emotional capabilities, 320–321
  social-emotional disabilities, 320–321
Social cognitive theory, 234
Social learning theory, 234
Social workers, *see* Child-oriented practitioners
Social-emotional capabilities, delays in development of, 327
Social and emotional capabilities that mind support
  confidence, 431
  emotional resilience, 432
  getting along, 431
  organization, 431
  persistence, 431
Social-emotional disabilities, 320–321
Socio-economic status and underachievement, 319
Socratic
  dialogue, 373
  disputing, 7
  style, 35
Special education, 283, 370
Special educators, 381–383
  common themes expressed by, 381–383
  assessment, 373–374
  disputation, 372–373
  program planning, 374–375
  rapport and relationship issues, 371–372
Specific age-related parenting goals
  for children 8-12, 188*t*
  for children 13-17, 191*t*
  for young children, 185*t*
Stages of change model, 397
Stimulant medications, 291–292
Structured diagnostic interviews, 286–287
SUD scale, 94
Summary of social and emotional learning standards, 416*t*
  positive social orientation, 416*t*
  positive work orientation, 416*t*
  resilience, 416*t*
Survey of person's social and emotional capabilities, 349*t*–350*t*

T

Talk therapy, 86
Targeted social and emotional capability, 343, 345*t*
The key of persistence, 442
The Rational Management of Children, 177
Therapeutic alliance in children and adolescent group, components of
  agreement on goals of therapy, 396–397
  agreement on tasks of therapy, 397
  relationship bond, 397
Therapeutic alliance, 292
  importance of, 317
Therapeutic interventions in treating depression
  act as if, 224
  away with the blues, 224
  concrete objects, 226
  depression tool box, 225
  doom and gloom glasses
  fortune telling, 225–226
  pros and cons analysis, 225
  silly songs, 224
  story time, 225
  when you need a helping hand, 224

Therapists, role of, 264–265, 318
Think first, 415
Thoughts for developing confidence, types of
  accepting myself, 366
  being independent, 366
  I can do it, 366
  taking risks, 366
Treatment for adolescents with depression study (TADS), 222
Treatment goals and methods, 32
Treatment of ADHD
  allied behavioral treatments, 296–297
  multimodal treatments, 297
  other cognitively based interventions, 297–298
  pharmacological treatments, 291–292
  REBT based interventions, 292–296
  self-instructional training, 298
  self-monitoring, 298–299
  self-reinforcement, 299
  social-problem solving, 298
Treatment of depression, 221–226
Tricyclic antidepressants, 291

U
Under achievement due to
  ADHD, 283
  anxiety, 328–329
  avoidance of responsibilities, 335
  chronic misbehavior, 332–333
  depression, 328–329
  general disorganization, 339
  pervasive low frustration tolerance, 335
  poor emotional regulation, 341
Underachievers, types of, with irrational negative habits of mind
  acting without thinking, 333
  being intolerant of limits, 333
  being intolerant of others, 333
  social irresponsibility, 333–334
Unfairness, child's perception of, 93
Unkind and firm child rearing practice, 12, 178
Unkind and not firm child-rearing practice, 13
Unpleasant visceral reaction, 133
Upward bound program, 407

V
Verbal
  mediational deficits, 21
  psychotherapy, 90
  self-instruction, 87
Vulnerability to depression, factors contributing to
  anxiety, 215
  cultural biases, 215
  depressed parents, 215
  extensive conflict, 215
  gender biases, 215
  genetics, 215
  poor conflict resolution and communication skills, 215
  strained family relationships, 215

W
Walker-McConnell scale elementary version, 172
Ways to incorporate YCDI in ethos
  assessing students' use of the 5 foundations, 443
  communicate behavior-specific feedback, 443
  display images and explicit statements, 441
  employ academic target setting, 447
  establish student understanding of the goals of YCDI education, 436
  provide written (and oral) feedback to students on homework assignments, 446
  take opportunities to teach the 12 habits of the mind, 445
  teach students about the importance thinking, 443
Well-being surveys, 172
Working with parents to alleviate children's anger
  case illustration, 201
  client-centered consultation, 202–203
  consultee-centered consultation, 201–202
  processes and outcome, 203
  psycho educating parents, 199–200
  steps for parents to help children, 200–201

Working with parents to alleviate children's anxiety
case illustration, 197
client centered consultation, 198
psycho educating parents about anxiety, 194–197
steps for parent to help child with their physiological responding, 196
steps for a parent to help child with anxiety, 196
Working with parents to alleviate children's depression
case illustration, 206
client-centered consultation, 206–207
consultee-centered consultation, 206
processes and outcome, 207
psycho educating parents, 204–206
steps for parents to help children, 205
Worries of parents, 374

Y

You Can Do It! Education, 6, 417–418, 429–430, 453
integration of social and emotional learning, 436
teaching, 436